PENGUIN BOOKS

THE VEDAS

Roshen Dalal was born in Mussoorie and studied in various schools across the country. After a BA (Hons) in history from the University of Bombay, she completed an MA and PhD in ancient Indian history from Jawaharlal Nehru University, New Delhi. She has taught at both school and university, and been involved in research in the fields of history, religion and philosophy, and education. Apart from books, she has written numerous articles and book reviews. After working for many years as an editor, she is now a full-time writer, living in Dehradun.

ALSO BY ROSHEN DALAL

The Religions of India: A Concise Guide to Nine Major Faiths

Hinduism: An Alphabetical Guide

The Illustrated Timeline History of the World

The Puffin History of India, Vols 1 and 2

The Puffin History of the World, Vol. 1

THE VEDAS

ROSHEN DALAL

AN INTRODUCTION TO
HINDUISM'S SACRED TEXTS

PENGUIN BOOKS

PENGUIN BOOKS
Published by the Penguin Group
Penguin Books India Pvt. Ltd, 11 Community Centre, Panchsheel Park,
New Delhi 110 017, India
Penguin Group (USA) Inc., 375 Hudson Street, New York, New York 10014, USA
Penguin Group (Canada), 90 Eglinton Avenue East, Suite 700, Toronto, Ontario, M4P 2Y3, Canada
(a division of Pearson Penguin Canada Inc.)
Penguin Books Ltd, 80 Strand, London WC2R 0RL, England
Penguin Ireland, 25 St Stephen's Green, Dublin 2, Ireland (a division of Penguin Books Ltd)
Penguin Group (Australia), 707 Collins Street, Melbourne, Victoria 3008, Australia
(a division of Pearson Australia Group Pty Ltd)
Penguin Group (NZ), 67 Apollo Drive, Rosedale, Auckland 0632, New Zealand
(a division of Pearson New Zealand Ltd)
Penguin Books (South Africa) (Pty) Ltd, Block D, Rosebank Office Park,
181 Jan Smuts Avenue, Parktown North, Johannesburg 2193, South Africa

Penguin Books Ltd, Registered Offices: 80 Strand, London WC2R 0RL, England

First published by Penguin Books India 2014

Copyright © Roshen Dalal 2014

10 9 8 7 6 5 4 3 2 1

The views and opinions expressed in this book are the author's own and the facts are as reported by her which have been verified to the extent possible, and the publishers are not in any way liable for the same.

ISBN 9780143066385

Typeset in Goudy Old Style by Eleven Arts, New Delhi
Printed at Replika Press Pvt. Ltd, India

For
Shahnaz Arni

CONTENTS

ACKNOWLEDGEMENTS

Among those who have contributed to this book, I would particularly like to thank Udayan Mitra of Penguin India for suggesting this book, and providing advice on its form and content; Mudita Chauhan-Mubayi for expertly editing it; and Tanvi Kapoor for carefully proofreading and finalizing the text.

INTRODUCTION

The Vedas are the most sacred books of Hinduism and, perhaps, the most controversial. There is no agreement on the nature and purpose of the texts, their date, or the origin of the people who composed them.

The controversies began almost as soon as the Vedas were translated and became known in the West. In the early 20th century, the great scholar Maurice Winternitz wrote, regarding the Rig Veda:

> In view of the very great divergence in the opinions of the specialists, it is not enough, even in a book intended for the general reader, merely to give some approximate date, for even the general reader must have an idea of the circumstances supporting the various opinions on the greater or lesser antiquity of the Vedas.
>
> (History of Indian Literature, vol. 1, p. 290)

The same principle holds true today both for controversies regarding the date and for other aspects of the texts. One of the most important points of dispute is the question of the homeland of the Vedic people. The other is the question of the region of composition of the Vedas. These two points are also related to the date of the texts.

There are four Vedas or Vedic Samhitas: Rig Veda, Yajur Veda, Sama Veda and Atharva Veda. There are also numerous related texts and commentaries. Based on both language and content, the Rig Veda is usually considered the earliest of the four Samhitas, which makes it the earliest known text in India.

This book begins with an overview of the contents of the four Vedas, and the different approaches used to understand them. This is followed by a summary of the related texts and commentaries. Among the important related texts are the Brahmanas, the Aranyakas and the Upanishads. Special texts that throw light on the Vedas include the *padapathas* (word texts) and *anukramanis* (indices). The Vedangas are a further group of early texts, which help in understanding the Vedas. These include texts on grammar and metre.

Where were the Vedas composed? And what was the origin of the Vedic people? Linguistics and archaeology are believed to provide the keys to answering these crucial questions. Since the late 18th century, it became clear that Sanskrit was related to several European languages including Greek and Latin. An assumption was then made that there must have been an earlier single language from which these languages later diverged. This hypothetical language has been termed Indo-European and its early form, Proto-Indo-European. If there was a single language, it is presumed that there was also a single homeland, from where all the groups speaking this language migrated and diverged, spreading across parts of Europe and Asia. Further, looking at the very close similarities between Rig Vedic Sanskrit and Old Avestan (earliest known language of Iran), it was presumed that one of the early divergent groups consisted of people speaking a language termed Indo-Iranian, which later diverged into the two languages referred to above. In addition, similarities were noticed in religion, myth and culture among the various Indo-European groups, and particularly between the two Indo-Iranian groups. Based on the linguistic theories, archaeologists began searching for an archaeological culture that would represent the early homeland, and various other such cultures that would represent the movements of the groups from the original homeland. In this book, the different Indo-European theories as well as theories regarding language change and diffusion are examined in detail, along with views that oppose or deny these theories. This is followed by a look at the Iranian material, which is essential for understanding the context of the Rig Veda. Despite the similarities in language, myth and ritual, the earliest Iranian texts, known today as the Gathas, provide an account of a very different monotheistic religion, later called Zoroastrianism. It is therefore important to understand the differences as well as the similarities in the Vedic and Avestan materials.

Against this background, what sort of information does the Rig Veda itself provide? What is the internal evidence of its date and origin? Can the Rig Veda and Later Vedic texts be equated with archaeological cultures and, if so, which ones? Is it possible, as many have claimed, that the Rig Veda belongs to the period of the Harappan civilization? An overview of the archaeological cultures in early India helps to situate the Vedas while an in-depth study of the texts provides some indications. The study includes a detailed analysis of peoples (tribes or clans), places and rivers mentioned, and their probable locations, as well as the likely identification of the numerous plants, trees and animals mentioned in the texts.

Apart from questions of location and origin, there is much of interest in the Vedas. There are beautiful prayers and hymns to deities, references to people, to wars and battles and to daily life, to nature, to crops and agriculture, and to wild and domestic animals. Among the deities are Indra, Vayu, Agni, Usha, Ratri, and many more. There are even some philosophical concepts. Early aspects of music are revealed in the Sama Veda and associated songbooks. Rituals are described in the Yajur Veda and associated texts, while the earliest account of medicine and healing occurs in the Atharva Veda.

The Vedas thus are rich texts, full of information of various kinds, written in a poetic and beautiful form. Yet there is a strange paradox: while the Vedas are considered eternal, supreme, and the most sacred of all texts of Hinduism, the contents are often mundane, or related to ritual.

This brings us to the question of translation. A single word in the Rig Veda can have multiple and divergent meanings. Can we be sure that the Rig Veda and other Vedas have been translated correctly? Among the earlier translators were H.H. Wilson, R.T.H. Griffith, A.B. Keith, Rudolf Roth, H. Grassman, Alfred Ludwig, and J. Stevenson. Newer translations include, among others, those of selected hymns of the Rig Veda by Wendy Doniger and of sections of the Atharva Veda by Arlo Griffiths. The newer translations have an easier and more modern style but, at the same time, are not wholly different.

It is instead the spiritual translators who provide a totally different meaning of the original hymns. Could they be correct and could all other interpretations be wrong? In Chapter 12 of this book, we look at the work of two spiritual leaders and scholars, who have interpreted the Rig Veda in a spiritual context. Another new translation that deserves mention is the complete Hindi translation by Pandit Shriram Sharma Acharya.

To summarize, this book presents an understanding of the texts both for the scholar and for the layperson. It ends with some unbiased and very tentative conclusions on their date and homeland based on a detailed analysis. The two appendices provide a list of hymns of the Rig Veda, and a selection of hymns from the four Vedas.

This book is based on my own original research, particularly on the Ganga–Yamuna Doab and surrounding areas, as well as on numerous other sources. Apart from the texts themselves, along with auxiliary texts and early commentaries, there are literally hundreds of books, and an even larger number of articles, on the Vedas, the so-called 'Aryans', the Indo-Europeans, the Indo-Iranians, and the relationship of the Vedic people with an archaeological culture.

A select bibliography provides a list of the main sources.

A NOTE ON SPELLINGS

Numerous Sanskrit words are used in this book. A standard system of spelling has been used, based on Monier-Williams's A Sanskrit–English Dictionary, though without diacritical marks.

CHAPTER 1

VEDIC LITERATURE: THE FOUR SAMHITAS

Vedic literature is very vast and is broadly divided into two parts: (1) the four Vedic Samhitas and (2) the related texts, including the Brahmanas, Aranyakas and Upanishads. Apart from these, there are three categories of texts known as Kalpa Sutras. There are also commentaries and *anukramanis* (indices) and associated literature—the Vedangas. All early texts and commentaries were composed in Sanskrit, though later interpretations use various languages.

THE SAMHITAS

The four Vedic Samhitas—Rig Veda, Sama Veda, Yajur Veda, and Atharva Veda—are considered the most sacred texts of Hindus. The word *veda* comes from the Sanskrit root *vid* ('to know') and implies 'divine knowledge'. These are said to be *shruti* or texts divinely revealed to the ancient *rishis* (sages).

DIFFERENT APPROACHES

These four Samhitas have been analysed and interpreted in different ways. Even early authors, such as Yaska (circa 7th–6th centuries BCE), recognized that the texts had many aspects. He described different interpretations of the Vedas by ritualists (*yajnikas*), etymologists (*nairuktas*), and traditional historians (*aitihasikas*). Other methods of interpretation traditionally referred to are *parivrajaka* (spiritual interpretation), *dharmashastrika* (pertaining to law) and *naidana* (etymological). The Vedas are also referred to in the six orthodox schools of Hindu philosophy, and are particularly important in the Mimamsa school.

The yajnikas emphasize the use of mantras in ritual and are less concerned with their meaning or context. Most commentaries on the texts also focus on their ritual use. Though this interpretation has its limitations, it has led to the preservation of the texts in their exact form over centuries.

The nairukta method is what is used by Yaska himself, based on earlier texts, and consists of analyses of the words used in the Vedas. It is actually not a complete method in itself but one of the six Vedangas, or sciences, used in Vedic analysis. The aitihasika method relates a Vedic mantra or hymn with a mythical story or account of an event in an ancient text. In one example regarding a hymn in praise of rivers (Rig Veda 3.33), the ancient event related to it is said to be that the rishi Vishvamitra addressed the rivers with these mantras. The aitihasika method thus is totally different from historical analysis as it is known today. The parivrajaka interprets every aspect of the text in a spiritual context. The dharmashastrika searches for aspects of law in the Vedas, while the naidana is little known but seems similar to the aitihasika. It focuses on the context in which the verses were composed.

Among the many approaches of the past and present, three major ones can be identified and, depending on the approach used, very different interpretations emerge.

In one approach, the Vedas are seen as ritual texts, containing mantras and prayers to be chanted and used both in yajnas or sacrifices, and at other times. This corresponds with the yajnika school referred to by Yaska. As they are ritual texts, it is recognized that they also contain descriptions of sacrifices and miscellaneous information. The Samhitas themselves, particularly the Sama and Yajur Vedas, as well as the Brahmanas and the later Kalpa Sutras, indicate their ritualistic use.

In a second approach, the Vedas are seen primarily as historical texts, through which information can be obtained on the composers of the texts, their society, economy and religion. This is a modern historical approach, very different from the traditional aitihasika method.

A third approach denies both the ritualistic and the historical contexts, and sees the Vedas as deeply spiritual texts whose true meaning is not immediately apparent. This is more or less the same as the parivrajaka approach. It bases itself on a paradox that arises through seeing the texts as either ritual or historical books, which negates the traditional viewpoint of the Vedic Samhitas as the most sacred of all Hindu literature, which had formed the basis of religious study from the time they were composed. Neither ritual nor historical interpretations reveal or bring out this sacredness, which was emphasized in ancient texts. New spiritual interpretations have gained ground in the last 150 years, though they are based on ancient accounts.

The concept that the Vedas are eternal and supreme was always widely accepted and recognized. However, right from the time the Brahmanas were composed and even from the time of the Sama and Yajur Vedas, the ritual aspects were emphasized, and a large body of literature grew around this. The historical aspects gained importance from the time of European inroads into India, and the study of the Vedas by both Western and Indian historians.

MYSTIC ORIGIN OF THE SAMHITAS

As mentioned earlier, traditionally, the Vedic Samhitas are considered shruti, that is, divinely revealed. 'Shruti' literally means 'that which is heard', hence these texts were 'heard' by the composers, conveyed to them from some divine source. The Samhitas themselves have various accounts of their mystical origin. The Rig Veda states that the origin of the three Vedas (the fourth was added later) was the mystical sacrifice of Purusha, the primeval person (10.90). The Atharva Veda, which was the fourth Veda, has different versions. One passage states that from Skambha (the supporting principle), they cut off the *rik* verses, and scraped off the *yajus*. The *saman* (song) verses are its hairs and the verses of Atharva and Angiras the mouth (10.7.20). In another, it says that the god Indra was born from the Rig verses, and the Rig verses were born from him (13.4.38). A third passage (19.54.3) says that Kala or time was the origin of the Rig verses and of the yajus. A fourth passage says that the Rig and saman verses, the metres, the Purana with the yajus, and all the devas arose from the remains of the sacrifice. All these verses indicate a belief in their divine origin.

The Brahmanas and Upanishads also refer to the divine origin of the Vedas. The Shatapatha Brahmana states that the Veda is the foundation of all that is (6.1.1.8), while the Brihadaranyaka Upanishad sees the Veda as the breath of the Supreme Being (4.5.11). There are other similar statements in these texts and in later Puranas.

SHAKHAS

The Samhitas have different recensions and schools (*shakhas*). The Vedas were studied by groups of rishis who belonged to different shakhas, each headed by a particular teacher. Shaunaka, Ashvalayana, Pippalada and Kaushika are some of the known teachers. There were once hundreds of different shakhas but now texts belonging to only a few of these are known. These shakhas were distributed across different geographical areas. Each shakha specialized in the study of one Vedic Samhita and seems to have had a slightly different version of the text.

Apart from the Samhita itself, shakhas studied various associated texts, which could include a Brahmana, an Aranyaka, an Upanishad, and texts in the category of Kalpa Sutras. This, however, was not essential.

Patanjali's Mahabhashya of about the 4th century BCE refers to twenty-one shakhas of the Rig Veda, 101 of the Yajur Veda, nine of the Atharva Veda, and 1000 paths of the Sama Veda. The Mahabharata and some of the Puranas also enumerate and describe a number of shakhas. Over one thousand shakhas are listed in various texts but, of all these, probably only ten are current today. Sometimes, two shakhas used some of the same texts.

A group of people who study one particular shakha of any Samhita, along with its associated texts, comprise a *charana*.

At one time, the Vedas in their various shakhas were studied across much of India. As communities of brahmanas moved from one place to another, when invited by kings or patrons to attach themselves to a temple or settle in a particular area, the shakhas and charanas moved to different geographical areas. The Upanishads indicate that members of different castes could engage in such study. Later, however, their study was confined to members of the brahmana caste, and the Vedas were not accessible to the general population. It was only in the 19th century that attempts began to be made to make them known and available to others.

VYASA

Though composed by or revealed to rishis and others, the Vedas were compiled and arranged by some unknown person. According to tradition, it was the rishi Vyasa who arranged all the Vedic Samhitas in their present forms, according to the requirements of sacrifice. He then taught each of the Samhitas to one of his students, who in turn taught it to others. Some of the Puranas provide the following names of these students. They state that Vyasa taught the Rig Veda to Paila, the Yajur Veda to Vaishampayana, the Sama Veda to Jaimini and the Atharva Veda to Sumantu.

Some later scholars presume that Shakala may have been the arranger of the Rig Veda, as the available recension carries his name.

COMPOSERS: RISHIS, KINGS, GODS

Over four hundred rishis are referred to as composers of the hymns in the Rig Veda. Twenty-one of these were *rishikas* (women). Wise and powerful rishis are also referred to in the hymns. Kings, gods and other people are also listed as composers.

A brief description of the four Vedic Samhitas is given below.

RIG VEDA

The Rig Veda has 1028 hymns, containing 10,552 *riks* (verses). A Rig Vedic hymn is known as a *sukta*. It comes from *su-ukta*, which can be translated as 'well-said' or 'wise saying' or 'song of praise'. Each sukta contains one or more riks.

These 1028 hymns are divided into ten *mandalas* (sections). Another type of later division was into *ashtakas* or eighths. Each ashtaka was again subdivided into eight *adhyayas* (sections or lessons) and each adhyaya into *vargas* or groups of five or six hymns. For practical purposes, the mandalas are also divided into *anuvakas* (recitations).

DATE

The date of the text is uncertain and is perhaps the most controversial aspect of studies on the Rig Veda. As there is no clear internal evidence for the date, many different suggestions have been put forward, with estimates varying from 11,000 BCE to 1000 BCE. These estimates are based on relative dating of various texts, language, and information within the text. Some have even dated it to millions of years ago though a range of 1500–1000 BCE is the most accepted. However, an analysis of the various theories (see Chapter 6 of this book) will show that it is very difficult to reach any definite conclusion on its date. Of the four Samhitas, linguistic analysis indicates that the Rig Veda is the earliest and forms the basis for the others. Some scholars feel that though the other three Vedas may be later than the Rig in their present form, they could have had earlier origins.

RIG VEDIC SHAKHAS

Though, as seen above, the Mahabhashya refers to twenty-one shakhas of the Rig Veda; according to the *Charana Vyuha* attributed to the rishi Shaunaka, there were five Rig Vedic shakhas: Shakala, Bashkala, Ashvalayana, Shankhayana, and Mandukeya. The only complete recension of this text known today is of the Shakala school.

The Shakala text is still studied in parts of Maharashtra, Karnataka, Kerala, Orissa, Tamil Nadu and Uttar Pradesh (UP), and may have also been studied in Punjab.

The Shankhayana and Bashkala shakhas are said to still be known in some parts of the country but this is uncertain. Some manuscripts of the Ashvalayana shakha are believed to have been found but the oral tradition no longer exists. Sometimes, Shakala texts are categorized as belonging to the Ashvalayana shakha. In Maharashtra, the Shakala shakha uses the related texts of the Shrauta Sutra and Grihya Sutra of the Ashvalayana.

Among the many lost shakha traditions of the Rig Veda are the Paingi, which existed in south India, and the Mandukeya, which was prevalent in Magadha, eastern and central UP and possibly farther north. The Shakala is, in fact, thought to be based on the Mandukeya.

THE PRIEST

Each Samhita had a priest specially trained in that text for use in the sacrificial ritual. The *hotr* was the main priest for the Rig Veda. His role is further explained in Chapter 10 of this book.

LANGUAGE

Panini's grammar, composed some time between the 7th and 4th centuries BCE, provides the standard for classical Sanskrit. The early language of the Rig Veda has a greater variety of grammatical forms, somewhat different *sandhi* rules (methods of joining words), and some of its letters or syllables are marked with accents. It is also uncertain if the meanings of the words used were the same as in classical Sanskrit. This has led to the Rig Veda being translated in different ways.

Vedic Sanskrit is classified as an Indo-Aryan language, part of the larger group of Indo-European languages. However, it includes some features, for instance retroflex phenomes, which do not occur in other Indo-European languages, and it has been suggested that these belong to local languages, or to certain lost languages. Linguistic analysis forms an important part of the theories of origin of the Vedic people, and of other groups in India at the time of the composition of the Rig Veda. The various theories and their implications will be looked at in more detail in subsequent chapters of this book.

METRE

The Rig Vedic hymns are composed in several metres. The Sanskrit term for metre is *chhanda* or *chhandas*. More details on the metres are provided in the section on Vedangas in Chapter 2 of this book.

SUMMARY OF THE TEXT

A summary of the ten mandalas of the Rig Veda is given below:

Mandala 1 has 191 suktas. Each hymn invokes one or more deities. In some, the gods are invited to attend the sacrifices, in others they are asked to confer blessings or particular benefits.

The mandala opens with a hymn to Agni. Thirty-six more hymns are dedicated to Agni in this mandala and, in addition, Agni is referred to along with other deities in several others. The god Indra first appears in the fourth hymn, but has forty-five hymns dedicated to him, and is mentioned in many more. Other gods to whom separate hymns are dedicated are Vayu, the Ashvins, Ribhus, Varuna, Maruts, Brahmanaspati, Pushan, Usha, Surya, Savitr, Soma, Rati, Vishnu and Brihaspati. Some gods are always worshipped together, such as Dyaus-Prithivi; others are often, but not always, joined together. Among pairs of deities in this mandala are Indra-Varuna, Indra-Agni, Indra-Vayu, Agni-Soma, Mitra-Varuna and Indra-Vishnu. Some hymns are dedicated to the Vishvedevas, which usually indicates a number of different deities, but sometimes seems to refer to a separate group. Even where a hymn is dedicated to a single deity, others are often mentioned in the course of the hymn. These include Ka, Rudra, Ratri, Romasha as well as several goddesses. Soma is frequently referred to, and many of the gods are asked to come and drink the Soma juice. There are hymns to the Ritus (seasons), to food, and against poisonous creatures (1.191). This last is similar to the magical spells found in the Atharva Veda. One hymn (1.164) talks of the year and months in symbolic language.

The second part of Mandala 1, hymns 51–191, is considered to be earlier that the first half, and just slightly later than mandalas 2–7. These hymns are in groups, each group said to be authored by one rishi. These rishis are Savya Angirasa, Nodha Gautama, Parashara Shaktya, Gotama Rahugana, Kutsa Angirasa, Kakshivan Dirghatamas, Paruchchhepa Divodasa, Dirghatama Auchathya, and

Agastya Maitravaruni. These groups are interspersed with some hymns composed by other rishis. The first part of Mandala 1 can be considered similar to Mandala 8. Over half its suktas are composed by the Kanva family, who are also composers of many of the hymns in Mandala 8.

Mandala 2 has forty-three suktas, almost all composed by the rishi Gritsamada. The opening hymns are to Agni; there are several to Indra. Among others are those to Rudra and the Maruts. There are also hymns to Brihaspati, Brahmanaspati, the Adityas, Varuna, the Vishvedevas, Dyaus-Prithivi, the Ashvins, Vayu, Savitr, Apam Napat, Rudra, the Maruts and to the seasons. There are two hymns to Shakunta, who represents augury.

Mandala 3 has sixty-two suktas, most composed by the rishi Vishvamitra and his family. The mandala opens with hymns to Agni, followed mainly by those to Indra and the Vishvedevas. Other deities include the goddess Usha, the Ribhus, Mitra, and the Ashvins. There are also hymns to the *yupa* (sacrificial post) and to rivers.

Mandala 4 has fifty-eight suktas, most of them composed by the rishi Vamadeva. The majority of the hymns are addressed to Agni and Indra. There are also hymns to Agni-Varuna, Rakshoha Agni, Vaishvanara Agni, Indra-Soma, Indra-Usha, Indra-Ashva, Indra-Brihaspati, Vayu, Usha, Savitr, the Ribhus, Dyaus-Prithivi, Surya, the Ashvins, the horse Dadhikra and Shyena, a falcon. One hymn has references to Kshetrapati, the lord of the fields, and to Sita (furrow).

Mandala 5 has eighty-seven suktas composed by various rishis, mainly Atri and his family. The suktas are to the gods Agni, the Vishvedevas, the Maruts, Indra, Dyaus-Prithivi, Mitra-Varuna, Savitr, Parjanya, Prithivi and others. There is one to induce sleep.

Mandala 6 has seventy-five suktas, most of them composed by the rishi Bharadvaja and his family. Many are prayers to Indra and Agni. Among others are hymns to Pushan, Dyaus-Prithivi, and the goddess Sarasvati. There is also a sukta in praise of cows. One hymn (6.75) refers to deified weapons of war, including drums, armour, bow, quiver, and arrows. There are hymns to Indra-Agni, Usha, the Ashvins, Savitr, Indra-Soma and Soma-Rudra.

Mandala 7 has 104 suktas, composed mostly by the rishi Vasishtha. They are mainly hymns to Indra and Agni, though there are also some to other deities including the Vishvedevas, Savitr, Rudra, Mitra-Varuna, the Ashvins, Vayu, Apah, Usha. Among others is a sukta in praise of Vishnu. There are hymns to Vasishtha and his family. There is one hymn to frogs as bringers of rain. Frogs are also compared here to those who sing praises. There is a hymn to Dadhikra, and two to Vastoshpati, the guardian of the house.

Mandalas 2 through 7 have some similarities: each is composed mainly by one family, and each begins with a group of suktas dedicated to Agni, followed by some to Indra, and after that to other deities. Another aspect of these mandalas is what seems to be a careful arrangement of the suktas, with longer hymns in the beginning, and a gradually diminishing number of verses in each. The names of the rishis are sometimes mentioned in these mandalas, whereas names of others are known from later sources. There are also some typical types of refrains within each mandala, reflecting the consistency in the style of composition.

Mandala 8 has 103 hymns and is composed by two rishi families, the Kanvas and Angirasas, as well as by other rishis. It includes eleven *valakhilya* (supplementary) hymns, which are later compositions, inserted after 8.48. This mandala does not begin with Agni hymns. The suktas include those to Indra, Agni, the Ashvins, the Adityas, Aditi, Ribhu, the Maruts, Soma and Indra-Agni. Some hymns are like riddles; thus one hymn (8.29) describes various gods without giving their names.

Mandala 9 has 114 suktas composed by more than sixty rishis. All except one are in praise of Soma, both as a deity and as the divine drink. The first half of this mandala has hymns composed mainly in the gayatri metre. In hymns 1–60, the number of verses in each stanza decreases from ten to four, but this pattern is not followed in the second part.

Soma here often refers to Soma Pavamana, the Soma juice while it is being pressed and clarified. These hymns were therefore probably collected together primarily for ritual purposes. However, there are indications that a different Soma was also meant, that which represented immortality and the divine *amrita*.

Mandala 10 has 191 suktas composed by various rishis. This is the same number of suktas as Mandala 1, showing how the whole text was carefully arranged. It has the greatest variety, both in the rishis who composed it and in its content. This mandala can be divided into three sections according to the content and type of hymn. Hymns 1–60 consist of thirteen groups composed by rishi families. Hymns 61–84 contain twelve pairs of hymns; each pair often invokes the same god, and has a certain unity. Hymns 85–191 include philosophical and other unique subjects.

Among the suktas are a mystical hymn on creation and cosmological speculations. Around six hymns have speculations on the origin of the world by a creator, different from other deities, but called by various names (10.129). Others contain various topics, including a dialogue between Yama and Yami (10.10), between Pururava and Urvashi (10.95), and other mythological dilaogues between divine beings (10.51, 52, 86, 108). There is a sukta praising the *havirdanas* (gifts of oblation), and another which attempts to call the spirit of man back from the other world. One refers to all the rivers known at the time. There is also the Purusha-sukta on the sacrifice of Purusha, the account of Sarama and the Panis, and other diverse hymns. This mandala also has some specific hymns including wedding hymns (10.85) and funeral hymns (10.14–18), and other unique hymns.

There are hymns against disease (10.163); against a demon who injured children (10.162); against enemies (10.166); against rival wives (10.145); to gain children (10.183); to preserve life (10.58.60). There are some hymns with secular topics. In one (10.34), a gambler regrets the sorrow he has brought to himself and his family. Two hymns explain the benefits of wise speech and good deeds (10.71, 117).

Most scholars agree that this mandala is the latest addition to the Rig Veda. This does not necessarily mean that they were all late compositions. Some of them may have existed earlier, but were the latest additions to the Rig. In others, the language seems to have later forms.

APRI HYMNS

These are hymns, appearing in various mandalas, that are specifically used during the sacrificial ritual.

DANASTUTIS

These are hymns or parts of hymns that refer to *dana* (gifts) given to priests. These give the names of patrons and provide socio-economic information.

SOME OTHER ASPECTS

The Rig Veda is primarily a religious text, consisting mainly of prayers to deities. Many of these prayers were used in rituals and sacrifices. Apart from numerous deities, other divine, semi-divine and demonic beings are referred to. In addition, there are several hymns which provide other information. There are indications of the geographical boundaries, rivers, mountains, plants and wild animals of those days. Different types of people as well as wars and conflicts are described. There are references to kings and rishis, and to some aspects of the politics, society and economy of those times, in the region of its composition.

The purely spiritual interpretation of the text sees these references differently.

The opening hymn of the Rig Veda is given below:

Mandala 1.1 Agni
1. I praise Agni, the chosen Priest, God, minister of sacrifice,
   The hotr, giver of wealth.
2. Worthy is Agni to be praised by living as by ancient seers.
   He shall bring the Gods here.
3. Through Agni man obtains wealth, increasing day by day,
   Most rich in heroes, glorious.
4. Agni, the perfect sacrifice which thou encompassest about
   Verily goeth to the Gods.
5. May the god Agni, sapient-minded Priest, truthful, most gloriously great,
   come here with the Gods.
6. Whatever blessing, Agni, you grant to your worshipper,
   That, Angiras, is indeed your truth.
7. To you, dispeller of the night, O Agni, day by day with prayer
   and with reverence, we come.

8. *Ruler of sacrifices, guard of Law eternal, radiant One,*
   Increasing in thine own abode.
9. *Be to us easy of approach, even as a father to his son:*
   Agni, be with us for our welfare.

(Based on the translation by R.T.H. Griffith)

The second hymn is dedicated to Vayu, and the third to the Ashvins. More examples of hymns are given in the Appendix.

THE OTHER SAMHITAS

YAJUR VEDA

The Yajur Veda consists of passages in verse and prose, arranged for the performance of yajnas (sacrifices). The term yajus can be distinguished from rik, a verse, and saman, a chant; yajus is that which is recited with the ritual. Many of the hymns in this text are taken from the Rig Veda, with some variations, but there are also some prose passages. It is the primary text for the whole sacrificial ritual. The Yajur Veda is mentioned frequently in the Brahmanas and Upanishads.

DATE

The Yajur Veda is considered later than the Rig Veda. However, the Matsya Purana and some other Puranas consider it the first Veda. While parts of it may be of ancient origin, its later date in comparison to the Rig Veda is indicated by the level of socio-economic development described in it. The caste system was further institutionalized by this time and there was a proliferation of occupations.

SHAKHAS

There are a number of different shakhas for this Veda, though they are nowhere near the original number of 101 referred to in the Mahabhashya. The two main versions of the Yajur are known as the Shukla (or 'White') Yajur Veda and the Krishna (or 'Black') Yajur Veda. The first is also known as the Vajasaneyi Samhita. Of this, texts of two shakhas are known, the Kanva and the Madhyandina, which are quite similar. Of the Black Yajur Veda, five shakhas are known: the Taittiriya (Apastamba), Kapishthala (Hiranyakesi), Katha, Kathaka, and Maitrayani (Kalapa), with four closely related recensions, known as the Kathaka Samhita, the Kapishthala–Katha Samhita, the Maitrayani Samhita and the Taittiriya Samhita.

The Vajasaneyi Madhyandina was originally prevalent in Mithila (north Bihar) while the Kanva was popular in Koshala (east UP).

PRIEST

The main priest for this text was the *adhvaryu*, and he was assisted by other priests.

TEXTS

The White and Black Yajurs differ somewhat and the outlines of both are given below.

VAJASANEYI OR SHUKLA SAMHITA (WHITE YAJUR VEDA)

This outline is based on a merging of the two recensions.

This text has prayers for the various sacrificial rituals. It has forty adhyayas, though some versions of the Kanva shakha have forty-one. In each adhyaya, there are subsections called *khandakas* or *khandikas*, each of which usually consists of a prayer or a mantra, which can be termed hymns for convenience. The prayers include riks or verses, and yajus or sacrificial formulas in prose. (Technically, both the verses and the prose passages can be termed yajus, as both are used in sacrifices.) There are frequent repetitions. A number of the riks or verses are from the Rig Veda, while some are from the Atharva Veda. Usually single verses of the Rig Veda are used, and grouped together in this text in a different way, for ritual use. The prose yajus are almost equal in number to the verse sections and are new compositions. There are approximately 1975 hymns in the Madhyandina and 2086 in the Kanva.

The prayers are grouped into anuvakas to be recited at sacrifices. Most of the first eighteen adhyayas of this text are part of the first nine sections of the Shatapatha Brahmana and are explained in detail there.

SUMMARY OF THE TEXT

Adhyayas 1 and 2 contain prayers for the Darshapurnamasa, that is, the new- and full-moon sacrifices, and the Pindapitrayajna, the offerings for *pitris* (ancestors), which is a part of them. Adhyaya 1 has thirty-one hymns and Adhyaya 2 has thirty-four.

Adhyaya 3 has the prayers for various fire sacrifices, for the laying of the fire, the morning and evening sacrifice (*agnihotra*), and the four-monthly sacrifices (*chaturmasya*). It has sixty-three hymns.

Adhyaya 4–8 have prayers for the Soma sacrifices including animal sacrifices. Some Soma sacrifices last for one day, others for several days. Several beautiful prayers are included here. The number of hymns is as follows: Adhyaya 4: thirty-seven; Adhyaya 5: forty-three; Adhyaya 6: thirty-seven; Adhyaya 7: forty-eight; Adhyaya 8: sixty-three.

Adhyayas 9–10 have prayers for the *vajapeya* and *rajasuya* sacrifices, both performed to increase the power of kings. They contain other topics, including comments on the use and efficacy of different metres.

Adhyayas 11–18 contain several prayers and sacrificial formulas for the *agnichayana* (the building of a special fire altar) and for other altars. These sections also include other topics. Among them, Adhyaya 12.1–4 refers to plants and the healing power of herbs. Adhyayas 13–14 describe various kinds of bricks used in constructing the altars, and include references to metres and songs. Adhyaya 15 deals with the fifth layer of the altar and refers to different *stomas*, *ukthas* and *samans*, all types of verses. Adhyaya 16 contains the Shatarudriya, the famous prayers to the god Rudra. Adhyaya 17 refers to bricks for building the altar, in millions and billions, and has prayers for taking possession of the altar. Adhyaya 18 ends with the symbolism of the altar. The number of hymns in these Adhyayas is as follows: Adhyaya 11: eighty-three, many with single verses; Adhyaya 12: 118; Adhyaya 13: fifty-eight; Adhyaya 14: thirty-one; Adhyaya 15: sixty-five; Adhyaya 16: sixty-six; Adhyaya 17: ninety-nine; Adhyaya 18: seventy-seven.

Adhyayas 19–21 have prayers for the Sautramani sacrifice. In this *sura* (a type of wine, not Soma) is used and is offered to the Ashvins, Sarasvati and Indra. Adhyaya 19 has ninety-five hymns, and Adhyaya 20 has ninety. Adhyaya 21, with sixty-one hymns, begins with a prayer to Varuna, and includes references to metres and songs.

Adhyayas 22–25 have prayers and instructions for the *ashvamedha*, the horse sacrifice. Only a powerful king or great conqueror could offer these prayers, which would enhance his glory. The number of hymns in these Adhyayas is as follows: Adhyaya 22: thirty-four; Adhyaya 23: sixty-five; Adhyaya 24: forty; Adhyaya 25: forty-seven.

Adhyayas 26–35 are somewhat later and are known in tradition as *khilas* (supplements or appendices). Of these, 26–29 have appendices to the prayers in the preceding sections. Adhyaya 26 has twenty-six hymns; Adhyaya 27 has forty-five; Adhyaya 28 has forty-six; Adhyaya 29 has sixty.

Adhyayas 30–31 include prayers for the *purushamedha*, the human sacrifice, and lists the people to be sacrificed. This sacrifice is generally believed to be symbolic. Each Adhyaya has twenty-two hymns.

Adhyayas 32–34 have prayers for the *sarvamedha*, the all-sacrifice or sacrifice of everything. The number of hymns in each are sixteen, ninety-seven and fifty-eight, respectively.

Adhyaya 35, with twenty-two hymns, has some funeral verses, mainly from the Rig Veda.

Adhyayas 36–39 have prayers for the *pravargya* (hot milk ceremony; explained in Chapter 10 of this book). Adhyayas 36 and 37 have twenty-one hymns each; Adhyaya 38 has twenty-eight; Adhyaya 39 has thirteen; and Adhyaya 40, the last part of the Vajasaneyi Samhita, contains the Isha Upanishad and has seventeen hymns. This is an important Upanishad and has no connection with the rest of the text.

KRISHNA OR BLACK YAJUR VEDA

The Krishna Yajur Veda only has the prayers of the first half of the Vajasaneyi Samhita. The prayers are interspersed with explanations and commentaries.

Taittiriya Samhita (Black Yajur Veda)

A summary of the Taittiriya Samhita, one of the recensions of the Krishna Yajur Veda, is given below. The text is divided into seven kandas or sections, further subdivided into prapathakas. These are subdivided into anuvakas for recitation, which for convenience can be called hymns.

Kanda 1 contains eight prapathakas.

Prapathaka 1 has prayers for the new and full moon sacrifices; these are basically for protection and abundance. They also indicate the steps of the sacrifice and the verses to be uttered as the sacrifice proceeds. In the last verse, Indra, Agni and Pushan are invoked. It has fourteen hymns.

Prapathakas 2–4 have prayers for the Soma sacrifice, including prayers for the victim for Agni and Soma and for the Soma cups, along with prayers to Indra, Soma, and other deities including Mitra, Varuna, the Ashvins, the Maruts, Parjanya, Savitr, Surya; Indra of the Shodashin, Tvashtr, Dhatr, and for the dakshina offerings. Prapathakas 2 and 3 have fourteen hymns each, while Prapathaka 4 has forty-six.

Prapathaka 5 deals with the rekindling of the fire. It has eleven hymns and begins with a story. While the devas and the asuras were in conflict, they left their riches with Agni, who desired these and made off with them. Hence, the devas had to find Agni and re-establish the fire. It describes how this is to be done, and also has prayers for this. It has eleven hymns.

Prapathaka 6 begins with prayers for the new and full moon sacrifices, and also comments on them. It has twelve hymns.

Prapathaka 7 continues with explanations of the new and full moon sacrifices. From the seventh hymn, prayers begin for the vajapeya sacrifice. There are a total of thirteen hymns.

Prapathaka 8 is concerned with the rajasuya sacrifice for kings. It includes explanations and prayers, and has twenty-two hymns. The last hymn also prays to remove evil from both the dwelling place, and from oneself.

Kanda 2, with six prapathakas, includes (in Prapathaka 1) aspects of the special animal sacrifices. It describes the animals to be offered depending on the results desired. For instance, the one who desires prosperity should offer a white animal to the god Vayu, while he who desires offspring should offer a hornless goat to Prajapati. The devas or gods too are described as making offerings. When the sun did not shine, an offering of ten bulls by the devas restored its brilliance or, on another occasion, the offering of a white cow. While the first ten hymns are descriptive, the eleventh and last is a prayer.

Prapathakas 2–4 deal with special sacrifices.

Prapathaka 2 includes descriptions of offerings that should be made for offspring, disputes, and various other occasions. Offerings are generally of a sacrificial cake (*purodasha*) on potsherds (*kapala*) to various deities. It has twelve hymns, the last being a prayer, the others descriptive.

Prapathakas 3 and 4 continue with the special sacrifices, describing the offerings to be made, interspersed with some prayers to be recited. These have fourteen hymns each.

Prapathakas 5 and 6 deal with the new and full moon sacrifices.

Prapathaka 5 explains how and why Indra performed these sacrifices. It begins with a description of Vishvarupa, son of Tvashtr, who was the domestic priest of the gods, and the son of the sister of the asuras. Vishvarupa has three heads, one which drank Soma, one which drank sura, and one which ate food. Indra feared his strength and cut off his heads, thus creating enemies. Indra then made these offerings to the new and full moons. This ritual is described as the chariot leading to the devas, which is the direct way to come in contact with them. There is a description of how the sacrifice should proceed and what is to be said during the ritual. Prapathaka 5 has twelve hymns and ends with a prayer.

Prapathaka 6 continues with the description and has twelve hymns, of which the last two are prayers.

Kanda 3 has five prapathakas.

Prapathaka 1 contains further comments on the Soma sacrifice and on how to proceed with it. It states that Soma is the king of metres and, apart from describing aspects of the sacrifice, it relates the metres to various deities. Soma is also the lord of plants. Among other things, this prapathaka describes the role of the adhvaryu, the special Yajur Veda priest, and how samans and *stotras* (basic unit of verses to be sung) are to be used, and when the *ukthya* or *atiratra* sacrifices (both Soma sacrifices, explained in Chapter 10 of this book) are to be performed. Some prayers are included. Prapathakas 2 and 3 are similar. The last few hymns of Prapathaka 3 focus on the special animal offerings. These three prapathakas have eleven hymns each.

Prapathaka 4 deals with the optional and occasional offerings. It begins by stating that if the sacrificial offering is too large, the sacrifice is rendered unsuccessful. It also describes conflicts between asuras and devas, and explains the power of the metres. It indicates when offerings should be made to minor deities such as Dhatr, Anumati, Raka, Sinivali and Kuhu. In one passage, it indicates that the gandharvas and apsaras are symbolic of different aspects of life—death is the gandharva, the apsaras are his offspring, or 'love is the gandharva, his apsaras are his thoughts'. It includes a prayer to Vastoshpati, god of the dwelling place, and has eleven hymns.

Prapathaka 5 has miscellaneous supplementary comments on sacrifices. One interesting passage (3.5.4) asks protection from the very gods who were destroying and stealing the sacrifice.

Kanda 4 has seven prapathakas, mainly concerned with the preparation of the fire altar.

Prapathakas 1 and 2, each with eleven hymns, focus on the placing of the fire in the fire pan made of clay, and the preparation of the ground for the fire. There are prayers and beautiful descriptions of Agni. There are references to the metres and to the healing power of plants.

Prapathakas 3 and 4 deal with the layers of bricks of which the fire altar is to built, and have comments and prayers. Importance is given to the metres and samans. Prapathaka 3 has thirteen hymns; Prapathaka 4 has twelve hymns. One of these gives the early names of the months, different from those used later.

Prapathaka 5 has prayers and offerings to Rudra and includes the Shatarudriya, a prayer to the god Rudra that is still popular. It has eleven hymns.

Prapathaka 6 begins with prayers for the preparation and piling of the fire. Indra and Agni are often invoked. From the sixth hymn, prayers for the ashvamedha begin. This prapathaka has nine hymns.

Prapathaka 7 continues with prayers for the piling of the fire altar, as well as for the ashvamedha. There are fifteen hymns.

Kanda 5 has seven prapathakas related to the building of the fire altar and the ashvamedha. It comments on the offerings to be made and how the rituals should proceed. Prapathaka 1, with eleven hymns, includes the apri hymn for the ashvamedha (5.1.11). Prapathaka 2 has twelve hymns, with the last two for the ashvamedha.

Prapathaka 3 describes how the second and later layers of bricks should be laid and what words or mantras should be uttered while laying them. It refers to conflicts between devas and asuras. It says that 'whatever the gods did, the asuras did', and that when the gods and asuras were in conflict, the gods were fewer, the asuras more. It also comments on the ashvamedha or horse sacrifice. It has a total of twelve hymns.

Prapathaka 4 continues with descriptions and comments on the piling of the fire altar. It refers to plants and food, including 'wild sesame and groats of *gavidhuka* grass'. It has twelve hymns.

Prapathaka 5 again continues with descriptions of the piling of the fire altar, the type of bricks to be used, and the animals to be offered to the altar and in the ashvamedha. It has twenty-four hymns. Hymns 11–24 are on the animals offered in the ashvamedha or horse sacrifice. Prapathaka 6 continues with the piling of the altar. Hymn 6 refers to Atharvan as Prajapati; it also says that Dadhyanch Atharvana is the fire, his bones are the bricks. Ashvamedha verses continue from Hymns 11–23, and there are a total of twenty-three hymns.

Prapathaka 7 continues with the piling of the altar, and points out the importance of the deity. It includes prayers to Agni. Hymns 11–26 continue with ashvamedha verses; there are twenty-six hymns in total.

Kanda 6, with six prapathakas, has an exposition of the Soma sacrifice and of the dakshina and other offerings.

Prapathaka 1 begins with the description of the making of a hall with beams pointing to the east, and the sacrificer purifying and consecrating himself for the ritual. There are again passages on metres. One verse states that metres are the descendants of Suparni (6.1.6). There is an interesting passage on musical instruments, which states 'speech went away from the gods, not being willing to serve in the sacrifice. She entered the trees. It is the voice of the trees that is heard in the drum, the lute and the flute' (6.1.4). There are also passages on Soma, and how it is bought in exchange for a cow or obtained from heaven. This prapathaka has eleven hymns.

Prapathaka 2 continues with the exposition of the Soma sacrifice, through descriptions and explanations of various aspects. One hymn recounts another conflict between devas and asuras. At this time, the devas themselves began to quarrel as they could not accept anyone as the chief deity. They then separated into five groups: Agni with the Vasus, Soma with the Rudras, Indra with the Maruts, Varuna with the Adityas, and Brihaspati with the Vishvedevas. The three citadels of the asuras—of iron, silver, and gold—are also mentioned. It is said that the devas made an arrow, of which Agni was the point, Soma the socket, Vishnu the shaft; it was shot by Rudra and the asuras were driven away. This prapathaka has eleven hymns.

Prapathaka 3 continues with the exposition of the Soma sacrifice. There are passages on the altars, the adhvaryu, and other priests, and on the sacrificial post; there is a reference to the Sadhyas, a group of gods who existed before any other living being. They offered Agni as a sacrifice to Agni for there was nothing else to offer. Another passage states that by means of Agni as hotr, the devas defeated the asuras. This prapathaka has eleven hymns.

Prapathaka 4 continues with explaining the Soma sacrifice. Once again, it states that 'whatever the gods did as the sacrifice, that the asuras did'. There are passages on the Soma cups to be offered to the deities. One passage refers to Brihaspati as the purohita of the devas, and Chanda and Marka as those of the asuras. Both the devas and the asuras had holy power, Brahman. Sacrifice is said to be a means for overpowering the asuras. This prapathaka has eleven hymns.

Prapathaka 5 continues with explanations and comments on the Soma sacrifice. In a reverse of the usual story of Indra killing Vritra, it states that Vritra bestowed the ukthya on Indra. On the cups (*grahas*) to be offered, it explains that 'the dhruva cup is the life of the sacrifice, it is drawn the last of the cups'. Aditi, the Adityas, and Vivasvant are mentioned. It also refers to the different types of cups to be offered and the results obtained. This prapathaka has eleven hymns.

Prapathaka 6 has explanations of the dakshina and other offerings, including the Shodashin sacrifice. In one passage, there is a suggestion that the sacrificial victim could be released and not killed. Thus 6.6.6 says that Indra caused Manu to sacrifice with his wife; after she had been encircled by fire, he let her go; therewith Manu prospered in that he lets go (the victim).

Kanda 7 has five prapathakas, concerning various sacrifices.

Prapathaka 1 deals with the Soma and other sacrifices, including the Pancharatra and the ashvamedha. It has twenty hymns.

Prapathaka 2 continues with the Soma sacrifices. From 7.2.11, the ashvamedha prayers continue. This too has twenty hymns.

Prapathaka 3 continues with the longer Soma sacrifices. The power of the sacrifice in overcoming the asuras is again mentioned. Thus one passage says that Indra was afraid of the asuras, but by the Agnistut he burned away the evil. The ashvamedha prayers are continued from the eleventh hymn. This prapathaka has twenty hymns.

Prapathaka 4 continues with explanations of longer Soma sacrifices. There are references to rites of twenty-four nights, thirty nights, thirty-two nights, as well as thirty-three, thirty-six, forty-nine nights and one year. There is a passage on the atiratra sacrifice while the twelfth hymn continues with the ashvamedha prayers. This prapathaka has twenty-two hymns. A riddle too is provided here.

Prapathaka 5 explains various sacrifices, including the *gavam ayana*, a Soma sacrifice that lasts for one year. Some samans are named. A passage says that when the gods had come to an end, their power and strength departed. They won them again by the *krosha* saman. One hymn (5.10) refers to a specific fire, the *marjaliya*. From the eleventh hymn, prayers and explanations for the ashvamedha are continued. Hymn 5.25 explains the symbolism of the ashvamedha horse, similar to that in the Upanishads.

The first hymn of the Yajur Veda, common to both texts, is given below. This is basically a prayer for protection and abundance.

1.1.1
For food thee, for strength thee!
Ye are winds, ye are approachers.
Let the god Savitr impel you to the most excellent offering.
O invincible ones, swell with the share of the gods,
Full of strength, of milk, rich in offspring, free from sickness, from disease.
Let no thief, no evil worker, have control over you.
Let Rudra's dart avoid you.
Abide you, numerous, with this lord of cattle.
Do thou protect the cattle of the sacrificer.

(Translated by A.B. Keith)

THE SAMA VEDA

The Sama Veda is usually the third in the list of Vedas but is considered second in importance to the Rig Veda. Its main purpose is to teach the musical method of chanting the verses (saman refers to 'melodies' or 'music'), particularly for the sacrifice. The Sama is more closely connected with the Rig Veda than the other two Samhitas. Its importance is indicated in the Bhagavad Gita (10.22), where Krishna says, 'Among the Vedas, I am the Sama.' The Sama chants form an essential part of Vedic ritual. The Chhandogya Upanishad (1.1, 2) states it is the essence of the Rig Veda. The Brihad-devata says, 'one who knows the samans knows the secret of the Veda'. The Rig Veda states, 'The samans go to him who are awake.'

However, some of the Dharma Shastras, for instance that of Manu, refers to the impurity of the Sama. That of Apastamba states that Veda study must be interrupted at the sound of the barking of dogs, the braying of donkeys, the howling of wolves and jackals, the hooting of owls, the sound of musical instruments, weeping, and the tone of samans. This probably does not refer to the Sama Veda as used in ritual but to a use of Sama tunes in a different context.

The Samavidhana Brahmana refers to the use of the Sama in magic, and magic was a practice that was often condemned.

The Sama has approximately 1800 riks in two parts: the Purvarchika and Uttararchika. Most of the verses are those found in the Rig Veda, with some variations. There are complete hymns, parts of hymns, and even single verses of the Rig Veda. However, these have been rearranged and grouped together differently, and are not in the order found in the Rig Veda. The Sama text is specially compiled for the Soma sacrifice. The method by which the samans are introduced in rituals is described in the section on sacrifices in Chapter 10 of this book.

ADDITIONAL TEXTS

The Sama has some additional texts. The Aranyaka Samhita is attached to the Purvarchika. There are also four *ganas* (songbooks), which indicate how the verses are to be sung and used in rituals.

MODIFICATION OF RIG VEDIC VERSES

In the Sama Veda, Rig Vedic verses are modified for chanting. This is done in several stages.

First, a mantra is chosen from the Rig Veda. In the Sama, it is placed in a different context. The words are not changed but the accents are marked as 1, 2, 3 whereas in the Rig, vertical and horizontal lines are used for accents. This first stage forms the Sama *yoni* or *adhar*, the base for further modifications from which the melody is developed. The text of the Sama Veda consists of these yonis.

The next stage in turning the yonis or basic verses into chants is indicated in the ganas or songbooks. This is done by modifications of the yoni. The existing syllables of the mantra are prolonged, modified or repeated. In addition, certain *stobhas* may be added. Stobhas are sounds without any particular meaning, such as *huva*, *hova*, *hoi*, and others. Hence the ganas, though based on the Sama Veda Samhita, are quite different from the yoni. Each song is given a name in the ganas.

A certain stanza or yoni is usually associated with a particular melody but, sometimes, can be used with other melodies. Thus, one Samayoni mantra can be transposed into several songs, with varying modifications. The first Sama Veda mantra has three tunes: Gotamasya *parka*, Kashyapasya *parhisha* and another Gotamasya *parka*. In this way, there are many more ganas than yonis, and theoretically any number of samans could be formed. The 585 riks of the Purvarchika are sung to at least double the number of tunes. The Uttararchika has verses which are often grouped in triads. Usually, each of the triads were sung together in one melody, though these melodies could vary. In the Kauthuma recension, 2722 melodies or songs have been counted and in the Jaiminiya, 3681. There may have been many more.

DATE

The Sama Veda is considered later than the Rig Veda as it reuses and rearranges parts of Rig Vedic verses. A few analysts and writers on the text believe that it is the Rig Veda that borrowed from an already existing Sama but this is unlikely. The Rig Veda represents an earlier stage when ritual use was not firmly established. However, some aspects of it may predate the Rig.

According to Maurice Winternitz, the origin of the melodies must have been much earlier than their codification, or their being attached to hymns for the sacrifice. Some may have been used in semi-religious songs, others by shaman-like magicians or priests. Frits Staal, among other scholars, also agrees that the melodies were probably already in use before they were attached to the Rig verses.

The Sama may be older than the Taittiriya and Vajasaneyi Yajur texts, as saman chants appear there, the same as those in the Sama but different from the Rig. However, Staal believes the Sama must have been composed 'in coordination with Yajurvedins' as it is for use in the Yajur Vedic *shrauta* ritual. He dates it to the 'Kuru period'—the time when the Kurus were the dominant kingdom.

Though the Purvarchika, the first part of the Sama Veda, is generally considered earlier than the Uttararchika or second part, W. Caland and some other scholars feel the Uttararchika can be placed before the Purvarchika, at least in its earliest version. According to this theory, initially the verses were taken from the Rig Veda, modified and set to tunes. The Uttararchika was then composed to collect the chants accompanying various rituals. This had many different versions in the various Sama Veda schools. To make memorization of the melodies and chants to be used easier, the Purvarchika listing the yonis was composed, along with the Aranyaka Samhita. The two ganas or songbooks, which had extensive rules, were probably later than the Brahmanas and the sutras.

Though the melodies could have been pre Rig Vedic, the majority, including all the village songs, had Sanskrit names such as Rathantara. But the names of some forest songs could have been non-Sanskrit in origin, indicating the existence and intermixture of different groups of people.

SHAKHAS OR RECENSIONS

The Sama Veda had a number of different recensions. Patanjali's Mahabhashya says the Sama Veda had 'a thousand paths'. The Puranas also mention a thousand paths. This may refer to the many different options and modes of singing in the ganas, which could have led to a number of different shakhas. Thirteen shakhas are listed in texts, but only three are known today. These are the Kauthuma, Jaiminiya or Talavakra, and Ranayaniya. The exact number of verses varies in the different recensions. The Ranayaniya recension was commented on by Sayana, and has been translated by several people from the 19th century onwards. The Ranayaniya has minor variations from the Kauthuma recension. In the 1930s a living Sama

Veda tradition of the Kauthuma branch was discovered in Baroda, Kumbakonam, Thanjavur, Chidambaram, and Trichinapoly; a rare Jaiminiya tradition has been found in Kerala, known to the Nambudiri brahmanas. These two traditions are different: the melodies had many insertions and replacements.

The Jaiminiya as used in chants by the Nambudiri brahmanas has ganas from unknown sources. Sabhapati's *Dharana-lakshanam*, a late text, provides information on their methods of singing and making notations.

COMPOSERS: ARRANGERS AND RISHIS

RISHIS

The rishis and others associated with the composition of the verses are listed in the anukramanis. As most of the verses are taken from the Rig Veda, the rishis too are generally the same.

ROLE OF THE PRIEST

The *udgatr* is the main priest for the Sama Veda. The Sama text provided the words for the udgatr priest but the music for the chants is indicated only in the ganas. The udgatr had to memorize the melody connected with the verses in the Purvarchika and the other verses connected with those melodies, found in the Uttararchika. He had to chant them as required, during the ritual. He was assisted by other priests.

METRE

The majority of verses are in the gayatri metre, or in mixed *pragatha* stanzas, which include gayatri and jagati lines.

SAMANS OR MELODIES

These are indicated in the attached ganas and referred to in the Yajur and later texts.

SUMMARY OF THE TEXT

As mentioned earlier, both the Kauthuma and Ranayaniya recensions have two parts, the Purvarchika (or Archika) and the Uttararchika. These two recensions are very similar, and some details regarding their nature and contents are given here.

Purvarchika

The Purvarchika, without the attached Aranyaka Samhita, has approximately 583–85 single stanzas (riks). The number varies slightly in different manuscripts. Of these, forty-five stanzas are not from the Rig Veda. These verses are grouped together in six prapathakas or sections, which are further subdivided. Each prapathaka is divided into two sections and has ten dashats (a dashat equals a decade, but not every dashat contains ten verses, though many do), except for the last prapathaka, which has nine. In reality, a prapathaka contains between ninety-six and ninety-nine single-line verses. The verses in the Purvarchika are arranged partly according to the metre used and partly according to the gods addressed.

Prapathaka 1 has ninety-six single stanzas, all dedicated to Agni. The first verse reads: 'agna-aa-yaahi-vitaye-grinaano-havyadaataye-ni-hotaa-satsi-barhishi.' (1)

This becomes the yoni or seed mantra. In chanting in Gotama's text, this becomes: 'Ognaai aayaahi voitoyaa i toyaa i grinaano ha-vyaadatoyaa i toyaa i naai hotaasaa tsaa i baa oau hovaa hishi.'

The song thus developed with the addition and change of syllables is known as Gotama's parka. Another different parka is attributed to Kashyapa.

To indicate how verses are taken from the Rig Veda, the correspondence between the first five mantras is given below:

Sama 1.1 = Rig 6.16.10
Sama 1.2 = Rig 6.16.1
Sama 1.3 = Rig 1.12.1
Sama 1.4 = Rig 6.16.34
Sama 1.5 = Rig 8.73.1

In Prapathaka 2, dashats 1 and 2 are dedicated to Agni, and the next eight to Indra along with some other deities. Prapathaka 3 is dedicated mainly to Indra, along with some other deities. Prapathaka 4 is again mostly dedicated to Indra, along with some other deities. Prapathaka 5 has verses mainly to Indra, Agni, and Soma, though other deities including the Adityas and the Maruts are mentioned. Prapathaka 6 has nine dashats, all dedicated to Soma. There are ninety-six verses in all, as in Prapathaka 1. The Aranyaka Samhita is attached to the end of this archika.

Uttararchika

The Uttararchika has between 1174 and 1225 single-line verses grouped together in varying combinations. Most of the groups have three stanzas each (triplets or triads). The others have varying numbers of stanzas, usually between one and ten. The verses are arranged in nine prapathakas, which are further subdivided into two to three sections known as *ardha* (half), with a total of twenty-two sections. Each section has between nine and twenty-three groups of verses. The total number of groups of verses is approximately four hundred.

Some of the single stanzas of Part 1 (Purvarchika) are repeated in the Part 2 (Uttararchika).

The first stanza in a group usually occurs in the Purvarchika, and has a connection with the other stanzas in the group. The Uttararchika verses are arranged according to the order in which they would be used in sacrifices, particularly in Soma sacrifices. In both sections, the melody is more important than the meaning.

Some more details are given below. The number of verse groups and of the triads in each section are given in brackets.

Prapathaka 1 has two sections. Section 1 has verses dedicated to Soma, Agni, Mitra-Varuna, Indra and Indra-Agni (twenty-three groups of which fifteen are triplets).

In Section 2, the first twelve triplets are dedicated to Indra. The thirteenth is to Agni, the fourteenth to Usha, and the sixteenth to the Ashvins, while the rest are to Soma (twenty-two groups, all triplets).

Prapathaka 2, Section 1, groups 1–5, 10–11, and 15–17 are dedicated to Soma with three verses each. Several are dedicated to Indra, and others to Agni, Mitra-Varuna, and Indra-Agni (nineteen groups).

In Prapathaka 2, Section 2, the majority of verses are to Soma, followed by those to Indra. There are two hymns to Agni and one each to Mitra-Varuna, the Maruts, and Indra-Agni (nineteen groups, seventeen triplets).

Prapathaka 3, Section 1 has verses mainly to Soma, followed by those to Indra. Other groups are to Agni, Mitra-Varuna, and Indra-Agni (twenty-two groups, with seventeen triplets).

In Prapathaka 3, Section 2, most verses are to Soma; others are to Indra, Indra-Agni, Agni, and Mitra-Varuna (twenty-two groups with seventeen triplets).

In Prapathaka 4, Section 1, most verses are dedicated to Soma. Agni, Mitra, Varuna, Aryaman, Indra, and Indra-Agni are other deities here (twenty-four groups; eighteen triplets; two groups are rather long with ten verses each).

In Prapathaka 4, Section 2, the majority of verses are to Soma, others are to Agni, Indra, Indra-Agni, Mitra-Varuna (fourteen groups, eleven triplets).

Prapathaka 5, Section 1 has verses mainly to Soma but also to Indra and Agni (twenty groups, fourteen triplets; three groups have nine verses each).

In Prapathaka 5, Section 2, the verses are mostly to Soma; there are some to Indra and one to Agni. There is a reference to Parjanya in hymn 13 (twenty-three groups, fourteen triplets).

In Prapathaka 6, Section 1, the verses are to various deities including Agni, Indra, Soma, the Adityas, and Surya (eleven groups, eight triplets).

Prapathaka 6, Section 2 has verses to Agni, Soma, and Indra (twenty groups, fourteen triplets).

Prapathaka 6, Section 3 has verses to Soma, Indra, Surya, Mitra-Varuna, Sarasvan, Sarasvati; group 10 has verses to Savitar, Brahmanaspati, and Agni (eighteen groups, ten triplets).

Prapathaka 7, Section 1 has verses mainly to Agni but also to Indra and Soma (sixteen groups, twelve triplets).

Prapathaka 7, Section 2 has verses to Agni (fifteen groups, twelve triplets).

Prapathaka 7, Section 3 has verses to Indra, Agni, Indra-Agni, Varuna, Vishvakarma, Soma, Pushan, the Maruts, the Vishvedevas, Dyaus-Prithivi; the Ribhus and the god Rudra are also mentioned (twenty-one groups; the lengths of the groups vary from one to four verses/lines).

Prapathaka 7, Section 1 has verses to Agni, Indra, Vishnu, Vayu, Soma; there are references to Vritra (fourteen groups, twelve triplets).

Prapathaka 7, Section 2 has verses to Indra, Agni, Indra-Agni, Vishnu, and Soma (nineteen groups, twelve triplets).

Prapathaka 8, Section 1 has verses to Agni, Indra, Vishnu, Vayu, and Soma; there are references to Vritra (fourteen groups, twelve triplets).

Prapathaka 8, Section 2 has verses to Indra, Agni, Indra-Agni, Vishnu, and Soma (nineteen groups, twelve triplets).

Prapathaka 8, Section 3 has verses to Agni, Soma, Indra, Usha, and the Ashvins (eighteen groups, fourteen triplets).

Prapathaka 9, Section 1 has verses to Soma, Indra, Agni, the Maruts, and Surya; it also refers to Mitra, Varuna, Aryaman, and Vayu; most of the verses are to Indra (eighteen groups, sixteen triplets).

Prapathaka 9, Section 2 has hymns mostly to Agni but also to Indra, Vata, Vena, Apah, and the devas; other deities including Surya are mentioned (thirteen groups, seven triplets).

Prapathaka 9, Section 3 has hymns mainly to Indra and Soma with references to other deities including Brihaspati, Varuna, the Maruts, Aditya and Pushan (nine groups, all triplets).

In another system of division, the Purvarchika is divided into kandas and the Uttararchika into adhyayas, as follows:

Purvarchika

1. Agneya Kanda: This has 114 verses mainly addressed to Agni but some to other deities. It is divided into twelve sections.
2. Aindra Kanda: This has 352 verses mainly addressed to Indra but also to some other deities.
3. Pavamana Kanda: This has 119 verses divided into eleven sections, addressed to Soma.
4. Aranyaka Kanda: This has fifty-five verses divided into five sections. It has verses to various deities but is more philosophical than the rest. (This is an addition to the Purvarchika, and corresponds with the Aranyaka Samhita.)

Uttararchika

This has twenty-one adhyayas, some of which are divided into sections. There are 1225 verses in total. They are addressed to various deities.

Ganas

The ganas or songbooks do not form part of the Sama Veda Samhita but, as indicated earlier, are essential for its use. The matter in them was perhaps once taught orally and later written down. There are four ganas. The first two are together called Purvagana (first songbook) or Prakritigana (principal songbook) and include the *Gramageyagana*, songs to be sung in the village, and the *Aranyakagana*, songs of the forest. Each of the Purvarchika verses forms the base of one or more chants in the Gramageyagana. In the Aranyakagana, verses of the Aranyaka Samhita are used interspersed with some based on the Purvarchika. Stobhas (syllables without meaning) are used in many chants and, at times, comprise entire chants. The Aranyakagana has five *parvans* or sections: *arka*, *dvandva*, *vrata*, and *shukriya*, with a supplementary *parishishta* at the end. The next two songbooks, Uhagana and Uhyagana, are known as Uttaragana (subsequent songbook) or Vikriti-gana, those derived from the first. The name Uhyagana is an abbreviated form of Uhyarahasyagana, and is related to the mystical songs of the Aranyakagana.

The two Uttaragana texts present Purvagana chants in a different form. Their organization and the order of the chants is based on their sequence and use in the Soma rituals. The Uha and Uhya ganas are each divided into seven sections. The first five are according to the length of the rituals, and are known by the names of the rituals for which they are used. They are: *dasharatra*, *samvatsara*, *ekaha*, *ahina*, and *sattra*. The next is the *prayashchitta*, which includes samans sung for expiation of sins, and *kshudra*, for the fulfilment of wishes. In some versions, there are only six sections.

The ganas are important in the history of music in India as they provide notes and melodies. The music form of Dhrupad traces its origin to the Sama Veda, though Dhrupad actually arose much later.

Several texts throw further light on the Sama, among them many of the Brahmanas attached to the Sama, as well as Upanishads and later texts. Some of these are described in Chapter 2 of this book.

ATHARVA VEDA

The Atharva Veda is the fourth and last Vedic Samhita. This Veda is also known by other names. It is sometimes called the Brahma Veda, though this is a late name. Atharvan-Angirasa is an early name of the Atharva Veda, which occurs once in the text and several times in the Brahmanas. The term Atharvana (Veda) occurs in the Chhandogya Upanishad, and is earlier than the term Atharva Veda, which came to be used later. Bhrigvangirasah is another name of this Veda, from Bhrigu and Angirasa.

Some of the Rig Vedic hymns are repeated in the Atharva and, according to estimates, around one-seventh of the verses are the same as in the Rig. Around one-sixth of the text is in prose.

Atharva hymns include a number of different topics and can be prayers to deities, or incantations and spells. There are some beautiful prayers to Rig Vedic deities, as well as to others. Overall, the text deals with health, prosperity, and the daily concerns of people, and not with grand sacrifices. A major part of the text consists of songs and spells. Several of these deal with the healing of diseases and include detailed descriptions of the body, and it is therefore considered the first text in India containing aspects of medicine. Diseases are sometimes personified, and hymns are addressed to them, while in other cases, there are spells to banish demons considered responsible for ill-health. There are prayers to curative herbs, or to healing waters and fires, chants for health and long life and for harmony within the family. There are spells to win someone's love, or for protection from demons and from people with evil intentions. There are hymns dedicated to the protection and blessing of kings, as well as hymns that are battle chants and songs of war.

There are also some philosophical hymns, which deal with creation and the origin of the world. Atharva Vedic prayers are used at births, marriages, funerals, and other ceremonies. Though the Atharva Veda is used in the sacrificial ritual, it does not have the same sanctity as the other three Vedas. The hymns and verses used in sacrifices were probably added so that the text could be used along with the other three Vedas, and recognized as a real Veda. Most of the hymns are used in *griha* or household rituals and not in shrauta or Soma sacrifices.

As Winternitz says: 'It is an invaluable source of knowledge of the real popular belief as yet uninfluenced by the priestly religion, of the faith in numberless spirits, imps, ghosts, and demons of every kind, and of the witchcraft, so eminently important for ethnology and for the history of religion.' Though brahmanical literature was generally against witchcraft or magic, according to the Manu Smriti (11.33): 'Without hesitation the brahmana shall make use of the sacred texts of the Atharva Veda; the word indeed is the weapon of the brahmana; therewith may he kill his enemies.' The Atharva has numerous hymns to protect brahmanas.

Parallels between the Atharva Veda and Shamanic, Mayan, and German Merseburg magic incantations and other magical traditions have been found, and aspects of the Atharva Veda later occur in the Tantras.

DATE

Most of the hymns have some similarity in language and metre to the Rig Veda, with later aspects. The metrical rules are not followed strictly, as they are in the Rig Veda. The prose sections are similar in language to those in the Brahmanas. However, language and metre alone cannot lead to a conclusion regarding a later date, as it could merely reflect a difference between popular and priestly compositions. However, its references to different regions and to later socio-economic aspects indicate a post–Rig Vedic date. There are also philosophical hymns, which almost reach the high philosophy of the Upanishads. Of the twenty kandas, the nineteenth and twentieth seem to be later.

The songs of magic and the various charms were probably very ancient but do not seem to appear in their original form here; rather, they appear in a version rewritten by brahmanas. Despite its rewriting, the text reflects popular tradition. Hermann Oldenberg felt that the oldest parts of the Atharva were the prose sections. According to Winternitz, 'numerous pieces of the Atharva Veda date back to the same dim prehistoric times as the oldest songs of the Rig Veda'. Maurice Bloomfield feels the charms can be dated to the Indo-European period. The text has also been related to an Indo-Iranian period. Athravan is a term for a fire priest in the Avesta, the literature of Zoroastrianism. Athar may also be related to *atar*, the Avestan (Iranian) term for fire. According to the scholar Martin Haug, the Avesta knows some Atharva collection under the name Apam Aivishtis.

Though the final version of the Atharva is certainly fairly late, one cannot refer to an Atharva Veda period, as there are both early and late elements. According to tradition, Paippalada and Vaidharbhi, who are associated with the text, lived at the time of Hiranyanabha of the Ikshvaku dynasty.

The later Kaushika Sutra describes the practices connected with the Atharva Veda hymns and complements the text.

SHAKHAS

Nine shakhas of the Atharva are listed in Shaunaka's Charanavyuha: Paippalada, Stauda, Mauda, Shaunakiya, Jajala, Jalada, Kuntapa, Brahmavada, Devadarsha. The Atharva Veda is known today in two recensions belonging to two shakhas, Shaunaka and Paippalada. The Shaunakiya recension consists of 731 hymns, with about six thousand verses, divided into twenty books or sections. The Shaunaka is known from various parts of India. Its oral traditions had been maintained in Gujarat, and recently revived in parts of south India. The Paippalada recension has been found both in Kashmir and in Orissa. The Paippalada is slightly longer, though it has very few vratya hymns, and excludes the funeral hymns.

COMPOSERS

The joint name Atharva-Angirasa is related to two aspects of the text, and connected with the names of two people, Bhishaj Atharvana and Ghora Angirasa. Atharvan is thought to refer to the healing practices described in this Veda, and Angirasa to its negative spells. Atharvan is also an ancient priest. In the Rig Veda, he is said to have produced Agni or fire, and brought order through sacrifices. He was the messenger of Vivasvat. According to the Atharva Veda, Atharvan was a companion of the gods. Possibly, he was the head of a family of real or mythical priests. Atharvan is also used as a generic term for a priest, while Atharvans, in plural, are a class of pitris or ancestors, who live in heaven. Dadhyanch was descended from Atharvan. According to the

Bhagavata Purana, Atharvan married Shanti, daughter of the rishi Kardama, and was responsible for spreading the practice of yajnas (sacrifices) in the world. Both Atharvan and Angirasa are considered mythic fire priests.

The first few suktas are attributed to Atharva. Some hymns are also ascribed to other rishis, among them Kaushika, Vasishtha and Kashyapa. The composers of the hymns are not mentioned in the text. The later Sarvanukramani provides a list of composers.

ARRANGER

The traditional arranger is Vyasa, as for the other Samhitas.

PRIEST

The brahman priest represents this Veda. He is assisted by other priests.

SUMMARY OF THE TEXT

A summary of the Shaunakiya recension of the text is given below. As mentioned earlier, this has twenty kandas. In the first eighteen kandas, hymns seem to have been arranged according to a plan. From Kanda 1 through 4, the number of verses in each hymn show a gradual increase in succession. Kandas 1–7 have short hymns with varied content. Kandas 8–12 have long hymns with varied content. From Kandas 13 through 18, each deals mainly with a specific topic.

In Kanda 1, most hymns have four verses each. There are a total of thirty-five hymns. The text begins with a prayer to Vachaspati for divine knowledge. Other deities mentioned in this section are the waters (Apah), Indra, Agni, Brihaspati, Soma, Parjanya, Prithivi, Mitra, Varuna, Pushan, the Adityas, the Vishvedevas, Aryaman, Savitr, and Dyaus-Prithivi. Many of the gods are invoked in prayers or charms against various diseases including fever, headache, cough, jaundice, and leprosy. The content of the hymns is quite varied. Some are prayers for the destruction of demons such as Yatudanas and Kimidins, and for enemies such as the dasyus (a group of people, discussed further in Chapter 7 of this book). There are prayers for protection, prosperity, health, and happiness made to various deities, as well as a specific prayer for protection from arrows and enemies. One hymn is a prayer to free a sinner from the anger of the god Varuna.

Interesting are two hymns, 1.29 and 1.30, which include a charm to secure the supremacy of a dethroned king and a benediction for a king at his consecration. Among other hymns are a spell for childbirth, a prayer for happiness for children, a woman's prayer against a rival, a young man's love-charm, a charm to become invisible and a prayer to ensure long life and glory.

In Kanda 2, most of the hymns have five verses each. There are thirty-six hymns in all, which again elucidate miscellaneous topics. The first hymn (2.1) looks at the highest element, the prime cause of all things. There are some general prayers for protection against enemies as well as prayers and charms for the cure of diseases. The prayers also indicate the use of amulets worn for protection, health, and freedom from disease. Among other interesting hymns are a prayer to ensure success in gambling, a beautiful prayer against fear, and a prayer for the long and happy life of a child. There is a prayer to bring a wonderful husband to an unmarried girl. The gods prayed to include Indra, Agni, Bhaga, Soma, Aryaman, Savitr, and others.

In Kanda 3, most of the hymns have six verses each. There are a total of thirty-one hymns on many diverse and interesting topics. There are prayers and charms for the cure of diseases, for prosperity, and against enemies. There are blessings for a newly built house, a newly dug water channel and a cattle pen. Other interesting hymns are a prayer for the new year, a morning prayer invoking blessings of various deities, a merchant's prayer for success in his business, and a prayer to the plough. There are other prayers for success in battle, and for the restoration or increase in the strength of a king. There are charms to secure love and submission, bring love or harmony in marriage, defeat rivals, cure a woman's sterility, ensure the birth of boys, and several other charms and prayers on varied topics.

In Kanda 4, most of the hymns have seven verses each. There are forty hymns in all. This section begins with a hymn which reveals cosmological and mythical ideas. Some hymns are in praise of various deities including Agni, Indra, Dyaus-Prithivi, Mitra-Varuna, Varuna alone as an omniscient god, the Maruts, Bhava and Sarva, Vayu, and Savitr. There are also hymns to Vak and Manyu, and to the Unknown God. There are charms and prayers for protection, health, freedom from enemies and from various evils. Among many others are a charm to heal broken bones, to bring rain, and against the effects of poison. Two interesting charms are against tigers, wolves, thieves and other dangers, and to acquire superhuman powers of sight. Two hymns are benedictions for a king, and one for cows. There is also a charm for success in gambling.

In Kanda 5, there are hymns with eight to eighteen verses. There are altogether 31 hymns. They include prayers to Agni, Indra, Trita, Varuna, Dyaus and Prithivi, and to the presiding deities of the four quarters. There are prayers for health, protection and prosperity, and for the increase of cattle, against emenies and demonic beings, and charms against fever, worms and other ailments and to mend broken bones and conceive a child. There are also charms against snakes and witchcraft. Two interesting hymns include a dialogue between Atharvan and Varuna, and one on the abduction and restoration of a brahmana's wife. There are other hymns that condemn harassing brahmanas in any way. Two hymns are to the war drum to secure victory.

Kanda 6 has 142 hymns. Several are prayers to various deities inluding Savitr, Agni, Brahmanaspati, Soma, the Maruts, Surya, and Apah. One prayer is to Agni and Indra for the well-being of a princely patron. This section has a number of prayers and charms against diseases, including against consumption, fever, wounds or bruises, eruptions, and against insanity. There are several love charms and others to banish jealousy. There are charms to ensure conception, the birth of a boy, and several to strengthen hair and promote its growth. There is a prayer to the rivers, which specifically refers to the Sindhu.

There are also prayers for peace, security, prosperity, power, health, and longevity, and blessings and charms against serpents, reptiles and insects, and to reconcile friends.

Kanda 7 has 118 hymns. The gods prayed to include Agni, Vayu, Aditi, the Adityas, the Ashvins, Vak, Sarasvati, Savitr, Vishnu, Brihaspati, Indra, and Ida. Pushan is prayed to for protection and the recovery of lost property. There are prayers in praise of Atharvan and others for long life, wealth, children, happiness, freedom from sin, and to bring rain. There are charms to win divine favour; to banish problems, enemies and demons; to achieve success in battle; to win love, and there are charms for the bride and bridegroom. There are prayers for the prosperity of a king and his kingdom, and some in praise of sacrifices as well as several other miscellaneous hymns. Some are for freedom from various diseases. There is a prayer for sacred knowledge and its fruit and a charm to obtain knowledge of the Veda. Some other interesting hymns are a funeral hymn, a blessing on cows, a charm for a king to make his subjects obedient. There are some verses to be used in sacrifices.

Kanda 8 has ten hymns, beginning with two for the recovery of a dying man. There are some prayers and charms for removing evil spirits and demons, restoring health, and one against a hostile army. Hymns 9 and 10 are the most interesting. The first deals with cosmological and ritual doctrines and the second is a glorification of the mystical concept of Viraj. Viraj can be considered a secondary creator. In the Rig Veda, Viraj was born from Purusha and Purusha from Viraj.

Kanda 9 has ten hymns on miscellaneous topics, beginning with a prayer to the Ashvins, followed by one in praise of Kama, as the god of desire and of all that is good. Hymns 9 and 10 provide an elaboration of cosmological doctrines.

Kanda 10, too, has ten miscellaneous hymns, beginning with a charm against witchcraft. The second hymn is on Purusha, the primeval man, while hymn 7 sees Skambha (supporting principle) as the basis or support for all existence. The eighth hymn has speculations on a supreme being, while the ninth contains the Sautadana or hundredfold oblation. The tenth glorifies the cow, which represents heaven.

Kanda 11 has ten hymns. The first consists of verses for the brahmaudana, the boiled rice mixture used in sacrifices, while the second is a prayer to Bhava, Sarva, and Rudra. Among other hymns are those which praise prana (breath) and the brahmachari (unmarried student). The last two hymns contain spells to destroy a hostile army, while the eighth is on the origin of certain gods and on creation.

Kanda 12 has five hymns beginning with a hymn to Prithivi, followed by a funeral hymn.

Kanda 13 consists of four hymns, which praise Rohita. Rohita is glorified as a form of fire and the sun, and praised as the highest being.

Kanda 14 has two hymns dealing with the marriage of Suryaa, daughter of Surya the sun god, and with marriage ceremonies in general.

Kanda 15 and most of Kanda 16 are in prose. Kanda 15 has eighteen hymns, all dealing with the *vratya*. This complex series of hymns and prose passages is very difficult to interpret. Vratya, a Sanskrit term, literally means 'one who has taken a vow'. Vratyas were a group of people, whose nature is uncertain. References indicate that vratyas did not follow the Vedas or observe brahmanical rules, and were often ascetic wanderers. The Yajur Veda includes a vratya in the list of victims for a Purushamedha.

In the Atharva Veda, vratyas are described in a mystical way, as pervading the whole world. The heavenly vratya is identified with Mahadeva, while the earthly vratya is his prototype. A vratya is also said to be a person who wandered to different places, a kind of religious mendicant.

The first hymn of this kanda is given here, indicating the complexity of the concept:

15.1
1. *There was a roaming Vratya. He roused Prajapati to action.*
2. *Prajapati beheld gold in himself and engendered it.*
3. *That became unique, that became distinguished, that became great, that became excellent, that became devotion, that became holy fervour, that became truth, through that he was born.*
4. *He grew, he became great, he became Mahadeva.*
5. *He gained the lordship of the gods. He became Lord.*
6. *He became chief Vratya. He held a bow, even that bow of Indra.*
7. *His belly is dark blue, his back is red.*
8. *With dark blue he envelops a detested rival, with red he pierces the man who hates him: so the theologians say.*

The Panchavimsha Brahmana describes sacrifices by which the vratya was absorbed into the brahmana caste. Their principles were said to be opposed by the brahmanas. The *grihapati* (leader or householder) wore a turban (*ushnisha*), carried a whip (*pratoda*), a kind of bow (*jyahroda*), wore black clothes, and had two skins (white and black). They owned a kind of wagon (*vipatha*) covered with planks. The leader wore an ornament (*nishka*) of silver. The others wore garments with red fringes, two each, skins folded double, and sandals (*upanah*).

Later references to vratyas are somewhat different, indicating they were people born from mixed castes, or from higher castes, but had not undergone initiations or purificatory rites. The Manu Smriti lists a number of vratya groups born from brahmana, kshatriya and vaishya vratyas. The names indicate that they were outside the main region of Aryavarta. The Brahmanda Purana states that vratya was a stage of life where *varna* and *ashrama* rules were not followed (3.48.47). Another Purana states that at Arbuda (a place identified with Mt Abu), those that were *divijas* (twice-born) became vratyas after the time of Puramjaya.

Textual references thus indicate there were different kinds of vratyas. In early days in the time of the Atharva Veda, they seem to have formed a separate religious cult which, however, was not totally alien, and they could be absorbed into the brahmanical fold through special rites. According to one theory, Vratyas were actually Vedic students who wandered around for six months before returning to their teacher. This may have been one category but most references to them do not support this. In later texts, vratyas were outsiders of some kind yet, again, not wholly alien.

Kanda 16 has nine hymns with various charms and blessings, beginning with a hymn on the purificatory aspects of water.

Kanda 17 contains only one hymn, which consists of a prayer to Indra. Here Indra is identified with Vishnu and the Sun. The prayer is for general protection, prosperity, and blessings.

Kanda 18 has four hymns connected with funeral ceremonies, partly taken from the Rig Veda.

Kanda 19 has seventy-two diverse hymns. These include philosophical hymns, hymns to various deities including Agni, Usha, Brahma, Kama, and Kala, as well as prayers for wealth and protection, and for victory in battle. There are charms for destruction of enemies and against diseases, and to gain a long life, and blessings for a newly elected king. Hymn 37 is a charm to secure a long life and dominion for a prince. There are hymns praising amulets and curative herbs, as well as some sacrificial formulas and a few prayers to be used with sacrifices. The Purusha-sukta, and a prayer to the twenty-eight *nakshatras* (constellations through which the moon passes), is included.

There are also prayers for final happiness in heaven, and to gain the love of both gods and people. A verse in the latter hymn reads: 'Make me beloved among the gods, beloved among the princes / Make me dear to everyone who sees, to Shudra and to Arya.'

Kanda 20 has 143 hymns, most of them from the Rig Veda. The new hymns are mainly 127–36, called Kuntapa Hymns, which are also part of sacrificial ritual.

The first of these, hymn 20.127, is in praise of the good government of King Kaurama. This is followed by sacrificial formulas and other verses. The last five hymns of this kanda praise the Ashvins.

The first verse of the Atharva Veda is given below:

To Vachaspati
1.1
Now may Vachaspati assign to me the strength and power of those
Who wearing every shape and form, the triple seven, are wandering round.
Come thou again Vachaspati
Come with divine intelligence.
Vachaspati repose thou here. In me be knowledge, yes, in me.
Here, even here, spread sheltering arms like the two bow arms strained with cord.
This let Vachaspati confirm. In me be knowledge, yes, in me.
Vachaspati has been invoked; may he invite us in reply.
May we adhere to sacred lore. Never may I be reft thereof.

(Based on the translation by R.T.H. Griffith)

CHAPTER 2

RELATED LITERATURE

BRAHMANAS

Among the numerous texts that throw light on the Vedic Samhitas, the most closely related are the Brahmanas. The Brahmanas are texts attached to the Samhitas—Rig, Sama, Yajur and Atharva Vedas—and provide explanations of these and guidance for the priests in sacrificial rituals.

The various Brahmanas are as listed below:

- Attached to the Rig Veda: Aitareya Brahmana (common to the Shakala and Ashvalayana shakhas); Kaushitaki Brahmana; Shankhayana Brahmana (almost identical with Kaushitaki).
- Attached to the Sama Veda: Tandya or Panchavimsha Brahmana; Shadvimsha Brahmana, which includes Adbhuta; Samavidhana Brahmana; Arsheya Brahmana; Devatadhyaya Brahmana; Chhandogya or Mantra Brahmana; Samhitopanishad Brahmana; Vamsha Brahmana; Jaiminiya or Talavakra Brahmana; Jaiminiya Upanishad Brahmana; Jaiminiya Arsheya Brahmana.
- Attached to the Black Yajur Veda or Taittiriya Samhita: Taittiriya Brahmana.
- Attached to the White Yajur Veda: Shatapatha Brahmana, which has two different recensions, Kanva and Madhyandina.
- Attached to the Atharva Veda: Gopatha Brahmana.

DATE

The Brahmanas are considered later than the Vedic Samhitas but contain some archaic elements. Their exact date would depend on that of the Samhitas and is, therefore, uncertain. Various scholars provide different relative dates for the Brahmanas. The prose portions of the Yajur (Taittiriya Samhita), which really constitute a Brahmana, are considered the earliest. The Panchavimsha Brahmana and Taittiriya Brahmana are probably next in date, followed by the Jaiminiya, Kaushitaki and Aitareya

Brahmanas, in that order. Sometimes, the Aitareya is considered older than the Kaushitaki, and the Jaimini older than the Panchavimsha. The Shatapatha is later than these, and the Gopatha and various short Brahmanas of the Sama, the latest. These views are based on linguistic analysis. These Brahmana texts are generally dated to between approximately 1000 BCE and 600 BCE, but they could be earlier.

LANGUAGE

In language, the Brahmanas demonstrate a more limited use of forms than the Rig Veda. But the syntax is said to represent the oldest stage of the language better than the Rig Veda, as the Brahmanas are mainly in prose while, in the Rig, the use of metres modifies the language. There are some passages in verse in the Brahmanas.

SUBJECT MATTER

The subject matter of the Brahmanas can be divided into two main topics of *vidhi* (rules) and *arthavada* (explanations). Thus the rules for conducting a sacrifice are supplemented by a commentary on aspects connected with the sacrifice, including stories and legends used to explain a point. They do not explain everything about the sacrifices but provide some details.

The symbolism of each item used in the sacrifice is explained in several texts. Rules for the sacrifice are laid out in minute detail, and any deviation is believed to lead to its failure. These complicated sacrifices gradually came to be conducted only by special priests, while earlier even householders could perform them. This led to the supremacy of the brahmana (caste) priests, who conducted the sacrifices.

Stories and legends in these texts include those of Manu and the flood, Harishchandra and Shunahshepa, and Pururava and Urvashi. There are early creation myths in which Prajapati, or sometimes Manu, is the creator. Some philosophical concepts are also mentioned. The Brahmanas are essentially similar but each emphasizes the role of specific priests. Thus the Rig Vedic Brahmanas emphasize the role of the hotr, the Sama Veda Brahmanas of the udgatr, and the Yajur Brahmanas of the adhvaryu.

The similarity of content among the different Brahmanas is marked, even though they must have been composed at different points in time over a long period. A brief description of the various Brahmanas is given below.

RIG VEDA BRAHMANAS

AITAREYA BRAHMANA

This Brahmana, attached to the Rig Veda, is used by the Shakala and Ashvalayana shakhas. It has forty adhyayas, arranged within eight *panchikas* or sections, and includes a number of topics.

The text provides a description of various sacrifices such as the Soma sacrifice, the agnihotra and the rajasuya. Mahidasa Aitareya is the traditional author of these texts. He is said to be the son of a brahmana from a shudra woman. However, Adhyayas 31–40 of the Aitareya Brahmana are assigned to Shaunaka.

Some details of this text are given below as indicative of the type of material contained in a Brahmana. The sacrifices themselves are described in Chapter 10 of this book.

Panchika 1, with Adhyayas 1–5, is on the Soma sacrifice, and begins with the agnishtoma, the consecration rites and the verses to be recited at these. It includes the introductory sacrifices, the buying and bringing of the Soma, welcoming Soma as a guest in the house of the sacrificer, and the first rituals, consisting of the pravargya. This is succeeded by the carrying forward of the fire, and the offerings to the high altar.

Panchika 2, with Adhyayas 6–10, continues with the agnishtoma Soma sacrifice. It includes the animal sacrifice, the cups of Soma to be offered to the deities, and their symbolism.

Panchika 3, with Adhyayas 11–15, continues with the agnishtoma Soma sacrifice. It includes a propitiation of the god Rudra, general considerations regarding the agnishtoma, and certain details regarding the sacrifice.

Panchika 4, with Adhyayas 16–20, continues with the agnishtoma Soma sacrifice in Adhyaya 16, and with the shodashin and the atiratra sacrifices. This is followed in Adhyayas 17 and 18, with the gavam ayana, which lasts 360 days. Adhyayas 19 and 20 describe the inauguration and the first two days of the *dvadashaha* or twelve-day Soma rite.

Panchika 5, with Adhyayas 21–25, continues with the dvadashaha rite of the Soma sacrifice from the third to the tenth days in Adhyayas 21–24. This is followed by comments on the agnihotra and on the brahman priest.

Panchika 6, with Adhyayas 26–30, continues with the agnihotra, dealing mainly with the specific verses of praise (shastras) to be uttered by the hotr and his assistants.

Panchika 7, with Adhyayas 31–35, continues with the agnihotra in 31 and 32, dealing with the animal offering, distribution of portions of the victim, and expiations of errors in the sacrifice. Adhyayas 33–35 begin an account of preparations for the royal consecration ceremonies (vajapeya and rajasuya).

Panchika 8, with Adhyayas 36–40, continues the account of the royal consecration. It describes the stotras and shastras of the Soma day, the anointing of the king, the great anointing of Indra, the great anointing of the king, and ends with a description of the role of the purohita, the chief priest of the king.

KAUSHITAKI BRAHMANA

Kaushitaki Brahmana, the other Brahmana attached to the Rig Veda, contains thirty adhyayas. The matter is similar to the Aitareya, with the Soma sacrifices being the central topic, but there are some differences. Adhyayas 1–6 deal with the fire sacrifices, including the laying of the fire, the agnihotra, the new- and full-moon sacrifices, and the four-monthly sacrifices. Adhyayas 7–30 describe the Soma sacrifices, in more or less the same way as the Aitareya Brahmana. The Shankhayana Brahmana is almost the same as the Kaushitaki.

SAMA VEDA BRAHMANAS

PANCHAVIMSHA BRAHMANA

The Panchavimsha Brahmana is one of the most important Brahmanas attached to the Sama Veda. It is named 'Panchavimsha' (twenty-five) because it has twenty-five prapathakas (sections). These are divided into 347 khandas or subsections. This is considered one of the oldest Brahmanas, and is also known as the Tandya-maha-Brahmana. The text describes the rituals and samans for the udgatr. It provides directions for various sacrifices including the Soma sacrifices. It incorporates various legends and stories. It is the main Brahmana for the Kauthuma and Ranayaniya shakhas of the Sama Veda.

SHADVIMSHA BRAHMANA

Shadvimsha Brahmana, or the twenty-sixth Brahmana, is actually a conclusion of the Panchavimsha, which has twenty-five books. This includes the Adbhuta Brahmana, which contains omens and miracles. The text has five sections, and the language seems to predate Panini, the composer of the classic Sanskrit grammar. It incorporates verses for the Subrahmanya priest, who was one of the assistants of the udgatr.

JAIMINIYA BRAHMANA

The Jaiminiya Brahmana is a long text with several legends and stories apart from the other typical Brahmana content. It has three main kandas. Kanda 1.1–65 deals with the agnihotra; this is followed by the agnishtoma (1.65–364), the gavam ayana (2.1–80), the *ekaha* Soma sacrifice (2.81–234), the *ahina* Soma sacrifice (2.235–333), the sattras (2.334–370), and then the gavam ayana again (2.371–442). Kanda 3 contains instructions for the dvadashaha as well as geographical and other miscellaneous material.

JAIMINIYA UPANISHAD BRAHMANA

The Jaiminiya Upanishad or Talavakara Upanishad Brahmana is available in fragmentary form. It is different from the Jaiminiya Brahmana and is considered an Aranyaka.

SAMAVIDHANA BRAHMANA

The Samavidhana is composed mostly in sutra style, that is, in terse verses. It explains how to use samans, which are more effective than just reciting the texts. The samans can be used both for healing and magic.

ARSHEYA BRAHMANA

The Arsheya belongs to the Kauthuma shakha; this Brahmana is in sutra style, and gives the names of the Sama melodies of the first two ganas, the Gramageyagana and Aranyakagana. The names are derived in various ways: from the name of the rishi composer; from the first or concluding part of a stanza, or a particular phrase in it; or from its aim or purpose. The names of the rishis connected with each song are provided, and can be different from the rishi who originally composed the underlying rik. The text has three prapathakas. It can be classified as an anukramani or index.

DEVATADHYAYA BRAHMANA

The first part of the Devatadhyaya is the most important as it provides rules to determine the deities to whom the samans are dedicated. Another section ascribes colours to different verses, possibly as aids to memory or for meditation. The Devatadhyaya includes some very late passages such as references to the four yugas or ages.

CHHANDOGYA BRAHMANA

The Chhandogya has ten prapathakas, of which the first two form the Brahmana, also known as the Mantra Brahmana or Mantra Parvan. Prapathakas 3–10 contain the Chhandogya Upanishad. The Chhandogya Brahmana is divided into eight khandas and has mantras that are used in grihya (household) sacrifices. The Khadira and Gobhila Grihya Sutras refer to these mantras.

SAMHITOPANISHAD BRAHMANA

The Samhitopanishad Brahmana belongs to the Kauthuma school. It has some older material and is composed in a mixture of prose and verse. It describes the nature of the chants and their effects, and how the riks or Rig Vedic verses were converted into samans. Thus it reveals some of the hidden aspects of the Sama Veda.

VAMSHA BRAHMANA

The Vamsha, a short Brahmana, has a list of fifty-three teachers of the Sama Veda. The earliest teacher, Kashyapa, is said to have received the teaching from the god Agni.

JAIMINIYA ARSHEYA BRAHMANA

This provides the names of Sama melodies. Thus it is similar to the Arsheya Brahmana of the Kauthuma school but for the fact that the names of the rishis in the two are different. Unlike the Kauthuma text, this lists only one rishi per saman.

KRISHNA YAJUR VEDA BRAHMANAS

TAITTIRIYA BRAHMANA

The Taittiriya Brahmana is a continuation of the Taittiriya Samhita, which also contains Brahmana portions. This Brahmana has three kandas. The first explains the *agnyadhana*, gavam ayana, vajapeya, some Soma sacrifices, the *nakshatreshti*, and the rajasuya sacrifices. The second kanda deals with the agnihotra, *upahomas*, *sautramani*, *vaisyasava*, and other sacrifices. The last kanda has additional details on various sacrifices such as the nakshatreshti and ashvamedha, and contains a description of the purushamedha. Some stories are included as well.

VADHULA BRAHMANA

Also known as the Anvakhyana Brahmana, this is a Brahmana type of text, though it is actually a part of the Vadhula Shrauta Sutra.

SHUKLA YAJUR VEDA OR VAJASANEYI SAMHITA (WHITE YAJUR VEDA) BRAHMANAS

SHATAPATHA BRAHMANA

This is the longest of the Brahmanas. The text has two main recensions, the Kanva and Madhyandina. The Madhyandina has 100 adhyayas in fourteen kandas. The first nine kandas form a commentary on the first eighteen sections of the Yajur Veda text of the Vajasaneyi Samhita. Kandas 1–5 seem closely connected. The kandas and their main topics are as follows:

Kanda 1: Haviryajna, dealing with the full- and new-moon sacrifices
Kanda 2: Ekapadika, on the installation of the sacred fires, agnihotra, pindapitrayajna, agrayana and chaturmasya
Kanda 3: Adhvara, on Soma sacrifices
Kanda 4: Graha, also on Soma sacrifices
Kanda 5: Sava, on the vajapeya and rajasuya
Kanda 6: Ukhasambharana, on the Agnichayana (laying of the fire altar), and Agnirahasya (fire altar mystery)
Kanda 7: Hastighata, as above

Kanda 8: Chiti, as above

Kanda 9: Samchiti, as above

Kanda 10: Agnirahasya, as above

Kanda 11: Ashtadhyayi, a recapitulation of previous chapters; in addition this has a description of the upanayana (initiation) and svadhyaya (self-study) of the Vedas; these last two topics usually do not appear in the Brahmanas

Kanda 12: Madhyama, on various sacrifices

Kanda 13: Ashvamedha, includes descriptions of the ashvamedha and purushamedha; it also refers to antyeshti (funeral ceremonies) and erecting a burial mound

Kanda 14: Brihadaranyaka, describes the pravargya ritual and includes the Brihadaranyaka Upanishad

The text thus has descriptions of the method of performing various sacrifices. Apart from those mentioned above, the sarvamedha (sacrifice of everything), and the duties of a student are also described.

The rishi Yajnavalkya is the traditional author and, in Kanda 14, is said to be the author of the entire text. However, in Kandas 6–9, Shandilya is the teacher and Yajnavalkya is not mentioned. Shandilya is also said to be the teacher of the agnirahasya in Kanda 10. In the last part of the text, the Brihadaranyaka Upanishad, sacrifices are only symbolic.

The Kanva recension has 104 adhyayas in seventeen kandas: Ekapad, Haviryajna, Uddhari, Adhvara, Graha, Vajapeya, Rajasuya, Ukhasambharana, Hastighata, Chiti, Samchiti, Agnirahasya, Ashtadhyayi, Madhyama, Ashvamedha, Pravargya, and Brihadaranyaka. The contents of the two recensions are largely the same but some adhyayas of the Madhyandina are here divided into two.

Apart from explaining Vedic sacrifices in detail, this Brahmana includes myths and legends, such as the stories of Pururava and Urvashi, and of Chyavana and Sukanya. Another interesting aspect is that various questions are framed as riddles.

The Shatapatha Brahmana has four *vamsha* (lineage) lists. The last states: 'We have received this from the son of Bharadvajo, the son of Bharadvaji, from the son of Vatsi Mandavi', followed by several people, all mentioned by their maternal names. The forty-fifth is Yajnavalkya, whose teacher is said to be Uddalaka, known from the Upanishads. The fifty-fifth is Kashyapa Naidhruvi, to whom the Shatapatha was revealed by the goddess Vach. 'She received it from Ambhrini (the voice of thunder) who obtained it from Aditya (the sun).'

The Shatapatha is one of the latest Brahmanas.

ATHARVA VEDA BRAHMANAS

GOPATHA BRAHMANA

The aim of this Brahmana seems to be to incorporate the Atharva in the Vedic ritual, and bring it in line with the other three Vedas. This Brahmana is the same for the Paippalada and Shaunaka shakhas, and is the only existing Brahmana of the Atharva Veda. It has two main sections, the Purvabhaga and the Uttarabhaga. The Purvabhaga is divided into five prapathakas, and the Uttarabhaga into six. Each is further divided into kandikas or subsections. The contents of the Purvabhaga are somewhat different from those of other Brahmanas. It praises the Atharva and its rishis. The Uttarabhaga is similar to other Brahmanas but contains some stories regarding Atharva Veda teachers such as Idhma Angirasa and Barhi Angirasa.

Within the text are Upanishads including the Pranava Upanishad.

The Atharvana Charanavyuha states that the Gopatha originally had 100 prapathakas. The Gopatha Brahmana says the one who knows this text knows everything.

ARANYAKAS AND UPANISHADS

Attached to the Brahmanas are the Aranyakas and Upanishads, in which the brahmana caste and the sacrifice do not have major roles. These texts focus instead on asceticism, knowledge and inquiry. Here is a brief look at these two categories of texts.

ARANYAKAS

The Aranyakas or 'forest texts' (*aranya* means 'forest') usually form the second part of the Brahmanas. They are generally believed to have provided instructions for *vanaprastha*, the traditional third stage of life, when the householder's life had been renounced and the person had retired to the forests. Alternatively, they are believed to have provided guidance for complex sacrifices that were meant to be practised outside the town area. The contents of the Aranyakas indicate that they form a bridge between the Brahmanas and Upanishads. They include descriptions of special sacrifices, along with comments on the mystical symbolism of sacrifices. There are philosophical sections as well as techniques of focusing on various symbols in order to attain the Absolute. The Aranyakas are closely linked with the Upanishads.

RIG VEDA ARANYAKAS

AITAREYA ARANYAKA

The Aitareya Aranyaka forms part of the Aitareya Brahmana, attached to the Rig Veda, and has five books or sections that describe sacrifices and philosophical concepts. It contains the Aitareya Upanishad. The first book focuses on the mahavrata and the Soma sacrifices. The second includes philosophical concepts and explains the meaning of uktha, while its last four chapters contain the Aitareya Upanishad. The third book discusses the Samhita, Pada and Krama texts, and mentions several rishis. The next two books, with miscellaneous topics, are attributed to the rishis Ashvalayana and Shaunaka. The fourth book includes the Mahanami verses, while the fifth incorporates the *nishkevalya* shastra (verses of praise) that form a part of the mahavrata ritual.

KAUSHITAKI ARANYAKA

The Kaushitaki Aranyaka, attached to the Kaushitaki Brahmana of the Rig Veda, has contents similar to the Aitareya Aranyaka. It has fifteen sections, of which the third to the sixth form the Kaushitaki Upanishad. It is also known as the Shankhayana Aranyaka. Its first two chapters are similar to a Brahmana.

KRISHNA YAJUR VEDA ARANYAKAS

TAITTIRIYA ARANYAKA

The Taittiriya Aranyaka is a continuation of the Taittiriya Brahmana, which is attached to the Krishna Yajur Veda and has ten prapathakas or sections. The first two prapathakas are known as Kathakani as they are based on the Kathaka shakha of the Yajur. They mainly deal with the agnichayana, or piling of the fire altar. The third prapathaka discusses various sacrifices. The fourth and fifth prapathaka include aspects of the pravargya ritual. The sixth has pitrimedha mantras, recited in funeral ceremonies. The prapathakas from seven to nine form the Taittiriya Upanishad. The tenth, known as the Mahanarayana Upanishad, is a late addition. It is a compilation of mantras from the the Vedic Samhitas.

KATHA ARANYAKA

This text mainly deals with the pravargya ritual.

SHUKLA YAJUR VEDA ARANYAKAS

BRIHADARANYAKA

The Brihad-Aranyaka, or Brihadaranyaka Upanishad, is attached to the Shatapatha Brahmana of the Shukla Yajur Veda, but is considered an Upanishad.

SAMA VEDA ARANYAKAS

The Chhandogya Upanishad of the Sama Veda has a first section similar to an Aranyaka. The Jaiminiya Upanishad Brahmana is really an Aranyaka, containing the Kena Upanishad. It is also known as the Talavakra Aranyaka and looks at the hidden or inner meanings of certain samans, and provides a spiritual interpretation of some Vedic mantras.

UPANISHADS

The Upanishads form the last part of the Samhitas. The word *upanishad* is said to mean 'sitting near the feet of a master' from *upa* or 'near' and *nishad* or 'sitting down'. Another interpretation takes *shad* as 'destruction' and *upanishad* as 'that which destroys ignorance'. The original meaning, however, was 'secret doctrine'.

These texts form the latter part of the Brahmanas and are attached to the Vedic Samhitas. They are called Vedanta, 'the end of the Vedas', both because they form the last part of the Vedas and because, in them, the Vedas reach the ultimate or highest philosophy. Philosophically, they are a great advance on the ritualistic nature of the Brahmanas. The earliest Upanishads in their present form, date back to the 6th or 7th century BCE, while altogether fourteen have been dated to before the 3rd century BCE. The earliest are said to be the Aitareya, Kaushitaki, Taittiriya, Brihadaranyaka, Chhandogya and Kena, while slightly later are the Kathaka, Shvetashvatara, Mahanarayana, Isha, Mundaka, Prashna, Maitrayaniya, and Mandukya. There are many later Upanishads and at least two hundred and eighty Upanishads are known today, of which 108 are recognized in classic texts. These 108 are uneven in quality and character.

Most of the early Upanishads have gone beyond all external forms of worship and seek the supreme goal through an exploration of ideas leading to ultimate knowledge.

The Upanishads indicate that anyone, from kings to shudras, could be involved in a philosophical quest, and that a spiritual search was not the preserve of brahmanas. The Vedic Samhitas retained their sanctity but, from an early date, several philosophers, scholars and commentators began to focus on the Upanishads. Badarayana's Brahma Sutra summarized the key features of the Upanishads, and this sutra was used as the base for all the schools of Vedanta, one of the six orthodox schools of Hindu philosophy. All six accept the sanctity of the Vedas.

The Vedic Samhitas were not rejected in the Upanishads, but a continuity was sought to be maintained between them and later ideas. As S. Radhakrishnan points out, passages from the Vedic Samhitas are often quoted in the Upanishads, but new meanings are given to them. Sri Aurobindo and others have pointed out numerous passages from the Samhitas that are explained in the Upanishads.

OTHER TEXTS

Additional texts were composed from an early date, which commented on, clarified, or explained aspects of the Vedas. Among these were the padapathas and anukramanis.

PADAPATHAS

Padapathas or 'word texts' were used for the study of the Vedas. Shakala, the compiler of the existing recension of the Rig Veda, is said to have composed one of the earliest for the Rig. The Samhita texts had words in their conjoined forms, whereas the padapatha gives the words separately, unaffected by sandhi. (Sandhi rules join words together in a particular way, changing the ending or beginning.) The *kramapatha* gives each word twice, once connected with the preceding word, and then with the succeeding word. Another type of arrangement was the *jatapatha*, where each pair of words was repeated twice, the second repetition being with the second word first. Hence if 'a' and 'b' represent the two words, the jatapatha had the order ab, ba, ab. With 'c' representing the next word, this would be followed by bc, cb, bc. A further type was the *ghanapatha*, in which the order of words was arranged in the following way: ab, ba, abc, cba, abc, bc, cb, bcd. These types of texts were aids to memory and ensured that the texts were transmitted correctly. The break-up of the words also helped in understanding the texts and the sandhi that was used.

ANUKRAMANIS

Anukramani is a Sanskrit term for a list, catalogue, or index. Some anukramanis classify and provide details that are not available in the Samhitas. They include lists of hymns, of rishis who composed the hymns, and of metres. The anukramanis are assigned to different authors. A number of anukramanis of the Rig Veda are assigned to Shaunaka. These include the Anuvakanukramani, Arshanukramani, Chandonukramani, Devatanukramani, Padanukramani and Suktanukramani. The Anuvakanukramani is still extant while parts of the others are quoted by Shadgurushishya, a 12th-century commentator on the Vedas. Katyayana composed the Sarvanukramani, a catalogue of everything in the Rig Veda. This incorporates the names of the deities, rishis, and metres of each of the Rig Veda hymns, and has been commented on by Shadgurushishya in his Vedarthadipika. The Anuvakanukramani states that there was a different sequence of hymns in the first mandala. While some feel these anukramanis record authentic names, others feel that family names may be correct in books 2–7, but the rest may not be authentic. Tradition, however, recognizes these as correct.

The Arsheya Brahmana and Jaiminiya Arsheya Brahmana are considered Sama Veda anukramanis. Two indices of the deities and composers of the Sama according to the Naigeya school have been preserved, indirectly providing information on the Kauthuma school.

The Samaveda-arsheyadipa is an anukramani text, assigned to Bhatta-Bhaskara-dhvarindra of a later date. It records metres, deities and rishis for the Sama chanters.

The Yajur Veda has three anukramanis. The Mantrashadhyaya belongs to the Charayaniya shakha of the Vajasaneyi Samhita. Another of the Madhyandina shakha of the Vajasaneyi is ascribed to Katyayana. A third is of the Atreyi shakha of the Taittiriya Samhita.

The Atharva Veda has the Brihatsarvanukramani and Atharvaveda-panchapatalika.

VEDANGAS

From very early times, the Vedas, that is the Vedic Samhitas, were considered difficult to understand. Hence another group of texts emerged, known as Vedangas. These associated texts deal with six subjects considered essential for an understanding of the Vedas: (1) *shiksha*, phonetics or the science of pronunciation; (2) *vyakarana*, grammar; (3) *chhandas*, metre; (4) *nirukta*, etymology or glossary; (5) *jyotisha*, astronomy and astrology, essential to fix the right time for ceremonies and sacrifices; and (6) *kalpa*, rules for sacrifices. There are several texts on these topics. Shiksha, vyakarana, and nirukta are connected, and the subject matter overlaps to some extent.

Most of the Vedangas are written in sutra style, that is in short aphorisms which provide information in a compressed form. The Shadvimsha Brahmana is the earliest text to state that there are six Vedangas, which are called the limbs of the goddess Svaha. The Apastamba Kalpa Sutra, the Manduka Upanishad and the Charanavyuha list the six Vedangas. The main concepts in the Vedangas are derived from the Samhitas, Brahmanas, and sutras, and have been compressed and grouped together.

Some details on the subjects elucidated in the six Vedangas are given below.

SHIKSHA

Shiksha, as a term for phonetics, is first used in the Taittiriya Upanishad, which gives its various components which include *varna* (individual sounds) and *svara* (accent).

The pratishakhyas are among the earliest texts on shiksha. *Pratishakhya* literally means 'belonging to each shakha' and there were pratishakhya texts for the various Vedic shakhas or schools. Pratishakhyas describe how the verses in the Vedas are to be pronounced, and also deal with sandhi rules, accents, vowels, and some aspects of grammar useful for pronunciation. They were composed later than the Vedas, and are related to the padapatha texts described earlier. Among the pratishakyas available today are the Rig Veda Pratishakhya, ascribed to Shaunaka. This is also known as the Shakala Pratishakhya, and is said to belong to the Shaishiriya shakha, a branch of the Shakala Shakha. Two pratishakhyas of the Yajur Veda are the Taittiriya Pratishakhya of the Black Yajur Veda and the Vajasaniya Pratishakhya of the Vajasaneyi Samhita or White Yajur Veda, said to be written by Katyayana. The former has references to the Mimamsakas (followers of the Mimamsa philosophy), who are not referred to in any other pratishakhya. Regarding the latter, the Katyayaniyas were a subdivision of the Madhyandina shakha, who were in turn a branch of the Vajasaneyis. Some sutras of this text are repeated in Panini, indicating its relatively early date. The Shaunakiya Chaturadhyayika of the Atharva Veda is attributed to Shaunaka. This is said to belong to the Shaunakiya shakha of the Atharva-vedis. In one source, this text is attributed to Kautsa.

Two pratishakhyas of the Sama Veda are considered to belong to a later date. These are the Riktantra-vyakarana and the Pushpa-sutra. The former is later than Panini, and its contents are related to grammar more than phonetics. The Pushpa-sutra is the main pratishakhya of the Kauthuma–Ranayaniya branch of the Sama Veda. It has both the text and the melodies of the Sama, along with comments on phonetics. It distinguishes between prakriti and vikriti—the basic forms of the chants as they appear in the first two ganas, the Gramageyagana and Aranyakagana, and the derivative form in the Uhagana and Uhyagana. The Pushpa-sutra was written long after the Sama Veda.

Among other related books, the Matra-lakshana deals with the time measurement of svara or a musical sound, and the various laws on the arrangement of notes for the melodies in the four ganas or songbooks. All the melodies in this and its commentary are derived from the Prakriti-gana.

The Panchavidha-sutra looks at chant construction.

Other Texts on Shiksha

There were other texts on shiksha, most of which were later than the pratishakhyas. At least sixty-five such texts on shiksha are known. The Paniniya Shiksha has *shloka*-type verses and is said to have been composed by Pingala, the younger brother of Panini. The text is much later than the pratishakhyas but quite comprehensive and has, therefore, influenced other shiksha texts. Two recensions of this text relating to the Rig Veda and Yajur Veda are known. Several other shiksha texts have borrowed from the Paniniya Shiksha. Some of them also deal with topics that are not found in the pratishakhyas. Among the other shiksha texts, the Svara-vyanjana Shiksha is important for the Rig Veda, and dates after Panini. The Yajnavalkya Shiksha, for the White Yajur Veda, probably dates to between the 5th and 10th centuries CE, much later than the presumed date of Yajnavalkya. For the Black Yajur Veda, the Vaidikabharana, composed by Gargya Gopala Yajvan around the 14th and 15th centuries, is a late but important work, including quotes from early texts that are unknown today. The Narada Shiksha of the Sama Veda is fairly old and deals particularly with accents and their relationship with musical notes. The Manduki Shiksha is important for the Atharva Veda.

Among some of the interesting aspects of shiksha texts are that they state that good health and a calm mind are necessary prerequisites for correct pronunciation. They also throw some light on the origin of the seven musical notes, stating that they evolved from the three Vedic accents, which were musical in nature.

NIRUKTA (ETYMOLOGY)

Nirukta, in the sense of etymology, is another of the Vedangas. Nirukta texts are important for understanding the archaic language of the Rig Veda. Aspects of etymology exist in earlier texts including the Samhitas, Brahmanas, Aranyakas, and Upanishads. About six hundred words are explained in these in different ways. There must have been several niruktas, but the one that is still extant is that of Yaska, who probably lived before Panini. These etymologies of Vedic words have been classified into three types: those based on both the phonetic and semantic history of the word; those based on semantic evolution, that is when the meaning or connotation of a word changes over time; and those based on phonetic similarities. Certain texts hold definitions of a nirukta. The Shabda-kalpa-druma says a nirukta explains five aspects of words, that is, how they are added to, transposed and modified, when certain letters can be omitted and, in addition, the meaning of the root word. Conjoined words with the same root, for instance *angara-angiras*, and homonyms are also used in explanations. Yaska's Nirukta presents clear insights into etymolgical and grammatical concepts.

Yaska summarizes the importance of nirukta, when he says: 'Without this (science) there can be no understanding of the Vedic mantras.' His Nirukta bases itself on an earlier text, the Nighantu, which had five chapters and could be classified into three parts. Part 1, the first three chapters, consisted of words with synonyms; Part 2, the fourth chapter, had words found only in the Vedas; and Part 3, the fifth chapter, had names of deities in the Rig Veda, and hymns and words connected with them. The important part of the Nirukta is the commentary, in which Yaska explains words with illustrative passages of how they were used.

Yaska's Nirukta has twelve chapters, divided into two parts of six each. The Purva-shatka, or first part, has two sections, Naighantuka Kanda and Naigama Kanda. The Naighantuka Kanda has three chapters, which comment on the first three chapters of the Nighantu. The Naigama Kanda, containing the next three chapters, comments on the fourth chapter of the Nighantu. The Uttara-shatka, or second part, with six chapters, is named the Daivata Kanda and comments on the fifth chapter of the Nighantu. Yaska's Nirukta thus includes some matter that already existed but was unified, commented on, and given a cohesive form. Yaska also refers to earlier Nirukta writers such as Shakapuni. The Rig Veda is the main text commented on.

VYAKARANA (GRAMMAR)

Vyakarana or grammar is another important topic necessary to study and understand the Vedas. The Brahmanas, Aranyakas, and Upanishads contain some aspects of grammar. The padapatha texts, and some of the pratishakhyas described above, also contain elements of grammar, as does Yaska's Nirukta. Yaska, in fact, mentions that in his time there were already two schools of grammarians, the eastern and the northern.

The earliest available complete Sanskrit grammar was written by Panini and is known as the Ashtadhyayi. Not much is known of his life but Panini is thought to have lived some time between the 7th and 4th centuries BCE. He was possibly born in the village of Shalatura in the north-west region of Gandhara, but lived mainly in Pataliputra. According to legend, he was inspired by the god Shiva, and the sound of his *damaru* or drum, which reveals the true word.

Panini was not, however, the first to write a grammar; he is believed to have had sixty-four predecessors. Among them were Apishali and Kashakritsna, who are said to have founded schools of grammar. Others include Gargya, Kashyapa, Galava, Bharadvaja, Shakatayana, Shakalya, Chakravarmana, Senaka, and Sphotayana.

Panini's Ashtadhyayi is said to be the most perfect grammar of any part of the ancient world. The text is divided into eight adhyayas, hence the name, which literally means 'eight parts'. The grammar has 4000 short aphorisms, which have been commented on and explained by others. Among notable commentaries on Panini are those by Patanjali and Katyayana or Vararuchi.

The Unadi-sutras and Phit-sutras are other grammatical texts. The former is assigned by Patanjali to Shakatayana, Panini's predecessor, but others assign it to Vararuchi who was later than Panini. The Phit-sutras are generally agreed to be later than Panini. Panini laid the foundation for all future grammatical works. His grammar was not exclusively on the Vedas, but included Vedic terms.

CHHANDAS (METRE)

Chhandas is a Sanskrit term with several meanings and is usually translated as 'prosody' but, in general, refers to metres occurring in sacred texts. The word chhandas is also used to refer to the hymns of the Atharva Veda or sometimes to other sacred hymns. In addition, it means intention, desire, or longing.

A knowledge of chhandas as metre is considered essential for the understanding of the Veda. Rig Vedic hymns are composed in several different metres. The line of a verse is known as a *pada*. A pada usually has eight, eleven or twelve syllables, and occasionally five, depending on the metre used. Generally short and long syllables alternate. The rhythm of the last four to five syllables follows a fixed pattern. A stanza or rik usually has three to four lines though there are variations, and some have five lines. Four is most common. There are seven main metres in the Rig Veda, as well as several more. These seven, in order of use, are *trishtubh, gayatri, jagati, anushtubh, ushnih, pankti,* and *brihati*. The three most commonly used metres in the Rig Veda are trishtubh also known as trishtup (4253 mantras), which has four lines with eleven syllables each; the gayatri (2467 mantras) of three lines and eight syllables per line; and the jagati (1350 mantras) with four lines and twelve syllables per line. Pankti and Mahapankti have five or six lines of eight syllables each. These seven metres are named in the other Samhitas as well. Among other metres is the *Divpada-viraj*, which has five syllables per line. The *Viraj* has thirty-three syllables. Usually a hymn is composed in a single metre but the last stanza is sometimes in a different metre. Some hymns are composed in several different metres. Hymns can have either single verses or groups of verses. A group often consists of three verses in the same metre, or two verses in different metres. Syllables in one stanza are between twenty and forty-eight, depending on the metre used. There are also stanzas or verses with mixed metres. The trishtubh and jagati, which have the same cadence, are sometimes found mixed together in one verse. *Pragatha* is a term used for mixed metres.

Aspects of metres are discussed in the Samhitas and some of the Brahmanas and Upanishads. References to the different metres occur even in the Rig Veda, which gives the names of deities who created various metres. Thus, gayatri was connected with Agni, and with transporting the Soma from heaven; ushnih was connected with Savitr; anushtubh with Soma; brihati with Brihaspati; and viraj with Maitravaruna. Indra is responsible for trishtubh and the Vishvedevas for jagati. The *shakvari* is another metre mentioned in the Rig, and it is said that the Vasishthas chanted praises to Indra in that metre. It has been suggested that Vedic metres were based on the natural modulations of the voice when speaking. This later developed into the music of the Sama Veda, which formed the basis for further developments in later times.

The Brahmana texts provide more details on types of metres, their usage, and their associations. They indicate that metres should be used according to the result desired. For instance, the Aitareya Brahmana (1.5) states that gayatri verses should be used as the invitatory and offering verses, for those who desire brilliance and splendour; ushnih verses are for those who desire life; anushtubh verses for those who desire heaven; brihati verses for prosperity and glory; pankti verses for the sacrifice; trishtubh verses for strength; jagati verses for cattle; and viraj verses for food. It is said that viraj means 'the glorious' and he who has the most food is the most glorious in the world. The text further explains how viraj contains the strength of all the other metres. The Shatapatha Brahmana states that metres were created by Prajapati.

The Chhandah-sutra of Pingala is among the texts dealing exclusively with Sanskrit metres. Though it is later than the Vedas, it has a section on Vedic metres.

Gayatri is revered as the goddess of metres. Thus texts indicate that the metres are believed to have a mystical origin. In some of the Dharma Shastras, sacrifices are offered to the metres, which are worshipped as deities.

The Nidana-sutra, a text on the Sama Veda, is an important text on metrics. It explains the musical aspects of uktha, stoma, and gana. It describes and names all the Vedic metres, mentioning those used in the ekaha, ahina and sattra sacrifices. It refers to several otherwise unknown Vedic texts.

A Rig Veda anukramani, Chandonukramani, lists all the metres of the Rig Vedic hymns. The Sarvanukramani summarizes the matter in other anukramanis. The anukramani of the White Yajur Veda, assigned to Katyayana, has a section on the metres of this text.

In post-Vedic times, though the gayatri was considered sacred, it was hardly used in texts. The anushtubh became the prominent metre, evolving into the classical shloka of the epics.

JYOTISHA (ASTRONOMY)

Elements of jyotisha and of a calendric system appear from the Rig Veda onwards. The times, dates, and duration of many of the sacrifices described in the Yajur Veda and later texts were based on a knowledge of the solar and lunar calendars.

The Yajur Veda texts as well as the Atharva Veda name the *nakshatras* (constellations), though the names differ. The Yajur Taittiriya Samhita says there are twenty-seven nakshatras, while the

Atharva and Yajur Maitrayani Samhita give twenty-eight. Listed in succession, the nakshatras formed a sort of lunar zodiac. Based on a passage in the Brahmanas, the early scholars B.G. Tilak and Hermann Jacobi felt the Krittikas (Pleiades) were the starting point of the nakshatra system. The Vedic texts also seem to refer to an older calendar, when the vernal equinox was Mrigashiras (Orion). In the Chhandogya Upanishad, the study and knowledge of nakshatras is considered worthwhile. The Grihya Sutras have references to astronomical phenomena.

The Vedanga Jyotisha, compiled by Lagadha, is the earliest known text on the subject. The date of this text is controversial. A sentence in it says that 'in the beginning of *shravishtha*, the sun and the moon turn towards the north'. By astrological calculation, this leads to a date of 1200 BCE, or to between 1300 and 1100 BCE. There are later elements in the work but the original could be of around this date. The entire text was probably composed before the 4th century BCE. It has thirty-six verses in its Rig Vedic recension and forty-three in the Yajur Vedic recension. Thirty verses in both versions are identical. The Vedanga Jyotisha was used to decide on the appropriate time for sacrifices, based on the position of the sun, moon, and nakshatras. It provides methods to calculate the *tithis* (lunar days), *parvans* (new- and full-moon days), and the *vishuvats* (equinox days). A five-year cycle termed a yuga was used for calculations, though the term yuga could be used in different ways. One solar year was taken as 366 days, hence five years came to 1830 days. Following the lunar calendar, this contained 124 parvans, which included sixty-two full moons and sixty-two new moons. To these parvans, one month added in the third year, and one in the fifth year, converted the lunar calendar into a solar calendar. The cycle began at the beginning of the six-month uttarayana period, on the first day of the bright fortnight of Magha, when the sun, moon, and nakshatra Dhanishtha came together. The Atharvana Jyotisha is post-Vedic. It has 162 verses on various topics, including muhurta (a division of time), karana (an astrological division of the day), yoga (this can refer to a time period, or to the main star in a lunar asterism), vara (a day of the week). It also looks at jataka (astrology) which forms a part of jyotisha. Later, the siddhanta system with twelve rashi divisions was introduced, and the Vedanga jyotisha was no longer used.

KALPA (RITUAL)

Apart from the Samhitas and Brahmanas, a special category of texts were concerned with ritual. These are broadly termed the Kalpa Sutras.

The Kalpa Sutras have three categories: the Shrauta Sutras, which provide instructions for the agnihotra and other sacrifices; the Grihya Sutras, which describe domestic sacrifices; and the Dharma Sutras, which explain laws and customs. Each of these are attached to one of the four Vedic Samhitas but are considered smriti (remembered) and not shruti (divinely revealed), that is, they have less sanctity than the Vedic Samhitas and other texts closely associated with them. Kalpa Sutras belong to different Vedic Samhitas and schools, and though each text is separate, some series of texts form a connected sequence. For instance, the Apastamba and Baudhayana schools of the Krishna Yajur Veda have closely related Shrauta Sutras, Grihya Sutras, and Dharma Sutras. For certain schools, only a single type of sutra is now available (Shrauta Sutra or Grihya Sutra) while some have only two.

Shrauta Sutras deal with the important Vedic sacrifices and further explain the sacrifices described in the Brahmanas. The method of laying the sacrificial fires, the agnihotra and the various Soma sacrifices, new- and full-moon sacrifices, are among those described. Shrauta Sutras are attached to each of the Vedic Samhitas. The Rig Veda has the Ashvalayana, Shankhayana, and Shaunaka Shrauta Sutras; for the Sama Veda, there are the Mashaka, Latyayana, and Drahyayana. The Taittiriya Samhita or Black Yajur Veda has the largest number, the Apastamba, Baudhayana, Satyasadha-hiranya-keshin, Manava, Bharadvaja, Vadhuna, Vaikhanasa, Laugakshi, Maitra, Katha, and Varaha; the Vajasaneyi Samhita or White Yajur Veda has the Katyayana; the Atharva Veda has the Kushika. Another Shrauta Sutra attached to the Atharva Veda is the Vaitana, which is anonymous.

Grihya Sutras describe household or domestic ceremonies, which are to be performed by Hindus at every stage in life, beginning from the time the child is in the womb. These ceremonies are known as samskaras. In addition, they describe the daily sacrifices a householder should perform, the morning and evening sacrifices, new- and full-moon sacrifices, and annual sacrifices. There are specific ceremonies related to agriculture and farming, house building, and protection from disease. Among the Grihya Sutras are the Ashvalayana, Apastambha, Baudhayana, Bharadvaja, Gobhila, Paraskara, Vaikhanasa, and Varaha. They were composed between about 400 BCE and 400 CE. Some of the Grihya Sutras have separate prayer books attached to them.

Dharma Sutras form the earliest sources of Hindu law and were originally composed between the 6th and 7th centuries BCE, with additions being made later. The customs and ethics described in these are written in short aphorisms and were later expanded and written in verse, forming the Dharma Shastras. Dharma Sutras are attributed to different authors, among them being the sages Apastambha, Baudhayana, Gautama, and Vasishtha. There are many Dharma Shastras probably composed from the 2nd century CE onwards, which expand on the Dharma Sutras. Some of these are idealistic, whereas others are used as legal texts and each is assigned to a mythical or real author. The Manava Dharma Shastra (of Manu), also known as the Manu Smriti, is the earliest, while those of Yajnavalkya, Vishnu, and Narada are probably of the 3rd to 5th centuries CE. There are several others.

Other types of kalpa texts are Shulva or Shulba Sutras, attached to the Shrauta Sutras. These contain information on the construction of fire altars, and include some basic principles of geometry. Shraddha Kalpas and Pitrimedha Sutras deal with ancestral rites; Parishishtas deal with additional material such as omens and practices to attain various powers. Later texts dealing with ritual include prayogas (handbooks), paddhatis (outlines), and karikas (descriptions in verse form).

UPAVEDA

Another category or branch of knowledge is known as Upaveda and includes several topics. Aspects of it are contained in the Vedic Samhitas and associated texts, but they were further developed as separate branches of knowledge. Four classes of Upavedas are Ayurveda, the science of medicine; Gandharvaveda, of music and dancing; Dhanurveda, of archery or military science; and Sthapatyaveda, of architecture.

OTHER TEXTS AND ASSOCIATIONS

There are also later texts and various commentaries, which throw light on the Vedas.

Several religious texts and schools of philosophy refer to the Vedas but there were also some specific commentaries. Some of the more important texts and commentaries are described below.

BRIHAD-DEVATA

The Brihad-devata is an important text assigned to Shaunaka, which provides an account of the Vedic deities. According to some scholars, the author of the Brihad-devata may not have been Shaunaka himself but a member of his school. The Brihad is composed primarily in the anushtubh metre but also has trishtubh stanzas. It has eight adhyayas. Each adhyaya has approximately thirty *vargas*, and each varga usually has five shlokas, though the numbers vary. The text begins by stating it is important to know every aspect of the Veda, including the deity addressed, the metre and nature of the verse. Only then can the mantras revealed to the rishis be understood. Adhyaya 1 and most of Adhyaya 2 provide a classification of the Vedic deities, with Agni, Indra or Vayu, and Surya representing the deities of the three worlds. The twenty-sixth varga of Adhyaya 2 begins a commentary, in successive order, on the deities of the Rig Vedic hymns. Some legends on the deities are also provided, many of them related to legends in the Mahabharata. The rishis, rishikas, steeds of the various deities, an account of the apri hymns, and a discussion on the Vishvedeva hymns are provided. The text is closely connected with the Rig Veda, the Naighantuka, the Nirukta, the Sarvanukramani, Arshanukramani, Anuvakanukramani, and Rigvidhana. It can be dated between the Nirukta and Saravanukramani. The Brihad also refers to several *khilas* or supplementary verses, some of which are not in the Shakala edition of the Rig Veda. The text quotes others including Yaska, Shakatayana, Shakapuni, Galava and the Aitareya Brahmana. It, in turn, is quoted in other texts. The Nitimanjari includes part of the text; Shadgurushishya and Sayana quote from it.

RIGVIDHANA

The Rigvidhana is also attributed to Shaunaka. It describes how the hymns or verses of the Rig Veda are to be used to obtain specific results.

COMMENTARIES

Over the centuries, there were numerous commentators on the Vedas, of whom a few are mentioned below. Skandasvami, who probably lived between the 6th and 7th centuries CE, composed a commentary on part of the Rig Veda. Udgitha and Venkata-Madhava were other commentators. The latter can be dated between the 10th and 12th centuries. Shadguru shishya, who lived in the 12th century, commented on Katyayana's Sarvanukramani. The Chhandogya Brahmana has a commentary by Gunavishnu.

Sayana is one of the most important commentators on the Rig Veda and other Vedic texts. He lived in the 14th century CE and was a minister of several kings of the Vijayanagara empire in southern India. Sayana wrote commentaries on the Rig Veda, the Yajur Veda text of the Taittiriya Samhita, the Sama Veda, Atharva Veda, a number of Brahmanas, and the Aitareya Aranyaka. He also wrote the Yajnatantra-sudhanidhi on Vedic rituals and a number of other texts, including some on grammar. Sayana's commentary on the Rig Veda is extensive and deals with each hymn, mentioning the rishi who is said to have composed it, the deity, the metre, and its use in sacrifice. Other texts and stories are used in explaining the verses. Sayana was probably assisted by other scholars, but was himself extremely learned. He is sometimes given the title *sarvajna*, 'one who has all knowledge'.

His work influenced all later scholars, including many European commentators and translators. Mudgala, who lived after Sayana, summarized some of Sayana's work. Mahidhara was a commentator of the 16th century. His commentary Vedadipa is on the Madhyandina recension of the Yajur Veda text of the Vajasaneyi Samhita. There were other commentators as well but these are the most important, up to the medieval period. Harisvamin and Dvivedaganga were among the others.

REFERENCES TO THE VEDAS IN OTHER SOURCES

References to the Vedas are found in many other sources, including the epics, Bhagavad Gita, Puranas, later regional literature, and in the six early systems of Hindu philosophy. A few aspects of these are provided here.

In the Epics

The two north Indian epics, the Mahabharata and the Ramayana, mention the Vedic Samhitas. Some Vedic myths are also retold or recast in the Mahabharata. On the whole, the Mahabharata has a closer connection with the Vedas than the Ramayana. Names mentioned in the Vedic Samhitas are also found in the Mahabharata. Several deities known in the Vedas are referred to and some of the same myths occur, though in a different form. The Mahabharata contains references to sacrifices and to sacrificial material such as *darbha* grass. Some scholars also suggest that events such as the Mahabharata war represent a kind of ritual or purificatory sacrifice.

In the Puranas

The Puranas have numerous references to the Vedas and Vedic deities. There are elaborations of old stories and new legends on Vedic deities and personalities.

VEDAS AND THE SIX SCHOOLS OF PHILOSOPHY

The six orthodox systems of philosophy—Nyaya, Vaisheshika, Samkhya, Yoga, Mimamsa, and Vedanta—were developing around the same time that the early Upanishads were composed, or just a little later. All six systems uphold the sanctity of the Vedas. Though Nyaya, Vaisheshika, Samkhya, and Yoga did not directly comment on them, they incorporated some aspects of the Vedic Samhitas.

Nyaya literally means that by which the mind reaches a conclusion, and is based on logic and analysis. Nyaya's methods of analysis have been used to understand the Vedas, and hence it has been called an *upanga* (auxiliary limb) of the Vedas.

Vaisheshika deals with physics, metaphysics, logic, and methods of knowledge, and its central feature is considered its theory on the atomic structure of the universe. As with Nyaya, its methods of analysis can be used to understand the Vedas.

Samkhya is said to have been founded by the sage Kapila. Elements of the Samkhya philosophy are found in the Upanishads and the Mahabharata and is also explained in the Bhagavad Gita. Samkhya sees the world as a result of two principles, Purusha and Prakriti. Prakriti is the active principle, the potentiality of all nature, through which the material and psychic world comes into being.

Purusha can be translated as soul. In each living being, there is a Purusha yet, essentially, all purushas are the same. The empirical self is the union of the free spirit, Purusha, and of Prakriti. Purusha is the knower, and the known is Prakriti. The purpose of Samkhya is to free the knower from the known. The Samkhya concept of Purusha can also be compared with the concept of Purusha in the Rig Veda.

However, Samkhya texts state that Vedic sacrifices do not lead anywhere and the path to liberation is only through knowledge and understanding. The later commentator Vijnanabhikshu attempted to reconcile Samkhya with theistic Vedanta, the philosophy contained in many Upanishads. He put forward the theory of a universal Purusha, which would be similar to Brahman.

The basics of Samkhya philosophy were accepted by the system of Yoga, with the addition of the concept of *ishvara* or god. It differs from Samkhya in its method of reaching the goal. In Yoga, a systematic effort is required to detach Purusha from Prakriti. Patanjali, in his Yoga Sutra, describes this unified system that has eight successive steps incorporating ethical, meditative and other practices.

Yoga is mentioned in some early Upanishads, and several later Upanishads deal with it too.

Of the six classical systems of philosophy, Mimamsa is most closely connected with the Vedic Samhitas. Jaimini (dated between the 4th and 2nd centuries BCE) is said to have founded this school; his work, Mimamsa Sutra, explains its philosophy. This early form of Mimamsa, known as Purva Mimamsa or Karma Mimamsa (analysis of action), focused on the Vedas as the ultimate source of divine knowledge, and the correct performance of rituals and sacrifices. As there were many different texts describing rituals, some guidelines or rules (nyaya) were required, and Jaimini's Sutra provided these. The interpretation of the Vedas was only possible through the understanding of each *shabda* or word, and thus the sutra focused on both sound and meaning. Other commentators elaborated on Jaimini's Sutras.

Later commentators began to deal with higher philosophical concepts; this philosophy became almost identical with Vedanta and was known as Uttara Mimamsa or later Mimamsa.

Vedanta too is closely linked with the Vedas, as it includes all those schools of philosophy that use the early Upanishads as their basic source, particularly as summarized by Badarayana (5th to 3rd century BCE) in the Brahma Sutra, also known as the Vedanta Sutra, a text reinterpreted by later scholars in varying ways.

The most notable school of Vedanta, Advaita, developed between the 7th and 9th centuries CE. Vaishnava Vedanta schools include Visishtadvaita, Dvaita, Dvaitadvaita, and Shuddhadvaita. A Shaiva school of Vedanta is Shivadvaita. These schools of thought agree on certain basic premises, for instance that Brahman, the Absolute, transcending time and space, is the ultimate cause of all creation, and that its true nature is concealed because of ignorance. However, they arrive at different understandings on the nature and relationship of Brahman, Ishvara or god, the Atman or Jiva (the individual soul), and the world.

Many philosophers of these schools of Vedanta referred to the Vedas while some wrote commentaries on them. Among them, Shankara, the greatest exponent of Advaita, did not believe in Vedic sacrifices but accepted shruti, that is, all revealed texts like the Vedas, as a source of knowledge (*jnana*).

Dvaita's founder was Madhva who lived in the 13th century CE. Among other works, he wrote a commentary on the first forty hymns of the Rig Veda. Dvaitadvaita's major exponent was Nimbarka, who probably lived in the 12th century. Nimbarka believed the person seeking Brahman should first study the literature on Vedic duties, and should understand that the enjoyments and beneficial results provided by these were only temporary and that only the realization of Brahman could lead to eternal bliss.

Other philosophers of these schools believed in the sanctity of the Vedic Samhitas but all saw the Upanishads as the highest aspect of Vedic literature. Vedanta literally means the 'last or ultimate part of the Vedas'.

Until the Europeans took an interest in the Vedas, the subject matter of the Vedic texts remained relatively unknown to the general public. Traditionally, the three upper castes could study the Vedas but, in practice, it remained a preserve of the brahmanas. Women were usually not allowed to listen to or chant the Vedas. Even among the brahmanas, many who used the texts in rituals did not understand the meaning. From the 19th century onwards, numerous Western scholars analysed and translated the Vedas. Notable among them were A.B. Keith, R.T.H. Griffith, A.A. Macdonell, and R. Roth. Indian scholars of the 19th and 20th centuries also began to study the Vedas along the same lines. Among them were Ram Mohan Roy, Bal Gangadhar Tilak, A.S. Altekar, F.E. Pargiter, and A.D. Pusalkar. While scholars were reading and interpreting the Vedas, they remained difficult for ordinary Indians to access. When the reformist Brahmo Samaj, founded by Ram Mohan Roy, attempted to introduce the Vedas to the general public, the brahmana pandits initially refused to allow non-brahmanas to listen to readings of the Vedic Samhitas, though they were allowed to attend readings of the Upanishads. In the late 19th century, Swami Dayananada Saraswati, founder of the Arya Samaj, attempted to make the Vedic Samhitas more easily available, and stated that they were meant for everyone. At the same time, he provided a new spiritual interpretation of the Vedas, which remains influential till today. In the early 20th century, Sri Aurobindo appreciated Swami Dayananda's efforts and provided a different spiritual interpretation of the Rig Veda. For both Swami Dayananda and Sri Aurobindo, the historical context of the text either did not exist or was irrelevant. New translations and commentaries, as well as new interpretations of the historical context of the Vedas, continue to emerge.

Today, the Vedas are accessible to everyone. New organizations such as the Gayatri Parivar, initiated in 1958 and now comprising over four thousand centres across the country, have made Vedic chanting and study available to all, including women.

CHAPTER 3

THE ORIGINS: THE INDO-EUROPEANS

Who were the people who wrote the Rig Veda? When was it written and where? There are innumerable controversies on these points, and no agreement.

Linguistic analysis forms an important part of the theories of origin of the Vedic people, and of other groups in India at the time of the composition of the Rig Veda. The various theories and their implications will be looked at in more detail in subsequent chapters; the focus here is on the classification of Vedic Sanskrit as an Indo-Aryan language belonging to the larger group of Indo-European languages. This theory owes its origin to William Jones, one of the first to discover the similarities between Sanskrit and Greek and Latin. Jones, who came to India in 1783 and became a judge of the Calcutta High Court, knew several languages including English, Persian, Latin, Greek, Gothic (an old form of German), and Welsh. In India, he began to study Sanskrit, to better understand local and customary laws. In 1786, he put forward his views, laying the base for hundreds of years of further study. He said:

The Sanskrit language, whatever be its antiquity, is of a wonderful structure: more perfect than the Greek, more copious than the Latin, and more exquisitely refined than either; yet bearing to both of them a stronger affinity, both in the roots of verbs and in the forms of grammar, than could possibly have been produced by accident; so strong indeed that no philologer could examine them all three, without believing them to have sprung from some common source, which perhaps no longer exists.

He stated that Persian, Celtic, and Gothic probably also belonged to the same family of languages. Jones provided the hints that later led to the theory of a group or family of Indo-European languages. This term was first used by an English scholar Thomas Young in 1813, and since then became the standard term for all these related languages. These languages are spread across Asia

55

and Europe, and are today spoken by about 3 billion people, more than any other language group. In addition, they include some extinct languages.

The Indo-European language pool is subdivided into twelve main branches, and also classified into the Centum and Satem groups based on the use of certain consonants. (*Centum* or kentum and *satem* are two different ways of pronouncing the word 'hundred'.)

Indo-European languages of the past and present, along with the areas where they are spoken, or were spoken in the past, are given below.

CENTUM GROUP

1. Celtic: British isles, Spain, across southern Europe to central Turkey; includes the extinct Gaulish and Manx, as well as Irish Gaelic, Scots Gaelic, Cornish, Breton, and Welsh.
2. Germanic: England, throughout Scandinavia, and central Europe to Crimea; includes Gothic, Flemish, Dutch, German, Afrikaans, Frisian, Old English, English, Yiddish, Scots, Old Norse, Icelandic, Faroese, Norwegian, Danish, and Swedish.
3. Italic: Italy, later throughout the Roman empire, including present Spain, Portugal, France, Romania; languages include the extinct Latin and Osco-Umbrian, and Catalan, French, Galician, Italian, Portuguese, Provencal, Romansch, Romanian, and Spanish.
4. Hellenic: In Greece and the Aegean islands, later in other areas conquered by Alexander, but mostly around the Mediterranean; languages include ancient and modern Greek.
5. Tocharian: In the Tarim basin of Xinjiang, in far-western China.
6. Anatolian: Languages in Anatolia or Asia Minor, modern Turkey; includes the ancient Hittite.

SATEM GROUP

1. Balto-Slavic: Baltic languages include Latvian, Lithuanian, and Old Prussian. Slavic can be divided into three groups of south, west and east Slavic. South Slavic includes Bosnian, Bulgarian, Serbian, Croatian, Macedonian, Slovenian and Old Church Slavonic; west Slavic includes the eastern European languages of Czech, Polish, Slovak, and Sorbian; east Slavic includes Belarusian, Ukrainian, and Russian. (Though these are classified as satem languages, they have some centum elements.)
2. Armenian: In Armenia and nearby areas, including eastern Turkey.
3. Indo-Iranian: In India, Pakistan, Afghanistan, Iran, and Kurdish areas of Iraq and Turkey; includes Sanskrit and all languages associated with or derived from it (Assamese, Bengali, Gujarati, Hindi, Marathi, Nepali, Punjabi, Romany, Sindhi, Singalese, Urdu); Dardic and Kashmiri languages; the Iranian group of Avestan, Sogdian, Old Persian, Persian, Baluchi, Kurdish, Pashto, and others, as well as Nuristani languages.
4. Albanian: Albanian, Gheg, and Tosk.
5. Extinct languages: Phyrgian, Thracian, Dacian, Illyrian.

Thus, most European languages and many in Asia belong to the Indo-European family. Among the European languages that are not Indo-European are Basque, Finnish, Estonian, and Magyar.

PROTO-INDO-EUROPEAN

All the Indo-European languages are believed to have been derived from a common language called Proto-Indo-European (PIE), a hypothetical language, reconstructed on the basis of key and root words in the various Indo-European languages. Having struggled with the problem for over two hundred years, linguists have carefully and painstakingly reconstructed around 1500 PIE roots, based on a comparison of words in all the Indo-European languages, known changes within the languages, and probable changes over time.

Thus, they have not only arrived at a probable initial language termed PIE but also, by calculating the rate of language change, have estimated the date around which such a language existed. They have also deduced an idea of the economy and society of the PIE people. When one examines or analyses all the words of a language, it presents a comprehensive picture of a people and their culture. For instance, food, clothes, relationships, the environment, economy, items available, and trade are all reflected in language. And yet, despite intensive analyses, archaeologists and linguists do not agree on the results.

RATES OF LANGUAGE CHANGE

Different methods have been used to calculate rates of change. It is thought that certain parts of a language, called a 'basic' or 'core' vocabulary, would change slower than others. This core vocabulary is believed to include kinship terms, aspects of nature, and terms for basic needs such as eating and sleeping.

In the early 1950s, the linguist Morris Swadesh listed a 100-word and 200-word basic core vocabulary. He was one of the first to use statistical methods to estimate the speed of language change. Though some criticized his theory, his ideas were utilized by later linguists, and the rate of change analysed through computer programs. A rate of change of 10–20 per cent per 1000 years was estimated for the core vocabulary. The American mathematician Joseph Kruskal, along with the linguists Isidore Dyen and Paul Black, was involved in a 'lexicostatistical' study of the core vocabulary. After comparing ninety-five Indo-European languages, they felt that PIE began to transform or split around 3000 BCE. Estimating its life between 1000 and 2000 years, it was thought that PIE must have existed between 5000 and 3000 BCE.

The British archaeologist Colin Renfrew put forward a different time frame. He suggested that Indo-Hittite was the source language, and that it predated PIE. This theory was in fact put forward in the 1920s by the American linguist Edgar Sturtevant. Renfrew believed that Indo-Hittite should be dated to around 7000 BCE. According to this theory, Indo-Hittite was spoken in Anatolia and, after reaching Greece around 6700–6500 BCE, it developed into PIE and spread across Europe and the Mediterranean basin with the expansion of agriculture. Renfrew also estimated the rate of change for various words differently, leading to this earlier date. He said that the various Indo-European languages of today already existed in their respective regions, possibly as earlier forms, by the Neolithic period. Several archaeologists support this theory.

Recently, numerous mathematical and computational models of language change have been generated. One such model estimates language change at the rate of 16 per cent per 1000 years.

PALAEOLITHIC CONTINUITY THEORY

However, there are some linguists who have challenged the very basis of these theories. Notable among these is the Italian linguist Mario Alinei, who put forward the Palaeolithic Continuity Theory (PCT) in a two-volume work in Italian, published in 1996 and 2000. Alinei argues that linguists have unfortunately been influenced by Darwinian theories, seeing 'language as a living organism, and language change an organic law'. He supports Noam Chomsky's theory of the innateness of language, holding that language is a social phenomenon, not some evolving organism governed by fixed rates of change. He divides language change into two broad categories of grammar and vocabulary, stating that language is basically conservative. Grammar changes occur in exceptional circumstances, usually through external influences, while vocabulary changes are responses to changes in the economy and society. Having said that, vocabulary changes are more evident in oral than in written language.

Alinei believes that language development can be traced to prehuman times, and that language diffusion took place along with the earliest migrations of *Homo sapiens* from Africa or, at the latest, during the Late or Upper Palaeolithic period. After reaching Europe, there was initially a very slow rate of change but, by the end of the Ice Age, Celtic, Italic, Germanic, Slavic and Baltic languages had developed. During the Neolithic period, language began to change at a faster pace.

This theory finds some support among linguists, though as Alinei pointed out, linguistics remained the one field that was trapped in Biblical chronology and failed to examine the distant past. In 1934, the German linguist Herbert Kuhn stated that the period of Indo-European unity must have been the Ice Age, specifically the Aurignacian period, estimated at circa 30,000 BCE. In 1958, the German archaeologist and botanist Gustav Schwantes proposed a similar theory. More recently, the Bulgarian linguist and philologist Vladimir I. Georgiev and the Italian linguists Marcello Durante, Gabrielle Costa, and Cicero Poghirc have worked on the same lines, while several others have expressed their agreement. Noted archaeologists who have supported this theory include the American Homer L. Thomas, the Belgian Marcel Otte, and the German archaeologist Alexander Hausler. These studies have been confined to Europe. However the PCT theory also has several critics.

Apart from the PCT supporters, the Russian scholar N.S. Trubetskoy (1890–1938), one of the founders of Eurasianism, who studied Indo-European and knew more than twelve languages, was among those who questioned the very idea of PIE. Trubetskoy instead put forward the 'sprachbund' theory of languages developing similarities through contact and influence. The French archaeologist Jean-Paul Demoule, in 1980 and later, has also questioned the existence of PIE and of an Indo-European language.

Most others accepted it but differed regarding the place and date of the homeland.

Some broad time schemes, based on suggestions of various scholars, are given below:

1. Theory of Indo-Hittite as the earliest language
    • Pre-PIE or Indo-Hittite, in Anatolia before 6500 BCE
    • Archaic PIE in Greece 6500–6000 BCE
    • 6500–5000 BCE, PIE spoken in most of Europe (In stage 2, 5000–3000 BCE, the language spread to the steppes.)
2. PIE: 4500 BCE
    • Pre-Anatolian breaks away, before 3500 BCE
    • Pre-Tocharian separates, though it also has some later traits
    • Pre-Celtic and Pre-Italic separate, before 2500 BCE; Germanic may have intially separated at the same time but had later influences of Celtic, Baltic, and Slavic, so this is uncertain
    • Pre-Greek separates: 2500–2000 BCE
    • Indo-Iranian separates: by 2000 BCE; common Indo-Iranian at the latest dates to circa 1700 BCE
3. Phylogenetic linguistic model
    This is based on the work of Russel D. Gray and Quentin D. Atkinson, of New Zealand, both with a background in biology and psychology. This analysis studied 87 IE languages and used evolutionary biology to construct a computational method.
    • Pre-Anatolian: 6700 BCE
    • Pre-Tocharian: 5900 BCE
    • Pre-Greek/Armenian: circa 5300 BCE
    • Pre-Indo-Iranian/Albanian: circa 4900 BCE
    • Ancestors of pre-Balto Slavic, pre-Italo-Celtic Germanic: 4500 BCE
4. PCT theory
    Most languages had developed and spread, at the latest by 10,000 BCE.

MIGRATION THEORIES

The spread of the Indo-European languages has usually been related to the migration of people, at the dates indicated above. These people were not genetically similar but are presumed to have once spoken the same language (PIE) and to have had certain cultural similarities. As the language spread to different regions due to the migration of this linguistic group, it changed and several languages arose. Where was its original home? And did such a migration take place at all?

There is no agreement on the answers to these questions but the main views are summarized below. Before looking at the theories of the original homeland, we will look at concepts of the spread or diffusion of languages.

LANGUAGE DIFFUSION

How languages diverge or converge are aspects of linguistic analysis. Theories of language diffusion are usually part of cultural diffusion theories. The Indo-European theory includes cultural diffusion—not merely language but also technology, ideas and styles spread to different regions. The Indo-Europeans are believed to have common socio-economic aspects as well as similarities in types of deities, in warfare, the use of the chariot and the horse, among others. To understand language diffusion, aspects of the environment as depicted in the language are also assessed.

At one time, conquest was believed to be a key aspect in the spread of language and culture. Later, the focus was on migration. Both conquest and migration can lead to cultural diffusion but these are no longer seen as the only—or even the main—methods by which languages and culture spread. Cultural diffusion can also take place via trade, merchants, and employment of artisans from distant lands or of mercenary soldiers. Explorers and diplomats can diffuse ideas. Diffusion can also take place when two groups live adjacent to each other and there is an interchange of various sorts, including marriage. Known as direct diffusion, this was more common in ancient times than indirect diffusion that takes place through an intermediary. The American linguist Benjamin W. Fortson points out that it is impossible to say whether a common linguistic feature in two adjacent areas is the result of development from a single language or of innovation in one region, later adopted by others. This could also apply to cultural diffusion and needs to be borne in mind while examining similarities in language and culture.

Another aspect to be kept in focus is that a social group need not form a linguistic group and, alternatively, that people speaking one language may belong to several different social groups—as is usually the case today.

LANGUAGE AND GENETICS

A problem here is the confusion over linguistic groups and race. While Max Müller in his later writings, and several others held that Indo-European was a group of languages not connected with race, others identified Indo-Europeans as a racial group. This evoked both nationalistic and imperialistic responses. Nationalists in several countries were against the concept that their culture was created by migrants. In the past, such theories have been misused by Hitler in his concept of the superior 'Aryan' race.

Recent genetic studies have been used by both linguists and archaeologists to arrive at ancient migration patterns. Luca Cavalli-Sforza, a geneticist of Italian origin who moved to the US in 1970, is a pioneer in the field of 'genetic geography', linking genes with patterns of migration, culture, and language. While genetics has been linked to race and nationality, Sforza does not connect genes with race, and is in fact totally against the concept of race.

While language and race can easily be separated, when one talks of a group speaking the same language—migrating and transporting their language and culture with them—it does become difficult to distinguish between a language group and a race or genetically identifiable group. However, in general, Indo-European refers only to languages, not to homogenous groups of people.

INDIGENOUS ORIGIN: CURRENT TRENDS

The current trend all over the world is to seek an indigenous origin for language and culture. This is the case in India and in several other countries. Some examples are given here.

In the context of Scotland, Katherine Forsyth, a British historian who specialized in Celtic studies, points out:

> Scottish archaeologists are now freeing themselves from the notion of recurring waves of people sweeping across the country, all but submerging older population groups, and are thus able to accord the indigenous inhabitants of Scotland a more active role in linguistic and cultural change. This fundamental shift is part of a more general trend in archaeological theory to down-play the role of invasion and wholesale population replacement in prehistoric cultural change.

Several scholars also propose an insider's view for Greek. For instance, Ernst Risch, a Swiss professor of Indo-European studies, stated that the Greek dialects arose in Greece from Proto-Greek and several dialects developed as the language spread over a large area. This explanation is now accepted by many.

While Proto-Germanic is generally thought to be an Indo-European language—actually believed to be the originator of the Germanic languages English and German—there are also theories that pre-Proto-German was different from PIE.

THE HOMELAND QUESTION

The concept of a homeland for PIE presumes that: (1) PIE did exist; (2) its time frame can be correctly estimated; and (3) language probably spread through migration or conquest, or through certain activities such as farming.

Despite the differences of opinion outlined above, many archaeologists and linguists believe that such a homeland did exist. The relationship between linguistics and archaeology is sometimes circular. The archaeologist depends on linguistic theories while searching for an appropriate culture, while the linguist seeks support for his theories from archaeologists. Linguistic theories, referred to above, have inspired several archaeologists to attempt to equate a Bronze Age archaeological culture with the early homeland, using the clues provided by linguists. The most likely date for the existence of a PIE homeland is taken as the period 5000–3000 BCE.

The search for a homeland is based on several factors including the cultural hints provided by the partially reconstructed PIE language. Such reconstruction indicates that the PIE people had a patrilineal society, with rights and duties inherited through the father. Women lived with their husband's family after marriage. Groups of people lived together under a chieftain, who had some authority over them.

The words for mountain, river, lake or sea, and for marshy land, are reconstructed, as well as that for boat, indicating that the PIE region was not a desert nor a totally flat plain. Among the names of wild animals, the words for bear, fox, otter, beaver, wolf, lynx, elk or deer, stag, horse, mouse, hare, and hedgehog have been reconstructed. Birds known included goose, crane, duck, eagle, falcon or hawk, sparrow, quail, thrush, vulture, blackbird, crow, raven, jay, kite, pheasant, stork, cuckoo, and possibly owl. (Linguists disagree on some of these animals and birds.) There are words for snake, turtle, frog, fish, and some specific fish including trout and salmon. Bees, honey and wax were also known, as were fly, wasp, hornet and louse, its egg or nit, and the flea. Among domestic animals were cattle (also cow, ox, steer), sheep, pig (and boar, sow, piglet), goat, and dog. Though numerous theories centre on the absence or presence of the horse, from the reconstructed language it is not clear if the horse was domesticated in the earliest times. The use of the horse was a characteristic of Indo-Europeans, as indicated by later available texts and inscriptions. Chariots were also used. Yet, others point out that use of the horse and chariot was not confined to Indo-Europeans.

These animals are found throughout Europe and much of Asia, though the beaver does not occur in Anatolia and Greece. The wild animals indicate that the PIE people lived in partly forested regions. Plant names are difficult to reconstruct, as very few are found in both western and eastern Indo-European languages. Birch is found in six branches; the next most common are willow, ash, and oak but these are mainly in the European branches of Indo-European. Hittite and Irish have a cognate word for hawthorn. In both cultures, hawthorn was used in rituals. Five branches have a word that means beech or elder. In the European languages, words for elm, juniper, alder, apple, hazel, and cherry have also been reconstructed. PIE words exist for berry, bean, and snow; the last is believed to indicate a temperate climate but this is not definite, as snowy mountains such as the Himalayas could be known, even if the people generally lived in the plains.

There seem to have been some common burial practices, and these have been projected back to the PIE period. Though details differ, it is thought that kings and warriors were buried in individual tombs, covered with earth mounds. Cremation was sometimes practised in the Indo-

Iranian world and as a special honour for Scandinavian heroes. Grave goods buried wth the dead included sacrificial animals.

Several Indo-European groups have some common religious practices, for instance, the worship of sky, earth and other nature deities, and fire sacrifices. All older Indo-European religions were polytheistic but this would be true of all religions across the world. Very few names of deities can be reconstructed in PIE. The general word for deity is from the root of the word 'shine'; the Vedic *deva*, Latin *deus*, Old Irish *dia* and Lithuanian *dievas* all come from the same root. The Greek *theos*, though it sounds similar, has a different root. There are also similarities in myths.

The French philologist G. Dumezil was among those who revealed some common aspects of the various Indo-European groups.

He believed in an Indo-European tripartite scheme of 'fonctions' that applied to social classes, deities, and other aspects. John Brough, a British professor of Sanskrit, is among the critics of this theory and says it can as well apply to the god of the Old Testament, as indeed every deity has these different aspects.

The search for a homeland is thus based on the quest for an archaeological culture of the appropriate date, with the characteristic culture believed to belong to PIE.

One problem is whether an archaeological assemblage that occurs across several sites, generally termed an archaeological culture, can be associated with a group of people. For instance, a particular pottery type can be found over a wide area but does not necessarily indicate a single group of people. Thus, a widespread change in pottery can take place without a change in the existing social group.

However, as Renfrew points out: 'If there were indeed major movements of early populations, which might have been responsible for this language distribution, then they should be reflected in the archaeological record.' In what way though? If pottery is not a reliable criterion, what other aspects could reflect this? Pottery as well as other artefacts could have been obtained through trade, or a particular artefact or pottery style adopted from another culture. Despite the uncertainty in date, type of culture, and what pottery or other artefacts, and structure or graves may indicate, various homelands have been suggested.

EUROPE

Several early and later scholars suggested a European homeland, dating to the Neolithic period. Before looking at particular suggestions, we will briefly survey the time frame of the European Neolithic. In Europe, the first evidence of agriculture and settled village life emerged around 7000 BCE. There were several different Neolithic cultures across the region. Radiocarbon dates suggest that Mesolithic cultures coexisted. Two major theories are that farming here developed independently from hunter-gatherer communities, or that it spread with migrating farmers from the region of Anatolia. The broad time frame for the Neolithic in Europe is between 7000 and 5500 BCE in south-east Europe; before 6000 BCE in the central and west Mediterranean; around

5500 BCE in central Europe; and about 4500 BCE in north-west Europe. The last region was associated with megaliths.

Among these various cultures, Linear pottery culture or LBK in central and north Europe is typified by a characteristic decorated pottery. It can be dated to 5500 BCE and later. It is often thought to result from the colonization of farmers from south-east Europe, though scholars such as Alasdair Whittle, professor of archaeology at Cardiff University and a specialist in the Neolithic period, feel it was an indigenous development. In 1902, the German linguist and archaeologist Gustav Kossina looked at north central Europe as the homeland of PIE. This could have been the core area of the Corded Ware (CW) culture, which began around 3000 BCE and is believed by some scholars to have spread through migration and to represent the Indo-Europeans. Kossina felt that the Linear pottery of Germany and Holland was displaced by Indo-European pressure from the north, and moved south and east, followed by the people of northern Europe who used Corded Ware. The CW culture was actually widespread across Europe from Switzerland in the north to the eastern Baltic, and from the Rhine to the east of the Vistula. Though the culture had regional differences, these people seem to have largely been cattle herders who engaged in some amount of farming and practised burial. Their core area could alternatively be between the western Ukraine to the south-east of the Baltic, or in part of Poland. Around this area, there were related cultures. In 1949, the Austrian linguist and anthropologist Wilhelm Schmidt proposed the theory of two waves of colonizers reaching Europe from the east. In 1960, P. Bosch-Gimpera, a Mexican archaeologist of Spanish origin, saw Central Europe as the homeland but felt that the IE people originated in the early Neolithic period, and spread to different areas in Europe in the later Neolithic. He equated their spread with that of various Danubian cultures. Marek Zvelebil, an archaeologist and historian of Czech origin, looked at northern Europe as the homeland. In 1995, he put forward what is known as the 'Neolithic creolisation' theory, in which migrating Neolithic famers mixed with indigenous hunter-gatherers in this region, resulting in the development of Indo-European.

SOUTH RUSSIAN STEPPES

The German philologist Otto Schrader (1855–1919) put forward the theory of a homeland in what is called the Pontic–Caspian steppes, that is, the region of South Russia near the Caspian and Aral seas, north of the Black Sea. The horse was native to the region, and Schrader felt that the Indo-European people domesticated as well as ate the horse.

In 1926, in his book *The Aryans*, Gordon Childe zeroed in on South Russia as the homeland after comparing various archaeological cultures. In a later book, *Prehistoric Migrations in Europe* (1949), Childe believed that the horse-drawn chariot and the war horse were related to the spread of Indo-European. He, among others, felt that the people of the Celtic Urnfield culture of the late Bronze Age were the main warrior migrants.

In the search for a homeland, the work of the Lithuanian archaeologist Marija Gimbutas has been influential. Gimbutas located the homeland in the South Russian steppes, and termed the archaeological complex the Kurgan culture, after the burial mounds found in the region. The Kurgan actually includes a number of Copper and Bronze Age cultures in the southern Russian steppes near the Black Sea and middle Volga that have burial mounds known as kurgans, from the original Russian term, which is the same. In 1970, Gimbutas wrote that, based on archaeology and the type of culture surmised from the recreation of PIE words and terms, 'The Kurgan culture seems the only remaining candidate for being Proto-Indo-European.' She used arguments from linguistics, based on common words, and significant features such as the kurgans or burial mounds that seemed to reflect Indo-European burial practices. She felt that excavations of Kurgan cultures indicated a pastoral economy, hierarchical society, indulgence in warfare, animal sacrifice, worship and/or use of the horse, existence of wheeled vehicles, and worship of a solar deity.

Gimbutas suggested successive waves of kurgan expansion, which could be related to various cultures, including the CW that Kossina had first referred to. The fourth expansion wave, she felt, influenced the Vucedol culture (3000–2200 BCE) in the Danube region, named after the site of Vucedol in Croatia. According to her, the Yamnaya culture then mixed with the Vucedol, leading to the Bell-Beaker culture. These people then spread over Europe in the second half of the 3rd millennium BCE, even reaching the British isles. However, archaeologists are not agreed on the origins of the Bell-Beaker culture.

According to Gimbutas, before the Indo-Europeans spread across Europe, 'Old Europe' as she called it, consisted of peaceful, women-centred, goddess-worshipping cultures. The Indo-Europeans brought in patriarchy and war. However, there is a problem with her viewpoint—warfare and forts existed in Europe well before her proposed dates for the Indo-European migration.

In addition, the 'Kurgan cultures' were not uniform; in fact, they had many differences. Several archaeologists now believe that the homeland was in Ukraine and southern Russia, known as the Pontic–Caspian steppes, but the focus is on a more specific culture rather than the kurgan burials in general. Some of the early cultures of this region are the Sredny Stog, Khvalynsk, and Dnieper–Donets. The Khvalynsk culture (5000–4000 BCE) and the Sredny Stog (4500–3500 BCE) are both identified with the PIE homeland. Sredny Stog was pre-Kurgan, with its main centres in what is now Ukraine. It had burials without mounds or kurgans, battleaxes of a type associated with the Indo-Europeans, and also some Corded Ware. It was succeeded by the Yamnaya culture, originating between the Pontic–Caspian steppes and the forest regions of the Dnieper and Volga steppes, dating to 3500 BCE and spread over a wide region. The earliest possible date for the break-up of PIE was thought to be 3500–3400 BCE, based on the first use of wheeled vehicles. The Yamnaya is connected with the later Andronovo, usually identified with the Indo-Iranian culture (see Chapter 5).

The Finnish Indologist Asko Parpola sees the origin of PIE in the Khvalynsk culture in the mid-Volga region. It spread east and west but PIE developed in southern Ukraine, in the later

Sredny Stog culture. The next stage was the Pit Grave culture (Yamnaya), followed by the Middle Dnieper and the Corded Ware cultures. Corded Ware spread to the north-west, where the Italo-Celtic, Proto-Baltic, Slavic, and Proto-Germanic languages developed.

ANATOLIA

As seen earlier, Renfrew places the homeland of Indo-European languages in Anatolia in a pre-PIE period. He provides two alternative hypotheses for the spread of Indo-European languages outside Europe. One suggestion is that, from Anatolia, PIE first spread with migrating farmers to northern Iran, and even to Turkmenistan. It then spread to the Iranian plateau and India–Pakistan, and this too was related to the adoption of farming. In another hypothesis, he believed that PIE spread to the south Russian steppes in its second phase, between 5000 and 3000 BCE, and from there to other areas. It probably reached there via the agricultural Cucuteni and Tripolye cultures of east Europe.

While pastoralism was once believed to have preceded agriculture, Renfrew and some other analysts believe that 'agriculture is a precondition for a pastoral economy', hence, the east European and Ukraine agricultural regions contributed to the development of pastoral nomadism in the steppes. These nomadic pastoralists succeeded the early agriculturalists and spread Indo-European languages as they migrated, just as farmers had spread it across Europe. The use of the horse was crucial to this spread, and warfare could have been a part of it. The spread of Indo-European to India and Iran may have been through two waves of migration. Based on Renfrew's theories, linguistically, the two waves would have differed. The first would have been a language directly developed from Indo-Hittite, which according to him was pre-PIE. The second would have been a post-PIE language, further getting transformed as it crossed Central Asia, Iran, Afghanistan, and finally reached north-west India.

Both theories are clearly hypothetical.

The Georgian linguist T.V. Gamkrelidze and the Russian philologist V.V. Ivanov are among those who see a relationship between PIE and the Kartvelian and Semitic languages. They have reconstructed the economic and cultural vocabulary of PIE, with names of different flora and fauna, and a homeland in a mountainous region. On the basis of their different reconstruction of PIE, they identify the Indo-European homeland in the 4th millennium BCE, in Anatolia or Armenia. They feel that the Indo-European area of origin extended south from Anatolia to the Balkans and north to the Caucasus mountains. According to them, from here, the Hittites and Greeks moved to the west and the Proto-Indo-Iranians moved to the east, towards the northern part of the Iranian plateau, from where some Indo-Aryans moved west to the Mittani kingdom (discussed later) and others farther east into India. The Tocharians, and those who spoke early Indo-European dialects, moved through Central Asia to the northern Caspian region, and from here across Europe.

INDIA

The German poet and Indologist Friedrich Schlegel (1772–1829) was one of the first to put forward this viewpoint. More recent proponents include Koenraad Elst, the conservative right-wing Belgian author; Nicholas Kazanas, a scholar and philosopher of Greek origin; Shrikant Talageri, the Indian scholar; and several others, who believe that India could be the Indo-European homeland. Elst placed the date for the migration out of India around the 6th millennium BCE.

BACTRIA–SOGDIANA

Johanna Nichols (1997), a linguist and specialist in Slavic languages, has a different view; she places the homeland in the 4th to 5th millennium BCE, to the east of the Caspian Sea, in the area of Bactria–Sogdiana.

OTHER HOMELANDS

The Irish–American archaeologist J.P. Mallory suggests four most likely homelands:

1. Pontic–Caspian: Chalcolithic, 5th to 4th millenniums BCE (Kurgan culture)
2. Anatolia: Early neolithic, 7th to 5th millenniums BCE
3. Baltics: Mesolithic to Neolithic (Ertebelle to CW, 6th to 3rd millenniums BCE)
4. Balkans: Neolithic, 5th millennium BCE

There are innumerable other identifications of the homeland. Lithuania, Armenia, and northern Europe are among the more credible options. Tibet too has been named.

NO CONSENSUS

After looking at the main theories, it is clear that there is no consensus on the date of PIE, or on how and when it spread. Some even doubt whether it ever existed. The accuracy of reconstructed terms and their meanings has also been doubted. It has been pointed out that a reconstructed term is 'a phonetic idealization', and one cannot definitely know the meanings of reconstructed words. But others feel that meanings can be assigned to such words. They believe that if one meaning is consistently attached to a word or its cognate in all languages, then it is likely that that meaning must have existed earlier as well.

Despite doubts and contradictions, the most accepted theory based on linguistics is that PIE did exist, that it originated in the Bronze Age (5000–3000 BCE), and that it subsequently spread through migrating groups, changing even as it spread. Renfrew's theory of its spread via agriculture and migrating farmers is perhaps the next most accepted version. But, in the light of new research, the PCT needs more serious examination.

WHAT WAS BEFORE PIE?

It is agreed that languages developed at a fairly early date. Dates for this vary between 1 million years and 40,000 years ago. Hence, if PIE or its antecedents developed in 7000 or 5000 BCE, why did it/they develop? What was the language people spoke before this? In what way was this language related to PIE or pre-PIE? The theory is that other languages were spoken in Europe before Indo-European languages replaced them. But the question is this: what was the language spoken before PIE by the very people with whom it originated?

WHERE? THE HOMELAND PROBLEM

As there is no consensus on the date or on whether there was any type of migration, there is obviously no agreement on the homeland of the PIE, if at all such a linguistic group existed. Despite this, the search for a homeland continues.

CHAPTER 4

THE IRANIAN CONNECTION

Indo-Iranian is one of the languages believed to be derived from Indo-European, from which both Iranian and Indo-Aryan languages are thought to have developed. The close similarities between the language of the most ancient Iranian text, the Gathas, and the Rig Veda, as well as similarities between Rig Vedic deities and *yazatas* or Zoroastrian deities, have led scholars to presume that Indians and Iranians were once a common people with a common homeland. Understanding the Iranian connection with the Vedas is an essential prerequisite to arrive at any conclusions regarding the origin of the Rig Vedic people.

The most accepted theory is that after the Proto-Indo-European language had emerged, and possibly after the first PIE speakers began to move out of their original homeland, the Indo-Iranian group lived together for some time, before separating. There are again many theories about their possible homeland and the date of separation. We have looked at some aspects of these theories in the preceding chapter.

THE INDO-IRANIAN LANGUAGES

This group of languages is usually subdivided into Iranian, Indo-Aryan (including Dardic), and Nuristani. Today, these are spoken not only in India–Pakistan, Afghanistan, and Iran but also over much of Asia from the Black Sea to western China.

INDO-ARYAN

Indo-Aryan, often referred to as Indic to avoid the use of the word Aryan, forms a large group of languages, mainly spoken in India, Bangladesh, and Pakistan. It includes Rig Vedic and classical Sanskrit and related languages. Linguists such as the American M.B. Emeneau point out that classical Sanskrit is not a linear descendant of Rig Vedic Sanskrit. There were probably several Sanskrit dialects in existence; one was used in the Rig Veda but classical Sanskrit developed from a different though related dialect. Related languages include many regional languages of India today, as well as Pali and Prakrits in the past. While we will look at Indo-Aryan and related material in chapters 6, 7, and 8, here we focus on understanding the Iranian material.

NURISTANI

Nuristani languages have been variously classified. They have been considered part of the Iranian languages, possibly influenced by Dardic (Indo-Aryan), or part of the Dardic group, or a separate and distinct branch of Indo-Iranian. Nuristani languages, formerly called Kafiri, have not been studied to the same extent as the others. These are spoken by tribal groups in the mountainous regions of north-east Afghanistan and north-west Pakistan. They comprise five or six main languages and several dialects, and seem to have existed in this area from remote times. Nuristani languages developed in relative isolation and reflect some ancient terms and forms.

BURUSHASKI

Burushaski is not part of the Indo-Iranian group but is included here as it belongs to the same region. It is spoken mainly in the Gilgit–Baltistan region of Kashmir (where several other languages are also spoken), and has three dialects. Though it has absorbed words from other languages, it is considered a language isolate—unrelated to any language family. Hence, its presence in this region is intriguing.

IRANIAN GROUP

Iranian has a number of related languages. The group includes Gathic Avestan and later or Younger Avestan; Old Persian; Middle Persian or Pahlavi in its various forms; Shaka dialects of ancient and early medieval times, in Central Asia, South Russia, and the Caucasus (among Shaka dialects are the old Khotani speech and the connected Ghalchah dialects of the Pamir plateau, which are still spoken); Ossetish in the Caucasus regions; various Kurd dialects; Pashto or Pashtu; Ormuri; and modern Persian dialects in Iran, Tajikistan, and Afghanistan.

The early Iranian languages, with which we are primarily concerned here, are Old Avestan (Gathic) and Younger Avestan. Old Avestan is also related to Old Persian, and the old eastern Iranian ancestor language of Pashto. Median seems to be another related language. There was probably a large group of old Iranian languages but those are not known today. Middle Persian, called Pahlavi, is a direct continuation of old Persian.

AVESTAN

Old and Younger Avestan are known from Avestan texts, which form part of the religion of Zoroastrianism. Avesta is the term used for both the texts as well as the language. According to the British scholar Mary Boyce, the term probably means 'the injunction' (of the prophet Zarathushtra). There are numerous similarities between Avestan and Vedic material, in terms of language and otherwise, but one very major difference is that the earliest Avestan text, the Gathas, record the creation of a new monotheistic religion by Zarathushtra.

Gathic or Old Avestan

Gathic Avestan, in which the Gathas are composed, is extremely similar to the language of the Rig Veda. The similarity is so marked that there can be no doubt that the two languages were once closely connected. In fact, minor changes enable one to 'translate' or transpose much of the text into Sanskrit. According to scholars such as Fortson, Gathic Avestan is more archaic than Rig Vedic Sanskrit in several ways. Others have also pointed out that the Gathic metre represents a stage earlier than the typical Rig Vedic metre. V.M. Apte, a well-known Sanskrit scholar from India, said that Vedic metres, particularly those of the Rig Veda, 'stand midway between the Avestan system and that of classical Sanskrit'. He stated: 'The Avesta has 8-syllable or 11-syllable lines, which ignore quantity but are combined into stanzas, which resemble those of the Rig Veda in all other aspects.' There are some who feel that Rig Vedic Sanskrit is earlier, though this is not generally accepted by linguists.

Younger Avestan

Younger Avestan is considered a simpler and later form of Old Avestan though, according to linguists, it did not evolve directly from Old Avestan and the two are different but related dialects of different times.

OLD PERSIAN

Old Persian is known from inscriptions of the Achaemenid (Hakhamanishya) dynasty, dating to the 6th century BCE. Its earliest use is not known. One theory is that it was spoken by a tribe called Parsuwash, which reached the Iranian plateau early in the 1st millenium BCE. Along with Matai of Median, Parsuwash is first mentioned in the area of Lake Urmia (ancient Chichast) in north-west Iran, according to the records of Assyrian king Shalmaneser III (859–824 BCE). Old Persian contains words from Median, another extinct language, and is written in a simple cuneiform script that probably developed in the 6th century BCE. The script differs from the one which was used for Avestan.

PASHTO

The ancestor dialect of Pashto is considered to have been close to that of the Gathas but it has no early written material.

MEDIAN

Median is an extinct language, known only from its loanwords in Old Persian.

EARLY IRANIAN TEXTS

The texts form part of the larger body of religious literature of Zoroastrianism. A brief account of these is provided here.

Old Avestan must have fallen out of use fairly early while Younger Avestan was probably used only till around 400 BCE. However, Avestan was still known up to Sasanian times and used by the priests. Several Avestan texts are said to have been destroyed at the time of Alexander's invasion in 331 BCE. Texts memorized by the priests were collated and written down at the time of the Sasanian dynasty between the 4th and 6th centuries CE. Like the Vedas, they had been conveyed for hundreds of years through the oral tradition. The script used to write the texts evolved from Pahlavi (Middle Persian), a script that had developed from Aramaic. The script was specially created for this purpose. It had fifty-three distinct charcters and was written from right to left. By this time, the written language of Iran under the Sasanians was Pahlavi, while the spoken language was known as Pazand.

Later Zoroastrian texts were composed in Pahlavi; as some of these are commentaries (zand) on the older texts, they are known as Zand-Avesta or Avesta-e-Zand.

According to tradition, many texts were again destroyed after the Arab invasion of the 7th century CE and the downfall of the Sasanian dynasty. After the Zoroastrians (Parsis) came to India, some of the texts they had brought with them were translated into Sanskrit. Here we are concerned with the two groups of Gathic and Younger Avestan texts, which may very broadly be taken to correspond with the time period of Rig and Later Vedic texts.

The known Avestan texts are as follows:

TEXTS IN OLD AVESTAN

THE GATHAS

The Gathas, or songs of the Prophet Zarathushtra, are among the earliest portion of these scriptures. The Gathas form part of the Yasna, a text with seventy-two chapters or haiti, and include seventeen hymns, divided into five Gathas, each with a different theme. These ancient verses are difficult to translate, as many words and aspects of grammar are unknown. Because of this, translations differ widely. But some texts of the Younger Avestan, as well as later Zoroastrian texts, help to explain the ideas contained in them. The verses are sometimes interpreted by comparing the words with those of Rig Vedic Sanskrit. The Gathas are the earliest texts of the Zoroastrian religion, and establish its main ideas, including the worship of one God—Ahura Mazda.

The five Gathas are:

1. Gatha Ahunavati, the Gatha of Free Choice (Yasna 28–34)

2. Gatha Ushtavati, the Gatha of Bliss and Enlightenment (Yasna 43–46)
3. Gatha Spenta Mainyu, the Gatha of the Holy Spirit (Yasna 47–50)
4. Gatha Vohu Khshathra, the Gatha of Sovereignty or the Good Kingdom (Yasna 51)
5. Gatha Vahishtoishti, the Gatha of the Highest Wish or Fulfilment (Yasna 53)

Note that while there are close language similarities between the Rig Veda and the Gathas, the religions described in them are different. Deities similar to those in the Rig Veda are found in other later parts of the Yasna, and in the series of hymns known as *yashts*.

YASNA HAPTANGHAITI

Literally 'worship of the seven sections', this part of the Yasna in Gathic Avestan is possibly, according to some scholars, older than the Gathas, but was revised in Gathic times. It is in praise of Ahura Mazda but could have praised other deities earlier. It is mainly in prose, and may have been used in ritual offerings to fire and water. However, its tone and content point to a post-Gathic composition.

DATE

The date of the Gathas is linked with the date of Zarathushtra. There are also certain socio-economic pointers of a simple lifestyle, accompanied by the use of metal (probably copper), the rearing of cattle, and the mention of horses, chariots, and camels. It can also be linked with the Rig Vedic date and, on the basis of linguistic analysis, could be earlier.

The date of Zarathushtra remains controversial. Some Greek sources refer to 6000 BCE while an esoteric Zoroastrian sect dates him around 7000 BCE. Western scholars once assigned him to around 600 BCE, based on a late Sasanian account, stating that he lived 258 years before Alexander. There were also accounts of Zarathushtra at the court of King Vishtaspa, once taken to be the father of the Achamenian king Darius (521–486 BCE). However, the close linguistic similarity with the Rig Veda makes a date later than 1500–1000 BCE improbable. In addition, the genealogy of Vishtaspa mentioned in association with Zarathushtra differs from that of the later Achamenian king. Most scholars now accept that Zarathushtra lived some time between 2000 BCE and 1000 BCE.

In his study of the language, Karl Hoffmann, the German specialist in Indo-European and Indo-Iranian studies, concluded that Gathic Avestan was the natural language of the composers of the Gathas, the Yasna Haptanghaiti, and the four sacred prayers (Y. 27, 54). Later changes were introduced by the method of slow chanting of the verses for ritual purposes. Further changes took place due to the transmission by speakers of Younger Avestan, who composed the younger texts.

TEXTS IN YOUNGER AVESTAN

There are a number of texts in Younger Avestan, of varying dates.

THE YASNA

This text, as noted earlier, has seventy-two sections or *haiti*. Apart from those described above, which are in Gathic Avestan, the rest is in Younger Avestan. These were probably compiled over a period of several hundred years. Later, 'yasna' was the term for a ritual in which the text was recited. Apart from the Gathas, the Yasna contains various invocations and prayers. Yasna has the same meaning as Sanskrit *yajna* (ritual, sacrifice).

The Yasna begins with a prayer to Ahura Mazda, followed by invocations to the yazatas (minor deities) to attend the yasna (ritual). There are other prayers and blessings, including some ancient and sacred prayers. Sraosha is among the important deities mentioned.

The Yasna hymns mention sacrifices, the use of *haoma*, the invigorating and intoxicating drink considered the same as Soma in the Vedas, and offerings to fire and water. The *daevas* (same as Sanskrit *devas*), seen as opposers to the religion, are condemned.

YASHTS: HYMNS TO SPECIFIC DEITIES

The origin of some of these may be earlier but they were written in Younger Avestan. The twenty-one Yashts are tabulated here:

Table 4.1

	Name	Main deity
1.	Ohrmazd Yasht	Ahura Mazda (the supreme god)
2.	Haft Ahmaraspand Yasht	Amesha Spentas
3.	Ardavahisht Yasht	Asha Vahishta
4.	Hordad Yasht	Haurvatat
5.	Aban Yasht	Aredvi Sura Anahita
6.	Khorshed Yasht	Hvare kshaeta (the sun)
7.	Mah Yasht	Maongha (the moon)
8.	Tishtar Yasht	Tishtriya (the star)
9.	Drvasp Yasht	Drvaspa (guardian of horses)
10.	Mihr Yasht	Mithra (similar to Rig Vedic Mitra)
11.	Sarosh Yasht	Sraosha
12.	Rashn Yasht	Rashnu
13.	Fravardin Yasht	Fravashis (souls of the ancestors)
14.	Varharan Yasht	Verethraghna (Skt Vritrahan, a name of Indra)
15.	Ram Yasht	Rama Hvastra (the good Vayu)
16.	Din Yasht	Chista (wisdom)
17.	Ard Yasht	Ashi (blessing)
18.	Ashtad Yasht	Khvarenah (divine glory)
19.	Zamyad Yasht	Zam (earth), Kavyan Khvarenah
20.	Hom Yasht	Haoma
21.	Vanant Yasht	Vanant (a star)

VENDIDAD: A BOOK OF LAWS

The name comes from the Avestan *vidaevadata*, meaning 'against the daevas'. It is also known as the Videvdad. It came to be recited in rituals along with the Yasna and this led to its survival, even as many other texts were lost. It is known from two sources; first, it is inserted into the yasna ritual along with the Visperad (see below), and second, it appears with a Pahlavi commentary or translation, which explains some aspects of it. The Vendidad also contains geographical information.

OTHER TEXTS IN YOUNGER AVESTAN

These texts provide information on the religion, but cannot be precisely dated.

Visperad

Another text used in rituals along with sections of the Yasna. The Visperad has twenty-four sections, and comes from the Avestan term *vispe ratavo*, 'all the ratus'. The term *ratu* is variously translated but can mean a lord, authority, or leader. The text was used during Yasna ceremonies at *gahambars* (five seasonal festivals). It invokes and praises the ratus of animals and people, and also praises some Gathas and special prayers. Its date is uncertain. It was known by Sasanian times but could contain earlier material.

Nyayesh

Five prayers in praise of Khvarshed (sun), Mithra, Mah (moon), Aban (water) and Atash (fire). These incorporate parts of some yashts. The Atash Nyayesh can be compared with prayers in praise of Agni in the Rig Veda.

Gah Prayers

Five prayers to be recited at the five *gahs* or parts of the twenty-four-hour day. The gahs are Ushahina (midnight to dawn), Havan (sunrise to midday), Rapithvina (midday to mid-afternoon), Uzaiyeirina (mid-afternoon to sunset), and Aivisruthrima (sunset to midnight).

Khordeh Avesta

Also known as the shorter Avesta, this text is used for personal prayers and includes matter from the above texts. Sections of the Nyayesh and Gah prayers and some of the yashts are part of it. In addition, there are short and longer prayers and blessings. These prayers are to be recited daily.

Apart from these, fragments of over twenty texts containing ritual and other information are known.

THE NASKS

At the time of the Sasanians, all known Avestan texts were compiled into twenty-one nasks or books. Only parts of these survive. The Vendidad is among them.

DATE OF YOUNGER AVESTAN

The date of the Younger Avestan texts is not clear. Some of the texts, particularly the Yasna and the Yashts, are believed to contain very old material. But, these were revised and rewritten later to bring them in line with Zarathushtra's ideas. All Younger Avestan texts are believed to contain later interpolations, dating up to at least one thousand years after the death of Zarathushtra. Minor changes probably continued to be made even after this. Some part of the Avesta may have been written in the late Parthian period but all available texts were compiled at the time of the Sasanians. The yashts in their present form have been attributed to the 5th century BCE, but this is only a guess; the scraps of evidence on which this was based have proved to be unreliable. According to Boyce, the Vendidad was compiled in the Parthian period. According to the Italian Iranologist Gherardo Gnoli, 'The period the text belongs to is uncertain: While the contents and lack of any reference to western Iran suggest that it should date back to the pre-Achaemenian period, the form in which it survives would seem to place it in the Parthian period.'

OTHER TEXTS

Zand, meaning 'interpretation' or 'commentary' as explained earlier, was important to understand Avestan texts. There were zands in Avestan but they no longer survive as complete texts. Some parts of these are incorporated into the later Pahlavi (Middle Persian) and many existing Avestan texts have zands in Pahlavi. There are also Pahlavi texts such as the *Bundahishn*, which are based on lost Avestan zands and provide information, sometimes legendary, on Zarathushtra and his times.

There are also Zoroastrian texts of later times, composed in Pahlavi, Persian, Sanskrit and Gujarati, and Pazand, that throw light on the past. Apart from these, there are now several modern translations of old texts into English and other languages, as well as accounts of rituals and ceremonies.

INSCRIPTIONS AND OTHER RECORDS

Inscriptions also throw light on the development of the religion, particularly of three major dynasties: the Achaemenian (circa 550–330 BCE), the Parthian (circa 141 BCE–224 CE), and the Sasanian (circa 224–651 CE).

ZARATHUSHTRA AND HIS RELIGION

Zarathushtra was probably the first to preach a monogamous religion—with one God—and to introduce the concept of good and evil and to underscore the importance of living an ethical life.

Briefly, the religion put forward by the Gathas is that there is one God, whose name is Ahura Mazda. Ahura Mazda represents truth and cosmic order, and guides the world through his powers, known as the Amesha Spentas. Ahura Mazda created twin spirits, Spenta Mainyu and Angra Maniyu (the good and the bad, respectively), and gave each person the freedom to choose between them. It is each person's responsibility to make the right choice in every situation and thus participate in the creation of a perfect world. In this struggle, the individual is helped by the Amesha Spentas, who are also personified as Asha (cosmic order), Vohu Mana (good mind), Armaiti (loving devotion), Khshathra (strength), Ameretat (immortality), and Haurvatat (perfection). The Gathas provide some other indications of religious practices, Zarathushtra's life, names of people who supported him, and some socio-economic data. There is much less information in it than one finds in the Rig Veda.

In the Gathas, Ahura Mazda says that Zarathushtra is the only man who 'listened to our decrees'. He is sent to the earth to guide the people on the right path (Y. 28). He refers to himself as a *zaotar* (Sanskrit *hotr*), a priest (Y. 33.6). He is a Master of Righteousness and an *erishi* (Sanskrit *rishi*) endowed with visionary insight (Y. 31.5, 10). He is also called a *manthran* (teacher of Manthras; Sanskrit, *mantras*), *ratu* (guide or leader) and *saoshyant* (saviour) and, in later texts, an *athravan* (priest; Sanskrit *atharvan*). Zarathushtra belonged to the Spitamid clan; his ancestor Spitama is mentioned several times in the Gathas. Haechataspa, who in later tradition was Zarathushtra's great grandfather, is mentioned as well. The marriage of his daughter Pouruchista is also mentioned (53.3) but no other members of his family are alluded to. According to Pahlavi tradition, Haechataspa was the fourth and Spitama the ninth ancestor of Zarathushtra. Zarathushtra seems to teach his new doctrine to the Spitamas. He says: 'Descendants of the Haechataspan Spitamas, to you I will proclaim . . .' (46.15).

Zarathushtra also refers to 'the heroic Maidhyomaongha Spitama', who becomes his follower (51.19). Among his greatest followers was Kavi Vishtaspa. Zarathushtra calls him his 'spiritual heir' (53.2) and, in another passage, says that through the power of the sacrament and by following the path of the good mind, Kavi Vishtaspa attained enlightenment (51.16). According to later texts, Kavi Vishtaspa was the ruler of Bactria. Two other people are mentioned in the Gathas as his followers: Frashaoshtra Hvogva (51.17, 53.2) and Jamaspa Hvogva (51.18). Later texts state that they were brothers. They seem to have been ministers at the court of Vishtaspa.

In parts of the Yasna and Yashts, Zarathushtra's father, Pourushaspa, and his three sons and three daughters are mentioned. His mother was Dughdova. Legendary accounts of his life, with some variations, are provided in later Pahlavi texts. At the age of fifteen years, he is said to have turned away from worldly life. A few years later, he went to Mt Ushidaran, where he lived in a cave, eating roots and berries, and drinking the milk of a goat who came there herself to feed him. There, around the age of thirty, he received enlightenment and conversed with Ahura Mazda in a vision. Thereafter, he returned to the world and began to convey his vision.

Zarathushtra is also said to have married Havovi and to have borne six children: three sons named Isatvastar, Urvatatnar, and Khurshid-chichar, and three daughters called Freni, Thriti, and Pouruchista. He travelled on horseback from place to place to spread his teachings and, according to tradition, even visited Tibet and China. He returned to Balkh, the capital of Bactria (Afghanistan), and settled there. At the age of seventy-seven, while he was praying in a temple, Tur-bara-tur, the leader of a hostile Turanian tribe, stabbed him. As Zarathushtra died, his attacker is said to have fallen dead too. Other legends regarding his death state that he died in his sleep, or that he ascended straight to heaven.

As for the Vedas, there are spiritual and esoteric interpretations of the Gathas. Among such interpretations, Tur-bara-tur is seen not as an individual but the embodiment of evil, which was shattered in Zarathushtra's last moments on earth, while his six children are believed to represent the six powers of Ahura Mazda.

EARLIER RELIGION

Attempts have been made by various scholars to analyse the pre-Zarathushtra religion of the Avestan people, based on material in the Gathas, Yasna, Yashts, and later texts. Comparisons have also been made with Vedic sources but some assumptions, on which comparisons are based, do not seem valid. The Gathas themselves convey very little about the pre-existing religion. They indicate that *ahura* (*skt asura*) was a term used for a deity, as well as *daeva* (*skt deva*). In the new religion, both ahuras and daevas were subordinate, or inferior, to Ahura Mazda. There was some opposition between daevas and ahuras, but this was not total. Hence, one passage says that even the daevas pray to Ahura Mazda for bliss (Y. 32.1) while another (Y. 32.2), in contrast, states that the daevas are dishonoured for ever in the seven regions of the earth.

Among deities, the Amesha Spentas are mentioned, each by name; the deity Sraosha is also referred to. There is a reference in negative terms to Yima, the son of Vivanghvant, who permitted the bull sacrifice (Y. 32.8). Yima is refferred to as a king rather than a deity. Animal sacrifices, which existed in the past, were obviously not a part of the new religion. The *karapans* and *kavis* are referred to in negative terms. Both are said to have acquired illicit wealth. Karapans seem to have been assistants of the zaotar (high priest) while kavis were perhaps priestly rulers.

Though haoma is not directly mentioned, passages in the Gathas indicate that it was used by some groups and condemned by Zarathushtra. There are several references to the problems Zarathushtra faced, as people refused to accept his teachings.

There are some concepts that reflect ideas in the Upanishads. Thus one passage in the Gathas (Y. 45.8) says, 'As an initiate, I see him clearly in my mind's eye through Truth'. There is also a reference to *tushnamaiti* or 'silent meditation' (43.15) and to *sava* or 'salvation' (45.7).

The terms *maga* as well as *magavan* are mentioned in the Gathas. Zarathushtra is said to belong to the magavan. Maga has been translated in different ways, as a 'difficult task', a 'gift' or 'reward', or a 'state of ecstasy'. But the term maghavan in the Vedas, referring to the god Indra, means 'the bountiful'. From the context, maga probably refers to a special group of followers of Zarathushtra.

If we include Younger Avestan texts, more details can be found on deities and the nature of the religion. But while some of these may be references to pre-Zarathushtra practices, others are clearly later. In general, the Yasna (Sanskrit yajna) and the yashts refer to rituals and have prayers to deities. Many of the deities are different from those in the Rig Veda. We will look at some similarities later, but will first look at the possible location of the Avestan people, which has a bearing on the Vedic homeland, as noted earlier.

LOCATION

It is very difficult to identify the region where the Avestan texts, particularly the Gathas, were composed. Austrian linguist P. Tedesco and some others felt that the Avestan homeland was in north-western Iran but many scholars of the later 20th century believe that it was in eastern Iran. Others feel the text was composed in the South Russian steppes or in Central Asia. As the Indo-Iranians are believed to have been one people, this homeland question is critical to an understanding of the location of the Vedic people. In this section, we look at the homeland of Zarathushtra and his people, not that of the Indo-Iranians.

In the Gathas, there are very few indications of their location and these too are not very clear. Two possible hostile tribes are mentioned: Grehma (Y. 31.12) and Bendva (Y. 49.1–2). However, not all translators agree; *grehma* has also been translated as 'illicit wealth' and *bendva* as 'corrupter and defiler'. The identity of these two opposing tribes, if they were such, is not known.

In one passage (Y. 46.12), the Turahya (Turanian) Frayana is mentioned as a supporter of Zarathushtra, along with his descendants. Where the Turans or Turanians were in this time period is unknown. The Younger Avestan mentions Tura at least twenty times, and refers to Yoisht Frayana (Fravardin and Aban Yashts). In the former, he is among 261 converts to the good religion. In general, the Tura are located in Central Asia but one can note the similarity of some names in Vedic literature. Turvayana is a name of a chieftain in the Rig Veda, who was helped and protected by the god Indra. Tura Kavasheya is mentioned in the tenth book of the Shatapatha Brahmana as a teacher. He erected a fire altar at Karoti, a place or a river. In the Aitareya Brahmana, he is the purohita (chief priest) of King Janamejaya Parikshita. Turashravas is mentioned in the Panchavimsha Brahmana, where it is said that he pleased Indra by composing two *samans*. Indra, in return, gave him the oblation of the Paravatas on the Yamuna. While these texts are dated later, the name could also be related to Turvasha, a clan in the Rig Veda (see Chapter 7). There is very little other information in the Gathas except that there were clans of kavis in Zarathushtra's homeland, most of whom opposed his teachings. The karapans and *usikh*, types of priests, were also against him. He recounts that he once had followers who 'now reverse the doctrine and their spiritual inheritance and inflict pain and torture'. In another passage, he seems to refer to earlier times, when he asks how the daeva worshippers could ever have been good rulers.

Karapans are not referred to in the Rig Veda but it is thought that the word may be related to the Sanskrit *kalpa* (ritual). Kavi is a term used in the Rig but for certain individuals, not for clans.

Usig, similar to usikh, occurs in this Veda, both in the singular and the plural, and seems to refer to priests. Some have interpreted them as mythical priests but this is not definite. According to the Gathas, the usig existed at the time of Zarathushtra.

There is one possible mention of a place named Pereta Zemo (Y. 51.12), which has been translated as 'Bridge of Winter' or 'Earth Bridge'. Not all agree but some scholars feel that this is the name of a place. Zemo is a common prefix or suffix of place names in Georgia, meaning 'upper' though the Georgian language is not Indo-European. Pereta is also a place name in Georgia. However, the antiquity of the name in Georgia is uncertain. The reference in the Gathas is to a place where Zarathushtra was refused hospitality along with 'his two shivering horses'. Alternatively *vazd* has been translated as two draught animals, and Zarathushtra is thought to have reached this place on a wheeled vehicle.

Thus, we have hardly any information on where Zarathustra lived. In all later sources, Kavi Vishtaspa, Zarathushtra's patron, is located in Bactria (northern Afghanistan). That was not Zarathushtra's homeland, but it may have been adjacent to it. His homeland has been variously thought to be in eastern Iran, Chorasmia (Uzbekistan), or some part of Central Asia bordering Iran. The most likely region is actually some part of Iran, from where Zarathushtra could have moved to Bactria. Ragha or Ray in northern Iran or Azerbaijan, is the traditional location of Zarathushtra's birthplace and homeland. This would be located in north-west Iran. Another place with a similar name is in eastern Iran. The Bactria–Margiana region and the South Russian steppes are among other suggestions. Richard Frye, the American scholar of Iranian and Central Asian studies, suggested Bactria or Chorasmia. The Russian scholar Igor N. Khlopin feels it could be the Tedzen delta in Turkmenistan. We will look at some of these suggestions later.

YOUNGER AVESTAN

Younger Avestan sources, which have several references to places and people, are also used to reconstruct Zarathushtra's homeland. But it needs to be kept in mind that these are later sources, though they may contain some earlier material.

Sometimes, Airyanem Vaejah mentioned in Younger Avestan sources, including the Vendidad and a yasht, is considered the homeland. It is said to be the best country in the world with a winter of ten months and a summer of two. The Vanghui Daitya, a river flowing through it, has been identified with the Amu Darya (Oxus) or Helmand. However, scholars have identified the region with central Afghanistan, Chorasmia, or even Siberia. It may be located north of Sogdiana, though Gnoli sees Airyanem Vaejah as a mythical land.

Younger Avestan traditions refer to Bactria, Media, and Azerbaijan, particularly the Median city of Raha (Ray, south of Tehran), as the home of Zarathushtra. Gnoli, based on Younger Avestan texts, looks at Sistan and Drangiana as the homeland.

Several yashts contain geographical material but the identity of the places/regions is often uncertain. The time period in which they can be placed is not clear either.

In the Mihr Yasht, the deity Mithra reaches Mt Hara. From there, he looks at the land of the Aryas (Airyo sayana), 'where the valiant chiefs draw up their many troops in array, where the high mountains, rich in pastures and waters, yield plenty to the cattle, where the deep lakes with salt waters stand, where wide flowing rivers swell and hurry towards Iskata and Paruta, Mouru (Margiana) and Harayu (Areia or Herat), Gava, Sughda (Sogdiana), and Havirizem (Khwarizm, Chorasmia)'. Ghur (Afghanistan) has been suggested as the location of Paruta. It has been suggested that Iskata may be Alexandria eschate (meaning the farthest Alexandria) set up by Alexander on the Jaxartes river (Syr Darya), but this is far too late to have any relevance for Zarathushtra's homeland.

The Farvardin Yasht, which glorifies the *fravashis* (divine souls) of people of the past, has references to places and people but these are difficult to identify. Among the places mentioned are Muza, Raozdya, Tanya, Anhvi, and Apaxsira. Muza is similar to the Sanskrit Mujavant, which several scholars locate in the area between the Hindu Kush and the Pamir. Fravashis belonging to various regions too are mentioned. The regions include Airia (Arya), Tuiria (Turanians), Sairima, Sainu, and Daha (Dahae).

The Zamyad Yasht refers to a number of mountains, both real and mythical. It also mentions rivers and lakes of the Helmand region. Among the rivers listed are Xastra, Hvaspa, Fradatha, Xaranahvaiti, Ustavaiti, Urvaba, Erezi, Zurenumaiti, and Haetumant. Based on later sources, Gnoli identifies six of these in Sistan. He also identifies some lakes, mountains, and places from other yashts in the same region.

Others find possible references to Central Asia and the region of the Jaxartes river.

The Vendidad contains a list of sixteen districts or regions; the original names have some explanations in the Pahlavi text and commentary and identifications are based on these. These regions were created by Ahura Mazda and threatened by Angra Mainyu (the evil spirit). For each of Ahura Mazda's beautiful creations, Angra Mainyu produced a counter-creation, with negative elements. It should be noted again that this is a relatively late text.

A brief idea of the sixteen lands and their identifications based on later commentaries is given here:

1. The first of the sixteen districts, Airyana Vaejah, is sometimes thought to represent the ancient Iranian homeland, and has been discussed above.
2. Gava has been explained as Sughdha, that is Sogdiana (Uzbekistan and Tajikistan).
3. Mouru is the same as Margiana (Turkmenistan).
4. Baxoi (Bakhdi) is the region of Bactria in Afghanistan and adjacent regions.
5. Nisaya is explained as lying between Mouru and Bakhdi; it has been suggested that it was the region around Maymana, in north central Afghanistan.
6. Haroiva (Haroyu) is Areia, Herat, in west Afghanistan; the Hari river (Harayu) flows here.
7. Vaekerata is the region of Gandhara (north-west Pakistan and Afghanistan).
8. Urva is probably the Ghazni region (Afghanistan).
9. Khnenta is a region explained as Vehrkano sayana (where the Vehrkana live). It has been identified with a river in Gorgan, and Vehrkana could be a people living in the Gorgan region of north

Iran or Hyrcania, which included but extended beyond Gorgan. The Vehrkana are mentioned in Old Persian as Varkana, and by Ctesias in early Greek sources as Barkanioi.

10. Haraxaiti (Harahvaiti) is the region of Arachosia (Afghanistan around Kandahar and Zhob).

11. Haetumant is the region of Helmand, the Achaemenian region of Drangiana (Zranka); Helmand is a province in south-west Afghanistan.

12. Raya (Ragha) is often identified with Ray, the traditional birthplace of Zarathushtra in Iran. However, Raya here is thought to be north of Haraxaiti and Haetumant, and close to Cakhra, and hence may not be a reference to the traditional birthplace. According to I. Gershevitch, scholar of Iranian studies at Cambridge, this cannot be the Median Raga because of its position in the list. It has been identified with Raga in an inscription of Darius I, the Rhagai of the Greeks, the al-Rayy of the Arabs, and Raya. Raya has also been identified with a place in eastern Iran.

13. Cakhra is Caex between Ghazni and Kabul, in the valley of the Logan river; alternatively, it has been identified with Mazandaran, a region in Iran.

14. Varena, described as four-cornered, is identified with Buner, or the Greek Aornos (possibly Pir Sar, north of Attock in present Pakistan).

15. Hapta Hindu is the same as Sapta Sindhava, the region of Punjab.

16. Ranha is akin to Rasa in the Vedas, a tributary of the Indus, probably in Afghanistan. Here, Angra Mainyu's counter-creation was winter, a work of the Daevas. This indicates its connection with north-west India–Pakistan. Others have located it in the Pamir, or identified it with the Syr Darya (Jaxartes) or even the Volga. In a yasht, the Ranha is the home of the mythical kara fish (Y. 16).

There is no agreement among Iranian scholars on the nature of these lands. The Swedish scholar H.S. Nyberg thought they represented the successive stages of the spread of Zarathushtra's ideas. O.S. Wikander, another Swedish scholar, related them to the spread of the worship of the god Vayu or of Vayu/Anahita. To A. Christensen, Danish orientalist and scholar of Iranian, it recorded the expansion of the territory of Aryan tribes in Iran. The French scholar Marijan Mole believed it represented a geographical structure and related it to Dumezil's tripartite ideology. The German historian and linguist Franz Altheim felt it was a projection into the future, when Zoroastrianism would spread to these lands. The German archaeologist, philologist, and historian E. Herzfeld saw the sixteen territories as a list of provinces in the Parthian kingdom.

According to Gnoli, these sixteen regions may have been territories acquired some time after Zarathushtra and before the advent of the Achaemenian empire. Therefore, he feels, the date when these territories existed could be between the 9th and 7th centuries BCE. However, they could even refer to a later period. The Vendidad reflects a period when the religion had become ritualistic, very different from that of the Gathas. Some aspects of the texts may be mythical but others have historical significance. The geographical horizon of the Younger Avestan thus extends over a very wide area, covering parts of Central Asia, Afghanistan, Iran, Pakistan, and north-west India. But as references in these texts could be as late as the Parthian period, they do not have much relevance for Vedic times. It is well known that the Achaemenians and Parthians had vast empires covering these regions.

However neither in this nor in the older Gathic material are there references to migration or movement from one region to another. The Younger Avestan material probably just indicates the regions where Zoroastrianism had spread, or the regions that were known, at a much later date.

GATHIC OR OLD AVESTAN ECONOMY AND SOCIETY

The information in the Gathas on polity, economy, and society is scanty. The kavis seem to have been rulers of clans. Based on the terms used by Zarathushtra to describe himself (see above), there were obviously priests or religious leaders in society. The community of animals and men, *pashu vira*, is mentioned. *Vira* could also imply a warrior. Other terms mentioned in the Gathas are *vastrya*, *vastar*, or *vastrya fshuyant*, which has been translated as 'herdsman, pasturer' or 'herdsman-farmer'. Cows and cattle were vital. *Pashu* is often translated as 'cattle' though, literally, it could refer to any animal, or to herds and flocks in general. There is, in fact, another term used for cows—*gaush*. Gaush Urva and Gaush Tasha are both mentioned in the Gathas. Gaush Urva, the soul of the cow, represents the suffering earth, and appeals to Ahura Mazda to save her. Gaush Tasha is called her creator. In Y. 31.9, Ahura Mazda is said to be the creator of Tasha, and hence of cattle. Butter and milk, the products of cows, are also mentioned. There are references to camels and horses. Y. 44.18 has a somewhat puzzling passage; Zarathushtra asks: 'How may I obtain, through Truth, that promised reward, namely ten mares, a stallion and a camel, so that perfection and Immortality may be mine?' According to Humbach, a German scholar and translator of the Gathas, this is the fee for a sacrificial ritual but this seems unlikely. Another interpretation is that the mares represent the ten senses; the stallion, his mind; and the camel, his faith. Whatever the interpretation, horses and camels were obviously known.

Chariots and horses are also referred to in religious imagery. Thus Y. 50.6–7 reads:

May the creator, as charioteer, teach me how to follow the directives of the good mind. So I will yoke for you O Mazda, the swiftest of steeds, far-reaching in victorious prayer, strong through Truth and the Good Mind.

Certain social groups are mentioned in the Gathas: *xvaetu* (family), *verezena* (community), *airyaman* (clan) (Y. 32.1, 33.3, 46.1, 49.7). Family and clan probably had a close relationship. In Y. 46.1, Zarathushtra refers to his unhappiness at being excluded from both.

A distinction is made regarding *demana* (dwelling), *vis* (settlement), *shoithra* (district), and *dahyu* (land). The last is thought to perhaps refer to a large area of land where related clans lived. Neither towns nor trade seem to be referred to though this does not mean they did not exist. There were obviously some different occupations—priest, warrior, charioteer, herdsman, as well as clan leader. Metal is mentioned, and was probably copper. Hence there must have been craftsmen who smelted and made copper implements; others must have made chariots and various weapons or implements.

Based on this limited information, scholars have different views on Gathic economy and society. Gathic society was initially seen as divided into two groups: priests, and the rest of the population, who were simple peasants. Each peasant could also act as a warrior. Later interpretations see them primarily as pastoralists, with a focus on cattle, and some elements of farming. Younger Avestan texts refer to three social divisions: priests, warriors, and herdsmen-farmers (*athravan*, *rathaeshtar*, *vastryo fshuyant*); and these have sometimes been projected back to the Gathic period, though such a projection may not be correct. In fact, comparing these to the brahmana–kshatriya–vaishya caste divisions of Later Vedic society, Dumezil dated these classes to the period of Proto-Indo-Iranian, which is not tenable, as these divisions appear in the late Rig Vedic period.

There was certainly a class of priests, though this may not have been hereditary at this time. Various words are used for priests. The term *karapan* seems to refer to priests who performed rituals, and are mentioned negatively by Zarathushtra. The term *zaotar* corresponds with the Sanskrit *hotr*, though the two may not have had the same functions. *Manthran* is another term related to the Sanskrit *mantra*. *Usig* occurs once.

Usually, gifts of cows or livestock were payments made for any services. The existence of a code of laws (*data*) is indicated and there are references to judgement. There are also references to killing, stealing, and theft.

YOUNGER AVESTAN ECONOMY AND SOCIETY

Though the Younger Avestan has many archaic elements, it reflects a more complex economy and society. As it was composed over a long period, it does not present a picture of a single time period. The people are believed to have been more warrior-like. The term for warrior was *rathaestar*, literally 'one standing in a chariot'. Bronze weapons and chariots were probably used.

In the Vendidad, there are references to a plough with share and yoke, a mortar of stone, a hand mill for grinding grain, and a spade for digging and tilling. In the same section, there are references to gold and silver being used for buying and selling, as the price of a stallion in silver, and of a camel in gold, are mentioned. In Vendidad 14.9, war implements are referred to—spear, knife, sword, bow, quiver with shoulder-belt and thirty bronze-headed arrows, sling with armstring and thirty sling stones, *hauberk* (shirt of chain mail), tunic, helmet, girdle, and a pair of greaves.

The Mihr Yasht indicates that not only were chariots used but horses were ridden too. A Yasna passage mentions the *huiti* (craftsmen or artisans); specialized crafts had probably developed, though town life is not described. The use of metals was increasing, and a metal (*ayah*) pestle and mortar are mentioned (Y. 22.2) but payments were still made at times with valuable animals, stallion, camel, bull, cow, or lamb. In the late Vendidad, a donkey (*kathwa*) is among items given as payment.

To summarize, despite the limited evidence available, it seems most likely that Zarathushtra lived somewhere in Iran, Afghanistan, or immediately north of these, and composed the Gathas in that region.

CHAPTER 5

THE INDO-IRANIAN HOMELAND

The Indo-Iranian homeland may have been different from the homeland of Zarathushtra and the Avestan people. Archaeology, inscriptions, and texts are used to try and arrive at a date for Indo-Iranian, its original homeland, its separation, and the route by which it reached Iran and India. The conclusions depend on which framework is followed.

The Avestan homeland, as seen in Chapter 4, could be somewhere in Iran or Afghanistan, or in the regions of Central Asia, immediately to the north. The Vedic homeland, based on references in the Rig Veda, was basically the region of Punjab and Haryana in Pakistan/India, extending into Afghanistan. The two regions were contiguous but not identical.

Did the two groups once speak the same language, and did they migrate to these regions from a common homeland? As we saw earlier, this is a major theory regarding their origin. Yet, the very uncertainties that arise when searching for the Indo-European homeland can apply to the Indo-Iranian homeland as well.

One difference is that there are more similarities between Avestan texts and the Vedas, than with any other Indo-European group. The first similarity is in language. Gathic Avestan and Rig Vedic Sanskrit are, as pointed out earlier, very similar. Younger Avestan also has similarities with the language of the Vedas.

Some language similarities are tabulated below:

Table 5.1

Vedic	Avestan	English
Ashva	aspa	horse
Ushtra	ushtra	camel
Asura	ahura	divine being
Deva	daeva	divine being/demon

Vedic	Avestan	English
Hotr	zaotar	priest
kshatra	khshathra	strength
Ratha	ratha	chariot
Yajna	yasna	sacrificial ritual
Yatha	yatha	as
Asti	asti	is
hiranya	zaranya	gold
Sukta	hukta	well said/good words

NAMES

There are also similarities in the names of people. Some examples of prominent names are given here. An intensive study of Younger Avestan and Later Vedic texts would reveal many more.

Table 5.2

	Vedic	Avestan
Similar/identical names	Kavya Ushana	Kavi Ushana
Names ending in tama	Dirghatama	Spitama, Haechastama
Names ending in rava	Pururava	Frahimrava
Names ending in gva	Atithigva	Hvogva
	Dasagva	
	Navagva	

RELIGION

Religion is another aspect used for locating the early Avestans. We have seen that the religion of Zarathushtra as depicted in the Gathas was unique, and different from that in the Rig Veda. Scholars, however, presume that an earlier substratum of the religion is revealed in what are actually later texts, those of Younger Avestan. These suggest a religion similar to the Vedas, with sacrificial rituals; reverence for fire, nature, and other deities; and the use of *haoma* (*soma*). There are also some common deities.

That Younger Avestan texts contain some material of a pre-Gathic date is an assumption based on an analysis of the texts. But, if we attempt to integrate these assumptions into a chronological sequence, difficulties arise. The sequence would be something like this:

1. Indo-Iranian religion, with multiple deities and a sacrificial ritual
2. Composition of the Gathas, rejecting the old religion (because, based on language and metre, the Gathas are thought to predate the Rig Veda)
3. Composition of the Rig Veda, reflecting a continuity with the old religion

4. Composition of Younger Avestan texts with multiple deities and developed sacrificial ritual, refecting a continuity of the old religion (deities mentioned have similarities with those in the Rig Veda)
5. Composition of the Later Vedic Samhitas, in which sacrificial ritual is fully developed.

The problem here is that the Gathas briefly mention and reject some sacrificial ritual but without any details. As Jean Kellen, the Belgian Iranologist, pointed out, actually there is no information on Old Avestan rituals. The Rig Veda refers to several rituals but does not have the fully developed rituals of the Yajur Veda or the Sama Veda. Hence, while the early joint Indo-Iranian religion (if it existed) must have had deities and rituals, the latter could not have been in the fully developed form of the yashts, Yasna, and Later Vedic Samhitas. (We are ignoring texts such as the Vendidad, which clearly refer to a much later stage of the religion.)

It is therefore possible that the early Indo-Iranian religion, including its deities and its rituals, is still largely unknown, and that the similarities between the Rig Veda, the Yasna and the yashts are the results of later influences and interaction. While keeping this possibility in mind, we will look at some of the similarities.

DEITIES

There are several divine beings in the yashts and in later texts. According to the noted scholar Mary Boyce these probably represent the original pantheon dating to the nomadic days of the joint Indo-Iranians. Others support her view but as most of the deities are not mentioned in the Gathas, there is no clear evidence for this (for deities in the Gathas, see Chapter 4). Some deity names are found on tablets and in inscriptions of later times while some are similar to those of Vedic deities. In 1938, Nyberg theorized that in Iran, the ancient Indo-Iranian pantheon was for a time broken up, with different Iranian peoples worshipping their own gods, but they came together again, subordinated by one God, in Zoroastrianism. However, Boyce and others feel that this is not correct.

In the Rig Veda, asura (ahura in Avestan) indicates a divine being, and only in some late passages does it acquire a 'demonic' character as in later Indian texts. Several Vedic gods are known as asura but only three Iranian deities are termed ahura: Ahura Mazda himself, Mithra, and Apam Napat. The Rig Vedic gods called asura include Agni, Brihaspati, Dyaus, Pushan, Savitr, and Varuna.

Mithra and Mitra

Mithra has a long yasht dedicated to him, and the Vedic Mitra is considered his counterpart. The Avestan noun mithra equals 'pact', 'contract', or 'covenant'. In the yasht, he oversees all covenants and judges. But, in Sanskrit, mitra equals 'friend', hence some feel that mithra too must have that meaning.

Ahura Mazda and Varuna?

In the Rig Veda, Mitra is closely associated with the god Varuna. Some Western scholars see Varuna as one of the two main gods of the Rig Veda but, based on the number of hymns addressed to him, he is not a major deity in this text. Their identification of him as such reflects their idea of what characteristics a major deity should have. Varuna, an ethical god who punishes misdeeds and who is prayed to for the removal of sins, corresponds with Western concepts of god. Western scholars also see him as the guardian of *rita*, along with Mitra. This is only partially correct, as several other deities were associated with or termed guardians of rita.

Rita is a complex concept. It has three aspects when used in different contexts: it usually means the 'course of nature' or order in the cosmos; in the context of sacrifice, it refers to the correct performance of it; and it also means moral conduct. Soma and Agni are also protectors of rita, and the Adityas are closely connected with it. The Vishvedevas' thoughts are fixed on rita; Vishnu is also associated with it in the Rig Veda. In some passages, rita seems personified as a deity. *Anrita* is the opposite of both *satya* (truth) and rita. As for forgiveness, or removal, of sins, not only Varuna but several gods are also invoked, including Indra, Agni, and Aditi.

There is no god called Varuna or Vouruna in the Iranian pantheon. One theory is that though his original name was forgotten, he was transformed into the supreme deity Ahura Mazda. But there is really little evidence to support this, except for Western concepts of Varuna being a great god.

Ahura Mazda and the Nameless Asura?

Another theory connects Ahura Mazda with a nameless asura that appears in the Rig Veda in a few passages as a higher being than Mitra-Varuna. The origin of the word *mazda* is not clear. Several feel it is similar to the Vedic *medha*, a feminine noun meaning 'mental vigour, perceptive power, wisdom'. Mazda is also considered to be related to a verb and noun meaning 'remember' in Avestan. The nature of Ahura Mazda in the Gathas (see Chapter 4) with the six Amesha Spentas, the powers inherent within him, actually has no counterpart in the Vedas. Despite the use of the term ahura/asura, it should be seen as an independent and separate development.

One view is that Ahura Mazda was a higher god even before Zarathushtra, recognized as such by Persians and Avestan peoples. This may be so but, overall, one can conclude that the origins of this supreme deity are unknown and unrelated to any other known deity.

Apam Napat and Varuna

Another theory is that the concept of the god Varuna was absorbed into that of Apam Napat in the Avesta. This is again unlikely as Apam Napat was the name of a deity in the Rig Veda, and should rather be related to this deity with the same name.

Several deities mentioned in Younger Avestan have Vedic counterparts, though there are many others who do not. Similar deities are listed here:

Table 5.3

Vedic	Avestan
Apam Napat	Apam Napat
Aramati	Armaiti
Aryaman	Airyaman
Bhaga	Baga (in old Persian, not Avestan)
Vritrahan, a name of Indra	Verethraghna, later the important deity, Behram
Mitra	Mithra
Puramdhi	Parendi
Soma	Haoma, later Hom
Surya (from root svar)	Hvare
Trita Aptya	Thrita or Thraetona
Vayu	Vayu
Vivasvat	Vivanhvant
Yama	Yima
Yami	Yimak
Narashamsa	Nairyosangha
	In the Vendidad
Nasatya	Nanhaitya
Indra	Indra
Sharva	Saurva

The rituals too had similarities. Agni, the sacred fire in the Vedas, had its counterpart in Atar or Atash in the Younger Avesta. Like the Apah, the Vedic water deities, there were feminine deities connected with water in the Avesta. Haoma, the counterpart of the Vedic Soma, was used in Younger Avestan rituals, and was even praised as a deity.

As seen earlier, in the Gathas, Zarathushtra was referred to as a zaotar (hotr), erishi (rishi), and manthran (teacher of mantras, or the sacred word). All these words are familiar from the Vedas. The Younger Avestan text Visperad lists eight priests who conducted rituals. Eight priests are also listed in the Rig Veda, though the names are different there. Athravans, descendants of Athravan (Vedic Atharvan), are mentioned several times in the yashts and later texts. Athravans are said to have travelled to preach the religion. In the Vedas, Atharvans are connected with the composition of the Atharva Veda.

Devas and Asuras

Devas (Avestan daeva) and asuras (Avestan ahura) are mentioned in both the Vedas and the Avestan texts. In the Yasna and yashts, the daevas are unequivocally condemned. The same is not true for the asuras in Vedic texts.

COSMOGRAPHY

Similarities between Indian and Iranian cosmography have also been pointed out, such as of the Iranian Mt Hara, or Haraiti, with the Indian Mt Meru. Texts of both countries also have mythical concepts of seven lands of the world. However, these concepts appear in texts of varying dates and may be the result of later interaction. Such interaction is well known at least from Achaemenian times, if not earlier.

COMMON MYTHS

Avestan and both Vedic and later Hindu texts contain certain common or similar myths.

Gaush Urva and Bhu Devi

In Zoroastrianism, Gaush Urva is a symbol of the suffering earth. Literally, it means 'the soul of the cow' but the cow represents the entire earth. In the Gathas, Gaush Urva's appeal is described thus:

> To you (the Divine), Gaush Urva (soul of the earth) cried out in anguish
> 'Why did you create me?
> Who made me?
> Anger and passion are everywhere,
> All around me are agression and violence,
> You are my only protector
> Therefore reveal to me, a saviour.'

> (Y. 29.1; translated by Piloo Nanavutty in *The Gathas*)

Ahura Mazda then sends Zarathushtra to protect the earth.

In the Puranas, a group of later Hindu texts, the goddess of the earth, Bhu Devi, appears to Varaha in the form of a cow and pleads for help for the oppressed earth. In the Bhagavata Purana, she appears to Indra, who sends Krishna to save the earth.

Similar myths of the cow representing the earth, attacked and oppressed in various ways and then provided with a saviour, occur in Georgia and in a Slavonic version of the *Book of Enoch*.

Manu and Yima: The flood and the vara

In the Shatapatha Brahmana and later texts, Manu, son of Vivasvat, saves the creatures of the earth from a great flood (see Chapter 6). In the Vendidad, Yima, son of Vivanhvant, saves the creatures of the earth from a fatal winter and fierce frost. He builds a *vara* (enclosure) where the seeds of two of every kind of living being and plant are preserved. People too lived there. The bird Karshipta brought the law of Mazda there.

Vritra and Azi Dahaka

In the Rig Veda, Vritra is an asura killed by Indra. This can be compared with the myth of Azi Dahaka in Avestan texts, where azi is the same as the Sanskrit *ahi*, a term used for Vritra.

It should be noted that these similarities are not unique. There are similar myths not only among other Indo-European groups, but also from Mesopotamia and other regions.

THE SACRED THREAD

Being initiated with a sacred thread is referred to in Younger Avestan texts and is similar to the *upanayana* of Hinduism. There is a conjecture that this dates to pre-Zoroastrian times but this is pure speculation. The upanayana is not mentioned in either the Rig Veda or the Later Vedic Samhitas, and the sacred thread is not referred to in the Gathas, hence similarities may be the result of later interaction. This inititiation ceremony, known in Zoroastrianism as the Navjote, still takes place today, and signifies an individual's formal acceptance of the religion.

THE FRAVASHI AND THE PITRIS

The Avestan people attached immense reverence to the souls (fravashis) of their ancestors while the Vedic people also worshipped their ancestors (pitris), though there is a difference in the concept of the fravashi and the pitri. The former is actually the perfect soul, closer to the concept of the *atman*, which in the Upanishads is identical to Brahman, the absolute.

SIMILARITIES IN RITUALS TODAY

Even today, there are striking similarities in the rituals performed in Zoroastrian temples in India and those of the Arya Samaj, which are based on the Vedic Samhitas.

SOCIO-ECONOMIC SIMILARITIES

As seen earlier, very little can be deduced about society and economy from the Gathas. Scholars have used Younger Avestan and Later Vedic sources to arrive at conclusions about the society and economy of the joint Indo-Iranians. This is not a valid method. Even by conservative estimates, the joint Indo-Iranians existed between 2000 and 1500 BCE. Younger Avestan texts have interpolations as late as the Parthian period. Later Vedic Samhitas were composed in the Gangetic plains and, whatever their date, were far removed in time and space from the supposed Indo-Iranians.

All early agrarian/pastoral societies would have certain similarities. The use of horses and chariots is thought to be a distinguising feature of the Indo-Iranians but there were many other groups, which also used horses and chariots.

THE REGION OF INTERACTION

Based on these and other similarities, archaeologists and linguists have attempted to identify a common Indo-Iranian homeland. Their origin is generally looked for in Western Asia and Central Asia, or alternatively within India. From ancient days, Western, Central and South Asia have been linked by sea and land routes. Boundaries in those days were more fluid and did not reflect the political concerns of today.

Western and Central Asia are variously defined. For instance, Afghanistan and Iran can be assigned to either region. The United Nations subregion of Western Asia lists the following countries: Armenia, Azerbaijan, Bahrain, Cyprus, Georgia, Iraq, Israel, Jordan, Kuwait, Lebanon, Oman, Palestine, Qatar, Saudi Arabia, Syria, Turkey, the United Arab Emirates (UAE), and Yemen. Of these, Armenia and Georgia are located adjacent to each other, west of the Caspian Sea. Azerbaijan, to the south of these, is historically linked with Iran. Turkey, Iraq, and Syria are in the region of ancient Anatolia and Mesopotamia. The Arab peninsula includes Saudi Arabia, the UAE, Yemen, Kuwait, Oman, and Qatar. Bahrain is an archipelago located in the Persian Gulf. Israel, Palestine, Jordan, and Lebanon are termed the Levant, or countries of the eastern Mediterranean. The island of Cyprus has some of the earliest towns of the world.

This region lies to the south of east Europe, and is surrounded by seas: the Aegean Sea, the Black Sea, the Caspian Sea, the Persian Gulf, the Arabian Sea, the Red Sea, and the Mediterranean Sea. There are high mountain ranges, plateaus, and arid as well as semi-arid regions.

Central Asia includes Kazakhstan, Kyrgyzstan, Tajikistan, Turkmenistan, and Uzbekistan. In a broader definition, other areas often included are central east Russia, Iran, Afghanistan, Mongolia, Tibet, the north-western regions of Pakistan, and within India, Punjab and part of Kashmir, including Ladakh. This area includes high mountains and passes, deserts, and grassy steppes. The main rivers are the Amu Darya (Oxus), Syr Darya, and Hari. The Aral Sea and Lake Balkash are large water bodies in the region.

Some of the old historical divisions of Central Asia are as follows:

1. Eurasian and Russian steppes (includes the northern part of this region)
2. Dzungaria and the Tarim Basin (in the north-east)
3. Zhegstu/Semirechye: West of Dzungaria with Lake Balkash to the north and Tien Shan mountains to the south
4. Khorazm (Chorasmia): South of the Aral Sea, along the Amu Darya
5. Transoxiana: North of the middle and upper Amu Darya
6. Maveranahr: Between the Amu Darya and Syr Darya, with the Aral Sea to the north-east
7. Bactria: Northern Afghanistan and the upper region of the Amu Darya
8. Sogdiana: North of Bactria (where Bukhara and Samarkand are located)
9. Khorasan: North-east Iran
10. Margiana: North-east Iran and Turkmenistan

11. Sistan/Seistan: a border region in eastern Iran (Sistan and Baluchestan provinces), south-west Afghanistan (Nirmuz province), and northern tip of south-western Pakistan (Balochistan province); derives its name from Sakastan of which it was once the westernmost region.

WEST ASIA

West Asia is one of the earliest areas with settled agriculture. It was once thought that agriculture and early animal domestication originated in this region and then spread into South Asia. But, as the American anthropologist and archaeologist G.L. Possehl points out, the emerging theory is that 'the near Eastern hearth of domestication was simply much larger than older hypothesis assumed. Rather than ending in the Zagros mountains of Iraq/Iran, it spread all the way across the Iranian plateau to the Indus valley'. Right across this huge area, stretching from the Mediterranean to the Indus, agriculture was beginnining around the same time—from 10,000 BCE or even earlier. Proto-agriculture, a stage of watering, weeding, and harvesting wild plants, represents an earlier stage. As Possehl says:

> This area can be seen as a large interaction sphere in prehistoric times. This is the expanded nuclear zone for Near Eastern, Iranian, Central and South Asian domestication. The domestication of those plants and animals on which Near Eastern, South and Central Asian civilizations were founded seems to have taken place in this nuclear zone. Interaction within it may have been so intense and regular that future excavations will find no predominant early centre of innovation within it, but that the ideas and products of early experiments with plants and animals, were rapidly disseminated within the interaction sphere. The forces of cultural change and adaptation were regional rather than local (Near Eastern, South Asian, Iranian, Afghan, etc). Rich communication and sharing of ideas and products were essential ingredients in the process of cultural change.
>
> The Indus Civilization: A Contemporary Perspective (p. 28)

Cultural interaction in this region is well known for later periods from historical sources. It would seem to have extended back to 10,000 BCE.

In West Asia by 9000 BCE there were village settlements in Anatolia, Cyprus, Jordan, and other areas. By 5000 BCE cities and city states had emerged in Sumer, the southern region of Mesopotamia, and the great Mesopotamian civilization soon developed. In 2334 BCE Sargon of Akkad took over Sumer. Other later groups and dynasties in the region were Hurrians, Hittites, Kassites, Assyrians, and Babylonians.

Jordan and Lebanon had early coastal settlements of the Phoenicians. The region of Palestine and Israel has evidence of occupation dating back to the Palaeolithic age. It was later occupied by the Cannanaites and the Hebrews. The Arab peninsula, with Saudi Arabia and other countries, also has early settlements dating back to Palaeolithic times. The Maqar civilization in Saudi Arabia has a suggested date of 7000 BCE.

LANGUAGES

As we have seen, West Asia was one of the main regions where scholars located the origins of pre-Indo-European, or Indo-Hittite, its precursor. However, early West Asian languages are diverse and numerous, and many were not Indo-European. They included the following:

- Sumerian, one of the languages of Mesopotamia, was used in Sumer from at least the 4th millennium BCE, and is known from inscriptions and texts. Around the 3rd millennium BCE, it began to be replaced by Akkadian. Ancient Sumerian was an isolate language—one that does not seem to be related to any other known language—though scholars have suggested that it was related to other language families. Such suggestions include the Munda, Dravidian, Nostratic, Dene-Caucasian, and Hurro-Urartian languages.
- Akkadian is the earliest known Semitic language. It is known from proper names in Sumerian texts in circa 2800 BCE, and later from thousands of other records. As it belonged to the same region as Sumerian, the two languages deeply influenced each other. From the 2nd millennium BCE, Assyrian and Babylonian were two languages that developed from Akkadian, which itself went into decline by the 8th century BCE and was gradually replaced by Aramaic.
- Hittite, an Indo-European language, is now extinct. It was the language of the Hittites, who ruled in Anatolia around 1900–1300 BCE with their capital at Hattusas.
- Hurrian and Urartian are related languages of ancient West Asia. They are neither Semitic nor Indo-European. Hurrian was the language of several states in north Mesopotamia, Syria, and south-east Anatolia between 2225 BCE and 1000 BCE. Urartian, an offshoot of Hurrian, is known from records of the state of Urartu between the 9th and 7th centuries BCE. Urartu was loacted in the mountainous areas near Lake Van (Turkey). Hurrian–Urartian are sometimes included, along with north Caucasian (Nakh-Daghestanian) languages, in a language family termed Alarodian, but this theory does not have much support.
- Kassite, Elamite, and Subarian were among other languages in the region.

There is evidence that some of these West Asian languages had Indo-Aryan connections.

AKKADIAN AND INDO-ARYAN

According to the Hungarian linguist Janos Harmatta, there is evidence of Indo-Aryan names in inscriptions of the Akkadian dynasty of Akkad in northern Mesopotamia. Harmatta points out two names, reconstructed as Arisen and Somasena, of the period 2300–2100 BCE. The Indian Indologist Malati Shendge has pointed out many more similarities in Akkadian and Indo-Aryan names, and suggested that even the Harappans were Akkadians. She provides a list of Sanskrit words for which she suggests Akkadian and, at times, Sumerian correspondences. She believes that the Harappans are those described in the Rig Veda as *asura*, *rakshas*, *yaksha*, *pishacha*, and *gandharva*. Of these, the asura is the most prominent and staunchest adversary of the aryas. She claims that the Harappans had different ethnic groups and may have been multilingual but only one language—the one understood by the majority—is on the inscriptions and this is Akkadian or a lineal descendant of it. It was the language of the asuras who migrated to the region from the Tigris–Euphrates in very early times. The script was developed in the Indus region. According to her, this very language became Vedic and, later, classical Sanskrit. She interprets names of the Rig Vedic composers through Akkadian and Semitic terms, and believes that many were asuras, that is Akkadians. Her views seem rather far-fetched and find little support, though there is some correspondence with Sanskrit and Akkadian names. This only indicates, as Harmatta pointed out, Indo-Aryan influence in the region.

KASSITE AND INDO-ARYAN

Indo-European or Indo-Aryan terms are found in Kassite inscriptions of around 1600 BCE from Babylon (Iraq area), which refer to Suryash and Marutash, similar to the names Surya and Marut. Kassite rule here began in the 18th century BCE. Their god of the wind, Buriash, could be related to the name Vayu. Buriash and, at times, Indash occur at the end of the names of Kassite kings. The horse was known in Mesopotamia, as an ideogram of circa 2500 BCE seems to refer to it, but it is thought it came into use in the region with the Kassites.

MITTANI INSCRIPTION

An important inscription, which has been used for dating, was found in the ancient region of Anatolia. This inscription of the 14th century BCE contains the names of Vedic deities. At this time, the area was occupied mainly by Hurrians and Hittites. The Hurrians occupied the Khabur river valley in the 3rd millennium BCE, with their capital at Urkesh, and were probably allied with the Akkadians. As seen earlier, their language was neither Semitic nor Indo-European. They adopted the Akkadian cuneiform script around 2000 BCE. The Hittites were located to the north-west of the Hurrians.

THE MITTANI KINGDOM

A new kingdom, known as the Mittani, arose in Hurrian territory around 1500 BCE in northern Syria and south-east Anatolia and existed till around 1300 BCE. Founded by a legendary king Kirta, it became a powerful state but seems to have ruled through a number of vassals. The Mittani kingdom probably came to power after the decline of Babylon following Kassite and Hittite invasions. Maittani, and later Mittani, was the term used by the people themselves. Hanigalbat was another name they used, also found in Assyrian, Babylonian, and Hattian texts. The Hattians were a pre-Hittite people of the same region. Another name was Nahrin (from the Assyro-Akkadian word for 'river').

Numerous Mittani kings are known though their chronology is not very certain. There is also some variation in names in different sources. It is suggested that they had rulers who were Indo-Aryan or had Indo-Aryan connections. Alternatively, they are thought to have been Indo-Iranian or early Iranian. The people were largely Hurrians. The Mittani king list (as given by the Belgian archaeologist Marc Van de Mieroop, and modified from other sources) is as follows, with alternative names in brackets:

- Before circa 1500 BCE: Shuttarna I;
- Circa 1500 BCE: Parrattarna (Barattarna, possibly the same as Parshatar);
- Saustatar (Shaushtatar);
- Followed by some unknown kings;
- The next king was known as Artatama I, who gave his daughter in marriage to Thutmose 1V (1400–1390 BCE) of Egypt;
- Circa 1380 BCE: Shuttarna II, whose daughter Kilu-hepa or Gilukhipa was married to Amenhotep III of Egypt;
- Succeeded by Artashuma (Artashumara), who was murdered by Udhi or Uthi;
- Succeeded by Tushratta, whose daughter Tadu-hepa or Tadu-khipa was sent to Egypt;
- Succeeded by Artatama II, a rival of Tushratta;
- Circa 1340 BCE: Shuttarna III, who succeeded Artatama II while the main line continued through Tushratta who was succeeded by his son Shattiwaza;
- 14th century BCE: Shattiwaza (Kurtiwaza);
- 14th–13th century BCE: Shattiwaza succeeded by Shattuara I;
- 13th century BCE: succeeded by Wasashatta;
- Succeeded by perhaps one unknown king;
- Followed by circa 1250 BCE: Shattuara II.

Parrattarna unified the smaller states, thus expanding the kingdom, and came in conflict with Egypt, probably at the time of Thutmose III. After Shuttarna II, there was political turmoil. Shattiwaza, a son of Tushratta, fled after his brother killed their father. He then made a pact with the Hittites who helped him defeat his rivals. This pact is recorded in an inscription on a cuneiform clay tablet found at Boghazkoy in ancient Hattusilas (present-day Turkey) and includes names of Rig Vedic deities. By this time, the Mittani kingdom was considerably diminished. Most, if not all, Hurrian states as well as Mittani states were conquered by the Assyrians in the mid-13th century BCE.

To corroborate Indo-Aryan connections, the names of some Mittani kings have been converted into Sanskrit in the following way: Tushratta (Tvesaratha, 'one who has an attacking chariot'); Artatama (Rita-dhaaman, 'one who has the abode of rita'); Artashumara (Ritasmara, 'remembering rita'); and Sattuara (Satvara, 'warrior'). Wassukanni, the capital, was said to be derived from Old Indic *vasu-khani*, 'wealth-mine'. However, this sort of conversion seems unwarranted. Arta, for instance, is a common beginning for a name in Old Persian. Artakhshassa I (Greek 'Artaxerxes') and Artakhshassa II were names of Achaemenian kings who ruled from 466–424 BCE and 404–358 BCE, respectively. The term developed from Avestan *asha* while 'khshassa' was a development from Avestan *khshathra*, the whole name meaning 'he who ruled with truth'. Asha and arta can be related to the Sanskrit rita but there is no reason to convert arta into Sanskrit as it was an independent development in a related but different language.

Tama and tamas are common name endings, both in Old Avestan and in the Rig Veda, for instance Spitama, Haechastama in Avestan, Dirghatama in the Rig. In fact, some scholars felt that the names and terms used in the Mittani inscription belonged to the Indo-Iranian period before the two groups separated. These names could thus indicate Indo-Aryan, Indo-Iranian, Iranian, or other links and cannot conclusively be assigned to Indo–Aryans alone. The name Tushratta is also equated with Hebrew or Assyrian kings.

The Mittani treaty, written in Hurrian language and Hittite cuneiform script, contains a long list of deities who are called upon as witnesses to the compact. Of these, only four can possibly have Indo-Aryan connections: Indara (Indra), Mitra, Urwana (Varuna), and the Nasatyas (Ashvins). The list of gods starts with Iskur, lord of heaven and earth, and continues with Sin; Shamash; Teshob, Lord of the town of Kahat; Nergel of Kurda; Teshob, Lord of Uhasuman; Eiasarri, Anu, and Antu; Enlil and Ninlil; and then the Indo-Iranian or Indo-Aryan gods, a few local gods, and finally the god Assur. A list of goddesses follows, then mountains, rivers, gods of heaven, and gods of earth.

The deities in this inscription thus include Hurrian and other deities. Anu/Antu and Enlil/Ninlil were Mesopotamian gods. To reiterate, the mention of a few Indo-Aryan deities, among so many others, does not indicate that the Mittani rulers were Indo-Aryan. In fact, the Russian historian and linguist I.M. Diakonoff, among others, is not convinced that Urwana refers to Varuna. In any case, the worship of a few deities could have spread through merchants or trade.

When describing this inscription, some Western scholars make a number of unfounded assumptions. The American archaeologist David Anthony, for instance, states that Indra, Varuna, and the Nasatyas were the three most important deities in the Rig Veda—and this is certainly not correct. The term *maryanna* used for chariot warriors of Mitanni is thought by some to be derived from Sanskrit *marya*. In the Rig Veda, marya is a term for both a man and a stallion. But, as a man, it usually refers to a 'young lover', not a warrior.

Other clay tablets of about the same time have Vedic numerals and references to the training of horses. Kikkuli (a Hurrian name) seems to have been a Mittani expert in horse training and wrote a text on horse training, which had some Indo-Aryan terms for technical details, including horse colours and numbers of laps. The term *aika* for 'one', as Manfred Mayrhofer, an Austrian professor specialized in Indo-European studies, has pointed out, is particularly Indo-Aryan (Skt: *eka*) and not Iranian. Other numerals it uses similar to Sanskrit are *tera* (*traya*), *panza* (*pancha*), *satta* (*sapta*), and *na* (*nava*). The colours of horses are given as *babru* (*babhru*), *parita* (*palita*), and *pinkar* (*pingala*). There are similar words in other Indo-European languages.

ASSYRIAN

Indo-Aryan or Iranian loanwords have also been identified in Assyrian inscriptions and texts. Diakonoff finds evidence of Zoroastrianism in Assyrian cuneiform inscriptions of the 9th–8th centuries BCE from the Median area. Iranian words include *masda* (*mazda*), *arta* (old Persian *arta*, Avestan *asha*), *satar* or *kastar/kistar* (Avestan *khshathra*, 'authority'), and *parna/barna* (Median *farnah*, Avestan *khvarenah*, 'glory'). He feels that Assara Mazas found in an Assyrian source in a list of gods from Assyria, Urartu, northern Syria, and Elam may be the name Ahura Mazda. He concludes: 'From such Iranian words and Assyrian texts referring geographically to Media, we can deduce Zoroastrianism was known in western Iran in the 9th century BCE.'

There is thus evidence of possibly Indo-Aryan or Indo-Iranian names and/or deities in the Anatolia region, first in Akkadian times and continuing up to the 8th century BCE.

THE HOMELAND

How did these names and terms come to be used in this region? There are several theories. Were these in continuity and evolution from the early Indo-Hittite or PIE that some scholars believe existed in the region? Though this may be possible, the intrusion of several other languages in the region needs to be explained.

David Anthony suggests that Hurrian kings may have hired mercenaries, perhaps charioteers, who 'regularly recited the kinds of hymns and prayers that were collected at about the same time far to the east by the compilers of the Rig Veda'. They then usurped the Hurrian throne and founded a dynasty. The dynasty became Hurrian in most ways but retained royal names, some Vedic deity names, and 'Old Indic technical terms related to chariotry long after its founders faded into history'. It is possible that mercenaries founded a dynasty, but unlikely that they were charioteers; chariots are generally not believed to be indigenous to India. In fact, one of the main pillars of the migration theory rests on the assumption that horses and chariots were imports to India. And, as seen above, the names of kings are more likely to have an Iranian origin.

Another theory links the Mittani rulers with Indo-Iranian- or Indo-Aryan-speaking migrants from the steppe regions, moving towards Iran and India.

THE RUSSIAN STEPPES

A number of scholars, particularly Russian, associated the Indo-Iranian homeland with the Yamnaya or Pit Grave culture, Timber Grave culture, or Andronovo culture of the Russian steppes. Genetic connections have also been established between the later Iranian-speaking Scythians, Sarmatians, and Shakas and the earlier Timber Grave and Andronovo cultures. The Abashevo, Catacomb, and Bishkent (Vaksh) cultures have also been connected with Indo-Iranians or Indo-Aryans. The Zaman Baba culture is another possibility.

Linguistic relationships with Finno-Ugrian and Indo-Iranian have been identified and are considered an additional reason to see this area as the homeland.

A steppe homeland is a popular theory both for Indo-European and Indo-Iranian languages. According to this theory, while Indo-European languages began to spread across Europe, Indo-Iranian developed in the Indo-European homeland of Ukraine and southern Russia. Alternatively, it reached here from Anatolia, and then began to cross Central Asia to Iran and India.

The second theory, based on the work of Renfrew and Gamkrelidze and Ivanov, sees one group reaching Iran and India directly from Anatolia, and another spreading to the South Russian steppes and on to other areas.

Based on Renfrew's theories, as discussed in Chapter 3, linguistically there were two waves of migration, which would have represented pre- and post-PIE languages. Thus, he felt, that in the 2nd millennium BCE, a population with Andronovo and Timber Grave characteristics spread into western Central Asia. The language they spoke had reached the Eurasian steppes through eastern Europe, and then was further transformed in its journey to the Iranian plateau, Afghanistan, and the Indus.

According to Boyce, the noted scholar of Zoroastrianism, in remote times, the Proto-Indo-Iranians possibly lived together on the South Russian steppes to the east of the Volga. At this time, she feels they were probably semi-migratory, with herds of cattle, sheep, and goats. They moved within a limited area on foot and used dogs to help herd the animals. This was a period when the horse had not yet been tamed. She sees their society as probably divided into two groups, priests and laity, the latter including herdsmen and hunters. The Proto-Indo-Iranians began to separate early in the 3rd millennium BCE. They had contacts with different areas: from Mesopotamia, they learnt to use wooden carts pulled by oxen and later the use of the war chariot; to draw these chariots, they tamed the wild horses of the steppes; bronze came into use about the same time; mountains flanking the inner Asian steppes, notably Altai, had rich deposits of copper and tin, hence they could equip themselves as fighting men.

Libations (*zaothra*) offered to life-giving water and to fire were part of the daily act of worship, *yasna* or *yajna*. They also sacrificed animals after consecration and worship, and used haoma. She believes that the Andronovo culture may represent the pre-Zoroastrian stage of the Iranians. Such imaginative reconstruction, based on limited evidence, is provided by other scholars as well.

The Andronovo had four subcultures:

1. *Sintashta-Petrovka-Arkaim in southern Urals and northern Kazakhstan (2200–1600 BCE):* Sintashta in southern Urals has graves along with grave goods including chariot burials in kurgans and all or part of animals, particularly horses and dogs. Sheep, goats, cattle, weapons, ornaments (including cheek pieces for horses), and scattered straw thought to represent *barhis* (used in Vedic sacrifices) were also buried. Excavations at Arkaim, located near Chelyabinsk in the southern Urals, have unearthed an area with three concentric walls.

2. *Alakul (2100–1400 BCE):* Lying between the Amu and Syr Darya in the Kyzylkum desert, the Alakul graves have a number of child burials.

3. *Alekseyevka (1300–1100 BCE)*: Lying in eastern Kazakhstan, this culture had contacts with Namazga VI in Turkmenistan.
4. *Fedorovo (1500–1300 BCE)*: Lying in southern Siberia, this has the earliest evidence of cremation and of a fire cult. There was handmade pottery and evidence of the *swastika*.

The Andronovo thus covers a huge area. The four subcultures and their inter-relationships have been analysed and defined in many ways. What is most important about the culture in terms of its connection with the Indo-Iranians is that aspects of the Andronovo have been traced in several cultures along a possible route of migration to Iran and Bactria.

Parpola traces the origin of the Indo-Iranians to the Pit Grave culture or the Hut Grave culture, which included the Poltavka and Abashevo cultures, dated to 2800–2200 BCE (or 2500–2000 BCE). These two cultures split between 2200 and 2000 BCE. One branch remained on the Volga steppes, and was known as the Poltova or Poltovka culture. This became the Timber Grave (Srubnaya) culture that continued till 1000 BCE. Another branch moved east between the Tobol and Ishim rivers, and became the early phase of the Andronovo or Sintashta-Petrovka-Arkaim culture. According to Parpola, it had two dialects. Poltavka in the west was pre-Proto-Iranian speaking while Abashevo in the east was pre-Proto-Aryan. These dialects became more distinct in 1800 BCE, and the Ural river formed the border between them. The Proto-Indo-Iranian speakers formed the Timber Grave culture and expanded through Central Asia using horses. The Proto-Indo-Aryan reached Mittani (Syria–Turkey) via southern Central Asia and northern Iran, using the horse-drawn chariot.

The Russian archaeologist Elena Kuzmina also identified Indo-Iranians with the Andronovo, partly on the retrospective method of seeing the evolution of the Andronovo elements in the later Sarmatian and Shaka of the 7th–6th centuries BCE. She also finds in the Andronovo a predominance of horses, cattle, chariots, and craft production for domestic use (handmade pottery, etc.) and no temples, no donkeys, no pigs, which, according to her, Indo-Iranians did not have. Instead, they had a camel and horse cult. In her book, *The Origin of the Indo-Iranians*, she says:

> The Andronovo is the only culture in which the Bactrian camel, horse, ox and sheep cults are combined, and there is no pig cult. In this culture horse-drawn chariots spread early, there was a chariot cult and ancient chariot warriors, the social strata was defined; the fire cult was well developed, (including a hearth and ash cult); the dead were buried in graves under a kurgan with a fence according to cremation or inhumation ritual; the economy involved mixed farming with stock-raising dominant. In other words, the economy, everyday life, social system, rituals and beliefs of the Andronovans corresponds completely to the picture that is reconstructed for the Indo-Iranians according to the evidence of language, which leads to the conclusion that the Andronovans spoke Indo-Iranian.

However, Rig Vedic evidence does not correspond with these theories. The social strata was not well defined at the time of the Rig Veda. The donkey was well known, and there was no camel cult.

Kuzmina also finds house styles similar to those described in the Atharva Veda but that is a later text, certainly composed in India, and cannot be projected back into a remote past and a remote land. In fact, others have identified the Sintashta with the Indo-Iranians because the remains, with large communal houses and pit graves of a single type, represented 'a lack of social classes'.

At least four Sintashta tombs had chariot remains, which is considered an additional reason to link them with Indo-Iranians. Wagon burials are found in the earlier Yamnaya culture. There is a chariot grave at Krivoye Ozero along with a horse. The archaeological culture at Krivoye Ozero, located north of Odessa along the Black Sea, is dated between 2012 and 1990 BCE. Chariot graves are found in China from circa 1200 BCE, in Europe from the 7th century BCE and in Iron Age England as well. They are not found in early Iran. And though there are many references to the chariot in the Rig Veda, there are no chariot remains in early north India.

Not all agree that the Andronovo culture represents Indo-Iranian speakers, or even any form of Indo-European. Among noted scholars, the Russian archaeologist and ethnologist V.N. Chernetsov as well as the Austrian anthropologist-archaeologist K. Jettmar initially considered Indo-Iranians as people of the Andronovo but later saw the people of the Andronovo culture as Finno-Ugrian speakers. This is a prominent theory.

Tracing the migratory route from here to India and Iran is not easy. The typical graves and burial mounds of the steppes do not occur south of the Amu Darya (Oxus). One possible route would be to move southwards towards Turkmenistan and north Iran, crossing through Afghanistan and south-east Iran into India.

Frits Staal, who has made a deep study of the Vedas, traces an alternative route of the Indo-Iranians to the Tarim Basin in Xinjiang, northern China. The Tarim mummies of this region are well known, and the people are generally believed to be Tocharian speakers. Staal feels they were Indo-Aryans and the Indo-Aryan language developed while they were here. Later, they moved and diverged; one group crossed through Afghanistan to enter India while another group, moving west, founded the Mittani kingdom.

TURKMENISTAN

Turkmenistan is one of the regions considered the Avestan and Indo-Iranian homeland. It could also have been along a route of migration from the steppe region. South Turkmenistan has a Neolithic culture named after the site of Djeitun, in the foothills of the Kopet Dag mountain range. Early agricultural villages in this region range in date from 7000 BCE to 6000 BCE, an era that gradually developed into the Bronze Age. Villages were also in the Tedzen or Hari Rud inland delta. From 4000 BCE, lapis lazuli and turquoise were found at these sites. Conch shells from India were found of a later date.

Metal also began to be used. Anau and Namazga are two sites with early metal use. At Namazga, circa 3500–3000 BCE, there was evidence of irrigation and both individual and collective burials in round brick structures. At this time, there is a suggestion of inroads from north-east Iran, which had numerous settlements in the Gurgan valley. Simultaneously, several sites were abandoned as the delta shifted east. By 2500 BCE, Namazga had an early Bronze Age culture. This was followed by an urban phase between 2500 BCE and 2000 BCE. Another urban centre at this time was Altyn Tepe, a fortified site. Crops grown included wheat, barley, chickpea, and grape. Among the domestic animals were cattle, sheep, goat, pig, and camel. Pottery and metallurgy were well developed. A number of seals belonging to this period have been found. There are remains of a pyramidal tower similar to the Mesopotamian ziggurat. Namazga also had objects of Indian ivory.

IRAN

Iran has been seen as the homeland of both the Avestan people and the Indo-Iranians. It was occupied from the Stone Age. Early agricultural settlements date to 8000 BCE, and there were urban settlements from the 4th millennium BCE. There seem to have been several different peoples in the region. In north-east Iran, there were Neolithic sites as well as later copper- and bronze-using sites. The latter include Tepe Hissar, Turang Tepe, and Yarim Tepe. Namazga V of Turkmenistan is of approximately the same time frame as Tepe Hissar III. Archaeological finds indicate contacts between the two areas. Cultural influences extended to central Iran, as indicated by the site of Tepe Sialk in the Kashan Oasis.

In north-west Iran, artefacts from Ray—Zarathushtra's traditional birthplace—date to at least 4000 BCE. In western Iran, there was the Elam civilization whose antecedents may go back to 7000 BCE. Elam had close connections with Mesopotamia and, at times, came under Mesopotamian dynasties. Its main centres were Anshan and Susa. Elam had its own unique language and script, unrelated to others in the region.

According to Boyce, an Elamite inscription refers to Mazdaka while Mazdafarnah is a name in an Elamite tablet. Elamites also have references to the veneration of Atar and to Mithra. She compares the Avestan Nairyosangha to the Elamite Narishankha, and the Avestan nature gods of the sun and moon to those in Elam. In the 1st millennium BCE, major gods in the region were Marduk in Babylon, Assur in Assyria, Humban in Elam, and Khaldi in Urartu. Boyce suggests that Ahura Mazda was revered by western Iranians before Zoroastrianism reached the area. She says, 'The surviving evidence thus suggests that the religion of the ancient Medes and Persians was essentially the same as of the Avestan, and the ethical ahuras dominated their pantheon,' though Zarathushtra brought in new elements. But it is more likely that the concept and name of Ahura Mazda was introduced by Zarathushtra.

In south-east Iran, there are a number of sites, including Shadad (east of Kerman), Tepe Yahya (about 150 km south of Kerman), and Shahr-i-Sukhteh in Iranian Sistan.

Other major sites include Konar Sandal near Jiroft, Tepe Bampur, and Iblis. The 'Jiroft' civilization is a term used for these settlements, believed to be a Bronze Age civilization, different from Elam to the west. However, not all agree that such a culture existed, though the settlements had many unique features.

Shahr-i-Sukhteh, on the south-east border of Iran, on the Helmand riverbank near the Zahedan–Zabol road, covers an area of 150 hectares. The name means 'the burnt city'. The first settlement is from around 3200 BCE, and it was burnt down three times before it was abandoned around 2100 BCE. Its huge graveyard covers 25 hectares, with graves of around 25,000–40,000 people. It was a very rich site, probably because of its proximity to sources of tin, and its involvement in trade. Shahr-i-Sukhteh had a large number of cattle figurines, bead production, work with lapis and turquoise, pottery, and other crafts. Women seem to have had a prominent position in the society, based on grave finds. There was an advanced system of medicine. A major find is the world's first artificial eyeball, probably made of bitumen and covered with gold. A central circle or iris was carved in it, and gold rays radiated outwards. A gold thread held it in place. It was worn by a woman, 1.82 m (6 feet) tall. Her skeleton is dated to 2900–2800 BCE. Another skull has evidence of brain surgery. There is a skeleton which from bone analysis can be deduced to be that of a regular camel rider, probably a messenger. The inhabitants were farmers and craftsmen, with no evidence of weapons. The route from Susa to the Indus region crosses through Tepe Yahya and Shahr-i-Sukhteh. Both places had evidence of interaction with Mesopotamia, Turkmenistan, the Persian Gulf, and the Indus region.

Shahr had contacts with Mundigak in Afghanistan as well as with Mehrgarh in Baluchistan, and the Quetta sites of the pre-Harappan period (see Chapter 8). Much of its pottery was similar to that of a contemporary period at Namazga.

South-east Iran's strategic location made it a zone of interaction between western Iran, Afghanistan, and north-west India. It may have been the region where Zoroastrianism emerged. This region also had contacts with the Arabian peninsula. The site of Bampur has fine black on grey ware (GW), and incised ware dated between 3500 BCE and 1800 BCE. Such ware has also been found on the Oman peninsula and Dubai at several sites. In addition, a seal found here has simlarities with those of the Bactria–Margiana Archaeological Complex or BMAC (see below).

Some specialists in Iranian archaeology, who have suggested that the homeland of the Indo-Iranians was in Iran, feel that they could be associated with the Early West Iranian Grey Ware (EWGW) also known as Monochrome Burnished Ware (MBW) and migrated into Central Asia from this region.

Critics of the indigenous origin theory point out that this region continued to be occupied by non-Iranians such as Hurrians, Kassites, Gutians, Lullubis, and Elamites.

INTO IRAN

Several others have supported the theory that Iranian-speaking people entered Iran from Central Asia. The Russian archaeologist I.N. Khlopin felt the Indo-Iranians were in Iran and south Central Asia by the 4th millennium BCE.

Their entry into Iran has also been associated with EWGW.

L. Vanden Berghe believed that Iranians reached Iran around 1200 BCE. Along with several others, he felt that images on Luristan artefacts from the 12th to 8th centuries BCE represented Zoroastrian divinities. Hasanlu in north Iran begins around 1300 BCE and, along with other sites in the region, is thought to mark the Iranian entry. West Iran has a new culture around the same time, in which three periods are identified: 1300–1000, EWGW with cultural uniformity; 1000–800, late GW with local trends; 750–500, red ware, sometimes painted or decorated.

The French archaeologist J. Deshayes dated the Iranian immigration to the end of the 3rd millennium BCE and the first quarter of the 2nd millennium BCE. He thought the culture on the south-west of the Caspian, termed the Gorgan culture, which made grey-black burnished ware on a potter's wheel, were the ancient Indo-Europeans or Iranians.

On the basis of comparison of the languages of Iran and Central Asia, I.M. Diakonoff felt that the Iranians came to Iran from the east through Central Asia, and the first groups were there by the end of the 2nd millennium BCE. The Russian archaeologist E.A. Grantovsky felt they followed a Caucasian route of migration from the Pontic steppes and reached Iran around 1100 BCE. Kuzmina believes that two routes were used.

Burials of horses and the existence of horse graves are thought to be indicators of Iranian entry. Horse burials at Hasanlu and other sites in west Iran are thought to belong to the 10th and 9th centuries BCE.

AFGHANISTAN

Afghanistan is another region identified as the possible homeland of the Avestan people or the Indo-Iranian people, or both. The Rig Veda refers to some rivers of Afghanistan (see Chapter 6), and Zarathushtra is believed to have spent his last days there (see Chapter 5). Though the region is mountainous and difficult to traverse, its location makes it a mid-point of several regions. To the north is Central Asia, to the east China, Pakistan and India, and to the west, Iran. Lapis lazuli, from its mines in the Badakshan region, was transported to Mesopotamia, Egypt, and the Harappan Civilization. Afghanistan thus had early connections with these regions.

Afghanistan too was occupied from the Stone Age. Palaeolithic tools have been found on river terraces, inhabited caves, and rock shelters, some dating to 100,000 BCE.

Upper Palaeolithic tools have been found at various sites, dating from 32,000 BCE to 10,000 BCE. Among notable sites is Aq Kupruk, 120 km south of Balkh, where over twenty thousand stone tools date between 18,000 BCE and 13,000 BCE. From this site, a face, either of a man or woman, carved on a limestone pebble, is one of the earliest in the world. From two different caves, there is evidence of domesticated sheep and goats of circa 10,000 BCE and circa 7500 BCE. Aq Kupruk also has indications of plant domestication by around 7000 BCE.

The next phase in north Afghanistan is marked by Mesolithic tools including microliths with geometric shapes, flints and microburins dating to 7000–6500 BCE.

With the intensification of agriculture, settlements developed in the plains. Deh Morasi Ghundai, 27 km south-west of Kandahar, and Said Qala nearby date to about 5000 BCE. Said Qala had mud-brick buildings with several rooms. Deh Morasi and Said Qala have similarities with pre-Harappan civilization sites, and with those of a similar date in the Iranian plateau and in Central Asia. It also has similarities with the large site of Mundigak, 51 km to the north. Excavations indicate that Deh Morasi possibly has a brick fire altar, in which goat horns, a goat scapula, a goblet, a copper seal, copper tubing, an alabaster cup, and a terracotta female figurine of Zhob type have been found. At Mundigak, the French archaeologist J.M. Casal suggested that a large pillared building, which had a doorway outlined with red, dating to the 3rd millennium BCE, was a temple.

Pottery, copper/bronze horse trappings, and stone seals were found at Shamshir Ghar, a cave in the limestone foothills near the Arghandab river dating to the 2nd millennium BCE. South-west of these Kandahar province sites are others of the same period.

Darra-i-Kur in Badakshan province dates back to 2000 BCE, and has similarities with sites in south Siberia and Kashmir. Three burials of domestic goats, one associated with fragments of children's skulls, suggest an association with the Vedic period. Such an association may date to a very early period, as at a Teshik Tash in Uzbekistan, the grave of a Neanderthal child was encircled by seven pairs of goat horns. In the Rig Veda, a goat is associated with funerals and with the god Pushan.

Khosh Tapa (Happy Mound) in north Afghanistan, was located on a route crossing from Central Asia to India, and to Mesopotamia. Fragments of a hoard of gold and silver, vessels, decorated with geometric designs and with bulls, boars and snakes, have been found here, probably dating to 2300 BCE. Similarities in designs can be seen with with the Indus Harappan civilization, as well as with Mesopotamian, Iranian, and Central Asian styles. There were several other settlements, some with evidence of fortifications, clay missiles, and bronze projectile points. Afghanistan also has settlements of the BMAC.

BACTRIA–MARGIANA ARCHAEOLOGICAL COMPLEX

The Bactria–Margiana Archaeological Complex dated to 2200–1700 BCE is also proposed as the Indo-Iranian homeland. Alternatively, it is thought to be a link region for the migration of the Indo-Iranians of the Andronovo culture. The BMAC culture covers present-day Turkmenistan, northern Afghanistan and part of Iran, southern Uzbekistan, and western Tajikistan, with its central region around the upper Amu Darya. Some of its elements extended to south-east Iran and Balochistan. It emerged at a time when Namazga and Altyn Tepe in Turkmenistan were declining.

There are different theories on the origin of the BMAC. According to one theory it was founded in Margiana (Turkmenistan) by people of the late Namazga V culture of the same region. From here, it spread to the Gurgan region of north-east Iran (represented by the site of Hissar IIIc) and farther south to Kerman (Shadad), Seistan, and east Balochistan. Another theory holds that Namazga Pd IV and V were the results of a population movement from north-west Iran. One more theory is that there were two routes, one from Tepe Hissar (Iran) along the Kopet Dagh foothills to Margiana, and another via a southern route to Bactria. This connected Tepe Hissar with the Elamite culture and moved through Shahr-i-Sukhteh to Bactria. An analysis of bones from the graves supports this theory.

Yet another possibility is a movement from the Indus in the east to Bactria and Margiana.

Settlements of the culture included Namazga, Altyn Tepe, Demarjin, Dashli Oasis, Togolok, Gonur, Kelleli, Sapelli, and Djarkutan.

Togolok 1 and Togolok 21 in Margiana had multi-roomed structures, which were possibly temples. Togolok 21 had a central area of 60 m by 50 m, enclosed by a thick wall and circular towers at each corner. Gonur (Margiana) had a fortified structure, whose surrounding wall had rectangular towers on each corner, and four such towers on each side. Within was a palace and administrative buildings and other structures.

The Dashli culture, north-west of Balkh, is part of the BMAC. Remains of buildings at this site include a mud-brick fort and a large temple complex with a circular building with inner and outer walls, and nine projecting towers. This is considered similar to that found at Arkaim. Nearby is a monumental palace with massive walls and a moat. Not far away are graveyards of the same date.

The BMAC had a number of other monumental buildings. Typical pottery included spouted vessels and others decorated with animals along the rim. There were objects of stone and semi-precious stone including carnelian, turquoise, and lapis lazuli. Metal objects included those of bronze, copper, silver, and gold. There were unique axes, decorated with human and animal figurines, which must have been used for ceremonial purposes. Sculptures of people and animals showed highly developed artwork. Stone, metal, and terracotta were used, combined with coloured or semi-precious stones. There were seals made of copper, bronze, and silver, and amulets of steatite. Cylindrical seals were carved with entire narrative scenes, while amulets depicted snakes, scorpions, eagles, Bactrian camels, and other items. Shells too were used, which must have been brought from the Indian Ocean or the Mediterranean Sea. Wheat and barley were among the crops grown, and irrigation was practised. No horse bones have been found at the BMAC sites but there are indications of horse presence as artefacts include axes with horse heads.

This brief survey indicates that the BMAC, which deserves a better name, was a separate and unique culture. It is not known who the people of this culture were, hence they have been linked to Indo-Iranians, Iranians, or Indo-Aryans. To support these links, early excavations in the BMAC found evidence for the preparation of Soma/haoma with remains of poppy, cannabis, and ephedra. However, later analysis by Dutch paleobotanist C.C. Bakels (2003) has disproved the alleged findings of ephedra.

The BMAC had links with other regions. Crested axes of the BMAC type have been found at Shadad and other sites in eastern and central Iran. A cemetery at Mehrgarh VIII in Balochistan contained a number of BMAC artefacts. BMAC-style sealings, ivory combs, steatite vessels, and pottery have been found in the Arabian Gulf from Umm-al-Nar on the Oman peninsula up the Arabian coast to Falaika island in Kuwait.

The language of the BMAC people is unknown but attempts have been made to reconstruct it.

The German–American indologist Michael Witzel and the Russian-origin specialist in Indo-European studies Alexander Lubotsky say there is a pre-Indo-European substratum in Proto-Indo-Iranian, which can be identified with the original language or languages of BMAC, later replaced by Proto-Indo-Iranian. Based on known langauges, Burushaski has been the proposed language. Words of this suggested BMAC language have been found in the Vedas. However, the French linguist G.J. Pinault finds BMAC words in Tocharian.

Parpola relates the BMAC to Dasa forts, conquered by the Rig Vedic Aryans. He connects the *dasa* with the *daha* mentioned in Younger Avestan texts and known from Persian and Greek accounts. These accounts indicate that the daha lived in the region circa 500 BCE. Parpola says that the BMAC was ruled by an early branch of Indo-Aryan speakers coming from the Andronovo culture. Later, another wave of Indo-Aryan migrants connected with the Rig Veda reached the region. Archaeologically, they were connected with the Bishkent culture (1700–1500 BCE) and the Yaz I culture (1500–1000 BCE). A different branch reached Mittani. This, according to him, 'postdates the Rig Vedic takeover of the dasas, as it includes Indra and Varuna, and Varuna was a god of the dasas'. The Rig Vedic people migrated into India towards the end of the BMAC circa 1700 BCE and, at the time of the early Gandhara grave culture, Ghaligai IV in Swat. According to him, finds at Mehrgarh, Sibri, Nausharo, and Quetta confirm the movement from the BMAC area into Balochistan (Pakistan). This theory has been challenged by several archaeologists, including B.B. Lal and V.I. Sarianidi.

Staal, as we saw earlier, felt that from the Andronovo culture, the Indo-Aryans reached Xinjiang. He traces their route to India from Xinjiang along the Amu Darya. They met inhabitants of, or passed through, the BMAC. He does not identify the BMAC with the Indo-Aryans but notes that Parpola found about three hundred and forty camp sites surrounding almost all known BMAC sites dating between 1550–1350 BCE. According to him, these may have been settlements of Indo-Aryan speakers who could not easily enter the BMAC forts. They then proceeded in two directions. One went east, crossed the Khyber Pass, and were the first Indo-Aryan speakers to enter India. Another route to India was via the Bolan Pass but another branch moving west became the Mittani.

The Russian archaeologist V.I. Sarianidi connected the BMAC with the Aegean and Anatolia, and saw Anatolia as the Indo-Iranian homeland, and Bactria as the homeland of Zoroastrianism.

According to another theory, cranial analysis from the BMAC cemeteries of Sapalli and Djarkutan indicates a population migrating from north-west Iran, and does not indicate any migration southwards towards Pakistan/India.

In Afghanistan, Shortughai and Mundigak were on trade routes to Indus. A migration from the north is suggested as Shortughai has skulls of Bishkent-type people.

SOUTH-EAST EUROPE

The French archaeologist of Ukranian origin R. Ghirshman placed the Indo-Iranian homeland in south-east Europe, saying their unity ended in the 4th millennium BCE, and Indo-Iranians then migrated to Mesopotamia and Iran. The Iranians reached Iran a little before 1000 BCE. He connected them with various archaeological complexes, including Sialk-A and B, Yaz I, and sites of ancient Dahistan.

OTHER REGIONS

Among other cultures with possible Indo-Iranian connections are the Zaman Baba, Bishkent, and Gandhara grave culture.

Zaman Baba

Zaman Baba is in the Zerafshan delta, close to the Amu Darya in Uzbekistan. The culture is located near lake Zaman Baba, in the dried-up Makhan river west of the Bukhara oasis. It can be dated to the late 3rd to early 2nd millenniums BCE. The agrarian settlement evolved from a local Neolithic culture. However, this culture had elements indicating the influence of the Pontic–Caspian steppe cultures and of those of south Turkmenistan. There was handmade pottery, burials, and items of bronze and semi-precious stones. Wheat and barley were grown, and cows, goats, and sheep were domesticated. Houses had floors slightly below ground level. Burials were in oval pits and catacombs.

Bishkent–Vaksh Culture

This culture, located mainly in Tajikistan, is known from the settlement of Tashguzor and numerous cemeteries in the Bishkent valley on the Kafirnigan river, and the valleys of the Vaksh and Kyzylsu rivers and beyond. There is both burial and cremation. Three phases have been identified: (1) corresponding to the Andronovo–Fedorovo, (2) early Bishkent, and (3) late Bishkent. In the third phase, there were catacomb burials. Archaeologists have identified Andronovo and Zaman Baba influences as well as BMAC influence. The culture has a large proportion of pottery from the BMAC or of BMAC types. Catacombs are known in both Zaman Baba and the BMAC. There were bones of cattle, donkey, and horse while sheep or goat bones were placed in graves. The Russian archaeologist A.M. Mandelshtam, in his study of the cemeteries, found correspondences with Indo-Aryan practices and felt these were cattle raisers, who were coming from the north-west (Andronovo) in transit to India. Others support this view. Similarities have also been seen with the Swat and Gomal cultures. But it has been pointed out that the Swat valley graves do not have catacombs.

Swat Valley

The Swat Valley, between Peshawar and Chitral, lies on a route from Central Asia to the subcontinent, and from Central Asia to China, through Gilgit. The Ghaligai rock shelter is one of the main sites, dating from 2500 BCE. In this region, what is known as the Gandhara grave culture emerged around 2000 BCE. Graves have been found at Ghaligai and other sites nearby.

There are different types of burials at these sites, including flexed and fractional burials. The site of Katelai has two burials of horses, with their riders. This culture shows both continuity with the earlier period as well as new elements. There are similarities with the BMAC, Bishkent culture, and sites in Iran and Central Asia, as well as with sites in Kashmir. The migration route has been traced through this culture farther into north-west India–Pakistan, and corresponds with the theory of migration from Central Asia.

CULTURAL INTERACTION

Despite the various theories on migration, there are other theories too. The French archaeologist J.F. Jarrige suggests that the entire region of Afghanistan, Iranian Seistan, west Balochistan, and Central Asia were involved in bidirectional exchanges around 2500 BCE. Hence, there were elements of similarity along with the existence of local cultures. Based on the analysis of available human bones, the American anthropologist Brian Hemphill and others suggest that this may be correct and such interactions continued to 1000 BCE and later. There were no great migrations but trade and cultural exchanges, including marriage.

MAIN THEORIES

Thus there are no conclusive results but the main theories regarding the Indo-Iranian homeland and possible migration are as follows:

1. The Indo-Iranians originated in Anatolia.
2. The Indo-Iranian languages originated in the South Russian steppes and the speakers of these languages migrated to Iran and India.
3. The Indo-Iranians originated from some other part of Central Asia.
4. The Avestan and Indo-Iranian homeland was in Iran, and migration started from here.
5. The Indo-Iranians belonged to the BMAC and migrated from there.
6. There was no migration but merely cultural and economic interaction across a vast area.

No single hypothesis correlating linguistic and archaeological evidence has so far been accepted. The picture will become clearer with an analysis of the Vedic material and a look at the theory of an Indo-Iranian homeland within India, in the context of archaeological cultures of India–Pakistan.

CHAPTER 6

THE RIG VEDA

In this chapter, we will look at the Rig Veda in greater depth, focusing on its possible date and the habitat and the people it describes.

DATE

As indicated earlier, the date of the text is uncertain and perhaps the most controversial aspect of studies on the Rig Veda. As there is no clear internal evidence for the date, many different suggestions have been put forward, with estimates varying from 11,000 BCE to 1000 BCE. These estimates are based on relative dating of various texts, language, information in the epics and Puranas, astrological information, references within the text to various phenomena, references from other sources including inscriptions and archaeology, as well as its relationship to Indo-European languages. Some have even dated the text millions of years ago, though a date lying within 1500–1000 BCE is the most accepted.

Rig Vedic Sanskrit differs from classical Sanskrit and is clearly of earlier origin, indicating the antiquity of the text. In addition, some words in it are borrowed from other languages. The hymns of the Rig Veda were probably composed over hundreds of years and transmitted orally. At some point of time, probably before 600 BCE, they were arranged in their present form. No early manuscript of the Rig Veda has been found. In fact, the earliest can be dated to around the 14th century CE. From this date onwards, there are numerous manuscripts. Because of the sacred nature of the text, it may have been memorized and written down several times. In ancient days, references indicate that palm leaves were used for writing—but these did not survive.

MAX MÜLLER'S THEORY: 1200–1000 BCE

Over the years, the most accepted estimate of the date became the one calculated by Max Müller in 1859, on somewhat arbitrary grounds. He based his theories on the date of the rise of Buddhism in the 6th century BCE. He felt that Buddhism arose as a reaction against Brahmanism and, hence, Vedic literature including the Samhitas, Brahmanas, Aranyakas and main early Upanishads must have existed before this. The Vedangas or Sutras, he believed, must belong to the same period as the early spread of Buddhism; hence he dated them between 600 and 200 BCE. Presuming the Brahmanas to be earlier than this, he placed their date between 800 and 600 BCE, as the long list of teachers mentioned in these would require at least two hundred years. The Samhitas are earlier than the Brahmanas, hence another 200 years, 1000–800 BCE, were added for the composition of the three later Samhitas: Sama, Yajur and Atharva Vedas. As the Rig Veda must be earlier than these, he allowed another 200 years, bringing its composition to between 1200 and 1000 BCE.

Max Müller only suggested these dates, stating that at the latest, the Rig Veda must have been composed by 1000 BCE. He did not believe that these dates were inviolable. In 1889, in his Gifford lectures, he rather prophetically said: 'Whether the Vedic hymns were composed in 1000, or 1500, or 2000, or 3000 BC, no power on earth will ever determine.' Yet, somehow, the dates of which he himself was not convinced gained acceptance by others. As Winternitz pointed out, 'Max Müller's hypothetical and really purely arbitrary determination of the Vedic epochs in the course of years, received more and more the dignity and character of a scientifically proved fact, without any new arguments or actual proofs being added.'

Winternitz actually disagreed with Max Müller, and said there was nothing against the assumption that Vedic literature was at least as old as the 3rd millennium BCE. The 19th-century German scholar Albrecht Weber also felt that the Rig Veda must be earlier than Max Müller's postulated date.

DATES BASED ON ASTRONOMICAL CALCULATIONS

Two early scholars, H. Jacobi in Bonn and B.G. Tilak in India, independently placed the Vedic texts between 6000 and 3000 BCE, using astronomical data. They calculated that in the time of the Brahmanas, the vernal equinox was in the Pleiades (Krittika), which began the *nakshatra* series. The date for this would be around 2500 BCE. Vedic texts refer to an earlier calendar, when the vernal equinox was in Orion (Mrigashiras), dated around 4500 BCE. Tilak placed some Vedic texts around 6000 BCE.

He felt that the Vedic hymns were composed around 4500 BCE and the Brahmanas in about 2500 BCE. Jacobi placed the Rig Veda towards the latter half of the period 4500–2500 BCE. The Grihya Sutras refer to Dhruva, the polestar. Dhruva, meaning 'the constant one', is mentioned in a marriage custom, where the bridegroom points this star out to the bride, asking her to be constant like Dhruva. It thus refers to a time when a 'constant' bright star could be seen in the sky. Over time, the position of the celestial equator and the North Pole change, hence the Pole star of the northern hemisphere today, Alpha of the Little Bear, was not the same 2000 years ago. In 2780 BCE, Alpha Draconis was the polestar, and must have appeared immovable for around five hundred years. As this custom does not appear in the Rig Veda, Jacobi placed the Rig Veda before 3000 BCE.

However, the use of such astronomical references to arrive at an authentic date has been challenged. It is said that, in ancient times, the nakshatras were related to the moon and not the sun, and the vernal equinoxes were unknown. Also the reference to Dhruva may be to some other less bright star.

In more recent times, many others have tried to date the Vedas on the basis of astronomy. Subhash Kak, who put forward his views in *The Astronomical Code of the Rig Veda*, connects the structure and arrangement of hymns in the Rig Veda with the five layers of the fire altar in Vedic times.

Through various calculations with the numbers of the hymns in each mandala, Kak believed he had discovered information about the distance between the earth and the sun, and the sidereal position and time of planets. On this basis, he dated the arrival of the Indo-Aryans to the 7th millennium BCE, and the composition of the Rig Veda to 4500–2500 BCE. His theories have been questioned, as this arrangement of hymns into mandalas was probably rather late and does not reflect the hymns at their original time of composition. Kim Plofker, an American historian of mathematics, in a critical review, states that Kak believes any number that appears in the text or related to it 'possessing possible astronomic significance implies that the number was deliberately chosen, in accordance with the Rig Vedic Code by authors fully aware of that significance'. Though Kak's theories and calculations are interesting, his conclusions seem unlikely. After going into the mathematical aspects of Kak's arguments, Plofker concludes: 'Dr Kak has, at best, seriously overinterpreted his data, and founded his sweeping chronological evidence upon a few interesting numerical coincidences, without sufficient regard for either the historical or the mathematical counterarguments.'

VEDIC CULTURE IN SOUTH INDIA

Another argument for an earlier date is in the context of the spread of Vedic culture to southern India. Some Vedic schools, such as those of Baudhayana and Apastamba, are believed to have originated in the south. The Rig Veda refers only to north-west India and it is argued that if the date were around 1200 BCE, Vedic schools could not have developed in the south in the space of a few hundred years.

MORE TIME NEEDED FOR DEVELOPMENT

It is also argued that a period of 700-odd years was grossly insufficient for the development of the entire Vedic literature. Buddhist texts presuppose the existence of even the Vedangas, hence all this complex thought must have taken a long time to develop.

DATES USING EPICS AND THE PURANAS

Certain scholars, such as the Indian historians F.E. Pargiter, A.D. Pusalker, and S.N. Pradhan, used Puranic and epic data to calculate the dates of some of the people mentioned in the Rig

Veda. These texts provide accounts of a great flood that took place in the time of Manu Vaivasvata, the seventh Manu or traditional world ruler. Manu is mentioned in the Vedic Samhitas but the first account of this flood dates to the Shatapatha Brahmana. The Puranas also have accounts of the first six Manus, and state that the first Manu, Svayambhuva, lived on the banks of the river Sarasvati. The Vayu Purana suggests that there was a ruler known as Ananda, prior to the first Manu. According to this theory, pre-flood traditions are represented by the first six Manus, Manu Vaivasvata being the seventh. But after the flood, the world was repopulated through the descendants of Manu Vaivasvata.

Based on later inscriptions and other sources, Pusalker calculates the date of the Mahabharata war as 1400 BCE. According to traditional accounts, Manu Vaivasvata flourished ninety-five generations before this. Taking eighteen years as the average reign of each king, he reaches a date of 3110 BCE for Manu, close to the traditional Kali yuga date of 3102 BCE. However, according to his calculations, the Kali yuga begins after the Mahabharata war, that is, in 1400 BCE. He feels one can trace the 'Aryan advance' during the four yugas or ages, the Krita, Treta, Dvapara, and Kali. Puranic accounts with lists of kings do not follow the mythical time scheme for these yugas, extending to hundreds of thousands of years, otherwise given in the same texts. Instead, they provide forty generations of kings for the Krita yuga, twenty-five for the Treta yuga, and thirty for the Dvapara yuga. Sagara, Rama, and Krishna are said to be the kings that lived at the end of the Krita, Treta, and Dvapara yugas, respectively.

Of Manu Vaivasvata's ten children, Ila, the eldest, was alternatively male and female. As a female, she married Budha or Soma and their son, Pururavas Aila, began the Chandravamshi or lunar dynasty. After analysing Puranic data and collating various accounts, Pargiter suggests the following as the names of Manu's other sons: Ikshvaku, Nabhaga, Sharyati, Narishyanta, Pramshu, Nabhagodishtha (or Nabhanedishtha), Karusha, and Prishadhra. Various dynasties can be traced from these and from Ila's sons after she was transformed into a man named Sudyumna. These three sons were Utkala, Gaya, and Vinatashva. All these dynasties ruled northern, central and eastern India but Pururavas, Nahusha, and Yayati soon displaced and conquered the rest. Ikshvaku was the first king of Ayodhya and ruled over Madhyadesha, initiating the Suryavamshi dynasty.

Yayati, fifth in descent from Manu Vaivasvata, is mentioned in the Rig Veda. By Pusalker's calculations, he would have lived ninety years after Manu, around 3010 BCE. He categorizes the period of 3000–2750 BCE as the Yayati period. Nahusha, son of Ayu who was the son of Pururavas, was the father of Yayati. Yayati's five sons in the Puranas were Yadu, Turvasha, Anu, Druhyu, and Puru who are mentioned as tribes in the Rig Veda but are not Yayati's sons in that text. It is notable that, according to the Puranas, Ayu married Prabha, the daughter of a *danava* (non-*arya*) king, Svarbhanu.

Pusalker calls the next era the Mandhatri period, dating from 2750 to 2550 BCE. Mandhatri, an Ikshvaku king of Ayodhya, was twenty generations later than Manu. He married Bindumati, daughter of Shashabindu of the Yadavas, and had three sons: Purukutsa, Ambarisha, and Muchukunda. Mandhatri conquered the areas of the Pauravas and Kanyakubjas, and was succeeded by Purukutsa. The Druhyus too were pushed out of Rajasthan and later lived in Gandhara, named after one of their kings. The Haihayas ruled in central India, the Anavas were powerful in the Punjab.

This was followed by the Parashurama period (2550–2350 BCE). At this time, the Bhrigus or Bhargavas were in Gujarat. This was the period of Arjuna Kartavirya, Vishvamitra, Jamadagni, Parashurama, and Harishchandra. Sagara of Ayodhya and Dushyanta and Bharata of Hastinapura also belong to this period.

The Ramachandra period (2350–1950 BCE) followed. Rama flourished sixty-five generations after Manu and, according to this scheme, lived at the end of this period, around 1950 BCE. This was succeeded by the Krishna period (1950–1400 BCE) when Sudasa of the north Panchalas was important. The Panchalas, Pauravas, and Yadavas dominated the scene. The Dasharajna war described in the Rig Veda occurred three or four kings after Rama in 1900 BCE.

If Pargiter's date for the Mahabharata war is taken, which is around 1000 BCE, these dates have to be reduced by 400 years. An interesting aspect of this scheme is that the Dasharajna is placed around 1900 BCE, which would not be far removed from other conventional views of its date. However, as Yayati is also mentioned in the Rig Veda, the Rig Vedic period would go back to around 3000 BCE, and according to traditional history, the whole of northern and central India was occupied by this time.

Pusalker thus reconstructs this early period with details that do not exist in the Vedas, but are found in later texts. The Bharata war then took place in 1400 BCE, after which the Kali yuga began. Using the Puranas to amplify Vedic texts is not a method that many agree on. However, Pargiter, Pusalker, and others find parallels between the two groups of texts, and also between the epics and the Vedas, but have different views on certain aspects.

The account of Samvarana in the Mahabharata has been equated with the battle of the ten kings in the Rig Veda, and Sudas has been identified with Sudasa of the Panchalas. Says Pargiter:

> Sudas drove the Paurava king Samvarana out of Hastinapura, defeating him on the Jumna [Yamuna]. His conquests stirred up a confederacy of the neighbouring kings to resist him—Puru (Samvarana), the Yadava (Yadava king of Mathura), Shivas (Shivis who were Anavas), Druhyus (of Gandhara), Matsyas (west of Shurasena), Turvasha (the Turvasu prince apparently in Rewa) and other smaller states. Sudas defeated them in a great battle near the Parushni (Ravi), and Puru (Samvarana) took refuge in the Sindhu (Indus) for many years.

Pradhan agrees with this analysis though Pusalker points out that the Mahabharata only refers to the driving out of Samvarana from his kingdom by the king of the Panchalas, and does not contain these other details.

These equations have inherent contradictions as among the kings or tribes that took part in the battle of the ten kings are those later referred to as Yayati's sons, who could not have been more than a thousand years later than him.

Another problem is that according to this theory, history begins around 3000 BCE, with Manu Vaivasvata repopulating the world. This has no relationship with the reality as revealed by archaeology.

Though there are discrepancies, it is to be noted that when Max Müller (1863-d. 1937), and some other early scholars were making conjectures about the date of the Rig Veda, the Harappan Civilization was unknown, and research in archaeology was limited.

OTHER DATES

There are still other views on the date, such as that put forward by Kazanas and supported by several others. According to him, the features of the Harappan civilization are found in the post–Rig Vedic texts, the Brahmanas, and the Sutras. The Brahmanas refer to and explain some Rig Vedic passages. The Brihadaranyaka Upanishad has long lists of teachers, indicating that considerable time had passed since the composition of the Rig Vedic hymns. In addition, the stars and planets referred to in the Mahabharata suggest a date for the core of that text of around 3000 BCE. Research shows that the Sarasvati river flowed to the ocean before 3200 BCE, hence the Rig Veda should be assigned to circa 3800–3500 BCE.

The entire text is not considered to be of the same date. In general, mandalas 2–7 are believed to be the earliest. Michael Witzel, a noted authority on the Vedas, identifies three chronological phases of the Rig Veda:

1. 1700–1500 BCE: Mandalas 4, 5, 6, 2
2. 1500–1350 BCE: Middle Vedic, mandalas 3, 7, 8
3. 1350–1200 BCE: Late Vedic, mandalas 1.1–50, 8.67–103, 10

There are other indications of the date of the text from the language used, inscriptions, texts, archaeology, and what is known about Rig Vedic and comparative cultures.

LINGUISTIC ANALYSIS FOR THE ORIGIN OF THE VEDIC PEOPLE

Linguistic analysis forms an important part of the theories of origin of the Vedic people, and of other groups in India at the time of the composition of the Rig Veda. We have already looked at some of the Indo-European and Indo-Iranian implications. But, within the Rig Veda, there are elements of non-Indo European languages, apart from the Sanskrit in which it was composed.

Suggestions for the languages that could have provided additional components include Dravidian, Proto-Munda, Proto-Burashaski, and other languages, now possibly lost. Various scholars have presumed the lost languages could belong to the Harappan Civilization or to the Bactria-Margiana Archaeological Complex of Central Asia, or some other unknown language cluster. Linguists who have analysed the text have come up with lists of non-Indo-European words. They themselves do not agree on the results of these studies, and whether these form a substratum or an adstratum of Indo-Aryan—were they included at the time of the composition of the Rig Veda, thus indicating that they were pre-existent in the region of its composition, or were they added later? The British Indologist and linguist Thomas Burrow listed twenty-five words from non-Indo-European languages in the Rig Veda while the linguist Koenraad Kuiper, a professor in New Zealand, listed 383, and the German linguist Thomas Oberlies identified 350. The noted linguist Emeneau felt that there may be a Dravidian language substratum in the Rig Veda, but actually pointed out only one word that he believed was definitely of non-Sanskrit origin. P. Thieme and H. Hock found no non-Sanskrit words. Other languages of the Indo-European group, such as Greek, are also thought to have non-Indo-European influences.

Apart from different types of words, the Rig Vedic language includes some features, for instance retroflex phenomes, which do not occur in other Indo-European languages. It has been suggested that these too are a result of the influence of local languages or of certain lost languages. Two opposing views concerning the retroflexes in the Rig Veda were whether they were borrowed from the Dravidian substratum as held by Krishnamurthy, or were innovated, as suggested by Hock.

Madhav M. Deshpande, professor of Sanskrit at the University of Michigan, brings out certain aspects of the Rig Veda. He points out that the version of the Rig Veda available to us was put together by editors. These were not the hymns in their original form. For instance, in the family books, large numbers of people from one family were the composers, separated in time by several generations, yet their hymns appear together in the same type of language. He says that Shakalya's edition, which is the one known to us today, is believed to be based on the Mandukya of Magadha in the east, even though the Rig Veda was composed in the north-west. The entire question of retroflexes thus gains a new dimension. Retroflexes do not exist in Iranian, hence they were acquired in India. Deshpande concludes that retroflexion was the result of changes in the text through centuries of oral transmission.

The linguist Fortson brings out another aspect. He points out that even in the Rig Veda, there are words that have undergone sound changes and belong to middle Indic or Prakrit.

There are different theories on the origin of Prakrit languages. One theory is that the various Prakrits developed from Sanskrit. Another is that Sanskrit and other languages, including Prakrits, must have always coexisted. Prakrits were the oral language of the common people, and Sanskrit of the priests, kings, and nobility. A third suggestion, put forward by Krishnamurthy and others, is that the Prakrits developed through a mixture of Dravidian and Indo-Aryan languages, Dravidian being the existing language of the subcontinent at the time of the so-called Aryan migration. Several linguists, including Andree F. Sjoberg of the University of Texas, have traced Dravidian influences in the later Indo-Aryan regional languages of Marathi, Gujarati, Odia (Oriya), and Bengali. However, this could be because of later influences. It seems plausible that Sanskrit was always the language of the elite, and that different vernaculars existed alongside, from the earliest times. We will look at other languages of the region in a later section.

THE HABITAT

Vedic texts have information on rivers, mountains, places, animals, birds, trees, and plants, as well as on clans, battles, and food and clothing, apart from gods and rishis. A look at all this will help in providing a picture of Rig Vedic life and culture and provide insights on its most likely date.

The exact locations of rivers, places, and tribes are uncertain but the general region can be deduced. The majority of all mentioned can be located in the northern region, to the west of the Yamuna up to eastern Afghanistan. Some can be located in the lower hills. The clans at that time did not have territories with fixed boundaries; many of them were merging with each other, forming more clearly demarcated boundaries by the Later Vedic period. Later Vedic texts also indicate a more extensive habitat.

RIVERS

Thirty-seven rivers are mentioned in the Rig Veda though, in some cases, there are doubts about whether the names actually refer to rivers. For some others the identification with known rivers is uncertain. The rivers mentioned are the Apaya, Amshumati, Anitabha, Arjikiya, Ashmanvati, Asikni, Asuniti, Brihadashva, Drishadvati, Ganga, Gomati, Hariyupiya, Kramu, Kubha, Mehatnu, Marudvridha, Parushni, Raka, Rasa, Sarasvati, Sarayu, Shipha, Shutudri, Shvetya, Silamavati, Sindhu, Sinivali, Susartu, Sushoma, Suvastu, Trishtama, Vibali, Vipash, Vitasta, Yamuna, Yavyavati, Urnavati.

The rivers provide the best indication of the region occupied. Many are mentioned in the Nadistuti, a Rig Vedic hymn in praise of rivers, in two verses in particular, 10.75.5–6. The rivers enumerated are the Ganga, Yamuna, Sarasvati, Shutudri, Parushni, Asikni, Marudvridha, Vitasta, Arjikiya, and Sushoma.

The rivers seem to be enumerated from east to west, and identifications are partially based on this. Many of these as well as other rivers are mentioned elswhere in the Rig Veda, sometimes in conjunction with those referred to above, or sometimes in other contexts.

Three Groups

The rivers can be classified into three groups: (1) the Parushni (Ravi), a tributary of the Indus, and those west of it; (2) the region between the Parushni and the Yamuna; and (3) the rivers east of the Yamuna. Different identifications of the rivers have been suggested by various scholars, but here the most likely identification is selected.

The Parushni and the Rivers West of It

Anitabha, Arjikiya, Asikni, Gomati, Krumu, Kubha, Marudvridha, Mehatnu, Parushni, Rasa, Sarayu, Shvetya, Silamavati, Sindhu, Sushoma, Susartu, Suvastu, Trishtama, Urnavati, Vitasta, Yavyavati (or Hariyupiya), Vibali.

Most of these rivers have been identified as tributaries of the Indus. The Indus rises in the Tibetan plateau at the confluence of the Sengge and Dar rivers, which flow from the Nganglong Kangri and Gangdise Shan mountain ranges. It crosses Ladakh in Jammu and Kashmir and enters Pakistan in the Gilgit–Baltistan region, south of the Karakoram range. The Shyok river and Shigar and Gilgit streams join it here. The river gradually turns south, emerging from the hills between Peshawar and Rawalpindi. Near Nanga Parbat (mountain), it passes through immense gorges that range from 4500 m to 5200 m in depth. Near Attock, it is joined by the Kabul river, coming from Afghanistan. On the west are a number of other tributaries, including the Kunar, Swat, Kurram, Toch, Gumal, Kundar, and Zhob.

It then flows south slowly through the plains of Punjab and Sindh, joining the Arabian Sea near Karachi. The Panjnad river joins it at Mithankot. It has a total length of 3180 km. The main tributaries of the Indus to the east of the river, in order from east to west, are the Satluj, Beas, Ravi, Chenab and Jhelum, and the small Sohan river.

The Sindhu (Indus) itself is mentioned. There are numerous references to this river, both in the Rig Veda and in the Atharva Veda. At times, the Sapta Sindhavah, 'the land of seven rivers', is mentioned. It seems to be used in two ways, referring to a region with seven streams or to seven rivers. Usually, these are taken to be the Indus, its five Punjab tributaries, and the Sarasvati.

The Parushni, referred to several times in the Rig Veda, was an important river. It was the scene of King Sudas's victory over the ten kings, and some of the kings seem to have drowned in it; in one passage, it is called a *mahanadi* (great stream). Yaska identified it as the Ravi (Iravati) mentioned in two other passages, and this identification is generally accepted. There is a possible reference to the river in the Atharva Veda.

The Asikni is recognized as a name of the Chenab, another major tributary of the Indus. The Vitasta has been identified with the Jhelum, a tributary of the Chenab. The name is rare in the Rig Veda, perhaps indicating that there was not much activity along its banks in Vedic times. The Marudvridha mentioned with the Asikni (Chenab) and Vitasta may be the combined waters of these, until it joins the Parushni.

Most of the other rivers in this region seem to be western tributaries of the Indus, extending into Afghanistan.

The Arjikiya has been variously identified; though Yaska identified it with the Beas, its most probable location is in south-east Afghanistan. Arjika and Arjikiya probably are a people or land, also mentioned in the Rig Veda. The river may be the Arghesan, which rises in the Sulaiman range, and after joining the Dori, flows into the Tarnak; or it could be the Tarnak, a tributary of the Arghandab, which rises north-west of Ghazni (Afghanistan) and flows south-west into the Helmand. The road from Kandahar to the Gomal Pass runs, for some time, along the Arghesan. The Dori rises on the western slopes of the Kohjak Pass, on the road from Quetta to Kandahar.

The Krumu, Kubha, and Gomati are identified with the Kurum, Kabul, and Gomal, western tributaries of the Indus, though the Gomati is also a tributary of the Ganga. There are three references to it and some have suggested that two different rivers are referred to, the Gomal and the eastern Gomati. The Suvastu is considered the same as the Soastos of Arrian, the modern Swat, a tributary of the Kubha.

The Rig Veda has three references to the Sarayu. As with the Gomati, two different rivers could be referred to. In one passage, it is mentioned with the Rasa, Anitabha, and Kubha and could refer to the Iranian Harayu, the river Hari in Herat. It also appears with the Sarasvati and Sindhu and it is not clear here which river is implied; in another passage, Chitraratha and Arna are said to have been defeated apparently by the Turvashas and Yadus who crossed this river, but this may refer to the other Sarayu, the tributary of the Ganga. The Rasa again has three references. Its position in the Nadistuti indicates a river in the north-west. The Vendidad mentions Ranha, or Rangha, the Avestan form of Rasa (see Chapter 4). As the Anitabha is listed in one passage with the Rasa, Kubha, Krumu, and Sarayu, it must be a river somewhere near them in the north-west. The Urnavati could be a tributary of the Indus. The Mehatnu, Shvetya, and Silamavati were probably other tributaries not precisely identified.

Sushoma may be the river Sohan while the Susartu refers to another tributary of the Indus, but it is not certain which. The Trishtama is another river sometimes identified with the Gilgit, but this too is uncertain. The Yavyavati is usually identified with the river Zhob. Hariyupiya is where the Vrichivants were defeated by Abhyavartin Chayamana; it may be a place or a river; it has been identified with a town on the river Yavyavati, or with another river, possibly the Iryab (Haliab), a tributary of the Kurum or the river Hari.

Between the Parushni (Ravi) and Yamuna

Apaya, Amshumati, Ashmanvati, Asuniti, Brihadashva, Drishadvati, Raka, Sarasvati, Shipha, Shutudri, Sinivali, Vipash, Yamuna.

The Vipash is the river Beas while the Shutudri (later Shatadru) is the Satluj. The Sarasvati and Drishadvati are the main rivers here. The Sarasvati itself is described as a very large river. Some equate it with the Haraqaiti in Afghanistan but there are many indications to show that the modern Sarasvati, also known as the Ghaggar, is meant. In the enumeration of rivers, it is listed in the following order: Ganga, Yamuna, Sarasvati, Shutudri, pointing to its identification with the Ghaggar. In one passage, it is said to reach the Indus. In the Rig Veda, there are three hymns in praise of the river and several other verses. She is the greatest of rivers, flowing from the mountains. With her swift flow and mighty waves, she flattens mountain peaks. She has seven sisters or streams, and is invoked to descend from the sky. She is the best of mothers, the best of rivers, and the best of goddesses. The Sarasvati was once a much longer river, and its ancient bed can be traced. It is referred to as a large river, on which many kings and the five tribes were located. The Purus were settled on its banks. The waters of the Satluj and Yamuna probably once flowed into it. The Ghaggar today is semi-dry, beginning in the Shivalik hills to the west of the Yamuna. Its dry bed crosses Rajasthan and flows onwards as the Hakra through the Cholistan desert. Explorations of its course indicate that the Ghaggar, ancient Sarasvati, once emptied into the sea. The Indian geologists V.M.K. Puri and B.C. Verma say that the Tons formed the upper part of the river, thus it was once fed by Himalayan glaciers but, by the Bronze Age, sediments from Himalayan glaciers were missing. The Drishadvati has been identified with the Chautang, which flows parallel to the Ghaggar.

Alternatively, the Sarasvati has been identified with a dry river flowing through Gujarat. Other identifications are with a river in Afghanistan, the Haraqaiti/Harahvati, whose name corresponds with Sarasvati. However, the most likely identification is with the Ghaggar.

In later times, the same name was used for different rivers. The historical importance of the original Sarasvati led to the name being used in a generic sense for a number of sacred rivers. This use is indicated in the Mahabharata and the Puranas. According to later texts, the Sarasvati joined the Ganga and Yamuna at Prayaga. As there is no such river here, this has been taken to have a symbolic, esoteric meaning.

The Apaya is a river located between the Sarasvati and the Drishadvati. It has been identified with a minor river flowing past Thanesar, or with the Indramati farther west, or the lower Khand river, a tributary of the Sarasvati. Other smaller streams here include the Asuniti, Amshumati, Ashmanvati, Brihadashva, Raka, and Sinivali. The Ashmanvati is possibly the Asmi or Asan, which flows in the hill regions to finally join the Yamuna. The Amshumati could be the Krishnavati, which extended from Narnaul to Rewari tahsil in Haryana. Its old course is marked by a dry riverbed. The Asuniti is probably a stream which branched off from the Yamuna near Panipat, and joined the Anumati near Gohana in district Rohtak (Haryana).

The Brihadashva has been identified with a stream that runs parallel between the Rakshi and Sarasvati. The Raka has been identified with the Rakshi which joins the lower Chautang, and the Sinivali, with the Soma or Sombh. It joins the Boli and West Yamuna canal. The Shipha is an unknown river.

The Yamuna and the Rivers to the East

Yamuna, Ganga, Sarayu, Gomati.

The Yamuna is mentioned three times in the Rig Veda, and several times later. In the Rig, the Tritsus and Sudas won a battle against their foes on the Yamuna.

The Ganga is mentioned in the Nadistuti. There is also a reference to Gangeyah, an epithet of Urukaksha, who may be a person from the region of the Ganga. The Ganga does not occur in the other Samhitas.

Two other rivers, which may have been in this region, are the Gomati and Sarayu. Each of these possibly refers to two different rivers in different contexts: as tributaries of the Indus in Afghanistan, and as tributaries of the Ganga.

It is interesting that the Yamuna probably once flowed to the west of the present river. According to Raikes, the old bed of the Yamuna divulged westwards near Indri (25 km north of Karnal in Haryana) to join the course now occupied by the Sirsa canal. Suraj Bhan traced a 400-m-wide depression of coarse grey sand similar to that of the Yamuna bed. This runs in a meandering course along the West Yamuna canal and continues south-east until it is obliterated by the desert. The Burhi Nadi, today a branch of the Yamuna to the west, was also once a much larger river.

A hymn to the Sarasvati, in which she is both a deity and a river, is given below:

1. *This stream Sarasvati with fostering current comes forth, our sure defence, our fort of iron.*
   As on a chariot, the flood flows on, surpassing in majesty and might all other waters.
2. *Pure in her course from mountains to the ocean, alone of streams Sarasvati has listened.*
   Thinking of wealth and the great world of creatures, she poured for Nahusha her milk and fatness.
3. *Friendly to man he grew among the women, a strong young steer amid the holy ladies.*
   He gives the fleet steed to our wealthy princes, and decks their bodies for success in battle.
4. *May this Sarasvati be pleased and listen at this our sacrifice, auspicious Lady,*
   When we with reverence, on our knees, implore her close-knit to wealth, most kind to those she loves.
5. *These offerings have we made with adoration: say this, Sarasvati, and accept our praises;*
   And, placing us under your dear protection, may we approach you, as a tree, for shelter.
6. *For you, O blessed Sarasvati, Vasishtha has here unbarred the doors of sacred order.*
   Grow, Bright One, and give strength to him who praises you. Preserve us forever, ye Gods, with blessings.

(Rig Veda 7.95; based on the translation by R.T.H. Griffith)

MOUNTAINS

Giri, the term for mountain or hill, occurs frequently in the Rig Veda. It also means height and is often combined with *parvata*, another word for mountain. In one passage in the Rig, a hill or *giri* is said to be tree covered (*vriksha-keshah*, literally 'with trees for hair'). Another passage says that streams proceed from the hills to the sea (*samudra*). Waters from the hills are also mentioned. Mountain names are rare.

In the Rig Veda, the Himalaya is referred to; Mujavant, one of its peaks, is said to be the source of Soma. Soma is said to be maujavata ('coming from the Mujavants') while Yaska takes it as coming from Mt Mujavant, equating it with Munjavant, a mountain in the Himalayas. Mujavant are a people in the Atharva and in the Yajur Veda. Mujavant has been identified with a low hill in Kashmir though Witzel identifies it with Muztagh Ata in Central Asia.

Sharyanavat is another mountain mentioned.

TREES AND PLANTS

The Rig Veda refers to trees in general and to parts of trees as well as to some specific trees. *Vriksha* is the general term for a tree. *Vaya* refers to a branch and *valsha* to a twig. *Daru* is a generic term for wood, such as the wood used to make a chariot pole or the wooden parts of anything, or even logs for fuel.

Among the specific trees mentioned are *ashwattha, khadira, kimshuka, shalmali, shimshapa, kakambira, spandana*, and *syandana*. The ashwattha is *Ficus religiosa*, the pipal tree. There are references to its berries (*pippala*) and to vessels made of its wood. This tree grows wild in the Shivalik hills and in the plains.

The nyagrodha (*Ficus indica*), the later banyan or *vata*, is not directly mentioned in the Rig Veda but seems to be referred to in one passage (1.24, 7). The khadira (*Acacia katechu*) is also mentioned. A hardwood tree, sacrificial ladles were made from it. Locally known as *khair* (or babul), it is a widespread tree, growing from the southern Himalayas to Andhra Pradesh in India and eastwards to Thailand.

The kimshuka (*Butea monosperma*) was a popular tree, also known as *palasha* or *parna*. The Rig Veda mentions that its flowers were used to decorate the bridal chariot. *Butea monosperma*, or the flame of the forest, is still known as palash. It is found all over the subcontinent, up to 1220 m in the Himalayas, and is native to tropical and subtropical parts of the subcontinent and to Southeast Asia. It is a dry-season deciduous tree. Palash forests once covered much of the Ganga–Yamuna doab but were cleared in the 19th century.

The shalmali (*Salmalia malabarica*) or silk cotton tree and its flowers (*shimbala*) are mentioned. Its wood was used to make bridal chariots. Shimshapa (*Dalbergia sissoo*), the shisham, is also known, growing up to sub-Himalayan tracts.

The identification of some trees is uncertain. Among these is the kakambira, a useful tree of some kind; according to Sayana, it literally means 'crow-bearer'. One identification is with *Anamirta cocculus*, a climbing shrub, but another suggested identification is *Neolamarckia cadamba* or the kadam, an evergreen tropical tree in South and Southeast Asia, which grows up to 45 m tall. Spandana and syandana are possibly names of trees, which have not been clearly identified.

There are also some general terms for plants. *Oshadhi* and *virudh* were two categories of plants, the latter usually inferior. *Vratati* was a term for a creeper or creeping plant. *Prasu* was a term for the young shoots of herbs or grass used in sacrifices.

In the Rig Veda, plants are said to be fruitful (*phalinah*), blossoming (*pushpavatih*), or having flowers (*pra-suvarih*). *Aratu* (*Colosanthes indica*) was a plant from which the wooden axle of a chariot was made.

Soma, of course, was well known. *Bhanga* was a term used for it in the Rig Veda, which at this time probably meant intoxicating. Later, by the time of the Atharva Veda, it came to mean hemp. *Madhu* is another term used for Soma, as for anything sweet used as food or drink. Numerous identifications have been made of Soma. Common identifications are with ephedra (*Amanita muscaria*), the fly agaric mushroom (*Perganum harmala*), the mountain rue or simply bhang (cannabis) that is still used today. Kholpin identifies the Iranian haoma with *Mandragora turcomanica*, a type of mandrake that grows in Turkmenistan, and the Indian Soma with the Himalayan mandrake.

Apart from this, not many plants are mentioned in the Rig Veda, and some of those that are, are connected with water. These include *kiyambu*, the name of one of the water plants which are to grow, according to a funeral hymn in the Rig Veda, on the place where the body of the dead was burnt; it could mean 'having some water'. Lotus flowers or blossoms known as *pundarika* or *pushkara* are referred to.

Shipala (*Blyxa octandra*) is another water plant that finds mention. *Pakadurva* (edible millet) is included with kiyambu and *vyalkasha* among plants to be grown on the spot where the corpse was burnt. *Urvara* (cucumber) is also mentioned.

Thus, the few trees and plants referred to in the Rig Veda, correspond well with those of the Indus plains and the submontane tract farther north, as well as the regions to the east and south. They are not the trees of mountainous regions and are not found in the mountainous regions of Afghanistan and Iran but could have existed in the north-western plains and plateaus extending into Iran.

These trees and plants are mentioned in later texts, in addition to many others.

ANIMALS

Pashu was a general term for animals, including people, but animals were also known as *chatushpad* (four-legged) as opposed to humans who were *dvipad* (two-legged). The Rig Veda also divides non-human animals into three groups: those of the air (*vayavya*), of the forest (*aranya*), and of the village (*gramya*).

The Rig Veda mentions a number of animals. Among the domesticated animals were goats, sheep, horses, cows and bulls, asses, dogs, buffaloes and, possibly, camels. Elephants and monkeys were also tamed. The cow was very important and there are several terms for it. *Go* was the word used for cow, and the many derivatives of it are discussed in Chapter 7. Among other words used were *stari* (barren cow), *tryavi* (calf, eighteen months old), and *vatsa* (calf).

The goat was usually known as *aja*, though the terms *basta*, *chaga*, and *chagala* were also used. Goats and sheep, *ajavayah*, are frequently mentioned together. The goat was associated with the god Pushan, and had a role in funeral ceremonies. *Mesha* (ram) or *meshi* (ewe) is mentioned in the Rig Veda; it can also indicate the wool of the sheep as used as a filter in the Soma sacrifice.

The horse was known as *ashva*, and by several other terms. References in the Rig Veda suggest that mares were preferred for drawing chariots, as they were swift and sure. *Ashu*, literally meaning 'swift', especially refers to the chariot horse. Apart from ashva, the commonest word for horse, it is also called *arvant*, 'the swift'; *atya*, 'the racer' or 'the runner'; *vajin*, 'the strong' (for pulling); *sapti*, 'the runner'; and *haya*, 'the speedy'. The mare is *ashvaa*, *atyaa*, *arvati*, *vadavaa*, etc.; there were horses of various colours, including *harita* or *hari* (dun), *aruna*, *arusha*, *pishanga*, *rohita* (all meaning ruddy); *shyava* (dark brown), and *shveta* (white).

Some individuals owned large numbers of horses, and one *danastuti* refers to a gift of 400 mares. On special occasions, horses wore ornaments of gold. Horses participated in races and, after racing, were cooled with water. They were kept in stalls and allowed to go out to graze.

The ass, known as *gardabha* or *rasabha*, is considered inferior to the horse but, among animals, the best bearer of burdens (*bhara-bharitama*). It is said to be *dvi-retas*, 'with double seed', which suggests its ability to produce offspring from either a mare or a female ass. It was said to have a great capacity to eat. Asses were given as gifts (*dana*), and hence must have been valauble. The *ashvatara* or mule was known as the offspring of an ass and a mare. The buffalo, *mahisha* ('strong'), is mentioned in the Rig Veda. It may have been wild or tame.

The domestic buffalo developed from the wild water buffalo after thousands of years of selective breeding, either in South or Southeast Asia. Asia is its native home.

The camel—*ushti* or *ushtra*—has one reference in the Rig Veda.

Gavaya (*Bos gavaeus*), a species of ox, is mentioned in the Rig Veda. It was probably tamed but could also be wild.

There are references to dogs. *Shvan* and *shuni* (female) are terms used for dogs. One passage indicates that dogs were used to guard houses. Dogs were also used for hunting. Sarama is mentioned as the god Indra's dog, who acted as his messenger. The Sarameyas, descendants of Sarama, were dogs of the god Yama.

The elephant is known as *mriga hastin* in the Rig Veda and even in the Atharva Veda. In the Rig, it was famous for its strength and was sometimes tamed. The elephant was also described as *mriga-varana*, a wild and dangerous animal. *Ibha* seems to have been another term for an elephant. Among later terms for elephant were *hastin* and *varana*, without the addition of mriga.

Kapi (ape or monkey) occurs only once in the Rig, with reference to *vrisha-kapi*, the man-ape in the dialogue of Indra and Indrani; it is termed *harita* or tawny.

Numerous wild animals are mentioned. Among these are deer, wild ass, rhinoceros, bear, lion, hyena, jackal, wild boar, elephant, wolf, weasel (or polecat), and hare. Mriga is used in the general sense of wild animal. *Eta* or *etah* (plural), the steeds of the Maruts, are swift deer, mentioned several times in the Rig Veda; it is not clear what kind of deer they are. *Harina*, probably gazelle, are also mentioned. *Pisha* and *ruru* were other terms for deer, while *rishya* is a stag. The *parasvant* was possibly a rhinoceros. *Riksha* is a bear. *Salavrika* (hyena) and *shasha* (hare) are also mentioned.

The jackal was known as *lomasha*. The *simha* or lion is mentioned many times. His thundering roar is referred to and he is said to live in the hills (*girishtha*) and to roam (*kuchara*). The boar (*varaha*) is known as well as the wild pig (*sukara*). *Vrika* (wolf) has several references—it was reddish in colour, an enemy of sheep, and considered dangerous. *Kashila*, a weasel or polecat, is also mentioned as well as mouse (*mush* or *mushika*).

Reptiles and amphibians are also referred to, including snakes, and the *godha*, probably a monitor lizard, as well as the frog (*manduka*). The *simshumara* or *shishumara* was an aquatic creature, possibly a crocodile or an alligator or a dolphin. The *vrischika* (scorpion) too was mentioned and its poison was said to be feared. *Suchika* was a type of stinging insect.

BIRDS

Pakshin is a general term for a bird. Birds mentioned in the Rig Veda are fairly common ones. The peacock or *mayura* is referred to. The god Indra's horses are said to have hair like peacock feathers (*mayura-roman*) and tails like peacocks (*mayura-shepya*).

Among birds of prey, the *gridhra* or vulture is mentioned as well as the *shyena* (eagle) and the *suparna* (either another term for eagle or possibly a falcon). However, in one passage (1.64.20), there is a possible reference to two types of suparnas, which have been identified as the golden oriole, with beautiful wings, and the eagle. The shyena is a strong bird, which attacks smaller birds and even herds but it is this bird that brings the mystical Soma from heaven. Shakuna is a large bird mentioned frequently in the Rig; shakuni is similar to shakuna, but smaller than the shyena or suparna. The Indian judge, civil servant, and Sanskrit scholar K.N. Dave, in his book on birds in Sanskrit literature, identifies shakuni with the common pariah kite, and *krishna shakuna* or *shakuni* with the all-black Punjab or Tibetan raven.

Among water birds is the *chakravaka* (*Anas casarca*), also known as the Brahmany duck; the *hamsa*, which is the gander or swan; and Ati, mentioned in the legend of Pururavas and Urvashi, which has been identified with the black ibis.

Other birds include the *chasha* or blue jay. *Kikidivi* could be another name for it, based on its calls, but kikidivi has alternatively been identified with the partridge. The *kapota* or pigeon is referred to; the *haridrava* is some yellow or green bird, which Sayana, the 14th-century commentator, identifies as the *gopitanaka* or wagtail. *Ropanaka* is some kind of a thrush or parrot. The *khargala* is a nocturnal bird, perhaps some kind of owl, though *uluka*, the usual name for owl is also mentioned. *Shushuluka* is thought to be a small owl. *Shakuntaka* or *shakuntika* means a small bird. *Vartika* or quail is also mentioned. It was saved by the Ashvins from a wolf's jaw. *Vayasa*, a large bird, could be the crow. *Kapinjala* is the grey partridge.

Unidentified birds include the *chichchika* and *vrishrava*. The former may be a nightjar, named for the sound it makes. The Rig mentions about twenty birds, though this does not mean that the composers did not know more.

In general, the fauna and flora of the Rig is thus compatible with what is available in the Indus Punjab–Sindh region.

LATER VEDIC

The Later Vedic texts include the other Vedic Samhitas (Sama, Yajur, Atharva) as well as the Brahmanas, Aranyakas, and Upanishads. Though this book is primarily concerned with the Samhitas, some aspects of the others are used to identify culture and location.

RIVERS

Among rivers, the Sindhu (Indus) and its tributaries continue to be mentioned in the three Later Vedic Samhitas, though its western or Afghanistan tributaries are hardly mentioned. In the post–Samhita Vedic texts, even the name Sindhu is not common. It is referred to as if it is far away. The Brihadaranyaka Upanishad mentions Saindhava horses, that is, horses that come from near the Indus. There are very few references to the rivers west of the Parushni.

The focus is on two regions, between the Parushni and Yamuna, and the region east of the Yamuna.

Between the Parushni (Ravi) and Yamuna

The Vipash (Beas) is mentioned in the Gopatha Brahmana, which says that Vasishtha-shila is in the middle of it. Panini too mentions it; and in post-Vedic literature it is known as the Vipasha. Its course has changed since ancient times. Vasishtha-shila can be connected with a place named Vasisht on the river Beas near Manali in Himachal Pradesh. According to the Nirukta, the Vipash was earlier known as Urunjira. The Shutudri was later known as the Shatadru, flowing through a hundred channels, a reference to its frequent course changes. It was known as Zaradros in the works of the Greek writers Ptolemy and Arrian and in those days seems to have flowed into the Rann of Kutch.

The most prominent river in this region is once again the Sarasvati. In the Brahmanas, Sarasvati is identified with Vach, the goddess of speech, indicating its continued importance. However, it is no longer known as a great river flowing to the sea. Instead it is said to disappear into the sands of the desert. The Drishadvati too is mentioned. According to the Panchavimsha Brahmana, special sacrifices were held on the banks of the Sarasvati and Drishadvati. But the Drishadvati too is said to disappear into the sands. As seen earlier, geologists believe the Sarasvati was once fed by Himalayan glaciers but began to dry up when a tectonic change made it a rain-fed river. The Panchavimsha Brahmana refers to the Parinah as another river in this region. It has been identified with the Parenos of Greek sources, a small tributary of the Indus.

The Yamuna and the regions to the east

The Yamuna is mentioned in the Atharva Veda and Later Vedic texts. In the Atharva, the salve (anjana) of the Yamuna is mentioned along with that of Trikakud. In the Aitareya and Shatapatha Brahmanas, the Bharatas won victories on the Yamuna. In the Mantrapatha, the Salvas live on its banks.

Strangely, the Ganga is not mentioned at all in the other Vedic Samhitas but is referred to in the Brahmanas. In the Shatapatha Brahmana, Bharata Dauhshanti gained victories on both the Ganga and the Yamuna. In the Taittiriya Aranyaka, special honour is given to those who live between the Ganga and Yamuna—probably the text originated here.

Some other rivers are mentioned that do not occur in the Rig Veda. There is a possible reference to the Reva, another name of the Narmada. In the Panchavimsha Brahmana, Revottaras is the name of a man and could refer to a person from the region of the Reva river. The Varanavati mentioned in the Atharva Veda (4.7.1) could be the name of a stream; Shipala (Shipalaa) in the same text is another possible river. The Sudaman is a river mentioned in the Panchavimsha Brahamana, and the Sadanira in the Shatapatha Brahamana. The latter meaning 'always with water', a perennial stream, is said to mark the boundary between the Koshalas and Videhas; it has been identified with the Karatoya, or with the Gandaki.

MOUNTAINS

In Later Vedic sources, the Himalayas continue to be referred to in several texts, including the Atharva Veda, and the Yajur texts of the Taittiriya Samhita and the Vajasaneyi Samhita. Though this is a generic term, it could include other mountains in the Himalayan range. Krauncha is a mountain referred to in the Taittiriya Aranyaka. It is thought to be in the region of Mt Kailash.

Trikakud or Trikakubh, 'having three peaks', is mentioned in the Atharva Veda, Shatapatha Brahmana and later texts, as the name of a mountain in the Himalaya; it is probably the modern Trikuta.

Nava-prabhramshana is one reading of a word in the Atharva Veda (19.39.8) but this is uncertain and may not be a proper name; literally 'the sliding down of the ship', it has been connected with Manor Avasarpana in the Shatapatha Brahmana, the northern mountain on which Manu's ship settled after the flood; however, a *pada* text (see Chapter 2 for an explanation of pada texts) and some commentators, including Sayana, read it as *na ava-prabhramshana*, 'no falling downward', and there is a dispute on the correct meaning of this term. Manor Avasarpana of the Shatapatha is known as Naubandhana in the Mahabharata.

Mahameru and Mainaga are two other mountains mentioned in the Taittiriya Aranyaka. Mahameru is a mythical mountain at the centre of the world. Mainaga could be the later Mainaka.

TREES AND PLANTS

Vana and *vriksha* are terms for trees. Plants in Vedic literature have two general terms, oshadhi and virudh, where oshadhi generally refers to plants with medicinal uses. The Yajur texts, the Taittiriya and Vajasaneyi Samhitas give the different parts of plants and trees and refers to roots (*mula*), panicle (*tula*), stem (*kanda*), twig (*valsha*), and flower (*pushpa*). In addition, trees have a corona (*skandha*), branches (*shakha*), and leaves (*parna*). The Atharva Veda divides plants into various types: those which expand (*pra-strinatih*), are bushy (*stambinih*), have only one sheath (*eka-shungah*), are creepers (*pra-tanvatih*), have many stalks (*amshumatih*), are jointed (*kandinih*), or have spreading branches (*vishakha*).

Most trees mentioned in the Rig Veda continue to be mentioned in the later Samhitas. In addition, other trees are referred to. In the Yajur texts, these include *karkandhu* (*Zizyphus mauritiana*) or the ber, a small tree which grows up to 1400 m. *Karshmarya* (*Gmelina arborea*), known as *gamari* or *gambhar*, is common in deciduous forests. It is an ornamental tree but its fruit can be eaten and its wood can be used to make musical instruments. *Badara* (jujube) is a kind of berry or jujube like *karkandhu* and *kuvala*. *Kharjura* (*Phoenix silvestris*) is a wild date palm; it is indigenous to the Tigris–Euphrates area and in the Indus region, where silicified date seeds have been found of the

6th millennium BCE. This deciduous evergreen tree still grows wild in the Indus basin, southern Pakistan, and most of India and Bangladesh, usually found in sub-Himalayan tracts along rivers, on low ground elsewhere, and up to 1350 m in Himachal. *Pitudaru* has been identified as either *devadaru* or deodar, or *khadira* or *udumbara* according to others. Deodar, *Cedrus deodara*, is a tall evergreen tree, that grows between 1200 m and 3300 m, in the region extending from Afghanistan to Garhwal. Another tree known as devidar in the western Himalaya is the Himalayan cypress, *Cupressus torulosa*. *Plaksha* (*Ficus infectoria*), known as *praksha*, is a wavy-leafed fig tree with small white fruit.

Putudru is probably the same as pitudaru. *Rohitaka* can be identified with the tree *Andersonia rohitaka* and is mentioned in the Maitrayani Samhita, as a tree, though in other texts it is the name of a place, probably modern Rohtak. *Tilvaka* (*Symplocos racemosa*), today known locally as *lodhra*, *rodhra*, and *srimata*, is used to treat dieases; it is a shrub or small tree that grows all over north-east India, up to 850 m. The Maitrayani Samhita refers to *tailvaka*—'something made of its wood'. In the Shatapatha Brahmana, it is inauspicious to construct a grave near it. *Vikankata* (*Flacourtia sapida*) is locally known as *katai*. *Krimuka* is a type of wood used for fuel, while *kramukha* is probably a variant of it.

The Atharva Veda mentions several of these trees as well as the following: *shami*, usually identified with *Prosopis spicigera* or *Mimosa suma*, but described in the Atharva as destructive to hair, broad-leaved and producing intoxication, which is not a characteristic of these; it may be what is locally known as *chonkar*.

Another tree is *bilva* (*Aegle marmelos*), later sacred to the god Shiva. This grows in the sub-Himalayan foothills, up to 1200 m; its fruit is eaten by animals, the fruit pulp can be made into sherbet, the leaves used for fodder, and the wood for agricultural implements. *Dashavriksha* in the Atharva is said to be a tree, which is not identified; alternatively it may refer to ten trees. *Arka* in an obscure passage possibly refers to a tree and if so can be identified with *Calotropis procera*, whose leaves are used in sun worship; it has healing properties but the juice is also used in infanticide.

Pilu (*Salvadora oleoides*) is still known by the same name. According to the Atharva, doves ate its fruit. *Sraktya* is used as an adjective describing an amulet (*mani*) and, according to commentators, it is derived from the sraktya or *tilaka* tree (*Clerodendron phlomoides*).

Talasha has been identified with *talisha* (*Flacourtia cataphracta*). In the Atharva, *tarshtaghi* is a term meaning 'derived from the tarshtagha tree'. *Tarshtagha* is mentioned in the Kaushika Sutra. It is not clear which tree is meant. *Varana*, still known by the same name (*varna* or *barna*), is mentioned as a tree in the Atharva and Brahmanas. It is *Crataeva magna*, or *Crataeva religiosa nurvala*, which grows in the Gangetic plains and peninsula, up to 600 m in shady areas near streams, and is a sacred tree planted near temples. The *udumbara* (*Ficus glomerata*) is another tree referred to in the Atharva and Brahamanas. *Abayu* has been identified with *Brassica nigra*. Alternatively, it may be the same as *Abhaya*, a tree also known as *haritaki* (*Terminalia chebula*), which has anti-ageing properties and grows all over the subcontinent.

The Later Vedic Samhitas thus mention several more trees including those found in higher regions, such as pine and deodar. In addition, the Brahmanas refer to a few more. These include *rajjudala* (*Cordia myxa* or *latifolia*); *sphurjaka* (*Diospyros embryopteris*); and *haridru* (*Pinus deodara*). The term *srekaparna* in the Brahmanas has been interpreted to mean 'like an oleander leaf'.

PLANTS

A number of plants are mentioned in the Later Samhitas, particularly in the Atharva Veda, which deals with the herbal treatment of diseases. Plants include those eaten as food and those used in diseases. Cultivated grains are in a different category. Food plants include cucumber, bottle gourd, lotus root and fibre, and citron fruit.

Plants in the Later Vedic Samhitas

- Urvara (cucumber plant) and *urvaruka*, its fruit, are mentioned even in the Rig Veda. *Priyangu*, in the Yajur and Brahmanas, is identified as foxtail millet (*Setaria italica*, formerly *Panicum italicum*). The earliest cultivation of this millet was in China in 6000 BCE. Priyangu has alternatively been identified with *Prunus mahaleb*, a type of cherry tree native to Iran and Central Asia, or with *Callicarpa macrophylla* which grows in north-eastern India and Kashmir up to 1800 m, or *Aglaia roxburghiana*. The above three are used in Ayurveda.
- *Bisa* (lotus fibre) and *shaluka* (edible lotus root) seem to have been delicacies.
- *Madavati* is the name of a plant, meaning 'intoxicating', while *madugha* or *madhugha* is a sweet herb or plant. Madavati has been identified with *Crataeva roxburghii* and may be the same as varanavati, though the latter is also identified with a river.
- *Alapu* or *alabu* (*Lagenaria vulgaris*) in the Atharva and Maitrayani Samhita is the bottle gourd; vessels too were made from it.
- *Jambila*, mentioned in the Yajur texts and in the Atharva, is probably the same as *jambira*, the citron (*Citrus medica*), which has medicinal uses. The early Greeks recorded that it grew in Media and Persia. It is believed to also be indigenous to India.
- Water plants including the lotus and lily are mentioned. *Kumuda* (*Nymphaea esculenta*), mentioned in the Atharva Veda, is the white water lily, known by this name in later Sanskrit texts.

Other plants with their probable identification are given below:

- *Ashvavavra* or *ashvavala* (*Saccharum spontaneum*), a species of reed, is mentioned in the Yajur texts and the Shatapatha Brahmana. It grows in the Himalayan foothills.
- *Karira* (*Capparis* or *Capparis decidua*), a leafless shrub or its fruit, is first mentioned in the Yajur Taittiriya Samhita amd Kathaka Samhita, and later in the Shatapatha Brahmana. Karira still grows along the banks of the river Yamuna.
- *Putika* is a plant often mentioned in the Kathaka Samhita, Shatapatha, and Panchavimsha brahmanas, as a substitute for the Soma plant. In the Taittiriya Samhita, it is used to make milk curdle, an alternative to *parna-valka* (*Butea frondosa*). It is most likely the same as *putikaranja*

(*Caesalpinia bonducella*), still used today as a remedy for fever. *Putirajju*, mentioned in the Atharva Veda, may be the same as this. *Adara* is another substitute for Soma and, in the Shatapatha Brahmana, is said to be the same as *putika*; it is also mentioned in other texts.

Among the large number of plants in the Atharva Veda, the following can be noted. Many are also mentioned in other Later Vedic texts.

- *Saphaka* seems to be an edible water plant or fruit.
- *Alasala*, *silanjala* (or *salanjala*), and *nilagalasala* may be some kind of grain or grass creepers. Silanjala is known as *shilanjala* in the Kaushika Sutra. It may be the same as *shilapushpa* (*Didymocarpus pedicellata*), a herb used to treat kidney stones.
- *Andika* is a plant similar to the lotus. An alternative reading is *paundarika*, similar to *pundarika*, the term for a lotus.

A number of plants have medicinal uses.

- *Avaka* (*Blyxa octandra* or *Vallisneria spiralis*) is an aquatic plant; the gandharvas are said to eat it. Later, it was known as *shaivala* and is identical to shipala. It still grows in watery areas. A related plant was *shitika* or four leaf clover (*Marsilea quadrifolia*). Both these plants, along with *jalasha* (unidentified), had cooling and soothing properties.
- *Ajashringi*, literally 'goat's horn', is referred to as a demon destroyer; according to the commentator, it is the same as *vishanin*; it is also known as *arantaki* or *arataki*. Various identifications have been suggested, including *Prosopis spicigera*, *Mimosa suma*, and *Odina pinnata*. However, vishani is a plant that is still used medicinally, known in Sanskrit as *meshashringi* or 'ram's horn', and is the same as *Gymnema sylvestre*. A woody climber, it is known as a remedy for snakebite and is also useful in diabetes. It has also been used for stomach and liver problems, and for water retention. It is found in the Deccan peninsula, extending to parts of northern and western India. The similarity in name indicates this is the most likely identification. *Vishanaka*, a plant used to cure the disease *vatikara*, is probably the same as this.
- *Amula*, literally 'without root', is described as a plant used to poison arrows. It has been identified with *Methonica superba*. Alternatively, it may be the same as *anantamul* (*Hemedesmus indicus*), a plant with antibacterial and anti-arthritic properties, found across most of India from the upper Gangetic plains to the east and south.
- *Aukshagandhi* is the name of an *apsara* as well as that of a plant. It is some fragrant plant but the exact identification is unclear.
- *Baja* is a plant used against the demon of disease; it may be some sort of a mustard plant.
- *Gugguli*, again an apsara and a plant, must be the same as the present Ayurvedic herb *guggulu*, which comes from the small tree (*Commiphora wightii* or *mukul*); guggul is the gum resin from the bark of this tree.
- *Nalada* is mentioned in the Atharva and other texts as a plant used for a garland. *Naladi*, the

feminine version, is the name of an apsara. It may be identified with *nala* (*Arundo donax*), a wild grass that grows to a height of 6 m and has medicinal uses. Another option is *Nardostachys jatamansi*, whose root is used in Ayurveda for insomnia and related ailments, while the leaves are used as stimulants and antispasmodics. The plant grows in the Himalayan regions, between 3000 m and 5000 m, and has pink or blue flowers. According to Greek writers the Ganga flowed from the mountain where it grew. However its use as a garland suggests it was used for its sweet scent. Perfumes are still made from it.

- *Nyastika* has been identified with *shankhapushpika* (*Andropogon aciculatus*).
- *Pata* in the Atharva Veda and Kaushika Sutra is probably the same as *patha* (*Cissampelos pareira*), a plant used in Ayurveda for women's ailments. Another alterantive is *Clypea hernandifolia*, also a medicinal plant.
- *Pila* in the Atharva is the name of an apsara and was probably originally the name of a fragrant plant like naladi and gugguli, two other apsara names in the same Atharva verse (4.37.3). Alternatively, it may be the same as pilu.
- *Pramandani*, an apsara in the Atharva, seems to be a sweet-scented plant known as *pramanda* in the Kaushiki Sutra.
- *Sahadevi*, mentioned in the Atharva, can be identified with *Vernonia cinerea* or Purple fleabane, a common weed found throughout India with a variety of uses. The juice is used to counter urinary incontinence; the leaves can be eaten; and its decoction is used to treat diarrhoea, stomach ache, colic, and cough. The plant *saha* may be the same as this.
- *Sahamana* may be the same as sahadevi or the Sanskrit *samanga*, the same as *manjishtha*, a medicinal plant, used in rheumatism, identified as *Rubia cordifolia*.
- *Shana* is a kind of hemp, probably *Cannabis sativa* or *Crotolaria juncea*; in the Atharva Veda, it is said to grow in the forest and is used like *jangida* as a remedy against the disease *vishkandha*.
- *Tuuli* seems to be the name of a plant; it is associated with *ghritachi*, 'dripping ghi'.
- *Vihalha* is also referred to as *vihamla* and *vihahla*.
- *Arundhati*, in the Atharva and other texts, is a medicinal plant. It was used to heal wounds, to fight fever, and to induce cows to give milk. It was a climber on trees such as *plaksha*, *ashvattha*, *nyagrodha*, and *parna*. Golden in colour (*hiranya-varna*), it had a hairy stem (*lomasha-vakshana*) and was also called *shilachi*; *laksha* seems to have been a product of it. Shilachi, like manjishtha (see above), has been identified with *Rubia cordifolia*, a herbaceous creeper that has medicinal uses and grows in the lower Himlayan ranges.
- Jangida is a healing plant; it is said to be produced from the juice (*rasa*) of ploughing (*krisha*); this may mean it was planted or that it grew in cultivated land; it is not clear what plant it is. The Dutch Indologist Willem Caland, based on the Kaushika Sutra, took it to be *Terminalia arjuna*. More recently, it has been identified with *ashvagandha* (*Withania somnifera*) which is extensively used in Ayurveda, or with a type of Himalayan mandrake, still used in magical rituals in Sikkim. It is considered the same as *kattuchooti* of Siddha medicine. However, Soma has also been identified with mandrake.

- *Kushtha* is mentioned many times as a healing plant. It grew mainly on the mountains, along with Soma, on the high peaks of Himavant, where the eagles nest, and was thence brought east to men. Like Soma, it grew in the third heaven under the famous ashvattha tree, where the gods used to assemble, and from there it was brought in a golden ship. It was a remedy for many diseases, and was also called *nagha-mara* and *nagha-risa*, and was said to be the offspring of Jivala or Jivanta and Jivalaa (the lively ones). It probably had aromatic qualities as it is classed with anjana or salve, and nalada or nard. Kushtha, still used in Ayurveda, is the same as *Saussurea lappa*; the dried roots yield oil with antiseptic, disinfectant, and anti-inflammatory properties; an extract of the herb is useful in bronchial asthma. It is generally found on the Himalayan hill slopes and in Kashmir. Jivala (*Laurus cassia* or *Cinamomum cassia*) and jivanta (*Desmotrichum fimbriatum*) are related plants.
- *Narachi* is perhaps a poisonous plant.
- *Prishniparni*, 'having a speckled leaf', was used as a protection against evil beings causing abortion. It has been identified with Uraria picta (*Hedysarum pictum*), an important herb in Ayurveda, or with *Hermionitis cordifolia* or a plant later called *lakshmana*, which is supposed to cure barrenness; or with *Glycine debilis*.
- *Apamarga* is an Ayurvedic herb, still in use, which can be identified with *Achyranthes aspera*, a weed found in dry places and wastelands from the seashore to 2100 m, throughout Asia, Africa, Australia, and America, known in English as the prickly chaff-flower. Apamarga has digestive, diuretic, and anti-inflammatory properties, and is especially used to treat inflammations of the internal organs.
- Tajad-bhanga is the name of a plant or tree, but its identification is unclear. It has been identified as the castor-oil plant known in Ayurveda as *eranda* (*Ricinis communis*) but it may be the Sanskrit *taja*, which is cinnamon.

Further plants mentioned in the Brahmanas include:

- *Ashmagandha* (*Physalis flexuosa* or *Withania somnifera*), the later ashvagandha, an important medicinal plant
- *Bimba* (*Momordica monadelpha*)
- *Praprotha*, another plant used as a substitute for Soma
- *Sahadeva*, probably the same as *sahadevi*
- *Sarshapa* (mustard)
- *Ushana*, another plant from which Soma was prepared. (In Ayurveda, ushana is another name for pippali, Indian long pepper or *Piper longum*; it is a climber, grows all over, including in the central Himalayas; the fruit is used for diseases of the respiratory tract. It is an analgesic when applied locally for pains and inflammation and also a general tonic and hematinic.)
- *Amala*, also called *amalaka*, identified with *amalaki* or *amla*, *Embilica officinalis*, the myrobalan tree. (The fruit of this deciduous tree is extremely nutritious and a rich source of vitamin C.)

Thus, by the Later Vedic period, a wide variety of trees, herbs, and plants were known. The area, even the mountainous regions, must have been extensively explored to discover these plants. Experiments must have been made to identify their medical uses. Other plants mentioned are either difficult to identify or were cultivated. The latter will be seen in Chapter 8.

ANIMALS

As in the Rig Veda, a division of animals into forest and village animals also occurs in the Atharva Veda, Yajur texts, and Brahmanas. There are other classifications of animals: as *ubhayadant* (with incisors above and below) and *anyatodant* (with incisors only on the lower jaw) and *eka-shapha* (whole-hooved) as well as *kshudra* (small), both referring to domestic animals. The horse and ass are eka-shapha; the sheep, goat, and ox are kshudra—this distinction corresponds with ubhayodant/anyatodant. Another classification is between those that hold with the hand (*hastadanah*) and those that cannot. The former include *purusha* or man, *hastin* or elephant, and *markata* or ape.

Pashu is a term used for both humans and animals. Thus, in the Yajur, five sacrificial animals (pashu) referred to are the horse, cow, sheep, goat, and man, to which the commentator adds the ass and camel.

The Later Vedic Samhitas also contain numerous references to animals, which can broadly be divided into domestic and wild. The Yajur refers to a number of animals in the context of the ashvamedha, and many of these are difficult to identify.

Animals in the Rig Veda continued to be known in the Later Vedic times. Thus domestic animals still included the cow, goat, sheep, horse, and dog. Cattle remained important. Goat milk was used and goats were said to have two to three young ones. Goats were looked after by an *ajapala* or goatherd. There were also cowherds and shepherds. A wild (*aranya*) sheep is mentioned in the Yajur Vajasaneyi Samhita, hence sheep must still have roamed wild. The dog was now also known as *kukkura*. Horses continued to be important and horse races were held. In the Atharva, a white horse with black ears is said to have special value. The Shatapatha Brahmana states that horses were sometimes used to draw carts. Horse attendants are referred to as *ashvapa*, *ashvapala*, or *ashvapati*. Horses were controlled with reins (*rashmayah*) and halters (*ashvabhidhani*). Valuable horses were obtained from the region of the Sindhu (Indus) and the Sarasvati. *Mahasuhaya* (great horse) is mentioned in the later Brihadaranyaka Upanishad. It came from the Indus region (Saindhava). Thus passages in the Vedas and later texts indicate that horses were found in the region west of the river Yamuna, and were not imported.

The camel, ox, ass, and buffalo were other domestic animals. The camel was still known as ushtra but *dhumra* was an additional term. The ox was called *gavaya* or *go-mriga*. *Gaura* (*gaur*) is also mentioned. Rasabha and gardhaba were terms for the ass or donkey. *Gardhabi*, a female ass, and *mahishi*, a female buffalo, are mentioned. Ashvatara or *ashvatari* were terms for a mule. *Kubhra* has been identified by Kuiper with a hump-backed bull. According to him, it is a word of Munda origin.

The monkey may have been tamed, and tamed elephants are known. A *hastipa* or elephant keeper is mentioned. Markata, *mayu*, and *purusha-hastin* were other terms at this time for an ape or monkey, in addition to the earlier term kapi.

Many wild animals too, mentioned in the Rig Veda, continue to be referred to. They include various kinds of deer and gazelle, jackal, rhinoceros, bear, hyena, hare, lion, wild boar, elephant, wolf, weasel, and mouse. Reptiles and amphibians such as the frog, iguana, crocodile or alligator, and snakes and poisonous insects such as scorpions are mentioned.

In addition, other animals are mentioned, while some are known by alternative names. Several are difficult to identify.

Nyanku and Kulunga are terms that possibly refer to gazelles, though kulunga has also been interpreted as a bird. Eni is a type of deer, possibly a female antelope. Prishata may be the spotted deer or chital. Harina, a deer or gazelle, is mentioned. Its horns were used for making amulets, and it was said to eat yava or barley. It was said to kill avaja or vipers. Ruru and rishya (stag) are terms still used for deer.

While the lion was known earlier, the tiger (vyaghra) and panther (dvipin, the spotted one) are mentioned in the later Vedas. Halikshna, an ashvamedha victim in the Yajur, is thought to be some kind of lion by the commentators Mahidhara and Sayana. It may be significant that Halikshan is a mountain in Xingjiang, China, in the Tarim region.

The rhinoceros was earlier known as *parasvant* (this identification is based on Pali sources, though others have suggested parasvant was a wild ass); in the later Vedas it was referred to as *khanga* or *khadga*. These animals were hunted; the Shankhayana Shrauta Sutra refers to a rhinoceros hide used as a covering for a chariot. *Vardhranasa* or *vardhrinasa* was, according to Sayana, another term for a rhinoceros.

Nakula, a mongoose, is mentioned in the Yajur and Atharva Vedas. Its ability to fight snakes was known, and it was believed to know a cure for snake poison. *Naga* and *mahanaga* are terms used for both snakes and elephants, from the Brahmanas onwards.

Other creatures mentioned in Later Vedic texts were tortoise (*kurma, kashyapa*), crocodile (*makara, nakra*), polecat (*jahaka*), a kind of wildcat (*shitputa*), porcupine (*shalyaka, shvavidh*), otter (*udra*), hyena (*tarakshu*), bat (*jati*), chameleon (*krikilasa*), boa constrictor (*vahasa*), python (*ajagara*), viper (*svaja*), and locust (*shalabha*).

Some other possible identifications are as follows:

- *Manthala*, *manthalava*, and *manthilava* is, according to Mahidhara, a kind of mouse, while Sayana feels it is an aquatic bird.
- *Panktra* is thought to be a field rat.
- *Kumbhinasa*, 'pot-nosed', could be a kind of snake. *Kundrinachi* could be a bird or, according to Sayana, a house lizard (*griha-godhuka*).
- *Ula* may be a term for a jackal or hyena.
- *Srijaya* has been interpreted as a kind of bird, 'black fly' or 'white serpent' or black buffalo, depending on the versions of the text used.
- *Nada* may be a term for a bull; *pashthavah* and *pashtauhi* refer to the ox and cow, respectively.
- *Kuririn* is thought to be some kind of horned or crested animal.
- *Makaka* and *mushkara* are small animals; mushkara could be a kind of mouse.

- Shashayu, 'following the hare', is the name of some animal, which must have chased hares; one suggestion is a tiger, but this is unlikely.
- Vrishadamshtra has been interpreted as a house cat by the German linguist Karl F. Geldner but others reject this; damshtra is a word used for teeth, particularly those of a snake.
- Vyadvara or vyadvari is the name of an animal that gnaws or eats.
- Sharkota, is possibly a term denoting a serpent or scorpion.

The Brahmanas mention a number of animals. Daka seems to mean 'a vicious ram'; durvaraha is a wild boar; dviretas ('having double seed') refers to both the ass and mare; gaja, a common name for the elephant in the epics and later, first appears in the Adbhuta Brahmna; shukladant in the Aitareya Brahmana, meaning 'white-tusked', refers to a wild elephant; machala is a type of dog found in Vidarbha; mahaja is a great aja or goat, probably a wild goat, larger than the domestic; and srigala is a term for a jackal in the Shatapatha Brahmana.

A number of animals listed as sacrificial victims in the Yajur Veda or mentioned in the Atharva and the Brahmanas are challenging to identify. These include balaya, bhaumi, bhaumaka, charachara, chilvati, ghrinivant, golattika, kasha, kirsha, nilashirshni, srimara, shaka, tarda, and tayadara.

Jasha, an aquatic animal or fish, has been equated with a makara. Jhasha, in the Manu story in the Shatapatha Brahmana, is a term for a great fish (maha-matsya). There is a reference to a horn on the fish, to which Manu's boat was tied. A horned fish today is the tusked narwhal whale. Narhwals are medium-sized whales, weighing up to 1600 kg, with a 2–3-m-long tusk, who live in the Arctic region near Canada and Greenland. As seen earlier, Tilak had once put forward the theory of an Arctic homeland for the Rig Vedic people.

BIRDS

Most of the birds mentioned in the Rig are also referred to in the Later Vedic texts. These include the haridrava (yellow water wagtail), ropanaka (thrush or parrot); kikidivi (blue jay or partridge), peacock, and others.

Further information is given on some of the birds. The shyena or eagle was one of the swiftest birds. From the heights where it flew, it could watch over people. Suparna was a term used for various birds. In one passage, it refers to a vulture. In the Atharva, the suparna is said to live in the hills. The uluka or owl was said to bring ill-fortune. In the ashvamedha, they were offered to the forest trees.

A number of birds are mentioned in the Yajur texts, many in the list of ashvamedha victims (around sixty), though this must be purely hypothetical. These include balaka (white egret); darvaghata (woodpecker); darvida (woodpecker); datyauha (a marsh bird, probably the same as datyuha, a moor hen, in later texts); dhunksha or dhunkshna (same as dhvanksha, the jungle crow); goshadi, 'sitting on a cow', possibly an egret; kalavinka (sparrow); kanka, identified by Dave with the fishing eagle, still known by the same name in Nepal; kapinjala (francolin or grey partridge); krunch or krauncha, curlew or snipe, said to be able to separate milk from water, later an attribute of the *hamsa*; *kukkuta* (cock); *kushitaka* (according to the commentary, it is *samudra-kaka*, a sea crow, possibly a gull); *kutaru* (cock), according to Mahidhara, the same as *kukkuta*; *laba* (quail, *Perdis chinensis*); *lopa*, which Sayana says is a bird, perhaps the carrion crow, *shmashana-shakuni*; *madgu* (diver), an aquatic bird; *paingaraja*, identified with the large, racket-tailed drongo found in the outer Himalayas from Nepal to Assam, in Madhya Pradesh, and south India; *paravata* (turtle dove); *pika* (Indian cuckoo); *pippaka*, could also be a type of cuckoo, perhaps the hawk cuckoo or brainfever bird; *plava* is an aquatic bird; it is a generic term for water birds in Ayurvedic texts; *pushkarasada*, 'sitting on the lotus', identified by Dave with the Indian whiskered tern, which nests on floating water plants and leaves of the lotus; *saghan*, is perhaps an eagle or vulture; *sari*, said to be *purusha vach*, 'of human speech', hence may be some kind of bird, possibly the later *sarika* or starling, though according to Dave, it is the hill myna; *sharishaka* may be a bird that Grill identifies with *sharika*, the hooded crow; *sharga*, according to Sayana is the 'wild *chataka*'; *shukra*, parrot; *vidigaya*, is thought to be a type of cock, *kukkuta-vishesha*; in the Taittiriya Brahmana, the commentator considers it it is a white heron, *shveta baka*.

Birds difficult to identify in the Yajur include *alaja*, *hamsasachit*, possibly a kind of duck; *kakara*, *kalaka*; *kulika* or *pulika*; *kaulika*; *kuvaya* or *kvaya*; *parushna*, *shayandaka*, *sichapu*, and *vikakara*.

Among birds in the Atharva were also *aliklava*, some kind of carrion bird; *dhvanksha*, the jungle crow; *krikavaku*, domestic cock; *patatrin*, an unknown bird; *raghat*, a falcon or other swift-flying bird; and *shakunta* and *vayas*, which may have been generic names for birds.

The Atharva also refers to *shyenau-sampatinau* or birds that hunt in pairs. In an interesting passage in this text, the god Indra is said to have helped a wounded pigeon (*kapota*) with food and water.

Among large birds, *bhasa* (a bird of prey) and *mahasuparna* (a great eagle) are referred to in the Brahmanas. The later Charaka and Sushruta Samhitas divide birds into four categories: *pratuda* (peckers), *vishkara* (scratchers), *plava* (water birds), and *prasaha* (birds of prey).

BIRDS AS FOOD

Birds, even wild ones, seem to have been caught and eaten. There was a belief that when a bird was consumed, its qualities were imbibed by the person who ate it.

The Paraskara Grihya Sutra has an interesting passage on the options for the first solid food for a boy of six months—*bhardvaji* or a female skylark if the father wanted the boy to have fluent speech; *kapinjala* or the grey partridge for abundant food; *krikasha* or the ringed plover for a long life; and *ati* or the black ibis for holy lustre.

LOCATION

All the plants, trees, birds and animals correspond with those found in the north India–Pakistan Indus–Ganga plains, and the hills and mountains to the north.

CHAPTER 7

THE TRIBES AND CLANS

Some places and many tribal groups have been mentioned in the Rig Veda, providing further indications of where the text was composed. Some aspects of the way of life at that time can be surmised from the text. Various scholars have different views on the general location of the different clans, and the region where the text was composed.

A few divergent views are given here. According to the *Vedic Index*, 'There is much evidence in placing the composition of the bulk of the Rig Veda, especially the books 3 and 8 in which Sudas appears along with Vasishtha and Vishvamitra, in the east, the later Madhyadesha.' This view was supported by the early scholars including Pischel, Geldner, and the American Sanskrit expert E.W. Hopkins. Another early German Sanskrit scholar, Alfred Hillebrandt, placed the sixth mandala in Iranian lands.

A few scholars of the past and present feel that all places mentioned should be located in Afghanistan but have not done a detailed identification of sites there. Most believe that the Rig Veda was composed mainly in the region of the river Indus and its tributaries. This is confirmed by the analysis in the previous chapter, where the location of the rivers, mountains, and the natural habitat, including trees, plants, animals, and birds, has been extensively analysed. This analysis indicates that the region of occupation corresponds with the north-west of India, the region to the west of the Yamuna, extending into Punjab, present-day Pakistan, and Afghanistan. Here, we will will look at the people and places as well as aspects of the society and economy.

ARYA, DASA, DASYU

These three terms are generally used to refer to groups of people. What exactly they meant, and whom they referred to, is controversial. *Arya* is considered to refer to the main group of people in the Rig Veda. The term *anarya* is used in contrast to it. In earlier times, these were considered racial or ethnic divisions but recent scholars feel such an interpretation has no justification. In the Rig Veda, arya refers to those who sacrifice properly as opposed to those who do not. The term came to mean noble, righteous, or morally superior, and is used in this sense even in the Rig Veda. In the 19th and 20th centuries, writers sought to derive its meaning from the root 'ar' and came up with different theories. For instance, Max Müller (1862) saw the root 'ar' as 'to cultivate or plough', hence arya was one who cultivated the land. Others interpreted the root as 'to go', 'to fit', 'to share', and 'to beget'. Based on this, various meanings were assigned to arya, such as 'companionable', 'hospitable', 'friendly', or 'one who roams like a nomad'. These theories were examined by Oswald Szemerenyi, the Hungarian specialist in Indo-European languages, who felt they were not conclusive, but the term could mean kinsman. The known later meaning of 'noble' probably fits the Rig Vedic period as well. Thus, in Buddhism, *arya satya* means the noble truths, and *arya marga* is the noble eightfold path. In the south, *ayya*, the term for arya, is used even for deities. The Indian scholar Shrikant Talageri, in his analysis of the text, finds the term arya has been used only thirty-six times in thirty-four hymns of the Rig Veda. He feels that the term initially referred only to a specific clan, the Bharatas. Though this may not be correct, it may be more limited in its application to various groups than is generally accepted.

Some other Indo-European languages have terms derived from the same root. The term *airya* was used in Iran but it does not occur in the earliest Avestan texts in Old Avestan. It had ethnic connotations from the 6th century BCE. There are also similarities with the German *ehre*, 'honour'; the Greek aristos, where 'ari' is 'very', 'super', 'extremely'; the Celtic arios, 'noble' or 'in advance' or 'leading', which comes from the old Irish *aire*, or *airech*, meaning 'freeman', 'nobleman', or 'leader'. However, according to recent studies, the Irish Eire is not cognate with arya; it comes from Proto-Irish Iueriu, with Welsh cognate Iwerddon, derived from the genitive form of Iueriu, Iuerionas, ultimately from Proto-Indo-European *pi-wer*, 'fat-fertile'.

Other groups are referred to as *dasa* or *dasyu*. The terms are used to describe people different from the aryas, who were often their enemies. Dasas or dasyus are said to be *avrata* and *akratu*, those who do not observe vows or perform sacrifices; they are said to be *mridhra-vach*, which has been interpreted as having different, strange, or hostile speech. In three passages, they are termed *krishna-tvach* or *asikni-tvach*. This has been interpreted as dark-skinned, or dark in a metaphorical sense. Sayana, however, saw the term tvacham-krishnam as the name of an asura. In one passage, dasas are said to be *anasa*. Again, this has been interpreted as flat-nosed, noseless (a-nasa), or even faceless, again perhaps in a metaphorical sense. It has also been interpreted as mouthless or speechless (an-asa), that is those with different or unintelligible speech. At one time, passages in the texts were interpreted to indicate conflicts, the dasas or dasyus being seen as the original inhabitants, and the aryas as immigrants. At that time, dasas and dasyus were generally seen as dark-skinned and flat-nosed, in contrast to the fair aryas. However, a re-examination of the text indicates that the picture is not so clear or simplistic, as the terms can be differently interpreted. In addition, even so-called aryas, such as the Purus, had names ending in dasyu. Trasadasyu was Purukutsa's son. Divodasa was Sudas's father or ancestor. The aryas were not a united group and conflicts took place across tribes, irrespective of their origin. Many with non-Sanskrit names were associated with arya groups. Some scholars feel that the dasas and dasyus were earlier Indo-Aryan migrants though, if that were the case, it is not clear why they should be considered alien. Others identify them with Dahae and Dahyu, two Iranian tribes. However, as we will see later, dahyu initially referred to a land or territory, and not to a tribe.

Based on various references, the arya and dasa/dasyu groups may have spoken different languages but it does not seem as if they were totally alien to one another. In the Rig Veda, Indra is referred to as lord of wealth to whom all aryas and dasas belong (3.51.9).

In a later Buddhist text, the *Bhaishajya-vastu* (part of the *Mula-Sarvastivada-vinaya*), the Sanskrit-speaking *arya-jatiya* and dasyu-speaking *dasyu-jatiya* are mentioned. Buddha had to teach them in arya and dasyu languages. However, it should be noted that this is a much later text.

PLACES

In the Rig Veda, Kurukshetra is said to be the region through which the Sarasvati, Drishadvati, and Apaya flow. It was the region of present Haryana, around the modern Kurukshetra and extending south. Sharanyavant, probably a lake and a mountain or hill, was located here. According to Sayana, Sharyanah was a region in Kurukshetra, in which the lake Sharyanavant was located.

In the Brahmanas, Kurukshetra is said to be a sacred area. Among places that can be located in the Kurukshetra region are Bharati Tirtha, Ilayaspada, the town Manusha, Pastyavani, and Sarasvati tirtha. Bharati tirtha has been located in the middle of the Kurukshetra region, at Kopar or Koer, east of Kaithal and south-west of Thanesar. Ilayaspada, or Ilaspada, has been connected with Ila and Manu but the verse where it is prominently used (3.23.4) indicates that it is located in the region of the Sarasvati, Drishadvati, and Apaya, that is, the region of Kurukshetra. A. Cunningham, the British archaeologist and first director of the Archaeological Survey of India, discovered a place, Iraspada (near Kaithal), with which it can be identified. Manusha has been identified with Mansa, also near Kaithal. Pastyavani, both a place and a stream, is referred to as the home of Soma. Its suggested location is in Patiala. Sarasvati Tirtha was a sacred site on the banks of the river Sarasvati, probably near Thanesar. Vivasvat Sadan was another place in the Kurukshetra region.

Bhajeratha could be a place but its location is not clear. Some see it as a corruption of the text, which should be read as Bhagiratha. Other places mentioned include Urjayanti and Chedi. Urjayanti possibly refers to a fort, the stronghold of Narmara, though there are other interpretations of the term. Chedi, mentioned in a *danastuti* (list of gifts), was in later times located in Bundelkhand, a region south of the river Yamuna. Its location in the time of the Rig Veda is not clear.

CLANS OR TRIBES

numerous clans or tribes are mentioned. It is not possible to locate them in a precise area but the broad region can be identified. Some information on their location and nature can be deduced from the descriptions of the battles fought.

SUDAS AND THE BHARATAS

King Sudas is frequently mentioned in the Rig Veda. A major battle was fought between this king and a confederation of ten opposing clans, on the banks of the river Parushni (Ravi). Sudas then fought another battle on the Yamuna. We could presume that Sudas was trying to establish control over this region. Earlier, with Vishvamitra as his *purohita*, he won battles on the Vipash and Shutudri (Beas and Satluj). These two rivers are broadly between the Parushni and the Yamuna. However, there were a number of other contenders for control in the Parushni–Yamuna region. This would seem to be the core area of this text.

Sudas is referred to as a Tritsu and a Bharata. While some scholars believe the Tritsus and Bharatas were the same, another view is that the Bharatas formed a clan (*jana*) while the Tritsus were their royal family. The Bharatas are referred to as *Tritsunam vishah*, that is, of the Tritsu family. Devavata and Devashravas, both Bharata chiefs, offered sacrifices on the Drishadvati, Sarasvati, and Apaya, that is, the Kurukshetra region. Perhaps this was also Sudas's stronghold from where he tried to expand to the west and the east.

Sudas's queen named Sudevi was given to him by the twin gods, the Ashvins, who are said to have helped Sudas in other ways too. However, Indra was the god who supported Sudas in all his battles.

Sudas is also called Paijavana, which Yaska explains as 'son of Pijavana'. Pijavana was either his father or another ancestor. Divodasa was another ancestor of Sudas. He was associated with the Bharatas. Another passage in the Rig states that the Bharatas were few and limited but as soon as Vasishtha became their priest or leader, the people of the Tritsus spread themselves everywhere. It is also said that the dwellers on the Yamuna and the Tritsus glorified Indra when he killed Bheda in battle.

SUDAS AND HIS ENEMIES

The hymns that mention Sudas's battles are not too clear about the sequence of events but it can be deduced that among the ten kings who fought against Sudas on the Parushni river, there was a confederacy of five janas (clans): the Anus, Yadus, Turvashas, Druhyus, and Purus. Others that joined this battle were the Alina, Paktha, Bhalana, Shiva, and Vishanin. The first five may be located somewhere west of the Parushni, or near it. The latter five could either be farther west, or north of Sudas's territory. The ten kings of these janas, who were led or organized by Sudas's former purohita Vishvamitra, were defeated in the battle.

Some more details of these clans are given below:

- Anus: The Anus are mentioned in the context of the battle, with the Druhyus in another passage, and elsewhere with the Turvashas, Yadus, and Dhruyus. After the battle, the Anu king seems to have drowned. One passage states that Indra gave the dwelling of the descendants of Anu to Tritsu. The Anus probably lived near the Parushni, and their territory was taken over by Sudas.
- Purus: A number of Purus are known, among them Durgaha, Purukutsa, Trasadasyu, and

Triksi Trasadasyava. Durgaha was the ancestor of Purukutsa, while Trasadasyu was Purukutsa's son. Triksi Trasadasyava was a later prince. Kurushravana was also a descendant of Trasadasyu. The king of the Purus is thought to have died after the battle of the ten kings. This king was possibly Purukutsa, who was involved in an earlier conflict with Sudas, in which Purukutsa was the victor. Trasadasyu, the son of Purukutsa, seems to have had friendly relations with Sudas, hence some sort of peace may have been made after the battle. In the later Aitareya Brahmana and Shankhayana Shrauta Sutra, Trasadasyu is said to be a great king with the rishi Vasishtha as his purohita. However, at the time of this battle, Vasishtha was Sudas's purohita. In another hymn, Agni of the Bharatas is said to be victorious over the Purus; but the Purus were also victorious over others.

- Turvashas: Turvasha is mentioned several times in the Rig Veda, either as a name of a man or of a people, usually together with Yadu. Kurunga, mentioned in a verse along with the Turvashas, could have been a Turvasha king. Alternatively, Kurunga could have been a king of the Anus. The Turvashas are said to have crossed the Parushni but it is not clear from which side they did so. The Turvashas were defeated by Sudas but their king was saved by Indra. In a hymn of the eighth mandala, Turvasha was a worshipper of Indra along with an Anu prince, who was probably the successor of the one who drowned.

- Yadu: This is a tribe or clan, and the name of its king, and is mentioned frequently with Turvasha; he seems to have survived the battle against Sudas, while Anu and Druhyu perished. Yadu may also have been involved in a raid across the Sarayu and the defeat of two kings, Arna and Chitraratha.

- Druhyu: This is mentioned many times in the Rig Veda, in singular and in plural. They were a clan defeated by Sudas. The leader or king, Druhyu, probably drowned after this battle. The Druhyus in the Mahabharata are connected with Gandhara, and may have been somewhere in this region or to the west of the Parushni.

- Alina, Paktha, Bhalana, Shiva, Vishanin: These five clans are mentioned together on the river Parushni. They probably fought against Sudas and were defeated by him, though one interpretation sees them as allies or a subdivision of the Tritsus. Regarding the Bhalana, there is a suggestion that their original home was around the Bolan Pass, because of the similarity in name, but this has no validity as Bolan is not an ancient name. Paktha is also referred to as a protégé of the Ashvins; a passage connects him with Trasadasyu, leader of the Purus. The Pakthas were allies of the Purus in the battle against Sudas. In another passage, Paktha is called Turvayana, the opponent of Chyavana. Paktha was probably a king of the Pakthas. The Shiva people can possibly be identified with the Shibis, who appear in the Anukramani as Shibi Aushinari. The Greeks refer to the Shibi or Shiboi as a people who lived between the Indus and Akesines (Asikni or Chenab). The Ushinaras referred to in the Rig were later associated with the Shibis. Vishanin seems to mean 'having horns'; perhaps they were a people who wore horn-shaped helmets, or headgear with horns.

SOME OTHER GROUPS CONNECTED WITH SUDAS AND THE BHARATAS

- Vasishthas: Connected with the Tritsus and Bharatas, they probably lived between the Parushni and the Yamuna.
- Kurus: The Kurus are not mentioned in the Rig Veda but there is reference to King Kurushravana, a descendant of Trasadasyu, who was known as a Puru king. The Purus and Kurus were thus probably associated. Kurushravana's son was Upamashravas; his father was Mitratithi; in one hymn, he is mentioned as if still alive. The Tritsu–Bharatas, along with the Purus, were probably among those who later formed the Kurus. Pakasthaman Kaurayana is another person mentioned in the Rig; his name associates him with the Kurus.
- Krivi: Mentioned in the Rig Veda, the Krivi were settled in the region of the Sindhu and Asikni (Indus and Chenab) or near the Parushni. The Kritvan, mentioned with the Arjikas and five peoples, could be connected with the Krivis.
- Vaikarnas: Sudas is said to have overthrown the twenty-one clans (janana) of the kings or people of the two Vaikaranas. One suggestion is that the Kurus and Krivis together formed the Vaikarnas. Vikarnas are known in the Mahabharata but their location is uncertain. The German Indologist and Sanskrit scholar Rudolph Roth placed them in Kashmir.
- Kavashas: The Kavashas may be connected with the Purus and the later Kurus. In the Rig Veda, Kavasha was overthrown by Indra for the Tritsus, along with the Druhyu king. According to the Anukramani, Kavasha was the author of some hymns, including those referring to Kurushravana. In a Brahmana text, Kavasha Ailasha was a brahmana born of a female slave.
- Kushikas: The Kushikas, a family of priests—the same as the Vishvamitras—helped the Bharatas in a raid on the Vipash and Shutudri.

OTHER CLANS

Also perhaps in this region were the Nahus, Shimyus, Srinjayas, Vrichivants, Parthavas and Jahnus, the priestly Atri family, as well as the Yatis and Bhrigus.

The Srinjayas were closely associated with the Tritsus. There are also references to a Abhyavartin Chayamana, a Parthava prince who may be the same as Srinjaya Daivavata, who was victorious over the Vrichivants and Turvashas; his sacrificial fire too is referred to. Sahadevya Somaka, Prastoka, and Vitahavya seem to have been other Srinjaya princes, who are mentioned in the Rig Veda. The Srinjayas and Tritsus were probably allied, while the Turvashas were enemies of both. In the Shatapatha Brahmana, Devabhaga Shrautarsha was the purohita of the Kurus and the Srinjayas.

As the Srinjaya king Daivavata conquered the Vrichivants, they may have been located somewhere in the vicinity.

The Shimyus were one of the peoples or kings defeated by Sudas; in another passage they are associated with dasyus. Jahnavi, mentioned in the Rig, could refer to the Jahnus, a group that later merged with the Bharatas. Among other people, Varashikha was a leader of a tribe defeated by Abhyavartin Chayamana. The Yati were an ancient clan connected with Bhrigus, possibly of the distant past. They are also mentioned with Bhrigu in the Sama Veda; in the Yajur and in the Atharva, they are given to the Salavrika by Indra. Though *salavrika* means a hyena, in this context it must be the name of a clan.

NEAR THE YAMUNA

The Paravatas, Shalvas, and Matsyas were perhaps adjacent to the Yamuna on the west. The Rushamas too may have been in this region. The identification of these tribes here is mainly based on later sources.

Not much is said about the Matsyas in the Rig but they seem to have been a people opposed to Sudas. The Paravatas, whose name suggests that they are a mountain people, are often mentioned in the Rig and are connected with the river Sarasvati. In the later Panchavimsha Brahmana, they are a people on the Yamuna.

Rushama is mentioned in the Rig Veda as a protégé of Indra. In another passage, the Rushamas are cited as having a generous king Rinamchaya. In the Atharva, Rushama is referred to with the king Kaurama. In the Panchavimsha Brahmana, Rushama is said to have run around Kurukshetra and defeated Indra. They probably lived near the Sarasvati.

The Panchajanah or 'five peoples' are frequently referred to in the Rig Veda and Later Vedic texts; the term has been variously interpreted. Aupamanyava, as quoted in Yaska's *Nirukta*, says they are the four *varnas* and the Nishadas; Sayana agrees with this interpretation. Yaska says they are the gandharvas, pitris, devas, asuras, and rakshasas. Roth and Geldner interpreted it as referring to all the people of the earth. The German Indologist and Sanskrit scholar Heinrich F. Zimmer believed it referred to the five tribes—Anus, Druhyus, Yadus, Turvashas, and Purus. Another theory is that it refers to five tribes that were the precursors of the later Panchalas.

EAST OF THE YAMUNA

King Sudas and the Tritsus won a great battle on the Yamuna. Their opponents—Ajas, Bhedas, Shigrus, Yakshus—were possibly located to the east of the river. Bheda may have been the leader of a tribe, who led his own people in the battle, apart from the other three groups. The Ajas may be connected with the Ajakeshins of Later Vedic sources, who were associated with the Kuru-Panchalas. Yakshu occurs in two places in the singular and plural, in the hymn celebrating Sudas's battle. They possibly took part in two conflicts, as indicated by the text—one on the Parushni, and one on the Yamuna.

The Panis were also possibly in this region; their identification with the Parnians of Strabo, located far to the west, does not seem correct in the Rig Vedic context. The Indian scholar M.L. Bhargava locates the Panis on the Ganga. *Pani* seems to refer to either a person or a group, who did not make offerings to the devas or give gifts to the priests. In a dialogue hymn, Sarama, a messenger of Indra, asks them to surrender and give up their cows but they refuse and instead invite her to stay with them! The name of the Panis (one meaning of *pani* is merchant) also indicates their connection with trade.

NORTH-WEST OF THE REGION

The Parshus and Parthavas may be located farther north-west and could have Iranian connections. References to them are only through names of people. In a danastuti of the Rig Veda, Parshu is the name of man. In the Vrishakapi hymn of the Rig, Parshu Manavi seems to be the name of a woman. Parthava is also a name in one hymn. Scholars have seen these as references to Persians and to the antecedents of the Parthians. This is possible, though later texts indicate they were different and had Indian connections. In the later Shankhayana Shrauta Sutra, Tirindira Parashavya, meaning 'Tirindira, a descendant of Parshu', was a patron of Vatsa Kanva. The Parshus in Panini's Ashtadhyayi were a warrior tribe. In the same text, the Parashavas are referred to as a tribe in south-west Madhyadesha. According to the 1st-century Greek text, *The Periplus of the Erythraean Sea*, the Parthoi were a tribe in north India. Both Panini and the Periplus are considerably later hence, in Rig Vedic times, there is really no indication of where these clans were located. Some scholars use these names along with references to dasa and dasyu, which they identify with *daha* and *dahyu* of Iranian, as proof that the Indo-Iranian and Iranian homeland was in India. This is a bit far-fetched though the similarity in names is another indication of early Iranian and Indian connections. However, dahyu in Gathic Avestan is usually interpreted as land, domain, or territory, and does not have the later connotation of a tribe or clan.

Prithu and Prithushravas are names of people in the Rig Veda, and have again been connected with the Parthavas. Prithu was a semi-mythical person who initiated agriculture. In the Panchavimsha Brahmana, Prithushravas Daureshravas (a descendant of Dureshravas) is mentioned.

Gandhara is not directly mentioned in the Rig Veda, but the good wool of the sheep of the Gandharis is referred to. In the Atharva, Gandharis are mentioned with Mujavants, Angas, and Magadhas, that is, as people who are rather distant.

THE LOW HILLS TO THE NORTH

The Shambaras, a mountain people, may be in the Shivalik foothills, somewhere west of the Yamuna. Shambara, a dasa chief, was an enemy of Divodasa Atithigva, a Tritsu. Indra defeated Shambara for Divodasa, and destroyed his ninety-nine forts. Shambara is mentioned in several passages in the Rig as an enemy of Indra. In one passage, he is called a dasa, son of Kulitara; in another, he is said to have made himself a devata or god. He is also referred to with Shushna, Pipru, and Varchin, and with Chumuri and Dhuni. All these were defeated by Indra, their forts destroyed. Chumuri and his friend Dhuni were also said to be defeated for Dabhiti, another king, by Indra. According to Asko Parpola, the dasas were in Bactria, part of the BMAC (see Chapter 5), but this is rejected by others.

FARTHER EAST

The Kikata are a people whose leader was Pramaganda and who are said to be hostile to the singer of the hymn. According to Yaska, they were not aryas. Later, Kikata were a people in Magadha, and the term Kikata is sometimes used as a synonym for Magadha. Whether they were already in this region at the time of the Rig Veda is uncertain. There are references to the Sarayu and Gomati and, as seen earlier, in different contexts these may be the rivers of eastern Uttar Pradesh or Afghanistan.

SOUTH OF THE YAMUNA

The Chedis, later located in Bundelkhand, are mentioned but their location in this period is unclear. On the Sarayu, Chitraratha and Arna were defeated by Indra for the Turvasha Yadus. Chitraratha was later known as a Chedi king.

Among other groups, whose nature and location are uncertain, are Sanaka, Shandika, and Shista, which could be tribes or clans. In the Jaiminiya Brahmana, Sanaka was one of the two Kapyas, the other being Navaka, who took part in the sacrifice of Vibhindukiyas. The Shistas are referred to in a Valakhilya hymn.

Many other people are mentioned as enemies, friends, or those involved in conflicts, as in this hymn below, where Indra speaks:

1. *I have enriched the singer with surpassing wealth; I have allowed the holy hymn to strengthen me.*
   I, furtherer of him who offers sacrifice, have conquered in each fight the men who do not worship.
2. *The people of the heavens, the waters, and the earth have established me among the gods with Indra's name.*
   I took for myself the two swift vigorous bays that speed on diverse paths, and the fierce bolt (vajra) for strength.
3. *With deadly blows I smote Atka for Kavi's sake; I guarded Kutsa well with these saving helps.*
   As Shushna's slayer I brandished the dart of death: I gave not up the arya name to dasyu foes.
4. *Smadibha, Tugra, and the Vetasus I gave as prey to Kutsa, father-like, to succour him.*
   I was a worthy king to rule the worshipper, when I gave Tuji dear inviolable gifts.
5. *I gave up Mrigaya to Shrutarvan as his prey because he ever followed me and kept my laws.*
   For Ayu's sake I caused Vesha to bend and bow, and into Savya's hand delivered Padgribhi.
6. *I crushed Navavastva of the lofty chariot, the dasa, as the Vritra-slayer kills the fiends;*
   When straightway on the region's farthest edge I brought the god who makes the lights to broaden and increase.
7. *I travel round about borne onward in my might by the fleet-footed dappled horses of the Sun.*
   When man's libation calls me to the robe of state I soon repel the powerful dasyu with my blows.
8. *Stronger am I than Nabhus, I who slew the seven: I glorified with might Yadu and Turvasha.*
   I brought another low, with strength I bent his strength: I let the mighty nine-and-ninety wax in power.

9. *Lord over all the streams that flow along the earth, I took the Sapta-sindhava as my own domain.*
   I, gifted with great wisdom, spread the floods abroad: by war I found for man the way to high success.

10. *I set within these cows the white milk which no god, not even Tvashtr's self, had there deposited,*
    Much-longed-for, in the breasts, the udders of the cattle, the savoury sweets of mead, the milk and
    Soma juice.

11. *Even so has Indra Maghavan, truly bounteous, sped Gods and men with mighty operation.*
    The pious glorify all these exploits, Lord of Bay Coursers, Strong, and Self-resplendent.

                    (Rig Veda 10.49; based on the translation by R.T.H. Griffith)

The general picture that emerges is that the Rig Vedic people, with their numerous tribes and clans, were located mainly in north-west India–Pakistan, extending from eastern and southern Afghanistan to the Yamuna. Some of the clans may have been located east of the Yamuna but that was not the primary location. Within this region, the concentration of clans seems to be between the Parushni or Ravi, and the Yamuna. The two rivers that are highly praised are the Sindhu (Indus) and Sarasvati. Before attempting to place the Rig Vedic people within an archaeological context, it is necessary to look at some other aspects of their culture.

At the same time, one should note that the Rig Veda is a single text, and a single text cannot be expected to provide complete information about a people or a culture.

KINGS

The kings, or leaders of the janas, were known as *raja* or *rajan*. Several such persons are mentioned in the Rig Veda, including Sudas and the ten kings of the Dasharajna. The danastutis refer to a number of rajas. Rajans may have been of different types, leading a number of clans, only one, or a part of one clan. Jana, *vish*, and *gana* are three terms used for the clan or group. Some have translated jana as tribe, vish as people or clan, and gana as lineage. However, jana seems to have been the term for the people in one clan or group, whereas vishah referred to all the people in the kingdom. There are some references to ganas headed by a *ganapati* or *jyeshtha* (elder) but these are not common. *Janasya-gopa* or *gopati*, 'protector of cattle', was another term used for the king or leader of the jana. Indra, the chief god, was also referred to as gopati. Most of the rajas probably controlled a very small area with flexible boundaries, or only controlled their own people, with no fixed territory. Sudas was perhaps fighting to establish a territory. One raja known as Kashu is said to have gifted ten kings to a rishi (Rig Veda, 8.5.38). Some passages refer to large palaces of the devas, and may reflect exaggerated accounts of royal palaces of the kings. The danastutis show that kings could possess wealth including cows, horses, chariots, gold, and other items. Some kings must have ruled over larger areas and may have been in the process of gradually bringing other areas under their control. The term *samrat* is mentioned, which later meant 'emperor'. One passage has the term *vishvasya bhuvanasya raja*, 'king of the whole world', indicating that the concept of powerful kings was emerging. Kingship seemed to have been hereditary, though sometimes kings were elected or selected, probably from within the members of the royal family.

Kings made alliances and seemed to have formed confederacies to fight battles. The people or leaders made some kind of offerings to the king, as the term *bali-bhrit*, 'paying tribute', indicates. This may not have been official taxation but could be voluntary offerings. A survivor king, defeated in battle, must have presented wealth and gifts to the victor.

SABHA AND SAMITI

Sabha and *samiti* are two institutions referred to, considered to be assemblies of people who had a say in governance though evidence for this is unclear, at least in the Rig Veda. The two have been distinguished; the samiti is thought to represent all the people of a village while the sabha is a special group of the elite. The term *sabheya* ('worthy of the sabha'), applied to a brahmana, has led to the view that it was a group of brahmanas and wealthy people but, in several passages, sabha is thought to refer to a house, hence its nature is uncertain. The sabha, which means 'assembly', also refers to a hall where people met for various activities, including to play dice. Another view is that the sabha was the place of meeting and the samiti was the people who met there. The role of these institutions in this early period is unclear. It would also be unreasonable to expect that the numerous tribes or clans, often at war with one another, had identical political or social systems, though there may have been some similarities.

WARS AND BATTLES

Numerous wars and battles were fought. Several kings and groups allied to fight major battles. The rajan led his warriors in battle. *Yodha* was the term for a warrior. The earliest term used in the Rig Veda for the class of warriors is *rajanya*. *Kshatriya* was also used and became more common later on. *Rana* was a term for battle, initially also meaning 'joy of battle'.

Warriors fought from chariots, armed with bows and arrows. Arrows, known as *shari*, *sharya*, or *sayaka*, had a shaft probably made of tall canes or reeds, and were tipped with a sharp point made of bone or horn. Poison could be placed on the tip. Arrows were kept in a quiver (*nishangin*). These were the primary weapons, though other weapons, including spears and knives, were known. A lance (*srika*) and spear (*srakti*) were also used. Warriors wore some kind of armour or breastplate, which may have been made of thick cloth, leather, metal or a material reinforced with metal. A guard (*hastaghna*) was worn on the left arm to avoid friction from the bowstring. A helmet (*shipra*) was probably worn but the use of a shield is uncertain. Sling stones may have been used. Foot soldiers probably accompanied the charioteers though *patti*, the term for a foot soldier, occurs only in the later Samhitas. The term *mushtihatya* for a hand-to-hand fight or fighter was known.

Apart from major battles, raids to gain wealth, cows, or booty seem to have been common. There is some indication that warriors also fought battles on horseback but this has been doubted. Warriors used *dhvajas* or banners in battle, and some sort of martial music was played. Troops must have been organized into groups under leaders such as the *vratapati* or ganapati. The *senapati* was the leader of the army.

TERRITORY

The territory of a king was known as *rashtra*. At this time, the king probably did not own the land but this is unclear. Grants of land are not referred to. On the other hand, in a danastuti, kings are given to a rishi, which must have been along with the land they ruled.

The *grama* was the basic village unit or settlement. Though its exact nature is not known, it may have been similar to later villages. It is referred to in contrast with *aranya* or forest. Its animals and plants were different from those of the forest. Cattle returned to the village every evening, after grazing on the outskirts. The grama is thought to have had several families (*kulas*), who were part of a particular clan. Settlements had barricades or fortifications of some kind. Stone and metal (*ayas*) forts (*pur*) are mentioned, though it is more likely that fortifications consisted of simple barricades. Pur has also been interpreted in different ways, and may not have referred to forts at all. Metal forts are certainly impossible and some of the references seem to be metaphysical. *Dehi*, or defences consisting of earthworks or dikes, are referred to. *Durga* was another term used for a fort. There do not seem to have been any cities or, at least, they are not referred to. Wood and bamboo were used to make houses, probably along with thatch.

OFFICIALS

The purohita or chief priest was an important official associated with the king. Like Vishvamitra or Vasishtha, he could even organize a battle. The purohita performed prayers and sacrifices and guided the king in all his actions, including in war and battle.

The headman or leader of the village was known as the *gramani*. The *vrajapati* may have been the same as the gramani. The kula or family was a smaller unit, headed by the *kulapati*. There is a reference to a kulapati fighting in a battle under the leadership of a vrajapati. The *senani* or senapati must have headed the *sena*, the army or group of warriors. There are references to spies (*spasha*) and to messengers (*duta*).

LAWS

Dharma is the term used for law or custom but it is not clear what kind of laws existed. Laws must have differed in the various kingdoms. Highway robbers and cattle thefts were common. People prayed to Pushan to safeguard their journeys and together fought battles for cattle. Playing dice often led people into debt and ruin. A debtor may have had to serve the person he owed money to, if he could not repay the debt. An interesting hymn in the Rig Veda refers to ruin caused through playing dice.

SLAVERY

Dasis or female slaves were gifted, according to the danastutis, but dasas were not always slaves. The terms seem to have been used in different ways—one for a category of people and the other for slaves.

CHARIOTS

Ratha, or chariot, is thought to be different from *anas* (cart) though the distinction is not always clear. *Sakata* was another term for a cart. The ratha usually had two wheels (*chakra*), each with a rim, felly, spokes (*ara*), and nave (*nabhya*). The rim and felly together were known as *nemi*. The axle (*aksha*) was sometimes made of *aratu* wood. The body was known as *kosha* or *vandura*. Usually there were two horses, with a pole on each side, and a yoke. Reins and a bit seem to have been used. Sometimes, the ass (*gardabha*) and mule (*ashvatari*) were used in chariots but usually it was the horse. Rathas are often vehicles of the gods, and some references can again be seen in a metaphysical sense. Rathas with one wheel are mentioned, and possibly referred to the sun.

CATTLE

Cattle raids seem to have been frequent causes of conflict, indicated by allusions to conflicts such as that with the Panis, and by the many words for war with a prefix derived from *go* or *gau*, the words for 'cow' and 'cattle'. Thus *gavishti*, *gaveshana*, *goshu*, and *gavya* were all words for battle. A hero was known as *gojit*, or one who had won cows, and a rich person was *gomat*, 'owner of cows'.

There were other domestic animals, including goats, sheep, horses, bulls, asses, dogs, and buffaloes, yet cows were obviously the most important. Cows went off in the morning to graze at a time known as *samgava* and returned in the evening at *godhuli*. (See Chapter 6 for more details on animals.)

AGRICULTURE

Agriculture was practised and was also important. *Kshetra* was a term for a cultivated field. Some lands were more fertile than others. Cereal grains were grown but it is not clear what these were. *Dhana*, *dhanya*, and *yava* are three types of grains mentioned. Though dhana is often translated as 'corn', it does not mean corn or maize, which was a late entrant into India. It only refers to a cereal grain, which was the earlier English meaning of 'corn'.

Dhanya is another general term for grain. Yava seems to be another generic term for any sort of grain and not only barley, which is its later meaning, though barley was probably cultivated at this time. *Priyangu* is probably a term for millet, *Setaria italica*, though it has also been interpreted differently (see Chapter 6). Some other plants, mentioned in Chapter 6, may have been cultivated, such as the cucumber, while others were probably collected from the wild. Both the plough (*hala*, *langala*, or *sira*) and hoe (*khanitra*) were used. Ploughing (*krish*) and sowing (*vap*) are referred to, as well as the ripening of grain. Grain is said to rejoice in the rain though some form of irrigation was also used. Crops were harvested with a sickle (*srini* or *datra*) collected in sheafs, threshed, and winnowed. The grain was then measured in a vessel termed *urdara* and stored in a granary (*khala*). The Ashvins are said to be connected with the sowing of grain with a plough. Ripe fruit is referred to; whether wild or cultivated is not clear. The first and tenth mandalas contain most of the references to agriculture, hence some have considered agriculture a late development for the Rig Vedic people. However, as the historian L. Gopal demonstrates, there are clear references to agriculture even in the family mandalas, indicating the agrarian character of the people. He points out a number of terms used: *vahah* (oxen in harness), *krishatu langalam* (plough in action), *varatrabhyantam*, (tying [the oxen] with strap), *sita* (furrow), *phalam vikrishantu bhumin* (ploughshare tearing the earth), *kinashah* (ploughman), and the metaphor of milking the earth by cultivation as one milks a cow. Kshetrasyapati, as the lord of the field, was worshipped.

FOOD

Food included milk and milk products such as butter and ghi as well as grain, vegetables, fruit, and sometimes meat. *Saktu*, in the Rig Veda, seems to mean grain before it is winnowed but it could mean coarsely ground cereal grains, as in the later Samhitas and Brahmanas.

Milk was often drunk straight from the cow but was also mixed with other substances. Soma and *sura* were intoxicating drinks. Soma was made from some sort of plant (for its possible identification, see Chapter 6) and used in rituals. The whole of Mandala 9 is in praise of Soma. There was an elaborate procedure to prepare it, including pressing the plant, sieving the juice, then mixing it with milk, sour milk, or yava. Sura was probably made with grain and seems to have been more intoxicating than Soma, as under its influence crimes were committed. *Madhu* is a term used for any sweet food or drink, including Soma and milk, but also meant honey. Grain was ground with a millstone and made into flour. Mixed with milk, ghi or butter, this was cooked and made into what is termed 'cakes'. The grain could also be roasted or parched. The meat of ox, sheep, and goat was eaten though it may not have been a regular practice. The cow was termed *aghnya*, 'not to be killed', indicating its importance.

METAL

Metal (*ayas*) is referred to. Whether this was copper, copper–bronze or even iron is uncertain.

CLOTHES AND JEWELLERY

Clothes and jewellery were worn. Clothes seem to have been woven from cotton or wool, or made from animal skins. *Vasa*, a lower garment, and *adhivasa*, an upper or outer garment, is mentioned in the Rig. *Drapi* was perhaps a shawl and *peshas* may have been an embroidered garment. Clothes were probably wrapped around the body and not sewn. *Vadhuya* was a special type of clothing worn by brides and was given to a brahmana after the marriage ceremony. Earrings, necklaces, head and breast ornaments, armlets, and anklets were evidently worn. Women and even men seem to have plaited their hair.

WEALTH

Danastuti hymns, in praise of gifts, refer to rishis and their patrons, and have references to wealth in terms of gold, horses, cattle, and female slaves.

TRADE

There are some references to trade. Long journeys are known to have been made. One passage refers to visiting faraway lands to gain a profit. The cow seems to have been an item used in barter while the *nishka*, a type of ornament, was also used as some sort of currency. Gains in battle included herds of cattle and sheep. Ships and boats are mentioned; the Ashvins rescued Bhujyu after sailing in the ocean (*samudra*) in a ship with a hundred oars. The term samudra has been variously interpreted but, at least in some cases, must refer to the sea or ocean.

OCCUPATIONS AND PASTIMES

Numerous occupations were known. There were kings or chieftains, warriors, priests, cattle herders, farmers, and traders. Despite the pastoral–agrarian economy, hunting was an occupation and hunters are referred to. All kinds of items were made; the *rathakara* (chariot-maker) must have existed, but is not mentioned in the Rig Veda. The term only occurs in Later Vedic texts. There were also cart-makers, carpenters, metal workers, leather and wood craftsmen, and those who made bows and bowstrings. Mats were made from reeds. Musical instruments too were made.

Chariot races, playing with dice and gambling, singing, and dancing were among the pastimes. The *vina* (a stringed instrument), *vana* (flute), and drums are mentioned. The dialogue hymns suggest an early form of theatre.

FAMILY

The family was usually a patriarchal joint family though there may have been other kinds as well. The wedding hymn suggests that the new wife had to establish her place in the household, and win over her brothers-in-law as well as her husband's parents. The son probably stayed with the parents even after he was married but this may have varied. One hymn suggests that the wife's mother sometimes lived in the joint family. This indicates that there were different customs prevailing among the various groups. There may have been some matrimonial groups too. *Vamsha* lists in the Brahmanas are often through the mother. The father could be authoritarian as indicated by the story of Rijrashva, who gave his father's sheep to a *vrika* (wolf) and was blinded by his father. Vrika here may not literally be a wolf but perhaps a person from a clan with a wolf totem.

CASTE

The general view is that there was no clear-cut caste system at this time and that it emerged in the Later Vedic period. Some differ, pointing out that hereditary succession was known in kings; brahmanas and purohitas had considerable importance; and families of rishis were known. *Varna*, which also literally means 'colour', was the later term for caste. Varna and other terms for colour are often used metaphorically. The *Purusha-sukta*, a late hymn in the Rig, refers to the four castes: 'When (the gods) divided *purusha*, into how many parts did they cut him? . . . The brahmana came from his mouth, the rajanya from his arms, the vaishya from his thighs, the purusha from his feet.' The terms rajanya, vaishya, and shudra occur only in this sukta. The terms brahmana and kshatriya are used but are not referred to as varna. The term 'brahman' sometimes refers to a priest and other times to anyone who was specially virtuous or distinguished. At this time, princes and householders could offer sacrifices themselves, indicating that the role of the brahmana had not yet crystallized. The various references indicate that the caste system was not well established.

MARRIAGE AND WOMEN

Several references indicate that girls reached maturity before they were married. At times girls may have had limited choice as to whom they married. One hymn refers to marriage through elopement; courtship and love are also referred to. On the whole, women definitely had an inferior position though the status would have differed among different classes and in different clans and areas. Marriage was important and was of various types, including polygamy and monogamy.

One indication of an inferior position of women is in the nature of the goddesses in the Rig Veda. Though goddesses are known, they are relatively few. Aditi and Usha are the most important but they do not have the same prominence as the gods. Around twenty hymns were composed by women in the Rig Veda, out of a total of 1028. Women accompanied their husbands in sacrifices but did not sacrifice on their own. No women priests conducted sacrifices. Several prayers in the Rig Veda are for children in general, and specifically for sons.

Some interesting hymns throw light on some aspects of society. In the dialogue hymn between Yama and Yami, incest between brother and sister is clearly forbidden. However, the concept of creation of life through twins is a common theme in different cultures. (In late Zoroastrian texts, the Iranian counterpart, Yima and Yimak, united and from them all people were descended. In India, Jain texts much later than the Vedas refer to a golden age when descent was through twins.) The Rig Veda has no reference to *sati* though, in one hymn, there is reference to a custom where a widow lies near her dead husband on the funeral pyre but gets up before the fire is lit.

EDUCATION

In this period, the *upanayana* is not mentioned. The Vedas, their language and metre, and other branches of learning must have been studied. The frog hymn suggests that repetition after the teacher was one method of study. Apart from book learning, there must have been practical learning too, in the context of warfare, agriculture, etc. The term *brahmachari*, in the sense of a student, is mentioned in one passage. Male students may have learnt from the father or from another teacher. Women also studied, as is clear from the fact that they were composers of hymns. Some feel there was writing at this time but no writing has survived.

Literature was quite advanced as seen from the complex and refined metres used in the Rig Vedic verses.

We thus get a picture of a fairly complex Chalcolithic society, in which the people prayed to numerous deities for success, wealth, progeny, and protection.

Two interesting hymns from the Rig Veda, which throw light on socio-economic aspects, are given below. Both are based on the translation by R.T.H. Griffith in *The Hymns of the Rig Veda*.

The gambler's hymn

1. *Sprung from tall trees on windy heights, these rollers transport me as they turn upon the table.*
    Dearer to me the die that never slumbers than the deep draught of Mujavan's own Soma.
2. *She never vexed me nor was angry with me, but to my friends and me in ever gracious.*
    For the die's sake, whose single point is final, my own devoted wife I alienated.
3. *My wife holds me aloof, her mother hates me: the wretched man finds none to give him comfort.*
    As of a costly horse grown old and feeble, I find not any profit of the gamester.
4. *Others caress the wife of him whose riches the die has coveted, that rapid courser:*
    Of him speak father, mother, brothers saying, We know him not: bind him and take him with you.
5. *When I resolve to play with these no longer, my friends depart from me and leave me lonely.*
    When the brown dice, thrown on the board, have rattled, like a fond girl I seek the place of meeting.
6. *The gamester seeks the gambling-house, and wonders, his body all afire, Shall I be lucky?*
    Still do the dice extend his eager longing, staking his gains against his adversary.
7. *Dice, verily, are armed with goads and driving-hooks, deceiving and tormenting, causing grievous woe.*
    They give frail gifts and then destroy the man who wins, thickly anointed with the player's fairest good.
8. *Merrily sports their troop, the three-and-fifty, like Savitr the God whose ways are faithful.*
    They bend not even to the mighty's anger: the king himself pays homage and reveres them.

9. *Downward they roll, and then spring quickly upward, and, handless, force the man with hands to serve them.*
    Cast on the board, like lumps of magic charcoal, though cold themselves they burn the heart to ashes.

10. *The gambler's wife is left forlorn and wretched: the mother mourns the son who wanders homeless.*
    In constant fear, in debt, and seeking riches, he goes by night unto the home of others.

11. *Sad is the gambler when he sees a matron, another's wife, and his well-ordered dwelling.*
    He yokes the brown steeds in the early morning, and when the fire is cold sinks down an outcast.

12. *To the great captain of your mighty army, who has become the host's imperial leader,*
    To him I show my ten extended fingers: I speak the truth. No wealth am I withholding.

13. *Play not with dice: no, cultivate your land. Enjoy the gain, and deem that wealth sufficient.*
    There are your cattle, there your wife, O gambler. So this good Savitr himself has told me.

14. *Make me your friend: show us some little mercy. Assail us not with your terrific fierceness.*
    Appeased be your malignity and anger, and let the brown dice snare some other captive.

(10.34)

Yama and Yami: A dialogue

Yami: 1. *Fain would I win my friend to kindly friendship.*
        So may the sage, come through the air's wide ocean,
        Remembering the earth and days to follow, obtain a son, the issue of his father.

Yama: 2. *Your friend loves not the friendship which considers her who is near in kindred as stranger.*
        Sons of the mighty asura, the heroes, supporters of the heavens, see far around them.

Yami: 3. *Yes, this the Immortals seek of you with longing, progeny of the sole existing mortal.*
        Then let your soul and mine be knit together, and as a loving husband take your consort.

Yama: 4. *Shall we do now what we never did before? We who spoke righteously now talk impurely?*
        Gandharva in the floods, the Dame of Waters (Saranyu)—such is our bond, such our most lofty kinship.

Yami: 5. *Even in the womb God Tvashtr, the shaper of forms, Creator, made us consorts.*
        None violates his holy ordinances: that we are his the heavens and earth acknowledge.

Yama: 6. *Who knows that earliest day of which you speak? Who has seen it? Who can here declare it?*
        Great is the law of Varuna and Mitra. What, wanton! will you say to men to tempt them?

Yami: 7. *I, Yami, am possessed with love for Yama, that I may rest on the same couch beside him.*
        I as a wife would yield me to my husband. Like chariot-wheels let us speed forward to meet each other.

Yama: 8. *They stand not still, they never close their eyelids, those sentinels of Gods who wander round us.*
        Not me—go quickly, wanton, with another, and hasten like a chariot wheel to meet him.

Yami: 9. *May Surya's eye with days and nights endow him, and ever may his light spread out before him.*
        In heaven and earth the kindred pair commingle. Oh Yama! Behave towards me as if you were not my brother.

Yama: 10. *Sure there will come succeeding times when brothers and sisters will act as if unrelated.*
         Not me, O fair one—seek another husband, and make your arm a pillow for your consort.

Yami: 11. *Is he a brother when no lord is left her? Is she a sister when destruction comes?*
Forced by my love these many words I utter. Come near, and hold me in your close embraces.

Yama: 12. *I will not fold my arms around your body: they call it sin when one comes near his sister.*
Not me—prepare your pleasures with another: your brother seeks not this from you, O fair one.

Yami: 13. *Alas! you are indeed a weakling, Yama we find in you no trace of heart or spirit.*
As round the tree the woodbine clings, another will cling about you girt as with a girdle.

Yama: 14. *Embrace another, Yami; let another, even as the woodbine rings the tree, enfold you.*
Win his heart and let him win your fancy, and he shall form with you a blessed alliance.

(10.10)

LATER VEDIC

Later Vedic literature refers to both places and people. The later Samhitas do not provide much information on this, hence the Brahmanas are also used, along with references to later sources.

We saw earlier that the rivers of Afghanistan are not mentioned in Later Vedic literature. However, people and places of the distant north and north-west are mentioned.

NORTH OR NORTH-WEST

Udichya, the northern region, is referred to. The brahmanas of Udichya are mentioned in the Shatapatha Brahmana; their speech was believed to be similar to that of the Kuru–Panchalas, hence the region was not considered alien.

Mujavant, already mentioned in the Rig Veda, is in the Atharva Veda, along with Mahavrishas, Gandharis, and Balhikas, a region where fever is to be banished. All these were probably far to the north or north-west. Whether they were in what has been termed udichya, or even beyond, is not clear. Mujavant is generally identified as a Himalayan mountain. Two kings of the Mahavrishas, Raikva-parna and Hritsvashaya, are referred to in the Chhandogya Upanishad and the Jaiminiya Upanishad Brahmana. The Balhikas are sometimes identified with the people of Balkh, that is, Bactria, though they are also located in the western region (see below). In the Shatapatha Brahmana, however, Balhika is the name of a Kuru prince, hence they may not have been so far north. Of course, it should be noted that Kuru or Kurush (the Greek Cyrus) were also names of kings of Iran. Gandhara is well known in later sources, with its capitals at Purushapura (Peshawar) and Takshashila. The Gandharis may belong to the same region. In the Aitareya Brahmana, Nagnajit of Gandhara is a teacher of the Vedas. Nagnajit is also known in the later Ramayana. Other northern people are mentioned in the Brahmanas and Upanishads, among them the Kekayas and Kambojas. Regarding these, Ashvapati, a king of the Kekayas and a teacher of brahmanas, is referred to. Kamboja Aupamanyu, another teacher, is mentioned. He may have been the son of Upamanyu of the Rig Veda. Kekaya and Kamboja are again well known in later sources.

Both can be located in the north-west, probably beyond Gandhara. These references seem to indicate that the Vedic people, by the time of the Brahmanas, lived in regions far north and north-west. Whether they were here even in Rig Vedic times, or reached the areas later, is not clear.

The Uttara Kurus and Uttara Madras were other people of the north and north-west but may not have been as far away as the former group. They may have lived in Himalayan regions and were different from the Kurus and the Madras but could have been their offshoots. The Aitareya Brahmana states that Janantapi Atyarati wished to conquer the Uttara Kuru region, which was the land of the gods. This suggests it may have been the region of the present state of Uttarakhand, still referred to as the land of the gods, or perhaps Himachal Pradesh. Kashmir has also been suggested as the home of the Uttara Madras.

Pratichya, the western region, is mentioned in the Brahmanas. It seems to refer to the Punjab region. The Nichya, Apachya, Ambasthas, and Balhikas lived here. Ambasthya was a king of the Ambasthas; his priest for the rajasuya sacrifice was Narada.

The Sparshu, who must be the same as the earlier Parshu, were another western people according to the Baudhayana Shrauta Sutra.

WEST OF THE YAMUNA

The region adjacent to the Yamuna on the west and the east is the most important region of the Later Vedic period, occupied mainly by the Kurus. This was part of the region of Madhyadesha, the 'middle country'.

The Sarasvati and Drishadvati still flowed in the region west of the Yamuna but they were not the great rivers of the Rig Vedic period. In the time of the Brahmanas, they disappeared into the sands of the desert. The time of the drying up of these rivers can be correlated to some extent from archaeology and geology. We will look at that and its implications for the date of the texts in Chapter 8.

Vinashana is mentioned in the Panchavimsha Brahmana and the Jaiminiya Upanishad Brahmana as the place where the Sarasvati is lost in the sands of the desert. Its probable location is the inland delta formed by the Ghaggar–Hakra near Derawar fort in the Cholistan desert. Alternatively, it can be located near Sirhind in the Patiala region, where the river temporarily disappears. Another place mentioned in connection with the Sarasvati, in the same texts, is Plaksha Prasravana, a place said to be a forty-four-day journey away from the spot where the Sarasvati disappears. Through references in later texts, it seems to mean the source of the Sarasvati. Triplaksha is a place mentioned in the Panchavimsha Brahmana, which can be located near the Yamuna. Here the river Drishadvati disappeared.

Several places in this region are mentioned in the Brahmanas too. These include Asandivant, said to be the capital of the Kuru prince Parikshit; it can be identified with Asandh in Karnal. Kurukshetra is the land of the Kurus. The Panchavimsha Brahmana gives Parinah as its western boundary and Turghna as its northernmost part. Turghna can be identified with Sugh, in Ambala district. Other places mentioned in this region in the Brahmanas and Aranyakas are Sachiguna, which seems to be a place in the territory of the Bharatas; Karoti, a place or a river, where Tura Kavasheya made a fire altar; Maru, referred to as the *utkara* (mound of earth thrown up from the excavation of the altar) at Kurukshetra; Nadapit, the birthplace of Bharata; Rohitaka, a locality after which a saman or chant was named, and which must be the Rohtak region of Haryana.

Many groups of people can possibly be located in this area. The Kurus were in this region but their territory also extended eastwards across the Yamuna.

The southern branch of the Madras could be located near Kurukshetra or farther north-west. The Paravatas and Rushamas seem to have been located in or near the Kurukshetra region in this period. The Panchavimsha Brahmana refers to the Paravatas on the Yamuna.

The Aitareya Brahmana states that the Ushinaras and Vashas were in Madhyadesha, along with the Kuru-Panchalas. However, the Gopatha Brahmana regards them as northerners. The Mahabharata refers to Ushinara performing a yajna (sacrifice) on marshy land on both sides of the Yamuna. In the Puranas, Drishadvati is one of the five wives of Ushinara, indicating the location of Ushinara near this river. Alternatively, the Ushinaras may have been in the Shivalik foothills, north of the Kuru region. According to the Buddhist text the Divyavadana, Ushinara was the northern boundary of Madhyadesha. The Baudhayana Shrauta Sutra refers to Shibi, son of Ushinara, as a protégé of Indra, who sacrificed for him on the Varshishthaya plain and saved him from fear of a foreign invasion.

The Vashas were located near the Ushinaras and seem to have united with them. The Kaushitaki Upanishad connects them with the Matsyas. The Shalvas and Matsyas were probably in the present region of Rajasthan. However, M.R. Singh places the Vedic Shalvas, Matsyas, Ushinaras, and Vashas in the northern part of the Kurukshetra region. In the Atharva Veda, the Shalvas are said to live on the banks of the Yamuna. In the Shatapatha Brahmana, Dhvasan Dvaitavana is a Matsya king. In the Gopatha Brahmana, the Matsyas are connected with the Shalvas and, in the Kaushitaki Upanishad, with the Vashas.

According to the Mantra Patha, the king of the Shalvas was Yaugandhari, at a time when they stayed their chariots on the banks of the Yamuna.

THE GANGA–YAMUNA PLAINS

East of the Yamuna, in the region between the Ganga and the Yamuna, both places and people are mentioned.

The most prominent people in this region were the Kuru-Panchalas, referred to together in the Kathaka Samhita and in several Brahmanas and Upanishads. Together, they seem to have occupied the area from the west of the Yamuna across the upper Ganga plains, up to Allahabad. A passage in the Kanva recension of the Kathaka Samhita shows that they had one king. The Kurus were within the western doab and to the west of the Yamuna in the Kurukshetra region. Kauravya in the Atharva enjoyed prosperity under Parikshit, who ruled at Asandivat.

Ibhiyagrama was a village in Kuru country, belonging to the owner or rider of elephants; it was probably the same place known later as Hastinapura. Karapachava in the Panchavimsha Brahmana is the name of a place on the Yamuna while Mashnara, mentioned in the Aitareya Brahmana, is the scene of victory of a Kuru king.

Both the Kurus and Panchalas were probably groups into which several different clans were amalgamated. The Kurus included the Bharatas and Purus.

In the Brahmanas and Aranyakas, the Bharatas are said to have won victories on the Ganga and the Yamuna, and must have been located between these rivers. At this time, the Bharatas seem to have merged with the Kurus. In the Vajasaneyi Samhita, Bharata appears as a variant for Kuru-Panchala. According to the Shatapatha Brahmana, Bharata Daushanta bound seventy-eight steeds on the Yamuna and fifty-five near the Ganga. The Jahnus had merged with the Bharatas. The Vasishthas and the Vishvamitras, who were the same as the Kushikas, were the priestly families associated with the Bharatas. The Vrichivants, who are said to have contested for sovereignty with the Jahnus, were also probably associated with the Bharatas.

Kurushravana is known as Trasadasyava, descendant of Trasadasyu, who was a king of the Purus. The Kurus are most important in Brahmana literature and the major Brahmana texts were probably composed in their region.

Parivakra (or Parichakra) and Kampila were in Panchala territory. According to the Shatapatha Brahmana, at Parivakra, the Panchala overlord of the Krivis seized a horse for sacrifice. It could be identified with Ahichchhatra of later literature, the same as Ahichchhatra in Bareilly district, or the later Ekachakra, which was probably Chakarnagar Kheda in Etawah district. Kampila, mentioned in the Taittiriya Samhita, can be identified with Kampil in Farrukhabad district.

The Shatapatha Brahmana indicates that Krivi was either the old name of the Panchalas, or was one of their tribes. The Jaiminiya Upanishad Brahmana (3.29.1, 7, 6; 8, 7; 4.7, 2) describes a close relationship between the Kurus and Panchalas. Ucchaishravas Kaupayeya was a Kuru king while Keshin Dalbhya, his sister's son, was king of the Panchalas. The Shatapatha Brahmna (13.9.3, 1) mentions that a Kuru king was opposed to the restoration of Dushtaritu Paumsayana to his hereditary kingdom over the Panchalas, but failed to prevent it from happening. One suggestion is that the Krivis, Turvashas, Keshins, Srinjayas, and Somakas were the five tribes that formed the Panchalas. This is also suggested by references in the Brahmanas. The Bharadvajas and Vaitahavyas were other families connected with the Srinjayas, and hence with the Panchalas, and the Shviknas and Vaitahavyas are suggested as other components of the Panchalas. The Shatapatha Brahmana mentions a king of the Shviknas, Rishabha Yajnatura.

Another passage in the Kathaka Samhita refers to a dispute between Vaka Dalbhya and Dhritarashtra Vaichitravirya, the former said to be a Panchala in origin, and the latter a Kuru.

In the Allahabad region, Kaushambeya, probably a native of the town of Kaushambi, is mentioned in the Shatapatha Brahmana. Kaushambi, identified with the present-day town of the same name, probably marked the eastern limits of Kuru–Panchala territory.

The Kapileyas and Babhravas, in the Aitareya Brahmana, were descendants of Devarata Vaishvamitra, who was the adopted son of Vishvamitra.

EASTERN GANGETIC PLAINS

Farther east were the Kashis, who can be identified with the later Kashis in the Varanasi region. Kashya was a king of Kashi. In the Shatapatha Brahmana, Dhritarashtra, another king of Kashi, was defeated by Shatanika Satrajita, a Bharata. Then the Kashis gave up kindling the sacred fire up to the time of that Brahmana. Ajatashatru and probably Bhadrasena Ajatashatrava were also kings of Kashi. The Koshalas, mentioned in the Brahmanas, can be located north of the Kashis. The Kashis and Videhas, who must have been in north Bihar, were connected.

The Magadhas, Angas, and Vangas were other groups in the eastern Gangetic plains. The Magadhas are not mentioned in the Rig but may have been the Kikatas of that text.

In the Yajur Veda, a man of Magadha is included in the list of victims of the *purushamedha* (human sacrifice). In the Atharva Veda, fever is wished away to the Magadhas and Angas, among other places. In the same text, Magadha is associated with the Vratya in a mystical way. Magadha is said to be his *mitra* (friend), his *mantra*, his laughter, and his thunder in the four quarters. (See Chapter 1, for more on the Vratyas.) In the Gopatha Brahmana, the term Anga–Magadha is used, indicating that they lived adjacent to each other. The Angas were later known to live in the region of the Son and Ganga, and were probably in this area earlier too.

Pundra is another region referred to in the Aitareya Brahmana, where the people are said to be oucasts. In the epics, Pundra was somewhere within Bengal and Bihar.

SOUTH OF THE YAMUNA

To the south of the Yamuna were the Kuntis, Satvants, and Kapeyas. The Satvants were defeated by the Bharatas, who frequently attacked them. The Kapeyas were the priests of Chitraratha, who was probably the king of Chedi. In the Rig Veda, Chitraratha is mentioned. The Kuntis were probably in the region of the Chambal river.

SOUTH OF THE VINDHYAS

Farther south were the Andhras and Pulindas. Vidarbha was a region in this area, probably the same as the Vidarbha region today.

OTHER PLACES AND PEOPLE

The Kiratas are mentioned as living in mountain caves. The Atharva Veda mentions a Kirata girl (*kairatika*) who digs up a herbal remedy on a mountain. The Kiratas were later a group in east Nepal but the term perhaps applied to a number of hill groups.

In the later Samhitas and Brahmanas, Nishada seems to be a general term for non-Aryan clans. The Karaskara, Muchipa/Mutiba/Muvipa, and Shabaras were among other people mentioned. Among places, Munimarana ('saint's death') was said to be the place where the Vaikhanasas were slain. Shaphala was the name of Rituparna's kingdom in the Baudhayana Shrauta Sutra.

THE KING AND HIS TERRITORY

Special sacrifices to increase the king's power are described in the Yajur Veda, Brahmanas, and Shrauta Sutras. These include the ashvamedha, rajasuya, and vajapeya. The Atharva Veda has many hymns, which consist of blessings for kings. Some accounts in the Brahmanas bring out the importance of kings. The Aitareya Brahmana says that once the devas and asuras fought against each other, and the devas were defeated because they had no king. Hence they elected a king, who led them to victory. Kings, at times, identified themselves with gods. Through the rajasuya, the king was identified with the god Prajapati. As tribes amalgamated and were grouped together, more powerful kings emerged, ruling over larger areas. Some powerful kings were known as samrat. Kingship was usually hereditary, though election or selection took place at times. There are references to ten successive hereditary kings. However, Dushtaritu Paumsayana, tenth king of the Srinjayas in the line of descent, was expelled from his kingdom. The Tandya Brahmana refers (6.6.5) to a sacrifice, which would help the people to destroy a king. The king was considered the protector of the people. In this context he could confer rewards and punishments. References indicate that some amount of agricultural produce had to be given to the king—the beginnings of a system of taxation.

Wars still existed but some sort of states seem to have started to form, with tribes joining together and settling in distinct areas. Buddhist texts dated to 600–200 BCE refer to great states or *mahajanapadas*. In this Later Vedic period, smaller states or *janapadas* were formed. States were known as *rajya*, those ruled by kings, or as *ganas* or *sanghas*, ruled by a group.

SABHA AND SAMITI

The two assemblies, the *sabha* and the *samiti*, continued to exist and, in this period, seemed to have more power, though there are not many details of how they functioned. They assisted the king in administration and justice. Women evidently did not attend the sabha. A *sabhapati*, 'lord or leader of the sabha', is mentioned. As earlier, there must have been variations in the system of government across regions.

OFFICIALS

The purohita was the chief priest who advised the king on an array of matters. The senani or senapati probably commanded the king's army. The *suta* was a charioteer or herald, the *samgrahitri* was the royal treasurer, while the *akshavapa* supervised dice playing, indicating the importance of this pastime. The gramani was the head of the village and supervised village affairs. There may have been different gramanis, one of whom was a representative at the king's court. In the Shatapatha Brahmana, the gramani is considered inferior to the suta. The *bhaga-dugha* was another official but his role is not clear; one suggestion is that he collected taxes. *Gramya-vadin* in the Yajur Veda seems to mean the village judge. The *kshattri*, the king's assistant or chamberlain, gonikartana/govikatrana or huntsman, and the palagala or messenger were other officials. Most of these officials are mentioned in the context of the rajasuya sacrifice, and were known as *ratnins* (jewels), a term used later too for important officials. Eight people are listed as *viras*, supporters or defenders of the king. These are the queen, the king's son, the king's brother, the purohita, the suta, the gramani, the kshattri, and the samgrahitri. Various other officials helped the king in his tasks and duties.

CITIES AND VILLAGES

Both villages and cities (or towns) now existed. The Taittiriya Aranyaka mentions *nagara* in the sense of a town. The Jaiminiya Upanishad Brahmana mentions *mahagrama*, or a large village. The Brihadaranyaka Upanishad records the storing of grain in villages.

HOUSES

The house, known as harmya, is described in the Atharva Veda. It had several rooms or spaces, as well as an area for cattle and sheep. The method of construction is not clearly known but bamboo and thatch, or some other kind of wood, were probably used. Bricks or *ishtaka* were used in the construction of the fire altar, but are not mentioned in the context of a house. The *dhana-dhani* mentioned in the Taittiriya Aranyaka may have been a granary. The Atharva mentions *patninam sadana* or separate women's quarters. A bed, couch, and seat with a cushion or cover are mentioned.

FAMILY

The kula (family) remained patriarchal. There were joint families where several generations lived together.

CASTE

The caste (varna) system began to increase in significance. Sacrifices became complex and the brahmanas' role was essential. However, the caste system was not rigid, and passages in both the Brahmanas and Upanishads indicate that each caste had importance.

The Brihadaranyaka Upanishad (1.4) suggests that each caste had a valuable role, and that each emerged out of Brahman, the Absolute. It states:

At first the kshatriya and other castes were Brahman, who was alone. Being alone, he did not prosper. He created a noble form, the kshatriya, consisting of those who are kshatriyas among the gods: Indra, Varuna, Soma, Rudra, Parjanya, Yama, Mrityu, Ishana. Therefore there is none superior to the kshatriya. Hence in the Rajasuya sacrifice, the brahmana adores the kshatriya from a lower seat.

However, the verse goes on to say that it is the brahmana who is the source of the kshatriya. Thus, though the king attains pre-eminence, he is ultimately under the brahmana. The next verse says that he (Brahman) still did not prosper, therefore he created the vaishyas, that is those gods who are in groups, the Vasus, Rudras, Adityas, Vishvedevas, and Maruts. As he still did not prosper, he created the shudra varna, Pushan. 'This earth indeed is Pushan for it nourishes all that exists.' He then created a noble form (*shreya rupam*), which is righteousness (*dharma*). He also equates dharma with *satya* (truth). Thus the four varnas were created through the divine varnas.

According to the Aitareya Brahmana (8.36.4), through the rajasuya sacrifice, different castes attained different qualities. The brahmana received *tejas* (ascetic fervour), the kshatriya, *virya* (bravery), the vaishya, *prajati* (power to have children), and the shudra, *pratishtha* (firmness or stability). Here, though the four castes are differentiated, each received something worthwhile.

Among the two higher castes, the brahmana and the kshatriya (or rajanya), the brahmana gradually gained importance though, at times, there was some ambivalence about their relative positions. In the Atharva Veda, brahmanas refer to themselves as devas or gods. The king's purohita was the most important brahmana in the kingdom. The office of the purohita was often hereditary. A number of brahmanas were village priests. Brahmanas received special privileges. Basically, the reverence for a brahmana was a reverence for the values they embodied—of learning, teaching, and simplicity. Not all brahmanas retained these values. Though brahmanas had religious authority, in the Upanishads, they were sometimes instructed by kings.

Kshatriyas consisted of the king's relatives, warriors, some nobles, and minor chieftains under his control. Vaishyas were artisans, traders, and agriculturalists. The practice of crafts was to some extent hereditary, thus creating castes.

In some passages, the shudras are considered inferior. The Aitareya Brahmana (35.3) says the shudra should obey the orders of others. The *chandalas* are mentioned in the Brahmanas and Upanishads but their status is unclear. Later Vedic texts also use the term *mleccha* for 'outsiders'. The first three castes were known as *dvija*, or 'twice born', as they were entitled to perform the upanayana, which was a kind of rebirth. The three upper castes could also install *agni* at the *agnyadheya*, 'first installation of the fire'. The vaishya is referred to as an arya in contrast to a shudra. The Shrauta Sutras indicate different methods of performing sacrifices according to the caste of the sacrificer (*yajamana*). In the Soma sacrifices, different results were sought for each caste. The Shatapatha Brahmana allots a place to the shudra in the Soma sacrifice. In the Upanishads, it is clear that a shudra could also study. But, according to the Kathaka Samhita, the shudra is not allowed to milk the cow for the *agnihotra* milk. In the purushamedha, different castes were offered to different deities.

OCCUPATION

Numerous occupations existed, including artisans and craftsmen of various kinds. Boats are mentioned and trade must have existed too. Farmer, animal rearer, teacher, officiator at sacrifices, warrior, service provider, hunter—a number of occupations are mentioned in the purushamedha list. Among them are also *anu-kshattri* (an attendant of some kind, probably doorkeeper or charioteer), *anuchara* (another type of attendant), drummer, maker of mats, metalsmith, ploughman, astrologer, butcher, herdsman, bowstring maker, carpenter, wood gatherer, dava-pa (fire-watcher), hand clapper, female embroiderer or basket-maker, jeweller, horse attendant (who yoked and unyoked horses), sura brewer, elephant keeper, and goldsmith. Other Later Vedic texts mention more occupations, including a ferryman or poleman, *malaga* (washerman), potter, moneylender, barber, boatman, cook, messenger, and an attendant who ran alongside a chariot. In addition, other art and craft specialists existed, such as the *rathakara* (chariot-maker).

Thus there was a wide array of diverse crafts, which could indicate an urban or late pre-urban economy, one on the verge of urbanization.

LAND

Individuals could own land, which was inherited by the sons after the father's death.

AGRICULTURE

More areas were cultivated and different types of crops were grown. According to the Brihadaranyaka Upanishad (6.3.22), there were ten kinds of cultivated (*gramyani*) grains: *vrihi-yava* (rice and barley); *tila-mashah* (sesamum and beans); *anu-priyangavah* (millets, *Panicum miliaceum* and *Setaria italica*); *godhuma* (wheat); *masurah* (lentils); and *khala-kulah* (khalvah and *Dolichos uniflorus*).

The Yajur and Atharva Vedas also mention wheat, rice, various types of beans and lentils, millets, and oilseeds as the crops grown. Different types of rice are described. While rice was known as *vrihi*, a term for rice and other seed grains was *tandula*; *karna* and *akarna* were husked and unhusked rice, respectively; and *nivara* was a type of wild rice. In the Taittiriya Samhita, black and white rice are contrasted; dark, swift-growing (*ashu*), and large rice (*maha-vrihi*) are mentioned; the swift-growing rice was probably later known as *shashtika*, which ripened within sixty days.

The Brahmanas too refer to *plashuka*, another fast-growing rice. Apart from anu and priyangu, *shyamaka* was a cultivated millet identified with *Panicum frumentaceum*; the Atharva Veda refers to the lightness of its seed that can be blown away in the wind and says it is the food of pigeons; in the Chhandogya Upanishad, shyamaka and its seed (tandula) are said to be very small; it has also been interpreted as canary seed.

Lentils too were of different kinds. Khalva is explained by the commentator Mahidhara as *chanaka* or chickpea while Shankara sees it as *nishpava*. Masura would be the *masur* of today, *Ervum hirsutum*. Mashah and *garmut* were types of beans.

Oilseeds included *til* (sesame), from which taila (oil) was made.

Other grains were *amba*, later called *namba*; *upavaka* was later known as *Indra-yava*. It was used to make gruel (*karambha*) and was also ground; *upavaka* groats (*saktavah*) are mentioned. Indra-yava has been identified as the seed of the medicinal plant *Wrightia antidysenterica*, still used in Ayurveda. Other identifications are with *Holarrhena antidysenterica*, or *Wrightia tinctoria*.

Gavidhuka, or *gavedhuka*, was a type of grass, identified with *Coix barbata*, which was boiled with rice or barley and made into a gruel.

Masusya, mentioned in the Taittiriya Brahmana, is a grain of the north country, according to the commentator.

Kulmasha is referred to in the Chhandogya Upanishad. The Nirukta explains it as sour gruel but the commentator feels it is bad or sour beans (masha).

Grain husk was used as fuel. Cucumbers (*urvaru*, *urvaruka*) and probably other vegetables were grown; fruit mentioned includes the jujube (*karkandhu*, *kuvala*, *badara*) but it is not clear if fruit was cultivated or collected from wild trees.

In the Atharva Veda and Kathaka Samhita, ploughs are mentioned, as drawn by six, eight, or twelve oxen, and even twenty-four, which would require a heavy ploughshare, possibly fashioned from iron. Plough land was referred to as *urvara* or *kshetra*; manure, known as *shakan* or *karisha*, was used; and irrigation (*khanitra*) was practised. In the Atharva, Prithi Vainya is said to have begun the use of the plough. In the Panchavimsha Brahmanas, it is said that the Vratyas did not cultivate the soil. The Shatapatha Brahmana describes the cycle of agriculture, consisting of ploughing, sowing, reaping, and threshing (*krishantah*, *vapantah*, *lunantah*, and *mrinantah*). The grain was cut with a sickle, known as *datra* or *srini*, tied into bundles or *parsha*, threshed, and then separated from the chaff. According to the Taittiriya Samhita, there were two harvests every year, and the Kaushitaki Brahmana states that the winter crop ripened in the month of Chaitra. Farmers faced quite a few difficulties; the seeds were destroyed by moles; birds as well as various reptiles (*upavasaka*, *jabhya*, *tarda*, *patanga*) destroyed the young shoots; and too much rain or drought could affect crops. The Atharva Veda refers to all this in its prayers and charms.

DOMESTIC ANIMALS

Animals that were domesticated included cows, sheep, goats, horses, and dogs. (For more details, see Chapter 6.)

FOOD AND DRINK

Apart from basic foods such as milk, butter, grain, fruit, and vegetables, various types of cooked food are mentioned. *Apupa* is a sort of cake made of rice or barley mixed with ghi. *Odana* was grain cooked with milk. Rice cooked with milk and beans is referred to in the Vajasaneyi Samhita and the Shatapatha Brahmana. Rice could also be fried. A gruel made of lightly roasted grain, barley, or unhusked sesame was known as *karambha*. *Yavagu* referred to barley gruel specifically. Meat was normally eaten on ceremonial occasions or in honour of a guest. As earlier, the sheep, goat, and ox were the animals usually eaten. Various milk products included sour milk (*dadhi*) and butter (*nava-nita*). *Amiksha* was clotted curds while *payasya* was curds mixed with sour milk; a blend of butter, fresh milk, and sour milk was known as *prisjad-ajya* ; *phanta* was creamy butter or the first lumps of butter produced by churning; and *vajina* was sour milk mixed with fresh, hot milk.

Sura, probably prepared from fermented grains, was kept in skins. People of the sabha drank it but, according to the Atharva, it sometimes led men on the wrong path and resulted in quarrels. The sautramani sacrifice was in expiation of drinking too much sura. The Yajur texts also refer to a drink called *masara*, made of rice, shyamaka, parched barley, and other items. Madhu indicates both honey and anything sweet. Soma was important but various substitutes and equivalents were used for the plant. It is suggested that the original Soma was difficult to obtain.

Pinda, the ball of flour offered to ancestors, is mentioned in the Nirukta and Sutras.

TRADE AND COMMERCE

Shreshthins (rich merchants) are referred to. *Vanija* was the term for a merchant. Moneylending was a good business. The term *kusida* indicated a loan while *kusidin* was a moneylender. Regular coinage is not referred to. The *krishnala*, a berry of the *gunja* (*Abrus precatorius*), was a unit of weight. The *mana* is mentioned as an equivalent of it. The *shatamana* was equal to 100 manas. The cow was a unit of barter. The *nishka* was also used. Bargaining in the market was known. Clothes, coverings, and goatskins were among the items bought and sold. Trade, including that via the sea, must have existed. Boats are mentioned.

Texts of this time clearly refer to iron as 'the black metal'—*krishna ayas*, *shyama ayas*, or *shyama*.

WOMEN

Women still seem to have married after puberty. Polygamy existed; two, four, or more wives are mentioned. The rishi Yajnavalkya had two wives whereas a king was said to have four wives, of whom *mahishi* was the chief queen while *vavata* was the favourite. Passages in the Atharva suggest that a widow could remarry and that polyandry too existed. The Vajasaneyi Samhita refers to illicit relationships and to the son of an unmarried girl (*kumariputra*). The father had some control over the daughter and there are instances where he gave her as an offering to a brahmana. Dowries were sometimes given. The marriage ceremony was probably much the same as in the Rig Vedic period, as the marriage hymn is repeated in the Atharva without much change. There is a reference in the Atharva (18.3.1) to the ancient practice of sati. Initially, the sacrificer (*yajamana*) was accompanied by his wife but she could not initiate a sacrifice on her own. Slightly later, the priest often replaced the wife in the sacrificial ritual, perhaps indicating a decline in her status. Most of the later types of marriage existed in this period, as they are referred to in the Grihya Sutras.

There are mixed references to women. The Shatapatha says that a wife is half her husband—without her, he is incomplete—but another passage suggests her inferior position when it states that she should eat after her husband. The Aitareya Brahmana says that a good woman does not talk back. In another passage, it says that a daughter is a source of misery and a son is a saviour for the family. Widow remarriage is permitted in some texts and prohibited in others. The Brihadaranyaka Upanishad (6.4) says that Prajapati created women and provides some instructions for the union of man and woman. At the time of procreation, there should be sublimation through meditation. Men who unite with their wives without this meditation destroy all their merit.

A man should try to win a woman over by giving her desired objects but if she refuses, he can curse her and hit her. If she does yield to him, he recites a mantra and then both become reputed parents. Instructions follow for what to do if the man's wife has a lover. Mantras are chanted and certain rituals undertaken so that the man whom the brahmana curses 'departs from the world, impotent and devoid of merit'. Men should therefore be very careful in their dealings with the wife of a Vedic scholar who knows these rites; they should not even joke with her. When the wife has her periodical impurity, she should drink from a bell metal vessel for three days; and no shudra man or woman should touch her. After this, she should bathe and wear fresh clothes, and the husband should ask her to thresh rice. (This is obviously related to fertility.) Next, there are instructions on what to eat to produce ideal sons, and even an ideal daughter. The Brihadaranyaka Upanishad (6.4.17) reads: 'He who wishes, "May a daughter be born to me who will be a scholar (*pandita*) and attain longevity" should have rice and sesamum cooked together, and with his wife eat it mixed with ghi. Then they would be able to produce such a daughter.'

The same Upanishad also says (1.4, 3) that the creator, Prajapati or viraj, was alone and not happy. Therefore he divided his body into two, and the husband and wife (*pati–patni*) came into being.

EDUCATION

A number of texts, including the Later Vedic Samhitas, the Brahmanas, Aranyakas, and early Upanishads, were composed at this time, and the entire sacrificial ritual was developed. Was all education oral or was there some writing too? Could all these texts have been transmitted orally? If so, were there specific methods and aids to memorize them? *Svadhyaya* or daily Vedic self-study is mentioned in the Yajur Veda. Kshatriya kings, such as Janaka and Ajatashatru, had studied the Vedas and even conveyed their philosophical understanding to others. Probably kshatriyas, and even vaishyas, underwent the upanayana, though both these must have had other practical or theoretical studies related to their profession. The upanayana as a *samskara* is described in the Shatapatha Brahmana, and instructions for a student are provided in other Brahmanas. The Tandya Brahmana indicates that studies included arithmetic, prosody, and grammar. Language was an important aspect of study. Those from the north are said to be experts in language. The system of a guru teaching students in his *ashrama* or residence is known. The Atharva refers to a brahmachari, a student, who gathered fuel for the sacred fire and begged for alms for his guru. Vedic schools or *charanas* already existed. Women of certain classes also studied but some were were taught singing and dancing.

DRESS

Weaving was known. Thread was woven from wool; *urva-sutra* or woollen thread is frequently mentioned. It is thought that this referred to sheep wool and perhaps goat hair. Embroidered garments were popular. Clothes included three garments: *nivi* or undergarment, *vasas* or main/ lower garment, and *adhi-vasas*, a mantle or upper garment. Sacrificial clothes are described in the Shatapatha. A *tarpya* or silk garment was worn close to the skin. A garment of undyed wool, an over-garment and a turban or *ushnisha* were also worn. The Shatapatha refers to a shoe or sandal made of boar skin. Skins were worn as clothing. Woven garments could be dyed or left in their natural colours. Fringes or borders were sometimes attached to garments. Among ornaments, *sthagara* was a sweet-smelling item worn. The *shankha* or conch shell was worn as an amulet. *Shalali* or a porcupine quill was used to anoint the eyes and part the hair. *Pravarta* may have been an earring. *Prakasha* was perhaps a metal mirror. A nishka (neck ornament) of silver is mentioned as an ornament worn by the vratyas.

ENTERTAINMENT

Music, singing, and dancing existed. *Aghati*, or cymbals, drums, flutes, and lutes are mentioned. *Shailusha*, a purushamedha victim, was possibly an actor or dancer. Chariot and horse racing, and dice playing were common. A *vamsha-nartin*, probably some kind of acrobat, is mentioned in the Yajur.

CHAPTER 8

THE ARCHAEOLOGICAL SETTING

As we have seen earlier, the Rig Veda, the earliest of the Vedic texts, is of uncertain date but was certainly composed by 1000 BCE. The area of its composition was north-west India, extending into present-day Pakistan, and possibly south and east Afghanistan. An increasing number of scholars today believe that an early date for the Rig Veda is a valid possibility. Some of the main theories regarding the Rig Vedic people are, as seen earlier, that the Vedic people formed part of the joint Indo-Iranians and moved to India after the decline of the Harappan civilization, around 1700–1500 BCE. This is still the most accepted theory, though it needs to be re-examined in the context of some serious challenges. Another theory is that they were indigenous people who predated the Harappan civilization. A third theory is that India was the home not only of the Indo-Iranians but also of the Proto-Indo-Europeans, who migrated from here to other parts of the world.

We have already looked at some theories of the Indo-Iranian homeland. Here we will look at the archaeology of early India, which could throw light both on the origin of the Rig Vedic people and their possible date. Arguments related to archaeology are used to prove or disprove theories of the date based on other sources.

India–Pakistan, which lies in South Asia, has the Himalayan ranges to the north. In the north-west, the land merges into Iran and Afghanistan. In Pakistan, the area of Balochistan has some of the earliest settlements. Pakistan Balochistan adjoins the Iranian province of Sistan and Baluchestan. The Afghan–Baloch area has a similar environment to the Iranian plateau, and the highlands near the Mediterranean. It has cold winters, and parts of it get snow. The Indus river system flows through Pakistan and north-west India. East of this are the vast alluvial Gangetic plains, through which the Ganga, its main tributary the Yamuna, and other tributaries flow.

In southern India, the peninsula is surrounded by water, with the Arabian Sea to the west, the Bay of Bengal to the east, and the Indian Ocean to the south. Archaeological sites in India–

Pakistan date to the Palaeolithic period, succeeded by the Mesolithic and the Neolithic. In the north-west, Neolithic cultures develop into the urban Harappan civilization (2500–1900 BCE). The urban centres then decline and new cultures emerge. This region corresponds, more or less, with that known from the Rig Veda.

AFGHANISTAN

As seen already, early Afghanistan had connections with Iran and Central Asia. In south-east Afghanistan, a route from Mundigak led to Balochistan. Mundigak is located in the Kushk-i-Nakhud valley, and was first settled from 4000–3500 BCE. Pottery dates back to this time, along with items of bone, stone, lapis lazuli, terracotta, and copper. There were houses and wells. Plant remains, including those of wheat and *ber*, along with bones of domesticated cattle, sheep, and goats were found in the succeeding occupation level. In the other direction, a route connected Mundigak to Shahr-i-Sukhteh in the Helmand valley of Iran, and through here to other parts of Iran and to Turkmenistan.

BALOCHISTAN–MEHRGARH

Balochistan in Pakistan has one of the earliest sites with settled agriculture, Mehrgarh, dating back to around 7000 BCE. The Kachi plain where Mehrgarh is located is on the eastern edge of the Iranian plateau. It is thought the Indus flowed here in the Pleistocene period. Even in the earliest period of occupation, circa 7000–5000 BCE, there were houses of mud bricks, tools of stone and bone, and evidence of the use of shell, lapis lazuli, and turquoise. Wheat and barley were grown; sheep, goats, and cattle were domesticated. Animal bones indicate that these were domesticated in this region, as they show a gradual reduction in the size of the animals, which happens with domestication from the wild. Graves have also been found, from the earliest period onwards. Human graves show the earliest evidence of drilling teeth. At least twenty more sites belong to this time frame, located in the North-West Frontier, Balochistan, Kachi, and Sindh. These were small sites, covering 2–3 hectares.

Mehrgarh in the next phase of occupation, termed the Burj Basket-Marked phase (dated 5000–4300 BCE) has handmade pottery, which is of a style and type also found across the Iranian plateau, at sites such as Tepe Yahya, and up to the Zagros mountains. There was continuity with the preceding period, and an increase in the number of sites in the Balochistan–Sindh region. Cotton was probably introduced at this time. Bodies in some graves were covered in red ochre. The next phase at Mehrgarh (4300–3800 BCE) sees the introduction of a different type of pottery termed Togau Ware. At least eighty-four sites with this ware were found in the region. Based on an analysis of skeletons found at Mehrgarh, those of this period, according to the American anthropologists B.E. Hemphill, J.R. Lukacs, and K.A.R. Kennedy, were similar to the type on the Iranian plateau, and to those of the Mature Harappan cemetery R37. Skeletons of the earlier period were different, suggesting similarities to the east of the subcontinent. At the same time, Mehrgarh showed continuity in the types of structures. Pottery was standardized, and copper and gold were used. Seals too were made, and there were domestic animals, wheat, and barley. From around 3800 BCE, settlements spread to other areas. At Mehrgarh, Balochistan, the north-west, and the Indus plains, there was a type of pottery termed Kechi Beg. At Mehrgarh, there was some continuity. Barley was the main crop and wheat was grown as well as grapes. Mehrgarh has connections with sites near Quetta and Kandahar including Mundigak, and with Shahr-i-Sukhteh. But these connections do not continue into the Mature Harappan period.

HAKRA WARES

Farther east, there were new settlements with a different type of pottery, named Hakra wares. Hakra wares include several types of pottery, some of which may have developed from styles at Mehrgarh and other western sites. Among them is a red pottery with a black slip. Hakra settlements were in Cholistan, in the region through which the dry bed of the Ghaggar–Hakra, the ancient river Sarasvati has been traced. The Hakra flows south-west and then south, ending in an inland delta. Most of the sites are in this delta. Hakra wares are also found on the Punjab plains, for instance at Jalilpur near the river Ravi, and extend into Haryana. Hakra sites have microlithic tools, stone mace heads, and finds of copper, carnelian, shell and other beads, bangles, and animal figurines. Some of them seem to be seasonal or temporary settlements.

Between 3200 and 2600 BCE, settlements had spread all over the north-western plains, extending into Haryana, Rajasthan, and Gujarat. These are termed Early Harappan as they culminate in the great urban Harappan civilization. Possehl identified four approximately contemporary, interrelated, archaeological assemblages that constitute the Early Harappan. These are the Amri-Nal, Kot Diji, Damb Sadat, and Sothi-Siswal, mainly differentiated by pottery types. Amri-Nal is in Sindh, north Balochistan, and north Gujarat. Amri types predominate in Sindh, and Nal types in Balochistan. Nal, in the Khozdar area linking north and south Balochistan, probably dates back to 3500 BCE, and so do Kulli and related sites in the Kalwa tract. Sites in north Gujarat have ceramics suggesting a combination of Amri-Nal and Kot Diji. These include Dholavira, Surkotada, Moti Pipli, the Santhli sites, and Nagwada. Other sites in Gujarat such as Padri, Somnath, and Loteshwar have ceramics that are different from Early Harappan and could be earlier.

Over one hundred Kot Diji sites are known, in northern Sindh and adjacent regions, which succeeded the Hakra ware settlements. The Damb Sadat type, with more than thirty-five known sites, represents a culture mainly in the Quetta valley of central Balochistan. The Quetta valley is linked to the Indus valley via the Bolan and Khojal passes. The largest site is Quetta Miri (23 hectares), located at a site occupied from prehistoric to modern times. Mundigak in Afghanistan,

200 km north-west of Miri, is another large site, with Damb Sadat pottery. Miri Qalat was probably occupied from 4500 BCE and, before 3000 BCE, had close contacts with south-east Iran and Afghanistan. Miri Qalat also had a Mature Harappan site. There was influence from the Indus region and Central Asia too.

The Sothi-Siswal culture is located in the valleys of the Ghaggar–Chautang, the ancient Sarasvati, Drishadvati and tributaries, with the addition of one site, Nawabans in the Ganga–Yamuna doab. There are at least one hundred and sixty-five Sothi-Siswal sites, two of them larger than 20 hectares. The Kot Diji and Sothi-Siswal regions seem to be the most important.

The site of Harappa also has an early phase dating to 3500 BCE. There is not much evidence in the Early Harappan phase for significant social differentiation, craft specialization, or, according to Possehl, 'the political and ideological institutions that produce public architecture'.

On the whole, Early Harappan sites were agricultural with domesticated animals, and some specialized crafts. Within a short period, the urban Harappan civilization, named after the type site of Harappa, emerged.

HARAPPAN CIVILIZATION

The Harappan Civilization, known as the Mature Harappan in contrast with the Early Harappan, extends from 2500 BCE to 1900 BCE, and evolves from the settlements and cultures of the preceding period. There were, at the same time, many new settlements, while some of the earlier ones were abandoned or temporarily deserted. Kot Diji, Gumla, Amri, and Nausharo have evidence of burning between Early and Mature Harappan phases. Kalibangan has signs of an earthquake at this stage.

The civilization extended over 1.3 million sq. km, an area larger than ancient Egypt and Mesopotamia. It was dominated by large cities with baked-brick structures and an intensive drainage network, extending from Afghanistan in the north-west through Balochistan, Punjab, and Sindh, and farther east through Haryana up to the Yamuna. It also extended into Rajasthan and Gujarat. Over one thousand sites have been found of this culture.

Harappa and Mohenjodaro (both in Pakistan today) were the earliest and largest cities discovered, with an estimated size of 100 hectares. Other large cities and their probable size were as follows: Rakhigarhi in Haryana, 80 hectares; Ganweriwala in West Punjab (Pakistan), Dholavira in Gujarat, 60 hectares each; Nagoor, Tharo Waro Daro, Lakhueenjo daro, all in Sindh, 50 hectares each; and Nandowari in Balochistan, 50 hectares. There are also some large sites in Bathinda district of Punjab (India), Lakhmirwala, Gurnikalan 1 and Hasanpur 2. Some of these cities had a population of 30,000–40,000 and were possibly the largest of those times. Other cities included Chanhudaro, Lothal, Kalibangan, Banawali, Sutkagendor, and Surkotada. Kot Diji, Amri and others may have been smaller cities. Some of these, such as Kalibangan, Amri, and Kot Diji, were occupied even in the Early Harappan period and prior to this.

GENERAL FEATURES

Harappan cities and towns had some common features. Several had a separate area where large buildings were built on raised brick platforms, with the whole area sometimes surrounded by a massive brick wall. At Mohenjodaro, these large buildings included the Great Bath, which was a swimming-pool-like complex; another structure that may have been a granary or storage room; and a pillared structure like an assembly hall. There was a large granary or storage building at Harappa as well.

The main town area was well planned. Several cities had houses made of baked brick or used some amount of baked brick in their structures. Some houses were two-storeyed, with several rooms, a courtyard, bathrooms, and wells to draw water from. Houses had their own drains connected to street drains that ran underground. Drains were made of brick and mortar. Street drains had manholes, so that they could be cleaned. It was the best drainage system of the ancient world.

Between the cities, crops were grown, with some variation by region. Crops included wheat, barley, millets, mustard, sesame, peas, and cotton. Millets included African millets, which must have been brought here at an early date. Rice was grown in western India, and rice grains were found at Harappa. Watermelon, dates, and grapes were also grown. Garlic was found at Balu in Haryana. The plough, probably made of wood, was used. At Kalibangan, there is evidence of a ploughed field of Early Harappan times.

Animals can be identified by bone remains or designs on seals or pottery. Domestic animals included cows, buffaloes, goats, sheep, pigs, dogs, donkeys, camels, and possibly the cat. The elephant was probably tamed. There is some controversy about whether the horse was known and domesticated. While excavators have identified horse bones at some sites, others feel the identifications are incorrect and the bones belong to the wild ass or onager. Horses are crucial to the Rig Veda, hence those who believe the Rig Veda belongs to the Harappan or pre-Harappan period accept the identifications of horse bones while those who would like to date the Rig Veda to a later period contradict these findings. Upinder Singh, a noted historian who specializes in ancient India, summarizes:

Horse remains have been reported at Harappa, Lothal, Surkotada, Kuntasi, and Kalibangan, and at superficial levels at Mohenjodaro. Sandor Bokonyi (1997) examined the equid bone samples from Surkotada and concluded that at least six of them probably belonged to the true horse. His conclusions were challenged by Meadow and Patel (1997). Brigadier Ross (1946) reported horse teeth at pre-Harappan levels at Rana Ghundai, but this identification was questioned by Zeuner (1963). While horse bones may not be completely absent at Harappan sites, they are not prolific either.

It should be added that Brigadier E.J. Ross of the British–Indian army was a veterenarian, hence his identifications are unlikely to be wrong. Horse bones have also been found at Shikarpur, a Harappan site in Gujarat, and at Mesolithic sites in other parts of the country (see below).

Wild animals known included several types of deer, such as black buck, nilgai, and gazelles; among other animals were elephants, tigers, leopards, monkeys, wild buffalos, rhinoceros, wild pigs and boars, wild sheep and goats, jackals, rabbits, and hare. Among birds, there were peacocks, wild fowl, ducks, and pigeons. There were also tortoises, crocodiles, snakes, and fish, both those with and without shells.

ARTEFACTS

Stone was used in buildings, and to make knives and sickles. Copper was crafted into numerous objects and also alloyed to make bronze. Copper and bronze items included cooking pots, vessels, tools, and weapons, including axes, saws, knives, arrowheads, and spears. There were copper mirrors, rings, and bangles. Jewellery was also made of gold, silver, semiprecious stones, and shell, and included necklaces, bangles, beads, and amulets. Carnelian, turquoise, and lapis lazuli were among the semiprecious stones used. Long carnelian beads were especially prized, even in Mesopotamia. There was wheel-made pottery, shiny red with black painting, as well as plain and other pottery. Baked bricks were made in standard sizes. Stone and terracotta images were made, as well as terracotta toys. Most notable is the sculpture of a bearded man, wearing a shawl. Wool and cotton were woven, and some woven material was also patterned.

The intricately carved stone seal was a hallmark of the civilization. Seals were small tablets, usually made of steatite stone, which left an impression when pressed into a soft substance like clay. Various images were carved into them, and they had short inscriptions in an undeciphered script. Boats and carts with wheels were constructed for long-distance trade by land and sea. Weights and measures were used. Weights were usually in multiples of sixteen.

ECONOMY

The economy was not entirely urban or city based. There were village settlements and pastoralists.

TRADE

Earlier land trade crossed through Mehrgarh in Balochistan and Mundigak in Afghanistan. During the Mature Harappan period, Shortughai in Afghanistan was a trade outpost on a route to the north-west. Harappan items have been found in Iran, Afghanistan, Turkmenistan, and

Mesopotamia. In Mesopotamian records, India is probably called Meluhha. From Meluhha came boats loaded with timber, copper, gold, carnelian, and ivory objects. Imports included turquoise and lapis lazuli.

RELIGION

As its script has not been satisfactorily deciphered, most of the evidence for its religion comes from its numerous stone or steatite seals. In addition, there are flat copper tablets as well as figures depicted in bronze and stone, and a number of terracotta figurines of humans and animals. There are also certain unique architectural structures. On the basis of these, scholars have formed tentative and varying conclusions about the nature of the religion of the civilization. Some of the key features are given below:

- *Horned deity*: Some seals and copper tablets of the Indus Valley Civilization depict a horned person, usually identified as a deity. The most well-known of these depictions is a seal with a figure with a horned headdress, seated in a yogic posture. On this seal, he appears to be ithyphallic, and possibly three-faced. It is not clear if the faces are human or animal. Under his seat are two goats or deer and around him are a rhinoceros, a buffalo, a tiger, and an elephant. The British archaeologist John Marshall, who first excavated Mohenjodaro, labelled it a deity, a proto or early form of Shiva. His identification with Shiva-Pashupati, the lord of animals, has been questioned as Pashupati was the guardian of domestic animals and not associated with wild animals. Others identified him with the Vedic Agni or Rudra. The Indian scholar Shubhangana Atre, using in addition other seals with a similar deity, is among those who saw this as a form of the goddess Diana. Jains identify this deity with an early Jain Tirthankara. Asko Parpola sees similarities to the sitting bull figures of the Elamite culture. The deity shows remarkable similarity to the early Celtic god Cernunnos, particularly to a possible image of him found on a cauldron at Gundestrup in Denmark, dated between the 6th and 2nd centuries BCE. (In new-age revivalism, Cernunnos is worshipped as the god of Wicca or witches, along with Diana as the goddess.) A. Hiltebeitel related the horns with the asura Mahisha, the buffalo demon. Later, there were other horned deities in India, including tribal deities, the Jain deity Naigamesha, and several others. There are horned and forest deities in other parts of the ancient world as well.
- *Mother goddess*: A small female figure in bronze has commonly been called the 'dancing girl' though some see her as a goddess. Female figurines in terracotta, found at several sites, are thought to represent worship of a mother goddess, though this too has been questioned. More questionable is the identification of 'ring stones' of various sizes, with the *yoni*, or feminine emblem.
- *Male images*: Sculptures of men have been found at Mohenjodaro and lately at Dholavira in Gujarat. The stone bust of an imposing bearded man is well known though it is not clear if this

was a deity or an important person. He has been thought by some to represent a priest-king. There are also phallic-like objects, sometimes identified as early lingas.

- *Animals*: There are numerous animal terracotta figurines. Animals are also depicted on seals. The terracotta figures include domestic animals and have generally been thought to be toys. On seals, the humped bull is the only domestic animal depicted, the rest being wild animals, including elephants, tigers, rhinoceros, buffalo, deer, antelope, a one-horned animal like a unicorn, crocodiles, and fish. On some seals, a bull or a 'unicorn' is shown in front of an altar or incense brazier. There are also birds and hybrid half-human, half-animal figures, which may have been deities.
- *Trees*: Trees, particularly pipal trees and and its leaves, are depicted. Some seals have figures in trees, including a horned figure, who may be tree deities. Tree worship could have taken place.
- *Other*: There is evidence of worship of fire and sacrifice of animals, from a series of 'fire altars' at Kalibangan. The Great Bath at Mohenjodaro may have been a sacred tank where people took a dip or wash before praying, just as today some people dip themselves in rivers or use water in other rituals. One structure in the citadel area of Mohenjodaro looks like a temple but this is not certain. Considering the large area covered, there were probably variations in religion in different areas.

Without the help of a written script, analyses of the religion of this civilization are many and varied. Some see in it Proto-Hinduism; others identify the culture with that of the Rig Veda or with an indigenous 'Dravidian' culture later displaced by the Vedic. Still others see indications of Shamanism, animism, or folk religions. No definite conclusions can be reached at present.

PEOPLE

The people portrayed in terracottas and various other material have been analysed. On this basis, The Dutch archaeologist Elisabeth (Inez) During Caspers concluded that there was a cosmopolitan population in Harappa and Mohenjodaro. Others feel that people are often not realistically depicted in ancient sculptures, and such deductions may not be valid. No one actually knows who ruled the area or who the inhabitants were but it is quite likely that the population included different types of people.

WRITING

The script, as we know, is undeciphered. There are actually over a hundred decipherments but none that is universally accepted. There are 4000–5000 inscriptions on various materials, mainly clay. The average length of 2905 inscriptions in the Indian epigraphist Iravatham Mahadevan's concordance is 4.6 signs. Hence the American historian Steve Farmer feels it is not a script as the inscriptions are too short. He is supported by the American linguist Richard Sproat and by

Michael Witzel. In fact, Farmer and Witzel refer to interpretations of the script as 'fantasies'. Jane McIntosh, a British specialist in Indian archaeology, is among those who rejected Farmer's theories. Short inscriptions of this sort are known from other early civilizations too, including the Minoan. In the Near East, according to Staal, they link families, clans, places, offices, professions, or festivals, to deities or various celestial and mythological figures. The seals seem to have mythological figures, hence it could be the same here.

The noted Indian historian Romila Thapar feels, 'They (the seals) could have been tokens identifying civic authorities, supervisory managers of long distance trade, merchants or those bringing raw materials to the cities, or clan affiliations.' The language of the inscriptions has been claimed to be Indo-Aryan by some, and Dravidian or Proto-Munda by others. Witzel relates the language with Munda or the larger group of Austro-Asiatic languages and refers to it as Para-Munda; he also proposed a southern dialect in the southern Indus or greater Sindh region termed Meluhhan. But current research suggests that Proto-Munda came from the north-east at a relatively later date (for more on Munda languages, see below). The script has a close connect with the Proto-Elamite script, which is also undeciphered. The linguist David McAlpin has proposed a link between Elamite and Dravidian, suggesting a Proto-Elamo-Dravidian language family (see below). Others suggest connections of the Harappan language with Altaic languages. As seen earlier, Akkadian too has been suggested.

It should be noted that a single script could be used for many languages. Even in the Harappan civilization, different languages may have been used. Further details of some of the settlements are given below:

In Afghanistan is the site of Shortughai, not far from the river Kokcha, a tributary of the Amu Darya or Oxus. It has typical brick structures, gold and carnelian beads, and a terracotta figure of a camel. Sources of lapis lazuli have been located nearby and were transported from here to other Harappan centres.

Harappa in the central Indus plains is near an earlier course of the Ravi but now 12 km away from this river. Under the citadel is evidence of a Kot Dijian culture level. Several periods of occupation have been identified. Period I has the 'Ravi' culture; Period 2, Kot Diji culture with mud-brick structures; above this, there are three levels of Mature Harappan, followed by a transitional level, and succeeded by what is known as the Cemetery H culture. Cemetery R, belonging to the Mature Harappan phase, lies further south; so far, thirty-seven graves have been excavated here. The bodies were mostly laid on the side with artefacts in pots, presumably to be used in the afterlife. There were some stone and bronze ornaments, and bronze mirrors. Some graves had wooden coffins and reed shrouds, similar to those found in Mesopotamia.

Sindh has the huge site of Mohenjodaro. It could be reached by a route through the Bolan Pass. Its lowest levels are underwater. Over three hundred houses or structures and seventy wells have been excavated. The most notable sculptures have been found here—the bronze 'dancing girl', the stone 'priest king', animal representations on pedestals, and others. In Sindh, fifty-two Early

Harappan (twenty-nine were abandoned by the Mature Harappan period) and sixty-five Mature Harappan sites (forty-three new ones) have been identified.

OTHER REGIONS

Some Mature Harappan sites are located in Sheikhupura district, opposite Lahore on the right bank of the Ravi river. Along the Hakra channel in Pakistan is the large site of Ganweriwala, with a separate citadel area. Early Harappan sites in Cholistan, which formed part of the Kot Diji cultural phase, amounted to thirty-seven, of which thirty-three were abandoned. In the Mature Harappan phase, there were 136 mostly new settlements in the region.

On the Ghaggar–Sarasvati in Haryana are Mitathal, Rakhi Garhi, and Banawali, and in Rajasthan, there was Kalibangan, which has a citadel and an Early Harappan fortification beneath. The residential area is made of mud bricks. The citadel has a dividing wall; one part has residences, the other what seem to be ritual structures including fire altars. The large site of Rakhigarhi has a number of terracotta animal figurines. Banawali has a citadel that is part of the city, and not separate. It is surrounded by a wall and a moat. Its lower levels are similar to the lowest levels of Kalibangan.

In Sindh, Chanhudaro has street drains and structures similar to Mohenjodaro. Nausharo to the west has a structure that could be a water storage tank and some drains.

Amiliano and Allahdino are small sites east of Karachi. Farther west is Balakot, which had structures mainly of mud bricks and contacts with the Kulli culture of south-east Balochistan. In southern Sindh are the small sites of Garho Bhiro and Kot Kori, along the Eastern Nara branch of the Indus. In northern Sindh are hills with sources of limestone and chert. A number of stone flaking sites have been found here, both of the Stone Age and of the Harappan period. The site of Kot Diji is nearby.

In Gujarat, Dholavira and Lothal are the main sites. Dholavira, in the Rann of Kutch, has surrounding walls of stone and brick. There are both Harappan and non-Harappan pottery and artefacts. A major find here is an inscription on a signboard. At Lothal, a 219-m-long and 37-m-wide brick basin, located near the estuary, could have been a dockyard for ships.

Lothal had a citadel-like area, and a structure similar to the granary, which has been termed a warehouse. Here, sixty-nine burnt clay sealings with string and cloth impressions were found. The seal impressions on these were not those of the steatite seals found at Lothal. It has been suggested that they were not local and that Lothal was a transit point for trade. One seal of the ancient Bahrain–Kuwait type has been found. There were also Early and post-Harappan levels. Lothal is spread across 10 hectares. There are other small sites in the region.

The Makran coast near the Iran border was vital to trade. A sea route from here reaches the Arabian peninsula. Sutkagen-dor is the main Harappan site here. It is not a port. In the upper regions of the Chenab–Satluj are the Harappan sites of Manda on the Chenab and Rupnagar and

Kotla Nihang Khan on the Satluj. There was both Harappan and local pottery, the latter termed Bara pottery.

In general, while discussing the Indus Civilization and the Rig Veda, the former is taken as a homogenous whole, which was not the case. There were several local cultures with just some Harappan elements. Some of these continued from the Early Harappan period. These are described below:

- In the Ghaggar–Chautang, or Sarasvati–Drishadvati system above Sirsa, the Sothi-Siswal of the Early Harappan period continued. There are some typical Harappan settlements such as Kalibangan, Mitathal, Banawali, and Rakhigarhi, but also contemporary late Siswal settlements with few Harappan elements.
- The site of Kunal, north of Hissar (Haryana), has local pottery and house styles as well as a treasure trove of gold-leaf and silver ornaments and beads of semiprecious stones in an earthen pot. This may have been through Harappan contacts.
- Farther north of the Sothi-Siswal on the Ghaggar–Chautang is the Bara culture, which extends to the Satluj region.
- The early Kot Diji culture of northern Sindh continued during Harappan times. Its sites extend to the north at this time. Sites of this culture had Harappan contacts but the main elements were different from the Harappan.
- The Kulli culture in southern Balochistan, represented by Kulli and related sites, was contemporary with the Harappan and had some Harappan influence, but was otherwise distinctive. Kulli material also occurs at some Harappan sites.
- Several sites in Gujarat too have some different and non-Harappan elements.

In Saurashtra, there are some sites such as Rojdi near Rajkot, which are contemporary with the Harappan and have similarities but do not have seals or writing; Possehl has named this regional culture Sorath Harappan. Lothal and Rangpur also have variants on the main Harappan tradition, and are called Sindh Harappan by Possehl. There are other non-Harappan sites on the Gujarat mainland with one or more local traditions.

DECLINE

The decline of the civilization began around 1900 BCE. At this time, some places were no longer occupied. In others, people still lived but the city culture and other typical elements of the Harappan culture had declined or ended. It is not clear why the urban civilization declined. The possible reason for the end is given as tectonic changes, causing earthquakes, floods, or the temporary blockage of rivers. (There is evidence that a natural dam once temporarily blocked the Indus at Sehwan.) Other reasons suggested include epidemics, fire, climate change accompanied by the drying up of rivers, ecological change caused by deforestation, economic decline accompanying a decline in trade, and invasions or warfare.

Another possibility is that the area was too large to be controlled indefinitely. It is not known what type of political control the civilization had but there would seem to be some centralization, along with local government. This is indicated by the broad uniformity accompanied by regional variations. Throughout history, many empires decline for a wide variety of reasons. In India, a few examples are the Mauryas, Guptas, and even the much later Mughals. There is no single factor that causes an inevitable decline.

POST-HARAPPAN

There are several post-Harappan or, rather, post-urban cultures, dating from 1900 BCE, which we will look at later.

Today, the climate in the whole region is somewhat dry. Rainfall varies from 5 cm to 60 cm a year. There is evidence that it was wetter in Harappan times. The Ghaggar–Hakra and Chautang rivers, which are today almost dry, once probably flowed up to the sea. Many Early and Mature Harappan sites are found along their dry beds. The Ghaggar–Hakra river probably started to dry up around 3500 BCE, as it already terminated in an inland delta in Early Harappan times. Dholavira in the Rann of Kutch is now 100 km from the sea—once it was close to the sea and may even have been a port. Thus there were not only climatic changes but changes in the coastline too.

ARCHAEOLOGICAL CULTURES IN OTHER PARTS OF INDIA

It is important to see what kind of culture prevailed in the rest of India. Though the north-west is the most important region for the Rig Veda, some scholars believe Vedic people reached here not through the north-western passes but from central north India, east of the river Yamuna.

MESOLITHIC

The Mesolithic Age marks the transition between the hunting–gathering economy of the Palaeolithic Age to the pastoral–agrarian economy of the Neolithic Age. Such changes took place throughout the world as well as in India. In India, Mesolithic sites can be broadly dated from 10,000 to 3000 BCE. These included permanent and semi-permanent settlements.

Mesolithic sites have been found in south Uttar Pradesh, Rajasthan, Gujarat, Bihar, and Bengal, central and south India, and Sri Lanka. Significant sites in Uttar Pradesh include Sarai Nahar Rai district, Mahadaha and Damdama in Pratapgarh district, Koldihwa in district Allahabad, Lekhakia and Baghai Khor in Mirzapur district. Among sites in Rajasthan are Bagor in Bhilwara district and Tilwara in Barmer district. Paisra in Bihar, Birbhanpur in Bengal, Laghnaj in Gujarat, and Adamgarh and Bhimbetka in Madhya Pradesh are other notable sites. Mesolithic people used various small stone tools, known as microliths, made of different materials such as quartzite, chert, chalcedony, jasper, or agate. Many microliths may have been attached to bone or wood handles, while some may have been used on their own. Bones of wild animals and shells/bones of fish were often found. Mesolithic people were mainly hunter-gatherers but some also domesticated animals. Cattle and sheep/goats were among the animals domesticated. Horse bones, possibly of the domestic horse, have been found from at least three Mesolithic sites, including Tilwara in Rajasthan, but the dates for these levels are uncertain. Mahagara had bones of two types of horses, one pony and one larger. Pottery is found at some Mesolithic sites. Some had simple structures with houses of wattle and daub. Human burials have been found as well as evidence of domesticated rice at Koldihwa and Damdama in early levels. In a burial at Sarai Nahar Rai, one male had an arrow embedded in his ribs, thus indicating warfare. An ivory pendant was found in one of the graves at Damdama. In the Deccan and south India, there are coastal sites, which must have used fish and their products. They include sites in Andhra Pradesh, Karnataka, and Tamil Nadu. Apart from coastal sites, others are found near low hills, on flat hilltops, in rock shelters, along river valleys, and near lakes. Southern sites used mainly milky quartz for microliths.

Dates for these sites vary. Koldihwa dates back to 7500 BCE. In Rajasthan, evidence near the salt lakes of Didwana, Lunkaransar, and Sambhar indicates an increase in cereal pollen around 7000 BCE. Small charcoal pieces nearby suggest the burning of forests, perhaps for agriculture. The Mesolithic phase of Bagor in Bhilwara district of east Rajasthan dates to 5000–2800 BCE. There were domesticated sheep and goats, which were not locally found in the wild, and may have been obtained from Balochistan. It was, otherwise, primarily a hunting site.

Cereal pollen, dated to circa 8000 BCE, has been found in the Nilgiri hills of south India. In Sri Lanka, in the Horton plains, there seems to have been some cultivation around 15,000 BCE, with oats and barley being grown from circa 11,000 BCE. Chert, agate, crystal, and other material for the microlithic tools must have been brought from hilly regions, indicating travel over fairly long distances for sites in the plains.

Mesolithic groups must have interacted. This is indicated by 'factory sites', where a number of tools were produced, which must have been distributed to other areas or exchanged for some produce. There is evidence of formal ceremonial burials, with bodies sometimes arranged in an east–west direction. Grave goods indicate some sense of an afterlife. Sometimes jewellery was placed on the body.

NEOLITHIC

Many of these Mesolithic sites continued into the Neolithic era. The characteristics of Neolithic sites are that they are settled village-type sites with evidence of agriculture, animal husbandry, and different crafts. Epineolithic is a term used for the transition stage between Mesolithic and Neolithic. Sites of the latter exist across India–Pakistan. Dates for the Neolithic in India vary from between 7000 BCE and 2000 BCE. In the north-west, as we have already seen, Neolithic sites evolved into the urban Harappan culture. Here we will look at some key sites and areas of Neolithic occupation in the rest of India. There was interaction between different types of sites.

In Kangra district of Himachal Pradesh, there are Neolithic tools at several sites but the dates are uncertain. In Ladakh, the Neolithic site Giak has a radiocarbon date of the 6th millennium BCE.

In Kashmir's Jhelum valley, Burzahom and other sites had a Neolithic culture dating to before 2900 BCE. The characteristics were pit dwellings, bone and stone tools, and mat-impressed pottery. Pit dwellings have also been found in Gufkral in Kashmir and in Loebanr III and Kalako-deray in the Swat valley. (For more on Swat valley settlements, see Chapter 5.) It is not clear if people actually lived in the pits, and if they did so all year round. They may have been seasonal dwellings, or could have been used for storage. In a later Neolithic phase, there were houses at the ground level and burials. Along with humans, wild and domestic animals were sometimes buried. Wild animals included the deer, wolf, ibex, snow leopard, and pig. There is also evidence of the hedgehog, beaver, and hare. Among domestic animals were cattle, buffaloes, dogs, sheep, and goats. Animals were also buried separately; in one case, there were five dogs buried together. Crops grown included wheat, barley, and lentils.

At least twenty-five similar sites are known. Burzahom had some remains that indicate contacts with Kot Diji, including a painted pot and several carnelian beads. A few copper arrowheads and fragments indicate that Harappans may have come here to search for mineral wealth. It has been suggested that Burzahom represents the southernmost region of a widespread north Asian complex. According to Possehl, it represents a movement that may have started in the Mesolithic of Europe and survived in the fertile valleys of Kashmir, and possibly Nepal, Tibet, Hunza, Baltistan, and Ladakh. The American linguist F.C. Southworth found evidence of languages of the Sino-Tibetan family in ancient South Asia, and these northern Neolithic sites may represent these.

In southern Uttar Pradesh, over forty Neolithic sites have been identified along the Ganga, and the Belan, Adwa, Son, Rihand, Lapari, and Paisuni rivers. Some of them continue from the Mesolithic and date back to 7000 BCE. The sites have simple structures of mud and thatch, and evidence of the use of stone and bone implements and pottery. Cattle, sheep, and goats were domesticated. Horse bones were found but it is not clear if these were wild or domestic. There were also bones of wild animals such as deer and boar, who may have been hunted for food. Rice was grown.

Neolithic settlements have also been found in the central Ganga plain. Excavations at Lahuradeva in Sant Kabir Nagar of east Uttar Pradesh show that it dates to the late 6th and early 5th millenniums BCE. The culture was similar to that of southern Uttar Pradesh.

Other settlements in the central Ganga plain include sites between the Ghaghara and Gandak rivers, extending up to the foothills of the Himalayas. Sohagaura in Gorakhpur district lies on a mound of 60 hectares, and begins with a Neolithic settlement. There are several Neolithic sites on the plains of north Bihar including Chirand, Senuar, Maner, and Taradih, some of which have settlements beginning before 2500 BCE. These sites generally had simple mud and reed structures, pottery, stone and bone tools, and beads of semiprecious stones, steatite, and faience. There were terracotta figurines including those of humped bulls, birds, and snakes. Crops grown included rice, wheat, barley, and lentils. Cattle, goat, and sheep were domesticated, and some sites had evidence of buffalo, dog, and pig domestication as well. Animal bones indicate hunting and fishing. Senuar, on the Kudra river in the foothills of the Kaimur range, even has evidence of a domestic cat, a rare occurrence. A copper-using culture followed. Farther east, Neolithic stone tools occur in various parts of West Bengal, while Kuchai is a Neolithic site in Orissa. The north-eastern states also have Neolithic tools but the dates are uncertain.

In central India, the Kayatha culture—with the type site of Kayatha in Ujjain district—dates back to 2500 BCE. It has at least three varieties of pottery, some of which are similar to that found in Early Harappan. The people seem to have lived in houses made of mud and reed, and reared cattle. It is significant that even bones of horses were found. Copper was used; copper artefacts and bangles were found as well as necklaces with beads of agate, carnelian, and crystal. There were thousands of tiny steatite beads strung on threads. Kayatha was deserted around 1800 BCE and reoccupied after about a hundred years. But, in this phase beginning around 1700 BCE, it was a part of the Ahar/Banas culture.

In Rajasthan, north of Jaipur and west of Alwar with the main area in Sikar district, is what is known as the Ganeswar–Jodhpura culture, with over eighty sites. Some of the settlements date to 3800 BCE, and copper began to be used from around 2800 BCE. There was some pottery similarity with Early Harappan. It is thought the Harappan culture may have obtained copper from here.

The Ahar/Banas culture is also located in Rajasthan, extending into the Malwa plateau. More than ninety sites have been found. Ahar, one of the excavated sites, has three settlement phases beginning at circa 2500, 2100 and 1900 BCE, respectively. In the first phase, there were house remains, a number of copper objects, some iron, semiprecious beads including one of lapis, spindle whorls, rice grains, and animal bones. Iron finds, which predate 2100 BCE, are not known elsewhere in India at such an early date. Other excavated sites are similar, though some have earlier dates. Wild animals were hunted and eaten. Deer bones were found, as well as those of fish, turtle, and fowl. Domestic animals included cattle, buffalo, sheep, and pig. Plants included wheat, barley, rice, two types of millet, black gram, green gram, pea, linseed, and ber. Grain seems to have been ground into flour. Later levels had connections with the Gujarat Harappan culture.

In the western Deccan, the Savalda culture, dating to the 3rd millennium BCE, is named after the type site of Savalda in the Tapi valley. There are several sites in north Maharashtra between the Tapi and Godavari rivers. Savalda has wheel-made, chocolate-coloured pottery. Paintings on the pottery include geometric designs as well as paintings of tools and weapons. Kaothe, a large Savalda site, covers 20 hectares. It has house remains, bone tools, and beads of shell, semiprecious stone, and terracotta. There are bones of wild and domestic animals, including deer, cattle, buffalo, sheep, goat, and dog. Plants included millet, and green and black gram.

There were several Neolithic cultures in south India, merging into the Chalcolithic; dates for these are broadly between 3000 BCE and 1000 BCE. In the early stages, there may have been a mix of nomadic pastoralism and farming in some areas, while others were settled village sites. Bone remains indicate that cattle were predominant among domestic animals though the sheep, goat, buffalo, and fowl were also kept. Horse bones are found but it is not clear whether they are from wild or domesticated horses. Wild animal remains included bones of the nilgai, blackbuck, antelope, monitor lizard, tortoise, birds, fish, crab, and molluscs. Millets seem to have been the main crop but pulses, Indian cherry, *amla*, and ber have also been found; betel nut (*Acacia catechu*) was found, the earliest such remains in South Asia, and probably grew wild. Horse gram was grown. Some sites had pottery, stone and bone tools, and items made of marine shells, semiprecious stones, as well as copper and bronze though there is no evidence of copper smelting. Animal and human terrcaotta figurines have been found.

A pair of gold earrings was found at Neolithic Tekkalakota; gold may have been obtained from the Kolar goldfields. The items found indicate that trade existed, including trade with coastal areas. There were human burials, including urn burials and extended burials.

Thus it can be seen that by around 2000 BCE, the whole of India was already occupied, though there must have been many forested and unoccupied regions. We now look at some settlements of a later period.

LATE HARAPPAN

To start with, we will look at sites classified as Late Harappan. This terminology indicates that there were Harappan elements but the typical Mature Harappan urban characteristics were missing. In the north-west, the number of sites in the Late Harappan period in Cholistan and Sindh showed a decline. The Mature Harappan was succeeded by the Jhukar and Jhangar cultures in Sindh and the Cemetery H culture in Punjab. The Jhukar culture is named after the site of Jhukar, north-west of Mohenjodaro, while the Cemetery H type of culture is found at Harappa and other sites. In both cultures, some of the pottery was similar to that of the Mature Harappan, but there were also new types. There was a general decline as well as a decline in the number of sites. The graves in Cemetery H contained extended burials with urn burials in upper levels. In eastern Punjab and Haryana, there was an increase in sites. In western Uttar Pradesh, there are several sites occupied for the first time, which have been classified as Late Harappan. Ochre Colour Pottery (OCP) sites and Copper Hoards (CH) are within the same time frame in this region. The Late Sorath Harappan can be identified in Gujarat.

Late Harappan sites can generally be dated after 1900 BCE. Structures are simple compared with the Mature Harappan but various crops including wheat, barley, and millet were still grown and animals were domesticated.

Late Harappan/OCP sites are found in large numbers in western Uttar Pradesh. The two representative types of pottery are often found mixed together in an unstratified context. OCP was so called because of its ochre colour. It was originally considered an ill-fired soft pottery, with a colour that rubbed off when touched. Later research and excavations revealed that the ochre colour only occurred under certain weather conditions, and was not an intrinsic part of the ware. Thus it often cannot be distinguished from Late Harappan pottery. Contemporary with these was the Copper Hoard culture.

In western Uttar Pradesh, Alamgirpur and Sanauli are among the important Late Harappan sites. Sanauli, in Baghpat district, seems to have a huge Late Harappan cemetery, and there must have been a habitation site nearby. Among the notable finds was the head of a goat in one of the graves, and a copper container with tiny copper objects shaped like arrowheads. Grave goods included copper and gold objects, bracelets, beads of semiprecious stones, as well as of glass, faience, and steatite. Another significant grave find is a copper antennae sword with a sheath, which provides a link with the CH culture. Another antennae sword was also found here. CH implements are also found in association with OCP sites.

The CH culture is so named because, typically, a large number of copper implements are found buried together in a hoard, though stray implements too have been found. The main region for such hoards is the Ganga–Yamuna region, extending to Orissa, Bihar, and Bengal. There are also some finds in Haryana, Rajasthan, Madhya Pradesh, and other parts of India but some of these are of different types. Bihar, Bengal, and Orissa had flat celts, shouldered celts, bar celts, and double axes. In Uttar Pradesh and Haryana, in addition, there are anthropomorphs, antennae swords, hooked swords, and harpoons. Rajasthan has mainly bar celts and flat celts. In Madhya Pradesh, the Gungeria hoard has 424 copper objects along with more than one hundred silver objects. Analysis of the CH objects shows that the composition and alloys were different from that of Harappan copper objects. Looking at the distribution pattern of these three cultures, which can be dated approximately between 1900 BCE and 1200 BCE, it would seem that the CH-using people entered the Ganga–Yamuna region from the east, and the Late Harappans from the west. The OCP culture has some elements, which are indigenous to the region, influenced by the Late Harappan culture. Both the OCP and the CH probably had an earlier level and could go back to 2500 BCE.

These three cultures are particularly significant for the Rig Veda, as some theories equate the Rig Vedic people with the Late Harappans, and some others with the CH culture. Alternatively, CHs have been attributed to the people represented in the Atharva Veda.

In Gujarat, Kutch, and Saurashtra, Late Harappan sites increased to 120 from eighteen in the Mature Harappan. Two phases have been identified on the basis of the pottery found, all varieties of Red Ware. In the first phase, there is some cultural decline, which intensifies in the second phase.

There are numerous other Neolithic/Chalcolithic sites in other parts of India.

CENTRAL GANGA REGION

In the central Ganga region is the site of Narhan, on the northern bank of the Sarayu (Ghaghara). Period I, known as the Narhan culture, was occupied from circa 1300 BCE to 700 BCE. The site was in continuous occupation till the 7th century CE.

The early period had simple structures, along with several varieties of pottery and bone, copper, and terracotta objects, with iron in the latter phase. A wide variety of plants were grown, including rice, barley, wheat, millets, mustard, and flax. There was also evidence of various trees including jackfruit, *mahua* (*Madhuca longifolia*), *sal* (*Shorea robusta*), tamarind, teak, Indian siris, babul (*Acacia nilotica*), mulberry, *ganiyari* (*Premna spinosa*), strychnine (*Strychnos nux vomica*), mango, and bamboo. Animal remains included domestic humped cattle, sheep/goat, wild deer, horse (possibly wild), and fish. There are several similar sites in the central Ganga plains, both north and south of the Sarayu, and others of the same period in adjacent regions. Among them, Imlidih Khurd near the Kuwana river had bone remains of both horse and dog.

In Bihar–Bengal, some sites continued from the Neolithic period and there were many new settlements, which can be dated between 1700 BCE and 1500 BCE.

In Rajasthan, the site of Ganeshwar continued to be occupied. From 2000 BCE, there were a number of copper objects and a variety of pottery types. Ganeshwar has also been linked with the CH culture. Ahar, after 2000 BCE, had a variety of pottery, microliths, terracotta objects, including animal figurines of bull, horse, and possibly elephant as well as objects of copper and semiprecious stones. Rice and millet were grown. The Chalcolithic agrarian Ahar people seem to have interacted with the Mesolithic hunter-gatherers.

The Ahar phase was followed by the Malwa culture, with the type site of Navdatoli. The earliest dates are between 2000 BCE and 1750 BCE. Maheshwar, Nagda, and Eran are other important sites. Malwa pottery has paintings of animals and, at times, people. Among the animals were tigers and panthers. A large pit in the floor of a house has been identified as a fire altar. Other evidence of some sort of religion is a storage jar decorated with a female figure, an alligator or lizard, and a shrine in between. Another human figure with wild hair is thought by some to be a Proto-Rudra. At Prakash, Maharashtra, was a shell amulet shaped like a tortoise, perhaps a precursor of the god Vishnu's Kurma avatara. At Azadpur, Indore, was a child buried without its feet, which seem to have been cut off after death.

In general, in the Deccan, the Savalda culture was followed by the Malwa and Jorwe cultures. The Jorwe culture, named after the site of Jorwe, begins around 1400 BCE. But some sites have Late Harappan influence. The site of Daimabad has the following sequence: Savalda, Late Harappan, Daimabad culture, Malwa, Jorwe. In the Late Harappan period, there was copper slag and copper smelting. Daimabad was known for its bronzes probably of this phase; these include a chariot yoked to oxen, with a man and a dog in it, as well as depictions of buffalo, elephant, and rhino. Also suggestive of Harappan connections are the number of bull figurines found at Malwa sites.

Imamgaon in Pune district begins with the Malwa period, circa 1600 BCE. More than one hundred and thirty-four houses have been excavated here. People at Imamgaon had a mixed culture of farming, fishing, and hunting. Cattle domestication was important, and other domestic animals included buffalo, goat, sheep, and pig. The Malwa period was followed by that representing the Jorwe culture. This was the richest period at the site, with pottery, items of semiprecious stone, and some gold and copper. Animal remains included those of horse and ass. In a slightly later period, one of the structures was thought to be a granary or a temple for fire worship. Burials were beneath the floor of the house or courtyard; the adults in the graves mostly had their feet cut off after death; children were interred in urns. Cutting off the feet of the dead is a mystical practice in some other cultures too, including the early Saxons of England, and is believed to prevent the dead from returning to haunt the living. It is also seen in some Moche (South American culture) graves. One urn burial at Imamgaon, dated circa 1000 BCE, had a painting of a boat with oars. Inside was an approximately forty-year-old male in a foetal position, with feet intact. Boats may have been used for trade.

At Walki in Pune district, another major site, a bone ploughshare was found. Around 1000 BCE, most of the north Deccan sites were deserted. In the four southern states, following the early Neolithic, some sites continued to be occupied, but there were also several new sites. Settlements were on granite hills, hillsides, and plateaus. There were simple wattle and daub structures with stone, copper and bronze tools, pottery and other items. In general, there was agriculture with cattle, sheep, and goats being domesticated. Possibly, chicken and water buffalo were also domesticated.

IRON USE

The use of iron is considered a transformatory factor in history. Among the early iron-using centres in India–Pakistan are places in the north-west and Balochistan; the Indo-Gangetic divide and upper Ganga valley; Rajasthan; Bihar and Bengal; Malwa and central India; Vidarbha, the Deccan, and south India. There is no evidence that iron use reached India from West Asia, or elsewhere; it seems to have been an independent development within the country. In northern India, iron is associated with the Painted Grey Ware (PGW) culture, dating to 1200 BCE. Ahar in Rajasthan probably has the earliest evidence of iron, dating to 2000 BCE. Recent excavations indicate that the central Ganga region also used iron fairly early. Radiocarbon dates for iron at Dadupur near Lucknow are circa 1700 BCE from Black and Red Ware (BRW) levels. The site of Malhar has evidence of iron, dating to the early 2nd millennium BCE. Also, iron has been found in levels dated to 1300 BCE at Raja Nal ka Tila in the upper Belan valley and at Jhusi near Allahabad.

Iron has been found in BRW levels of the Malwa culture of central India, dated back to 1300 BCE. In Assam, Orissa, and Gujarat, there is no evidence of the use of iron before the historical period. In south India, the first evidence of iron is between the Neolithic and Megalithic levels.

MEGALITHS

Megaliths, known in Europe from around 4000 BCE, existed in India from 2000 BCE, though in most parts of the country, they occur after 1300 BCE. They continued to be constructed up to the early centuries CE and still are, in some parts of the country. Megaliths are of different kinds but all include the use of large stones and usually, but not always, cover or mark grave sites. They include tombs made of granite slabs, partly or wholly underground, pit or urn burials surrounded by circles of tall stones, sometimes with cap stones on top, and sarcophagus burials. Megalithic burials are usually away from habitation sites. Within the tombs, bodies are arranged in different ways; there are also fractional burials while some are buried after cremation. There are joint and common burials, many with grave goods. Some are only memorials without burials. Megaliths are not of the same culture or period.

There are several megalithic sites in the Aravallis in Rajasthan, in Mirzapur of south Uttar Pradesh, in Almora and other northern hill regions, at Burzahom and Gufkral in Kashmir, in Balochistan, and in most upland areas of the peninsula.

Megalithic sites with habitation areas in Maharashtra have iron in levels that can be dated to 800–400 BCE. Horse remains, with iron bits and wearing copper ornaments, have been found in stone circles at Mahurjhari and Naikund. One grave at Mahurjhari had a full horse skeleton along with a human. The horse bones had cut marks, suggesting a sacrifice. In another grave, the human male had an arrow stuck in his collarbone. One male was buried with a copper-hilted iron dagger placed on his chest. Megaliths in different areas of south India can be dated to 1300–200 CE. The people were agriculturalists, and practised hunting, fishing, animal husbandry, and different crafts. Cattle, sheep, dog, and horse were domesticated. There was inter-regional trade. Kudatini in Bellary district has a child burial in a sarcophagus. At Kodumanal in Erode district of Tamil Nadu, dated 3rd century BCE to 1st century CE, is a cist with a deer buried in an urn, along with carnelian beads, a sword, and axes. There were rock paintings at megalithic sites. At Paiyamapalli were scenes of fighting and horse raiders, among others. The Tamil *sangam* (*cankam*) literature has sometimes been correlated with southern megaliths.

B.B. Lal finds similarity with Nubian, upper Egypt megaliths, and those in India. The megalithic or early or pre-literate societies of the south were based, according to Kamil Zvelebil, an Indologist of Czech origin, on successful warfare with iron weapons and the use of the horse and horse chariots in fertile rice-growing regions. There is a suggestion that the Dravidian culture moved from south to north, and not vice versa.

Before ending this section, we will look at two more cultures that have been associated with the Later Vedic Samhitas.

BLACK AND RED WARE CULTURE

BRW does not represent a single culture. Various types of this pottery are widely distributed. However, it is found in the Ganga–Yamuna region, in the core area of the Kuru country. In this region, it is often in a stratified context above OCP and below the succeeding PGW culture and, therefore, could be within a time frame approximately between 1500 BCE and 1200 BCE, though it also occurs in later levels.

PAINTED GREY WARE CULTURE

PGW is a fine grey pottery with black painting. It has a wide area of distribution, including the hill regions of Garhwal and Kumaon, the Himalayan foothills, and the northern plains from the Bahawalpur region in Pakistan to Kaushambi near Allahabad. It extends into the Malwa plateau in central India and stray sherds also occur in other areas. There are numerous sites near the upper region of the Ghaggar–Chautang (Sarasvati–Drishadvati of the Vedas), the small tributaries of these rivers, and the West Yamuna canal, which must have been an old course of the river Yamuna. At a few sites, particularly the site of Bhagwanpura (Haryana), there is an overlap with the Late Harappan strata. The earliest dates for PGW are 1300–1200 BCE. In general, there were: houses made from wood posts and thatch, sometimes of mud bricks and occasionally of baked brick; agriculture and domestication of cattle, goats, sheep (and sometimes horses); and a variety of crafts. Objects of copper, iron, semiprecious stone, bone, terracotta, glass, and occasionally of ivory have been found in association with this culture; the fine grey painted pottery actually forms a small percentage of other pottery types found.

Once again, it should be noted that similar pottery does not always indicate a similar culture and, even if it does, different types of people could have occupied the sites of a single culture. It is interesting that PGW sites have been associated with the Later Vedic culture, and are also believed to represent the core area of the Mahabharata. However, they cannot represent both.

LANGUAGE GROUPS

Before making suggestions of the possible identity of Rig Vedic people, we will also look at the languages of India. India has four main language groups: Indo-Aryan, which is part of the Indo-European group; Dravidian; Austro-Asiatic; and Tibeto-Burman. In addition, there are some languages unrelated to these groups, for instance, Andamanese. It is thought that language itself originated around 40,000 to 1 million years ago. How and when these groups of languages developed and arose within India is not very clear. This also has to be linked with the origin of people within India. Some analysis has been done by looking at the different language groups, and linking the results with the theory of the original spread of population from Africa. The chronological sequence of the other language groups in India has not been established. For all these languages, there are different theories regarding their advent and diffusion in India. These languages are often linked to racial groups or subgroups but, once again, it should be emphasized that language and race are not connected.

We cannot go into an in-depth study of the research in all these languages but let us take a look at the main viewpoints.

ANDAMANESE

Andamanese includes languages spoken in the Andamans, which are unrelated to others in India. It is thought to represent one of the earliest languages in South Asia. Two language families here are Great Andamanese and Ongan, and one little-known language, Sentinalese. Great Andamanese is spoken by the Aka-Jeru people who are also known as the Great Andamanese. It had thirty-six speakers in 1997; they were bilingual and could also speak Hindi. Ongan includes Jarawa and Ongan, and does not seem related to the Great Andamanese group. They have about three hundred speakers currently.

The American anthropologist and linguist Joseph Greenberg and the Australian linguist Stephen Wurm felt that these languages are related to West Papuan languages, part of a larger group termed Indo-Pacific; Wurm added that they are also close to certain Timor languages but this could be because of a linguistic substratum. The American phonologist and linguist Juliette Blevins has traced connections between the Ongan language and Austronesian.

The Andaman people remained isolated from other groups for centuries, and thus preserved their original language. They may have been part of a very early migration from Africa, at least 60,000 years ago, though others have linked them with Oceanic peoples.

DRAVIDIAN

These languages are unique to the subcontinent but have some similarities with other languages of the ancient world. The main Dravidian languages are Tamil, Telugu, Malayalam, and Kannada, with Tamil being the oldest literary language. However, there are numerous other languages or dialects, and these can broadly be divided into three groups. The northern group consists of Brahui, spoken in the Brahui Hills in Balochistan, as well as Kurukh and Malto spoken in Bengal and Orissa. The central group consists of Telugu and a number of dialects including Kui, Khond, Holani, Konda, Gondi, Naiki, Parji, and Koya. The southern group consists of Tamil, Kannada, Malayalam, Tulu, Badaga, Toda, Kota, and Kodagu. Tribes such as the Irulas, Kadars, Paniyans, and Kurumbas also speak Dravidian languages, though it is thought that their earliest languages may be related to East African languages, and that they may constitute some of the earliest inhabitants of India.

There are Austric elements in Dravidian languages. As already seen, scholars such as McAlpin (1975) suggested similarities between Elamite and Dravidian. He estimated 20 per cent vocabulary cognates and 12 per cent probable cognates. Though many support this theory, the Russian linguist Georgiy Starostin, among others, denied that there were major similarities while the Russian linguist Vaclav Blazak connected Elamite with Afroasian languages. The Elamo-Dravidian hypothesis is related to the theory that agriculture, along with the language, spread to the Indus region from Elam in Iran. However, the British archaeobotanist Dorian Fuller analysed archaeobotanical and archaeozoological data, and felt that Proto-Dravidian already existed in the Indian peninsula. Based on plant remains, the beginnings of agriculture in this region was a local development. The distribution and dispersion of Dravidian languages in this context dates to the Neolithic period, around 4000 BCE, and is unconnected with the north-west or north-east.

Dravidian has also been related to Japanese (Japanese Tamil scholar Susumu Ohno and Sri Lanka professor A. Shanmugadas) not due to the migration of Japanese speakers to India but, as per Ono, due to the eastward migration of Tamil people, which he at first dated to around 3500 BCE but then revised it to a much later date.

Brahui

This is part of the Dravidian group of languages. Today it has only 15 per cent Dravidian words but retains its Dravidian morphology. Brahui speakers are believed to number 2,066,000 in Pakistan; 260,000 in Afghanistan; 16,000 in Iran; and 400 in India. There are numerous Brahui tribes, and they are now mainly Sunni Muslims. There are three main theories of their origin: (1) that they were descendants of Elamite–Dravidians of the Indus civilization; (2) that they came to the region from north India, either before or after the Indo-Aryan migration, but before the arrival of the Baloch; and (3) that they migrated to the area from inner India in the 11th or in the 13th to 14th centuries CE. Though the first theory has been proposed by archaeologists, it is the third theory that is favoured by linguists.

There are no Avestan loanwords in Brahui, suggesting its origin in India at a later date. It is related to Kurukh (Oraon) and Malto of the northern group of Dravidian languages. The traditional origin of these is from farther south, not from the north.

AUSTRO-ASIATIC LANGUAGES

This is a group of about one hundred and fifty languages spoken in South-East and East Asia, India, and Vietnam. As far as India goes, the main subdivisions are Munda and its variants. There are a number of Munda languages, generally subdivided into northern and southern braches. Munda languages include Korku, Santhali, Mundari, Kharia, Savara, and others.

They have been influenced by contact with other Indian languages. Remo is another language, spoken in southern Orissa, with a basic vocabulary inherited from Proto-Munda and Proto-Austro-Asiatic languages. All Austro-Asiatic languages have certain aspects in common. They have a large number of vowels, between thirty to thirty-five, and a number of prefixes and infixes but no suffixes (except in Nicobarese). Mon-Khmer languages form part of this group and include Khasi (spoken in Meghalaya) and Nicobarese (spoken in the Nicobar Islands). Beyond India, the other languages of this family are Vietnamese, Khmer, Muong, Mon, Khmu, and Wa.

There are various theories of how the Austro-Asiatic languages entered India. One theory is that they originated in Indo-China and south China, spread east to India and south to Malaya, and then to the islands beyond. Another theory linking language with race, is they are associated with very old offshoots of the Mediterraneans, who came into India from the north-west, before typical Mediterranean features with light or brown skin and long heads had developed. This theory states that Austric tribes, along with their languages, spread over India and then went to Myanmar, Malaya, and the Southeast Asian islands. In Myanmar and Indo-China, they mixed with Sino-Tibetans. An Austric group from India reached Sri Lanka, where they survive as the Veddahs, and then went to Australia where their descendants are the Australian aborigines. In the plains, they were displaced by Dravidian and Aryan speakers but Austric languages survive in the hills and forests of central and eastern India. On the Himalayan slopes, Austric languages mixed with and modified prevailing Sino-Tibetan dialects. This explains how Khasis speak an Austric language.

There is still insufficient data for Proto-Austric but, based on linguistic data, a homeland north of eastern Eurasia is suggested, with a split into different languages around 9000–8000 BCE. Reconstructions of Proto-Munda suggest its existence at an early date in Orissa. Para-Munda is suggested by Witzel as predating Proto-Munda, and existing in the Indus region, but this has been questioned.

Recent genetic studies indicate that Austro-Asiatics posssibly originated in India and spread through Tibet and Myanmar to China, but once again these studies are insufficient. Fuller believes current archaeobotanic evidence provides pointers but is not adequate to reach a conclusion, though he favours the theory of language spread into India from the north-east.

Nihali or Nahali is considered an isolate language in central India, though it may be related to Munda.

TIBETO-BURMAN LANGUAGES

This group, sometimes considered a part of Sino-Tibetan languages, is thought to comprise 350 or more languages. (There are several divergent classifications of Sino-Tibetan.) These are spoken in central, east, south, and south-east countries including Myanmar, Tibet, northern Thailand, part of Vietnam, Laos, parts of central China, part of Nepal, Baltistan in Pakistan, and many areas in India, including Himachal Pradesh, Uttarakhand, Ladakh, and Kargil in Jammu and Kashmir, and north-east India; within north-east India, the Naga languages, Manipuri, Bodo, Garo, Lushai, Lepcha, Chakma, and Tripuri are part of this group. Within this broad grouping, there are several sub-classifications of Tibeto-Burman; recent research in this area includes the work of David Bradley, an American-origin linguist and professor at La Trobe University, Melbourne, and George Van Driem, a linguist at the University of Berne. It is thought that Sino-Tibetan had developed by 4000 BCE in western China between the Yangtze and Hwang. Here, a language developed from which Chinese, Tibetan, and Burmese evolved, and also perhaps Thai, though Thai is possibly of different origin. It is interesting that Proto-Indo-European and Sino-Tibetan languages have been connected by a scholar of Taiwanese origin, Tsung-tung Chang.

It is not clear when these languages reached India. According to some accounts, they could have been spoken by the Vedic Kiratas and were in the region by Vedic times.

INDO-ARYAN

Most research work in this sphere has been done on the Indo-Aryan languages but here too there are no conclusions on their date. Indo-Aryan has also been considered a racial group. It is presumed that the other three groups were here before the Indo-Aryans. This racial grouping was the result of prevalent British ideas; research from 1990–2010 suggests that there is no Aryan–Dravidian division as north and south Indians are genetically similar.

In any case, anthropologists no longer believe in racial classifications, and the Indo-Aryan theory, in the context of the Rig Veda, is related to langauge, not to race. The relationship of Indo-Aryan and Indo-European as well as Indo-Iranian languages has already been discussed. Several languages of this group are spoken today, of which the base language is Sanskrit, with other additions. Indo-Aryan languages are spoken across north India, extending east to Assam and towards the south till Maharashtra. It is thus the largest language group within India.

Regional and colloquial variants of Sanskrit began to develop from early days, and included Pali, various Prakrit languages, including Ardha Magadhi, Maharashtri, and other variants. Languages of this group today include Hindi and its dialects, including Hindustani, Rajasthani, Avadhi, Bagheli, Chhattisgarhi, Bihari, Garhwali, Kumaoni, other hill dialects, Punjabi, Sindhi, Marathi, Konkani, Gujarati, Odia (Oriya), Bengali, and Assamese. All of these also have local variants.

Kashmiri is also considered Indo-Aryan. Some feel it is derived from Dardic, not Sanskrit, but Dardic too is usually thought to be a branch of Indo-Aryan. Dardic is also, at times, considered a separate division of Indo-Iranian. These languages are spoken by mountain communities within north India, Pakistan, and Afghanistan. They are divided into two branches: (1) Shina, including Kashmiri; Shina proper; Kohistani and (2) Khowar or Chatrarai or Chitrali. Nuristani languages were once thought to belong to this group but are now considered a separate branch of Indo-Iranian (see Chapter 4).

Bangani

Bangani, an Indo-Aryan language of Garhwal in Uttarakhand, is believed to have a centum substrate (see Chapter 3 for centum and satem languages), according to various scholars including Claus Peter Zoller of the University of Oslo, and the Indian linguist Anvita Abbi. This has, however, been challenged by Dutch linguist George van Driem and Indian linguist Suhnu R. Sharma (1997). The debate on this continues.

LANGUAGES OF BALOCHISTAN

As Balochistan is a key area in the early history of north-west India–Pakistan, we will briefly look at the languages spoken there today. These include Balochi, Saraiki, Brahui, Pashto, Sindhi, Hazaragi, and Urdu. The Baloch claim that they left their original home in the far north-west Zagros mountains near Aleppo in the mid-1st millennium CE, and moved to Balochistan. They are considered an Iranian group with some Semitic, Indic, and other genes. In the north-west Zagros, the district and tribe of Belijan or Beluchan still exist. These identify themselves as Kurds, who are culturally and linguistically cousins of the Baloch. The migrating Baloch tribes absorbed the locals of Makran, southern Sistan, and the Brahui region. Pashtuns are the other large group in the area. There are also some Sindhis.

GENETIC STUDIES

Scientists such as Stephen Gould, Richard Lewontin, Leonard Lieberman, and others have argued that race is not a valid method to classify humans, and anthropologists have moved away from categorizing people according to race. However, though the term 'race' may not be used, recent studies on genetics, genome decoding, and paleo-analysis of bones have again brought the question of types of people to the forefront. Such studies have come up with various theories. Among them are the following:

On the basis of genetic analysis, the American geneticist David Reich and others suggested that Indians are a mixture of two groups, termed Ancestral North Indians (ANI) and Ancestral South Indians (ASI). ANI are similar to western Eurasians, including Europeans, and account for 40–80 per cent of the Indian genome; ASI are not linked with any other group. Today only Andaman islanders have exclusive descent from ASI; the rest are mixed.

Reich also suggests that Dravidians are related to people from the eastern Mediterranean; they are thought to be of the same stock as the people of Asia Minor and Crete, as well as the pre-Hellenic Greeks (Aegeans).

Other genetic studies suggest that there was no large inflow of genes into India after 10,000 BCE. Paleo-analysis of bones from graves in the north-west suggests that there were two periods of discontinuity—between 6000 and 4500 BCE, and after 800 BCE. These studies may have some basis but should not be taken as conclusive. For instance, Reich's conclusions have been arrived at with samples of only 132 people, from twenty-five groups across thirteen states; the majority of people selected were tribals or lower castes. Haryana, Punjab, Bihar, Maharashtra, West Bengal, Assam, and even Tamil Nadu are among the states totally excluded from this study. Gujarat, Kerala, Karnataka, and Madhya Pradesh are represented only by samples from tribal populations. The limited nature of such a study is clear.

Whatever genetic studies may show, historically we do know of population movements into India from 600 BCE onwards, even before the medieval period. Early Persians, Greeks, Parthians, Kushans, Huns, and even Sasanians all had a presence in north India.

ARCHAEOLOGY AND THE VEDAS

The challenge in identifying the Rig Vedic culture with one or more of the archaeological cultures described above will be summarized in the conclusion to this book.

CHAPTER 9

RELIGION

Religion is the most important aspect of the Vedic texts. The earliest strand in Vedic religion is represented in the Rig Veda, which has several types of hymns. In some of them, there are references to various theories of creation. According to early hymns, creation was a result of a cosmic battle or of the cosmic separation of heaven and earth. Later hymns include the theory that all creation emerged from the sacrifice of Purusha (primeval man) or from some other form of sacrifice. Alternatively, there was creation through Hiranyagarbha, the golden egg or embryo, or through an unkown god (Ka) or Prajapati. A late hymn in the Rig Veda (10.129) ponders on creation, introducing an element of philosophical inquiry. One of its verses states:

No death was there, nor was there life immortal
Of day and night there was then no distinction
That One alone breathed windless by itself
Than that, forsooth, no other thing existed.

In early texts, there is no clear concept of a supreme creator. In some verses in the Rig Veda, Indra is seen as the ruler of all; in others it is Varuna. In the late hymns of the Rig, there is Prajapati, often identified with Brahma. Prajapati was the primeval man or Purusha.

The Atharva Veda too has several philosophical hymns on creation. Some of the myths in the Rig Veda are expanded in the Brahmanas. In the Shatapatha Brahmana, a myth of creation through sacrifice follows that of the great flood. After the flood, when Manu was the only survivor, he offered a sacrifice, from which Ida was born. From her, the human race came into being. In another myth in this Brahmana, Prajapati is responsible for creation, again through offering a sacrifice. In a third, and probably later, myth in the same text, it said that once nothing existed but water. The waters wanted to propagate their kind, and practised *tapas*, from which a golden

195

egg (Hiranyagarbha) appeared. Prajapati emerged from this and created the earth, the middle regions, and the sky. Through further tapas, he created the devas (gods) from his mouth, and daylight was associated with them. Then, with the breath of life that is below he created the asuras, and night and darkness came into being. Another myth says that in the beginning there was *asat* (unreality, non-being). But in this were *rishis*, who were Prana (breath), and created seven Purushas, who then became Prajapati. Then he created Brahman, the threefold knowledge (*trayi-vidya*). This *veda* ('knowledge') was the foundation from which Prajapati created water and then an egg, from which Agni, the earth, and other things came.

The Upanishads take the concept of creation to a new level, which is beyond the scope of this book.

THE GODS

IN THE RIG VEDA

Though a large number of deities are referred to, the text states that there are thirty-three gods: eleven in heaven, eleven on earth, and eleven in the waters or air. Based on this, Yaska, compiler of the Nirukta on the Vedic Samhitas, classifies the main Vedic deities into three categories: terrestrial, celestial, and atmospheric. Among the terrestrial deities are the rivers Sindhu, Vipasa, Shutudri, and Sarasvati; Prithivi, the earth; Agni, fire; Brihaspati; and Soma. Celestial deities include Dyaus, Varuna, Mitra, Surya, Savitri, Pushan, Vishnu, Vivasvat, the Adityas, Usha, Ratri, and the Ashvins. The atmospheric deities are Indra, Trita Aptya, Apam Napat, Matarishvan, Ahi Budhnya, Aja Ekapad, Rudra, the Maruts, Vayu-Vata, Parjanya, and Agni. Agni is a deity that belongs to several categories.

Other gods include Yama, Dhatr, Vidhatr, Tvashtr, Dhartr, Tratr, and Netr. Though female deities are not very important, many are mentioned apart from Sarasvati, Prithivi, and Usha. Ratri and Aranyani have separate hymns dedicated to them. Aditi was another female deity, considered the mother of the gods, while Diti seems to have been her counterpart. Varunani, Indrani, and Agnayi—the wives of Varuna, Indra, and Agni, respectively—are referred to. Sita, a goddess connected with agriculture, is prayed to for crops and blessings. Male and female deities who personify abstract nouns or qualities include Manyu, Shraddha, Anumati, Sunrita, Asuniti, and Nirriti (see below for more on these deities). Among other deities, Vastoshpati was the lord of the house while Kshetrasyapati was the lord of the fields. Deities such as the Rudras, Adityas, and Maruts were also worshipped in groups. Other groups of divine beings were Vasus and Ribhus. The Ribhus were skilful beings, who became deities because of their great feats.

There were also *gandharvas* and *apsaras*. The Rig refers to gandharva in the singular, an apsara being his wife. Gandharva is said to guard Soma in the celestial sphere. Apsaras are also mentioned in the plural while one apsara, Urvashi, is named in the text. Some hymns, mainly in Mandala 10, have a concept of one supreme being but, on the whole, the deities are personifications of nature, or of an attribute or ideal. At the same time, several hymns consider the various deities as aspects of one. Prajapati, Brihaspati, Ka, Hiranyagarbha, and Vishvakarma are some of the names by which a supreme deity is referred to.

Deities are also referred to in pairs. Mitra-Varuna and Dyava-Prithvi are often referred to together. Among other pairs are Indra-Varuna, Indra-Agni, Indra-Vayu, Agni-Soma, and Indra-Vishnu. Some hymns are dedicated to the Vishvedevas, which usually indicates a number of different deities but, at times, seems to refer to a specific group.

The gods are described in human form, with arms, legs, and bodies. Some are said to be earlier than the others, others the offspring of earlier deities. The gods cross the sky or atmosphere in their *rathas* (chariots), drawn by horses or other animals. They taste the offerings prepared at the sacrifices and confer blessings on the people who have made the offerings. They are powerful, and help their followers to overcome their enemies. The deities know what goes on in the world and want people to follow the right path. These deities are elaborated on in later texts.

There are numerous references to demonic beings, who may be purely mythical or real people of opposing groups. Danu's son Vritra, who was defeated by Indra, is mentioned most frequently. Vala, who guarded a cave filled with cows, was driven out by Indra and his allies. Arbuda, the three-headed Vishvarupa, and Svarbhanu were others defeated by Indra. Some individuals referred to as Dasas were also Indra's victims. These are believed to have been either kings of rival groups or mythical beings. The Panis were a particular group in this category.

Other beings are asuras, rakshas (rakshasas), and *pishachas*. While the latter two are usually demonic, in the Rig Veda, asura is often used interchangeably with deva, indicating a divine being. *Yatu* or *yatudhana* (probably sorcerer) are also mentioned.

SAMA VEDA

The Sama and Yajur Vedas are focused on sacrifices. They are the songbook and the prayer book for the practical use of the special priests, the *udgatr* and *adhvaryu*. The Sama Veda, as noted earlier, is composed almost entirely of verses selected from the Rig Veda and rearranged. Thus there are no different deities mentioned here but all Rig Vedic deities do not have the same importance in the Sama. The three main deities are Agni, Indra, and Soma, associated primarily with the sacrifice, though other Rig Vedic deities are mentioned in the hymns.

YAJUR VEDA

The Yajur Veda also has prayers to gods but the emphasis is different. The prayers are to be used during sacrifices. Prayers such as the series of hymns to Rudra are not found in any other Samhita. Rudra gained importance from this time onwards.

ATHARVA VEDA

The Atharva Veda has many unique and different features concerning religion. Some aspects of this were indicated in Chapter 1 while its information on diseases is dealt with in Chapter 11. Many of the deities are the same, including Agni and Indra, but their nature is different. Cosmological and philosophical concepts are mentioned too. The Atharva has the concept of a supreme god, identified with Prajapati, and also of a creative principle. Terms such as Brahman, asat, and tapas are found in the text. The concept of Rudra-Shiva is somewhere between that of the Rig Veda and the Shvetashvatara Upanishad. In different hymns, Kala, Kama, and Prana are described as the first cause of the universe. There are prayers to Rig Vedic deities, among which are hymns not found in the Rig. These include hymns to Varuna, the Ashvins, Prithivi, and others. The Shaunakiya text begins with a prayer to Vachaspati for divine knowledge. Other deities mentioned in this section are the waters (Apah), Indra, Agni, Brihaspati, Soma, Parjanya, Prithivi, Mitra, Varuna, the moon, and Surya, the sun. Kama, Kala, and Pushan are among the other Rig Vedic deities referred to. The text mentions some deities that are not known in the Rig, such as Arbudi, Nyarbudi, and Rohita. The Rohita hymns glorify a supreme being. In various other hymns, the ox, bull, cow, and *vratya* are each in turn glorified as the highest being. Sarva and Bhama, known in the Yajur, are also mentioned.

Magic and religion initially had the same aim. Magic spells are given, though these are not really different from the purpose and aim of the sacrificial ritual. One difference is that the gods are not necessarily invoked in these spells. The main aims of the Atharva are said to be to appease, to bless, and to curse. Some philosophical aspects are similar to those expounded in the Upanishads.

Ritual texts and great sacrifices also have some formulas for the priest to destroy enemies. Magic rites are found in most other parts of the ancient world. Some hymns (such as 4.16) combine two aspects: the first on the power and glory of god, the second on a magical rite.

BRAHMANAS AND ARANYAKAS

The Brahmanas have several creation legends. The old gods still existed but the focus in some texts was on different ones. Prajapati was seen as a supreme god in the Brahmanas. Rudra was an important deity from the Yajur onwards. As Bhutapati, in the Aitareya Brahmana, he became the god of cattle. By this time, he was developing into a complex god—the later Shiva. Vishnu became more important. In the Taittiriya Aranyaka, Vishnu is identified with Narayana. Gandharvas, apsaras, *nagas*, etc. were seen as semi-divine. Naga worship gained importance. Deva–asura wars began to be described. The concept of Brahman developed. In the Vedas, the term Brahman referred to prayer verses and formulas, and to some kind of spiritual power. It also referred to the *trayi vidya* or the first three Vedas. By the time of the Brahmanas and Upanishads, it came to signify the first and ultimate principle.

There are also some ethical principles. All activities which form part of daily life are considered a duty and a responsibility. Life has to be lived according to the customary norms and Vedic injunctions. Selflessness, prayer, and truthfulness are important qualities.

THE MANY GODS ARE ONE

In the Rig Veda, some hymns indicate that though the gods had different names, they actually represented one reality. This concept is further developed and brought out in the Brihadaranyaka Upanishad. In this text (3.9), it says that Vidagdha, son of Shakala, asks Yajnavalkya about the number of gods, and the latter says there are 303 and 3003 as given in the laudatory hymns, but then shows how these can be reduced to one. He also says that there are basically thirty-three gods, the others only being their manifestations. These thirty-three are the eight Vasus, eleven Rudras, twelve Adityas, along with Indra and Prajapati. The Vasus are aspects of nature, the Rudras are aspects of the mortal body or person, the Adityas represent the twelve months of the year; Indra represents the thunder cloud and thunderbolt, and Prajapati the sacrifice. The thirty-three gods can be reduced to six, which are fire (Agni), earth (Prithivi), the air (Vayu), the sky (Antariksha), the sun (Aditya), and heaven (Dyaus). He then reduces these to three, which are the three worlds (*loka*) in which all these are contained; then to two: matter (*annam*) and the life force (*prana*); then to one and a half, which is that (*ayam*) which blows (*pavate*); and finally to one, the cosmic *prana* that is Brahman.

DEITIES

The main Vedic deities are described here, while some hymns on creation and prayers to various deities are provided in Appendix II.

ADITI

A goddess in the Rig Veda, she is the mother of the Adityas, a group of gods, and is said to nourish and sustain all existence. There is no separate hymn to her but she is mentioned almost eighty times in this text. She is said to be bright and luminous, a supporter of all creatures, invoked in the morning, at noon, and at sunset. Her name means 'unbinding', 'without bonds', or 'unbound', hence Aditi is worshipped to provide freedom from the bonds of suffering. She is the sky and space or air, the mother, father, and son, all the devas, the five clans or tribes, and all that has been, and will be, born. In one passage in the Rig Veda, she is said to be both the mother and the daughter of Daksha. Yaska, in his Nirukta, comments that it is part of the nature of gods, that they can be born from each other. According to the Taittiriya Samhita, Aditi contains the whole world. In the Mahabharata and Puranas, she is the daughter of Daksha and wife of Kashyapa, the mother of the thirty-three devas, including twelve Adityas, eight Vasus, eleven Rudras, and two Ashvins. (Though thirty-three devas is a standard number, the lists of gods included in this differ.) As a goddess, one of the main characteristics of Aditi is that of motherhood, while the other is her connection with the Adityas, and therefore with light and the sun.

ADITYAS

A group of gods. In the Rig Veda, there are six hymns dedicated to them and they are mentioned in others. They are said to be seven or eight but six names are listed together: Mitra, Aryaman, Bhaga, Varuna, Daksha, and Amsha. The three most commonly mentioned are Mitra, Varuna, and Aryaman. In one hymn (10.72), Martanda is mentioned as the eighth Aditya. The Adityas are said to protect the universe, see the good and evil actions of people, and punish the wicked. They are bright, golden, animisha (unblinking) and provide a long life, good health, and offspring to their worshippers. The Atharva Veda mentions the eight sons of Aditi (8.9) while the Taittiriya Brahmana (1.1.9) lists eight Adityas: Mitra, Varuna, Aryaman, Amsha, Bhaga, Dhatr, Indra, and Vivasvat. The Shatapatha Brahmana refers to Martanda as the eighth Aditya, but, in some passages, mentions twelve Adityas, who can be identified with the twelve months. In the Mahabharata and some later texts, twelve Adityas are listed: Dhatr, Mitra, Aryaman, Shakra (that is, Indra), Varuna, Amsha, Bhaga, Vivasvat, Pushan, Savitr, Tvashtr, and Vishnu. Indra is said to be the most important, and Varuna the oldest and best. Various later texts provide different lists of Adityas, who later came to be worshipped along with the Navagraha (nine planets). They are specifically linked with Surya worship.

AGNAYI

A goddess mentioned in the Rig Veda, who is the wife of Agni.

AGNI

The personification of the sacrificial fire, Agni is the second most important god in the Rig Veda (the first being Indra) where over two hundred hymns are dedicated to him, while he is mentioned in many more. Agni is sometimes linked with other deities who are jointly worshipped, for instance Agni-Indra or Indra-Agni, Agni-Maruts, Agni-Soma, Agni-Varuna, Agni-Parjanya, and Agni-Surya. Agni-Soma together light up the sky and grant wealth, cattle, horses, and children.

His consort, who is briefly mentioned, is Agnayi. Adjectives used to describe Agni are related to sacrificial ceremonies, in which offerings of butter and ghi are made. Thus he is described as butter-backed, butter-faced, or butter-haired. He has sharp or burning jaws, golden or shining teeth, and resembles gold. His main food is wood or ghi (clarified butter) and he drinks melted butter. Sometimes, he drinks Soma. He removes darkness and brings light everywhere. He is brilliant and shines like the sun. His chariot is made of lightning, luminous and golden, and his horses are tawny and ruddy, but the path he makes in his journey is black. Agni has a threefold nature—born of heaven, men, and the waters—a precursor of the later trinity of Brahma, Vishnu, and Shiva. He protects his worshippers behind one hundred metal walls, preserves them from calamities, and is the deliverer and friend of those who worship him. He bestows every kind of boon, particularly in the sphere of domestic welfare, offspring, and property. He is compared with various animals, including a bull, a calf (*vatsa*), and an agitated horse. Like an excited horse, Agni can be tamed and pacified. He is also called an eagle of the sky and a divine bird, and is compared with various birds. Agni is the son of Dyaus and Prithivi, or of Tvashtr, or sometimes of other deities. At the same time, other gods were descended from him. As he was constantly reborn, Agni could be both old and new, and has many births. He is sometimes identified with other deities, particularly Mitra and Varuna. Agni, or individual Agnis, is specifically associated with some people and families, including Vasishtha, Angiras, Bhrigu, Bharata, Vadhryashva, Devavata, Divodasa, and Trasadasyu.

Agni takes on many forms, just as fire does, and exists wherever there is fire on earth, or lightning in the heavens. He is the god of fire sacrifices and of the domestic hearth. As such, he is also important in the ritual texts, the Sama and Yajur Vedas, and is frequently called the *hotr* or chief priest, and also *ritvij*, *purohita*, *adhvaryu*, and *brahman* (the priest of the Atharva). In him are the aspects of all the priests, and he is also a rishi. A passage in the Taittiriya Samhita says that Agni is the messenger of the devas, while Kavya Ushana (see below) or Daivya is the messenger of the asuras.

Agni is also referred to as Jataveda Agni and Agni Vaishvanara, among other names. The name Jataveda is mentioned over one hundred and twenty times in the Rig and is explained as one who knows the births of all. Agni Vaishvanara has a semi-independent status. The term Agni Vaishvanara occurs at least sixty times in the Rig Veda, and indicates the Agni that belongs to all. In the Shrauta Sutras, Vaishvanara is a special form of Agni.

As Agni is associated with the sacrificial ritual, he has an important role in the Sama and Yajur Vedas. Agni represents fire and is, at the same time, its personification. Numerous legends are narrated about Agni in the Mahabharata, Ramayana, and later texts. The term Agni has Indo-European roots, similar to the Latin *ignis* and the Slavonic *agni*. The sacred fire is also important in Zoroastrianism, another shared aspect.

AHI BUDHNYA

A deity in the Rig Veda, who is the serpent of the deep or of the atmospheric ocean, and is invoked as a divine being. In this text, his name is mentioned twelve times in hymns to the Vishvedevas. He is associated with Aja Ekapad, Apam Napat, and other deities. In the Vajasaneyi Samhita and

Brahmanas, he is connected with Agni Garhapatya. In later texts, it becomes the name of Rudra or Shiva. In the Mahabharata, Ahi Budhnya is one of the eleven Rudras, and is also mentioned as one of the Maruts. According to the Vishnu Purana, Ahi Budhnya was a son of Vishvakarma, the divine architect.

AJA EKAPAD

A deity in the Rig Veda, he is associated with Ahi Budhnya and has been equated with the sun, or with a form of Agni. In one passage, he is invoked along with the 'thundering Paviravi', the daughter of lightning. Literally, his name means 'the one-footed goat', while the commentator Yaska explains it as 'he who protects with one foot'. Other interpretations are 'the one-footed driver or stormer' or 'the goat who goes alone', indicating the moon, or 'the unborn, who has only one foot', meaning he who inhabits an isolated, mysterious world. It is also thought to refer to lightning, which is swift like a goat and strikes the earth with one foot (single streak). The god is referred to in the Atharva Veda, and is said to have made the two worlds firm. The name later evolved into Ajaikapad who, in the Mahabharata and Puranas, is one of the eleven Rudras. It is also a name of the god Shiva.

AMBIKA

The goddess Durga, so popular later on, is not known in the Rig Veda. One of her names, Ambika, appears in some Later Vedic texts. In the Taittiriya Aranyaka, Ambika is also called Durga Vairochani, Katyayani and Kanyakumari. Some other names associated with her, such as Uma Haimavati, or Kali, are mentioned in the Upanishads. Durga is fully described for the first time in the Mahabharata, and later in several Puranas.

AMSHA

A god in the Rig Veda, who is one of the Adityas, similar to Bhaga. The term occurs only twelve times in this text, and may not always refer to a god. In one passage, Agni is equated with Amsha. Amsha is mentioned in the Puranas both as an Aditya, and as a god of the Tushita group.

ANUMATI

Anumati, a minor goddess in the Rig Veda, literally means 'the favour of the gods'. In the Atharva Veda and Vajasaneyi Samhita, she is a goddess of love, prayed to for children. In later texts, she is a lunar deity, and also a Shakti-devi, a personification of Shakti.

APAH

A group of deities, who in the Rig Veda, are water goddesses. Four hymns are dedicated to them, and they are mentioned elsewhere as well. They are mothers and wives, bestow boons, and come to the sacrifice. They follow the path of the gods and flow in channels, with the sea as their goal. Indra made channels for them with his *vajra*. They cleanse and purify worshippers and grant strength and immortality. Their waters are said to be filled with honey, and pleasing to the gods, indicating their link with Soma. They are also specifically mentioned as carrying ghi, milk, and honey, like the priests who carry Soma for Indra. Apah are later mentioned in the Mahabharata and Puranas.

APAM NAPAT

A deity in the Rig Veda, where one entire hymn is dedicated to him (2.35) and he is in addition mentioned in other hymns. He is the son of the waters, golden in form and appearance, always shining. He comes from a golden womb and shines in the waters without any fuel. His food is ghi and the *vrishanah* (steeds) carry him, swift as thought, through the waters. He is connected with rivers (*nadya*) and is sometimes equated with Agni. Apam Napat in the Avesta is a spirit of the waters.

ARAMATI

Aramati, literally 'devotion' or 'piety', is personified as a goddess in the Rig Veda. She is a minor deity in the Rig, and is similar to Armaiti, who represents loving devotion in Zoroastrianism.

ARANYANI

A goddess of the forest, who has one hymn dedicated to her in the Rig Veda. She is described as a spirit of the forest, who cannot be seen. Her voice is like that of a man calling his cattle, or of a tree falling. She does not come to the village but if one stays in the forest in the evening, she can be heard like a voice crying, far away. She is perfumed and fragrant, and the mother of wild things: Aranyani has some parallels with the Roman goddess Diana. She is not known in later times, though there are other goddesses associated with forests.

ARBUDI

In the Atharva Veda, Arbudi is a god who, along with Nyarbudi, is a companion of Indra. The two are prayed to for success in battle.

ARYAMAN/ARYAMA

In the Rig Veda, Aryaman is one of the Adityas, similar to Mitra. He is mentioned around a hundred times, usually with Mitra and Varuna, but has no exclusive hymns. His nature seems similar to Mitra. Aryaman is said to represent chivalry, honour, and nobility while Mitra incorporates the concepts of friendship, and of honouring promises and contracts. As an Aditya, he is connected with the sun and with light. Aryaman or Airyaman is also a yazata, a lesser deity in Zoroastrianism.

ASHVINS

The twin Ashvins are prominent in the Rig Veda, and are the most important deities after Indra, Agni, and Soma. Fifty hymns are dedicated to them, as well as parts of several others, and their name occurs more than four hundred times. They are said to be young but ancient, honey-hued, and with a golden brilliance. Their name indicates their connection with horses (*ashva* means 'horse'). They ride in a three-wheeled golden chariot, drawn by horses or sometimes by deer, birds, buffaloes (*kakuha*), or a single ass. They are also known as Nasatyas, *na-asatya*, usually interpreted as 'no untruth'. They are helpers in distress, and there are numerous stories of the people they helped. Particularly, they rescue people from the ocean, and also draw treasures out of the ocean. They rescued Bhujyu, son of Tugra, from the ocean (*samudra*) or from a water cloud (*udameghe*). In one passage, it is said that they rescued him in a ship with 100 oars, while others refer to flying boats or chariots. Bhujyu is also said to have been rescued after clinging to a log or branch (*vriksha*). They rescued and restored to life the sage Rebhu, who had been stabbed, tied up, and left in the waters for ten days and nine nights. They also rescued Vandana, either from a deep pit or from old age. They helped the rishi Atri Saptavadri when he was burnt in a fire, by healing and restoring him to health. Their help extended to the animal kingdom, and they rescued a quail who prayed to them from the jaws of a wolf.

Another story connected with the Ashvins is that of Rijrashva. He gave 101 sheep to a female wolf to eat and, therefore, was blinded by his father. He prayed to the Ashvins, who restored his eyesight. They are great healers of those on earth, and are the physicians of the gods. They protect their worshippers and prevent an early death. They restored the youth of the rishi Chyavana, a story mentioned in the Rig Veda, and elaborated on in the Shatapatha Brahmana. They cured Paravrij, who was both blind and lame. Vishpala, who had lost a leg in battle, was given a new one made of metal. They also gave a husband to Ghosha, a wife to Vimada, and a son to the wife of a eunuch. Another interesting story is of the blessings they bestowed on Kakshivat who belonged to the family of Pajra. Because of these blessings, 100 jars of sura (wine or honey) flowed 'from a strong horse's hoof, as from a sieve' (1.116, 117). They also placed a horse head on the rishi Dadhyanch, son of Atharvan, who then revealed where the *madhu* (honey or mead) of Tvashtr was. There are many other such stories regarding them. The Ashvins were married to Surya (Suryaa), daughter of the sun god.

It is thought their name (Ashvin) and the fact that they were said to be owners of horses (ashva) was actually related to the term ashva in its sense as 'rays of light'. Yaska, in his Nirukta (12.1), says that some considered them to be heaven and earth, others day and night, while 'legendary writers' thought they were two kings. The Shatapatha Brahmana (4.1.5) considers them to be heaven and earth. However, their nature and the various kind actions they are said to have performed indicate that they may have been real people of the distant past. On the other hand, there are other twin gods in ancient cultures, some of whom have similar characteristics, pointing to the Ashvins' evolution from ancient myths. Among ancient twin gods are Castor and Pollux of Greek mythology, the Lithuanian Asvieniai, the Latvian Dieva deli, the Alcis gods, the Roman Romulus and Remus, the Germanic Hengest and Horsa, and the Slavic Volos and Veles. Michael Shapiro, an American specialist in Slavic languages, points out some common aspects of several twin deities, which include their association with horses and their healing skills. Many of these twins were also associated with the sea, and were helpers of people. Castor and Pollux were associated with horses, and were widely worshipped by Greeks, later by the Etruscans and Romans, and even by the Celts; they were the special gods of sailors. The Lithuanian pair is depicted as twin horses, who draw the sun's chariot. The Ashvins are frequently mentioned in the Mahabharata and Puranas.

ASHVINI

The goddess known as Ashvini, mentioned in the Rig, must be the same as Suryaa, the daughter of Surya and the wife of the Ashvins.

ASUNITI

A minor goddess in the Rig Veda, who occurs only in one passage (10.59), she is prayed to for strength and longevity.

BHAGA

In the Rig Veda, Bhaga is one of the Adityas. Usha (dawn) is his sister. One hymn in the Rig (7.41) is dedicated to his praise, though other gods too are mentioned. As an Aditya, Bhaga is associated with the sun; according to Yaska, he presides over the forenoon. The name means 'dispenser', 'gracious lord', or 'patron', and the god is considered the distributor of wealth and the bestower of divine blessings. He also presides over love and marriage. The French historian, musicologist, and Indologist A. Danielou interprets the name as representing the 'inherited share', which provides wealth and status. However, Bhaga could be derived from *bogu*, a term for god in Indo-European languages. Baga is a deity with a similar name in Zoroastrianism. In the Mahabharata, Bhaga was a member of the god Indra's assembly. In some later texts, he is one of the eleven Rudras.

BHARATI

A goddess in the Rig Veda, she is mentioned in some hymns, usually along with Sarasvati and Mahi.

BRAHMA

In the Vedic Samhitas, many names are given to a creator god, one of which is Brahma. Other names of the creator are Vishvakarman, Brahmanaspati, Hiranyagarbha, and Prajapati. Brahma is mentioned in the Shatapatha Brahmana as the creator of the gods, and the source of all. In the Mahabharata, Brahma is said to be the same as Prajapati.

BRAHMANASPATI

In the Rig Veda, this is one of the names of a creator god. It is considered another Z name of Brihaspati.

BRIHADDIVA

A goddess in the Rig Veda, she is mentioned a few times and referred to as a mother. The Brihaddiva is also a river.

BRIHASPATI

A deity who has eleven hymns dedicated to him in the Rig Veda, and two more jointly with Indra. He is mentioned around one hundred and twenty times as Brihaspati and about fifty times as Brahmanaspati, which is considered one of his names. He is described in the Rig as being born from light in the highest heaven. He is said to drive away the darkness with thunder. He has seven mouths, seven rays, and 100 wings, and he is blue-backed. His voice is clear, he is bright and pure. His bow has *rita* or cosmic order as its string, his chariot is drawn by reddish horses. He is the friend of Indra, and associated with him in his actions. In some hymns, he is identified with Agni. In the Yajur Veda and Brahmanas, he is connected with Vedic rituals and invoked as a priest. The Maitrayani Samhita says that his *shloka* reaches heaven (1.190) and that *chhandas* or metre is his creation. In the Vajasaneyi Samhita, he is said to use the octosyllabic metre to win the gayatri metre. He is also praised in the Atharva Veda. In later times, Brihaspati was identified with the planet of the same name, equated with Jupiter, and became the lord of the planet. He is thus one of the Navagrahas or nine planets.

DAKSHA

In the Rig Veda Daksha is mentioned around six times as a deity, but otherwise is an adjective meaning 'dexterous, strong, clever or intelligent'. In the Taittiriya Samhita, the gods are called *daksha-pitarah*, 'fathers of daksha'. In the Shatapatha Brahmana (2.4.4), Daksha is identified with

Prajapati. In later texts, Daksha had a very important role as the father of Sati, and of Aditi and other daughters who married Kashyapa and gave birth to all living beings.

DESHTRI

A deity mentioned in the Rig Veda (10.85). She is referred to here along with Matarishvan and Dhatr.

DEVAGANA

The gods (devas) are frequently mentioned together in the Rig Veda, as a group (*gana*).

DEVA-NETR

Literally, 'the leader god', he occurs in the Rig Veda (5.50), probably as an independent deity. He provides guidance to attain prosperity.

DEVANAM-PATNIH

A collective term for the wives of the devas, who are referred to in the Rig Veda and later texts. Varuni, wife of Varuna; Indrani, wife of Indra; and Agnayi, wife of Agni, are among those that this refers to.

DHARTR

Literally meaning 'supporter', this term is usually applied to various deities, including Indra, but in one place (7.35), he is an independent deity in the Rig Veda.

DHATA/DHATR

Dhatr, literally 'creator', appears about twelve times in the Rig Veda as a creator god. He is said to have created the sun, moon, heaven, earth, and air, and to be the lord of the world. According to the Naighantuka, he is a deity of the middle regions. In post-Vedic texts, he is the creator and preserver of the world, the equivalent of Prajapati or Brahma. In the Mahabharata and Puranas, Dhatr is also one of the Adityas. He is considered the same as Dhata. Dhatr is also later the name of other deities including Surya, Shiva, and Vishnu.

DHISHANA

A goddess in the Rig Veda, she seems to be connected with nourishment, particularly the kind received from the cow in the form of milk and butter.

DITI

A goddess associated with Aditi, Diti is referred to three times in the Rig Veda. In one passage, it is said that from their chariot in the sky, the gods Mitra and Varuna can see Aditi and Diti. This has been interpreted in various ways. The commentator Sayana says it refers to the indivisible earth and the creatures on it; others believe it could refer to all visible nature. In another passage, Agni is asked to 'grant diti, and save from aditi'. These words may not refer to the goddess, and could mean 'wealth' and 'penury', respectively. Sayana however interprets it as 'liberal giver' (Diti) and 'illiberal giver' (Aditi). In a third passage, Diti is mentioned with Agni, Savitr, and Bhaga, and said to give that which is desirable. In the Later Vedic Samhitas, she is mentioned with Aditi. In the Atharva Veda, her sons are said to be the *daityas*, but there seems to be no negative connotation of daityas at this time. In the Mahabharata and Puranas, she was one of the daughters of Daksha, and was married to Kashyapa. Her children included several daityas.

DYAUS OR DYAVA

Dyaus is a term used both for the sky, and for the god of the sky or heaven. In some contexts, it also means day. He is called a roaring bull, and a black horse decorated with pearls—a poetic reference to the night sky. There is no separate hymn in the Rig Veda to Dyaus, but he is often associated with Prithivi, the earth; together, they are known as Dyava-Prithivi. Usha, the dawn, is said to be his daughter. Other descendants are the Ashvins, Agni, Parjanya, Surya, the Maruts, and the Angirasas. Dyaus is also referred to as an asura, which in the Rig was a term for a great god. Dyava-Prithivi have six hymns dedicated to them, and are mentioned in many others. Heaven and earth are celebrated together in many ancient cultures. In the Rig, they are called father and mother, or parents who sustain the world and all creatures in it. They are also the parents of the gods, and they came from the head and feet of Purusha. Tvashtr made their forms though, according to the Atharva Veda, they were made by Vishvakarma. They are said to be wise and righteous. By the Later Vedic period, Dyaus had lost his importance. His counterpart in Greek mythology is said to be Zeus.

GANGA

The river Ganga, along with other rivers, is praised as a deity in one hymn.

GARUTMAN

The Rig Veda mentions a celestial deity Garutman, who has beautiful wings. He can be identified with the later Garuda, the vehicle of Vishnu. According to the Unadi Sutra, Garuda comes from the root 'gr', 'to speak'. He thus represents sacred speech. In the Shatapatha Brahmana, Garuda is said to personify courage. In the Mahabharata, Garuda is said to be the same as Garutman. He is also known as Tarkshya. Garuda appears in Buddhist sculptures and, in Jainism, is the *yaksha* of the Tirthankara Shantinatha. A winged Garuda is associated with Surya images and is similar to Zoroastrian depictions of the Fravashi (divine aspect of an individual).

HIRANYAGARBHA

A deity first referred to in the Rig Veda, where he is mentioned only once and said to be the supreme god. He is also mentioned in the Atharva Veda and Brahmanas. In the Taittiriya Samhita, he is identified with Prajapati and, in later texts, with Brahma. Hiranyagarbha means 'golden womb' and is the cosmic womb from which all life originates. Hiranyagarbha is also identified with Brahman, the ultimate reality.

ILA/IDA

A goddess, mentioned in the Rig Veda. The name means 'nourishment' and she was the personification of the offering of milk and butter, representing the nourishment provided by the cow. In the Rig Veda, she is called 'butter-footed' and 'butter-handed', and Agni is once said to be her son. In the Shatapatha Brahmana, she is the daughter of Manu or of Mitra-Varuna. According to the Taittiriya Samhita, Manu sent her to see whether the sacrifice of the devas and asuras had been conducted properly. She said their sacrifice was incorrect and described the correct way, as a result of which the devas attained prosperity. Through Ila, Manu gave birth to the human race. In later texts, she was a mythical person, both a woman and a man.

INDRA

The most important deity in the Rig Veda, Indra has approximately two hundred and fifty hymns addressed to him in that text. Along with other deities, he is praised in at least another fifty hymns. He is the god of thunder and the dominant deity of the middle region, pervading the air. He is also invoked in wars and battles, and helps warriors and kings in their struggles. Indra's form and weapons are described. His weapon is the *vajra* or thunderbolt, also the name of lightning, and it is described as golden and metallic. Indra is sometimes described as golden-coloured but, more often, is said to be tawny, with tawny hair and a tawny beard. He can take on different forms and radiates light like the sun. Apart from his vajra, he uses bows and arrows and carries an ankusha (hook or goad). He rides in a golden chariot drawn by two bay or tawny horses, or sometimes by even 1000 horses. Their hair is like peacock feathers and they have golden manes.

His Family and Dog

He is said to have been born and his mother is in one passage said to be a cow (grishti), and in another is called Nishtigri. The later commentator Sayana identifies this with Aditi, his mother in later texts. In the Atharva Veda, the mother of Indra and Agni is known as Ekashtaka, who was the daughter of Prajapati. Indra's father is mentioned as Dyaus or Tvashtr. Indra is married to Indrani, who is known as Shachi and Pulomaja. According to the Aitareya Brahmana, his wives were called Prasaha or Sena, who have been identified with Indrani. Sometimes other female consorts are mentioned. He was the most powerful of gods and is, therefore, known as Shakra (mighty), Shachivat (possessed of might), and Shachipati, (lord of might, or husband of Shachi). He had a female dog named Sarama, who assisted him as his messenger to the Panis. Indra is said to be huge in size, greater than heaven, earth and air, and than the two worlds. The other gods were subordinate to him, and he was king of the whole world, the ruler of the universe.

Indra's Helpers or Associates (Gods)

Indra is associated with the Maruts and loves drinking Soma. Indra's love of Soma is reflected particularly in hymn 10.119. The first three verses are given here:

1. *This, even was my resolve, to win a cow, to win a steed:*
   Have I not drunk of Soma juice?
2. *Like violent gusts of wind the draughts that I have drunk have lifted me:*
   Have I not drunk of Soma juice?
3. *The draughts I drank have borne me up, as fleet-foot horses draw a chariot:*
   Have I not drunk of Soma juice?

But, as A.A. Macdonell, the British-origin Sanskrit scholar, points out, 'The exhilaration of Soma partook of a religious character in the eyes of the Vedic poets.' Agni is sometimes considered his twin brother, and Pushan is also called his brother. In one hymn in the Rig Veda (4.26), Indra says he was, in earlier times, both Manu and Surya. He is sometimes considered the same as Surya and, in one passage, is referred to as Savitr (2.30).

Indra Kills Vritra

He was the slayer of Vritra, the chief of dragons or serpents (*ahi*), who was obstructing the waters. When Indra struck Vritra with his vajra, heaven and earth trembled, and streams of water were released. References to him releasing the waters are frequent. He then used his bolt to dig out channels for the waters to flow in, and they reached the sea. One passage connects him with ninety rivers (1.80). The imagery of cows is often used in Indra's release of the waters, and it is thought they may represent rain clouds. Indra is called Vritrahan, killer of Vritra, at least seventy times. The Shatapatha Brahmana (1.6.4) identifies Indra with Surya, and Vritra with the moon.

Another possibility is that Vritra actually represents some natural obstruction, which had temporarily blocked the flow of one or more rivers. This could have been caused by tectonic change.

Indra's location and association with natural forces

Mountains (*parvata, giri*) are frequently referred to in connection with Indra. Indra defeats enemies or demons from the mountains (1.130) or shoots his arrows from the mountains (8.66). He has also opened the rock (*adri*) to release the cows.

Other Aspects of Indra

He defeats other minor demons, including Urana who has ninety-nine arms, Vishvarupa who has three heads and six eyes, and Arbuda.

Indra is also known as Purandara or 'breaker of forts'. He was the friend and defender of his worshippers, and was invoked in battles. He helped the *aryas* who worshipped him and defeated their enemies. He destroyed the forts of the *dasas*. He made the *dasyus* subject to the aryas (6.18) and gave land to the aryas (4.16). He deflected dasyu weapons from the aryas in the land of the seven rivers (8.14). Agni, the Ashvins, and other devas are also protectors of the aryas. Indra helps and protects those who worship him, and is their friend and brother. He is once called Kaushika indicating he favoured the Kushika family. He provides his worshippers with wealth, cows, and horses. He is called *gopati*, 'lord of cows', and his battles are termed *gavishti*, 'desire for cows'. The Panis kept the cows in a cave far away beyond the river Rasa. Indra desiring the cows pierced Vala's unbroken ridge and defeated the Panis. There are other passages concerning Vala who confined the cows and was driven out by Indra, where the Panis are not mentioned. The Angirasas help Indra in defeating Vala and releasing the cows. Indra defeats dasas and dasyus, who may be both human enemies or demons. Shambara, son of Kulitara, was defeated for Divodasa Atithigva, father or ancestor of Sudas.

Among his many battles, Indra helped Sudas in his battle against the ten kings, brought Yadu and Turvasha across the rivers, and crushed twenty chiefs and their 60,099 warriors along with Sushravas.

One dialogue hymn concerns Indra, Indrani, and Vrishakapi; this has been variously interpreted but the German scholar Peter von Bradke sees it as a satire, in which Indra and Indrani represent a king and his wife. Another interesting hymn (8.80) recounts the story of Apala, a woman who finds Soma near a river, presses it with her teeth, and presents it to Indra, receiving a reward from him.

Though Indra was not so powerful later on, he was frequently mentioned in other texts, and there are numerous stories about him in the Mahabharata and Puranas. In later times, Indra became secondary to Brahma, Vishnu, and Shiva, and is one of the Dikapalas, the guardian of the eastern quarter. However, his worship as an independent deity continued to some extent. In the Zoroastrian Avesta, his name occurs twice as that of a demon but also as a deity, Verethraghna, the same as the Sanskrit Vritrahan, defeater of Vritra.

Indra is known by a number of different names. Maghavan is one of his names in the Vedas. In the Rig Veda, he is referred to in dual forms such as Indra-Agni, Indra-Ashva, Indra-Brahmanaspati, Indra-Parvata, Indra-Pushan, Indra-Ribhu-gana, Indra-Soma, Indra-Usha, Indra-Varuna, Indra-Vayu, Indra-Vishnu, and Indra-Brihaspati. Indra-Varuna are together called universal gods, who provide riches and fame. They drink Soma and defeat and kill Vritra. Indra-Agni drink Soma together and sit together at the time of the sacrifice. They too are the killers of Vritra, and destroyed ninety-nine forts of the dasas. Two hymns are dedicated to Indra-Brihaspati who are prayed to for wealth and prosperity. They, as well as the pairs Indra-Vayu and Indra-Vishnu, are invited to drink Soma and attend the sacrifice. Indra-Soma together destroy all enemies and fill the world with light. Indra-Pushan are praised together in one hymn.

Indra is one of the main deities in the Sama Veda.

INDRANI

The wife of Indra, she is mentioned in the Rig Veda and the Brahmanas. In the Puranas, she is the daughter of Puloman and the mother of Jayanta and Jayanti. She is also known as Shachi, Pulomaja, Shakrani, Mahendrani, and Paulomi.

INDU

A name sometimes applied to Soma. It can be translated as 'drop' or 'moon'.

KA

A Sanskrit word, which means 'who?', and came to mean a deity, particularly Prajapati. A hymn in the Rig Veda (10.121) poses the question: which god (Ka) should be adored? It begins:

> In the beginning rose Hiranyagarbha, born only lord of all created beings. He fixed and holdeth up this earth and heaven. What god shall we adore with our oblation?
> Giver of vital breath, of power and vigour, he whose commandments all the gods acknowledge: The lord of death, whose shade is life immortal. What god shall we adore with our oblation?
>
> (Translated by R.T.H. Griffith)

Each verse ends with this question until, at the end of the hymn, it provides the answer: 'Prajapati! Thou only comprehend all these created things, and none beside thee.' In the Later Vedic Samhitas and Brahmanas, Ka is used both as a name of Prajapati and a name in itself, that of the supreme deity. In the Puranas, it is a name of the god Vishnu.

KALA (KAALA)

A Sanskrit term for 'time'. In the Atharva Veda, Kala or time is said to be the 'first god' and the creator of heaven and earth. Kala is also time, which destroys all things, and later the god Shiva as the destroyer as well as Yama as the god of death are associated with Kala. Other gods too are sometimes referred to as Kala. The concept of Kala was extensively analysed in various schools of philosophy including Nyaya, Vaisheshika, Samkhya, and Vedanta. The idea of it as the creator and first god can be compared to the concept of Zurvan in later Zoroastrianism.

KAMA

The god of love. The term, originally meaning 'desire', is mentioned in the Rig Veda but is first clearly recognized as a deity in the Atharva Veda. A verse in this text states that Kama is a supreme deity, unequalled by gods, *pitris* (ancestors) or men. Kama is believed to fulfil all desires and is also identified with Agni, the god of fire. In the Taittiriya Brahmana, he is said to be the son of Dharma Deva, by his wife Shraddha. There are more accounts of him in later texts as well as numerous myths and legends. In these texts, Kama is known by several names and is, at the same time, a name of other deities, including Shiva and Vishnu.

KSHETRASYAPATI

A protector deity of the fields, first mentioned in the Rig Veda. The Grihya Sutras state that he should be worshipped before ploughing a field.

KUHU

A goddess, who represents the new moon. She is mentioned in the later Samhitas and Brahmanas.

KUNAMNAMA

A female deity, she is mentioned in one Rig Vedic hymn (10.136). However, several translators do not see this as a name.

MADHUKASHA

In the Atharva Veda (9.1), Madhukasha is the mother of the Adityas. She is golden coloured and the daughter of the Vasus.

MAHI

A goddess in the Rig Veda, she is mentioned in the Apri hymns, usually along with Sarasvati and Bharati.

MANU

A term referring to the first, or archetypal, man. In the Rig Veda, the term is used both for 'man' and as a proper name. Manu is said to be a father and the creator of the sacrifice. Both Manu Vivasvat and Manu Samvarani are mentioned in the late Valakhilya hymns. Manu Vivasvat is also mentioned in the Atharva Veda. In later texts, Manu is the name or title of fourteen mystical rulers of the earth. Of them Samvarani or Savarni is the eighth and Manu Vaivasvata, son of Vivasvat, is the seventh, and the current ruler of the earth. Manu is said to be the first of men living on the earth. The Shatapatha Brahmana has a story of a flood in which Manu is saved in a ship drawn by *matsya*, a fish. This story is probably known at the time of the Atharva Veda, as it is suggested in one passage (19.39). In later texts, Matsya is an incarnation of the god Vishnu. According to Hindu myths and cosmological stories in the Puranas and other texts, Brahma, creator of the world, also has a beginning and an end. One lifetime of his is known as a *mahakalpa*, at the end of which there is a *mahapralaya*, or 'great deluge'. One day of his is known as a *kalpa*, and consists of fourteen *manvantaras*, each presided over by a Manu.

MANYU

A deity, he is the personification of anger, and is mentioned in the Rig Veda and praised in two hymns. He glows like fire, protects his worshippers, and defeats their enemies. He also grants wealth and is said to be united with *tapas*, 'ascetic fervour', which gives him great power. Manyu is mentioned in later texts as the name of an Agni or fire.

MARTANDA

A deity, a name of Surya, or the sun god. Martanda is one of the eight Adityas in the Rig Veda.

MARUTS

A group of deities prominent in the Rig Veda. Thirty-three hymns are dedicated to them in addition to nine along with another deity. According to this text, they were the sons of Rudra, associated with thunder, lightning, and rain. They formed a *gana* or group, and their number was said to be three times seven, or three times sixty. They were closely connected with the goddess Rodasi, and were probably married to her. They are also mentioned with the goddesses Indrani and Sarasvati. They wore spears on their shoulders, anklets on their feet, golden ornaments on their breasts, and golden helmets on their heads. They rode across the sky in golden chariots, drawn by horses with golden feet, as swift as thought. They were invoked not only for rain but also to bring healing remedies from seas, mountains, and rivers. They were called singers and were associated with the god Indra. They were helpers of Indra but, at times, seem to have been in conflict with him. They were self-luminous, shining and brilliant, of the same age, and born at the same place. In the Vedas, they seem to be primarily storm gods but later represent winds. Some scholars see the Maruts as personifications of souls of the dead, but there is no evidence of this in the Rig Veda. Marut-Agni is a joint deity in some hymns, whereas Indra is referred to as Marutvan. The Maruts are also mentioned in the Ramayana, Puranas, and other texts. According to a Puranic story, they consisted of forty-nine gods, the sons of Kashyapa and Diti. In later accounts, these forty-nine Maruts are divided into seven ganas or groups of seven deities each.

MATALI

Matali is mentioned in the Rig Veda and is said to have been 'made strong by the Kavyas' (10.14.3). He could have been a semi-divine being. Later, he was the charioteer of the god Indra. According to the Mahabharata, Matali took Arjuna to Indra's heaven in his chariot. In the Ramayana, he carried Rama in it for his fight with Ravana.

MATARISHVAN

A deity mentioned in the Rig Veda, who is sometimes equated with Agni. There is no separate hymn to him in the Rig Veda but he is mentioned twenty-seven times. He seems to have been a personification of Agni. In some passages, he is connected with the Bhrigus. In the Atharva Veda, Matarishvan is connected both with Agni and with Vayu, and Yaska feels it is another name of Vayu.

MITRA

A deity associated with the god Varuna, usually referred to along with him as Mitra-Varuna. In the Rig Veda, there is only one hymn, which is to him alone (3.59). Here he is said to 'bring men together uttering his voice', and the same phrase occurs in other hymns as well. Some hymns state that he supports heaven and earth and sustains all gods. In the Atharva Veda, in two hymns, Mitra is connected with the morning and sunrise, and Varuna with evening and darkness. In the later Brahmanas, he is considered a god of the daytime. Mitra is referred to in the Yajur Veda (Taittiriya Samhita and other texts), where he is to be offered a white victim, and Varuna a dark one. In the

Mahabharata and Puranas, he is one of the Adityas. Mitra is similar to the Zoroastrian Mithra, god of light and sun, guardian of friendship and faithfulness, who developed into the deity of a major cult in the Roman empire. In the Mahabharata, Mitra also appears as a name of the god Shiva.

MITRA-VARUNA

Twenty-three hymns, and parts of several others, are dedicated to the two deities together. In their dual form, they are said to be young, shining, and bright.

NARASHAMSA

A deity in the Rig Veda, he is associated with Agni and occasionally with Pushan. He is also considered a form of Agni, and Agni is said to be Narashamsa when he is born. The Naighantuka takes him as a separate deity.

NIRRITI

A deity first mentioned in the Rig Veda, where his name occurs twelve times, sometimes in association with Yama, god of death. He is recognized there as a god of death or destruction. Later, he becomes one of the Dikapalas, the guardian of the south-west. He is also described as one of the eleven Rudras, and is said to be the son of Sthanu and grandson of Brahma. In later texts, Nirriti is also a female deity of destruction.

PARJANYA

A deity described in the Rig Veda, he has three hymns dedicated to him in this text. He is the god of rain clouds and sheds rain. He brings thunder and lightning, and is rich in clouds and water. His chariot is watery, and he nourishes vegetation. He is often called a bull, or a roaring bull. More important rain gods in the Vedas are the Maruts and Indra. Parjanya is associated with Vata and is sometimes considered a name of Indra. The Atharva Veda (4.15) has a hymn to him, where some Rig Vedic verses are repeated. He is also referred to in other Atharva hymns. Parjanya is sometimes identified with Perkunas, the Lithuanian god of thunder. Later, Parjanya was a name of the god Vishnu, and of a Deva Gandharva.

PRAJAPATI

A deity in the Vedas. In the Rig Veda, he is described in a hymn in the tenth or latest book, where he is praised as the creator of heaven and earth, of the waters and of all that lives, of the one god above all other gods. He is prayed to for children (*praja*). In the Vajasaneyi Samhita, Atharva Veda, and Brahmanas, he is often called the chief god, or father of the gods, the creator of the devas and asuras, and the first sacrificer. He is also known as Ka or 'who', as the verse praising him in the Rig Veda uses this pronoun to ask who the greatest god is.

The Maitrayani Samhita (4.2) states that he loved his daughter Usha, and when he approached her, she turned herself into a gazelle. He then became a male gazelle, but the god Rudra threatened to shoot an arrow at him. Prajapati then offered to make Rudra the lord of the beasts, if he refrained from shooting him.

Later, Brahma replaced Prajapati, and the two names became interchangeable. The gods Shiva and Vishnu and some other deities are sometimes called Prajapati in later literature.

PRISHNI

A goddess in the Rig Veda, where she is the mother of the Maruts. The term also refers to something that is speckled. In the context of the Maruts, it is thought to mean a speckled cloud.

PRITHIVI/PRITHVI

A deity, the goddess of the earth, she is described in the Rig Veda where she is usually mentioned along with Dyaus. One hymn is dedicated to her alone. She supports the mountains and forests, and scatters rain. She is said to be firm or steady, great (*mahi*), and shining. She is also the kind mother, to whom the dead man goes. Literally, Prithivi means 'one who is broad or wide', and this term reflects the extensive nature of the earth. Prithivi is described in the Yajur Veda. In the Atharva Veda, a hymn of sixty-three verses is dedicated to her. A few verses of this hymn are given below:

> Truth, high and potent Law, the consecrating Rite,
> Fervour, Brahma and Sacrifice uphold the Earth,
> May she, the queen of all that is and to be, may
> Prithivi make ample space and room for us. (1)
> O Prithivi, auspicious be thy woodlands, auspicious be thy hills and snow-clad mountains.
> Unslain, unwounded, unsubdued, I have set foot upon the Earth,
> On Earth, brown, black, ruddy and every-coloured, on the firm earth that Indra guards from danger. (11)
> Supporting both the foolish and the weighty, she bears the death both of the good and the evil.
> In friendly accord with the boar, Earth opens herself for the wild swine that roams the forest. (48)
>
> (Translated by R.T.H. Griffith)

In later texts, Prithivi is an alternative name for Bhudevi, a consort of Vishnu. In the Puranas, there are several stories about Prithivi as the earth. One narrates how she allowed King Prithu to milk her, and then seeds, vegetables, and various crops came into being. Another famous story is regarding the rescue of Prithivi by Vishnu in his form of Varaha.

PURAMDHI

A goddess whose name appears a few times in the Rig Veda, she is probably one who grants wealth and abundance. In a Zoroastrian Yasht, Parendi is a similar deity, believed to provide riches.

PURUSHA

A Sanskrit term, meaning 'man' or 'person'. In different contexts, it refers to the soul or to god. Purusha represents the eternal principle, the passive or fixed aspect of creation. It is the Truth that sets creation in motion. It is beyond form and shape, the subtle essence of creation. In the Rig Veda (10.90), Purusha represents the primeval person from whom creation emerged. This famous hymn states that Purusha pervades the earth and has 1000 heads, 1000 eyes and 1000 feet. Purusha is the past, present and future, and all creatures are a part of him. Viraj was born from him, and he again from her. Purusha was the sacrificial offering, and spring was the clarified butter, summer the fuel, and autumn the oblation. The four castes arose from him, as well as the sun and moon, Indra and Agni, the elements and space. Thus, here Purusha is similar to the concept of Brahman. The Brihadaranyaka Upanishad (1.4) states that Purusha was the first, but feeling lonely, he swelled his body and divided it into two parts, male and female. These united, and from them human beings and other creatures were born. Purusha as the creative principle is further described in later texts and in Samkhya philosophy, while Prakriti is the female principle.

PUSHAN/PUSHA

A deity in the Rig Veda, who later declined in importance. Pushan means one who makes something prosper, grow, and thrive. There are eight hymns dedicated to him in the Rig Veda while he is mentioned at least another one hundred and twenty times. He is also mentioned jointly with Indra and with Soma. He is described as the lord of all things, and the guardian of all. He has braided hair and a beard, and carries a golden spear along with an awl or a goad. His chariot is drawn by goats, and he eats gruel. He is referred to in the marriage hymn, and was married to Surya (Suryaa), daughter of the sun god, Surya. He is described as 'glowing' and leads the dead to the distant abode of the fathers. He has golden ships that move in the oceans of the air. He is a messenger of Surya and a helper of Savitr. He makes hidden things easy to find, and protects cattle and horses, and weaves and smoothens the wool of sheep. He is known as Pashupa, 'protector of animals', the only deity in the Vedas with this title. He is the guardian of roads and is prayed to for protection from all dangers on the way, including wolves. He is called *vimucho napat* or 'son of deliverance' and Vimochana, 'deliverer'. Pushan's goat is connected with the ashvamedha or horse sacrifice and leads the horse to the other world. He is referred to in the Atharva Veda (16.9, 18.2), where he guides the dead to the world of the gods. The Vajasaneyi Samhita refers to him as a guide (*prapathya*) on roads. In both Grihya and Shrauta Sutras, prayers are offered to him before the beginning of a journey. He is one of the Adityas, and is mentioned in the Mahabharata and Puranas. He is sometimes compared with the Greek god Pan, who is also associated with goats, and it is suggested that Pushan and Pan had a common origin. Pan, Roman Faunus, in turn, has been equated with the Celtic Cernunnos (also spelt Kernunnos), and the horned god of Wicca. In India, Naigamesha is a later goat-headed deity. It is interesting that the famous horned yogi depicted on a Harappan Civilization seal is similar to a later depiction of a horned deity often identified with Cernunnos.

RAKA

A goddess mentioned in the Rig Veda, she is associated with fertility and wealth. According to the Vishnu Purana, she is the presiding deity of the day of the full moon.

RATRI

A goddess of the night, but not of the dark night, she is the daughter of heaven and the goddess of the starlit night. Only one hymn in the Rig Veda is addressed to her. Ratri fills the valleys and heights, driving away the darkness with her light. Ratri is also mentioned in the Mahabharata.

RIBHUS/RIBHU-GANA

A group of semi-divine beings. Eleven hymns are dedicated to them in the Rig Veda and they are mentioned in that text at least one hundred times. There are three Ribhus, whose names are Ribhu or Ribhukshan, Vaja, and Vibhuvan. They are known as Saudhanvana (sons of Sudhanvan) and are helpers of Indra. They are also said to be descendants of Manu, with Agni as their brother. They have a 'sunlike appearance', and wear helmets and necklaces. They possess horses and are prayed to for prosperity. They made their old parents young again. They made prayer, sacrifice, and the two worlds. They went around the sky and, after wandering for a long time, reached the house of Savitr, who made them immortal. Then they went to the house of Agohya, and after sleeping for twelve days, they made fields and grass, caused the streams to flow in the right direction, and brought water into the lowlands. 'Twelve days' may actually mean twelve months, as another passage suggests they slept for one year, and then asked who awakened them. Some scholars think the twelve days refers to the time of the winter solstice, when the earth is dormant. Savitr or Agohya refers to the sun. According to some passages, they were originally men, but because of their skilful deeds became immortal. The Ribhus are also mentioned in the Mahabharata and later texts.

RODASI

A goddess mentioned in the Rig Veda, associated with the Maruts. As she is always mentioned with them, she is thought to have been their wife.

ROHITA

A god in the Atharva Veda, he is a creator deity. He is said to be the highest being, representing fire and the sun. The name means 'red' or 'reddish'.

RUDRA

A deity, usually regarded as a storm god, and an early form of the god Shiva. In the Rig Veda, three full hymns are dedicated to him. He is also invoked jointly with Soma in one hymn, and in part of another. His name appears seventy-five times in this text. Rudra is described as dazzling, shining like the sun or like gold, and wearing golden ornaments. His weapons include a thunderbolt, a lightning shaft, and bows and arrows. The Maruts are his sons, and he is sometimes identified with Agni. The Atharva Veda states that he is copper-coloured and red, with a blue neck and blue tufts. Rudra is called Mahadeva, a name of Shiva, in the Yajur Veda. This text has the Shri Rudram or Shata-Rudriya (Vajasaneyi Samhita, Chapter 16; Taittiriya Samhita 4.5, 4.7), believed to be one of the most powerful Vedic chants used in the worship of Shiva. The chant has two parts, known as Namakam and Chamakam, which have been put together, each divided into eleven *anuvakas* (sections). According to this, he dwells in mountains and is clothed in skin. He is young, fierce, strong, unassailable, and wise, and though benevolent, his anger is to be feared. He has a fierce and formidable nature, but is also a healer. Rudra was accepted as a name of the god Shiva and usually represents the fierce or destructive aspect of Shiva. Some have interpreted the Shri Rudram as referring to Vishnu or to a universal deity.

SADHYAS OR SADHYA-GANA

A class of semi-divine beings, in the Rig Veda, they are called the 'gods of old' and in the Taittiriya Samhita are said to have existed before creation. According to the Puranas, they are the sons of Dharma and Sadhya, who was a daughter of Daksha. They were associated with the ashvamedha sacrifice, and with the Pushyasnana, the sacred bath before the annual consecration ceremony of a king. Seventeen Sadhyas are listed in some Puranas. Sadhyas are frequently mentioned in the Mahabharata. They are said to rule the creatures through the virtue of yoga.

SARAMA

In the Rig Veda, she is the dog and messenger of the god Indra. She was the mother of the Sarameya, who accompanied the god Yama. In the Bhagavata Purana, Sarama is one of the daughters of Daksha, from whom all wild animals were descended.

SARAMEYA

Two watchdogs of the god Yama, the god of the dead, the Sarameya had four eyes each and their names were Shabala and Shyama. Their mother was Sarama, the dog of Indra. In several ancient religious myths, dogs are associated with the underworld and the dead. In Zoroastrianism, Yima, the counterpart of Yama, had four dogs. In the *Arda Viraf Namah*, a Zoroastrian text, Zerioug Goash is a dog who guards the Chinvat Bridge that connects this world with the other. In Greek myths, the dog Kerberos (Cerberus) guards the underworld and has three heads, a dragon's tail, and snakes on his back. His name is thought to be similar to Shabala. In Egyptian myths, Anubis, with a jackal or dog's head, was called the 'opener of the way' to the land of the dead.

SARANYU

A goddess mentioned in one hymn in the Rig Veda (10.17), where she is said to be the daughter of Tvashtr and wife of Vivasvat. The term is also an adjective meaning 'swift'.

SARASVAN OR SARASVAT

A male deity associated with Sarasvati in two Rig Vedic hymns. In one hymn (7.96), there are three verses dedicated to Sarasvat, after those praising Sarasvati. He is prayed to by those who want children, wives, riches, and protection. In another passage (1.64), he is said to refresh worshippers with rain. His nature has been interpreted as a guardian of the celestial waters. He is sometimes considered the same as Apam Napat.

SARASVATI

A sacred river personified as a goddess, first mentioned in the Rig Veda as a great river flowing into the sea. In the Rig, there are three hymns in praise of the river, and several other verses.

She is the best of mothers, the best of rivers, and the best of goddesses. As Amba, 'mother', she gives renown to those who are unknown. She gave a son called Divodasa to Vadhryashva (6.61). She defeats enemies and protects her worshippers. She is connected with other deities including Pushan, Indra, the Maruts and the Ashvins, with the goddesses Ida and Bharati, and occasionally with Mahi and Hotra (Hotraa). Sarasvat is a male deity associated with Sarasvati in two Rig Vedic hymns. In the Brahmanas, Sarasvati is identified with Vach, goddess of speech, and later becomes a great goddess of wisdom.

SAVITR

A solar deity to whom eleven hymns are dedicated in the Rig Veda. In addition, there are over one hundred and fifty other references to him. Almost everything about Savitr is golden. He is said to be golden-eyed, golden-tongued, and has golden hands and arms. He drives in a golden car, which has a golden pole, and is drawn by radiant horses (in one passage, brown, white-footed horses). Golden in colour, he is said to light up the air, heaven, and earth. It is easy to travel on his ancient pathways. Savitr provides immortality to the devas and is said to have made the Ribhus immortal. He is prayed to take the spirit of the dead to the place where the righteous live. His light constantly shines in the east, and he protects people from evil spirits and bad dreams. Savitr is among those termed an asura, here meaning a great deity. He follows the laws of the universe, and even the wind and waters move according to his orders. He is praised by various gods including the Vasus, Aditi, Varuna, Mitra, and Aryaman. Other gods, including Indra, have to follow his will. He is associated with Prajapati, Pushan, Mitra, and Bhaga, and sometimes seems identical with Surya, but in other passages is distinctly different. He stimulates or arouses all that lives, protects worshippers, and bestows immortality. Some scholars feel that Savitr in the Rig Veda reflects the divine power of the sun in a personified form, while Surya represents the sun in a more concrete way. The sacred Gayatri Mantra is recited to this deity. In the Mahabharata, Savitr is one of the twelve Adityas, often identified with Vivasvat. Savitr is later a name of the god Shiva and of Vishnu. Savitr is also referred to as Savita.

SHACHI PAULOMI

A name of Indrani (see above), the wife of Indra.

SHRADDHA

A goddess, whose name means 'faith'. She was personified as a deity in the Rig Veda, where one hymn (10.151) is dedicated to her. Through her, the sacred fire burns and the offering of ghi is made. The deity also grants wealth to her worshippers. In the Brahmanas, she is said to be a daughter of the sun god, Surya, or of Prajapati. In the Mahabharata, she is said to be a daughter of Daksha and wife of Dharma, or a daughter of Vivasvat (Surya).

SHRI OR SHRIDEVI

A goddess, a name of Lakshmi, who was the consort of Vishnu. Literally, it means 'auspicious' or 'prosperous'. The name Shri occurs in the Rig Veda, while the Shatapatha Brahmana states that Shri emerged from Prajapati. There are several references to Shri in the Mahabharata, and in later texts.

SINDHU

A river identified with the Indus, who is also considered a goddess. In the Rig Veda, hymn 10.75 is mainly in praise of the Sindhu, though it also lists a number of other rivers. Another hymn (3.33) is dedicated to the Vipash and Shutudri, tributaries of the Sindhu. There are several other references to the river.

SINIVALI

A goddess mentioned in the Rig Veda, she is prayed to for children and is said to be a sister of the gods. The Atharva Veda (8.46) says she is the wife of Vishnu. In the Brahmanas, she is a deity connected with the moon. Three other moon goddesses were Kuhu, Anumati, and Raka. They are connected with different phases of the moon and are all related to childbirth, fertility and, also in Vedic days, to cattle.

SITA

A goddess, she is later known as the wife of the god Rama. The story of Rama and Sita is first narrated in the Ramayana of Valmiki, a Sanskrit text of around the 1st century CE or earlier. However, Sita as a fertility deity and goddess of the earth existed even before Valmiki's Ramayana, and is mentioned in the Rig Veda. In hymn 4.57 to agricultural deities, Sita (furrow) is prayed to for blessings and good crops. In the Kaushika Sutra, she is the wife of Parjanya. In the Paraskara Grihya Sutra, she is the wife of Indra.

SKAMBHA

A deity praised in the Atharva Veda (10.7, 8), he is said to uphold or support the world. Some verses from 10.7 are given here to indicate the nature of Skambha.

7. *Who out of many, tell me, is that Skambha,*
   On whom Prajapati set up and firmly established all the worlds?
8. *That universe which Prajapati created, wearing all forms, the*
   highest, midmost, lowest,
   How far did Skambha penetrate within it? What portion did
   he leave unpenetrated?
9. *How far within the past has Skambha entered? How much of*
   him has reached into the future?
   That one part which he set in a thousand places, how far did
   Skambha penetrate within it?
10. *Who out of many, tell me, is that Skambha in whom men*
    recognize the Waters, Brahma,
    In whom they know the worlds and their enclosures, in whom
    are non-existence and existence?
11. *Declare that, Skambha, who is he of many,*
    In whom, exerting every power, Fervour maintains her loftiest
    vow;
    In whom are comprehended Law, Waters, Devotion and Belief
12. *Who out of many, tell me, is that Skambha*
    On whom as their foundation earth and firmament and sky are
    set;
    In whom as their appointed place rest Fire and Moon and Sun
    and Wind?
13. *Who out of many, tell me, is that Skambha*
    He in whose body are contained all three-and-thirty Deities?

(10.7)

SOMA

A deity, god of the moon, who originated in the Rig Veda, where he also represented a divine drink, made from the Soma plant.

In the Rig Veda, Soma is one of the most important deities. All the 114 hymns of the ninth book are dedicated to him, both in his realistic form as a plant and as a deity. There are also six other hymns dedicated to him, and he is mentioned and praised in many more. On the basis of the number of times he is mentioned, he is the third-most important deity in the Rig Veda. The method of extracting juice from the plant is described in detail, as well as the nature of the juice, which is said to be the equivalent of *amrita*, the drink of immortality. The drink had an exhilarating and invigorating effect, as well as medicinal properties, and this led it to be considered divine. It is probably the same as the Avestan Haoma, from the Haoma plant. Soma is also the lord of the plants, or of the woods (Vanaspati). He is a king of the rivers and of the earth, and the father of the gods. Soma is also known as Indu.

One hymn (8.48) states: 'We have drunk Soma, we have become immortal, we have entered into light, we have known the gods.' Soma is called a wise rishi, who has 1000 eyes. He is the soul of Indra, and his auspicious friend, and sometimes even his vajra. Soma is also invoked jointly with other deities. Thus we have Indra-Soma, (discussed under Indra); Agni-Soma (under Agni), Soma-Pushan who together provide wealth and remove darkness, and Soma-Rudra who remove sickness and free their worshippers from sin.

As Soma sacrifices form an important part of Vedic ritual, Soma is frequently referred to in the Sama and Yajur Vedas. The method of pressing and straining it, and it being mixed with water and milk is described. Soma is pressed three times a day. (This can be linked to sacrificial rituals that take place in temples today). It can be mixed with milk (*gavashir*), sour milk (*dadhyashir*), or barley (*yavashir*).

Soma's abode is said to be heaven or the highest heaven, from where an eagle brought the Soma. In the Brahmanas, Gayatri brings the Soma. Soma is called a god, a king of rivers, a king of the whole earth, and of gods and people. The Soma plant has been variously identified, the most common identification being with *Ephedra*. Its identification has been discussed in Chapter 6.

In post-Vedic literature, Soma is the name of the moon. Some scholars feel Soma is connected with the moon even in the Rig Veda while others feel the identification is made only in later texts. Like the Soma plant, the moon is drunk by the gods, thus explaining the waning of the moon.

SUNRITA

A goddess, literally 'bounty', she is a minor deity in the Rig Veda, mentioned three times.

SURYA

A name for the sun as well as a deity, the sun god. There are ten hymns to Surya in the Rig Veda, mostly in mandalas 1 and 10, and references in many more. In some cases, Surya refers only to the sun, not to its personification as a deity. In the Rig Veda, it is said that Surya shines for the whole world, prolongs life, and drives away sickness, disease, and evil dreams. He is the face of Agni, or the eye of Mitra and Varuna. He is born of the gods, and the seven horses who draw his chariot represent the rays of the sun. He is a bird traversing space or a brilliant white steed. Sometimes his chariot is drawn by a single horse, called Etasha. He is the *asurya purohita* of the gods, that is, their special priest. He is a brilliant *ayudha* or weapon, and is also called a chakra or wheel, probably referring to the wheel of time. In the Atharva Veda, he is referred to as the 'lord of eyes' and the eye of created beings, which can see the whole world and beyond. In the Vedas,

Savitr, Pushan, Bhaga, Mitra, Vivasvat, and Aryaman are sometimes considered synonyms of Surya, though these were also individual deities. Surya is also known as Aditya, son of Aditi. His father is said to be Dyaus. Sometimes he is said to be born of the gods, who placed him in heaven, or to have come from the eye of Purusha. Various gods including Dhatr, and the pairs of Indra-Vishnu, Indra-Soma, and Indra-Varuna had a hand in his creation. In one passage (RV 10.62), the prayers of the Angirasas are said to have caused Surya to reach his position in the sky. In some passages in the Rig Veda, Indra is said to have defeated Surya.

In the Rig Veda, Surya is sometimes invoked with the moon as Suryamasa or Suryachandramasa. The term 'surya' is derived from the Sanskrit root *svar* and in the Avesta the sun is known as *hvare*, from the same root. Drawn by swift horses, it is the eye of Ahura Mazda. Sun gods and goddesses are worshipped in other ancient cultures, and the Hittite word for sun was *surias*.

In India, Surya continued to be worshipped after the Vedic period. In fact, a hymn in the Mahabharata begins with a description of the deity similar to that in the Vedas: 'You are the eye of the universe and the soul of all material creation.'

SURYAA

The daughter of the god Surya. Her marriage is referred to in a wedding hymn in Mandala 10 of the Rig Veda. In various other parts of the text, she is said to be married to Soma, the Ashvins, or Pushan.

TANU NAPAT

A deity who is associated with Agni—or alternatively, a name of Agni. The name, which appears eight times in the Rig Veda, is generally in the second verse of the Apri hymns, where Agni is invoked under different names. The Naighantuka sees him as a separate deity. Tanu Napat is said to distribute or disperse the benefits of the sacrifice.

TRITA APTYA

A deity in the Rig Veda, he has no separate hymn dedicated to him but is mentioned forty times in twenty-nine hymns. His name *aptya* signifies his connection with water. He is usually associated with Indra and also with Agni, the Maruts, and Soma. Along with Indra, he was involved in killing Vritra, Vala, Vishvarupa, and Arbuda. Trita is said to live in a secret, faraway place but, when born in a house, he comes as a youth surrounded by brightness. In one passage, he is said to be the centre of wisdom. The concept of him being a distant god is revealed in a passage where prayers are made to the Adityas and Usha to send evil dreams and actions to Trita Aptya. In one hymn he is said to have been deep in a well, and was rescued by Brihaspati; in another, he is in a pit (*vavre*) but comes out after praying to his father. In the Atharva Veda, Trita is mentioned as a god to whom dreams or guilt can be transferred. In the Taittiriya Samhita, he is said to grant a long life. His name signifies 'the third'.

In the Brahmanas, Trita was a rishi, the brother of Ekata (one) and Dvita (two). The Rig Vedic reference to him being in a well is elaborated on by Sayana who quotes a story where it is said that his brothers pushed him in, but he prayed to the gods and was rescued. Yaska, in his Nirukta, explains the term Trita, as 'one who has wisdom' and, in another passage, says that Trita is Indra in three abodes—heaven, earth, and air.

His counterpart in the Avesta is Thrita, the third man to prepare haoma (Soma) or Thraetona, who slew the serpent Azi Dahaka. In the Yashts, Thrita is called the son of Shayuzdri; in the Vendidad, he is stated to have received 10,000 healing plants, which grew near the white haoma plant, from Ahura Mazda. Trita has been considered a god of lightning, or of wind and water, or of the moon. Others feel he was a healer, who was later deified.

TRATR

A protector deity in the Rig Veda, and also a name of other deities including Indra and Agni. Roth felt the name referred to Savitr or Bhaga.

TVASHTR/TVASHTA

A Vedic deity whose nature is somewhat obscure. He has been considered a solar deity, a god of the year, or an abstract god. Most commonly he is considered the divine artisan. Though there is no entire hymn dedicated to him in the Rig Veda, his name occurs about fifty times.

Tvashtr is described as holding an axe. He gave all beings their form, fashioned the bolt of Indra, sharpened the axe of Brahmanaspati, and formed a new cup which held the food of the asura (here meaning a divine being). He is said to be agraja, or the first born, one who goes in front, and a companion of the Angirasas. His daughter was Saranyu, wife of Vivasvat, from whom Yama and Yami, as well as the Ashvins, were born. Tvashtr also had a son, Vishvarupa, who was attacked by Indra. The Vajasaneyi Samhita states he is a universal father, who made the whole world. In the Atharva Veda, he is described as an old man, carrying a bowl of Soma. The Shatapatha Brahmana states that he produced and nourishes a great variety of creatures. In the Puranas, he is identified with Vishvakarma, and sometimes with Prajapati.

In the Mahabharata he is one of the Adityas and was the creator or father of Vritra. In later texts, Tvashtr is a name of various deities including Surya, Shiva, and Vishnu. He is thought to belong to an earlier group of gods along with Trita and others, or to be different from the other Vedic deities.

USHA/USHAS

A deity mentioned in the Rig Veda, she is the goddess of the dawn. Forty hymns in the Rig Veda are dedicated to her, and she is mentioned over three hundred times.

In the Vedic hymns, Usha is said to be shining and bright, ancient yet young, as she is born again and again. She is the one who drives away the darkness and awakens all life. Clothed in light, she appears in the east. She chases away evil dreams and evil spirits. At the same time, she reveals the hidden treasures of the dark. Her chariot radiates light and is drawn by reddish horses, or by bulls or cows. These are thought to represent the rays of the morning sun, or the red clouds at morning. In one passage, she is said to arrive in 100 chariots, reflecting the way the dawn lights the sky with hundreds of rays. Her radiant rays are like herds of cattle, hence she is called the mother of cattle. She awakens the devout worshippers, leaving others to sleep. She herself was first awakened by the Vasishthas. She travels thirty yojanas in a day. She is closely associated with Savitr and Surya, and is the sister of Bhaga, an Aditya. She is mentioned together with Ratri as Ushasanakta (Usha + Ratri) and is her sister. She is associated with Agni, and related to Varuna. Soma, Agni, and Brihaspati are among those mentioned as being responsible for the birth or discovery of Usha. The Naighantuka provides sixteen descriptive names of Usha, and she is known by several more. The term *ushas* comes from the root *vas*, to shine, and is related to the Greek goddess Eos, the Roman Aurora, and perhaps the Germanic Ostara or Austron, Baltic Ausra, and Lithuanian Ausrine. In PIE, the name has been reconstructed as Hewsos or Hausos, though other reconstructions are also suggested.

VACH/VAK

A goddess in the Rig Veda, later identified with Sarasvati, Vach is the personification of speech, through whom divine knowledge is communicated. One hymn (10.125) is dedicated to her, and she is mentioned in others. She is called the queen of the gods and is said to accompany other deities. She is also associated with water. In the Naighuntaka, she is referred to as *madhyamika-vach*, or the 'voice or sound of the middle region'. In the Taittiriya Brahmana, she is the wife of Indra and the mother of the Vedas, while in the Shatapatha Brahmana and Kathaka Upanishad, she is associated with Prajapati. In the Mahabharata and most of the Puranas, Vach is identified with Sarasvati. However, according to the Padma Purana, Vach was one of the daughters of Daksha, and a wife of Kashyapa.

VARUNA

A deity, he is usually mentioned along with Mitra in the Rig Veda. Only twelve hymns are exclusively dedicated to Varuna in this text, and twenty-four to Varuna-Mitra. Varuna was a moral and ethical deity. His face is similar to Agni; his eye through which he observes the world is like Surya, the sun.

He has 1000 eyes and can see far into the distance. His chariot, drawn by horses, shines like the sun. Both Mitra and Varuna lived in a golden residence in the highest heaven. Varuna was omniscient—he knew the flight of the birds, the path of ships, the course of the wind, and all the secrets of the world. A highly ethical god, he punished those who broke his laws, which were fixed or permanent. Like the other great gods, he too was known as an asura, a word which in early days meant a divine being. He is important even in the Atharva Veda where a hymn (4.16) dedicated to him says that the god knows all secrets, and there is nothing in heaven and earth unknown to him. One verse states:

Whatever exists in heaven and earth,
Whatever beyond the skies,
Before the eyes of Varuna, the king,
Unfolded lies.

(4.16.5)

The Shatapatha Brahmana (11.6.1) says that Varuna sits in the middle of heaven and is the lord of the universe. His nature and character have led scholars to see him as similar to Ahura Mazda, the name of God of Zoroastrianism (asura is paralleled by ahura in Persian) though there is no similarity in the name, and the concept too is somewhat different. He has also been compared with Semitic concepts of god.

In post-Vedic times, though there are numerous stories about Varuna, he was a more minor deity, the lord of the waters and guardian of the western quarter.

VARUNANI/VARUNI

A goddess in the Rig Veda, she is the wife of Varuna.

VASTOSHPATI

A deity who is the protector of the house. In the Rig Veda, one hymn is dedicated to the deity, who is mentioned seven times more. He is prayed to for protection, blessings, prosperity, and freedom from disease. His name means 'Lord of the dwelling' and, according to the Grihya Sutras, he should be propitiated before entering a new house. There are also prayers to him in the Atharva Veda.

VASUS

A group of gods mentioned in the Rig Veda, though their number is not given here. Later, Agni is said to be their leader. The Taittiriya Samhita states that they numbered 333 but, in the Brahmanas, they are said to be eight. In most later texts too, they are said to be eight, and to represent aspects of nature.

VATA

In the Rig Veda, a name of the wind god, Vayu. *Vata* literally means 'wind' or 'air'. The name Vata is sometimes thought to come from the same root as that of the Germanic god, Odin.

VAYU

The god of the wind, first mentioned in the Rig Veda, where he is also known as Vata. Here, Vayu seems to be the personified form of Vata, the wind. Vayu has one hymn solely dedicated to him, and six jointly with Indra. In addition he is invoked in parts of other hymns. Vata has two separate hymns to him, and is sometimes mentioned with Vayu. His chariot is said to have a golden seat, touches the sky, and is drawn by reddish horses. As Vata, he is the breath of the gods, goes where he likes, and cannot be seen. He is a healer, who can prolong life. Vayu bestows fame and wealth on his worshippers, disperses or scatters their enemies, and protects the weak. In the Mahabharata, Vayu is the father of Bhima, the second Pandava brother. In the Ramayana, he is known as the father of Hanuman. In the Puranas, he is one of the Dikapalas, the guardian of the north-west.

VENA

A deity mentioned in both the Rig Veda and the Atharva Veda. In the Atharva, Vena is part of a hymn on creation that begins: *'Eastward first the prayer was generated: Vena disclosed bright flashes from the summit . . .'* (4.1)

VIDHATR

A Sanskrit word, meaning 'the creator'. In the Rig Veda, it is both an independent deity, and a name of Dhatr, Indra, and Vishvakarma. In later texts, it is a name of various deities, including of Brahma and Vishnu.

VIRAJ

A Sanskrit term that indicates sovereignty, excellence or splendour. Viraj is often personified as a secondary creator, or is associated with creation. Viraj can be either male or female. According to the Rig Veda (10.90.5) Viraj is born from Purusha, and Purusha in turn from Viraj. In the Atharva Veda, Viraj is a female, identified with a cow, or with Prana, the life breath. In the Mahabharata, Viraj is the name of the primeval being, Purusha, and is at times identified with Shiva or with Vishnu.

The Manu Smriti (1.32) states that Brahma divided his body into two, one male and one female, and from the female, Viraj was born. Viraj then produced Manu Svayambhuva, who in turn created the ten Prajapatis.

VISHNU

Later one of the most important deities, Vishnu has five hymns dedicated to him in the Rig Veda, and is mentioned around one hundred times. His three strides or steps are frequently referred to and he is said to be young, with an immense body. Two of his steps could be seen by men, that is, they were on the earth, but with the third he went beyond the world of mortals, or into the region where birds fly. His third name is in heaven, and his highest step is like an eye in heaven. Agni, in this highest point of Vishnu, guards the cows. Here, where Indra and Vishnu live, there are swiftly moving cows with many horns. Both these references to cows are thought to imply clouds. Vishnu guards and lives near the highest place of his third step, and all beings live in his three steps. Vishnu's three steps are thought to refer to the course of the sun. Aurnabhava, Yaska's predecessor mentioned in the *Nirukta*, says it is the rising, traversing, and setting sun, while Shakapuni, another of Yaska's predecessors, says Vishnu represents a solar deity, moving through the three parts of the universe. Vishnu sets in motion his ninety steeds (days) with four names (seasons), like a revolving wheel (*chakra*). This probably refers to the solar year of 360 days. In the Atharva Veda, Vishnu's head becomes the sun. In the Rig Veda, Vishnu is said to live on the mountain (*girikshit, girishtha*). In another passage, Vishnu and Indra are together called the two who cannot be deceived, who stand on the peak (*sanuni*) of the mountains 'as it were with an unerring steed'. In the Taittiriya Samhita, Vishnu takes on the dwarf form, to redeem the earth from the asuras. This also occurs in the Taittiriya Brahmana and the Shatapatha Brahmana. In the Rig Veda, Indra and Vishnu are often referred to together and, in some hymns, Vishnu helps Indra in his fight against Vritra. Vishnu and Indra together conquered the dasa, destroyed the ninety-nine forts of Shambara, and defeated Varchin. Indra drinks the Soma pressed by Vishnu in three cups. In one passage (6.17), Vishnu cooks 100 buffaloes for Indra, referred to elsewhere as well. In other passages, Vishnu carries away 100 buffaloes and a milk mixture belonging to the boar (*emusham*); Indra shoots across the mountain and kills the boar. In a hymn (8.15), Vishnu, Mitra, Varuna, and the Maruts praise Indra with their songs. Vishnu is also associated with the Maruts. In the Brahmanas, Vishnu is often identified with the sacrifice. The myths of Vishnu's three steps and of his killing the boar were further developed in the Brahmanas, before they reached their final form in the epics and Puranas. The Brahmanas also narrate the story of Manu and the flood, but here the fish is an incarnation of Prajapati. Prajapati is also referred to as a tortoise. These stories formed the base of two of the later incarnations of Vishnu.

In the Avesta ritual, the Amshaspands (Amesha Spentas) also take three steps from earth to heaven.

VISHVAKARMA/VISHVAKARMAN

The divine architect. In the Rig Veda, there are two hymns in his praise (10.81, 82) as well as a few other references. He is considered an all-seeing god, four-faced and four-armed, the creator of heaven and earth. He is the lord of speech (*vachaspati*) and gives other gods their names. He is also referred to as *dhatr* and *vidhatr*, 'establisher' and 'disposer'. In the Brahmanas, he is identified with Prajapati. In post-Vedic times, he is considered both the architect of the universe and the artificer of the gods. He also made their weapons and chariots.

VISHVEDEVA/VISHVADEVAS

A class of semi-divine beings. In the Vedas they are said to be preservers of men and bestowers of rewards. Forty hymns are dedicated to the Vishvedevas in the Rig Veda, which are meant to refer to all the gods together. Sometimes they are mentioned as a separate group in the Vedas. In the Mahabharata, they are a distinctive group of sixty-four Vishvedevas, whose names are listed.

VIVASVAT/VIVASVAN

In the Rig Veda, Vivasvat does not have a hymn specially dedicated to him but is referred to at least thirty times. He is the father of the Ashvins and of the god Yama. Manu is referred to as Vivasvat, indicating he too is the son of Vivasvat, as in later texts. In the Atharva Veda and Shatapatha Brahmana, he is called Manu Vaivasvata. The Rig Veda states the gods were born from Vivasvat, and the Taittiriya Samhita says that people were descended from Vivasvan Adityah. Indra and Soma are closely connected with Vivasvat, and he is often mentioned in Mandala 9 in connection with Soma. Vivasvat is a god of light or of the rising sun. Vivasvat's wife is Saranyu. In both the Rig and the Atharva, the Adityas pray that Vivasvat's arrow should not kill them before they become old. In the Atharva, Vivasvat protects people from Yama. In the Yajur texts and in the Brahmanas, he is known as an Aditya. In later texts, Vivasvan is a name of the sun, similar to the Iranian Vivanhvant, father of Yima. Some scholars feel that in the Vedas he cannot be considered a deity, only the ancestor of human beings. He is included in the list of the 108 names of Surya in the Mahabharata. In the Bhagavad Gita, Krishna says, 'I revealed this Yoga to Vivasvat'.

YAMA

A deity, the god of the dead. According to the Vedas, the spirits of those who died went to his abode. He was the son of Vivasvat or Vivasvan, and had a twin sister named Yami or Yamuna. In some passages, it is said that all people were descended from them. Another hymn (10.14) states that Yama was the first of men who died and the first to find his way to the other world, so that others could later follow his path. This funeral hymn also connects Yama with the Angirasas. It asks the dead man to proceed to the house of Yama, past the two four-eyed dogs, the Sarameyas. The hymn also states that the dead man takes on a new and glorious body. An offering of Soma is made to the deity. In the Mahabharata, he was the son of the god Surya by Samjana, and the brother of Vaivasvata, the seventh and present Manu. By this time Yama became known as the judge of the dead. In later texts, he is the guardian or Dikapala of the southern quarter and is therefore named Dakshinapati. In Zoroastrianism, his counterpart is Yima.

YAMI

The twin sister of the god Yama, she is mentioned in the Rig Veda. In later texts, she was also known as Yamuna and was a personification of the river Yamuna. In the Rig Veda, there is a dialogue between her and her brother Yama in which she asks him to unite with her and says that she loves him. Yama however refuses and says that such an action would not be correct (see Chapter 7).

OTHER DIVINE BEINGS

APSARAS

Apsaras or divine nymphs, who are frequently mentioned in later literature, are not prominent in the Rig Veda, where there are very few references to them. An apsara, living in the highest heaven, is said to smile at her beloved (a gandharva). Vasishtha is said to be born from an apsara, and to sit close to them. Another passage states that apsaras of the sea flow to Soma. One hymn (10.136) describes a long-haired ascetic, whose powers included being able to move on the path of apsaras and gandharvas. A wife of a gandharva, referred to as Apyayosha, or 'nymph of the waters', is probably also a reference to the apsaras. Thus, in the earliest text, the apsaras are associated with water. In the Rig Veda, the apsara Urvashi is the mother of Vasishtha. The most famous story regarding Urvashi is her relationship with Pururavas. This is first narrated in the Rig (10.95) and later elaborated on in several texts. The Rig Veda hymn is a dialogue between the two. Urvashi has spent four autumns with the human Pururavas, son of Ila. After she goes back to her heavenly abode, Pururavas asks her to return but, in the Rig Veda this does not seem to happen, though Pururavas is promised bliss in heaven.

In the Atharva Veda apsaras are associated with water, rivers, and with trees. They live in the *nyagrodha* (banyan), *ashvattha* (pipal), and in the *udumbara* and *plaksha* (other fig trees). Some names of apsaras are mentioned, which are the same as those of herbs or plants. These include Gugguli and Naladi. Among other apsaras mentioned in the Atharva Veda are Ugrajit, Ugrampashya, and Rashtrabhrit. The Vajasaneyi Samhita refers to Urvashi and Menaka. The Atharva says apsaras bring luck to the dice player but they can also negatively affect the mind, hence sometimes they are feared. Apsaras are said to be very beautiful. According to the Shatapatha Brahmana, they could assume any form they liked, and frequently appeared as aquatic birds. In post-Vedic texts, both apsaras and gandharvas also live in mountains. The Mahabharata states that warriors who died in battle were transported by the apsaras, in brightly coloured chariots, to Indra's heaven. A similar legend occurs regarding the Valkyries. There are various later accounts of the origin of apsaras. Later texts indicate there were thousands or even millions of apsaras.

GANDHARVAS

The Rig Veda refers to gandharva mainly in the singular, an apsara being his wife. The term appears twenty times, and only three times in the plural. He was a deity like the sun, who generated rain. He knew the secrets of heaven and the divine truths. In this text, gandharvas are associated with water but there is no indication of their later association with music and dance. The Rig Veda does not have a clear description of them though it says they are wind-haired and wear *surabhi* (fragrant clothes). In the Atharva Veda, they are mentioned thirty-two times, half in the plural. In the Atharva and Taittiriya Samhita, gandharvas are referred to in a group. The Atharva says they numbered 6333. Gandharva is said to guard Soma in the celestial sphere. In the Rig, the gandharva is said to live in the region of the sky or air. In the Atharva, he is said to live in heaven. In the Rig, he is also connected with light, the sun, and a golden-winged bird who is called the messenger of Varuna. In the Vajasaneyi Samhita, he is connected with the *nakshatras* and, in the Atharva, particularly with Rohini. In Mandala 9 of the Rig Veda, he is associated with Soma. He guards Soma and protects the devas. The Maitrayani Samhita says the gandharvas preserved the Soma for the devas but then it was stolen, and therefore they were later excluded from drinking it. In the Taittiriya Samhita, Soma is requested to take the form of an eagle and evade the gandharva Vishvavasu. The Yajur texts and the Aitareya Brahmana say that Soma was bought from the Gandharvas in exchange for the goddess Vach. In the Avesta (Yasht 5.38), the Ganderewa, who lives in the sea Vourukasha where white Haoma is found, was defeated by Kereshaspa. In the Rig Veda (4.27), Krishanu, an archer, shoots at the eagle that carries off Soma. In the Taittiriya Aranyaka, Krishanu is said to be a gandharva. The Atharva says they are shaggy, with half animal forms, and the *gandha* (smell) of the earth rises to them.

There is no conclusion on the early nature of the gandharvas. In the Mahabharata, they seem to be a people living in hilly and forested areas, though they are also described as celestial beings. The Puranas and other texts state that they lived in the sky or atmosphere, and prepared Soma for the gods. Their food is the scent of fragrant herbs, and the smell of water, and they wear sweet-smelling clothes. They love women, are very handsome, and are divine singers, dancers, and musicians.

ASURAS

Originally a divine being, the word later came to mean a demon. In the Rig Veda, several deities are referred to as asura, including Agni, Brihaspati, Dyaus, Pushan, Savitr, and Varuna but by the Later Vedic period, asuras were at war with the devas (gods). They were supernatural beings with considerable powers, which the devas recognized. In some texts, devas and asuras are not actual beings but represent different aspects of a person. In the Brihadaranyaka Upanishad the asuras and devas are usually said to be in conflict, though they both originated from Prajapati. In later texts, there are mixed references to asuras.

At times, the devas temporarily entered into a pact with them, as when churning the ocean of milk for *amrita* or divine nectar. In the Mahabharata, the Asura Maya was a great architect and was well respected. He built a magnificent palace for the Pandavas at Indraprastha. Shukracharya, the guru of the asuras was extremely learned, and is mentioned with respect in several texts.

Some Puranas state that the asuras ruled the earth for ten yugas, after which it was returned to the devas. The terms daitya and danava are used as synonyms for asuras. They were two different categories of asuras but are often used interchangeably. Asuras have also been seen as a historical group.

DIVINE ANIMALS

Some animals are considered divine or are symbols of certain attributes or qualities. Cows, for instance, often symbolize clouds. Sarama and the Sarameyas are divine dogs. Horses or other animals such as deer, buffaloes, or asses—who draw the chariots of the gods—also have divinity. A few divine horses are described here.

Dadhikra

A divine horse, described in the Rig Veda, where there are four hymns in praise of him. He is swift, and speeds like the wind, flying through the air like a swooping eagle. He fights against thousands and wins. He was given by the gods Mitra and Varuna to the Purus. He is also known as Dadhikravan, and is associated with Usha, the dawn. He is said to be symbolic of knowledge, or the morning sun, or, alternatively, a real horse, who was deified.

Etasha

In the Rig Veda, the name of a divine horse of the sun god Surya.

Paidva

A mythical horse mentioned in the Rig Veda, which was given by the Ashvins to Pedu. The horse is described as white (*shveta*), praiseworthy, and to be invoked by men. He is powerful like Indra and a slayer of dragons or snakes (*ahihan*). Invincible in battles, he is a conqueror who seeks heaven. Paidva is thought to be either a real horse or symbolic of the sun.

Tarkshya

A divine horse in the Rig Veda, described in terms similar to Dadhikra. He is swift as a bird, and in later texts, is identified with Garuda, the eagle-vehicle of the god Vishnu. Tarkshya was later the name of a rishi.

COWS

In the extracts below, it is clear that references to cows are not always to them as animals. The term can also have an esoteric or symbolic meaning.

I

1. *Not men of magic skill, nor men of wisdom impair the gods' first steadfast ordinances.*
   Never may the earth and heaven which know not malice, nor the fixed hills, be bowed by sage devices.
2. *One, moving not away, supports six burdens; the cows proceed to him the true, the highest.*
   Near stand three mighty ones who travel swiftly; two are concealed from sight, one is apparent.
3. *The bull who wears all shapes, the triple-breasted, three-uddered, with a brood in many places,*
   Rules majestic with his triple aspect, the Bull, the everlasting ones' lord.

(Rig Veda 3.56)

II

1. *My thought with fine discernment has discovered the cow who wanders free without a herdsman,*
   Her who has straightaway poured me food in plenty: Indra and Agni therefore are her praisers.
2. *Indra and Pushan, deft of hand and mighty, well-pleased, have drained the heaven's exhaustless milk.*

(Rig Veda 3.57)

III

1. *The ancient's milch-cow yields the things we long for; the son of Dakshina travels between them.*
   She with the splendid chariot brings refulgence. The praise of Ushas has awoken the Ashwins.

(Rig Veda 3.58)

IV

One should meditate on the Vedas as a cow. Her four teats are the sounds svaha, vashat, hanta and svadha. The devas live on two of her teats, the sounds svaha and vashat; men on the sound hanta; the pitris on the sound svadha; the vital force (prana) is her bull (rishabha), and the mind her calf (vatsa).

(Brihadaranyaka Upanishad 5.8.1)

SOMA

Though there are concrete references to Soma as a plant, the term also refers to amrita, the divine nectar of immortality, and is used this way even in later texts.

In the Rig Veda, many passages indicate this sense, and not that of an intoxicating drink of the material world. Translations do vary but all versions also indicate the divine nature of Soma, different from that of a drink from a plant that grows in the high mountains or elsewhere. Common interpretations are that the ecstasies produced by Soma the drink led to it being worshipped as a deity. However, it seems more likely that Soma was a name of amrita, the mystical nectar of immortality. Amrita, as various myths and texts indicate, is the divine element in a person that is revealed when the layers of consciousness are purified. It is possible that Soma was a name given to an actual drink, only at a later date. At a still later stage, this was used in sacrificial ritual, and sacrifices became associated with Soma the drink instead of Soma the divine element. Here are some passages from Griffith's translation (spellings and punctuation slightly modified) that show that Soma is not just a drink.

I

1. *O Soma, flowing on thy way, win thou and conquer high renown; and make us better than we are.*
2. *Win thou the light, win heavenly light, and, Soma all felicities; and make us better than we are.*
3. *Win skilful strength and mental power, O Soma drive away our foes; and make us better than we are.*

(Rig Veda 9.4, verses 1–3)

II

7. *Aid us in holy rites; O Pavamana, drive away*
   Dark shades that must be met in fight.
8. *Give, Pavamana, high renown, give kine and steeds and hero sons;*
   Win for us wisdom, win the light.

(Rig Veda 9.9, verses 7–8)

III

1. *Like chariots that thunder on their way, like coursers eager for renown,*
   Have Soma drops flowed forth for wealth.
2. *Forth have they rushed from holding hands, like chariots that are urged to speed, like joyful songs*
   of singing men.
3. *The Somas deck themselves with milk, as kings are graced with eulogies,*
   And with seven priests, the sacrifice.
4. *Pressed for the gladdening draught, the drops flow abundantly with song, the Soma juices in a*
   stream.
5. *Winning Vivasvan's glory, and producing morning's light, the suns pass through the openings of*
   the cloth.
6. *The singing men of ancient time, open the doors of sacred songs, for the mighty to accept.*
7. *Combined in close society sit the seven priests, the brotherhood, filling the station of the One.*
8. *He gives us kinship with the gods, and with the Sun unites our eye; the sage's offspring has appeared.*
9. *The sun with his dear eye beholds that quarter of the heavens which priests*
   Have placed within the sacred cell.

(Rig Veda 9.10)

IV

1. *Pleasant to Indra's, Mitra's, Pushan's and Bhaga's taste, speed onwards Soma, with thy flowing stream.*
2. *Let Indra drink, O Soma, of thy juice for wisdom, and all deities for strength.*
3. *So flow thou on as bright celestial juice, flow to the vast immortal dwelling place.*
4. *Flow onwards, Soma, as a mighty sea, as father of the gods to every form.*

(Rig Veda 9.109)

DIVINE METRE

All the poetic metres used in the Rig Veda are considered divine and associated with various deities. Later, the gayatri metre was identified with a goddess named Gayatri. One verse in this metre that occurs in the Rig Veda is considered the most sacred and a powerful mantra. An invocation to the sun as Savitr, it reads: *Om bhur bhuva svaha, tat savitur varenyam, bhargo devasya dhimahi, dhiyo yo nah prachodayat.* This verse has been variously translated. One version is: 'We meditate on that excellent light of the divine sun; may he illumine our minds' (H.H. Wilson). According to the Mahabharata, the twenty-four *aksharas* (syllables) of the gayatri metre represent the universe, containing nineteen classes of beings and five elements. In the Bhagavad Gita, Krishna says, 'Among metres, I am the Gayatri'. Other verses too can be composed in this metre, and are referred to with a qualifier, such as Vishnu Gayatri or Surya Gayatri.

Gayatri is also one of the names of the god Shiva, who is said to have made Gayatri and Savitri his reins.

RISHIS

Numerous rishis or sages are mentioned in the Rig Veda, as well as the other Samhitas and the anukramanis. Some of the main rishis and rishi families are described here.

AGASTYA

The rishi Agastya is first mentioned in the Rig Veda. Here he is referred to as a Mana or Manya and the son of Mana. He is known as Maitravaruni, as he is said to be the son of the gods Mitra and Varuna. His brother was the rishi Vasishtha, and both were born through the apsara Urvashi. His wife was Lopamudra, whom he himself had created. In one passage in the Rig Veda, he cured the leg of Vishpala with the help of the Ashvins. Agastya appears in all the four Vedas, as well as in the Brahmanas, Aranyakas, epics, and Puranas. He was one of the seven main rishis. The later texts recount several stories about him, and he is said to have settled in south India.

Agastya Shishyagana, a group of students of the rishi Agastya, along with the rishi himself and his wife Lopamudra, are the authors of one Rig Vedic hymn (1.179). The Anukramani gives the names of two students as Antye and Brihatya. Another Agastya mentioned as the author of one Rig Vedic hymn is Dalhachyuta Agastya (9.25).

ANGIRASA

A great rishi, described in the Rig Veda and later texts. He is the first of the Agni-devas or fire gods, the first sacrificer associated with fire rituals, and a teacher of divine knowledge (*brahma vidya*). Angirasas were the descendants of the rishi Angiras, or sometimes of the god Agni. In the Rig Veda, Angirasas are mentioned over sixty times, two-thirds of these in the plural. Also, there are an additional thirty, which are derivatives of the word. They are mentioned as *pitris* along with Atharvans and Bhrigus and are associated with Yama. They are said to have become immortal through sacrifice and to have gained Indra's friendship. They are closely associated with Indra, and helped Indra in getting the cows from the Panis. They are also associated with song. Thus one hymn (1.62) says, singing they found the cows, while another (1.72) says that they burst the rock with their song and found the light. Brihaspati is once called Angiras. Some scholars feel they were priests of the ancient past, dating to the Indo-Iranian period.

As descendants of Angiras, some Angirasas represented various types of agnis.

The anukramanis attribute several Rig Vedic hymns to members of the Angirasa family. They are said to be authors of some hymns in mandalas 1, 5, 8, 9, and 10. Among the Angirasas mentioned are Abhivarta, Amahiyu, Ayasya, Baru, Bhikshu, Bindu, Brihanmati, Brihaspati, Dharana, Dhruva, Divya, Harimanta, Hiranyastupa, Krishna, Murdhanvan, Nrimedha, Pavitra, Prabhuvasa or Prabhuvasu, Pracheta, Priyamedha, Purumila, Purushamedha, Putadaksha, Rahugana, Samvarta, Saptagu, Savya, Shishu, Shrutakaksha or Sukaksha, Suditi, Tiraschi, Uchathya, Vihavya, and Virupa. Some of these are also referred to in later texts including the Mahabharata and Puranas, as sons or descendants of Angirasa.

Angirasa or his descendant Ghora Angirasa is associated with the composition of the Atharva Veda. In later texts, he is one of the mind-born sons of the god Brahma. He is also said to be one of the sixteen Prajapatis created by Brahma, who then created the universe.

ASHVALAYANA

An ancient scholar and composer of Sanskrit texts, Ashvalayana is said to have been the disciple of Shaunaka and the author of a Shrauta Sutra, a Grihya Sutra, and of other texts, as well as the originator of a Rig Veda Shakha (branch or school). He is not mentioned as the author of any Rig Vedic hymn.

ATHARVAN

An ancient priest, his name is found fourteen times in the Rig Veda, three times in plural, and several times in the Atharva Veda, which was once known as Atharvana Veda. In the Rig, Atharvan produced Agni or fire, who became the messenger of Vivasvat. Atharvan also brought order through sacrifices. Indra is said to be his helper. According to the Atharva Veda, Atharvan was a companion of the gods. He gave a cup of Soma to Indra and received a Kamadhenu ('wish-fulfilling cow') from the god Varuna. Possibly, he was the head of a family of real or mythical priests. Atharvan is also used as a generic term for a priest, while Atharvans in plural are a class of pitris, who live in heaven. He was the father of Dadhyanch, a rishi known for his knowledge (see below). Two people mentioned as composers of hymns in the Rig Veda are Bhishaj or Bhishak Atharvana (10.97) and Brihaddiva Atharvana (10.120).

Bhishaj Atharvana is one of the traditional composers of the Atharva Veda. The name Bhishaj refers to his connection with medicine and healing.

In the Shatapatha Brahmana, Atharvan is an ancient teacher. Atharvan originally meant 'fire-priest', corresponding with Athravan of the Avesta, therefore this text may have an Indo-Iranian origin, though in its present form is later than the Rig Veda. The name may be related to the Avestan word for fire, *atar*.

As a group Atharvans are associated with the Angirasas, Navagvas, and Bhrigus.

ATRI

An ancient rishi, Atri is described in the Rig Veda and later in the Mahabharata, Puranas, and other texts. He is mentioned around forty times in the Rig Veda, six times in the plural. He is a rishi of the five tribes and, along with Manu, an ancient ancestor. Atri is mentioned with Indra and Agni but is mainly connected with the Ashvins, who are said to have saved him from a deep pit, from darkness, and from a demon. The Ashvins prevented him from burning in fire and are said to have made him young again. Atri, or the Atris together, found the sun that was hidden by Svarbhanu and placed it in the sky. This is also referred to in the Atharva Veda. In the Shatapatha Brahmana, Atri, a priest who removed darkness, was the same as Vach, or originated from her. Atri is once given as a name of Agni (Rig Veda 2.8). In four passages, Atri is mentioned in connection with the rishi Saptavadhri, who is connected with the Ashvins and also referred to as Atri Saptavadhri. Mandala 5 of the Rig Veda is attributed to Atri and his descendants. In the same text, he is one of the ancestors of the human race. In later texts, he was one of the sons of the god Brahma, and was married to Anasuya.

Atreya is a collective name for the sons or descendants of the rishi Atri. The anukramanis mention a number of rishis known as Atreya or Atri, mainly in Mandala 5, but also in mandalas 8 and 10. Among them are: Archanana, Arishtanemi Tarkshya, Aruchakri, Avasyu, Babhru, Bahuvrikta, Dhyugna Vishvacharshani, Evayamarut, Gatu, Gaya, Gopavana, Kumar, Mriktavaha Dvita, Paura,

Pratikshatra, Puru, Ratahavya, Sadaprina, Saptavadhri, Sasa, Satyashrava, Shrutavrita, Shyavashava, Sutambhara, Svasti, Vasuyu, Vavri, Vishvasama, Vishvavara, Yajata, Budha, Gavishthara, Vasushruta, Apala, Bhauma, Sankhya, Prayasvan Atrigana, and Isha.

BHARADVAJA

An ancient rishi, to whom several hymns in the Rig Veda are attributed. The entire Mandala 6 is said to be composed by Bharadvaja or the family of Bharadvajas. He is also known as Bharadvaja Barhaspatya, that is, 'Bharadvaja, descendant of Brihaspati'. According to the Panchavimsha Brahmana, Bharadvaja was the purohita of Divodasa, a king mentioned in the Rig Veda, who was the ancestor of Sudas. He is also mentioned in the Ramayana, Mahabharata, Puranas, and other texts. In the Puranas, his love for Vedic study is described. One lifetime was not sufficient, so he obtained a boon from the god Indra, to live for thousands of years to continue his study. Others of the Bharadvaja family mentioned in the Rig or anukramanis include Nara, Payu, Rijishva, Shasa, Shunahotra, Suhotra, Vasu, Garga, and Shirimbitha.

Shamyu Barhaspatya is said to be the composer of some hymns in Mandala 6 and Tapumurdha Barhaspatya of one in Mandala 10 (10.182). Bharadvaja was also the name of other rishis.

BHRIGU

An ancient rishi whose name occurs twenty-one times in the Rig Veda, Bhrigu means 'shining', from the root *bhraj*, and is thought to have originally been a name of fire.

In the Rig Veda, Bhrigu is said to have received Agni (fire) from heaven. In the Brahmanas, he is referred to as Varuni, that is, a son of Varuna. The Bhrigus were a family of priests related to the Angirasas, descended from Bhrigu. Even in the Rig, the Bhrigus seem to have been priests of olden times. Both the Bhrigus and Matarishvan are connected with fire. Matarishvan brought it as lightning but the Bhrigus kindled the fire on earth. Bhrigus are mentioned with the Yatis and Praskanva and, in another passage with the Dhruyus and Turvasha, as the enemies of Sudas. Thus in some passages they seem to be a historic group. In one Rig Vedic hymn (8.35) they are invited to drink Soma, along with the thirty-three devas, the Maruts, Apah, Ashvins, Ushas, and Surya. In the Atharva (5.19), Bhrigu is a rishi, a leader of a clan or group, and also in the Brahmanas. In later texts there are several stories relating to Bhrigu.

The Bhargavas are those descended from Bhrigu. The Anukramani lists some Bhargavas as composers of hymns in mandalas 8, 9, and 10. Among them the most important is Jamadagni Bhargava, also known as Rama Jamadagnya. Others include: Bharga Pragatha, Bhriguvaruni, Syumarashmi, Ita, Kavi, Nema, Somahuti, and Vena. Shukra in later texts is known as Bhrigu and was the priest of the asuras. In the Puranas Bhrigu was one of the Prajapatis.

DADHYANCH

An ancient rishi, first mentioned in the Rig Veda where his name occurs nine times, he was the son of Atharvan (6.16, 1.116–117) and kindled Agni. The Ashvins wanted the secret knowledge of Soma (*madhuvidya*) revealed to him by the god Indra. They replaced his head with that of a horse, as he had promised not to reveal the knowledge. After the horse's head had told the Ashvins what they wanted to know, his real head was restored. The horse head fell on a lake on Mt Sharyanavat, where it remained, granting boons to men. Indra used them to kill ninety-nine Vritras (1.84). Here again the horse, or the horse head, is symbolic of knowledge.

DASHAGVAS

A group mentioned seven times in the Rig Veda, thrice in the singular, and twice associated with the Navagvas. They are also associated with Indra. Together with Indra, the Navagvas and Dashagvas broke open the rock and defeated Vala. In one hymn (10. 62), Dashagva, mentioned with Navagva, is said to be chief Angiras. The commentators see it as a numerical variation of Navagva.

GOTAMA

An ancient rishi, Gotama Rahugana is referred to as a composer of several hymns in Mandala 1 and of one hymn in Mandala 9. Nodha Gautama, of the same family, also composed several hymns.

GRITSAMADA

A rishi, the composer of most of the hymns in Mandala 2, he was also known as Gritsamada Bhargava Shaunaka (later Angirasa Shaunahotra). Kurma Gartsamada is alternatively mentioned as the composer of some of the hymns in this mandala.

KANVA

An ancient rishi. The name Kanva is mentioned in both singular and plural around sixty times in the Rig Veda. In plural, it refers to his descendants. Kanva is said to be the son of Nrishad and was known as Narshada both in the Rig and Atharva. He is listed with other ancestors including Manu and Angiras. Agni was his friend, helping him in battle along with Trasadasyu, Atri, and others. Indra gave gold and cattle to Kanva, Trasadasyu, and others (Valakhilya hymns). The Maruts helped Kanva, Turvasha, and Yadu while the Ashvins helped Kanva several times. He was blind but they restored his eyesight. Most of the hymns of the eighth book of the Rig Veda are attributed to him and his family, and he is sometimes mentioned as one of the seven great rishis. Kanva himself is not mentioned as existing at the time of the Rig, hence he was either a distant ancestor or a mythical figure, but the Kanvas were a real family. His descendant Medhyatithi is mentioned nine times in the Rig. Priyamedha is referred to a few times with Kanva but his descendants also call themselves Priyamedhas and Priyamedha in the anukramanis is referred to as Angirasa. In later texts, Kanva is described as the rishi who took care of Shakuntala, daughter of Vishvamitra and Menaka, in his ashrama. Members of Kanva's family listed in the anukramanis as authors of hymns, mainly in Mandala 8 but also a few in 1 and 9 include: Ghaura, Ayu, Brahmatithi, Devatithi, Irimbathi, Krisha, Kusidi, Matarishva, Medatithi, Medhya, Nabhaka, Nipatithi, Pragatha, Praskanva, Prishadra, Punarvatsa, Pushtigu, Sadhvansa, Shashkarna, Shrushtigu, Sobhari, Suparna, Varusuti, Vatsa, and Vishoka.

KASHYAPA

An ancient rishi. Some of the Vedic hymns are attributed to him, and in Vedic texts, he is also a mythical being associated with the sun. He is one of the seven great rishis, later said to be the grandson of the god Brahma, and the progenitor of human beings, as he was the father of Vivasvat and grandfather of Manu. He is also called Prajapati.

In the Mahabharata and Puranas, he is a rishi who married a number of daughters of Daksha, through whom all beings in the world were descended.

Kashyapa Maricha is mentioned as the author of some hymns in mandalas 1 and 9. Other Kashyapas listed as authors in mandalas 5, 8, 9, and 10, include Asita, Avatsara, Bhutasha, Devala, Nidhuvi, Rebha, Rebhusunu, and Vivriha.

KAVYA USHANA

Ushana is mentioned eleven times in the Rig Veda. He is called Kavi twice, and Kavya five times. He is wise, and Soma in his wisdom is compared with him. In one hymn, Kavya Ushana made Agni the hotr. In another, he is referred to in the same verse as Atharvan. Indra is once identified both with Ushana and with Kutsa. Kanva is also associated with Kutsa and Indra in the defeat of Shushna. He made the bolt for Indra to kill Vritra.

Kavya Ushana is similar to Kava-Ushan of Zoroastrian texts, who was also a legendary king of the Kayanian dynasty.

Shukracharya, the preceptor of the asuras, is also known as Kavya Ushana. In some Puranas, Shukra is said to be the strongest of the seven sons born to the rishi Bhrigu and Puloma. He is therefore referred to as Bhrigu.

The Mahabharata states that he had four sons, who were priests of the asuras: they were Tashtadhara, Atri, and two others of fierce deeds; they were like the sun in energy and had set their hearts on acquiring the region of Brahman.

Ushana or Shukra is also the name of the planet Venus, or of its regent.

KRISHNA

Krishna of the Rig Veda is a rishi, composer of a hymn (8.74). In the Chhandogya Upanishad, Krishna, son of Devaki, is a great scholar and student of Ghora Angirasa. In the Mahabharata Anukramani, Krishna is descended from Angirasa. In a few passages, Krishna is described as a *ritvij*, a priest. At the same time, Krishna was a great warrior. In later texts, there are several myths and stories relating to Krishna as an incarnation of the god Vishnu but he may not be the same as Krishna the rishi.

KUSHIKAS

A family of rishis, they were the same as the Vishvamitras (see below).

KUTSA

A rishi and heroic figure mentioned forty times in the Rig Veda, Kutsa is associated with the god Indra. In one hymn, Kutsa is called Arjuneya, son of Arjun. In another, Indra helped a son of Kutsa in a fight with a dasyu. Once Kutsa is invoked with Indra as Indra-Kutsa. Kutsa is young, bright, and similar to Indra. Shushna is often mentioned as his enemy and Indra helps Kutsa to defeat him. Tugra, Snadibha, and Vetasu were also defeated by Indra for Kutsa. Indra removed the wheel of the sun for Kutsa. Kutsa is also called Indra's charioteer. In a few passages, Kutsa is defeated by Indra, along with Ayu and Atithigva. In a hymn (1.53), these three are delivered by Indra to the young king Turvayana. Thus Kutsa was possibly a historical figure. The Kutsas are referred to in plural as a family of singers, in a hymn praising Indra. In the Naighantuka, Kutsa is a synonym of the vajra (Indra's thunderbolt).

Several hymns in Mandala 1 are attributed to Kutsa Angirasa, and one in the eighth to Kutsa Bhargava. In Mandala 10, a hymn is attributed to Durmitra or Sumitra Kautsa (10.105), that is, a descendant of Kutsa.

MADHUCHHANDAS

Jeta Madhuchhandas and Adhamarshana Madhuchhandas are mentioned as composers of hymns.

NAVAGVAS

A group of rishis mentioned fourteen times in the Rig Veda, sometimes with the Angirasas, Bhrigus, and Atharvans, and along with them are said to be ancient pitris. They are referred to with the Angirasas as helping Indra release the cows from the Panis. In one hymn, they are said to press Soma, sing praises of Indra, and break open the cow stall. Navagva, in singular form, seems to be a name of Angiras or of Dadhyanch. According to Macdonell, Navagva probably means 'going in a company of nine' and refers in plural to 'a group of nine ancient priestly ancestors'.

It may be significant that in late Zoroastrian texts, nine ancestors of Zarathushtra are mentioned.

PARASHARA SHAKTYA

An ancient rishi who is mentioned in the Rig Veda along with the rishis Shatayatu and Vasishtha. According to the Anukramani, he composed some hymns in Mandala 1 of the Rig. The Nirukta states he was the son of Vasishtha. In the Mahabharata and Puranas, he is described as the son of Shakti and Adrishyanti, the grandson of Vasishtha, and the father of Vyasa.

PIPPALADA

An ancient rishi, who founded a school of the Atharva Veda, which was named after him. In the Prashna Upanishad, he guides other rishis on the path to enlightenment.

SHUNAHSHEPA AJIGARTI (LATER DEVARATA VAISHVAMITRA)

A rishi to whom some hymns of the Rig Veda are attributed, his story is narrated in later texts, including the Brahmanas, Ramayana, Mahabharata, and Puranas, with some variations. According to the Aitareya Brahmana, Raja Harishchandra was childless. He prayed for a son, and promised the god Varuna to offer him as a sacrifice. However, after his son Rohita was born, he kept putting off the sacrifice. When he finally decided to sacrifice him, Rohita refused and went into the forest. He came across a poor rishi Ajigarta, who had three sons, and bought his second son Shunahshepa for 100 cows, to offer him as a sacrifice in his place. Ajigarta received 200 more cows to bind Shunahshepa to the post and kill him but, as Shunahshepa recited verses in praise of deities, he was saved. He was adopted by the rishi Vishvamitra who treated him like his son.

VAIKHANASA

The Vaikhanasas were a group of rishis. Two are specifically referred to in the anukramanis as authors of one hymn each in mandalas 9 and 10: Shata Vaikhanasa and Vamra Vaikhanasa.

VAMADEVA

A rishi, the composer of a number of hymns in Mandala 4, he was also known as Vamadeva Gautama. Brihaduktha Vamadevya, the composer of some hymns in Mandala 10, seems to have been a member of his family.

VASISHTHA

An ancient rishi, he has many hymns of the Rig Veda ascribed to him, including those of Mandala 7 as well as some others. He is said to be one of the seven great rishis, and also one of the ten Prajapatis. In one of the hymns of the Rig Veda, he and the rishi Agastya are described as the offspring of Mitra and Varuna. When these two gods saw the beautiful apsara Urvashi, their seed fell and the two rishis were born from it. In another account, Vasishtha was Varuna's son, associated with the Tritsus, a Rig Vedic clan, and was the priest of King Sudas. One hymn of his consists of a sleep spell, which according to some commentators was uttered when he entered the house of Varuna to get some food, and a dog barked at him.

The rivalry between him and the rishi Vishvamitra is often described, right from the time of the Rig Veda. In the Mahabharata, Vasishtha is said to be the purohita or priest of several kings. There are several stories about Vasishtha in the epics and Puranas, as well as a number of local legends.

The rishi Vasishtha was one of the mildest and most pious rishis described in texts. He had all powers but never used them to benefit himself.

Some members of his family, including Chitramaha Vasishtha and Mrilika Vasishtha, are also said to be authors of Rig Vedic hymns. Parashara Shaktya was his grandson.

VIRUPAS

A group of rishis connected with the Angirasas. In the Rig Veda, they are mentioned three times in the plural. They are said to be born from Agni or from heaven.

Descendants of the Virupas mentioned as authors of hymns include Nabha Prabhedana Vairupa, Sadhi Vairupa, and Shata Prabhedana Vairupa.

VISHVAMITRA

An ancient rishi. In the Rig Veda, the hymns of Mandala 3 are assigned to him, and he is said to be the son of Kushika. According to later texts, he was the son of Gadhi, King of Kannauj, a descendant of Puru, and a king himself. His intense rivalry with the rishi Vasishtha is described in several texts. This rivalry is even mentioned in the Rig Veda, though here Vishvamitra is not described as a king. There are several stories about Vishvamitra in the epics and Puranas. Vishvamitra was an immensely powerful rishi but was always prone to anger.

Members of his family or descendants are also mentioned in the anukramanis as the authors of hymns. These include Ashtaka, Kata, Madhuchhanda (see above), Purana, Renu and Rishabha, Kushika Saubhara, Gadhi Kaushika, Kushika Aishirathi, and Prajapati Vaishvamitra.

VYASA

A rishi of ancient days. According to tradition, Vyasa arranged the Vedas, compiled the Mahabharata, and was the author of the Puranas. His life is described in the Mahabharata and other texts. He was the son of the rishi Parashara and Satyavati. Parashara was the grandson of the rishi Vasishtha.

Several Vyasas are mentioned in the Puranas as incarnations of Vishnu or of Shiva. According to the Vishnu Purana, in every Dvapara Yuga, Vishnu (in the form of Vyasa) divides the Veda, which is actually one, into many, to adapt it to the capacities of the people. Thus Vyasas are born in successive ages to arrange and propagate the Vedas and other texts. While this is the traditional view scholars feel Vyasa is a title used by many of the authors and compilers of ancient texts.

YAJNAVALKYA

An ancient rishi, who is said to have composed the Vajasaneyi Samhita or White Yajur Veda as well as the Shatapatha Brahmana, the Brihadaranyaka Upanishad, and the Yajnavalkya Smriti. It is unlikely that he was the author of all these texts, as they are of different dates.

SAPTA RISHIS

A group of seven rishis, who are referred to four times in the Rig Veda. They are said to be ancient and divine, associated with the gods. One hymn refers to seven hotrs with whom Manu made the first offering to the gods. In later texts, these rishis are mentioned by name, though the names listed sometimes differ. The seven rishis referred to as a group are: Bharadvaja, Kashyapa, Gotama, Atri, Vishvamitra, Jamadagni, Vasishtha.

ANCIENT RISHIS

The most ancient rishis, said to have lived in the distant past, seem to have been the Angirasas, Bhrigus, Navagvas, and Atharvans.

RISHIS AS DEVAS

One or more rishis who were devotees of the god Indra adopted Indra as their own name. This rishi name has been found both in the Rig Veda and Yajur Veda, and is commented on by Sayana. Agni and several other gods are also named as authors of hymns; this could be when the rishi name is not known or when a rishi deliberately adopted the name of a deity.

CHAPTER 10

RITUAL AND SACRIFICE

The Vedas are often seen as ritual texts. Both ritual and sacrifice form important parts of these. According to the French Indologist Louis Renou, 'Vedic religion is first and foremost a liturgy, and only secondarily a mythological or speculative system; we must therefore investigate it as a liturgy.'

The sacrifice, known in Sanskrit as *yajna*, is of many different types. There are cosmic sacrifices resulting in creation, ritual sacrifices to propitiate a deity or gain some desire, and internal sacrifices, which is the offering of oneself for a divine purpose.

Vedic rituals are still performed in India. Apart from abbreviated birth or marriage or other domestic rites, Soma and Shrauta rituals are still performed.

AIMS OF A SACRIFICE

The sacrifice is considered supremely important, as a creative power to harness nature, and is identified with Prajapati, the creator, or with Vishnu. Agni, fire, is identified with Prajapati, and with the fire altar, as well as the time taken to build it.

Here, we will look mainly at ritual sacrifices in the four Vedic Samhitas, with reference to the details provided in the Later Vedic texts. Broadly, all ritual sacrifices were performed with the aim of gaining the object of one's desire, be it wealth, prosperity, happiness, strength and victory, or something more definite. The sacrifices aimed to do this either through rituals which involved propitiating and praying to the gods, or through rituals that, people believed, would compel the gods to grant the desires or compel certain events to take place. All rituals are believed to provide occult connections with the divine. In several places, the symbolic nature of the sacrifice is indicated, as when a cooking pot is said to represent the sky and the earth, as well as the god Matarishvan (Vajasaneyi Samhita 1.2), and the fire brought for the fire altar is called a beautiful winged bird, representing different melodies and chants.

TEXTS

References to the sacrifices can be traced to the Rig Veda and Atharva Veda. The Sama Veda and Yajur Veda were specially compiled for the sacrificial ritual. The Brahmanas both describe and explain the sacrifices. Later texts on sacrifices include the Grihya Sutras and Shrauta Sutras.

TYPES OF SACRIFICES

There were both simple and complex types of ritual sacrifices. All power and accomplishment was linked with sacrifice, and thus sacrifice came to be identified with the gods and with a supreme creator. As the sacrificial system became well-established, a sacrifice had to be performed according to the precise and exact directions laid down by tradition, and only by the brahmana caste. Among the sacrifices conducted, in ancient days in India, there were several to increase or assert the power of a king, such as the *ashvamedha* (horse sacrifice), *rajasuya*, *vajapeya*, *punar abhisheka*, and *aindra mahabhisheka*. Other sacrifices included fire sacrifices of the *agnihotra* and *agnishtoma*, and daily household sacrifices.

Later, a short form of this sacrifice was devised, which consists of reciting the Gayatri Mantra five times, while focusing on the five objects of worship of the *pancha-maha-yajna* (see below). Other types of sacrifices included offering lights, incense, flowers, etc., along with ritual prayers.

TERMS USED IN THE SACRIFICIAL RITUAL

The sacrificial ritual had a special terminology. Some of the terms commonly used are given here:

- *Yajya*: (invocatory) verses
- *Purovakya*: the verse to a deity, requesting him or her to attend the sacrifice
- *Anuvakya*: verses to invite the gods to the sacrifice
- *Nivid*: proclamation; the name assigned to eleven prose formulas, each of about sixty-five words; some Rig *suktas* seem versified and amplified nivids; the nivids were inserted in the shastras or suktas which were verses of praise
- *Vashat* call (*vashatkara*): the summons to the sacrifice
- *Shastra*: hymns or verses of praise
- *Stutis*: laudations; traditionally some Rig Vedic hymns are known as stutis
- *Ajya*: the ghi offering
- *Sruc*: spoon
- *Darvi*: ladle used to pour ghi, etc. on the fire.
- *Graha*: cup
- *Savana*: pressing

- *Sada*: the ritual arena
- *Ishti*: a sacrifice to fulfil a wish; ishtis are still performed to fulfil specific wishes

  Here are some terms related specifically to chanting:

- *Rik*: an entire verse or mantra
- *Girah*: words of a *pada* or quarter
- *Uktha*: recitation of certain verses
- *Shamsa*: a mantra praising the power of a deity
- *Stotra*: the term for the basic unit of verses to be sung, usually a triplet, though there are also longer units
- *Stoma*: the form in which the stotra is chanted; can have varying numbers of verses, but often indicates the chanting of three riks in different ways
- *Sama*: song or tune

  Homa, havana, or *yaga* are later post-Vedic terms for yajnas.

SACRIFICES IN THE RIG VEDA

The Rig Veda has many passages, which were later used both in rituals and sacrifices, and some which were from the beginning connected with various rituals. According to some scholars, the Rig Veda was a liturgical text from its inception while others feel it came to be used later in rituals, and was not originally meant for this purpose. The Sanskrit scholar V.M. Apte believed that there must have been a separate Rig Veda for ritual use.

The Rig Veda refers to various priests and aspects of rituals. Many priests associated with sacrifices are mentioned. One passage refers to the following priests: *hotr, potr, neshtr, agnidh, prashastr, adhvaryu,* and *brahman*. Another passage mentions the *udgatr* and *samaga* (saman singer). Initially, possibly, the hotr alone invoked the gods and prepared the offering. Later the adhvaryu, assisted by the agnidh, performed the second function. One hymn also shows that the rituals even at this time were initiated with the adhvaryu requesting the hotr permission to begin. In the late Mandala 10 (10.141.3), a brahman priest (associated with the Atharva Veda) was known and worshipped along with various deities, Soma, and the king. Some verses in Mandala 4 also refer to the brahman.

The purohita was different from the sacrificial priests but references in the Rig indicate that initially the purohita and the hotr performed the same functions. In two passages, the divine hotrs of the Apri hymns are also referred to as purohitas. From the priestly families described, it would seem that priesthood was usually hereditary. The different priestly families may once have had different rituals but gradually they became formalized. One passage refers to the ceremony of choosing and formally inviting the priests.

The Rig Veda also refers to several sacrifices. Items connected with sacrifices are revered, and these include the *yupa* or sacrificial post, *barhis* or sacrificial grass, and *dvaro devih* or the divine doors said to lead to the sacrificial area. There are several *anuvakya* or verses to invite the gods to the sacrifice. There are also hymns, which refer to the agnishtoma, ashvamedha, Soma, and other sacrifices. The wedding and funeral hymns of the Rig Veda form part of *grihya* rituals.

The fire is kindled by friction and only one altar is referred to but the fire from this is placed at three sites, corresponding to the three later fires. Only the *garhapatya* (domestic fire) is named, but the Vaishvanar and Narashamsa (or *kravya-vahana*) could be the precursors of the *ahavaniya* (sacrificial fire for the devas) and *dakshina* (sacrificial fire for the pitris and others, later used in rituals). Barhis were gathered from the east and spread on the sacrificial ground for the gods to sit on. Sacred fire wood (*samidh*) was placed in the fire and offerings were made three times a day. Some verses (3.27, 5.28) must have been used from the beginning at the time of lighting the fire. Offerings to the fire consisted of milk, butter, grain, barley, or wheat cakes, and at times meat, including that of the cow, bull, goat, sheep, or horse. Honey was also offered. Sruc and darvi were used to pour ghi on the fire. Grahas or special cups were used for the offerings.

The Rig also knows the process of heating the milk in a pot, which later became part of the *pravargya* (hot milk) ceremony, and the conclusion of the ritual with offering a cake made of grain to Agni Svishtakrit. The ten Apri hymns were probably from the beginning used as yajya (invocatory) verses in the animal sacrifice. One hymn in Mandala 3 (3.8) is meant for preparing the yupa (sacrificial post) for the sacrifice. The ashvamedha was a major ceremony even in the Rig, with separate hymns for its various stages.

The Soma sacrifice was, however, the most important. Its essentials were known in the Rig Veda. The three savanas or pressings (morning, midday, evening) are referred to. The gayatri, trishtubh, and jagati metres are used in the three savanas. The evening pressing is especially for the Ribhus, though Indra has a share in it; the afternoon for Indra, along with the Maruts. The morning savana is for several deities including Indra. The Soma was usually pounded with *adri* (pressing stones) to extract the juice, then mixed with water in the *kosha* (tub or vat), then poured into two *chamus* (bowls), where it was mixed with milk and poured into the *kalasha* (vessel), ready for the sacrifice. The sautramani sacrifice seems to be known though it is not named.

The Rig Veda refers to several words used in chanting: rik, girah, uktha, shamsa, stuti, stoma, sama, and others. These have related meanings (see above).

ATHARVA VEDA

The Atharva Veda originally seems to have been a separate text, not a part of the three Vedas, which were grouped together. Later verses and hymns were added, which brought it in line with the other three texts. This was done perhaps to incorporate different groups into the whole sacrificial system. In its later sections, the Atharva repeats, with some variations, many of the marital, funeral, and sacrificial hymns of the Rig, though it has other magical formulas and spells. Its Kuntapa hymns (20.127–136) form part of the sacrificial ritual.

SAMA VEDA

The Sama Veda takes most of its hymns from the Rig Veda. However, these are arranged differently, specially for the performance of the sacrifice, particularly Soma sacrifices.

YAJUR VEDA

The Yajur is the most important of the four Samhitas in the sacrificial ritual. It has been called 'the prayer book' of the Vedas, as it provides the prayers to be recited with the sacrifices. The prayers and sacrificial formulas have both verses and prose passages but even the latter is sometimes rhythmic and poetic. The verses are known as rik, the prose as *yaju*, from which the text gets its name.

Most of the verses occur in the Rig Veda but are not quite the same; they are modified to suit the sacrifices. Single verses from the Rig are mostly used, entire hymns are rare.

The Vajasaneyi Samhita of the Shukla Yajur Veda provides prayers for the *darshapurnamasa* (new- and full-moon sacrifices); *pindapitrayajna* (offerings for *pitris*), which is a part of the former; the various fire sacrifices, including the laying of the fire, morning and evening sacrifices (agnihotra), and *chaturmasya* (four-monthly sacrifices); the Soma sacrifices, including animal sacrifices, vajapeya, and rajasuya; for the *agnichayana*, the building of the fire altar, which could take one year; the sautramani sacrifice; and the ashvamedha and *purushamedha*.

The Taittiriya Samhita of the Krishna Yajur Veda has the prayers of only the first half of the Vajasaneyi Samhita. It also contains some explanations and descriptions of the sacrifices.

By the time of the Later Vedic Samhitas, the whole sacrificial system was in place.

PRIESTS

There were four groups or categories of priests, each assigned to a different Samhita. The four categories were headed by the hotr for the Rig, the udgatr for the Sama, the adhvaryu for the Yajur, and the brahman for the Atharva.

The number of priests was expanded to sixteen, and classified into four groups:

1. *hotr, maitravaruna, achavaka, gravastut*
2. *udgatr, prastotr, pratihartr, subrahmanya*
3. *adhvaryu, pratiprasthatr, neshtr, unnetr*
4. *brahman, brahmnachchhamsin, agnidhra, potr*

Thus, elaborate yajnas had a total of sixteen *ritviks* (priests), at times even seventeen. These priests were assisted by other workers who carried out menial tasks. The purohita, spiritual adviser to the king, was usually a different priest though, as seen earlier, he may have carried out the functions of the hotr in Rig Vedic times. The priest needed to be an expert in the text. He had to have a knowledge of the rishi to whom it was revealed, the deity to which it was addressed, the metre (*chhandas*), as well as its ritualistic application (*viniyoga*). Several texts explained and provided guidance for these additional aspects (see Chapter 2).

SHRAUTA AND GRIHYA SACRIFICES

Sacrifices can be divided into two categories: *shrauta* and *grihya*. Shrauta rituals usually used three fires, or one of the three, instead of the domestic fire. The sacrificial rituals developed over time; the Brahmanas and Shrauta Sutras provide methods and steps which may not have existed at the time the Samhitas were composed. There were also variations in the way the sacrifices were performed. The Jamadagnis and Bhrigus had five divisions or layers of offerings, while others had four. Some invoked Tanunapat in the Apri hymns for the animal sacrifice, while others invoked Narashamsa. According to the Sutras, the basic aspects of the sacrifice are known as *prakritis* while the variations superimposed on these are *vikritis*. Thus the new- and full-moon sacrifices are the prakriti or model for all sacrifices of the *ishti* type (performed to obtain various results) while the agnishtoma is the prakriti for the Soma sacrifices. The elements of each sacrifice were classified as *angas* and *pradhanas*. Angas were aspects that provided the framework for the sacrifice, and which could be common to other sacrifices. Pradhanas were specific to a sacrifice.

The type of prayer and formula varies from the simple to the complex. An item may be dedicated with the simple words: 'This (or you) for Agni' or 'for Indra' or 'for Agni/Indra hail'! For the morning and evening agnihotra, milk is offered with the words 'Surya is Light, Light is Surya, Hail' (morning) and 'Agni is light, Light is Agni, Hail' (evening). Various actions and objects used are accompanied by sacrificial formulas. Taking a piece of wood, the sacrificer (*yajamana*) says, 'This Agni is your igniter. Through it, may you grow and thrive! Through it, may we also grow and thrive.' Items are also addressed with prayers that they do not injure the sacrificer or transform into something harmful. Items are also compared with the attributes of deities. For instance, the sacrificer ties a girdle made of hemp and grass while reciting, 'You are the strength of Angiras, soft as wool, lend me strength.'

The two sacrificial fire sticks, to create friction to ignite a fire, were said to be male and female, mother and father, who produced the child, Agni. Pururavas, Urvashi, and their child Ayu are identified with these sticks and their product in the Soma sacrifice. The sticks are twirled with the following formula: 'I twirl you with the gayatri metre, I twirl you with the trishtubh metre, I twirl you with the Jagati metre'.

A number of prayers were offered along with the sacrifice, for instance:

You, Agni, are the protector of bodies, protect me!
You, the giver of life, give me life.
You, the giver of strength, give me strength.
Agni, make complete whatever is incomplete in my body!

(Vaj. 3.17)

There are also question-and-answer sessions among the priests, indicating the mysteries of the universe. For instance, the hotr asks:

Who wanders lonely on his way?
Who is constantly born anew?
What is the remedy for cold?
What is the great corn vessel called?

And the adhvaryu replies:

The sun wanders lonely on its way,
The moon is constantly born anew,
Fire is the remedy for cold,
The earth is the great grain-vessel.

(Vaj. 23, 45–46; based on the translation by R.T.H. Griffith)

There are, in addition, prayers that form magical spells, some elements of devotional prayers, and the use of sacred words with prayers such as 'Om' and 'Svaha'. The sacrifices are not really about praying to the gods but more about compelling them, via rituals, to grant the wishes of the sacrificer.

THE RITUAL

The entire sacrificial ritual and the exact sequence of each step of the sacrifice is not fully explained even in the Sutras, but is found in later texts and oral traditions. Based on these, the main steps of the sacrifice can be reconstructed. Along with the priests, each Samhita had a special role in the sacrifice. The hotr verses of the Rig were different from the verses to be sung by the saman priests. The Rig Vedic verses to be used in the sacrifice had different categories. Among them were yajya (invocatory) and purovakya (invitation to the deity) verses. The hotr recited the yajya when the adhvaryu was about to throw the offerings into the fire. The shastra, translated as a song of praise or a weapon, was also from among the Rig verses.

The adhvaryu, the Yajur priest, measured the ground, built the altar, and prepared the sacrificial vessels, as well as performing other rites. While doing this, he recited verses from the Yajur Veda. The adhvaryu was concerned with conducting rituals in the right way. He also uttered prose yajus or sacrificial formulas, which were different from the Yajur mantras. Samans were sung with Soma sacrifices and formed a complicated part of the ritual. The saman was divided into different parts to be sung by various priests. There were various methods for this but the most common was the following:

1. The prelude or *prastava*, sung by the *prastotr*, who faced west. This was initiated with the mantra 'hum' (*humkara*).
2. The *udgitha*, sung by the udgatr who faced north. This was introduced by the mantra 'Om'.
3. The *pratihara*, sung by the pratihartr, who faced south. This too began with the mantra 'hum'; this could also be divided into two, the second part or *upadrava* being sung by the udgatr.
4. The *nidhana*, the final part, sung by all together. The upagatrs accompanied the song with the word 'ho'.

Several rituals accompany the chants. The whole system of combining verses from different texts in the sacrificial ritual was quite complicated. Before beginning a stotra, the saman priests asked for permission from the brahman and Maitravaruna, who gave it with the words 'om stuta'. The brahman recited one of the *stomabhagas*, a ritual formula.

The stotra recitation began and, as it ended, the hotr would ask the adhvaryu's permission to recite. The adhvaryu would assent and the hotr would recite a shastra (Rig Veda).

According to some ritual sutras, before the chanting, the adhvaryu gave the udgatr some blades of grass, with the words, 'You are the bed for coupling Rik and Saman for the sake of procreation.' The udgatr may have had to sing a sequence of chants, and to mark the number sung he would wind the grass blades around his fingers and later attach them to a pole.

THE SACRIFICES

The main sacrifices are described here.

AGNICHAYANA

Agnichayana is a Sanskrit term for the construction of a fire altar, where sacrifices can be performed. A detailed description of this is given in the Shatapatha Brahmana. The fire altar for the Soma sacrifice had five layers. According to this Brahmana, merely the act of constructing the altar includes all the sacrifices: the first layer is the Soma sacrifice, the second the rajasuya, the third the vajapeya, the fourth the ashvamedha, and the fifth the *agnisava*. At the lowest level, the heads of five sacrificial animals were buried and the bodies thrown into the water to be used in the clay for making the bricks. A man is included among the victims. The head of a man killed by lightning or by an arrow could be used. However, the Shatapatha says that this was not an ancient custom and, after some time, substitutes were used. The Vajasaneyi Samhita (Yajur Veda) provides prayers and mantras to be recited while constructing the altar—a process that took a whole year. It was built with a large number of bricks, many of them with special shapes and names. The fire altar also represented the body of Prajapati, the creator, and symbolized the universe. The commonest variety of altar was built in the form of a *shyena*, a hawk or large bird with outstretched wings.

It could be built in a number of other shapes, including *drona* (trough) and *ratha-chakra* (chariot wheel). This elaborate altar was used in special Soma sacrifices.

As seen earlier, the sacrifices or rituals can be divided into Shrauta, the more important and sacred sacrifices, and Grihya (household sacrifices). A further division is between *havir* and Soma sacrifices. Havir sacrifices are those where *havis* or oblations are offered, while Soma sacrifices must have offerings of Soma. Havir sacrifices include both Shrauta and Grihya sacrifices. Shrauta havir sacrifices include, among others, agnihotra, darshapurnamaseshti, chaturmasya, agrayana-ishti, and some animal sacrifices. Shrauta Soma sacrifices include the ekaha, ahina, sattra, and others. The main sacrifices and rituals are summarized here.

SHRAUTA HAVIR SACRIFICES

ESTABLISHING THE FIRE

The sacrificial fire was an important part of daily rituals. For shrauta sacrifices, three sacred fires have to be first set up. This takes two days and has to be begun either on a new-moon day or a full-moon day, or in a particular season, depending on the caste of the person. Two temporary structures are made; in one, a round altar or hearth is made for the garhapatya fire, and a semicircular one to the south for the dakshina fire. In the other structure, a square altar is prepared for the ahavaniya fire. The *yajamana*, along with his wife, stays awake the whole night, listening to the music of flutes and lutes. In the morning, a fire is created by friction or borrowed from an already-lit fire. The garhapatya is first lit while remembering the pitris and more wood is added. From the garhapatya, the other two fires are lit. If, at any time, the fire is believed to have brought bad luck to the practitioner, it can be allowed to go out and relit using kusha grass as the fuel.

There are daily, fortnightly, and four-monthly sacrifices among the shrauta, all offered to more than one deity.

AGNIHOTRA

The agnihotra is a sacrifice to Agni, that is, a fire sacrifice. It usually consists of offerings of milk, oil, or other substances to the fire. According to the Mahabharata, it is the best of the Vedic sacrifices. It consists of daily offerings to the garhapatya and ahavaniya fires. In this, the main offering is hot milk mixed with water. In the evening, the *agnyupasthana* (worship of Agni concluding the agnihotra) takes place, with prayers for the fire and the cow that supplied the milk. Performing the agnihotra is said to bring great merit and leads to a life in Pitriyana, the realm of the ancestors.

In the Puranas, Agnihotra is personified as the son of Prishni and Savita.

DARSHAPURNAMASESHTI

The *darshapurnamaseshti* consists of the new- and full-moon sacrifices, which are of the ishti type. It is both a shrauta and a grihya rite. The new-moon sacrifice takes two days. The full-moon sacrifice is similar but lasts for one day. On the first day of the new-moon sacrifice, the sacrificer takes certain vows and prepares the fires. On the second day, the sacrificial cakes to be offered are made. The altar is prepared and the wood is laid on it while reciting the *samidheni* verses. Two *agharas* or libations of butter are added and the hotr is formally chosen by the adhvaryu. Various deities are invited to attend, *ajya* offerings are made to Agni and Soma, and cake offerings to Indra and Agni (or Agni and Soma at the full moon). Then an offering is made to Agni Svishtakrit in which all gods are invoked. The priests taste the offering and the libation of holy milk (*ida*). The pitris are invited and the dakshina is given. Then the anuyajyas or after-offerings are made to the barhis, Narashamsa, etc. Next is a prayer, and then the bundle of sacred grass is thrown in the fire.

CHATURMASYA OR FOUR-MONTHLY SACRIFICES

Three such four-monthly sacrifices are performed in the spring, monsoon, and autumn. The Maruts are the most important deities here, along with a set of deities that are different for each sacrifice. At the beginning of each sacrifice, Agni, Soma, Savitr, Sarasvati, and Pushan are worshipped. The wood used in each sacrifice is selected from a tree that blossoms at the time and, for the barhis, from the plants that sprout at the time. The first of the sacrifices is the *vaishvadeva*. After offerings to the five deities, a cake is offered to the Maruts, followed by a milk dish to the Vishvedevas, and a cake to Dyaus-Prithivi. The second is the *Varuna-praghasa* at the beginning of the rains. In this, a ram and an ewe are represented in dough, placed in milk, and offered to Varuna and the Maruts, respectively. This is believed to bring an increase in flocks. Karira fruits are offered for rain and a good harvest. An odd aspect of this sacrifice is that the wife of the sacrificer worships Varuna, confesses the names and number of her lovers (if any), and offers plates of gruel to the southern fire. The third is the *sakamedha* sacrifice, which takes place in autumn. The *pitriyajna* (ancestor rituals) form an important part of it, and the *dakshinayana* fire is prominent. An offering is made to Rudra Tryambika, who is then supposed to depart for the safety of the flocks. After this festival, an offering is made to two deified parts of the plough, the *shuna-sirau*.

AGRAYANA-ISHTI

The *agrayana-ishti* is another sacrifice of both shrauta and grihya rituals. In this, the first fruit of the harvest is offered twice a year. A barley cake is presented in spring and a rice cake in autumn, to Indra and Agni. Offerings are also made to the Vishvedevas, Dyaus, and Prithivi. The *dakshina* (gift to the priest) is the first calf born during the year.

There are several other ishti-type sacrifices, which can be performed to fulfil desires or to gain one's aims.

ANIMAL SACRIFICES

Animal sacrifices were performed both separately and as part of the Soma sacrifice.

Nirudha-pashubandha is a sacrifice that can be performed by an *ahitagni*, that is, 'one who has established the three fires via the correct procedure'. The first performance is before the sacrificer first eats meat. Then it can be repeated once or twice a year, during the *uttarayana* (northern course) of the sun. The sacrifice is similar to the new-moon sacrifice, except that an animal is offered to Indra instead of milk. The sacrificial post is erected on the edge of the altar, half within and half outside. The post is sanctified and mantras are recited. The animal is then tied to the post, bathed, and anointed with butter. After the *ajya* offerings, the usual new-moon sacrifice procedure is followed, including the preliminary offerings.

The *paryagni-karana* then follows. In this, three circles are made around the animal with a fire brand, to sanctify it. As the animal is taken to the sacrificial spot, the sacrificer touches it with two spits, which will later be used to roast it; these are known as the *vapashrapani*. With these, he transfers the divine essence now embodied in the sacred animal, unto himself. Then mantras are recited praying for forgiveness of the sin of killing. Prayers are also offered stating that the animal does not die but goes straight to god. The animal is first strangled by the *samitr* priests. All present look at the *ahavaniya* fire, not at the victim. When the animal is dead, the caul or *vapa* is first removed, cooked, and offered to the gods. The blood is poured out for *rakshasas* and *bhutas*. The spits are then placed in the fire to be burnt. Three cows are given as dakshina.

There is a second phase, which involves making the rice cake and cutting the body of the animals, after which offerings are made to gods and priests. After this are the eleven *anuyajyas*, where offerings are made to the barhis, dvaro devih, and other items, according to the order in the Apri hymns. Certain items related to the sacrifice, including the *prastara* or grass and the remaining ghi or butter, are thrown into the fire, whereas, the various implements are buried. This marks the completion of the sacrifice.

SAUTRAMANI SACRIFICE

This sacrifice is considered a *havir yajna*, not a Soma sacrifice. In this, *sura* (a type of wine) is used instead of Soma. The sacrifice is dedicated to Indra, the Ashvins, and Sarasvati. According to the associated legend, Indra drank too much Soma and became intoxicated. He was then cured by the Ashvins and Sarasvati. The sacrifice could be performed for various purposes: by a brahmana who wished for success; by a king who had lost his throne and wanted to regain it; by a Vaishya who wished to get rich.

SHRAUTA SOMA SACRIFICES

Soma sacrifices are the most important. Rich people and kings performed these but others also watched. A number of Vedic rites are classified as Soma sacrifices. Each sacrifice has four preliminary preparatory days:

1. *Ekaha*: This has one *sutya* day, the day on which Soma is extracted and the sacrifice performed.
2. *Ahina*: This has a varying number of sutya days, between two and twelve.
3. *Sattra*: This has more than twelve sutya days, and can last for a year or longer. The priests conducting it are considered the sacrificers. It is basically of the same form as the *dvadashaha*, the ahina sacrifice with twelve pressing days, which is further extended in the sattra type. Theoretically, a sattra sacrifice can last for many years, even 1000 years!

Among the various Soma sacrifices are seven forms together known as jyotishtoma. These are (1) agnishtoma, (2) atyagnishtoma, (3) ukthya, (4) shodashin, (5) vajapeya, (6) atiratra, and (7) aptoryama. Among these, the atyagnishtoma, vajapeya, and aptoryama are not part of the jyotishtoma in older texts, and must have been added later to reach the mystical number of seven. Descriptions of these sacrifices in various texts are not identical but the main aspects are given here.

AGNISHTOMA

Agnishtoma is one of the seven jyotishtoma sacrifices, which comprises offerings of Soma to the god Indra and other deities. This is an ekaha, that is, a one-day Soma sacrifice. Though the rituals are spread over several days, Soma is offered only on one day, in the morning, midday, and evening. It is performed at the request of a householder for religious merit. According to the Puranas, performing the agnishtoma is equivalent to honouring the pitris. The sacrifice can also be performed for general welfare, fame, health, good rainfall, and a bumper harvest. The entire ritual usually takes five days though some of its stages can be extended. It is conducted by sixteen priests. It is not commonly practised today but does take place occasionally.

The sacrifice has several stages. First, the priests are chosen, next the venue. The person initiating the sacrifice, that is the householder, and his wife are consecrated, after which they maintain purity, and do not eat or drink anything but boiled milk. A ritual is carried out consisting of acquiring Soma in exchange for a cow (though the cow is then returned) and this Soma is taken to the place of sacrifice, where it is given a ceremonial reception. Three *upasad* days follow, which are ceremonial days preceding the sutya day. On each of these, the pravargya ceremony takes place twice. On the second day, the altar is prepared. On the third day, a goat is offered to the gods Agni and Soma. The sons, grandsons, and relatives of the sacrificer participate in this. Next is the sutya day, the day of the Soma offerings. This begins with offerings to Agni, Usha, and the Ashvins. Soma juice is pressed and removed in an elaborate ritual involving several priests. There is another animal sacrifice, which is offered to Indra and Agni. Other offerings, including those of sacrificial cakes, take place and various verses are recited. The second or midday pressing takes place, accompanied by more rituals, after which the sacrificer distributes fees, including his possessions, to the priests. The third evening pressing takes place, again with several rituals. Finally, the Agni-Maruta shastra (verses) is recited and the *avabhritha*, 'carrying of the items to the water', takes place. Items left over from the sacrifice are thrown into the water. The yajamana and his wife bathe and wear new clothes. The god Varuna is then praised with offerings.

The pravargya ceremony forms part of the agnishtoma, though it was once possibly a separate rite. In this, a vessel is heated till it becomes red-hot and represents the sun. Milk is boiled in it and offered to the Ashvins. The entire ceremony has great mystery. All the sacrificial implements and utensils are finally arranged to represent a man. The head is the cauldron of milk. A bit of sacred grass is the tuft of hair. Two gold leaves are the eyes, two milk pails the ears, two cups the heels. Flour is sprinkled over it, representing the marrow; a mixture of honey and milk represents the blood. Prayers are recited along with these ceremonies. According to the Aitareya Brahmana, through this ritual, the sacrificer receives a new body, new energy, new life.

ATYAGNISHTOMA

This sacrifice is actually similar to the shodashin described below, but the three stotras and shastras of the ukthya and the ukthya cup are omitted.

UKTHYA

The ukthya sacrifice is similar to the agnishtoma but, in the third Soma pressing, the number of shastras and stotras recited is increased, thus reaching a total of fifteen. Additional and different samans are sung, and offerings are made to other deities. A second animal, a male goat, is offered in sacrifice on the pressing day.

SHODASHIN

This sacrifice is similar to the ukthya but a ram is offered to Indra, and the shastras, stotras, and offering cups increase to sixteen, leading to its name. The sacrificial fees differ and the shodashin cup receives special care. It is placed in another vessel, made of khadira wood.

VAJAPEYA

A consecration rite for kings, vajapeya literally means 'drink of strength' and this sacrifice conferred a superior status on the king. The vajapeya sacrifice included a chariot race, with seventeen chariots, after which the royal sacrificer and his wife had to ascend a pole and worship mother earth from above. The significance of this is explained in the Shatapatha Brahmana, which states that he who gains a seat in the air, gains a seat above others (5.2.1.22). Descending from the throne, the sacrificer is seated on a throne covered with goatskin. The adhvaryu then tells him, 'You are the ruler, the ruling lord, firm and steadfast. Here I seat you for tilling, for peaceful dwelling, for wealth, for prosperity (of the people).'

ATIRATRA

This sacrifice has twenty-nine stotras and shastras. Recitation continues through the night, with the last verse recited after sunrise. At daybreak, the sandhi stotra (twilight stotra from Sama Veda 2) with nine verses is sung to the Rathantara tune (one of the tunes found in the Sama ganas). Following this is the *prataranuvaka* (morning litany), which is modified to form a special recitation to the Ashvins, which has at least 1000 verses, and then 1000 Brihati (metre) verses. Then the adhvaryu takes the cup of the hotr. A cup is offered to the Ashvins containing the Soma of the last evening's pressing; the *pratiprasthatr* (an assistant of the adhvaryu) offers the cake. A male goat is sacrificed to Sarasvati. As it extends beyond one day, it can be classified as an ahina sacrifice.

APTORYAMA

This is similar to the atiratra. After the sandhi stotra and Ashvina shastra, it has four more stotras and shastras, with four sets of cups for the priests. According to some texts, these are for Agni, Indra, the Vishvedevas, and Vishnu. According to others, these are for the deities to whom offerings of Soma are made in the Sandhi graha or cups.

OTHER SACRIFICES

BRIHASPATI-SAVA

This sacrifice is described in some texts. The Taittiriya Brahmana states that, by its performance, a priest attained his aim of becoming a purohita (chief priest). According to the Ashvalayana Shrauta Sutra, a priest usually performed this after the vajapeya. In some texts, it is considered the same as the vajapeya but, in an earlier period, the two must have been different.

ASHVAMEDHA

The horse sacrifice, one of the main sacrifices in early India, was conducted to increase the power of the king. It was the greatest of sacrifices performed by a king. It is considered an ahina Soma sacrifice, with more than one sutya day. After certain purificatory ceremonies, a horse—marked with the king's name—was set free to roam, accompanied by warriors and nobles. The territory through which it wandered was claimed by the king; anyone who challenged this had to defeat the accompanying warriors in battle. After a period of time, usually a year or more, the horse returned to the kingdom and was sacrificed, often along with hundreds of other animals. During the time it wandered, many rituals were performed at court. Prayers were offered, and the hotr narrated stories of ancient, powerful kings. There was also music and chanting.

After the horse returned, a Soma sacrifice was held, with three sutya days; the horse was sacrificed on the second day. The sacrificial ritual, involving the priest, king, and queen is described in detail in several texts. Some of the flesh of the horse was consecrated to the gods, some eaten by participants in the sacrifice. Before this, the queen had to spend one night near the dead horse, during which some rituals were prescribed. A priest recited riddles, for which the answers are given by another priest. On the third sutya day, the participants bathe, thus concluding the ceremonies.

There are some controversies about the nature of the ashvamedha in early times. The sacrifice is first mentioned in the Rig Veda and described in detail in the Yajur Veda, Brahmanas, and other texts. The Rig has verses on the ashvamedha but does not describe the entire ritual. The offering of a goat to Pushan is mentioned but no other animal sacrifice is cited. The Yajur provides a list of animals to be sacrificed but some feel it was a symbolic list, not meant to be taken literally. Some of the animals, such as various goats to be offered, were certainly symbolic; at times, the entire sacrifice was symbolic. In the Brihadaranyaka Upanishad, the symbolism of the sacrifice is described, with the horse reflecting the cosmos.

The Mahabharata describes an ashvamedha performed by King Uparichara Vasu where no animals were sacrificed (Shantiparva Chapters 335–339). Usually, however, it seems to have involved an actual sacrifice, and such animal sacrifices certainly took place in later times.

Inscriptions recording ashvamedhas occur from the 2nd century BCE, though it was practised even earlier. It indicated the power and glory of the king; in fact, important kings performed several ashvamedhas. The Guptas, the Chalukyas, and the Cholas are among the many dynasties whose kings performed the sacrifice; by the time of the Cholas, however, the practice was rare and gradually died out, though one was conducted in Jaipur in the 19th century.

Horse sacrifices took place in other ancient cultures as well including Greece and China. For instance, the Greeks and Cretans sacrificed horses to the god Poseidon Hippios. Horse sacrifices in ancient Rome were connected with agriculture and the harvest. In recent times, the ashvamedha has been recreated and performed according to Vedic rites without any animal sacrifices.

A few verses from the Vajasaneyi Samhita (Yajur Veda) related to the ashvamedha are given below. These show that many aspects of the ashvamedha cannot be taken literally. The complete verses can be read in Appendix II.

1. *Horse, hornless goat, Gomriga, these belong to Prajapati.*
   A black-necked goat, devoted to Agni, (is to be bound)
   in front to the forehead (of the horse); Sarasvati's ewe
   below his jaws; two goats belonging to the Ashvins, with
   marks on the lower parts of the body, to his fore-legs; a
   dark-coloured goat, Soma's and Pushan's, to his navel; a
   white and a black, sacred to Soma and Varuna, to his sides;
   Tvashtr's two, with bushy tails, to his hind feet; Vayu's
   white goat to his tail; for Indra the Good Worker a cow
   who slips her calf; a dwarf belonging to Vishnu.

2. *The red goat, the smoky-red, the jujube-red, these belong to*
   Soma. The brown, the ruddy-brown, the parrot-brown,
   these are Varuna's. One with white ear holes, one with
   partly white, one with wholly white, belong to Savitar.
   One with fore feet white, partly white, wholly white,
   belongs to Brihaspati. She-goats speckled, with small spots,
   with big spots, these belong to Mitra-Varuna.

3. *The bright-tailed, the wholly bright-tailed, the jewel-tailed,*
   these belong to the Ashvins. The white, the white-eyed,
   the reddish, these are for Rudra Lord of Beasts. Long-eared
   goats are for Yama; proud ones for Rudra; cloud-coloured
   ones for Parjanya.

(Vajasaneyi Samhita 24.1–3)

PURUSHAMEDHA

A term for a human sacrifice, this is described in early texts such as the Yajur Veda, Taittiriya Brahmana, Shatapatha Brahmana, Shrauta Sutras, and others. The sacrifice was performed to gain prestige, prosperity, and power in the world. The Shatapatha Brahmana states that it is the highest of the sacrifices while the Katyayana Shrauta Sutra says that a performer of this sacrifice excels over everyone else in the world. Though human sacrifices are mentioned in ancient stories and legends, some feel that the complex Purushamedha described in these texts could not actually have taken place and must be symbolic. According to these, 184 human beings were to be offered to various deities or personifications of qualities. Many different types of people were to be sacrificed, including a brahmana, a kshatriya, a vaishya, a shudra, a murderer, a eunuch, a blind man, a deaf man, a washerwoman, a barren woman, a vina player, a flute player, a cripple, a bald man, and many more. It is unlikely that all these were actually located and sacrificed. An additional reason for considering it symbolic is that in the Yajur Veda section on the purushamedha, a version of the Purushasukta hymn of the Rig Veda is given, in which Purusha is the highest being, from whose sacrifice creation emerges. Purusha is also identified with Prajapati and Brahman. However, G.R. Sharma, the excavator of Kaushambi, felt he had discovered the site of an ancient purushamedha site there. He describes the *shyenachiti* (hawk-shaped) *agnichayana* (fire altar) with the remains of human and animal bones and human skulls, as well as with the different types of bricks described in texts.

RAJASUYA

One of the four main consecration rituals for kings in ancient days, the rajasuya sacrifice is described in detail in the Shatapatha Brahmana. It was inaugurated and initiated by the king. In form, it followed a Soma sacrifice. A diksha (consecration) ceremony was followed by upasad days and other rituals that lasted over a year. The main rituals began after thirteen months, with presents to the chief queen and court officials, followed by the *abhisheka* or sprinkling with consecrated water. This was a mixture of seventeen different types of water, including that from the river Sarasvati, from a pond, a well, a whirlpool, seawater, and dew. After invoking the gods and sprinkling the water, the king walked towards the different directions, indicating that his rule extended everywhere. Next he trod on a tiger skin, to gain the strength of a tiger. After this, the hotr recited the story of Shunahshepa, following which a mock battle or cattle raid was enacted. The king was then enthroned and played a game of dice, which he was made to win. These rituals blessed the king and were symbolic of his rule over the four quarters, and the strength and luck he required for his successful rule. The sacrifice is mentioned in the Mahabharata and other texts, as performed by Yudhishthira and several others. Other consecration rituals were the vajapeya, punar abhisheka, and aindra mahabhisheka.

SARVAMEDHA

Another sacrifice of ahina type is the sarvamedha. At the end of this, the sacrificer gives away all his possessions to the priests and retires to the forest.

The gavamayana is an interesting sattra sacrifice, lasting for one year.

All the above are shrauta sacrifices.

GRIHYA SACRIFICES

Grihya rituals, performed by the householder, were simpler than Shrauta sacrifices. While Shrauta sacrifices used three fires, the householder used one. This is mentioned even in the Rig Veda.

The domestic fire was initiated and used in rituals, and maintained without interruption during marriage or the death of the head of the family.

Some Shrauta sacrifices were also grihya rituals but conducted slightly differently, and not in such an elaborate manner. Among these were the morning and evening sacrifices, the new- and full-moon sacrifices, and some animal and other sacrifices. But Soma sacrifices were exclusively part of shrauta ritual, and personal and family rites are purely part of the grihya ritual. Soma is never used in a grihya ritual.

The best time for the first lighting of the fire was on an auspicious morning at the time of the uttarayana, the northern course of the sun. The householder could perform the rituals himself but a brahmana was required at the *shulagava* (see below) and *Dhanvantari* sacrifices or offerings. (Dhanvantari is a deity, a divine physician, and the traditional founder of medicine in the world.) In the morning and evening sacrifices, the wife could represent her husband. All the people in the house helped maintain the fire. At the end of most such rituals, the *yajna-vastu* ceremony took place. This included a prayer to the god Rudra, while some kusha grass which had been dipped in the ajya and sprinkled with water, was thrown into the fire.

MORNING AND EVENING SACRIFICES

Morning and evening sacrifices were daily rituals. In the daily morning sacrifice, barley or rice was offered to Surya and Prajapati, and in the evening to Agni and Prajapati.

PANCHA-MAHA-YAJNA

Apart from these two, five sacrifices—the *pancha-maha-yajna*—were to be performed daily. These were the deva yajna, an offering to the gods; bhuta yajna, an offering to the four elements, and to some minor deities and demons, as well as to non-human living beings; pitr-yajna, an offering to the ancestors; brahma-yajna, which consists of self-study or *svadhyaya*, and here involves the reading of Vedic texts; and *manushya-yajna*, a sacrifice to people, which refers to food offered to a guest or beggar.

SHRAVANA OFFERING TO SNAKES

Periodic grihya rituals include the *shravana* offering to snakes. It must have originated because of the danger from snakes in the rainy season. On the full-moon day of the month of shravana, an offering of barley flour or cooked food is made to the month of shravana, the god Vishnu, and to the rainy season. Next, grain and barley flour mixed with butter are offered to snakes. Snakes are not necessarily present at the time of the offering. Next, water is filled in a new pot, which is said to be for the snakes to have a wash. A comb, perfume, flowers, collyrium, and mirror are presented, so that snakes may decorate themselves. Finally an offering is made to the Nagas (divine snakes). After this, people sleep on high beds until the end of the rainy season, as this provides protection from snakes on the ground. An offering is made every night until the full moon of the month of *margashirsha*, when another ceremony takes place, known as the *pratyavarahona* (re-descent) or *agrahayani* festival.

AGRICULTURAL RITES

Agricultural rites are other rituals. Two of these take place before the shravana festival: one, a ceremony for the first ploughing, which should take place at the time of a particular nakshatra, usually *rohini* or *jyeshtha*, and two, an offering to Sita (deity of the furrow). Other rituals are performed when sowing, harvesting, threshing, storing the threshed grain, and eating the first produce of the harvest.

RITES FOR CATTLE

There are several rites for cattle. Some of these are explained here:

- *Shulagava*, an ox sacrifice, had two forms. In one form, an ox was sacrificed and dedicated to the god Rudra. In another form, no animal was killed but boiled rice was offered to a bull, a cow, and a calf—or to representations of these. These also represented the deities Sharva, Madhushi, and Jayanta.
- In *baudhyavihara*, boiled rice, sprinkled with ajya, was placed in a basket of palasha leaves and hung on a tree as an offering for Rudra.
- *Sthalipaka* was an offering to Kshetrapati, lord of the fields, represented by a bull. The offering was wrapped in leaves, and placed in the path of the cows.
- *Vrishotsarga* was a ceremony where a bull was loosened on the full-moon night of the month of Karttika. It was said to ensure that cows bred well.
- On several occasions, mantras for the protection and safety of cattle were recited.

OCCASIONAL CEREMONIES

Guest Reception

This is for special guests, more elaborate than the daily manushya-yajna. A special area is prepared, and the guest is welcomed and seated. First the guest's feet are washed, next the guest is offered *arghya* (water and items for worship), *achamaniya* (water for sipping), and *madhuparka* (a honey mixture). A cow is presented to the guest, after which food is offered.

House Construction

Various rituals are performed during the building of a house. When the building is complete, the vastu-shanti rite is performed, and special food is offered to Vastoshpati, the deity of houses. Brahmanas and relatives are then fed. Two Grihya Sutras state that an animal is to be sacrificed as part of the vastu-shanti ritual but others do not.

Chaitya Sacrifice

This is a special ritual where offerings are made to a religious shrine or a memorial monument.

FAMILY SAMSKARAS

Apart from these formal grihya sacrifices, there are the personal or family *samskaras* and rituals. Some of these are referred to in the Rig Veda while others came into use later. At a still later time, some authorities selected sixteen main samskaras to be practised: (1) *garbhadana* (conception), (2) *pumsavana* (quickening, ensuring a male offspring), (3) *simantoyana* or *simantonnayana* (ritual parting of the hair of the woman during pregnancy), (4) *jatakarma* (birth ceremony), (5) *namakarana* (naming ceremony), (6) *nishkarmana* (first outing), (7) *annaprashana* (first solid food given), (8) *chudakarana* (shaving the head of the child, normally between the first and third year; can be later for a kshatriya or vaishya), (9) *karnavedha* (piercing the ears), (10) *vidyarambha* (beginning to learn the alphabet), (11) *upanayana* (initiation), (12) *vedarambha* (beginning of Vedic study), (13) *keshanta* or *godana* (the male student's first shaving or cutting of his beard, indicating maturity, accompanied by a gift to the teacher), (14) *samavartana* (end of studentship, and return to the parent's home; he has a ceremonial bath, followed by other rituals, and is now ready for marriage and a life in the world; he is known as a *snataka*, 'one who has taken a bath'), (15) *vivaha* (marriage ceremonies, several beginning with the betrothal), and (16) *antyeshti* (funeral ceremonies).

Not all these are observed today, except by the very traditional. However, namakarana, annaprashana, chudakarana, and upanayana are usually observed by many, while marriage and funeral ceremonies are performed by most. There are regional and caste-based variations of these ceremonies. In some regions, Vedic verses are recited at marriage and funeral ceremonies. All rituals conducted according to Arya Samaj rites use verses from the Vedas. Some details on marriage and funeral rituals are given here.

MARRIAGE

The vivaha or marriage was an important custom from ancient days, and is described in the Vedas, epics, Puranas, and other texts. Marriages took place not merely among ordinary people but also among the gods, and these are described in great detail.

In Vedic times, marriage seemed to be between two adults. Polygamy was known but polyandry was rare. Elder children were supposed to get married before younger siblings. Prohibitions regarding marriage are not clear, though brother–sister marriages were prohibited. Incest of any kind was frowned upon.

Acceptable forms of marriage are described in the Smritis and Sutras. *Grihastha ashrama*, the stage of a householder, was important in the fourfold scheme of Hindu life, and in the Grihya Sutras, marriage is the most important of the Samskaras. The Gobhila Grihya Sutra and the Dharma Sutras prohibit marriage within the *gotra* (extended family) within six degrees on the mother's or father's side, though earlier such prohibitions did not seem to have existed.

In later texts, there were recommendations that the girl be married at very young age, though this did not always happen. There were several different forms of marriage. According to the Ashvalayana Grihya Sutra, there were eight forms of marriage. Though other Grihya Sutras do not describe all these, they are referred to in stories in various texts, and described in the Smritis. The Manu Smriti states that, of these, four methods are approved or good (*prashasta*) and four are not approved (*aprashasta*).

Prashasta Forms of Marriage

1. *Brahma*: This is the best form, according to the Shastras. Here the girl is given by the father to a man who is learned and has a good character. The girl is gifted by the father with ornaments he can afford, and nothing is taken in return.
2. *Daiva*: In this form, the girl is given to a brahmana as dakshina (sacrificial fee) after he has conducted a sacrifice. This form was common in the old days when kings or rich and powerful people gave their daughters to prominent rishis.
3. *Arsha*: A form common among brahmanas and rishis of olden days, in this marriage, a pair of cattle was given by the groom to the brahmana father of the bride for the performance of a sacrifice. Another type of Arsha consisted of the marriage of a girl to a rishi in honour of his learning.
4. *Prajapatya*: In this form, the aim of the marriage is that both husband and wife together perform their social and religious duties. The father gives away his daughter to a man who will be suitable for this.

Aprashasta Forms of Marriage

The four aprashasta forms were at one time quite common but later frowned upon by Shastra writers.

1. *Asura*: According to the Manu Smriti, this was when the husband paid money to the bride and her relatives. Some ancient writers call this the *manusha* (human) form. The custom was criticized by Shastra writers, who said that selling a daughter led one into hell.

2. *Gandharva*: This form was when a man and a woman chose each other. The Manu Smriti states that a gandharva type is 'where the bride and the bridegroom meet each other of their own accord, and the meeting is consummated in copulation born of passion' (3.32). Kings, rishis, and others often had this type of marriage in ancient days, but it gradually fell into disfavour.

3. *Rakshasa*: In this form, a girl was captured by force while weeping and crying and her relatives were injured or killed (Manu Smriti 2.21). It was considered a good form for Kshatriyas (3.24). However, several instances of capture in the Mahabharata and other texts involved the consent of the woman, even though the relatives were against it. Thus Arjuna captured Subhadra with the support of Krishna, though Balarama and others were opposed to it. Later, they were formally married. Sita's capture by Ravana in the Ramayana was in a different category, as she was already married. In times of war, Kshatriyas continued to capture women but otherwise this form became uncommon.

4. *Paishacha*: Shastra writers considered this the worst. It involved carrying away or ravishing the woman when she was alone, asleep, senseless, or intoxicated.

There were other forms of marriage in later times. Child marriage also became common.

FUNERAL CEREMONIES AND CUSTOMS

One of the main samskaras of Hindu life is the funeral ceremony, known as antyeshti. Cremation is the most common form of funeral ceremony performed today. However, certain groups are not cremated. Ascetics and children are generally buried or given a 'water burial' (floated down a river). Dalits and certain castes such as Lingayats also bury their dead.

Historically, both cremation and burial existed. The Indus Civilization has evidence of burial as well as post-cremation burial and symbolic burial. The Rig Veda seems to refer to both burial (10.18.10–13) and cremation (10.16.1–6), though cremation soon became the norm. Archaeological excavations indicate burial existed in various areas at both Neolithic and Mesolithic sites. Another early funeral practice was the erection of megaliths over graves or over ashes placed in urns.

Funeral ceremonies are described in different places in the Atharva Veda, the Aranyaka of the Krishna Yajur Veda, and later in some Grihya Sutras. Further texts on funeral practices termed Paddhatis and Prayogas were written in medieval and modern times. These were based on early sources but added some new elements.

For funeral ceremonies and offerings to the ancestors, only one fire, the dakshina, is used in both grihya and shrauta rituals. In the shrauta ceremonies, the other two have a nominal presence. There are two types of ancestral rites. The first are for the distant or ancient ancestors, the pitris, and the second for those recently dead, known as *pretas*. The Grihya Sutras describe shraddha ceremonies for both categories. For the pitris, there is the daily *pitri yajna*, the monthly *shraddha*, as well as offerings at the *ashtaka* and *anvashtakya* rituals. Ashtaka rituals take place on the eighth day of the dark fortnights after the full moon of certain months (more details below). The anvashtakya is performed the day after the ashtaka. Immediately after a person dies, there are funeral rituals and others come later. According to the Grihya Sutras, several Rig Vedic verses are to be recited during the funeral ceremonies. In a custom described in the Rig Veda, when a man dies, the wife lies down beside him on the funeral pyre, and then is asked to rise by someone from her husband's family with the recitation of the verse 10.18.8. While the body of an *ahitagni* (one who has established the sacred fire) is being burnt, the following Rig verses are recited: 10.14.7, 8, 10, 11; 10.16.1–6; 10.17.3–6; 10.18.10–13. These ask him to follow the ancient paths of the pitris, which lead to Yama and Varuna, the two kings. He should leave behind all faults and go past the Sarameyas. If the dead person is not an ahitagni, no verses are recited when the body is burning. After the body is burnt, milk and water are sprinkled on the spot, and Rig Vedic verses 10.16.13 onwards are chanted. Either on the third or on the tenth day, the bones are collected and placed in an urn, which is buried in a pit. At this time, the verses (Rig 10.18.10) are recited, beginning, 'Approach mother earth . . .' Some of the Rig Vedic mantras indicate that with the burning of the body and the chanting of verses, the preta (spirit of the dead person) went directly to abode of the pitris. But in the later sutras the *sapindakarana* (*shraddha*) leads the preta to this region. During this ceremony, the Rig Veda verses 10.191.3–4 are recited. The Shatapatha Brahmana and the Katyayana Shrauta Sutra state that a memorial is to be erected, after removing the bones from the place where they were buried, and reburying it outside the village. Then a mound was erected and a barrier placed on the mound, to separate the dead from the living. Rig 10.18.3–4 says a stone can be a barrier.

After the sapindakarana, offerings are made usually for one year after death, when the preta is considered a pitri and offerings are made accordingly. A monthly shraddha is performed. As this takes place in the afternoon of the day of the new moon, it is called *parvana* (both new-moon and full-moon days are called parvan). In the Shrauta cult, the equivalent is the pinda pitri yajna, in which only the dakshina fire is lit. Food, mainly rice, is cooked, and at least three brahmanas are invited, to represent the father, grandfather, and great-grandfather. Offerings are made to these three, along with the recitation of the Vedic verse 10.15.15. Various other rituals conclude the ceremony, which is followed by the *ashtakas* or eighth-day ceremonies. Usually, three ashtakas take place, on the eighth day following the full moon in the months of Pausha, Magha, and Phalguna. In the second ashtaka, part of the Rig Vedic hymn 10.15 is used. There are also other shraddha ceremonies described in the sutras.

Rites for cremation vary in different regions and among the various communities, and have been modified and simplified over time.

Some early sutras prescribe that a cow or goat should be sacrificed along with the dead person, as it was supposed to guide them over the Vaitarani river, the mythical river separating life and death. The sacrifice may have been only symbolic. According to later texts, a cow was made to walk around the funeral pyre, and then set free or gifted to a brahmana. Modern times have led to a modification or elimination of this practice.

CHAPTER 11

THE BEGINNINGS OF MEDICINE

Dhanvantari, an incarnation of Vishnu, emerged from the *kshir-sagara*, the ocean of milk, carrying the vessel of *amrita*, the divine drink of immortality. Dhanvantari is said to be the physician of the gods, and the first of all physicians on earth. Though this is a later legend, medicine can be traced back to the Vedas and even earlier.

IN THE ANCIENT WORLD

Even in the Palaeolithic age, people would have suffered from diseases and injuries and attempts must have been made to cure them, to help them heal. We don't know what these early attempts were but, by the Bronze Age, medicine and systems of healing, including surgery, use of herbs, and spiritual methods, were used in ancient Egypt, Iran, India, Mesopotamia, and other parts of the ancient world.

HARAPPAN CIVILIZATION

Some Harappan seals and artefacts have been interpreted from the standpoint of medicine. Kenneth G. Zysk, an Indologist at the University of Copenhagen, suggested that the extensive drainage system in Harappan cities indicates 'a concern for public health and sanitation', and that the Great Bath at Mohenjodaro could indicate the use of hydrotherapy as a therapeutic measure, though the latter seems unlikely. Some seals and sealings may have been used as amulets to ward off disease and ill-fortune. The short inscriptions on them may have been mantras. A seal of a woman standing in a pipal tree with seven devotees below suggests a tree goddess, and a reverence for plants that were used extensively to cure diseases in the Atharva Veda and later texts. The horned deity in another famous seal (see Chapter 8) could have been a *shaman* or medicine man. There are other possibilities too but, without the script having been deciphered, nothing can be said with certainty.

THE VEDAS

The Rig Veda and Later Vedic Samhitas, particularly the Atharva Veda, have references to the healing and curing of ailments. *Bheshaja* is the term used for medicine or a remedial measure in the Vedic texts; remedies included plants, water, and spells. A *bhishaj* or physician is frequently mentioned, right from the time of the Rig Veda. Among the gods, the Ashvins, Varuna, and Rudra are known as bhishaj. One hymn in the Rig Veda (10.97) refers to a physician with his plants and healing powers. In the same text, the Ashvins are the greatest healers, who could heal the lame and the blind, restore youth, and even replace a leg with a metal one. These miraculous cures may have been mythical or based on ancient stories and legends. They do not exist in the Atharva Veda, which describes different methods to treat illness and disease. However, the practice of medicine seems to have been a profession by the time of the Rig Veda. In the Yajur Veda, a physician is included among the *purushamedha* (human sacrifice) victims.

In the Dharma Shastras, the profession of physician is looked down upon; this attitude can be seen even in the Yajur Veda, where the Ashvins are condemned for practising medicine.

The Vedic texts also reflect a knowledge of the body and its functions, and some knowledge of the human anatomy.

The Atharva Veda provides information on the body, mentions diseases, and also indicates the plants and herbs used to cure these. Herbs that can cure disease are also praised in prayers and invocations. There are prayers to water, which has healing powers, and to fire, which is believed to guard against demons. Both *pishachas* and *rakshasas* are believed to cause diseases. Healing rituals, accompanied by chants, are described. Diseases, personified as demons, were sent to far-off countries or peoples, carried away by birds, or transferred to the ground. These were not unusual practices. Even in the New Testament of the Holy Bible, people are said to be possessed by devils and, in one instance, these are transferred to a herd of swine.

Healing rituals were conducted at specific times, some performed when the stars were in a particular alignment, indicating the use of astrology. Amulets of wood and other items are referred to in the Atharva Veda.

The later texts, the Rigvidhana and the Kaushika Sutra, perhaps of the 3rd and 2nd centuries BCE, elucidate some aspects of medicine mentioned in the Samhitas. The Kaushika Sutra (25–36) has a *bhaishajya* (medical section), which classifies the spells and charms.

SPIRITUAL HEALING

The magic songs and magic rites of the Atharva are said, in the Kaushika Sutra, to form the oldest system of medical science. Though Ayurveda is a scientific system that is increasingly gaining ground, spiritual healing systems such as reiki and pranic healing proliferate today, both in India and other parts of the world. Belief in disease being caused by negative thoughts of others, or by tantric practices, is still widespread in India. Amulets are still used for protection. Pujas are often conducted in the hope of restoring the health of loved ones. Thus, the ancient ideas cited in the Atharva have not gone out of circulation, and are still relevant today.

DISEASES

Many diseases are described in the Vedas. The major ones are described here.

Yakshma

A term in the Rig, Yajur, and Atharva Vedas, yakshma indicates 'disease'. In later texts, yakshma is a term for consumption but, in the Samhitas, it is not used in such a specific way. For instance, the Vajasaneyi Samhita refers to 100 kinds of yakshma (12.97). The Kathaka Samhita (17.11) contains the term *a-yakshma* indicating 'free from disease'. In addition, in the Yajur Veda Samhitas, *raja-yakshma* (royal yakshma) and *papa-yakshma* (evil yakshma) are referred to. The latter probably indicates a serious disease. *Ajnatayakshma* or 'unknown sickness' is mentioned in the Rig Veda, Atharva Veda, and Kathaka Samhita in connection with raja-yakshma. Yakshma is also identified with a demon or demonic force.

Yakshma occurred in both human adults and children, and in cattle, causing pain, fever, and debility. In one passage, it is said to be caused by sin (*enas*) and to have been sent by the gods. Among the gods prayed to for its prevention and cure were Agni, the Adityas, Vayu, and Savitr. The healing ointment (*anjana*) and amulets of wood from the *varana* tree, and of *shatavara* were used. The *gugguli* plant was burnt and its fumes were helpful. Certain powerful spells were used, along with herbs such as *kushtha*, *chipudru*, and *arundhati*. The Rigvidhana and Kaushika Sutra recommend sprinkling water and ghi on the patient, along with other rituals. A chant from the Atharva Veda on yakshma is given here:

A spell to banish yakshma
1. *From both nostrils, from both eyes, from both ears, and from your chin,*
   From your brain and tongue I root out yakshma, seated in your head.
2. *From the neck and from the nape, from dorsal vertebrae and spine.*
   From arms and shoulder blades I root out yakshma seated in your arms.
3. *From your heart and from your lungs, from your gall bladder and your sides,*
   From kidneys, spleen and liver, yakshma we eradicate.
4. *From bowels and intestines, from the rectum and the belly, I*
   Extirpate your yakshma, from flanks, navel and mesentery.
5. *From your thighs and from your knees, heels and the fore-parts of your feet.*
   From your loins and hips I draw out yakshma.

6. *From your marrows and your bones, from your tendons and veins*
   I banish yakshma, from your hands, your fingers, and your nails.
7. *In every member, every hair, in every joint wherein it lies,*
   We with the exorcising spell of Kashyapa drive far away yakshma settled in your skin.

(Atharva Veda 2.33; based on the translation by R.T.H. Griffith in
The Hymns of the Atharva Veda)

Jayenya

Jayenya or *jayanya* is mentioned in the Atharva Veda and in the Taittiriya Samhita, as some kind of disease; in one passage in the Atharva, it is mentioned with jaundice and pain in limbs. If these are its symptoms, it could be some kind of liver disease. It has also been mentioned with yakshma and with *apachit* ('skin sores'). Like yakshma, it pervades the whole body. It also leads to a swollen belly. It is said to have two types: *akshita* and *sukshita*. Scholars have interpreted the disease in different ways. Sayana feels it is an inherited or venereal disease. According to the American philologist and Sanskrit scholar Maurice Bloomfield, based on references in the Kaushika Sutra, it must be syphilis. Several scholars support this. It has also been interpreted as gout, though this seems unlikely. Prayers and anjana or ointment were used to cure it.

Takman

Takman, or fever, has several hymns related to it in the Atharva. The term takman for fever is used only in this text. Takman had several different varieties. Some of the fevers described are clearly malarial, while others are associated with rashes. Extracts of a prayer against takman, which indicates its different types, is given below. This is a prayer that may have been recited by a physician to rid everyone of all kinds of fever that affected people throughout the year.

1. *May Agni drive the takman away from here, may Soma, the press-stone, and Varuna, of tried skill; may the altar, the straw (upon the altar), and the brightly flaming faggots (drive him away)! Away to naught shall go the hateful powers!*
2. *You that makes all men sallow, inflaming them like a searing fire, even now O takman, you will become void of strength: do now go away down, aye, into the depths! The takman that is spotted, covered with spots, like reddish sediment, him you, (O plant) of unremitting potency, drive away down below!*

The prayer continues, requesting takman to go to the far-off northern countries, the land of the Mujavants, Mahavrishas, and Balhikas. The last few verses are:

10. *When you, being cold, and then again deliriously hot, accompanied by cough, did cause the (sufferer) to shake, then O takman, your missiles were terrible: from these surely exempt us!*

11. *By no means ally yourself with balasa, cough and spasm! From there do not return here again: that O takman, do I ask of you!*

12. *O takman, along with your brother balasa, along with your sister cough, along with your cousin paman (itch), go to yonder foreign folk!*

13. *Destroy the takman that returns on (each) third day, the one that intermits (each) third day, the one that continues without intermission, and the autumnal one; destroy the cold takman, the hot, him that comes in summer, and him that arrives in the rainy season!*

14. *To the Gandharis, the Mujavants, the Angas and the Magadhas, we deliver over the takman, like a servant, like a treasure!*

(Atharva Veda 5.22; based on the translation by M. Bloomfield in
The Hymns of the Atharva Veda)

There are several other hymns regarding takman in the Atharva. Takman is associated with Agni, as it is burning hot. Lightning too is prayed to, as its flashes are associated with fever. One verse asks takman to pass into a frog, which is known to be cool and moist. The kushtha plant is prayed to, to drive away takman, and must have been used as a practical remedy for fever. An amulet from the *jangida* tree is also cited as being used. Takman was also known as *hrudu*; this is a word applied to takman but its meaning is not clear. According to Weber, it could mean 'cramp' but there are also other interpretations, such as 'greenish-yellow' or 'gold'. Perhaps this indicates a pallor or change in complexion.

The Kaushika Sutra actually states that a frog should be tied to the patient. A frog was also used in healing rituals for fever in early Europe. The Kaushika also states that the kushtha plant was crushed, mixed with fresh butter, and rubbed on the patient. In later Ayurveda, the kushtha root is used to counter cough, and fever, and for fumigation.

Some ailments associated with takman in the Atharva Veda are *kasha* (cough); *paman*, a skin disease, which could be an itch, eruptions, or scabs that occur with fever; *prishtyamaya*, a pain in the sides or ribs; and *asharika*, possibly the pain in limbs that accompanies fever.

Balasa

Balasa is mentioned in the Vajasaneyi Samhita and also several times in the Atharva and occasionally later. The commentators Mahidhara and Sayana interpret it as consumption; it is said to be a kind of yakshma, because of which bones and joints fall apart; and can be caused by love, or aversion, and the heart; similar statements are made in later Ayurvedic texts. It causes lumps in the armpits, suggesting a disease associated with the lymph glands. Swellings and abscesses are also associated with it. It is called the 'brother' of takman. However, it has also been interpreted as dropsy, or a sore or swelling that accompanies a fever caused by dropsy. The salve or ointment (anjana) from Trikakud, a mountain, and jangida plants are used in its cure, as well as chipudru, which may be *palasha*.

In one hymn in the Atharva, balasa is described as an internal disease, which crumbles the bones, and joints. There is a suggestion that it is removed through surgery: 'the balasa of him who is afflicted with balasa do I remove, as one gelds a lusty animal. Its connection do I cut off as the root of a cucumber [gourd]' (6.14.2). V.W. Karambelkar, an Ayurvedic physician, thought it was a skin disease as it was related to *kilasha* (leucoderma). However, the various references suggest that it could be cancer, which was known to exist in the ancient world. Two prayers against balasa (both based on the translation by R.T.H. Griffith) are given below:

1. *Remove all balasa that lurks within the members and the joints,*
    The firmly settled heart disease that racks the bones and rends the limbs.
2. *From the balasa victim I pluck balasa as 'twere a severed part.*
    I cut the bond that fetters him, even as a root of cucumber.
3. *Begone, balasa, hence away, like a young foal that runs at speed.*
    Then, not pernicious to our men, flee, yearly visitant like grass!

(Atharva 6.14)

1. *Of abscess, of the red balasa, of inflammation. O plant,*
    Of penetrating pain, you herb, let not a particle remain.
2. *Those two withdrawn testicles, balasa! which stand closely hidden in your armpits*
    I know the balm for that disease: the magic cure is chipudru.
3. *We draw from you piercing pain that penetrates and racks your limbs,*
    That pierces ears, that pierces eyes, the abscess, and the heart's disease.
    Downward and far away from you we banish that unknown yakshma.

(Atharva 6.127)

Jaundice

Hariman mentioned in the Rig Veda, Atharva Veda, and elsewhere indicates yellowness in a disease, and that is clearly jaundice. A charm to banish jaundice is given below:

A charm against jaundice and heart disease
As the sun rises, let your heart disease (hridyota) and yellowness depart.
We compass and surround you with the colour of a red bull.
With red tints we surround you, so that you may live a long life;
So that this man be free from harm, and cast his yellow tint away.
Devatyas that are red of hue, and the reddish-coloured cattle,
Each several form, each several force—with these we surround you.
To parrots and to ropanakas (thrush), and to haridravas (yellow wagtail) we transfer your sickly yellowness;

Now in the yellow-coloured birds we lay this yellowness of thine.
(Atharva Veda 1.22; based on the translations by
R.T.H. Griffith and M. Bloomfield)

Heart disease

Hridroga or heart disease is mentioned in the Rig Veda. It seems to be the same as the *hridayamaya* and hridyota cited in the Atharva. However, it is not clear why jaundice and heart disease are mentioned together (see above).

Kshetriya

Kshetriya is mentioned in the Yajur Veda and several times in the Atharva Veda as well as in the Taittiriya Brahmana. Kshetriya seems to be an internal disease with multiple symptoms. It is associated with yakshma, and with seizure (*grahi*) and evil spirits. References suggest that it was either inherited or caused by eating or drinking something. Apart from spells and prayers, barley, sesame, *apamarga* (a plant) and deer horn were used in its cure. Tying of an amulet, either filled with herbs or fashioned from antelope horn, and sprinkling of water were among methods referred to in later texts. According to Sayana, it is some kind of an inherited disease, though Bloomfield and others think it may be scrofula or syphilis. Karambelkar, after an extensive analysis of the term in later texts, feels it is caused by grass poisoning.

The term comes from kshetra, field, and the hymn below indicates it had some relationship with fields and crops.

Hymn to kshetriya
1. *Twin stars of happy omen, named releasers, have gone up.*
   May they loosen, of kshetriya, the uppermost and lowest bond.
2. *Vanish this night, extinct in dawn! Let those who weave their spells depart.*
   So let the kshetriya-destroying plant remove kshetriya.
3. *With straw of barley tawny-brown in colour with its silvery ears,*
   with stalk and stem of sesamum—
   So let the kshetriya-destroying plant remove kshetriya.
4. *Let homage to your ploughs be paid, our homage to the pole and yokes.*
   So let the kshetriya-destroying plant remove kshetriya.
5. *Homage to men with blinking eyes, homage to those who hear*
   and act! To the Field's Lord (Kshetrasyapati) be homage paid.
   So let the kshetriya-destroying plant remove kshetriya.
(Atharva 2.8; based on the translation by R.T.H. Griffith)

Rapas

Rapas is mentioned in the Rig and the Atharva, and seems to be a term for a disease, though it has also been translated as 'wound'. The disease attacked the foot and joints, particularly knees and ankles. A crawling creature known as *ajakava* was said to live under the skin and cause this. Alternatively, it was caused by polluted water or by a creature living in water. It was associated with yakshma and jaundice. Barley was used in its cure, possibly as a poultice. Zyst suggests it was dracunculiases or guinea-worm disease.

A hymn against rapas
1. O Mitra-Varuna, guard and protect me here: let not that come to me which nests within and swells.
    I drive afar the ajakava hateful to the sight: let not the winding worm touch me and wound my foot (or cause foot-rapas).
2. Eruption that appears upon the twofold joints, and that which overspreads the ankles and the knees,
    May the refulgent Agni banish far away; let not the winding worm touch me and wound my foot.
3. The poison that is formed upon the salmali, that which is found in streams, that which the plants produce,
    All this may all the gods banish and drive away: let not the winding worm touch me and wound my foot.
4. The steep declivities, the valleys, and the heights, the channels full of water, and the waterless—
    May those who swell with water, gracious goddesses, never afflict us with the shipada disease, may all the rivers keep us free from shimida.

> (Rig Veda 7.50; based on the translation by R.T.H. Griffith
> in *The Hymns of the Rig Veda*)

Eye Diseases

Among the eye diseases mentioned in the Atharva Veda are *alaji* and *dushika*. In later texts, alaji is a discharge from the eye while dushika is a disease connected with rheum of the eyes. Alaji has also been interpreted as an abscess or boil.

Malnutrition

Amiva in the Rig Veda (10.162) is a disease personified as a demonic being who kills the unborn child. In the Atharva, amiva is a disease associated with poverty (amati), hunger, and malnutrition. It may have been a disease like anaemia, caused by malnutrition. It was treated with prayers, herbs, and amulets.

Anaemia, Blood Flow

Vilohita is mentioned as a disease and literally means 'flow of blood'. It has been interpreted as anaemia, nosebleed, or 'decomposition of blood'.

Swellings and Skin Disorders

Several terms in the Atharva Veda refer to swellings and skin disorders. The term *apachit* is mentioned several times; Bloomfield believes it refers to scrofulous swellings while according to Zyst, it is a rash with pustules. *Upachit* is a term in the Vajasaneyi Samhita, which Roth believes means 'swelling', while Bloomfield thinks it is a variant of apachit. *Galunta* is a term that probably also means 'swelling'; *graivya* seems to denote tumours on the neck; *glau*, also mentioned in the Vajasaneyi Samhita and Aitareya Brahmana, is a symptom of a disease, and possibly refers to a boil. Kilasha is discolouration of the skin or leucoderma.

Hair Loss

Hair loss is mentioned in the Atharva Veda. There are herbs, charms, and prayers to prevent hair loss and have abundant, long, and healthy hair.

Stomach

Some diseases are related to the stomach. Apva is mentioned both in the Rig Veda and in the Atharva. In the Rig, it is located in the stomach and is said to confuse the mind, seize the limbs, and burn the heart. Yaska suggested it was a disease, or that it was fear. It is thought to be dysentery or diarrhoea, perhaps that induced by fear.

Asrava

Mentioned several times in the Atharva, it is literally 'discharge'; the context indicates a disease. Bloomfield feels it is diarrhoea; others suggest painful urination, unhealed wounds, diabetes, or sickness and cold. *Vishuchika*, mentioned in the Vajasaneyi Samhita, other Yajur Samhitas and Shatapatha Brahmana, is a disease caused by drinking too much Soma; it seems to mean dysentery or, literally, 'evacuations in both directions'. *Vishthavrajin* is referred to in the Shatapatha Brahmana; based on the Kathaka recension, Julius Eggeling, Sanskritist and translator of this Brahmana, suggests that it is a disease and means 'one afflicted by dysentery' but others disagree.

Urine Retention and Constipation

The converse of diarrhoea and dysentery was urine retention and constipation. Reference to the reed in the hymn below suggests the use of a catheter-like object. Later commentaries indicate treatments with herbs and by physically opening the bladder and administering an enema.

> Opening the channels
> 1. *We know the father of the reed, Parjanya strong with hundred powers:*
>   *By this may I bring health to your body: let the channels pour their burden freely as of old.*

2. *We know the father of the reed, Mitra, the Lord of hundred powers:*
   By this, may I bring health to your body: let the channels pour their burden freely as of old.
3. *We know the father of the reed, Varuna, strong with hundred powers:*
   By this, may I bring health to your body: let the channels pour their burden freely as of old.
4. *We know the father of the reed, the Moon endowed with hundred powers:*
   By this, may I bring health to your body: let the channels pour their burden freely as of old.
5. *We know the father of the reed, the Sun endowed with hundred powers:*
   By this may I bring health to your body: let the channels pour their burden freely as of old.
6. *Whatever has gathered, as it flowed, in bowels, bladder, or in groins,*
   Thus let the conduit, free from check, pour all its burden as of old.
7. *I lay the passage open as one cleaves the dam that bars the lake:*
   Thus let the conduit, free from check, pour all its burden as of old.
8. *Now has the portal been unclosed as, of the sea that holds the flood:*
   Thus let the conduit, free from check, pour all its burden as of old.
9. *Even as the arrow flies away when loosened from the archer's bow,*
   Thus let the burden be discharged from channels that are checked no more.

(Atharva 1.3; based on the translation by R.T.H. Griffith)

Paralysis

Graha and *grahi* are two terms probably related to paralysis or seizures. Grahi occurs in both the Rig Veda and the Atharva Veda and is personified as a female demon of disease; her son is *svapna*, 'sleep' or 'dream'.

Akshata

Akshata, *akshita*, and *sukshuta* are related terms. They may be related to the term *kshata*, which in later texts is a wound or ulcer in the lungs.

Haemorrhoids

Arshas, a term that occurs in the Vajasaneyi Samhita, probably refers to haemorrhoids.

Jambha

Jambha in the Atharva Veda is a disease or demon of disease; in one passage, it is said to be cured by the jangida plant, in another it is said to 'bring the jaws together'. It has been interpreted as convulsions, tetanus, or (based on a passage in the Kaushiki Sutra), as a child's ailment, probably teething.

Vishkandha

Vishkandha is mentioned several times in the Atharva Veda, as a disease. It has been interpreted as something that draws the shoulders apart (vi–skandha). *Samskandha* is mentioned with vishkandha and means 'having the shoulders together'. Zysk interprets the two terms together, and feels that they refer to tetanus; Weber suggested vishkandha is rheumatism; Sayana saw it as a *vighna*, an impediment by which the body dried up. Karambelkar saw it as progressive muscular dystrophy. It is said to be very painful and to be associated with wounds. Amulets of lead or of the jangida plant, as well as an ointment, and the plants *karshapha* and *vishapha* were used to cure it.

Leprosy

Shvitra, literally, 'white', is a term used in the Panchavimsha Brahmana for a person afflicted with white leprosy; in some other texts, it refers to a type of snake. *Sidhmala* or 'leprous' also refers to a person with leprosy. In the Vajasaneyi Samhita and Taittiriya Brahmana, a sidhmala is one of the victims of the purushamedha.

Krimi

Krimi in the Atharva Veda is a term for worms or parasites, which affected people and cattle. Many types of worms have been identified, some probably mythical. Different types of worms were known by a number of names such as *kururu*, *algandu*, or *yevasha*. Worms lived in mountains, forests, and water, and were found in plants, animals, and people. Worms were removed by prayers and spells and those outside were crushed. Worms were known as causes for diseases in later medical texts too. The prayer below indicates the many different kinds of worms.

A prayer against worms
1. *I have called Heaven and Earth to aid, have called divine Sarasvati,*
   Indra and Agni have I called: Let these destroy the worm, I prayed.
2. *O Indra, Lord of treasures, kill the worms that prey upon this boy.*
   All the malignant spirits have been smitten by my potent spell.
   We utterly destroy the worm, the worm that creeps around the eyes.
   The worm that crawls about the nose, the worm that gets between the teeth.
3. *Two of like colour, two unlike, two coloured black, two coloured red.*
   The tawny and the tawny-eared, the vulture-like and the wolf-like, all these are killed.
4. *Worms that are white about the sides, those that are black with black-hued arms,*
   All that show various tints and hues, these worms we utterly destroy.
5. *Eastward the sun is mounting, seen of all, destroying things unseen,*
   Crushing and killing all the worms invisible and visible.
6. *Let the yevashas, kashkashas, ejatkas, sipavitnukas,*
   Let both the worm that we can see, and that we see not, be destroyed.
7. *Slain the yevasha of the worms, slain too is the nadaniman.*
   I have reduced them all to dust like vetches with the pounding stone.
8. *The worm saranga, white of hue, three-headed, with a triple hump,*
   I split and tear his ribs away, I wrench off every head he has.

9. *I kill you, worms, as Atri, as Kanva and Jamadagni killed.*
   I crush the worms to pieces with a spell that formerly Agastya used.
10. *The king of worms has been destroyed, he who was lord of these is slain.*
    Slain is the worm whose mother, whose brother and sister have been slain.
11. *Destroyed are his dependants, those who dwell around him are destroyed,*
    And all the worms that seem to be the little ones are done to Death.
12. *Of every worm and insect, of the female and the male alike,*
    I crush the head to pieces with a stone and burn the face with fire.

(Atharva 5.23; based on the translation by R.T.H. Griffith)

Mental Diseases

Not merely physical but mental diseases too were known. Insanity of two types is referred to: *unmadita*, probably that which was self-created or circumstantial, and *unmatta*, 'demonic possession'.

A charm against mania
1. *Release for me, O Agni, this person here who, bound and well-secured, loudly jabbers! Then shall he have due regard for your share (of the offering) when he shall be free from madness!*
2. *Agni shall quiet down your mind, if it has been disturbed! Cunningly do I prepare a remedy, that you shall be freed from madness!*
3. *(Whose mind) has been maddened by the sin of the gods, or been robbed of sense by the rakshas (for him) do I cunningly prepare a remedy, that he shall be free from madness.*
4. *May the apsaras restore you, may Indra, may Bhaga restore you; may all the gods restore you, that you may be freed from madness!*

(Atharva Veda 6.111; based on the translation by M. Bloomfield)

OTHER DISEASES IN THE VEDAS

Skandhya is a term in the Atharva Veda for some disease of the shoulders. *Pakaru*, mentioned as a disease in the Vajasaneyi Samhita, along with vishuchika and arshas, probably refers to ulcers or sores. *Pramota* mentioned in the Atharva Veda as some sort of disease, possibly means 'deaf and dumb'. *Viklindu* possibly means catarrh; *vidradha* could refer to abscesses; *vishara, visharika, vishalya*, and *vishalyaka* seem to be terms for pain, probably associated with various diseases. *Vishras* refers to decay, old age, decrepitude, or senility. *Sipada* and *shimida* are unidentified diseases mentioned in the Rig Veda. *Shirshakti* and *shirshashoka* refer to headaches, while *shirshamaya* is a disease of the head. *Slonya* in the Taittiriya Samhita probably refers to lameness, though according to the commentator it is a skin disease. *Vilishta* is a term for a sprain, and *asthnah chinnasya* for broken bones. Wounds of different kinds are mentioned. *Surama* is referred to in the Rig Veda as sickness caused by drinking too much sura, though the term surama also had other meanings, as sura could refer to a deity. This hymn below is a broad-based prayer to cure several diseases.

A charm for the cure of various diseases

1. *Each pain and ache that racks the head, earache, and vilohita,*
    All malady that wrings your brow we charm away with this our spell.

2. *From both your ears, from parts thereof, your earache, and the throbbing pain,*
    All malady that wrings your brow we charm away with this our spell.

3. *So that yakshma may depart forth from your ears and from your mouth,*
    All malady that wrings your brow we charm away with this our spell.

4. *The malady that makes one deaf (pramota), the malady that makes one blind,*
    All malady that wrings your brow we charm away with this our spell.

5. *The throbbing pain in all your limbs that rends your frame with fever throes,*
    All malady that wrings your brow we charm away with this our spell.

6. *The malady whose awful look makes a man quiver with alarm,*
    Fever (takman) whom every Autumn brings we charm away with this our spell.

7. *Yakshma that creeps about the thighs and, after, reaches both the groins,*
    yakshma from your inner parts we charm away with this our spell.

8. *If the disease originates from love, from hatred, from the heart,*
    Forth from the heart and from the limbs we charm balasa.

9. *The yellow jaundice from your limbs, and apva from the parts within,*
    And phthisis from your inward soul we charm away with this our spell.

10. *Let wasting malady (balasa) turn to ash, become jalasha (the water of disease).*
    I have evoked the poison-taint of all yakshmas out of thee.

11. *Forth from the hollow let it run, with rumbling sounds from within you.*
    I have removed the poison-taint of all yakshmas out of you.

12. *Forth from your belly and your lungs, forth from your navel and your heart.*
    I have drawn out the poison taint of all yakshmas from you.

13. *The penetrating stabs of pain which rend asunder crown and head,*
    Let them depart and pass away, free from disease and harming not.

14. *The pangs that stab the heart and reach the breast bone and connected parts,*
    Let them depart and pass away, free from disease and harming not.

15. *The stabs that penetrate the sides and pierce their way along the ribs,*
    Let them depart and pass away, free from disease and harming not.

16. *The penetrating pangs that pierce your stomach as they shoot across,*
    Let them depart and pass away, free from disease and harming not.

17. *The pains that through the bowels creep, disordering the inward parts,*
    Let them depart and pass away, free from disease and harming not.

18. *The pains that suck the marrow out, and rend and tear the bones apart,*
    May they speed forth and pass away, free from disease and harming not.

19. *Yakshmas with their fierce pains which make your limbs insensible*
    I have evoked the poison-taint of all yakshmas out of you.

20. *Of piercing pain, of abscesses, rheumatic ache, alaji (ophthalmia or boils)*
    I have drawn out the poison-taint of all yakshmas from you.
21. *I have dispelled the piercing pains from feet, knees, hips, and hinder parts,*
    And spine, and from the neck and nape the malady that racked the head.
22. *Sound are the skull bones of your head and your heart's beat is regular.*
    you, Aditya (sun) arising with your beams has chased away the head's disease, has stilled the pain
    that racked the limbs.

(Atharva 9.8; based on the translation by R.T.H. Griffith)

REMEDIES

Jalasha

Apart from water, fire or fumigation, prayers, and charms, various other remedies have been suggested. Among them is jalasha. There are contradictory views on what this is. It has been interpreted as a herb or plant, water, water mixed with something, a leech that lives in water, or urine therapy. It is mentioned as Rudra's healing remedy.

Trees, Herbs, Plants

Various trees, herbs, and plants were also used as medicine. The trees and plants of the Atharva Veda have been identified, analysed, and described in Chapter 6. A few of them, particularly important in the treatment of diseases, are given below:

• Ajashringi (probably *Gymnema sylvestre*) was used in the treatment of *vatikara*, a disease of the eyes.

• Apamarga (*Achyranthes aspera*) was a plant used frequently in witchcraft and as medicine, and specially against kshetriya.

• Jangida (*Terminalia arjuneya* or *Withania somnifera* or *Himalayan mandrake*) was used as an amulet for protection against diseases or symptoms of disease, including takman, balasa, visharika, prishtyamaya, fevers and rheumatic pains, vishkandha, samskandha, jambha, etc. It is also used against all diseases and considered the best of healing powers.

• Kushtha (*Saussurea lappa*) cured headache (shirshamaya), diseases of the eyes, bodily afflictions, and especially fever, hence it was also called fever-destroyer (takma-nashana) and also cured yakshma. It had general healing qualities, hence was known as *vaishva-bhrishaja*, 'all-healing'; it is a plant still used in Ayurveda.

• Arundhati (identified with *Rubia cordifolia*) was used to heal wounds, combat fever, and to induce cows to give milk.

The Atharva Veda thus provided the basis for the later medical science of Ayurveda.

AYURVEDIC TEXTS

The earliest Ayurvedic texts date to the first few centuries CE and include the works of Bhela, Charaka, and Sushruta. These texts include not only the theory and practice of medicine but also look at disease from a philosophical viewpoint, and address the relationship between karma and disease.

IN BUDDHISM

Medicine was also extensively studied in Buddhism, and taught in its monasteries. The Buddhist story of Jivaka is well known. In the Mahavagga, Jivaka excises worms from the head by making an incision. Bhaishajya guru is the Buddha of healing.

CHAPTER 12

TWO SPIRITUAL INTERPRETATIONS

In the 19th and early 20th centuries CE, the Vedas were analysed by two spiritual leaders, Swami Dayananda and Sri Aurobindo.

Swami Dayananda (1824–83), founder of the Arya Samaj, provided a purely spiritual interpretation of the Vedas, which is still accepted and followed by members of the Arya Samaj.

Born at Tankara in Kathiawar, Gujarat, he was originally named Mulasankar. He took *sannyasa* and was named Dayananda Saraswati, as he joined the Sarasvati order of ascetics. In 1860, after wandering through different parts of India, meeting gurus and sannyasis, he met Guru Virajananda at Mathura and became his disciple. Though blind, Virajananda was very learned and encouraged Dayananda to reveal the true Vedic knowledge to the world. Dayananda inaugurated the Arya Samaj at Mumbai (Bombay) in 1875, to teach people to follow the Vedas and lead a life of nobility (arya means 'noble'). In 1877, the Samaj headquarters shifted to Lahore, and Punjab became the centre of his teachings. His ideas spread across north India and several branches (*samajs*) were set up in present-day Uttar Pradesh, Punjab, and Rajasthan. Gradually the number of followers increased, numbering 39,952 by 1891 and almost two million by 1947.

Dayananda also tried to bring about reforms in Hindu society, believing that the Vedas represented true Hinduism. He felt that the focus on texts such as the Puranas had led to a corruption of Hinduism. He was against the caste system, child marriage, and oppression of widows. He opposed idol worship, reverence for deities, unnecessary rituals, and the exalted position of brahmanas. He wrote several books, including the *Rigvedadi-bhashya-bhumika*, a commentary on the Vedas in nine volumes; *Samskara Vidhi*, a treatise on the philosophy behind sixteen important Hindu ceremonies; and his most famous work, *Satyartha Prakasha*, which explains the philosophy of the Arya Samaj. His followers opened schools, colleges, and orphanages, as well as homes for widows. Several of his followers participated in the freedom movement. The Arya Samaj is still a popular organization, with thousands of followers in all countries.

In his book *Satyartha Prakasha* Swami Dayananda begins with a Vedic prayer and states that though the Vedas name various deities, they are all aspects of one god. He says:

> *I believe in a religion based on universal and all-embracing principles which have always been accepted as true by mankind and will continue to command the allegiance of mankind in the ages to come. Hence it is that the religion in question is called the primeval eternal religion, which means that it is above the hostility of all human creeds whatsoever.*

Out of the vast body of Hindu literature, Dayananda accepted as authentic only the Vedas, Brahmanas, Yaska's commentary, and some Vedangas. He said that the true Puranas are the Brahmanas (texts) while the eighteen traditional Puranas (including the Bhagavata) are not the real Puranas. Apart from the Vedas and Brahmanas, he used the Manu Smriti extensively in his writings but reinterpreted a number of passages. All these texts, he stated, had numerous interpolations, which had to be ignored and sifted through, while the works of the commentators Sayana, Mahidhara, and others, were too late to have any value.

However, the memorization of the Vedas by brahmanas and their use in *yajnas* had one positive aspect—it helped to preserve the texts in an unchanged form.

Swami Dayananda's basic beliefs were that there is only one god, who is the creator of the world. God, the soul, and Prakriti are the three eternal aspects. The nature of god and the soul is as of a father to a son, or of the pervader and the pervaded. Salvation or *moksha* can be obtained through right knowledge and right action.

Dayananda did not believe in idol worship but said that sixteen *samskaras* (rituals related to family life) should be performed as well as yajnas, particularly the *agnihotra*, which purifies air and water and promotes the well-being of all sentient creatures. He was absolutely against animal sacrifices. He stated that the passages in the Vedas describing these sacrifices were inserted by Vama Margis (Tantrics). Quoting passages from some Brahmanas, he added that the actual *ashvamedha* was the king who governed his people righteously, a learned man who offered knowledge or the burning of clarified butter (*ghi*) and similar substances in the fire.

Dayananda also proffered advice on the best ways to bring up children and discussed the duties of man in the four stages of life, the role of women, and the specifics and repercussion of the caste system.

In his commentaries on the Vedas, Swami Dayananda said that the supreme god, Parabrahman, produced the four Vedas. At the beginning of creation, there was no system of teaching and learning, nor were there any books—hence no person could acquire knowledge without the intervention of god. He also stated that there is nothing that can be called 'innate knowledge' and no man can accomplish anything without divine knowledge and the learning of learned men. He said:

> *God, in his great mercy, revealed the Vedas for the benefit of all men. If he had not done so, gross ignorance would have been perpetuated and men could not have achieved righteousness, worldly prosperity, enjoyment and emancipation, and would have been deprived of the highest bliss. When*

the most merciful God created bulbous roots, fruits and herbs etc., for the good of His creatures, why should he not have revealed the Vedic knowledge that brings to light all kinds of happiness and contains all sciences? The pleasure one experiences in enjoying the best things of the world does not equal the one-thousandth part of the pleasure one feels after acquiring knowledge. It is, therefore, certain that the Vedas were revealed by God.

He believed that the gods and rishis mentioned in the Vedas had different meanings depending on the context in which the words were used. At times, the words referred to the One God, at other times to people, or to certain physical forces. Thus, in one context Agni, Vayu, Aditya, and Angirasa were people of ancient times to whom the Vedas were revealed. To support this theory, he quoted a statement in the Shatapatha Brahmana (11.2.8.3), which says that when Agni, Vayu, and Surya (Aditya) meditated, they produced respectively the Rig, Yajur, and Sama Vedas. This meant that God conveyed it to them—not that they were the composers. Similarly the god Brahma, Vyasa, or the rishis mentioned in the Puranas were not composers of the Vedas.

Based on the theory of the vast cosmic ages of *kalpas*, *manvantaras*, and *yugas*, he calculated that 1,960,852,976 years had elapsed from the beginning of creation and the year in which he was writing (1876) was the 1,960,852,977th. Six manvantaras were over and this was the seventh, in which 4796 years of the Kali Yuga had been completed. The year 1876 was the 4797th.

To Dayananda, the Vedas contain eternal words. These words have always existed—and always will exist. Eternal words, according to him, are pre-existent and initially unmanifested. Hence even when they are not known through writing or speech, they still exist in their unmanifest forms.

Dayananda reinterpreted the Vedas in what he believed was their original intent. He said that all words in the Vedas were in the *yaugika* (derivative) sense and could not be interpreted as proper names. There were no historical references. Words had to be interpreted in the context in which they were used and thus had different meanings. According to him, a correct interpretation revealed that the Vedas contained the germs of all the sciences—of the past, the present, and the future. All physical laws, mathematics, inventions, and other aspects of the material universe, in essence, were contained in the Vedas. This concept again has to be understood in a metaphysical sense, in that all aspects of creation had an eternal existence in the unmanifested Supreme principle, and this was reflected in the eternal words of the Vedas.

Swami Dayananda completed his commentary on the Yajur Veda, and three-quarters of that on the Rig Veda before his death. To him, the eternal Vedas revealed the only true religion in the world.

SRI AUROBINDO

Sri Aurobindo (1872–1950) was a multifaceted personality whose work was not limited to the Vedas. In fact, he evolved a new and distinctive philosophical system, which he called Integral Yoga. Born at Kolkata (Calcutta) in India on 15 August 1872, as Aurobindo Ghose, at the age of seven, he was sent to England to study. Returning to India as a young man in 1893, he worked for some time in the state of Baroda but gradually got involved in the freedom movement against the British, who ruled most of India at the time. He had already begun certain yoga practices and, when in prison for his actions in the struggle for freedom (1908), he received a divine revelation. He left British India and entered the small territory of Puducherry (Pondicherry) in south India, which was then under the French. Here he could not be pursued by British authorities, and giving up politics he founded an ashram, and developed his own philosophy.

His philosophical works include *The Life Divine*, *The Synthesis of Yoga*, *The Integral Yoga*, the epic *Savitri* (a poem with 24,000 lines) and several other works, as well as commentaries on all major ancient texts.

In developing his philosophy, Sri Aurobindo undertook an in-depth study of Hindu texts, including the Vedas. His work on these texts culminated in a book, *The Secret of the Veda*. In this book, he wrote:

> In the fixed tradition of thousands of years, they have been revered as the origin and standard of all that can be held as authoritative and true in Brahmana and Upanishad, in Tantra and Purana, in the doctrines of great philosophical schools and in the teachings of famous saints and sages. The name borne by them was Veda, the knowledge—the received name for the highest spiritual truth of which the human is capable. But if we accept the current interpretations, whether Sayana's or the modern theory, the whole of this sublime and sacred reputation is a colossal fiction.

He felt that the great philosophy of the Upanishads must have had its origin in the Rig Veda, where the profound ideas were concealed by 'a veil of concrete and material figures and symbols which protected the sense from the profane and revealed it to the initiated'. But even by the time of the Brahmanas and Upanishads, the great truths had been obscured, and 'the material aspects of Vedic worship had grown like a thick crust over the inner knowledge and were stifling what they had once served to protect'.

He traced three main attempts to understand the Vedas. The first was the fragments preserved in the Brahmanas and Upanishads. The second was the interpretation of Sayana, and the third of European scholarship. According to him, the latter two 'present one characteristic in common, the extraordinary incoherence and poverty of sense which their results stamp upon the ancient hymns'.

He felt that the Vedic Samhitas should be understood at two levels—the outer and the inner. The outer rituals and ceremonies were for the common people whereas, for the initiate, there were hidden, inner mysteries in the same words. Later, the Brahmanas [texts] preserved the form, while the Upanishads revealed the secrets.

Sayana focused on the material and ritualistic aspects. According to Sri Aurobindo, 'It is the final and authoritative binding of the Veda to this lowest of all its possible senses that has been the most unfortunate result of Sayana's commentary.' And Sayana 'became in the European mind the parent of fresh errors'.

Sri Aurobindo's comments on European scholarship are worth quoting. He says:

Vedic scholarship of Europe has really founded itself throughout on the traditional elements preserved in Sayana's commentary and has not attempted an entirely independent handling of the problem. What it found in Sayana and in the Brahmanas it has developed in the light of modern theories and modern knowledge; by ingenious deductions from the comparative method applied to philology, mythology and history, by large amplifications of the existing data with the aid of ingenious speculation, by unification of the scattered indications available it has built up a complete theory of Vedic mythology, Vedic history, Vedic civilisation which fascinates by its detail and thoroughness and conceals by its apparent sureness of method the fact that this imposing edifice has been founded, for the most part, on the sands of conjecture.

Sri Aurobindo commends Swami Dayananda's efforts at reinterpretation but does not agree with them. He states:

Dayananda's interpretation of the hymns is governed by the idea that the Vedas are a plenary revelation of religious, ethical and scientific truth. Its religious teaching is monotheistic and the Vedic gods are different descriptive names of the one Deity; they are at the same time indications of His powers as we see them working in Nature and by a true understanding of the sense of the Vedas we could arrive at all the scientific truths which have been discovered by modern research. Such a theory is, obviously, difficult to establish.

Sri Aurobindo goes on to examine the symbolism of terms in the Vedas. Quoting various passages on the cow (go), he observes: 'The Vedic cow was an exceedingly enigmatic animal that came from no earthly herd.' *Ashva*, or horse, was also symbolic. Go and ashva, to him, were symbolic of light and energy, consciousness and force. Thus wealth in terms of cows and horses, signified mental illumination and energy. Every word in Sanskrit had numerous possible interpretations and, in this, Sri Aurobindo retranslates several hymns according to his own interpretation. One such hymn to Soma is given below. According to him, 'The wine of Soma is the intoxication of the Ananda, the divine delight of being.'

A hymn to Soma
l.   *Wide spread out for thee is the sieve of thy purifying, O
     Master of the soul; becoming in the creature thou pervadest
     his members all through. He tastes not that delight who is
     unripe and whose body has not suffered in the heat of the
     fire; they alone are able to bear that and enjoy it who have
     been prepared by the flame.*

2. *The strainer through which the heat of him is purified is*
    spread out in the seat of Heaven; its threads shine out and
    stand extended. His swift ecstasies foster the soul that purifies
    him; he ascends to the high level of Heaven by the
    conscious heart.

3. *This is the supreme dappled Bull that makes the Dawns to*
    shine out, the Male that bears the worlds of the becoming
    and seeks the plenitude; the Fathers who had the forming
    knowledge made a form of him by that power of knowledge
    which is his; strong in vision they set him within as a child
    to be born.

4. *As the Gandharva he guards his true seat; as the supreme*
    and wonderful One he keeps the births of the gods; Lord
    of the inner setting, by the inner setting he seizes the enemy.
    Those who are utterly perfected in works taste the
    enjoyment of his honey-sweetness.

5. *O Thou in whom is the food, thou art that divine food,*
    thou art the vast, the divine home; wearing heaven as a robe
    thou encompassest the march of the sacrifice. King with
    the sieve of thy purifying for thy chariot thou ascendest to
    the plenitude; with thy thousand burning brilliances thou
    conquerest the vast knowledge.

(Rig Veda 9.83)

It is obvious to any translator that all the references in the Vedas to material items—cows, horses, wealth—are not always literal. It has often been pointed out that cows represent clouds at times, and ashva has different meanings, including knowledge. Soma, as indicated in Chapter 6, probably also had two different meanings: of divine amrita and an intoxicating drink.

But, at the same time, it does not seem possible to deny all material and historical references, or to presume an inner meaning that could be understood only by initiates.

In his later works, Sri Aurobindo did not focus on texts. Instead, he stated that no religion revealed the whole Truth. He said, 'The Divine Truth is greater than any religion or creed or scripture or idea or philosophy.' He ceased to identify with Hinduism, and wrote:

The Ashram has nothing to do with Hindu religion or culture or any religion or nationality. The Truth
of the Divine which is the spiritual reality behind all religions and the descent of the supramental
which is not known to any religion are the sole things which will be the foundation of the work of
the future.

CONCLUSION

In this book, we have steered a path through the innumerable theories on the Vedas to arrive at some pointers on their possible date, the origin and nature of the people who composed the texts, and the region in which these people lived.

Linguistic analyses indicate that the Rig Veda is the earliest of the four Vedic Samhitas, and that it forms the basis for the other texts. One theory is that though the other three Vedas may be later than the Rig in their present form, they could have had earlier origins.

Among the various theories regarding the date of the Rig Veda is that it was composed millions of years ago—at the beginning of creation. This theory has to be understood in a spiritual and not a historical sense. It implies that the first sound, the first aspect of creation, is the eternal word.

In a historical context, the Rig has been dated on the basis of its relationship with other languages, astronomical references, references in later texts, and socio-economic references.

To begin with, one should reiterate that the Rig Veda is a single text and, that too primarily a religious one. It cannot be expected to provide a complete picture of a culture.

In addition, the Rig Veda was a text in which hymns were put together and carefully arranged. The version that we have today, though carefully preserved over centuries, is not the original version. Another aspect to be kept in mind is that the time period, to which the Rig Veda refers, was not necessarily the period in which it was composed; in fact, it is unlikely to have been the same. The time period could also have been quite vast, and there could be some references to very ancient times.

The language of the Rig Veda was certainly connected with Avestan and Indo-European languages. There are also some similarities in religion, myths, and legends. There is, however, no agreement on either the date or origin of Indo-European languages or their method of diffusion. One can identify three main theories about the homeland of Indo-European languages:

1. An Anatolian homeland, dating perhaps to before 6500 BCE, from where the spread was through the migration of farmers
2. A homeland in the Pontic–Caspian steppes, dating to between 5000 BCE and 3000 BCE, with the spread through migration
3. A homeland either in Europe or Central Asia within the same broad timeframe (5000–3000 BCE), with the spread through migration again

Another major theory is the Palaeolithic Continuity Theory, which states that language development can be traced back to pre-human times, and that language diffusion took place along with the earliest migrations of *Homo sapiens* from Africa or, at the latest, during the Late or Upper Palaeolithic period.

All the homeland theories presume that there was once a common language, either Indo-Hittite or Proto-Indo-European, which gradually modified as the languages diffused through migration. After looking at the main theories, it is clear that there is no consensus on the date of PIE or on how and when it spread. Some, in fact, even doubt whether it ever existed.

Language did not originate in 6000 BCE, 5000 BCE, or even 10,000 BCE. By Neolithic times, most of Asia and Europe were occupied, and languages must have been spoken throughout the region. The single homeland theory presumes that groups of nomads replaced almost the entire population, or were dominant enough to replace existing languages, particularly in Europe, where there are very few surviving non-Indo-European languages. Is it logical to look for a small pocket for the origin of each language group? Originally, it was thought that conquest led to the spread of languages but this theory was later discarded. The theory of language spread through migrating farmers or farm techniques is equally uncertain, as recent theories indicate that farming was an independent and simultaneous development in different areas. Hock points out that apart from some Avestan theories, and the Roman legend of migration from Troy, other Indo-European groups do not have migration legends or myths. Frits Staal, in the context of India, suggests that very few people (representing the Rig Veda) crossed the high mountains and passes and entered India, but became a dominant group through 'the power of mantra'. Even supposing that this suggestion has some validity, it can hardly be applied to other Indo-European groups.

For Indo-Iranian, the most prominent theory is of its origin in the Andronovo culture. From here, migration routes have been traced into Iran and India. But it has been doubted that the Andronovo culture represented Indo-Iranian speakers, or even any form of Indo-European. There are several other Indo-Iranian homeland theories, including its origin in west Turkmenistan, Iran or in India. Another theory is that the entire region of Afghanistan, Iranian Seistan, west Baluchistan, north-west India–Pakistan and Central Asia was involved in bidirectional exchanges. According to this, there were no great migrations but trade and cultural exchanges, including marriage, and this led to similarities in language.

It is a long-held assumption that Indo-Iranian people once formed a single group, which later separated. What really is the evidence for this? There are certainly close similarities between Rig Vedic Sanskrit and Gathic Avestan. There is also some similarity between deities of the Younger Avestan texts and the Rig Veda though, at the same time, there are many differences. The homeland for Gathic and Younger Avestan speaking people is considered to be somewhere between Central Asia and Eastern Iran. The homeland of the Rig Vedic people, or rather the region referred to in the Rig Veda, is clearly between Afghanistan and the river Yamuna within India. Why presume that either group migrated to these regions? All the noted similarities could be due to their long coexistence in contiguous regions, where they spoke a similar but slightly different language. There is really no need to look for an original homeland somewhere in the steppes of South Russia, or in Anatolia, or elsewhere.

Both groups of texts provide little idea of their dates. In fact, the Gathas are dated on grounds that they must be approximately of the same date as the Rig Veda. The Rig Veda itself is dated on somewhat arbitrary grounds.

Here, we will try and date some of the socioeconomic data, and examine in particular the question of the horse. However, it should be pointed out that dates such as when horses were first tamed or ridden, or when copper was first used, are constantly changing based on new discoveries and excavations.

Both the Rig Veda and the Gathas mention the use of copper. Copper has a history of use that dates back at least ten thousand years. A copper pendant of north Iraq dates to 8700 BCE. Copper smelting sites date back to about 4500 BCE in the Middle East (present-day Egypt, Israel, and Jordan). Copper was known in Iran and India around the same date. Even today, Iran has rich copper deposits.

Another pointer to the possible date are the domestic animals in the region. How did animals reach the area where they were domesticated? A number of them may have been indigenous and were found in the wild and gradually tamed. Some, both tamed and wild, may have reached the region from different lands. Seasonal animal migrations are known even today. In the past too, animals migrated across continents, both with and without humans. Research shows that when herds of wild animals are domesticated, they gradually diminish in size.

Cattle, goats, and sheep were domesticated between 10,000 BCE and 7000 BCE in Iran, Afghanistan, and north-west India–Pakistan. Analysis of bone remains suggests that domestication was local.

In the Gathas, the term *ushtra*, used also in the name Zarathushtra, is believed to mean 'camel', based on Sanskrit usage of the same term. Ushtra is mentioned in the Rig Veda but is not a common term. Camels known today are of two types: the Bactrian (*Camelus bactrianus*) with two humps, in Central Asia, and the dromedary (*Camelus dromedarius*) with one hump, in north Africa and the Near East. Dromedaries were probably domesticated along the southern Arabian coast between 3000 BCE and 2500 BCE. A camelid bone, probably that of a wild dromedary, was found at Sihi, a Neolithic site in Yemen, dating to 8000–7000 BCE. Evidence for domesticated Bactrian camels dates to at least 2600 BCE at Shar-i-Sukhteh, Iran, and such evidence has also been found in Afghanistan. A Bactrian camel figurine of the Harappan period was found in Shortughai, Afghanistan. Another such figurine was found at Kalibangan. Dromedary bones have been found from Harappan sites, mainly in Gujarat, but also from Harappa, Mohenjodaro, and Kalibangan, and these can be dated to 2000 BCE or later. Such camels may have reached there through trade.

Aspa is another term used in the Gathas, signifying 'horse'. It is the equivalent of the Sanskrit *ashva*. In the Rig Veda, the word ashva is frequently used though there are also other terms for horse, such as *ashu*, *vajin*, and *sapti* (see Chapter 6 for more).

Horses are believed to have been hunted in Palaeolithic times and are depicted in paintings dating as early as 30,000 BCE. Horse taming was earlier dated to around 4000 BCE, and is believed to have first taken place in Central Asia. According to some scholars, it could be pushed back to 5500 BCE. Discoveries in Saudi Arabia (Maqar Civilization) suggest an earlier date of 7000 BCE, though more studies are necessary to confirm this. Considering Harappan and even earlier contacts with these regions, horses could have been imported into India. Horse bones have been recorded from some Harappan sites though it has been doubted whether they were bones of the horse or the onager. Horse bones have also been recorded from Mesolithic and Neolithic sites in other parts of India, as pointed out in Chapter 8, and from some Painted Grey Ware (PGW) sites.

At no early period in north India are horse remains numerous or prolific. Horse burials at Hasanlu and other sites in west Iran are thought to belong to the 10th–9th centuries BCE period. However, in the Gathas, cattle are predominant, not horses or camels, though the latter were probably known. It is not the suffering horse but the suffering cow that appeals to Ahura Mazda for help.

It should be noted that aspa and ushtra may have had meanings different from horse and camel, just as the Vedic ashva meant both horse as well as knowledge or light. Ushtra in the name of Zarathushtra has also been interpreted as light, derived from the root *us*.

One other aspect of ashva is that in the *ashvamedha*, a horse with thirty-four ribs has been mentioned, whereas the horse generally has thirty-six. There have been numerous discussions and theories on this, including the theory that the Indian horse is different and unique. However, the number thirty-four may have some symbolic significance. In this context, here are some verses of a hymn, from the Yajur Veda, related to animal sacrifices:

To gods, to sky, the sacrifice has gone! Come riches thence to me!
To men, to air, the sacrifice has gone! Come riches thence to me!
To fathers, to earth, the sacrifice has gone! Come riches thence to me!
Whatever sphere the sacrifice has reached, may wealth come thence to me!
The threads (sacrificial formulas) that have been spun, the four and thirty, which establish this our sacrifice with svadha,
Of these I join together what is broken. All hail! To gods go the warm milk oblation!

(Vajasaneyi Samhita, 8.60–61; verses 54–58 contain 34 sacrificial formulas)

Ratha, the word for 'chariot', is common in the Rig. As seen earlier, ratha is thought to be different from *anas* (cart) but the distinction is not always clear. *Sakata* was another term for a cart. The wheels of the ratha are referred to as *chakra*, the rim and felly are known as *nemi*, the spokes are *ara*, the nave *nabhya*, and the body *kosha*. Some references can again be interpreted in a metaphysical sense. Rathas with one wheel are mentioned too, and possibly referred to the sun. Ara also refer to time periods as in *manvantara* or the Jain system of cosmography. Chakra, kosha, and nemi also have different and metaphysical connotations. Chakra refers to the wheel of time or to metaphysical centres of energy within the human body, which is also known as kosha.

Chariots are known from Andronovo burial sites. At least four Sintashta tombs had chariot remains, and this is considered an additional reason for linking them with Indo-Iranians, though neither Iran nor India have early chariot burials. There is a chariot grave at Krivoye Ozero along with a horse. The archaeological culture at Krivoye Ozero, located north of Odessa on the Black Sea, is dated between 2012 BCE and 1990 BCE. Chariot graves are found in China circa 1200 BCE, in Europe from the 8th century BCE and in Iron Age England, dating between 800 BCE and 100 CE.

However, chariot remains are not found in north India. The earliest chariot remains are from a Megalithic site in peninsular India, dating to 800–400 BCE. A terracotta seal depicting a horse-drawn cart of a slightly earlier period was found at Daimabad in central India. The earliest evidence for chariots in southern Central Asia is from the Achaemenid dynasty. Earlier petroglyphs have ox-drawn chariots. As Staal points out, chariots could not have entered India through the high mountains and narrow passes. He therefore suggests that it was only their idea or concept, which was imported. But the term *rathakara*, or 'maker of chariots', is not mentioned in the Rig Veda. Scholars who have analysed ratha-related terms in this text point out that descriptions do not match those of the two-wheeled chariots of Europe or Central Asia.

The ass or donkey is another animal mentioned in the Rig Veda. After collecting and analysing donkey and wild ass DNA from across the world, scientific studies conclude that wild asses in north-east Africa are ancestors of all modern donkeys, *Equus asinus*. By the 4th millennium BCE, the donkey had spread to south-west Asia. In this context, it may be significant that B.B. Lal has pointed out Nubian similarities with Indian megaliths.

The use of donkeys is believed to signify a transition to a more trade-oriented society, as the donkey had a crucial role in travel and transport. The onager (*Equus hemionus*), also known as the wild ass, is native to the deserts of Syria, Iran, Pakistan, India, Israel, and Tibet; onager bones have been found in India. However, it is unlikely to have ever have had domestic use, as it is known to be almost impossible to tame.

Sheep (*Ovis orientalis*) were first domesticated circa 8000–7500 BCE in eastern Anatolia, western Iran, Afghanistan, and north-west India–Pakistan. However, early domestic sheep did not have a woolly coat, as they do today. This probably developed through a genetic alteration that took place around 4000–3500 BCE. Hence, references in the Rig Veda that refer to the use of wool would indicate a date of around or after 4000 BCE.

Another aspect is the wheel (chakra, as earlier), which seems to have been invented around 4000 BCE. The question of spoked wheels in India is another controversial aspect. Staal feels that spoked wheels were depicted only in Mauryan times while others have found evidence of spoked wheels even in Harappan times. In any case, no one is suggesting that the Rig Veda belonged to the Mauryan period, hence if references to spokes and wheels in the Rig Veda are to be taken literally, they must have existed at least by 1000 BCE.

Using this socio-economic data, we come to an outer date of 4000 BCE for the Rig Veda. There are no two-wheeled chariots of this date discovered in an archaeological context but, as we saw earlier, the Rig Veda does not refer to a single time period. It may have been composed at a time when chariots were used but could simultaneously refer to an earlier period. For instance, most scholars accept that the war described in the Mahabharata possibly took place in a more limited form around 1000 BCE or 1400 BCE, but that the text of the Mahabharata was compiled between 400 BCE and 400 CE. One also has to keep in mind that ratha too had many meanings.

Next, we try to understand the presence of Indo-Aryan or Indo-Iranian names and/or deities in Anatolia, first in Akkadian times, continuing up to the 8th century BCE.

How did these names and terms come to be used in this region? There are several different theories. Did these signify a continuity and development from the early Indo-Hittite or PIE, which is believed by some scholars to have existed in the region? Though this may be possible, there are other possibilities too. Let us look at the zone of interaction during the 3rd millennium BCE. The entire region from Mesopotamia and the Arabian Gulf to Central Asia, Afghanistan, Iran, and the Indus region had trade and interaction during this period, both over land and via sea. African millets reach South Asia at this time, possibly by boat. In addition, Mesopotamian records refer to ships reaching there from Dilmun, Magan, and Meluhha. Meluhha is mentioned even earlier but it is an inscription of Sargon of Akkad (2334–2279 BCE), that refers to the three lands. Dilmun is generally identified with Bahrain, Magan with Oman or south-east Iran, and Meluhha with the Indus region. Meluhha is referred to in several inscriptions and texts. Even a translator of the Meluhha language is referred to. The most obvious conclusion on references in Akkadian, and Kassite records, and in the later Mittani inscription, and Assyrian, is that traders of Meluhha and Magan, possibly identified with India and Iran, settled in the region at this time, and stayed on there. This, however, challenges the assumption of migration of Indo-Aryans into India in the 2nd millennium BCE. This migration theory may account for the Mittani references but not for those dated to an earlier time. Another option is that traders and mercenaries regularly travelled between these regions. In any case, references to names similar to those in Sanskrit date to before 2000 BCE in this region, and indicate that the language existed by that time.

To sum up, we can conclude that the Rig Vedic people were located in the region of north-west India–Pakistan possibly extending into eastern Iran and southern Afghanistan. Detailed analyses of the locational references in the Rig Veda rule out other theories such as the primary location area being in Afghanistan, the Gangetic plain, Rajasthan, central India, or the Deccan, which are among the various suggestions that have been made.

Though one cannot rule out migration into India, both evidence for this and for a possible date of migration is unclear and uncertain, and is primarily based on linguistic theories. Genetics and palaeoanthropology are among the additional methods that have been used to prove or disprove this. As seen earlier, Kenneth Kennedy's analyses of skeletons in the north-west found two periods of discontinuity—one between 6000 BCE and 4500 BCE, and the other after 800 BCE. Another pointer is Togau Ware, found at Mehrgarh and several other sites in the region, dated 4300–3800 BCE. Skeletal analyses of sites related to this pottery indicate new types similar to those on the Iranian plateau. However, one cannot come to any definite conclusions based on limited studies of genes or of skeletons. It needs to be reiterated that language dispersion is not necessarily related to ethnicity. New cultural elements and new settlements also appear in the Mature Harappan period, and in the Post or Late Harappan period. But these new elements could be due to internal changes. As S. Cleuziou, the French archaeologist, pointed out, migrationists believe that pottery moves along with people, but this is just a theory that has never been proved.

Among others, Jim Shaffer and Diane Lichtenstein state that the archaeology of the subcontinent suggests indigenous developments within the region, along with cultural interaction with neighbouring regions. They believe there is a need to reassess the migration/invasion hypothesis in the light of new archaeological data. Other archaeologists confirm that there is no clear evidence from archaeology for migration into India.

The theory that India was the homeland of the Indo-Europeans and that migration occurred out of India to spread the Indo-European languages across Europe and Central Asia seems unlikely. There are two main versions of this theory. Koenraad Elst feels that PIE originated in north-west India–Pakistan and spread across Central Asia, Europe, and into China. However, in an article titled 'Linguistic Aspects of the Aryan Non-invasion Theory', Elst himself says: 'This chapter will give a sympathizing account of the prima facie arguments in favour of the Out of India Theory of IE expansion. I am not sure that this theory is correct, indeed I will argue that the linguistic body of evidence is inconclusive, but I do believe that the theory deserves a proper hearing.'

The other version of this theory is based on the work of Johanna Nichols, who proposed a Bactrian–Sogdiana homeland. Nichols, basing herself on linguistic analysis, suggests that this represents 'a linguistic epicentre'. The OIT (Out of India) theory proponents move this linguistic centre southwards to north-west India–Pakistan but without the detailed linguistic analysis undertaken by Nichols. Most linguists do not favour the OIT theory.

Apart from the lack of supporting archaeological data or literary records, the theory raises other questions. If PIE spread from India, why did it not also spread to south, central, and east India, and replace the existing languages there? If it could spread right across Europe, replacing earlier European languages, why not across India? If representatives of Indo-European languages could cross the high mountains and passes of the north and north-west towards Central Asia and Europe, why did they not cross the much lower Vindhyas? The concept of the Sanskritization of south India does exist but is assigned to a later period and, even then, it did not result in the total replacement of other languages.

Regarding theories on the date of the Rig Veda, it would seem that the probable date—not of the text itself but of the period it refers to—could be between 4000 BCE and 1000 BCE.

At the earlier end of the spectrum, it could belong to the pre-urban phase, possibly reflected in the Kot Diji or Sothi-Siswal culture. The Rig Vedic culture does not reflect the urban Harappan civilization though some scholars have identified aspects of the Mature Harappan civilization in the Rig Veda. One suggestion is that the animals on Harappan seals were totemic clan symbols, which can be identified with Rig Vedic clans. There is no horse on the seals but no cow either or lion, only the tiger; and yet, lions and panthers must have existed in the Harappan region. Thus, many animals that must have been there are not portrayed on the seals. In the same way, the tiger is not mentioned in the Rig Veda but was probably known. If the Rig Vedic people were present in Mature Harappan times, they must have existed as a subculture with local elements. It may be significant that the Kot Diji culture continued to exist independently of the Mature Harappan culture, and that other local cultures also coexisted. But even if the Rig Vedic people coexisted with the people of the Mature Harappan Civilization, the question remains: who were the latter?

Alternatively, the period the text refers to belonged exclusively to a Post or Late Harappan phase. This theory fits most of the other socioeconomic criteria but does not explain the absence of references in the Rig Veda to cities, writing, and long distance trade, which should at least have been known in the Post Harappan period, even if all these elements were declining.

As for the Later Vedic Samhitas, analyses of the places mentioned indicate that their core area was the region of the upper regions of the Sarasvati-Drishadvati rivers extending into the Gangetic plains. Archaeologically, the Later Vedic could be identified with the Late Harappan/ Ochre Colour Pottery (OCP) cultures, or with the even later Painted Grey Ware (PGW) culture. But the PGW has been identified with Mahabharata sites, and the Later Vedic clearly refers to an earlier period. There are no Kauravas and Pandavas in the Later Vedic Samhitas, and even Hastinapura was not known by that name. Hence if the Late Harappan/OCP are Later Vedic, the Rig Vedic period must be earlier. However, it is most unlikely, as suggested by N. Kazanas and endorsed by several others, that the Mature Harappan civilization is represented in the Brahmanas and Sutras.

Another aspect of the date is the drying up of the Ghaggar-Chautang rivers, which have been identified with the Sarasvati-Drishadvati of the Vedic period. As seen earlier, the disappearance of these rivers into the sands of the desert is mentioned in the Brahmanas but not in the Rig Veda or Later Samhitas. Though geological research throws up various dates for this, archaeology suggests that the rivers had begun to diminish even before the Mature Harappan period, and had certainly dried up substantially by the time of the PGW culture, when sites in the lower courses were located in the old riverbeds.

There are some who challenge the entire exercise of attempting to correlate literary texts with archaeological cultures, and believe that it cannot have any validity. And yet, despite the pitfalls, it is an attempt that needs to be made, as archaeology can best provide a date and context.

Finally, I would like to say that the suggestions made in this chapter are what seemed to be the most logical, based on existing evidence and theories. It has not been possible to go into every single theory in detail but the main theories have been discussed in the course of this book. Given the limited nature of the Rig Veda, and the still undeciphered Harappan script, no final conclusions are possible.

It would also be useful if studies ceased to focus on a specific time period and went into the larger question of migration into the subcontinent beginning with Palaeolithic times. To arrive at a better understanding of this problem, it is not just the Indo-Aryan languages but all the languages of the subcontinent that need to be understood and analysed in terms of their origin and distribution from the earliest times. In this process, it should be kept in mind that language and genetics are not necessarily related.

Regardless of the time frame and historicity of the Vedas, their magnificent poetry and imagery can be appreciated by everyone.

APPENDIX I

A list of the hymns in the Rig Veda is given here:

MANDALA I

Sukta	Main deity/deities	Rishi composer
1	Agni	Madhuchhanda Vaishvamitra
2	Vayu	Madhuchhanda Vaishvamitra
3	Ashvins	Madhuchhanda Vaishvamitra
4–10	Indra	Madhuchhanda Vaishvamitra
11	Indra	Jeta Madhuchhandas
12	Agni	Medhatithi Kanva
13	Agni and others	Medhatithi Kanva
14	All or many gods	Medhatithi Kanva
15	Ritus, along with various deities	Medhatithi Kanva
16	Indra	Medhatithi Kanva
17	Indra-Varuna	Medhatithi Kanva
18	Brahmanaspati and others	Medhatithi Kanva
19	Agni and Maruts	Medhatithi Kanva
20	Ribhus	Medhatithi Kanva
21	Indra-Agni	Medhatithi Kanva
22	Ashvins and others	Medhatithi Kanva
23	Vayu, Indra-Vayu and others	Medhatithi Kanva

Sukta	Main deity/deities	Rishi composer
24	Ka, Agni, Savitr, Varuna and others	Shunahshepa Ajigarti, later Devarata Vaishvamitra
25	Varuna	Shunahshepa Ajigarti
26	Agni	Shunahshepa Ajigarti
27	Agni, other devatas	Shunahshepa Ajigarti
28	Indra and others	Shunahshepa Ajigarti
29	Indra	Shunahshepa Ajigarti
30	Indra and others	Shunahshepa Ajigarti
31	Agni	Hiranyastupa Angirasa
32–33	Indra	Hiranyastupa Angirasa
34	Ashvins	Hiranyastupa Angirasa
35	Savitr and others	Hiranyastupa Angirasa
36	Agni, yupa (sacrificial post)	Kanva Ghaura
37–39	Maruts	Kanva Ghaura
40	Brahmanaspati	Kanva Ghaura
41	Varuna, Mitra, Aryaman	Kanva Ghaura
42	Pushan	Kanva Ghaura
43	Rudra, Mitra-Varuna, Soma	Kanva Ghaura
44	Agni, Ashvins, Usha	Praskanva Kanva
45	Agni and others	Praskanva Kanva
46–47	Ashvins	Praskanva Kanva
48–49	Usha	Praskanva Kanva
50	Surya	Praskanva Kanva
51–57	Indra	Savya Angirasa
58–60	Agni	Nodha Gautama
61–63	Indra	Nodha Gautama
64	Maruts	Nodha Gautama
65–73	Agni	Parashara Shaktya
74–79	Agni	Gotama Rahugana
80–84	Indra	Gotama Rahugana
85–88	Maruts	Gotama Rahugana
89–90	All or many gods (Vishvedevas)	Gotama Rahugana
91	Soma	Gotama Rahugana
92	Usha, Ashvins	Gotama Rahugana
93	Agni-Soma	Gotama Rahugana
94	Agni and others	Kutsa Angirasa

Sukta	Main deity/deities	Rishi composer
95–98	Agni	Kutsa Angirasa
99	Agni	Kashyapa Maricha
100	Indra	Varshagira, Rijashva, Ambarisha, Sahadeva, Bhayamana, Suradhasa
101–04	Indra	Kutsa Angirasa
105	All or many gods (Vishvedevas)	Kutsa Angirasa or Trita Aptya
106–07	All or many gods (Vishvedevas)	Kutsa Angirasa
108–09	Indra-Agni	Kutsa Angirasa
110–11	Ribhus	Kutsa Angirasa
112	Ashvins	Kutsa Angirasa
113	Usha, Ratri	Kutsa Angirasa
114	Rudra	Kutsa Angirasa
115	Surya	Kutsa Angirasa
116–20	Ashvins	Kakshivan Dairghatamas (Aushija)
121	Indra	Kakshivan Dairghatamas
122	Many gods	Kakshivan Dairghatamas
123–24	Usha	Kakshivan Dairghatamas
125	Svanaya danastuti	Kakshivan Dairghatamas
126	Svanaya Bhavyavya, Romasha	Kakshivan Dairghatamas
127–28	Agni	Paruchchhepa Daivodasi
129	Indra, Indu	Paruchchhepa Daivodasi
130–33	Indra	Paruchchhepa Daivodasi
134	Vayu	Paruchchhepa Daivodasi
135	Vayu, Indra-Vayu	Paruchchhepa Daivodasi
136	Mitra-Varuna, other gods	Paruchchhepa Daivodasi
137	Mitra-Varuna	Paruchchhepa Daivodasi
138	Pushan	Paruchchhepa Daivodasi
139	Many gods	Paruchchhepa Daivodasi
140–41	Agni	Dirghatama Auchathya
142	Apri sukta	Dirghatama Auchathya
143–50	Agni	Dirghatama Auchathya
151	Mitra, Mitra-Varuna	Dirghatama Auchathya
152–53	Mitra-Varuna	Dirghatama Auchathya
154	Vishnu	Dirghatama Auchathya
155	Vishnu, Indra-Vishnu	Dirghatama Auchathya
156	Vishnu	Dirghatama Auchathya

Sukta	Main deity/deities	Rishi composer
157–58	Ashvins	Dirghatama Auchathya
159–60	Dyava-Prithivi	Dirghatama Auchathya
161	Ribhus	Dirghatama Auchathya
162–63	Ashva, the horse	Dirghatama Auchathya
164	Many gods	Dirghatama Auchathya
165	Maruts, Indra	Indra, Maruts, Agastya Maitravaruni
166	Maruts	Agastya Maitravaruni
167	Indra, Maruts	Agastya Maitravaruni
168	Maruts	Agastya Maitravaruni
169	Indra	Agastya Maitravaruni
170	Indra	Indra, Indra or Agastya, Agastya Maitravaruni
171–72	Maruts	Agastya Maitravaruni
173–78	Indra	Agastya Maitravaruni
179	Rati	Lopamudra, Agastya Maitravaruni, Agastya Shishya Brahmachari
180–84	Ashvins	Agastya Maitravaruni
185	Dyava-Prithivi	Agastya Maitravaruni
186	Many gods	Agastya Maitravaruni
187	Anna-deva (food)	Agastya Maitravaruni
188	Agni and others	Agastya Maitravaruni
189	Agni	Agastya Maitravaruni
190	Brihaspati	Agastya Maitravaruni
191	Aptrina-Surya (water, grass, sun) (against poisonous creatures)	Agastya Maitravaruni

MANDALA 2

Sukta	Main deity/deities	Rishi composer
1–2	Agni	Gritsamada Bhargava Shaunaka (later Angirasa Shaunahotra; below listed as Gritsamada)
3	Apri sukta, various deities	Gritsamada
4–7	Agni	Somahuti Bhargava
8–10	Agni	Gritsamada
11–22	Indra	Gritsamada

Sukta	Main deity/deities	Rishi composer
23	Brihaspati	Gritsamada
24	Brahmanaspati, Brihaspati, Indra-Brahmanaspati	Gritsamada
25–26	Brahmanaspati	Gritsamada
27	Adityas	Gritsamada or Kurma Gartsamada
28	Varuna	Gritsamada or Kurma Gartsamada
29	Vishvedevas (many gods)	Gritsamada or Kurma Gartsamada
30	Indra and others	Gritsamada
31	Vishvedevas (many gods)	Gritsamada
32	Dyava-Prithivi and others	Gritsamada
33	Rudra	Gritsamada
34	Maruts	Gritsamada
35	Apam Napat	Gritsamada
36–37	Various gods	Gritsamada
38	Savitr	Gritsamada
39	Ashvins	Gritsamada
40	Soma-Pushan, Aditi	Gritsamada
41	Vayu, Indra-Vayu and others	Gritsamada
42–43	Shakunta (Indra in form of Kapinjala)	Gritsamada

MANDALA 3

Sukta	Main deity/deities	Rishi composer
1	Agni	Vishvamitra
2–3	Vaishvanara Agni	Vishvamitra Gathin
4	Apri sukta	Vishvamitra Gathin
5–7	Agni	Vishvamitra Gathin
8	Yupa, etc.	Vishvamitra Gathin
9–11	Agni	Vishvamitra Gathin
12	Indra-Agni	Vishvamitra Gathin
13–14	Agni	Rishabha Vaishvamitra
15–16	Agni	Utkila Katya
17–18	Agni	Kata Vaishvamitra
19	Agni	Gathi Kaushika
20	Agni, others	Gathi Kaushika

Sukta	Main deity/deities	Rishi composer
21	Agni	Gathi Kaushika
22	Agni, Purishya Agniya	Gathi Kaushika
23	Agni	Devashrava, Devavata Bharata
24–25	Agni	Vishvamitra Gathin
26	Vaishvanara Agni and others	Vishvamitra Gathin, Atmaa
27	Agni, Ritus	Vishvamitra Gathin
28	Agni	Vishvamitra Gathin
29	Agni	Vishvamitra Gathin
30	Indra	Vishvamitra Gathin
31	Indra	Vishvamitra Gathin or Kushika Aishirathi
32	Indra	Vishvamitra Gathin
33	Rivers, others	Vishvamitra Gathin, rivers (rishis)
34–35	Indra	Vishvamitra Gathin
36	Indra	Vishvamitra Gathin, Ghora Angirasa
37	Indra	Vishvamitra Gathin
38	Indra	Vishvamitra Gathin or Prajapati Vaishvamitra
39–52	Indra	Vishvamitra Gathin
53	Indra, mountains, others	Vishvamitra Gathin
54–56	Vishvedevas	Prajapati Vaishvamitra or Prajapati Vachya
57	Vishvedevas	Vishvamitra Gathin
58	Ashvins	Vishvamitra Gathin
59	Mitra	Vishvamitra Gathin
60	Ribhus, Indra	Vishvamitra Gathin
61	Usha	Vishvamitra Gathin
62	Indra and others	Vishvamitra Gathin, Jamadagni

MANDALA 4

Sukta	Main deity/deities	Rishi composer
1	Agni, Agni-Varuna	Vamadeva
2–3	Agni	Vamadeva Gautama
4	Rakshoha Agni	Vamadeva Gautama

Sukta	Main deity/deities	Rishi composer
5	Vaishvanara Agni	Vamadeva Gautama
6–12	Agni	Vamadeva Gautama
13–14	Agni (Lingokta devata)	Vamadeva Gautama
15	Agni and others	Vamadeva Gautama
16–17	Indra	Vamadeva Gautama
18	Indra and others	Vamadeva Gautama, Indra, Aditi
19–22	Indra	Vamadeva Gautama
23	Indra and others	Vamadeva Gautama
24–25	Indra	Vamadeva Gautama
26–27	Indra, Shyena	Vamadeva Gautama
28	Indra, Indra-Soma	Vamadeva Gautama
29	Indra	Vamadeva Gautama
30	Indra	Vamadeva Gautama
31	Indra	Vamadeva Gautama
32	Indra-Ashva	Vamadeva Gautama
33–37	Ribhus	Vamadeva Gautama
38	Dadhikra, Dyava-Prithivi	Vamadeva Gautama
39	Dadhikra	Vamadeva Gautama
40	Dadhikra, Surya	Vamadeva Gautama
41	Indra-Varuna	Vamadeva Gautama
42	Trasadasyu (atmastuti); Indra-Varuna	Trasadasyu Paurukutsya
43–44	Ashvins	Purumila Sauhotra, Ajamila Sauhotra
45	Ashvins	Vamadeva Gautama
46–47	Indra-Vayu, Vayu	Vamadeva Gautama
48	Vayu	Vamadeva Gautama
49	Indra-Brihaspati	Vamadeva Gautama
50	Brihaspati, Indra-Brihaspati	Vamadeva Gautama
51–52	Usha	Vamadeva Gautama
53–54	Savitr	Vamadeva Gautama
55	Vishvedevas	Vamadeva Gautama
56	Dyava-Prithivi	Vamadeva Gautama
57	Kshetrapati, Shuna, Sira, Sita	Vamadeva Gautama
58	Various deities, Ghrita	Vamadeva Gautama

MANDALA 5

Sukta	Main deity/deities	Rishi composer
1	Agni	Budha and Gavishthara Atreya
2	Agni	Kumar Atreya, or Vrisha Jana (Jara) or both
3	Agni, Maruts, Rudra, Vishnu	Vasushruta Atreya
4	Agni	Vasushruta Atreya
5	Apri sukta	Vasushruta Atreya
6	Agni	Vasushruta Atreya
7–8	Agni	Isha Atreya
9–10	Agni	Gaya Atreya
11–14	Agni	Sutambhara Atreya
15	Agni	Dharana Angirasa
16–17	Agni	Puru Atreya
18	Agni	Mriktavaha Dvita Atreya
19	Agni	Vavri Atreya
20	Agni	Prayasvan Atrigana
21	Agni	Sasa Atreya
22	Agni	Vishvasama Atreya
23	Agni	Dhyugna Vishvacharshani Atreya
24	Agni	Bandhu, Subandhu, Shrutabandhu, Viprabandhu Gaupayana or Laupayana
25	Agni	Vasuyu Atreya
26	Agni, other gods	Vasuyu Atreya
27	Agni, Indra-Agni	Trayaruna Traivrishna, Trasadasyu Paurukutsya, Ashvamedha Bharata or Atri Bhauma
28	Agni	Vishvavara Atreyi
29	Indra, Ushana	Gauriviti Shaktya
30	Indra, Rinanchaya (king)	Babhru Atreya
31	Indra, Kutsa, Ushana	Avasyu Atreya
32	Indra	Gatu Atreya
33–34	Indra	Samvarana Prajapatya
35–36	Indra	Prabhuvasa Angirasa

Sukta	Main deity/deities	Rishi composer
37–39	Indra	Atri Bhauma
40	Indra, Surya, Atri	Atri Bhauma
41	Vishvedevas	Atri Bhauma
42	Vishvedevas, Rudra	Atri Bhauma
43	Vishvedevas	Atri Bhauma
44	Vishvedevas	Avatsara Kashyapa
45	Vishvedevas	Sadaprina Atreya
46	Vishvedevas, Devapatnis	Pratikshatra Atreya
47	Vishvedevas	Pratiratha Atreya
48	Vishvedevas	Pratibhanu Atreya
49	Vishvedevas	Pratiprabha Atreya
50–51	Vishvedevas	Svasti Atreya
52–59	Maruts	Shyavashva Atreya
60	Maruts or Agni Maruts	Shyavashva Atreya
61	Maruts, others	Shyavashva Atreya
62	Mitra-Varuna	Shrutavrita Atreya
63–64	Mitra-Varuna	Archanana Atreya
65–66	Mitra-Varuna	Ratahavya Atreya
67–68	Mitra-Varuna	Yajata Atreya
69–70	Mitra-Varuna	Aruchakri Atreya
71–72	Mitra-Varuna	Bahuvrikta Atreya
73–74	Ashvins	Paura Atreya
75	Ashvins	Avasyu Atreya
76–77	Ashvins	Atri Bhauma
78	Ashvins	Saptavadhri Atreya
79–80	Usha	Satyashrava Atreya
81–82	Savitr	Shyavashva Atreya
83	Parjanya	Atri Bhauma
84	Prithivi	Atri Bhauma
85	Varuna	Atri Bhauma
86	Indra-Agni	Atri Bhauma
87	Maruts	Evayamarut Atreya

MANDALA 6

Sukta	Main deity/deities	Rishi composer
1–6	Agni	Bharadvaja Barhaspatya
7–9	Vaishvanara Agni	Bharadvaja Barhaspatya
10–14	Agni	Bharadvaja Barhaspatya
15	Agni	Bharadvaja Barhaspatya or Vitahavya Angirasa
16	Agni	Bharadvaja Barhaspatya
17–20	Indra	Bharadvaja Barhaspatya
21	Indra, Vishvedevas	Bharadvaja Barhaspatya
22–26	Indra	Bharadvaja Barhaspatya
27	Indra, Abhyavarti Chayamana (danastuti)	Bharadvaja Barhaspatya
28	Indra, cows	Bharadvaja Barhaspatya
29–30	Indra	Bharadvaja Barhaspatya
31–32	Indra	Suhotra Bharadvaja
33–34	Indra	Shunahotra Bharadvaja
35–36	Indra	Nara Bharadvaja
37–43	Indra	Bharadvaja Barhaspatya
44	Indra	Shamyu Barhaspatya
45	Indra, Bributaksha	Shamyu Barhaspatya
46	Indra	Shamyu Barhaspatya
47	Indra and others	Garga Bharadvaja
48	Agni and others	Shamyu Barhaspatya
49–52	Vishvedevas	Rijishva Bharadvaja
53–56	Pushan	Bharadvaja Barhaspatya
57	Indra, Pushan	Bharadvaja Barhaspatya
58	Pushan	Bharadvaja Barhaspatya
59–60	Indra-Agni	Bharadvaja Barhaspatya
61	Sarasvati	Bharadvaja Barhaspatya
62–63	Ashvins	Bharadvaja Barhaspatya
64–65	Usha	Bharadvaja Barhaspatya
66	Maruts	Bharadvaja Barhaspatya
67	Mitra-Varuna	Bharadvaja Barhaspatya
68	Indra-Varuna	Bharadvaja Barhaspatya
69	Indra-Vishnu	Bharadvaja Barhaspatya

Sukta	Main deity/deities	Rishi composer
70	Dyava-Prithivi	Bharadvaja Barhaspatya
71	Savitr	Bharadvaja Barhaspatya
72	Indra-Soma	Bharadvaja Barhaspatya
73	Brihaspati	Bharadvaja Barhaspatya
74	Soma-Rudra	Bharadvaja Barhaspatya
75	Weapons of war	Payu Bharadvaja

MANDALA 7

Sukta	Main deity/deities	Rishi composer
1	Agni	Vasishtha Maitravaruni
2	Apri sukta	Vasishtha Maitravaruni
3–4	Agni	Vasishtha Maitravaruni
5–6	Vaishvanara Agni	Vasishtha Maitravaruni
7–12	Agni	Vasishtha Maitravaruni
13	Vaishvanara Agni	Vasishtha Maitravaruni
14–17	Agni	Vasishtha Maitravaruni
18	Indra, Sudasa Paijavana	Vasishtha Maitravaruni
19–31	Indra	Vasishtha Maitravaruni
32	Indra	Vasishtha Maitravaruni, possibly with Shakti Vasishtha
33	Vasishtha Putragana, Vasishtha	Vasishtha Maitravaruni, Vasishtha Putragana
34	Vishvedevas, Ahi, Ahirbudhnya	Vasishtha Maitravaruni
35–37	Vishvedevas	Vasishtha Maitravaruni
38	Savitr, Bhaga ($^1/_2$ verse), Vajin	Vasishtha Maitravaruni
39–40	Vishvedevas	Vasishtha Maitravaruni
41	Lingokta devata (Agni, Indra, Maitravaruna, Ashvins, Bhaga, Pushan, Brahmanaspati, Soma, Rudra, Usha)	Vasishtha Maitravaruni
42–43	Vishvedevas	Vasishtha Maitravaruni
44	Dadhikra, others	Vasishtha Maitravaruni
45	Savitr	Vasishtha Maitravaruni
46	Rudra	Vasishtha Maitravaruni

Sukta	Main deity/deities	Rishi composer
47	Apah	Vasishtha Maitravaruni
48	Ribhus, Vishvedevas	Vasishtha Maitravaruni
49	Apah	Vasishtha Maitravaruni
50	Mitra-Varuna, other gods, rivers	Vasishtha Maitravaruni
51–52	Adityas	Vasishtha Maitravaruni
53	Dyava-Prithivi	Vasishtha Maitravaruni
54	Vastoshpati	Vasishtha Maitravaruni
55	Vastoshpati, Indra	Vasishtha Maitravaruni
56–58	Maruts	Vasishtha Maitravaruni
59	Maruts, Rudra (Mrityu Vimochani)	Vasishtha Maitravaruni
60	Mitra-Varuna, Surya	Vasishtha Maitravaruni
61	Mitra-Varuna	Vasishtha Maitravaruni
62–63	Surya, Mitra-Varuna	Vasishtha Maitravaruni
64–65	Mitra-Varuna	Vasishtha Maitravaruni
66	Mitra-Varuna, Adityas, Surya	Vasishtha Maitravaruni
67–74	Ashvins	Vasishtha Maitravaruni
75–81	Usha	Vasishtha Maitravaruni
82–85	Indra-Varuna	Vasishtha Maitravaruni
86–89	Varuna	Vasishtha Maitravaruni
90–91	Vayu	Vasishtha Maitravaruni
92	Vayu, Indra-Vayu	Vasishtha Maitravaruni
93–94	Indra-Agni	Vasishtha Maitravaruni
95–96	Sarasvati, Sarasvan	Vasishtha Maitravaruni
97	Brihaspati, Indra, Indra-Brahmanaspati, Indra-Brihaspati	Vasishtha Maitravaruni
98	Indra, Indra-Brihaspati	Vasishtha Maitravaruni
99	Vishnu, Indra-Vishnu	Vasishtha Maitravaruni
100	Vishnu	Vasishtha Maitravaruni
101–02	Parjanya	Vasishtha Maitravaruni or Kumara Agneya
103	Manduka (frogs, representing those who sing praises)	Vasishtha Maitravaruni
104	Indra, Soma, others	Vasishtha Maitravaruni

MANDALA 8

Sukta	Main deity/deities	Rishi composer
1	Indra, Asanga	Pragatha (Ghaura) Kanva, Medhatithi and Medhyatithi Kanva, Asanga Playogi, Shashvati Angirasi Rishika
2	Indra, Vibhindu	Medhatithi Kanva, Priyamedha Angirasa
3	Indra, Pakasthama Kauryana	Medhyatithi Kanva
4	Indra, Indra or Pushan, Kurunga	Devatithi Kanva
5	Ashvins, Chaidya Kashu	Brahmatithi Kanva
6	Indra, Tirindara Parshvya	Vatsa Kanva
7	Maruts	Punarvatsa Kanva
8	Ashvins	Sadhvamsa Kanva
9	Ashvins	Shashakarna Kanva
10	Ashvins	Pragatha Kanva
11	Agni	Vatsa Kanva
12	Indra	Parvata Kanva
13	Indra	Narada Kanva
14–15	Indra	Goshukti and Ashvasukti, Kanvayan
16–17	Indra	Irimbithi Kanva
18	Adityas, Ashvins, Agni, Surya, Anila	Irimbithi Kanva
19	Agni, Adityas, Trasadasyu Paurukutsa	Sobhari Kanva
20	Maruts	Sobhari Kanva
21	Indra, Chitra Raja	Sobhari Kanva
22	Ashvins	Sobhari Kanva
23	Agni	Vishvamana Vaiyashva
24	Indra	Vishvamana Vaiyashva
25	Mitra-Varuna, Vishvedevas	Vishvamana Vaiyashva
26	Ashvins, Vayu	Vishvamana Vaiyashva, or Vyashva Angirasa
27–28	Vishvedevas	Manu Vaivasvata
29	Vishvedevas	Manu Vaivasvata or Kashyapa Maricha
30	Vishvedevas	Manu Vaivasvata
31	Yajnastuti, various deities	Manu Vaivasvata

Sukta	Main deity/deities	Rishi composer
32	Indra	Medhatithi Kanva
33	Indra	Medhyatithi Kanva
34	Indra	Nipatithi Kanva, Sahastra Vasurochisha Angirasa
35	Ashvins	Shyavashva Atreya
36–37	Indra	Shyavashva Atreya
38	Indra-Agni	Shyavashva Atreya
39	Agni	Nabhaka Kanva
40	Indra-Agni	Nabhaka Kanva
41	Varuna	Nabhaka Kanva
42	Varuna, Ashvins	Nabhaka Kanva or Archanana Atreya
43–44	Agni	Virupa Angirasa
45	Indra, Indra-Agni	Trishoka Kanva
46	Indra, Prithushrava Kanita, Vayu	Vasha Ashvya
47	Aditya, Usha	Trita Aptya
48	Soma	Pragatha Kanva
49	Indra	Praskanva Kanva
50	Indra	Pushtigu Kanva
51	Indra	Shrushtigu Kanva
52	Indra	Ayu Kanva
53	Indra	Medhya Kanva
54	Indra, Vishvedevas	Matarishva Kanva
55	Praskanva danastuti	Krisha Kanva
56	Praskanva, Agni, Surya	Prishadhra Kanva
57	Ashvins	Medhya Kanva
58	Vishvedevas, Ritvij	Medhya Kanva
59	Indra-Varuna	Suparna Kanva
60	Agni	Bharga Pragatha
61	Indra	Bharga Pragatha
62	Indra	Pragatha Kanva
63	Indra, Deva-gana	Pragatha Kanva
64–65	Indra	Pragatha Kanva
66	Indra	Kali Pragatha
67	Adityas	Matsya Sammada or Maitravaruni

Sukta	Main deity/deities	Rishi composer
		Manya, or another Matsya Jalanadha
68	Indra, Riksha Ashvamedha	Priyamedha Angirasa
69	Indra, Vishvedevas, Varuna	Priyamedha Angirasa
70	Indra	Puruhanma Angirasa
71	Agni	Suditi and/or Purumilha Angirasa
72	Agni or havistuti	Haryata Pragatha
73	Ashvins	Gopavana Atreya or Saptavadhri
74	Agni, Shrutava Arkshya	Gopavana Atreya
75	Agni	Virupa Angirasa
76–78	Indra	Varusuti or Kurusuti Kanva
79	Soma	Kutsa Bhargava or Kritnu
80	Indra, Deva-gana	Ekadyu Naudhasa
81	Indra	Kusidi Kanva
83	Vishvedevas	Kusidi Kanva
84	Agni	Ushana Kavya
85	Ashvins	Krishna Angirasa
86	Ashvins	Krishna Angirasa or Vishvaka Karshani
87	Ashvins	Krishna Angirasa or Dyumnika Vasishtha or Priyamedha Angirasa
88	Indra	Nodha Gautama
89–90	Indra	Nrimedha Angirasa and Purumedha Angirasa
91	Indra	Apala Atreyi
92	Indra	Shrutakaksha Angirasa or Sukaksha Angirasa
93	Indra, Ribhus	Sukaksha Angirasa
94	Maruts	Vindu or Putadaksha Angirasa
95	Indra	Tirashchi Angirasa
96	Indra, Maruts, Indra-Brihaspati	Tirashchi Angirasa or Dhyutana Maruta
97	Indra	Rebha Kashyapa
98–99	Indra	Nrimedha Angirasa
100	Indra, Vak	Nema Bhargava

Sukta	Main deity/deities	Rishi composer
101	Mitra-Varuna and others	Jamadagni Bhargava
102	Agni	Prayoga Bhargava, or Agni Barhaspatya, or Agni Pavaka or son of Sahasa, Grihapati, and/or Yavishtha
103	Agni, Maruts	Sobhari Kanva

MANDALA 9

Sukta	Main deity/deities	Rishi composer
1	Pavamana Soma	Madhuchchhanda Vaishvamitra
2	Soma	Medhatithi Kanva
3	Soma	Shunahshepa Ajigarti
4	Soma	Hiranyastupa Angirasa
5	Apri sukta	Asita Kashyapa or Devala Kashyapa
6–24	Soma	Asita Kashyapa or Devala Kashyapa
25	Soma	Drilhachyuta Agastya
26	Soma	Idhmavaha Drilhachyuta
27	Soma	Nrimedha Angirasa
28	Soma	Priyamedha Angirasa
29	Soma	Nrimedha Angirasa
30	Soma	Vindu Angirasa
31	Soma	Gotama Rahugana
32	Soma	Shyavashva Atreya
33–34	Soma	Trita Aptya
35–36	Soma	Prabhuvasu Angirasa
37–38	Soma	Rahugana Angirasa
39–40	Soma	Brihanmati Angirasa
41–43	Soma	Medhyatithi Kanva
44–46	Soma	Ayasya Angirasa
47–49	Soma	Kavi Bhargava
50–52	Soma	Uchathya Angirasa
53–60	Soma	Avatsara Kashyapa
61	Soma	Amahiyu Angirasa
62	Soma	Jamadagni Bhargava

Sukta	Main deity/deities	Rishi composer
63	Soma	Nidhruvi Kashyapa
64	Soma	Kashyapa Maricha
65	Soma	Bhriguvaruni or Jamadagni Bhargava
66	Soma, Agni	Shata Vaikhanasa
67	Soma, Agni, others	Bharadvaja Barhaspatya and several others
68	Soma	Vatsapri Bhalandana
69	Soma	Hiranyastupa Angirasa
70	Soma	Renu Vaishvamitra
71	Soma	Rishabha Vaishvamitra
72	Soma	Harimanta Angirasa
73	Soma	Pavitra Angirasa
74	Soma	Kakshivan Dairghatamas (Aushija)
75–79	Soma	Kavi Bhargava
80–82	Soma	Vasu Bharadvaja
83	Soma	Pavitra Angirasa
84	Soma	Prajapati Vachya
85	Soma	Vena Bhargava
86	Soma	Akrishtamasha Rishigana, Sikatanivavari Rishigana, Prishni-Aja Rishigana, Atri Bhauma, Gritsamada Bhargava
87–89	Soma	Ushana Kavya
90	Soma	Vasishtha Maitravaruni
91–92	Soma	Kashyapa Maricha
93	Soma	Nodha Gautama
94	Soma	Kanva Ghaura or Angirasa
95	Soma	Praskanva Kanva
96	Soma	Pratardana Daivodasi
97	Soma	Vasishtha Maitravaruni and several others
98	Soma	Ambarisha Varshagiri and Rijishva Bharadvaja
99–100	Soma	Rebhusunu Kashyapa
101	Soma	Andhigu Shyavashvi, Yayati

Sukta	Main deity/deities	Rishi composer
		Nahusha, Nahusha Manava, Manu Samvarana, Prajapati (Vachya or Vaishvamitra)
102	Soma	Trita Aptya
103	Soma	Dvita Aptya
104	Soma	Parvata Kanva and Narada Kanva or Shikhandini (Kashyapa's two apsara daughters)
105	Soma	Parvata Kanva and Narada Kanva
106	Soma	Agni Chakshusha, Chakshu Manava, Manu Apasva
107	Soma	Saptarishi-gana (Bharadvaja Barhaspatya, Kashyapa Maricha, Gotama Rahugana, Atri Bhauma, Vishvamitra Gathin, Jamadagni Bhargava, Vasishtha Maitravaruni
108	Soma	Gauriviti Shaktya, Shakti Vasishtha, Uru Angirasa, Rijishva Bharadvaja, Urdhvasadma Angirasa, Kritayasha Angirasa, Rinanchya
109	Soma	Agnidhishnya Aishvara
110	Soma	Trayaruna Traivrishna, and Paurukutsya Trasadasyu
111	Soma	Ananata Paruchchhepi
112	Soma	Shishu Angirasa
113–14	Soma	Kashyapa Maricha

MANDALA 10

Sukta	Main deity/deities	Rishi composer
1–7	Agni	Trita Aptya
8	Agni	Trishira Tvashtra
9	Apah (water deities)	Trishira Tvashtra or Sindhudvipa Ambarisha
10	Yama Vaivasvata, Yami Vaivasvati	Yami Vaivasvati (rishika), Yama Vaivasvata

Sukta	Main deity/deities	Rishi composer
11–12	Agni	Havirdhana Agni
13	Havirdhana	Vivasvan Aditya
14	Yama, Lingokta devata (Angira, Pitara, Atharva, Bhrigu, Soma), Lingokta devata or Pitrigana, Shvanadvaya	Yama Vaivasvata
15	Pitri-gana	Shankha Yamayana
16	Agni	Damana Yamayana
17	Saranyu, Pusha, Sarasvati, Apo devata, Soma	Devashrava Yamayana
18	Mrityu, Dhata, Tvashta, Pitrimedha, Prajapati	Sankusuka Yamayana
19	Apo devata (or cows), Agni-Soma	Mathita Yamayana or Bhriguvaruni or Chyavana Bhargava
20–21	Agni	Vimada Aindra or Vimada Prajapatya or Vasukrit Vasukra
22–24	Indra	Vimada Aindra or Vimada Prajapatya or Vasukrit Vasukra
25	Soma	Vimada Aindra or Vimada Prajapatya or Vasukrit Vasukra
26	Pushan	Vimada Aindra or Vimada Prajapatya or Vasukrit Vasukra
27	Indra	Vasukra Aindra
28	Vasukra Aindra, Indra	Indrasnusha Vasukra Patni (rishika), Indra (rishi), Vasukra Aindra
29	Indra	Vasukra Aindra
30	Apah or Apam Napat	Kavasha Ailusha
31–32	Vishvedevas, Indra	Kavasha Ailusha
33	Various deities	Kavasha Ailusha
34	Dice	Kavasha Ailusha or Aksha Maujavan
35–36	Vishvedevas	Lusha Dhanaka
37	Surya	Abhitapa Saurya
38	Indra	Indra Mushkavan
39–40	Ashvins	Ghosha Kakshivati

Sukta	Main deity/deities	Rishi composer
41	Ashvins	Suhastya Ghausheya
42-44	Indra	Krishna Angirasa
45-46	Agni	Vatsapri Bhalandana
47	Indra Vaikuntha	Saptagu Angirasa
48-50	Indra Vaikuntha	Indra Vaikuntha
51	Deva-gana, Agni Sauchika	Deva-gana, Agni Sauchika
52	Deva-gana	Agni Sauchika
53	Agni Sauchika, Deva-gana	Deva-gana, Agni Sauchika
54-55	Indra	Brihaduktha Vamadevya
56	Vishvedevas	Brihaduktha Vamadevya
57	Vishvedevas	Bandhu, Subandhu, Shrutabandhu, Viprabandhu, Gaupayana or Laupayana
58	Mana Avartana	Bandhu, Subandhu, Shrutabandhu, Viprabandhu, Gaupayana or Laupayana
59	Nirriti, Soma, Asuniti, other gods	Bandhu, Subandhu, Shrutabandhu, Viprabandhu, Gaupayana or Laupayana
60	Asamati, Indra, Jiva, Hasta	Bandhu, Subandhu, Shrutabandhu, Viprabandhu, Gaupayana or Laupayana, Agastya-bhagini
61	Vishvedevas	Nabhanedishtha Manava
62	Vishvedevas or Angirasa, Savarni	Nabhanedishtha Manava
63	Vishvedevas, Pathya Svati	Gaya (son of Plati)
64	Vishvedevas	Gayaplati
65-66	Vishvedevas	Vasukarna Vasuka
67-68	Brihaspati	Ayasya Angirasa
69	Agni	Sumitra Vyaghryashcha
70	Apri sukta	Sumitra Vyaghryashcha
71	Jnana (knowledge)	Brihaspati Angirasa
72	Deva-gana	Brihaspati Laukya or Brihaspati Angirasa or Aditi Dakshayani
73-74	Indra	Gauriviti Shaktya
75	Nadi *samuha* (rivers)	Sindhukshit Priyamedha
76	Grava (press-stones)	Jaratkarna Airavata (sarpa)

Sukta	Main deity/deities	Rishi composer
77–78	Maruts	Syumarashmi Bhargava
79–80	Agni	Agni Sachika or Agni Vaishvanara or Saptivajambhara
81–82	Vishvakarma	Vishvakarma Bhauvana
83–84	Manyu	Manyu Tapasa
85	Soma, Suryaa-vivaha, other gods	Suryaa-Savitri (rishika)
86	Indra	Indra, Vrishakapi Aindra, Indrani
87	Rakshoha Agni	Payu Bharadvaja
88	Surya, Vaishvanara Agni	Murdhanvan Angirasa or Murdhanvan Vamadevya
89	Indra, Indra-Soma	Renu Vaishvamitra
90	Purusha	Narayana
91	Agni	Aruna Vaitahavya
92	Vishvedevas	Sharyata Manava
93	Vishvedevas	Tanva Partha
94	Grava	Arbuda Kadraveya (sarpa)
95	Pururava Aila, Urvashi	Pururava Aila, Urvashi
96	Indra, Hari	Baru Angirasa or Sarvahari Aindra
97	Herbs	Bhishaj
98	Deva-gana	Devapi Arshtishena
99	Indra	Vamra Vaikhanasa
100	Vishvedevas	Duvasyu Vandana
101	Vishvedevas	Budha Saubhya
102	Drughana (mace) or Indra	Mudgala Bharmyashva
103	Indra, other gods	Apratiratha Aindra
104	Indra	Ashtaka Vaishvamitra
105	Indra	Durmitra or Sumitra Kautsa
106	Ashvins	Bhutamsha Kashyapa
107	Dakshina or Dakshinadata Yajamana	Divya Angirasa or Dakshina Prajapatya
108	Sarama, Pani Samuha	Pani, Sarama Devashuni (rishika)
109	Vishvedevas	Juhu Brhamajaya or Urdhvanabha Brahma
110	Apri sukta	Jamadagni Bhargava or Rama Jamadagnya
111	Indra	Ashtradamshtra

Sukta	Main deity/deities	Rishi composer
112	Indra	Nabha Prabhedana Vairupa
113	Indra	Shata Prabhedana Vairupa
114	Vishvedevas	Sadhri Vairupa or Gharma Tapasa
115	Agni	Upastuta Varshtihavya
116	Indra	Agniyuta Sthaura or Agniyupa Sthaura
117	Dhana-anna dana prashansa	Bhikshu Angirasa
118	Rakshoha Agni	Urukshaya Amahiyava
119	Lava Aindra (atmastuti)	Lava Aindra
120	Indra	Brihaddiva Atharvana
121	Ka (Prajapati)	Hiranyagarbha Prajapatya
122	Agni	Chitramaha Vasishtha
123	Vena	Vena Bhargava
124	Agni, Varuna, Soma, Indra	Agni, Varuna, Soma
125	Vak or Vagambhrini (atmastuti)	Vak or Vagambhrini
126	Vishvedevas	Kulmalabarhisha Shailushi or Amhomuk Vamadevya
127	Ratri	Kushika Saubhara or Ratri
128	Vishvedevas	Vihavya Angirasa
129	Bhavavrita (creation)	Prajapati Parameshthi
130	Bhavavrita (creation)	Yajna
131	Indra, Ashvins	Sukirti Kakshivata
132	Mitra, Varuna, other gods	Shakaputa Narmedha
133	Indra	Sudas Paijavan
134	Indra	Mandhata Yauvanashav, Godha (rishika)
135	Yama	Kumara
136	Keshins (Agni, Surya, Vayu)	Vatarashana munigana (Juti, Viprajuti, Vrishanaka, Karikrita, Etasha, Rishyashringa)
137	Vishvedevas	Sapata-rishi-gana (Bharadvaja, Kashyapa, Gotama, Atri, Vishvamitra, Jamadagni, Vasishtha)
138	Indra	Anga Aukha
139	Savitr, Vishvavasu Devagandharva (atmastuti)	Vishvavasu Devagandharva

Sukta	Main deity/deities	Rishi composer
140	Agni	Agni Pavaka
141	Vishvedevas	Agni Tapasa
142	Agni	Sharngagana (Jarita, Drona, Sarisrikva, Stambamitra)
143	Ashvins	Atri Sankhya
144	Indra	Suparna Tarkshyaputra or Urdhvakrishana Yamayana
145	Sapatni badhana (removing a rival wife)	Indrani
146	Aranyani	Devamuni Airammada
147	Indra	Suvedas Shairiksha
148	Indra	Prithuvainya
149	Savitr	Archan Hairanyastupa
150	Agni	Mrilika Vasishtha
151	Shraddha	Shraddha
152	Indra	Shasa Bharadvaja
153	Indra	Indra's mothers (sisters of the gods)
154	Bhavavrita (new life)	Yami Vaivasvati
155	Alakshmighna, Brahmanaspati, Vishvedevas	Shirimbitha Bharadvaja
156	Agni	Ketu Agneya
157	Vishvedevas	Bhuvana Aptya or Sadhana Bhauvana
158	Surya	Chakshu Saurya
159	Shachi Paulomi	Shachi Paulomi
160	Indra	Purana (Poorana) Vaishvamitra
161	Indra or Raja-yakshma	Yakshmanashana Prajapatya
162	Garbhasanstrava prayashchitta	Rakshoha Brahma
163	Yakshma-nashana	Vivriha Kashyapa
164	Duhsvapnashana (dream charm)	Pracheta Angirasa
165	Vishvedevas (kapotopahataprayashchitta)	Kapota Nairrita
166	Sapatnanashana	Rishabha Vairaja or Rishabha Shakvara
167	Indra, Soma, Varuna, and others	Vishvamitra and Jamadagni
168	Vayu	Anila
169	Cows	Shabara Kakshivata

Sukta	Main deity/deities	Rishi composer
170	Surya	Vibhraj
171	Indra	Ita Bhargava
172	Usha	Samvarta Angirasa
173	Raja (kings or rulers)	Dhruva Angirasa
174	Raja	Abhivarta Angirasa
175	Grava	Urdhvagrava Arbudi (sarpa)
176	Ribhus, Agni	Sunu Arbhava
177	Mayabheda	Patanga Prajapatya
178	Tarkshya	Arishtanemi Tarkshya
179	Indra	Shibi Aushinara, Pratardana Kashiraja, Vasumana Rohitashva
180	Indra	Jaya Aindra
181	Vishvedevas	Pratha Vasishtha, Sapratha Bharadvaja, Gharma Saurya
182	Brihaspati	Tapumurdha Barhaspatya
183	Yajamana, Yajamana Patni, and Hota-ashisha	Prajavan Prajapatya
184	Lingokta devata (Vishnu, Tvashtr, Prajapati, Sinivali, Sarasvati, Ashvins)	Tvashta Garbhakarta or Vishnu
185	Adityas	Satyadhriti Varuni
186	Vayu as Vata	Ula Vatayana
187	Agni	Vatsa
188	Jatavedas Agni	Shyena
189	Sarparajni or Surya	Sarparajni
190	Bhavavrita (creation)	Aghamarshana
191	Agni, Samjnana	Samvanana

APPENDIX II:
A SELECTION OF HYMNS FROM THE FOUR VEDAS

The translations used here are based mainly on the work of R.T.H. Griffith, unless otherwise mentioned. The selected hymns have been arranged in the order in which they appear in the texts.

RIG VEDA

MANDALA 1

To Indra
1. *All sacred songs have magnified Indra expansive as the sea,*
   The best of chariot-borne warriors, the Lord, the very Lord of
   strength.
2. *Strong in your friendship, Indra, Lord of power and might, we have*
   no fear.
   We glorify you with praises, the never-conquered conqueror.
3. *The gifts of Indra exist from the earliest times, his saving grace, never fails,*
   To those who give gifts to the praise singers he gives the boon of substance rich in
   cattle.
4. *Crusher of forts, the young, the wise, of strength unmeasured, was*
   he born
   Sustainer of each sacred rite, Indra, the Thunderer, much extolled.

5. Lord of the thunder, you burst the cave of Vala rich in cows.
   The gods came pressing to your side, and free from terror aided you.
6. I, Hero, through your blessings have come to the flood addressing you.
   Song-lover, here the singers stand and testify to you.
7. The wily Shushna, Indra! You overthrew him with your wondrous powers.
   The wise saw this deed of yours: now go beyond their eulogies.
8. Our songs of praise have glorified Indra who rules by his might,
   Whose precious gifts in thousands come, yes, even more abundantly.

(1.11)

To Agni

1. Like the sun's glance, like wealth of varied sort, like breath which is the life, like one's own son,
   Like a swift bird, a cow who yields her milk, pure and refulgent to the wood he speeds.
2. He offers safety like a pleasant home, like ripened grain, the conqueror of men.
   Like a seer lauding, famed among the people; like a steed friendly he guarantees us power.
3. With flame insatiate, like eternal might; caring for each one like a woman at home;
   Bright when he shines forth, whitish amidst the people, like a car, gold-decked, thundering to the fight.
4. He strikes with terror like a dart shot forth, even like an archer's arrow tipped with flame;
   Master of present and of future life, the maidens' lover and the matron's Lord.
5. To him lead all your ways; may we attain the kindled god as cows their home at eve.
   He drives the flames below, as floods push down their swell; the rays rise up to the fair place of heaven.

(1.66)

To Usha, the dawn

1. This light is come, amid all lights the fairest; born is the brilliant, far-extending brightness.
   Night, sent away for Savitr's uprising, has made space for the morning to be born.
2. The Fair, the Bright has come with her white offspring; to her the Dark One has resigned her dwelling.
   Akin, immortal, following each other, changing their colours both the heavens move onward.
3. Common, unending is the Sister's pathway; taught by the Gods, alternately they travel.
   Fair-formed, of different hues and yet one-minded, Night and Dawn clash not, neither do they tarry.
4. Bright leader of glad sounds, our eyes behold her; splendid in hue, she has opened the portals.
   She, stirring up the world, has shown us riches; Dawn has awakened every living creature.
5. Rich Dawn, she sets afoot the curled-up sleeper, one for enjoyment, one for wealth or worship,
   Those who saw little for extended vision. All living creatures has the Dawn awakened.

6. One to high sway, one to exalted glory, one to pursue his gain, and one his labour;
   All to regard their different vocations, all moving creatures has the Dawn awakened.

7. We see her there, the Child of Heaven apparent, the young Maid, flushing in her shining raiment.
   Sovereign Lady of all earthly treasure, glow on us here, auspicious Dawn, this morning.

8. She, first of endless morns to come hereafter, follows the path of mornings that have departed.
   Dawn, at her rising, urges forth the living; him who is dead, she wakes not from his slumber.

9. As you, Dawn, has caused Agni to be kindled, and with the Sun's eye has revealed creation.
   And has awakened men to offer worship, you have performed, for Gods, a noble service.

10. How long a time, and they shall be together—Dawns that have shone and Dawns to shine thereafter?
    She yearns for former Dawns with eager longing, and goes forth gladly shining with the others.

11. Gone are the men who in the days before us looked on the rising of the earlier Morning.
    We, we the living, now behold her brightness and they come near who shall hereafter see her.

12. Foe chaser, born of Law, the Law's protectress, joy-giver, waker of all pleasant voices,
    Auspicious, bringing food for God's enjoyment, shine on us here, most bright, O Dawn, this morning.

13. From days eternal has Dawn shone, the goddess, and shows this light today, endowed with riches.
    So will she shine on, in days to come; immortal, she moves on in her own strength, undecaying.

14. In the sky's borders has she shone in splendour; the goddess has thrown off the veil of darkness.
    Awakening the world with purple horses, on her well-harnessed chariot Dawn approaches.

15. Bringing all life-sustaining blessings with her, showing herself she sends forth brilliant lustre.
    Last of the countless mornings that have vanished, first of bright morns to come has Dawn arisen.

16. Arise! The breath, the life, again has reached us; darkness has passed away and life approaches.
    She for the Sun has left a path to travel; we have arrived where men prolong existence.

17. Singing the praises of refulgent mornings, with his hymn's web, the priest, the poet rises.
    Shine then today, rich maid on him who praises you, shine down on us the gift of life and offspring.

18. Dawns giving sons all heroes, cattle and horses, shining upon the man who brings oblations—
    These let the Soma presser gain when ending his glad songs louder than the voice of Vayu.

19. Mother of Gods, Aditi's form of glory, symbol of sacrifice, shine forth exalted.
    Rise up, bestowing praise on our devotion; all bounteous, make us chief among the people.

20. Whatever splendid wealth the Dawns bring with them to bless the man who offers praise and worship,
    Even then may Mitra, Varuna protect us, and Aditi and Sindhu, Earth and Heaven.

(1.113)

MANDALA 2

Apri (hymn for sacrifices)

1. Agni is set upon the earth well kindled; he stands in the
   presence of all beings.
   Wise, ancient, God, the priest and purifier, let Agni serve the Gods
   for he is worthy.

2. May Narashamsa lighting up the chambers, bright in his majesty through threefold heaven,
    Steeping the gift with oil diffusing purpose, bedew the Gods at the chief time of worship.

3. Adored in heart, as is your right, O Agni, serve the Gods first today before the mortal.
    Bring the Marut host here. O men worship Indra seated on the grass, eternal.

4. O grass divine, increasing, rich in heroes, strewn for wealth's sake, well laid upon this altar,
    On this bedewed with oil sit you, O Vasus, sit all you Gods, you Holy, you Adityas.

5. Wide be the Doors, the Goddesses, thrown open, easy to pass, invoked, through adorations,
    Let them unfold, expansive, everlasting, that sanctify the maghavans, rich in heroes.

6. Good work for us, the glorious Night and Morning, like female weavers, waxen from an earlier time,
    Yielders of rich milk, interweave in harmony the long-extended thread, the web of worship.

7. Let the two heavenly Heralds, first, most wise, most fair, present oblation duly with the sacred verse,
    Worshipping God at ordered seasons decking them at three high places at the centre of the earth.

8. Sarasvati who perfects our devotion, Ila divine, Bharati all surpassing,
    Three goddesses, with power inherent, seated, protect this holy grass, our flawless refuge!

9. Born is the pious hero swift of hearing, like gold in hue, well formed, and full of vigour.
    May Tvashtr lengthen our line and kindred, and may they reach the place which Gods inhabit.

10. Vanaspati shall stand near and start us, and Agni with his arts prepare oblation.
    Let the skilled heavenly Immolator send to the Gods the offering thrice anointed.

11. Oil has been mixed; oil is his habitation. In oil he rests; oil is

his proper province.
Come as you wish: O you Steer (Agni), rejoice; carry away the
oblation duly consecrated.

(2.3)

NOTE: The doors: of the place of sacrifice; Narashamsa: a name of Agni.

To various deities
1. *Graciously further, O Heaven and Earth (Dyaus and Prithivi), this speech striving*
   to win reward, of I, your worshipper.
   First rank I give to you, Immortal, high extolled! I, in order to win me
   wealth, to you the mighty pair.
2. *Let not man's guile annoy us, secret or by day; give not us up a*
   prey to these calamities.
   Sever not our friendship: think thereon for us. This, with a
   heart that longs for bliss, we seek from you.
3. *Bring here with benign mind the willing cow teeming with*
   plenty of milk, full, inexhaustible.
   O you invoked by many, day by day I urge you with my word, a
   charger rapid in his tread.
4. *With eulogy I call on Raka swift to hear; may she, auspicious, hear*
   us, and herself observe.
   With never-breaking needle may she sew her work, and give us a hero son
   most wealthy, worthy of praise.
5. *All your kind thoughts, O Raka, lovely in their form, with which you*
   grant wealth to him who offers gifts—
   With these come you to us this day, benevolent, O Blessed One,
   bestowing food of a thousand sorts.
6. *O broad-tressed Sinivali, you who are the sister of the gods,*
   Accept the offered sacrifice, and, Goddess, grant us progeny.
7. *With lovely fingers, lovely arms, prolific mother of many sons—*
   Present the sacred gifts to her, to Sinivali, Queen of men.
8. *Her, Sinivali, her, Gungu, her, Raka, her, Sarasvati, Indrani to*
   my aid I call, and Varunani for my welfare.

(2.32)

NOTE: Verse 8 lists various goddesses.

To Shakunta (Indra in the form of *kapinjala*, a partridge)

1. Announcing his message aloud with repeated cries, he sends his voice
    out as a steersman sends his boat.
    O Shakuni, you bring good fortune to all; from no side let calamity befall you.
2. Let not the falcon kill you, nor the eagle; let not the
    arrow-bearing archer reach you.
    Still crying in the region of the Fathers, let your speech here be auspicious,
    bearing joyful tidings.
3. O Shakuni, you are the one who brings good tidings; therefore, bird of good fortune, call out loudly
    southward of our dwellings,
    So that no thief, no sinner may oppress us. Loud may we together, with
    heroes, celebrate you.

(2.42)

NOTE: Kapinjala: francolin partridge (in this hymn, the god Indra is said to be in the form of kapinjala, representing Shakunta, where Shakunta or Shakuni refers to a bird as an omen of good fortune; later scholars identify Shakuna and Shakuni with kites or ravens but in this hymn it has a specific connotation).

MANDALA 3

To Indra

1. Come to the juice that we have pressed, to Soma, Indra, blessed
    with milk:
    Come, favouring us, with your Bay-drawn chariot!
2. Come, Indra, to this gladdening drink, placed on the grass,
    pressed out with stones:
    Will you not drink your fill of it?
3. To Indra have my songs of praise gone forth, thus rapidly sent
    hence,
    To turn him to the Soma-draught.
4. Here with songs of praise we call Indra to drink the Soma juice:
    Will he not come to us by these hymns?
5. Indra, these Somas are pressed. Take them within your stomach, Lord
    Of Hundred Powers, Prince of Wealth.
6. We know you as winner of the spoil, and resolute in battles, Sage!
    Therefore your blessing we implore.

7. Borne here by your stallions, drink, Indra, this juice which we
   have pressed,
   Mingled with barley and with milk.

8. Indra, for you, in your own place, I urge the Soma for your
   drink:
   Deep in your heart let it remain,

9. We call on you, the Ancient One, Indra, to drink the Soma juice,
   We Kushikas who seek your aid.

(3.42)

To Mitra

1. Mitra, when speaking, stirs men to labour: Mitra sustains
   both the earth and heaven.
   Mitra watches men with eyes that never close. To Mitra bring, with
   holy oil, oblation.

2. He is foremost who brings you food, O Mitra, who strives to keep
   your sacred Law, Aditya.
   He whom you help is never killed or conquered, on him, from near
   or far, no affliction falls.

3. Rejoicing in sacred food and free from sickness, with knees bent
   low on the earth's broad surface,
   Following closely the Aditya's statute, may we remain in Mitra's
   gracious favour.

4. Auspicious and adorable, this Mitra was born with fair dominion,
   King, Disposer.
   May we enjoy the grace of him the Holy, and rest in his propitious
   loving kindness.

5. The great Aditya, to be served with worship, who stirs men,
   is gracious to the singer.
   To Mitra, him most highly to be praised, offer in fire, oblation that
   he loves.

6. The gainful grace of Mitra, god, supporter of the race of man,
   Gives splendour of most glorious fame.

7. Mitra whose glory spreads afar, he who in might surpasses heaven,
   Surpasses earth in his renown.

8. All the Five Races have repaired to Mitra, ever strong to aid,
   For he sustains all the gods.

9. *Mitra to gods, to living men, to him who strews the holy grass,*
    Gives food fulfilling sacred Law.

(3.59)

To Usha, the dawn

1. *O Usha, strong with strength, endowed with knowledge, accept the*
    singer's praise, O wealthy Lady.
    You, goddess, ancient, young, and full of wisdom, move,
    all-bounteous, as the Law ordains.
2. *Shine forth, O Morning, you auspicious goddess, on your bright chariot*
    awaking pleasant voices.
    Let docile horses of far-reaching splendour convey you here,
    the golden-coloured.
3. *You, Morning, turning towards every creature, stands on high as*
    a sign of the immortal,
    To one same goal ever and ever moving now, like a wheel, O
    newly born, roll here.
4. *Letting her reins drop downward, Morning comes, the wealthy Lady,*
    the Lady of the dwelling;
    Bringing forth light, the Wonderful, the Blessed has spread her
    from the bounds of earth and heaven.
5. *Here invoke the radiant Goddess Morning, and bring with*
    reverence your hymn to praise her.
    She, dropping sweets, has set in heaven her brightness, and, fair
    to look on, has beamed forth her splendour.
6. *From heaven, with hymns, the Holy One was wakened: brightly to*
    both worlds came the wealthy Lady.
    To Morning, Agni, when she comes refulgent, you go forth
    soliciting fair riches.
7. *On Law's firm base the speeder of the Mornings, the Bull, has*
    entered mighty earth and heaven.
    Great is the power of Varuna and Mitra, which, bright, has spread
    in every place its splendour.

(3.61)

To the Vishvedevas

1. *Not men of magic skill, nor men of wisdom, impair the gods' first*
    steadfast ordinances.

Never may the earth and heaven which know not malice, nor the fixed
hills, be bowed by sage devices.

2. One, moving not away, supports six burdens: the cows proceed to
him the true, the Highest.
Near stand three Mighty Ones who travel swiftly: two are concealed
from sight, one is apparent.

3. The bull who wears all shapes, the triple-breasted, three-uddered,
with a brood in many places,
Rules majestic with his triple aspect, the bull, the Everlasting
Ones' Lord.

4. When near them, as their tracer he observed them: he called aloud
the dear name of the Adityas.
The goddesses, the Waters, stayed to meet him: they who were
wandering separate enclosed him.

5. Streams! The wise gods have thrice three habitations. Child of
three mothers, he is Lord in assemblies.
Three are the holy Ladies of the Waters, thrice here from heaven
supreme in our assembly.

6. Do you, O Savitr, from heaven thrice here, three times a day,
send down your blessings daily.
Send us, O Bhaga, triple wealth and treasure; cause the two worlds
to make us prosperous, Preserver!

7. Savitr thrice from heaven pours down abundance, and the
fair-handed Kings, Varuna, Mitra;
And spacious Heaven and Earth, yes, and the Waters, solicit wealth
that Savitr may send us.

8. Three are the bright realms, best, beyond attainment, and three,
the asura's heroes, rule as sovereigns,
Holy and vigorous, never to be injured. Thrice may the gods from
heaven attend our assembly.

(3.56)

MANDALA 4

To Indra and Shyena

1. I was before Manu, I was Surya: I am the sage Kakshivan, holy
singer.
I am greater than Kutsa the son of Arjuni. I am the wise Ushana, behold me!

2. I have granted the earth to the arya, and rain to the man who
    brings offerings.
    I guided forth the loudly roaring waters, and the gods moved
    according to my pleasure.

3. In the wild joy of Soma I demolished Shambara's forts,
    ninety-and-nine, together;
    And, utterly, the hundredth habitation, when helping Divodasa
    Atithigva.

4. Before all birds be ranked this bird, O Maruts; supreme of falcons
    be this fleet-winged Shyena,
    Because, strong-pinioned, with no chariot to bear him, he brought to
    Manu the god-loved oblation (Soma).

5. When the bird brought it, he swiftly went on the wide path, fleet as thought, he hurried.
    Swift he returned with sweetness of the Soma, and hence the Shyena
    has acquired his glory.

6. Bearing the stalk, the falcon sped onward, the bird bringing from
    afar the drink that gladdens,
    Friend of the gods, he brought, grasping fast, the Soma which he had
    taken from the highest heaven.

7. Shyena took and brought the Soma, bearing a thousand libations
    with him, yes, ten thousand.
    The Bold One left all enemies behind him, wise, in the wild joy of Soma,
    he left the foolish.

(4.26)

NOTE: In the first three verses, the god Indra speaks; the remaining verses refer to Shyena,
the falcon.

To the Ribhus

1. The chariot that was not made for horses or for reins,
    three-wheeled, worthy of hymns of praise, rolls round the firmament.
    That is the great announcement of your godhood, that, O you Ribhus, you
    sustain the earth and heaven.

2. You Wise Ones who made the lightly rolling chariot from your mind,
    by thought, the chariot that never errs,
    You, being such, to drink of this drink offering, you, O you Vajas,
    and you Ribhus, we invoke.

3. O Vajas, Ribhus, reaching far, among the gods this was your
    exaltation gloriously declared,

In that your aged parents, worn with length of days, you brought
again to youth so that they moved at will.

4. The chalice that was single, you have made fourfold, and by your
wisdom brought the cow forth from the hide.
So quickly, amidst the gods, you gained immortal life. Vajas and Ribhus,
your great work must be extolled.

5. Wealth from the Ribhus is most glorious in renown, that which the
heroes, famed for vigour, have produced.
In assemblies must be sung the chariot which Vibhvan wrought: that which you
favour, gods! is famed among mankind.

6. Strong is the steed, the man a sage in eloquence, the bowman is a
hero hard to beat in fight,
Great store of wealth and manly power has he obtained whom Vaja,
Vibhvan, the Ribhus, have looked kindly on.

7. To you has been assigned the fairest ornament, the hymn of
praise: Vajas and Ribhus, joy therein;
For you have lore and wisdom and poetic skill: as such, with this our
prayer we call on you to come.

8. According to the wishes of our hearts may you, who have full
knowledge of all the delights of men,
Fashion for us, O Ribhus, power and splendid wealth, rich in high
courage, excellent, and vital strength.

9. Bestowing on us here riches and offspring, here create fame for
Us, befitting heroes.
Grant us wealth of splendid sort, O Ribhus, that we may make us
more renowned than others.

(4.36)

To Kshetrapati and others

1. We through Kshetrapati, the master of the field, even as through a friend,
Obtain what nourishes our cattle and horses. In such may he be good to us.

2. As the cow yields milk, pour for us freely, Lord of the Field,
the wave that bears sweetness,
Distilling mead, well-purified like ghi, let the Lords of
holy Law be gracious.

3. Sweet be the plants for us; the heavens, the waters, and full of
sweetness for us be air's mid-region.
May Kshetrapati for us be full of sweetness, and may we follow
after him uninjured.

4. *Happily work our oxen and men, may the plough furrow happily.*
    Happily be the traces bound; happily may he ply the goad.

5. *Shuna and Sira, welcome this hymn of praise, and with the milk which you*
    have made in heaven
    Bedew you both this earth of ours.

6. *Auspicious Sita, come near: we venerate and worship you*
    That you may bless and prosper us and bring us fruits abundantly.

7. *May Indra press the furrow down, may Pushan guide its course*
    aright.
    May she, as rich in milk, be drained for us through each succeeding
    year.

8. *Happily let the ploughshares turn up the ploughland, happily let the*
    ploughers go with the oxen.
    With mead and milk Parjanya make us happy. Grant us prosperity,
    Shuna and Sira.

(4.57)

NOTE: Sita: furrow; Shuna, Sira: parts of the plough, which were deified.

MANDALA 5

To the Maruts

1. *Sing boldly forth, Shyavashva, with the Maruts who are loud in song,*
    Who, holy, as their wont is, joy in glory that is free from guile.

2. *For in their boldness they are friends of firm and sure heroic*
    strength.
    They in their course, bold-spirited, guard all men of their own
    accord.

3. *Like steers in rapid motion they advance and overtake the nights;*
    And thus the Maruts' power in heaven and on the earth we celebrate.

4. *With boldness to you Maruts let us offer praise and sacrifice:*
    Who all, through the ages of mankind, guard mortal man from injury.

5. *Praiseworthy, givers of good gifts, heroes with full and perfect*
    strength—
    To Maruts, Holy Ones of heaven, will I extol the sacrifice.

6. *The lofty heroes cast their spears and weapons bright with*
    gleaming gold.

After these, the Maruts followed close, like laughing lightning from the
sky, a splendour of its own accord.

7. *They who were strong on the earth, they who are in the wide*
   mid-air,
   Or in the rivers' compass, or in the abode of ample heaven.

8. *Praise you the Maruts' company, the brave and truly strong,*
   The heroes, hastening, by themselves have yoked their deer for
   victory.

9. *Fair-gleaming, on Parushni they have clothed themselves in robes of*
   wool,
   And with their chariot tires they cleave the rock asunder in their
   might.

10. *Whether as wanderers from the way or speeders on or to the path,*
    Under these names the spreading band tend well the sacrifice for me.

11. *To this the heroes well attend, well do their teams attend to*
    this.
    Visible are their varied forms. Behold, they are Paravatas.

12. *Hymn-singing, seeking water, they, praising, have danced about*
    the spring.
    What are they to me? No thieves, but helpers, splendid to behold.

13. *Sublime, with spears of lightning, Sages and Orderers are*
    they.
    Rishi, adore that Marut host, and make them happy with your song.

14. *Rishi, invite the Marut band with offerings, as a maid invites her friend.*
    From heaven, too, Bold Ones, in your might come quickly here, glorified
    with songs.

15. *Thinking of these now let him come, as with the escort of the*
    gods,
    And with the splendid princes, famed for rapid courses, to the gifts.

16. *Princes, who, when I asked their kin, named Prishni as their*
    mother-cow,
    And the impetuous Rudra they, the Mighty Ones, declared their father.

17. *The mighty ones, the seven times seven, have singly given me a*
    hundred gifts.
    I have obtained on the Yamuna famed wealth in cows and wealth in horses.

(5.52)

NOTE: In this hymn, the Maruts could be people. Parushni: a river; Paravatas:
people of the mountains.

To Agni

1. Agni is awakened by the people's fuel to meet the Dawn who arrives
   like a milch cow.
   Like young trees shooting up on high their branches, his flames are
   rising to the vault of heaven.

2. For worship of the gods the priest was awakened: at morning
   gracious Agni has arisen.
   Kindled, his radiant might is made apparent, and the great deity set
   free from darkness.

3. When he has stirred the line of his attendants, with the pure
   milk pure Agni is anointed.
   The strength-bestowing gift is then made ready, which spread in
   front, with tongues, erect, he drinks.

4. The spirits of the pious turn together to Agni, as the eyes of all
   turn to Surya.
   He, when both Dawns of different hues have borne him, springs up at
   daybreak as a strong white charger.

5. The noble One was born at the days' beginning, laid red in colour amid
   the well-laid fuel.
   Yielding in every house his seven rich treasures, Agni is seated,
   Priest most skilled in worship.

6. Agni has sat him down, a Priest most skilful, on a sweet-smelling
   place, his mother's bosom.
   Young, faithful, sage, preeminent over many, kindled among the people
   whom he sustains.

7. This singer excellent at sacrifices, Agni the Priest, they glorify
   with homage.
   To him who maintains both worlds by eternal Law they offer oil, he is like a
   strong horse who never fails.

8. He, worshipful House-Friend, in his home is worshipped, our own
   auspicious guest, praised by sages.
   That strength the Bull with a thousand horns possesses. In might, O
   Agni, you exceed all others.

9. You quickly pass by all others, Agni, for him to whom you
   have appeared most lovely,
   Wondrously fair, adorable, effulgent, the guest of men, the darling
   of the people.

10. *To you, most youthful god! To you, O Agni from near and far the*
    people bring their tribute.
    Mark well the prayer of him who praises you best. Great, high,
    auspicious, Agni, is your shelter.

11. *Ascend today your splendid chariot, O Agni, in splendour, with the*
    Holy Ones around it.
    Knowing the paths by mid-air's spacious region bring the gods here to
    feast on our oblation.

12. *To him adorable, sage, strong and mighty we have sung our*
    song of praise and homage.
    Gavishthira has raised with prayer to Agni this far-reaching hymn,
    like gold light to heaven.

    (5.1)

To the Ashvins

1. *Agni, the bright face of the Dawns, is shining; the singers'*
   pious voices have ascended.
   Borne on your chariot, Ashvins, turn towards us and come to our
   full and rich libation.

2. *Most frequent guests, they do not scorn what is ready: and even now the*
   lauded Ashvins are beside us.
   With the promptest aid they come both morning and evening, the worshipper's
   most blessed guards from trouble.

3. *Yes, come at milking-time, at early morning, at noon of day and*
   when the sun is setting,
   By day, by night, with favour most auspicious. Not only now has the
   draught (Soma) drawn the Ashvins.

4. *For this place, Ashvins, was formerly your dwelling, these were your*
   houses, this your habitation.
   Come to us from high heaven and from the mountains. Come from the
   waters bringing food and vigour.

5. *May we obtain the Ashvins' newest favour, and gain their*
   health-bestowing happy guidance.
   Bring riches here to us, and heroes, and all felicity and joy,
   Immortals!

   (5.76)

MANDALA 6

To Pushan

1. O Pushan, bring us to the man who knows, who shall direct us
   straight,
   And say to us, It is here.

2. May we go forth with Pushan who shall point the houses out to us,
   And say to us, These same are they.

3. Unharmed is Pushan's chariot wheel; the box never falls to the
   ground,
   Nor does the loosened felly shake.

4. Pushan forgets not the man who serves him with offered gift:
   That man is first to gather wealth.

5. May Pushan follow near our cows; may Pushan keep our horses safe:
   May Pushan gather gear for us.

6. Follow the cows of him who pours libations out and worships you;
   And ours who sing to you songs of praise.

7. Let none be lost, none injured, none sink in a pit and break a
   limb.
   Return with these all safe and sound.

8. Pushan who listens to our prayers, the strong whose wealth is never
   lost,
   The Lord of riches, we implore.

9. Secure in your protecting care, O Pushan, never may we fail.
   We here are they who sing your praise.

10. From the distance, far and wide, may Pushan stretch his right
    hand forth,
    And drive our lost again to us.

(6.54)

To Usha, the dawn

1. The radiant Dawns have risen up for glory, in their white
   splendour like the waves of waters.
   She makes paths all easy, fair to travel, and, rich, has shown
   herself benign and friendly.

2. We see that you are good: far shines your lustre; your beams, your
   splendours have flown up to heaven.
   Decking yourself, you make yourself seen, shining in majesty,
   you Goddess Morning.

3. *Red are the cows and luminous that bear her the Blessed One who*
    spreads through the distance.
    The foes she chases like a valiant archer, like a swift warrior she
    repels darkness.
4. *Your ways are easy on the hills: you pass Invincible!*
    Self-luminous, through waters.
    So lofty goddess with your ample pathway, Daughter of Heaven, bring
    wealth to give us comfort.
5. *Dawn, bring me wealth: untroubled, with your oxen you bear*
    riches at your will and pleasure;
    You who, a goddess, a child of heaven, has shown yourself lovely through
    bounty when we called you early.
6. *As the birds fly forth from their resting places, so men with store*
    of food rise at your dawning.
    Yes, to the liberal mortal who remains at home, O Goddess Dawn,
    much good you bring.

(6.64)

MANDALA 7

To Vastoshpati

1. *Acknowledge, O Vastoshpati, guardian of the home; bring no disease,*
    and give us happy entrance.
    Whatever we ask of you, be pleased to grant it, and prosper both
    quadrupeds and bipeds.
2. *Protector of the home, be our promoter; increase our wealth in*
    cows and horses, O Indu.
    May we be ever-youthful in your friendship: be pleased in us as a father in
    his sons.
3. *Through your dear fellowship that brings welfare, may we be*
    victors, Vastoshpati!
    Protect our happiness in rest and labour. Preserve us forever, you
    Gods, with blessings.

(7.54)

NOTE: Indu: drop (refers to Soma).

To the rishi Vasishtha

1. *These who wear hair knots on the right, the movers of holy*
    thought, white-robed, have won me over.

   *I warned the men, when from the grass I raised me, not from afar can
   my Vasishthas help you.*

2. *With Soma they brought Indra from a distance, over Vaishanta, from
   the strong libation.*
   *Indra preferred Vasishthas to the Soma pressed by the son of Vayata,
   Pasadyumna.*

3. *So, truly, with these he crossed the river, in company with these
   he slaughtered Bheda.*
   *So in the fight with the Ten Kings, Vasishthas! did Indra help Sudas
   through your devotions.*

4. *I gladly, with prayer prayed by our fathers have fixed your
   axle: you shall not be injured:*
   *Since, when you sang aloud the Shakvari verses, Vasishthas, you
   invigorated Indra.*

5. *Like thirsty men they looked to heaven, in battle with the Ten
   Kings, surrounded and imploring.*
   *Then Indra heard Vasishtha as he praised him, and gave the Tritsus
   ample room and freedom.*

6. *Like sticks and staves with which they drive the cattle, stripped
   bare, the Bharatas were found defenceless:*
   *Vasishtha then became their chief and leader: then were the
   Tritsus' clans extended.*

7. *Three fertilize the worlds with genial moisture: three noble
   creatures cast a light before them.*
   *Three that give warmth to all attend the morning. All these have
   they discovered, these Vasishthas.*

8. *Like the Sun's growing glory is their splendour, and like the
   sea's is their unfathomed greatness.*
   *Their course is like the wind's. Your heights, Vasishthas, can never be
   attained by any other.*

9. *They with perceptions of the heart in secret, resort to that which
   spreads a thousand branches.*
   *The apsaras brought the Vasishthas here wearing the clothes spun
   for them by Yama.*

10. *You were a form of lustre springing from the lightning, when
    Varuna and Mitra saw you.*
    *Your one and only birth was then, Vasishtha, when from your stock
    Agastya brought you here.*

11. Born of their love for Urvashi, Vasishtha you, priest, are the son of
Varuna and Mitra;
And as a fallen drop, in heavenly fervour, all the gods laid you on
a lotus-blossom.

12. He, thinker, knower both of earth and heaven, endowed with many a
gift, bestowing thousands,
Destined to wear the vesture spun by Yama, sprang from the apsaras
to life, Vasishtha.

13. Born at the sacrifice, urged by adorations, both with a common
flow bedewed the pitcher.
Then from the midst thereof there rose up Mana, and thence they say
was born the sage Vasishtha.

14. He brings the bearer of the laud and Saman: first shall he speak
bringing the stone for pressing.
With grateful hearts in reverence approach him: to you, O Pratridas,
Vasishtha comes.

(7.33)

NOTE: This hymn refers to the battle of the ten kings against King Sudas.
Vaishanta: possibly a river; Pasadyumna: a king.

To Savitr
1. On high has Savitr, this god, extended the golden lustre which
he spreads around him.
Now, now must Bhaga be invoked by mortals, Lord of great riches who
distributes treasures.

2. Rise up, O Savitr whose hands are golden, and hear this man while
sacrifice is offered,
Spreading afar your broad and wide effulgence, and bringing mortal
men the food that feeds them.

3. Let Savitr the god be praised in song, to whom the Vasus,
even, all sing glory.
Sweet be our praises to him whose due is worship: may he with all
protection guard our princes.

4. Even he whom Aditi the goddess praises, rejoicing in god Savitr's
incitement:
Even he who praise the high imperial rulers, Varuna, Mitra, Aryaman,
sing in concert.

5. They who come eagerly to our oblation, dispensing bounty, from the
    earth and heaven.
    May they and Ahibudhnya hear our calling: guard us Varutri with the
    Ekadhenus.
6. This may the Lord of Life, entreated, grant us—the wealth which
    Savitr the god possesses.
    The mighty calls on Bhaga for protection, on Bhaga calls the weak to
    give him riches.
7. Bless us the Vajins when we call, while slowly they move, strong
    singers, to the gods' assembly.
    Crushing the wolf, the serpent, and the demons, may they completely
    banish all affliction.
8. Deep-skilled in Law eternal, deathless, singers, O Vajins, help us
    in each fray for booty.
    Drink of this mead, be satisfied, be joyful: then go on paths which
    gods are wont to travel.

(7.38)

NOTE: Varutri: the protectress, goddess of speech; Vajins: group of deities (according to Sayana) and the horses that draw the god's chariots (according to Mahidhara).

MANDALA 8

To the Adityas

1. Now let the mortal offer prayers to win the unexampled grace
    Of these Adityas and their aid to cherish life.
2. For no enemy molests the paths which these Adityas tread:
    Infallible guards, they strengthen us in happiness.
3. Now soon may Bhaga, Savitr, Varuna, Mitra, Aryaman
    Give us the shelter widely spread which we implore.
4. Along with the gods are you, O goddess Aditi, who nourishes us with your fostering care,
    Come, dear to many, with the Lords who guard us well.
5. For well these sons of Aditi know to keep enemies away,
    Unrivalled, giving ample room, they protect us from sorrow.
6. Aditi guard our herds in the day, Aditi, free from guile, guard them at night,
    Aditi, ever strengthening, save us from grief!
7. And in the day our hymn is this: May Aditi come near to help,
    With loving kindness bring us wealth and chase our foes.

8. And may the Ashvins, the divine pair of physicians, send us health:
    May they remove iniquity and chase our foes.

9. May Agni bless us with his fires, and Surya warm us pleasantly:
    May the pure Wind breathe sweet on us, and chase our foes.

10. Drive all disease and strife away, drive away malignity:
    Adityas, keep us ever far from sore distress.

11. Remove from us the arrow, keep famine, Adityas! far away:
    Keep enmities afar from us, Lords of all wealth!

12. Now, O Adityas, grant to us the shelter that lets man go free,
    Yes, even free the sinner from his sin, you bounteous gods.

13. Whatever mortal with the power of demons tries to injure us,
    May he, impetuous, suffer harm by his own deeds.

14. May sin overtake our human foes, the men who speak evil,
    those who cause our misery, whose hearts are false.

15. Gods, you are with the simple ones, you know each mortal in your
    hearts;
    You, Vasus, can distinguish the false from the true.

16. Grant us the sheltering aid of mountains and of water-floods:
    Keep us far from us iniquity, O Heaven and Earth.

17. So with auspicious sheltering aid do you, O Vasus, carry us
    Beyond all trouble and distress, borne in your ship.

18. Adityas, you most mighty ones, grant to our children and their
    descendents an extended term of life so that they may live long days.

19. Sacrifice, O Adityas, is your inward monitor: be kind,
    For in the bond of kindred we are bound to you.

20. The Maruts' high protecting aid, the Ashvins, and the god who
    saves,
    Mitra and Varuna we appeal to you for our welfare.

21. Grant us a home with triple guard, Aryaman, Mitra, Varuna!
    Unthreatened, Maruts! Grant us peace and give us fame.

22. And as we human beings, O Adityas, are mortals, prone to death,
    Graciously lengthen our lives that we may live long.

(8.18)

To Varuna

1. To make this Varuna come forth sing you a song to the band of
    Maruts wiser than yourself,

This Varuna who guards well the thoughts of men like herds of
cattle.
Let all the others die away.

2. Him altogether I praise with the song and hymns our fathers sang,
and with Nabhaka's eulogies,
Him dwelling at the rivers' source, surrounded by his Sisters Seven.

3. The nights he has encompassed, and established the mornings with
magic art; visible over all is he.
His dear Ones, following his Law, have prospered the Three Dawns for
him.

4. He, visible over all the earth, established the quarters of the sky;
He measured out the eastern place, that is the fold of Varuna: like
a strong herdsman is the God.

5. He who supports the worlds of life, he who well knows the hidden
names mysterious of the morning beams,
He cherishes much wisdom, Sage, as heaven brings forth each varied
form.

6. In whom all wisdom centres, as the nave is set within the wheel.
Haste you to honour Trita, as cattle haste to gather in the fold, even
as they muster steeds to yoke.

7. He wraps these regions as a robe; he contemplates the tribes of
gods and all the works of mortal men.
Before the home of Varuna all the gods follow his decree.

8. He is an ocean far-removed, yet through the heaven to him ascends
the worship which these realms possess.
With his bright foot he overthrew their magic, and went up to
heaven.

9. Ruler, whose bright far-seeing rays, pervading all three earths,
have filled the three superior realms of heaven.
Firm is the seat of Varuna: over the Seven he rules as king.

10. Who, after his decree, overspread the Dark Ones with a robe of
light;
Who measured out the ancient seat, who pillared both the worlds
apart as the Unborn supported heaven. Let all the others die away.

(8.41)

MANDALA 9

To Soma Pavamana

1. Here, in this direction, have the Soma streamed,
   the drops while they are purified:
   When blended, in waters they are rinsed.
2. The milk has run to meet them like floods rushing down a
   precipice:
   They come to Indra, being cleansed.
3. O Soma Pavamana, you are flowing to be Indra's drink:
   The men have seized and led you forth.
4. Victorious, to be hailed with joy, O Soma, flow, delighting men,
   To him who rules over mankind.
5. You, Indu, when, effused by stones, you run to the filter,
   Ready for Indra's high decree.
6. Flow on, best Vritra-slayer; flow worthy to be hailed with joyful
   hymns of praise.
   Pure, purifying, wonderful.
7. Pure, purifying is he called the Soma of the drink effused,
   Slayer of sinners, dear to gods.

(9.24)

To Soma Pavamana

1. Pour down the rain upon us, pour a wave of waters from the sky,
   And plenteous store of wholesome food.
2. Flow onward with that stream of yours, whereby the cows have come
   to us,
   The cows of strangers to our home.
3. Chief friend of gods in sacred rites, pour on us fatness with your
   stream,
   Pour down on us a flood of rain.
4. To give us vigour, with your stream run through the fleecy
   straining-cloth
   For truly the Gods will hear.
5. Onward has Pavamana flowed and beaten off the rakshasas,
   Flashing out splendour as of old.

(9.49)

MANDALA 10

Surya

1. Pray to Varuna's and Mitra's eye: offer this solemn
   worship to the mighty god,
   Who sees far away, the ensign, born of gods. Sing praises to
   Surya, to the son of Dyaus.

2. May this my truthful speech guard me on every side wherever heaven
   and earth and days exist.
   All else that is in motion finds a place of rest: the waters ever
   flow and the Sun forever rises.

3. No godless man from the remotest time can draw you down when you are
   driving forth with winged dappled steeds.
   One lustre waits upon you moving to the east, and, Surya, you
   arise with a different light.

4. O Surya, with your light you scatter gloom, and with
   your ray impel every moving thing,
   Keep far from us all feeble, worthless sacrifice, and drive away
   disease and every evil dream.

5. Sent forth, you guard well the universe's law, and in your
   wonted way arise free from anger.
   When Surya, we address our prayers to you today, may the gods
   favour our purpose and desire.

6. This invocation, these words of ours may Heaven and Earth, and Indra
   and the Waters and the Maruts hear.
   Never may we suffer want in presence of the Sun, and, living happy
   lives, may we attain old age.

7. Cheerful in spirit, evermore, and keen of sight, with store of
   children, free from sickness and from sin,
   Long-living, may we look, O Surya, upon you rising day by day,
   You are as great as Mitra is!

8. Surya, may we live long and look upon you still, O
   Far-seeing One, bringing the glorious light,
   The radiant god, the spring of joy to every eye, as you are
   mounting up high, over the shining ocean.

9. You, by whose lustre all the world of life comes forth, and by your
   beams again returns to its rest,
   O Surya with the golden hair, ascend for us day after day, still
   bringing purer innocence.

10. Bless us with shine, bless us with perfect daylight, bless us
    with cold, with fervent heat and lustre.
    Bestow on us, O Surya, varied riches, to bless us in our home and
    when we travel.

11. Gods, to our living creatures of both kinds provide protection,
    both to bipeds and to quadrupeds,
    That they may drink and eat invigorating food. So grant us health
    and strength and perfect innocence.

12. If by some grievous sin we have provoked the gods, O deities,
    with the tongue or thoughtlessness of heart,
    That guilt, O Vasus, lay upon the Evil One, on him who ever leads us
    into deep distress.

                                                              (10.37)

Manas or the Inner Spirit

1. Your spirit, that went far away to Yama, to Vivasvan's son,
   We cause to come to you again so that you may live and sojourn here.

2. Your spirit, that went far away, that passed away to earth and
   heaven,
   We cause to come to you again that you may live and sojourn here.

3. Your spirit, that went far away, away to the four-cornered earth,
   We cause to come to you again that you may live and sojourn here.

4. Your spirit, that went far away to the four quarters of the world,
   We cause to come to you again that you may live and sojourn here.

5. Your spirit, that went far away, away unto the billowy sea,
   We cause to come to you again that you may live and sojourn here.

6. Your spirit, that went far away to beams of light that flash and flow,
   We cause to come to you again that you may live and sojourn here.

7. Your spirit, that went far away, went to the waters and the plants,
   We cause to come to you again that you may live and sojourn here.

8. Your spirit, that went far away, that visited the Sun and Dawn.
   We cause to come to you again that you may live and sojourn here.

9. Your spirit, that went far away, away to lofty mountain heights,
   We cause to come to you again that you may live and sojourn here.

10. Your spirit, that went far away into this All, that lives and moves,
    We cause to come to you again that you may live and sojourn here.

11. Your spirit, that went far away to distant realms beyond our knowledge,
    We cause to come to you again that you may live and sojourn here.

12. *Your spirit, that went far away to all that is and is to be,*
We cause to come to you again that you may live and sojourn here.

(10.58)

Nirriti and others

1. *His life has been renewed and carried forward as two men,*
chariot-borne, by the skilful driver.
One falls, then seeks the goal with quickened vigour. Let Nirriti
depart to distant places.

2. *Here is the holy song for wealth, and food, in plenty: let us do many*
deeds to bring us glory.
All these our doings shall delight the singer. Let Nirriti depart to
distant places.

3. *May we overcome our foes with acts of valour, as heaven is over*
earth, hills over lowlands.
All these our deeds the singer has considered. Let Nirriti depart to
distant places.

4. *Give us not up as prey to death, O Soma still let us look upon*
the Sun arising.
Let our old age with passing days be kindly. Let Nirriti depart to
distant places.

5. *O Asuniti, keep the soul within us, and make the days we have to*
live yet longer.
Grant that we still may look upon the sunlight: strengthen your body
with the oil we bring you.

6. *Give us our sight again, O Asuniti, give us again our breath and*
our enjoyment.
Long may we look upon the Sun uprising; O Anumati, favour you and
bless us.

7. *May Earth restore to us our vital spirit, may Heaven the Goddess*
and mid-air restore it.
May Soma give us once again our body, and Pushan show the Path of
peace and comfort.

8. *May both worlds bless Subandhu, young Mothers of everlasting Law.*
May Heaven and Earth uproot and sweep iniquity and shame away: nor
sin nor sorrow trouble you.

9. *Health-giving medicines descend sent down from heaven in twos and*
threes, or wandering singly on the earth.
May Heaven and Earth uproot and sweep iniquity and shame away: nor sin nor sorrow trouble you.

10. *Drive forward you the wagon ox, O Indra, which brought*
    Ushinarani's wagon here.
    May Heaven and Earth uproot and sweep iniquity and shame away: nor
    sin nor sorrow trouble you.

                                                                    (10.59)

NOTE: Nirriti is a god representing destruction. According to Sayana, the first line of this hymn refers to the rishi Subandhu; Ushinarani: wife of Ushinara; the Ushinaras are a clan mentioned in later texts.

The Vishvedevas
1. *What god, of those who hear, is he whose well-praised name we may*
   record in this our sacrifice; and how?
   Who will be gracious? Who of many give us bliss? Who out of all the
   Host will come to lend us aid?
2. *The will and thoughts within my breast exert their power: they*
   yearn with love, and fly to all the regions round.
   None other comforter is found save only these: my longings and my
   hopes are fixed upon the gods.
3. *To Narashamsa and to Pushan I sing forth, unconcealable Agni kindled*
   by the gods.
   To Sun and Moon, two Moons, to Yama in the heaven, to Trita, Vata,
   Dawn, Night, and the two Ashvins.
4. *How is the Sage extolled whom the loud singers praise? What voice,*
   what hymn is used to praise Brihaspati?
   May Aja-Ekapad with Rikvans swift to hear, and Ahi of the Deep listen
   to our call.
5. *Aditi, to the birth of Daksha and the vow, you summon the kings*
   Mitra and Varuna.
   With course unchecked, with many chariots, Aryaman comes with the
   seven priests to tribes of various sorts.
6. *May all those vigorous coursers listen to our cry, hearers of*
   invocation, speeding on their way;
   Winners of thousands where the priestly gift is won, who gather of
   themselves great wealth in every race.
7. *Bring you Puramdhi, bring Vayu who yokes his steeds, for friendship*
   bring Pushan with your songs of praise:
   They with one mind, one thought attend the sacrifice, urged by the
   favouring aid of Savitr the god.

8. The thrice-seven wandering rivers, yes, the mighty floods, the
   forest trees, the mountains, Agni to our aid,
   Krishanu, Tishya, archers to our gathering place, and Rudra strong amid
   the Rudras we invoke.

9. Let the great streams come here with their mighty help, Sindhu,
   Sarasvati, and Sarayu with waves.
   You Goddess Floods, you mothers, animating all, promise us water rich
   in fatness and in balm.

10. And let Brihaddiva, the mother, hear our call, and Tvashtr,
    father, with the goddesses and women.
    Ribhukshan, Vaja, Bhaga, and Rathaspati, and the sweet speech of him
    who labours, guard us well!

11. Pleasant to look on, as a dwelling rich in food is the blessed
    favour of the Maruts, Rudra's sons.
    May we be famed among the people for wealth in cows and ever come to
    you, ye Gods, with sacred food.

12. The thought which you, O Maruts, Indra and you Gods have given to
    me, and you, Mitra and Varuna,
    Cause this to grow and swell like a milch cow with milk. Will you not
    bear away my songs upon your chariot?

13. O Maruts, do you never, never recollect and call again to mind
    this our relationship?
    When next we meet together at the central point, even there shall
    Aditi confirm our brotherhood.

14. The Mothers, Heaven and Earth, those mighty goddesses, worthy of
    sacrifice, secure with the race of gods.
    These two with their support uphold both gods and men, and with the
    Fathers pour the copious genial stream.

15. This invocation wins all good that we desire Brihaspati,
    highly praised Aramati, are here,
    Even where the stone that presses mead rings loudly out, and where
    the sages make their voices heard with hymns.

16. Thus has the sage, skilled in loud singers' duties, desiring
    riches, yearning after treasure,
    Gaya, the priestly singer, with his praises and hymns contented the
    celestial people.

17. Thus has the youthful sage the son of Plati, praised you,
    O Aditi and all Adityas.

Men are made rich by those who are Immortal: the Heavenly People have been extolled by Gaya.

(10.64)

Purusha

1. A thousand heads has Purusha, a thousand eyes, a thousand feet.
   On every side pervading earth he fills a space ten fingers wide.
2. This Purusha is all that has been and all that will be;
   The Lord of immortality which grows larger through food.
3. So mighty is his greatness; yes, greater than this is Purusha.
   All creatures are one-fourth of him, three-fourths is eternal life in heaven.
4. With three-fourths Purusha went up: one-fourth of him again was here.
   Then he strode out to every side over what eats and what does not eat.
5. From him Viraj was born; again Purusha from Viraj was born.
   As soon as he was born he spread eastward and westward over the earth.
6. When gods prepared the sacrifice with Purusha as their offering,
   Its oil was spring, the holy gift was autumn; summer was the wood.
7. They consecrated as victim on the grass Purusha born in earliest time.
   With him the deities and all Sadhyas and rishis sacrificed.
8. From that great general sacrifice the dripping fat was gathered up.
   He formed the creatures of the air, and animals both wild and tame.
9. From that great general sacrifice the Riks and Sama-hymns were born:
   Therefrom were spells and charms produced; the Yajus had its birth from it.
10. From it were horses born, from it all creatures with two rows of teeth:
    From it came cows, from it the goats and sheep were born.
11. When they divided Purusha how many portions did they make?
    What do they call his mouth, his arms? What do they call his thighs and feet?
12. The brahmana was his mouth, of both his arms was the rajanya made.
    His thighs became the vaishya, from his feet the shudra was produced.
13. The moon emerged from his mind, and from his eye the sun was born;
    Indra and Agni from his mouth were born, and Vayu from his breath.

14. *From his navel came mid-air; the sky was fashioned from his head;*
    Earth from his feet, and from his ear the regions. Thus they formed
    the worlds.

15. *Seven fencing sticks had he, thrice seven layers of fuel were*
    prepared,
    When the Gods, offering sacrifice, bound, as their victim, Purusha.

16. *Gods, sacrificing, sacrificed the victim; these were the earliest*
    holy ordinances.
    The Mighty Ones attained the height of heaven, there where the
    Sadhyas, Gods of old, still live.

(10.90)

NOTE: Purusha is both the universal soul and the individual soul. The sacrifice is manasa yajna—of the mind.

Creation

1. *Then there was neither non-existence nor existence: there was no realm of*
   air, no sky beyond it.
   What covered it, and where? And what gave shelter? Was water there,
   unfathomed depths of water?

2. *Death was not there then, nor was there anything immortal; no sign was*
   there, of the day's and night's divider.
   That One Thing, breathless, breathed by its own nature; apart from
   it there was nothing whatsoever.

3. *Darkness was there; at first concealed in darkness this All was*
   indiscriminate chaos.
   All that existed then was void and formless: by the great power of heat was born a unit of life.

4. *Thereafter arose Desire in the beginning, Desire, the primal seed*
   and germ of Spirit.
   Sages who searched with their heart's thought discovered the relationship of
   existence with the non-existent.

5. *Transversely was their severing line extended: what was above it*
   then, and what below it?
   There were begetters, there were mighty forces, free action here and
   energy up above.

6. *Who truly knows and who can say, from where it was born*
   and from where this creation came?
   The gods are later than this world's creation. Who knows then from where it first came into being?

7. He, the first origin of this creation, whether he formed it all or
   did not form it,
   Whose eye controls this world in the highest heaven, he only knows,
   or perhaps even he does not know.

(10.129)

Aranyani

1. Goddess of the wilderness and forest who seems to vanish from sight.
   How is it that you do not seek the village? Are you perhaps afraid?
2. When the grasshopper replies and answers the shrill cicada's
   call, with a sound like tinkling bells, then Aranyani rejoices.
3. And, far away, one can catch a glimpse of her, as if cattle seem to graze, or a distant house appears:
   Or else in the evening Aranyani is heard, like the sound of moving wagons.
4. Here she is heard as if one is calling to his cow, or as if another there has felled a tree:
   At evening the dweller in the wood hears her faintly, but fancies that someone has screamed.
5. The Goddess never kills, unless some murderous enemy approaches.
   She eats savoury wild fruit and then whenever she wants, she rests.
6. Now have I praised Aranyani, the Forest Queen, sweet-scented, redolent of
   balm,
   The mother of all wild things, who tills not but has stores of
   food.

(10.146)

To Vayu, in the form of Vata

1. O the Wind's (Vata's) chariot, O its power and glory! Crashing it goes and
   has a voice of thunder.
   It makes the regions red and touches heaven, and as it moves the
   dust of earth is scattered.
2. Along the traces of the Wind they hurry, they come to him as women
   to an assembly.
   Borne on his chariot with these for his attendants, the god speeds
   forth, he is the monarch of the universe.
3. Travelling on the paths of air's mid-region, there is not a single day when he
   rests or sleeps.
   Holy and earliest-born, friend of the waters, where did he spring from
   and from what region did he come?
4. Germ of the world, the deities' vital spirit, this god moves always
   according to his will.

His voice is heard, his shape can never be seen. Let us adore this
Wind with our oblation.

(10.168)

Cows

1. *May the wind blow upon our cows with healing: may they eat*
   herbage full of vigorous juices.
   May they drink waters rich in life and fatness: to those that move
   on feet be gracious, Rudra.
2. *Like-coloured, various-hued, or single-coloured, whose names*
   through sacrifice are known to Agni,
   Whom the Angirasas produced by fervour, grant to these, Parjanya,
   great protection.
3. *Those who have offered to the gods their bodies, whose varied*
   forms are all well known to Soma,
   Those grant us in our cattle pen, O Indra, with their full streams
   of milk and plenteous offspring.
4. *Prajapati, bestowing these upon me, one-minded with all gods and*
   with the Fathers,
   Has to our cow pen brought auspicious cattle: so may we own the
   offspring they will bear us.

(10.169)

Creation

1. *From heat and fervour (tapas) Eternal Law and Truth (rita and satya) were born;*
   From that too, the night was produced, and from that the billowy flood of sea
   arose.
2. *From that same billowy flood of sea the year was afterwards*
   produced,
   Ordainer of the days and nights, Lord over all who close the eyes.
3. *Dhatr, the great creator, then formed in due order the sun and the moon.*
   He formed in order Heaven and Earth, the regions of the air, and
   light.

(10.190)

YAJUR VEDA

As explained in Chapter 1, the Yajur Veda had two main versions. We begin with some verses and passages from the Taittiriya Samhita. These are based on the translation by A.B. Keith.

TAITTIRIYA SAMHITA

These two prayers from Kanda 1 form part of the Soma sacrifice.

1.
May the waters wet (you) for life,
For length of days, for glory.
O plant, protect him.
Axe, hurt him not.
Obedient to the gods I shear these.
With success may I reach further days.
Let the waters, the mothers, purify us,
With ghi let those that purify our ghi purify us,
Let them bear from us all pollution,
Forth from these waters do I come bright, in purity.
You are the body of Soma, guard my body.
You are the milk of the great ones, you are the giver of
splendour; splendour place in me.
You are the pupil of Vritra's eye, you are the guardian of the
eye, guard my eye.
Let the lord of thought purify you, let the lord of speech purify
you, let the god Savitr purify you
With the flawless purifier,
With the rays of the bright sun.
O lord of the purifier, with your purifier for whatsoever I purify
myself, that may I have strength to accomplish.
We approach you, O gods,
You that have true ordinances at the sacrifice
What O gods you can assent to,
For that we ask you, O holy ones.
Indra and Agni, heaven and earth, waters, plants.
You are the lord of consecrations, guard me that am here.

(1.2.1)

2.
In thought divine we meditate,
Merciful, for our help,
That gives glory, and carries the sacrifice.
May it guide us safely according as we will.

The gods, mind-born, mind using,
The wise, the sons of wisdom,
May they guard us, may they protect us,
To them honour! To them hail!
O Agni be you wakeful;
Let us be glad;
Guard us to attain prosperity;
Grant us to wake again.
You, O Agni, are the guardian of vows,
Among the gods and men.
You are to be invoked at our sacrifices.
All the gods have surrounded me,
Pushan with gain, Soma with a gift,
The god Savitr the giver of brightness.
O Soma, give so much, and bear more hither.
May he that fills never lack fullness. Let me not be parted with life.
You are gold; be for my enjoyment. You are raiment; be for my enjoyment. You are a cow;
be for my enjoyment. You are a horse; be for my enjoyment. You are a goat; be for my
enjoyment. You are a ram; be for my enjoyment.
To Vayu hail; to Varuna hail; to Nirriti hail; to Rudra hail!
O divine waters, son of the waters, the stream
Fit for oblation, mighty, most exhilarating,
That stream of yours may I not step upon.
Along an unbroken web of earth may I go.
From good to better do you advance.
May Brihaspati be your leader;
Then set him free, on the chosen spot of earth;
Drive afar the foes with all your strength.
We have come to the place on earth for sacrifice to the gods,
Where in olden days all the gods rejoiced.
Accomplishing (the rite) with Rik, Saman, and Yajus,
Let us rejoice in fullness of wealth, in sustenance.

(1.2.3)

From prayers for the optional and occasional offerings
Agni, overlord of creatures, may he help me;
Indra of powers,
Yama of the earth,

Vayu of the atmosphere,
Surya of the sky,
Chandrama of the nakshatras,
Brihaspati of holy power,
Mitra of truths, Varuna of waters,
The ocean of streams,
Food of lordship overlord,
May it help me;
Soma of plants,
Savitr of instigations,
Rudra of cattle,
Tvashtr of forms,
Vishnu of mountains,
The Maruts of troops overlords,
May they help me.
O you fathers, you grandfathers, you who are further, you who are nearer,
Do you here help me.
In this holy power,
This worldly power,
This prayer,
This purohitaship,
This rite,
This invocation of the gods.

(3.4.5)

Instructions and prayers for placing the fire in the fire pan
Yoking mind first,
Extending his thoughts, Savitr
Discerning the light,
Has brought Agni from the earth.
Yoking with mind the gods,
Going to the heaven, the sky, with thought,
Those that are to make great light,
Savitr instigates.
With mind well-yoked are we
In the instigation of god Savitr,
For strength to go to the heaven.
They yoke their minds, they yoke their thoughts,

The priests of the mighty wise priest,
He alone, who knows the way, appoints their functions.
Great is the praise of the god Savitr.
I yoke with honour your ancient prayer;
The praises go like Suras on their way;
All the sons of immortality hear (it),
Who have achieved dwellings divine.
He whose advance others followed,
Gods, of the god praising might,
He who meted out the regions of earth,
He is the brilliant god Savitr in greatness.
O god Savitr, instigate the sacrifice,
instigate the lord of the sacrifice, to good luck;
may the divine gandharva,
who purifies thoughts, purify our thought;
may the lord of speech today make sweet our utterance.
This sacrifice for us, O god Savitr
Do you instigate, serving the gods,
Finding comrades, ever victorious,
Winning booty, winning heaven.
By the Rik make the stoma (song of praise) to prosper,
By the Gayatra the Rathantara,
The Brihat with the Gayatri for its metre.
On the impulse of the god Savitr,
with the arms of the Ashvins,
with the hands of Pushan,
with the Gayatri metre,
I take you, in the manner of Angiras.
You are the spade, you are the woman,
from the abode of the earth I bear Agni of the dust in the manner of Angiras;
with the Trishtubh metre I grasp you in the manner of Angiras.
You are the bearer, you are the woman;
through you may we be strong to dig Agni of the dust in his place;
with the Jagati metre I grasp you in the manner of Angiras.
Grasping in your hand, Savitr,
Bearing the spade of gold,
Therewith digging Agni

Do you bring for us light unperishing.
With the Anushtubh metre I grasp you in the manner of Angiras.

(4.1.1)

NOTE: These verses correspond to the first eleven verses of Adhyaya 11 of the Vajasaneyi Samhita.

A passage from the section on the preparation of the ground for the fire
Headed by Vishnu the gods won finally these worlds by the metres; in that he strides the strides of Vishnu, the sacrificer becoming Vishnu wins finally these worlds. 'You are the step of Vishnu, overcoming hostility,' he says; the earth is connected with the Gayatri, the atmosphere with the Trishtubh, the sky with the Jagati, the quarters with the Anushtubh; truly he wins in order these worlds with the metres. Prajapati created Agni; he being created went away from him.

He followed him with this (verse), 'He has cried'; with it he won the home dear to Agni; in that he repeats this (verse), he wins thereby the home dear to Agni. Now he who steps the strides of Vishnu is apt as he goes away to be burnt up; he turns with four (verses); the metres are four, Agni's dear body is the metres; truly he turns round on his dear body.

He turns round from left to right; truly he turns round on his own strength; therefore the right side of the body is the stronger; truly also does he turn with the turning of the sun. Varuna seized Shunahshepa Ajigarti, he saw this verse addressed to Varuna, by it he freed himself from the noose of Varuna; Varuna seizes him who takes the fire pan; 'From us the highest knot, O Varuna,' he says; truly thereby he frees himself from Varuna's noose.

'I have drawn you,' he says, for he draws him. 'Be thou firm and motionless', he says, for support. 'Let all the people desire you,' he says; truly with the people he unites him. 'In him establish the kingdom', he says; truly in him he makes the kingdom to abide. If he desire of a man, 'May he be a ruler', he should think of him with his mind; truly he becomes a ruler.

'In greatness he has risen erect in the van of the dawns,' he says; truly he makes him the first of his peers. 'Emerging from the darkness,' he says; truly he smites away darkness from him. 'He has come with the light,' he says; truly he bestows light upon him. He places him with four (verses); the metres are four; truly with the metres (he places him); with an Atichhandas as the last; the Atichhandas is the highest of metres; truly he makes him the highest of his peers; it contains the word 'sit' (sad); truly he makes him attain reality (sat-tvam).

With (the hymn) of Vatsapri he reverences (him); by that did Vatsapri Bhalandana win the home dear to Agni; truly by it he wins the home dear to Agni. It has eleven (verses); truly in eleven places he bestows strength on the sacrificer. By the stoma the gods prospered in this world, by the metres in yonder world; the hymn of Vatsapri is the type of the stoma; in that he pays reverence with (the hymn) of Vatsapri, he wins with it this world; in that he strides the steps of Vishnu, he wins by them yonder world. On the first day he strides forth, on the next day he pays reverence; therefore the minds of some creatures are set on energy, those of others on rest; therefore the active lords it over him who takes his ease therefore the active fixes upon a man who takes his ease. He clenches his fist, he restrains his speech, for support.

(5.2.1)

NOTE: Vatsapri: a rishi, son of Bhalanda; Gayatri, Trishtubh, Jagati, Anushtubh, Atichhandas: the names of metres used in the Vedas.

A passage from recitations for the Ahina sacrifices

Atri gave offspring to Aurva who was desirous of children. She deemed herself empty, without strength, weak, worn out. He saw the four night rite; he grasped it, and sacrificed with it. Then indeed were four sons born for him, a good hotr, a good udgatr, a good adhvaryu, a good councillor. He, who knowing thus offers the four-night rite, has four sons born for him, a good hotr, a good udgatr, a good adhvaryu, a good councillor.

The Pavamana (stomas) which are twenty-fourfold are splendour; the increasing stomas are prosperity. Atri who had faith as his deity and offered sacrifices was not visited by the four strengths, brilliance, power, splendour, food. He saw these four Soma libations with the four stomas; he grasped them and sacrificed with them. He won brilliance with the first, power with the second, splendour with the third, food with the fourth. He, who knowing thus, grasps the four Soma libations with the four Stomas and sacrifices with them, wins brilliance with the first, power with the second, splendour with the third, food with the fourth. With the success which Atri had, the sacrificer prospers.

(7.1.8)

Vajasaneyi Samhita
The two passages below are based on the translation by R.T.H. Griffith.

Adhyaya 18
These verses are recited for the benefit of the sacrificer by the adhvaryu in the ceremony known as Vasordhara. The sacrificer offers 401 oblations of ghi while the recitation takes place. The first twenty-nine out of seventy-seven verses are given here.

1. *May my strength and my gain, and my inclination and my*
    influence, and my thought and my mental power, and
    my praise and my fame, and my renown and my light,
    and my heaven prosper by sacrifice.
2. *May my in-breathing and my out-breathing, and my*
    through-breathing and my vital spirit, and my thought and my
    reflection, and my voice and my mind, and my eye and

my ear, and my ability and my strength prosper by
sacrifice.

3. May my energy and my force, and my self and my body,
    and my shelter and my shield, and my limbs and my
    bones, and my joints and my body, and my life and
    my old age prosper by sacrifice.

4. May my pre-eminence and my overlordship, and my wrath
    and my angry passion, and my violence and my impetuosity,
    and my victorious power and my greatness, and my
    breadth and my width, and my height and my length,
    and my increase and my improvement prosper by sacrifice.

5. May my truth and my faith, and my cattle and my wealth,
    and my goods and my pleasure, and my play and my
    enjoyment, and my children and my future children, and
    my hymn and my pious act prosper by sacrifice.

6. May my religious rite and my immortality, and my freedom
    from consumption and my freedom from disease, and my
    life and my longevity, and my freedom from enemies
    and my freedom from danger, and my happiness and my
    lying down, and my fair dawn and my fair day prosper
    by sacrifice.

7. May my controller and my supporter, and my security and
    my firmness, and my goods and my pleasure, and my
    knowledge and my understanding, and my begetting and
    my propagation, and my plough and my harrow prosper
    by sacrifice.

8. May my welfare and my comfort, and what I hold dear and
    what I desire, and my love and my gratification, and my
    enjoyment and my substance, and my happiness and my
    felicity, and my higher bliss and my fame prosper by
    sacrifice.

9. May my vigour and my pleasantness, and my milk and my
    sap, and my butter and my honey, and my meal in company
    and my drinking in company, and my ploughing and my husbandry, and my superiority and my
    pre-eminence prosper by sacrifice.

10. May my wealth and my property, and my prosperity and
    my growth, and my pervading power and my lordship,
    and my abundance and my greater abundance, and my

bad harvest and my unwasted crop, and my food and
my satiety prosper by sacrifice.

11. May my gain and my future gain, and what I have and
     what I shall have, and my good road and my good path,
     and my success and my succeeding, and my achievement
     and my contrivance, and my thought and my good counsel
     prosper by sacrifice.

12. May my rice plants and my barley, and my beans and my
     sesamum, and my kidney beans and my vetches, and my
     millet and my Panicum milliaceum, and my Panicum
     frumentaceum and my wild rice, and my wheat and my
     lentils prosper by sacrifice.

13. May my stone and my clay, and my hills and my mountains,
     and my pebbles and my trees, and my gold and my bronze,
     and my copper and my iron, and my lead and my tin
     prosper by sacrifice.

14. May my fire and my water, and my creepers and my plants,
     and lily plants with culture-ripened fruit and my plants
     with fruit ripened without culture, and my domestic
     animals and my wild animals, and my substance and my
     future substance, and my belongings and my power be
     produced by sacrifice.

15. May my treasure and my dwelling, and my religious service
     and my ability to perform it, and my object and my
     course, and my way and my going prosper by sacrifice.

16. May my Agni and my Indra, and my Soma and my Indra,
     and my Savitr and my Indra, and my Sarasvati and my
     Indra, and my Pushan and my Indra prosper by sacrifice.

17. May my Mitra and my Indra, and my Varuna and my Indra,
     and my Dhatr and my Indra, and my Maruts and my
     Indra, and my All-Gods and my Indra prosper by sacrifice.

18. May my Earth and my Indra, and my Air and my Indra,
     and my Sky and my Indra, and my half-months and my
     Indra, and my Lunar Mansions and my Indra, and my
     Sky-regions and my Indra prosper by sacrifice.

19. May my Amshu and my Rashmi, and my Adhipati and my
     Upamshu, and my Antaryama and my Aindra-Vayava, and

my Maitra-Varuna, and my Ashvina and my Pratiprasthana,
and my Shukra and my Manthin proper by sacrifice.

20. May my Agrayana and my Vaishvadeva, and my Dhruva and
my Vaishvanara, and my Aindragna and my Mahavaishvadeva,
and my Marutvatiya and my Nishkevalya, and my Savitra
and my Sarasvata, and my Patnivata and my Hariyojana
prosper by sacrifice.

21. May my ladles and my cups, and my Vayu vessels and my
Soma reservoirs, and my pressing stones and my two press boards,
and my Putabhrit and my Adhavaniya, and my
altar and altar grass, and my Avabhritha and my cries of
Svaga prosper by sacrifice.

22. May my Agni and my charms, and my Arka and my Surya,
and my Prana and my Ashvamedha, and my Prithivi and
my Aditi, and my Diti and my Sky, and my fingers, powers,
and sky regions prosper by sacrifice.

23. May my vow and my seasons, and my austere devotion, and
my day and night, thighs and knees, and two Great
Rathantaras prosper by sacrifice.

24. May my One and my Three, and my Three and my Five,
and my Five and my Seven (and similarly up to thirty-three)
prosper by sacrifice.

25. May my Four and my Eight and my Twelve (and similarly
up to forty-eight) prosper by sacrifice.

26. May my eighteen-months steer and my eighteen-months
heifer, and my two-year bull and cow (and similarly up
to four-year) prosper by sacrifice.

27. May my six-year bull and my six-year cow, and my bull and
my barren cow, and my young bull and my calf-slipping
cow, and my ox and my milch cow prosper by sacrifice.

28. To strength, Hail! To Gain, Hail! To After-born, Hail! To
Power, Hail! To Vasu, Hail! To the Lord of Days, Hail!
To the Failing Day, Hail! To the Final Sprung from
the Transitory, Hail! To the Transitory sprung from the
Final, Hail! To the Final Mundane, Hail! To the Lord
of the World, Hail! To the Sovereign Lord, Hail! To Prajapati,
Hail! This is your kingdom. You are a guiding controller

for the friend. You for vigour, you for rain,
you for the sovereign lordship of creatures.

29. May life succeed through sacrifice. May life-breath thrive
by sacrifice. May the eye thrive by sacrifice. May the
ear thrive by sacrifice. May the voice thrive by sacrifice.
May the mind thrive by sacrifice. May the self thrive by
sacrifice. May Brahman thrive by sacrifice. May light
succeed by sacrifice. May heaven succeed by sacrifice.
May the hymn thrive by sacrifice. May sacrifice thrive
by sacrifice; And hymns of praise and sacrificial text, and verse of
praise and Sama chant, the Brihat and Rathantara.
Gods, we have gone to light. We have become the children
of Prajapati. We have become immortal.

NOTE:
Verse 16: Ardhendra or half-Indra oblations are offered to twelve deities, jointly with Indra.
Verse 19: This and the succeeding two verses list the pairs of Soma cups and the sacrificial
implements.
Verse 22: These are two sets of oblations known as yajnakratus.
Verse 24: This refers to the hymns of praise (stomas) with an uneven number of verses.
Verse 25: This refers to stomas with an even number of verses.

Adhyaya 24
This lists the animals for the ashvamedha and the gods to whom they are dedicated. There are 327
domestic animals and 282 wild animals (including birds and insects). The wild animals were later freed.

1. Horse, hornless goat, gomriga, these belong to Prajapati.
A black-necked goat, devoted to Agni, (is to be bound)
in front to the forehead (of the horse); Sarasvati's ewe
below his jaws; two goats belonging to the Ashvins, with
marks on the lower parts of the body, to his fore-legs; a
dark-coloured goat, Soma's and Pushan's, to his navel; a
white and a black, sacred to Soma and Varuna, to his sides;
Tvashtr's two, with bushy tails, to his hind feet; Vayu's
white goat to his tail; for Indra the Good Worker, a cow
who slips her calf; a dwarf belonging to Vishnu.

2. The red goat, the smoky-red, the jujube-red, these belong to
Soma. The brown, the ruddy brown, the parrot-brown,

these are Varuna's. One with white ear holes, one with
partly white, one with wholly white, belong to Savitr.
One with forefeet white, partly white, wholly white,
belongs to Brihaspati. She-goats speckled, with small spots,
with big spots, these belong to Mitra-Varuna.

3. *The bright-tailed, the wholly bright-tailed, the jewel-tailed,*
   these belong to the Ashvins. The white, the white-eyed,
   the reddish, these are for Rudra, Lord of Beasts. Long-eared
   goats are for Yama; proud ones for Rudra; cloud-coloured
   ones for Parjanya.

4. *Goats speckled, transversely speckled, upward speckled are*
   for the Maruts. The reddish she-goat, the red-haired, the
   white, these belong to Sarasvati. The goat with diseased
   ears, the short-eared, the red eared are Tvashtr's. The
   black-necked, the white-flanked, one with bright-coloured
   thighs belong to Indra and Agni. Those with black marks,
   small marks, large marks belong to Usha (Dawn).

5. *Parti-coloured female victims belong to the Vishvedevas (All-Gods);*
   red-coloured, eighteen months old to Vak; victims without
   distinguishing marks to Aditi; those of one same colour
   to Dhatr; weaned kids sacred to the Consorts of the Gods.

6. *Black-necked victims for Agni; white browed for the Vasus;*
   red for Rudra; bright ones for the Adityas; cloud-coloured
   for Parjanya.

7. *The tall goat, the sturdy, the dwarf, these are Indra-Vishnu's;*
   the tall, the white fore-footed, the black-backed,
   Indra-Brihaspati's; parrot-coloured the Vajins'; speckled
   Agni-Maruts'; dark-coloured Pushan's.

8. *Variegated, Indra-Agni's; two-coloured, Agni-Soma's; dwarf*
   oxen, Agni-Vishnu's; barren cows, Mitra-Varuna's; partly
   variegated, Mitra's.

9. *Black-necked ones, Agni's; brown, Soma's; white, Vayu's;*
   undistinguished, Aditi's; self-coloured, Dhatr's; weanlings,
   the Gods' Consorts'.

10. *Black ones for Earth; smoke-coloured for Firmament; tall*
    ones for Sky; brindled ones for Lightning; blotched ones
    for Stars.

11. *Smoke-coloured ones he sacrifices to Spring; white to*

Summer; black to the Rains; red ones to Autumn;
speckled to Winter; reddish-yellow to the Dewy Season.

12. Calves eighteen months old to Gayatri; steers of two and
a half years to Trishtup; two-year-old steers to Jagati;
three-year-olds to Anushtup; four-year-olds to Ushnih.

13. Four-year-old steers to Viraj; full grown bulls to Brihati;
strong bulls to Kakup; draught oxen to Pankti; milch cows
to Atichhandas.

14. Black-necked victims sacred to Agni; brown to Soma; spotted
to Savitr; weaned she-kids to Sarasvati; dark-coloured
goats to Pushan; speckled victims to the Maruts;
many-coloured to the All-Gods; barren cows to Heaven
and Earth.

15. Called contemporary, the dappled belong to Indra-Agni;
black ones to Varuna; speckled to the Maruts; hornless
he-goats to Ka.

16. To Agni foremost in place he sacrifices firstling goats; to
the consuming Maruts those born of one mother; to the
Maruts who perform domestic rites those born after a long
time; to the sportive Maruts those born together; to the
self-strong Maruts those born in succession.

17. Called contemporaneous, the dappled belonging to Indra-Agni;
those with projecting horns to Mahendra; the many-coloured
to Vishvakarman.

18. Smoke-coloured, those of brownish hue, to be offered to the
Soma-possessing Fathers (Somavantah); the brown and the smoky-looking
to the Fathers who sit on sacred grass (Barhishadah); the black and
the brownish-looking to the Fathers who have been tasted
by Agni (Agnishvattah); the black and the spotted belong to Tryambaka.

19. Called contemporaneous, the dappled belong to Shuna and
Sira; white ones to Vayu; white ones to Surya.

20. To Spring he offers kapinjalas; to Summer sparrows; to
the Rains partridges; to Autumn quails; to Winter kakaras; to the Dewy Season vikakaras.

21. To the Sea he sacrifices porpoises; to Parjanya frogs; to
the Waters fishes; to Mitra kulipayas; to Varuna nakra (possibly crocodiles).

22. To Soma he sacrifices wild geese; to Vayu female cranes;
to Indra-Agni curlews; to Mitra divers; to Varuna chakravakas.

23. To Agni he sacrifices cocks; to Vanaspati owls; to Agni-Soma
    blue jays; to the Ashvins peacocks; to Mitra-Varuna pigeons.

24. To Soma he sacrifices quails; to Tvashtr, kaulikas; mynas
    to the Gods' Consorts; kulikas to the Gods' Sisters;
    parushnas to Agni, Lord of the Homestead.

25. To Day he sacrifices doves; to Night sichapus; to the Joints
    of Day and Night (evening and morning twilight) bats; to the Months gallinules; to the
    Year great eagles.

26. To Ground he sacrifices rats; to Firmament field-rats; to Day voles; to the Quarters mongooses;
    to the Intermediate Spaces brownish ichneumons.

27. To the Vasus he sacrifices blackbucks; to the Rudras stags;
    to the Adityas nyanku deer; to the All-Gods spotted deer;
    to the Sadhyas kulinga antelopes,

28. To Ishana he sacrifices wild asses; to Mitra gauras; to Varuna
    buffaloes; to Brihaspati gayals; to Tvashtr camels.

29. To Prajapati he sacrifices male elephants; to Vak white ants;
    to Sight flies; to Hearing black bees.

30. To Prajapati and to Vayu a gayal is to be offered; to Varuna
    a wild ram; to Yama a black ram; to a human king a
    monkey; to the Tiger a red doe; to the Bull a female
    gayal, to the Kshiprasyena a quail; to the Nilangu a
    worm; to the Sea a porpoise; to the Snowy Mountain an
    elephant.

31. The kinnara belongs to Prajapati; the Ula, the Halikshna,
    the cat (vrishadamsha) belong to Dhatr; the heron belongs to the Quarters;
    the dhunksha to Agni; sparrow, red snake, saras, these are Tvashtr's; the curlew belongs to Vak.

32. To Soma an antelope is to be offered; wild goat, mongoose,
    saka, these are Pushan's; the jackal is the Mayu's; the
    gaura Indra's; pidva, antelope, cock, these are Anumati's;
    the chakravaka is for Echo.

33. The female crane is Surya's; sarga, srijays, sayandaka,
    these are Mitra's; to Sarasvati belongs the human-voiced
    myna; to Ground the porcupine; tiger, wolf, viper belong
    to Passion; to Sarasvan the human-voiced parrot.

34. The eagle is Parjanya's; the ati (ibis), the vahasa, the woodpecker,
    these are for Vayu; for Brihaspati Lord of Speech is the paingaraja; the alaja belongs to Firmament;
    pelican, cormorant, fish, these belong to the Lord of Rivers; the tortoise belongs to Heaven and Earth.

35. *The buck belongs to the Moon; iguana, kalaka, woodpecker,*
    these belong to the Vanaspatis; the cock belongs to Savitar;
    the swan is Vata's; crocodile, dolphin, kulipaya, these belong to the Sea; the porcupine to Modesty.

36. *The black doe belongs to Day; frog, female rat, partridge,*
    these belong to the Serpents; the jackal belongs to the Ashvins; the Blackbuck to Night; bear, bat,
    sushilika, these belong to the Other Folk (that is, fairies); the polecat belongs to Vishnu.

37. *The cuckoo belongs to the half-months; antelope, peacock, eagle, these are the Gandharvas'; the*
    otter belongs to the Months; tortoise, doe-antelope, iguana, golathika
    belong to the apsaras; the black snake belongs to Death.

38. *The frog belongs to the Seasons; the vole, the rat, the mouse,*
    these are the Fathers'; the python, the balava belong to
    the Vasus; kapinjala, pigeons, owl, hare belong to Nirriti;
    the wild ram to Varuna.

39. *The white animal belongs to the Adityas; the camel, the ghrintivan, the rhinoceros to Mati*
    (Thought or Devotion); the srimara belong to the Forest-God; the Raru buck is Rudra's; kvayi,
    cock, gallinule, these are the Vajins'; the cuckoo belongs to Kama.

40. *The khanga is the All-Gods'; the black dog, the long-eared,*
    the ass, the hyena, these are the rakshasas; the boar is
    for Indra; the lion is for the Maruts; the chameleon,
    the pippaka, the vulture, these belong to Sharavya; the
    spotted antelope belongs to the All-Gods.

NOTE: Sharavya: arrow, regarded as a deity; sacrifices: literally takes and ties up; for more on the ashvamedha and for an identification of animals and birds mentioned here, see chapters 10 and 6.

SAMA VEDA

FROM THE PURVARCHIKA

To Agni
1. *Come, Agni, praised with song, to feast and sacrificial offering: sit*
   as hotr on the holy grass!
2. *O Agni, you have been ordained hotr of every sacrifice,*
   by gods, among the people.
3. *Agni we choose as envoy, skilled performer of this holy rite,*
   hotr, possessor of all wealth.
4. *Served with oblation, kindled, bright, through love of song may Agni, bent*
   on riches, smite the Vritras dead!

5. I praise your most beloved guest like a dear friend, O Agni, him
   who, like a chariot, wins us wealth.
6. O Agni, with great might guard us from all malignity, and from the hate of mortal man!
7. O Agni, come; I will sing other songs of praise to you.
   grow mighty with these Soma drops!
8. May Vatsa draw your mind away even from your loftiest dwelling place!
   Agni, I yearn for you with song.
9. Agni, Atharvan churned you from the sky, for the benefit of all who offer sacrifice.
10. O Agni, bring us radiant light to be our mighty help, for
    you are our visible deity!

(1.1.1.1; based on the translation by R.T.H. Griffith)

NOTE: Each verse in this and other dashats is by a different rishi, put together from different parts of the Rig Veda.

To Indra
1. Our praises moving towards Indra, go and reside in him, and beg of him superior might.
2. O ye Gods, we slaughter no victim, we use no sacrificial stake, we worship by the repetition of sacred verses.
3. I have now come while the night is departing. O offerer of praise, sing loudly and well. O you, who walks within the sacred enclosure, praise the (generative) god Sarita.
4. The matchless lovely Dawn has just come to take up her abode in the heavens. I praise you, twin sons of Ashvini, with all my might.
5. The invincible Indra slew ninety times nine of his foes with the bones obtained from the rishi, Dadhicha's head.
6. Come, O Indra, delight in our food, along with our preparations of Soma; for you are the mighty one that excels in strength.
7. O Indra, slayer of our enemies, come to our sacred enclosure. O mighty god, come with all prevailing aids.
8. His might, whereby he encircles heaven and earth, as the skin does the body, appears in all its splendour.
9. You approach the sacrifice with the eagerness the male pigeon does his mate; let then these prayers of mine reach your ear.
10. Let him come as our medicine, and the conferrer of happiness, and the inspirer of vigour into our breasts; and let him prolong our lives.

(1.2.2.4; based on the translation by J. Stevenson)

To Soma
1. O dripping, purifying divinity, sit down speedily among our guests, strain the strengthening liquid.

The purifiers lead you, the supplier of nourishment, with cords to the place where the sacred grass is spread, as men lead a horse.

2. The orator divinity (Soma) narrates the illustrious actions of you as well as Shukra himself, and he, the brother of the pure, the purifier, the assumer of the form of a boar, marches to us on foot, singing holy songs.

3. Agni, the sacrifice attracting divinity, produced the three Vedas, the rite of sacrifice and the Brahmanical incantations; and as the cows approach the lord of the herd, so do the inquisitive, loving intelligences approach the god Soma.

4. The god who passionately desires the sacrifice, the purifier, the golden one, and who, along with the gods, prepares the liquor and the pressed juice, the singer of holy hymns, the inviter of the gods, comes to his state of purity with the eagerness the officiating priest goes to the house where there is an animal sacrifice.

5. Soma is being purified; he is the father of intelligences, the father of heaven, the father of fire, the father of the Sun, the father of Indra, the father even of Vishnu.

6. The moon-plant (Soma) is being sprinkled with waters as copious as from the sea in the place where are the three daily sacrifices, the procurers of rain, the stay of bread, the support of multitudes—here are the lovely voices of the chanters, and the much desired gifts.

7. The great, overflowing, indestructible sea of Soma juice proceeded forth in the beginning, creating and producing all beings. It is the lord of the world, produced on the mountain tops, and dripping near the sacred increase-causing goats' skins.

8. The purifying, green coloured Soma juice, uttering its own praise, rests upon the womb of its water-containing receptacle, and drawn out by men, is prepared for our solemnities, and then brings forth native intelligence, as well as sustains bodily vigour.

9. O Indra, that sweet-flavoured moon-plant of yours, the drencher of him who drenches (the earth) is being distilled into the holy receptacle: it, the giver of thousands as well as the giver of hundreds, the giver of manifold gifts, that is stationed on the eternal, food-providing, sacrificial grass.

10. O sweet, truth inspiring liquid, O overshadowing Soma, be purified, you who are produced on the mountains, and prepared over the goats skins; do you, most sweet, inebriating liquor, of which Indra drinks, descend into the sacred receptacle.

(1.6.1.4; based on the translation by J. Stevenson)

NOTE: In this hymn, Soma is described as the supreme spirit.

Uttararchika
All translations in this section are based on the translation by R.T.H. Griffith.

To Soma Pavamana
Om. Glory to the Sama Veda! To Lord Ganesha glory! Om. (This invocation is a late addition.)

1. *Sing forth to Indu, O you men, to him who now is purified,*
   Gladly to pay worship to the Gods!
2. *Together with your pleasant juice the Atharvans have mixed milk.*
   Divine, God-loving, for the God.
3. *Bring health to cattle with your flow, health to the people, health to horses,*
   Health, O King, to growing plants!

(2.1.1.1)

To Mitra-Varuna

1. *Varuna, Mitra, wise pair, pour rain on our pastures, pour*
   Mead on the regions of the air!
2. *Gladdened by homage, ruling far, you reign by majesty of might,*
   Pure in your ways, for evermore.
3. *Praised by Jamadagni's song, sit on the sacrificial seat:*
   Drink Soma, you who strengthen Law!

(2.1.1.5)

NOTE: Here, Jamadagni could refer to the famous rishi of that name or to Vishvamitra, who in the Rig Veda is the author of these verses.

To Indra

1. *Sing a song, to make him glad, to Indra, Lord of tawny steeds,*
   the Soma-drinker, O my friends!
2. *To him, the bounteous, chant the hymn of praise, and let us glorify, as men*
   may do, the giver of true gifts!
3. *O Indra, Lord of boundless might, for us you seek spoil and cattle,*
   you seek gold for us, good Lord!

(2.1.2.2)

Agni

1. *Agni we choose as envoy, skilled performer of this holy rite,*
   Hotr, possessor of all wealth.
2. *With constant calls they invoke Agni, Agni, Lord of the house,*
   Oblation-bearer, much-beloved
3. *Bring the Gods here, Agni, born for him who trims the sacred grass:*
   you are our Hotr, worthy of praise!

(2.2.1.6)

Soma Pavamana

1. *Impetuous, bright, have they come forth, unwearied in their speed, like bulls,*
   Driving the black skin far away.

2. *May we attain the bridge of bliss, leaving the bridge of woe behind:*
   The riteless dasa may we quell!

3. *The mighty Pavamana's roar is heard as 'twere the rush of rain*
   The lightning flashes move in heaven.

4. *Indu, pour out abundant food with store of cattle and of gold,*
   Of heroes, Soma! And of steeds!

5. *Flow onward, dear to all mankind! Fill the mighty heaven and earth,*
   As Dawn, as Surya with his beams!

6. *On every side, O Soma, flow round us with your protecting stream,*
   As Rasa flows around the world!

(2.3.1.3)

NOTE: Rasa is a river, both mythical and real.

Soma Pavamana

1. *Flow, Soma, Indu, dear to Gods, swift through the purifying sieve,*
   And enter Indra with your strength

2. *As mighty food speed here, Indu, as a most splendid steer:*
   Sit in your place as one with power

3. *The well-loved mead was made to flow, the stream of the creative juice:*
   The Sage drew waters to himself.

4. *The mighty waters, yes, the floods accompany you mighty one,*
   When you will clothe yourself with the milk.

5. *The lake is brightened in the floods. Soma, our friend, heaven's prop and stay,*
   Falls on the purifying cloth.

6. *The tawny Bull has bellowed. Fair as mighty Mitra to behold*
   He gleams and flashes with the Sun.

7. *Songs, Indra, active in their might, are beautified for you, wherewith*
   you deck yourself for rapturous joy.

8. *To you who gives ample room we pray, to win the wild delight,*
   That you may have exalted praise.

9. *Winner of cattle Indu, you are, winner of heroes, horses, and spoil:*
   Primeval soul of sacrifice.

10. *Pour on us, Indu! Indra-strength with a full stream of sweetness, like*
    Parjanya, sender of the rain!

(2.4.1.3)

Soma Pavamana

1. Guard of all being, generating creatures, loud roared the sea as highest law commanded. Strong in the filter, on the fleecy summit, pressed from the stone, Soma has become mighty.

2. Make Vayu glad, for furtherance and bounty: cheer Varuna and Mitra, as they cleanse you! Gladden the Gods, gladden the host of Maruts: make Heaven and Earth rejoice, O God, O Soma!

3. Soma, the mighty, when, the water's offspring, he chose the Gods, performed that great achievement. He, Pavamana, granted strength to Indra; he, Indu, generated strength in Surya.

(2.5.2.1)

Surya

1. May Surya, the bright God drink glorious Soma-mingled mead, giving
   the lord of sacrifices, unbroken life;
   He who, wind-urged, in person guards our offspring well,
   nourishes them with food and shines over many a land.

2. Radiant, as high Truth, cherished, best at winning strength,
   Truth based upon the statute that supports the heavens,
   He rose, a light that kills Vritras and enemies, best slayer of the dasyus, asuras, and foes.

3. This light, the best of lights, supreme, all conquering, winner of riches, is exalted with high praise.
   All-lighting, radiant, mighty as the Sun to see, he spreads wide unshaken victory and strength.

(2.6.3.5)

Agni

1. Invincible is Agni, he who goes before the tribes of men,
   A chariot swift and ever new.

2. By bringing offerings unto him the mortal worshipper obtains
   A home from him whose light is pure.

3. Inviolable power of Gods, subduing all his enemies, Agni is mightiest in fame.

(2.7.2.9)

Heaven and Earth (Dyaus-Prithivi)

1. To both of you, O Heaven and Earth, we bring our lofty song of praise,
   Pure pair! to glorify you both.

2. You sanctify each other's form, by your own proper strength you rule:
   Further the sacrifice evermore!

3. Promoting and fulfilling, you, mighty ones, perfect Mitra's law:
   You sit around our sacrifice.

(2.7.3.14)

Vishnu
1. *What, Vishnu, is the name that you proclaimed when you declared, I am Shipivishta?*
   Hide not this form from us, nor keep it secret, since you did wear another shape in battle.
2. *This offering today, O Shipivishta, I, skilled in rules, extol, to you the noble.*
   Yes, I, the poor and weak, praise you, the mighty, who live in the realm beyond this region.
3. *O Vishnu, to you I cry Vashat! Let this offering of mine, Shipivishta, please you!*
   May these my songs of eulogy exalt you! Do preserve us for ever with your blessings!

(2.8.1.4)

NOTE: Shipivishta: 'clothed with rays of light' (according to the commentator, the name Vishnu took when he helped Vasishtha in battle); Vashat: a sacred exclamation.

Dawn
1. *This Lady, excellent and kind, after her sister shining forth, Daughter of Heaven, has shown herself.*
2. *Red, like a mare, and beautiful, holy, the mother of the cows, the Dawn became the Ashvins' friend.*
3. *Yes, and you are the Ashvins', friend, you are the mother of the cows; O Dawn, you rule over wealth.*

(2.8.3.6)

Ashvins
1. *Now Morning with her earliest light shines forth, dear daughter of the Sky:*
   High, Ashvins, I extol your praise
2. *Children of the Ocean, mighty ones, discoverers of riches, Gods,*
   Finders of treasure through our prayer!
3. *Your lofty coursers hasten over the everlasting realm, when your chariot flies with winged steeds.*

(2.8.3.7)

Gods
1. *Praise to the friends who sit in front! to those seated together, praise*
   I use the hundred-footed speech.
2. *I use the hundred-footed speech, I sing what has a thousand paths,*
   Gayatri, Trishtup, Jagat hymn.
3. *Gayatri, Trishtup, Jagat hymn, the forms united and complete,*
   Have the Gods made familiar friends.

(2.9.2.7)

NOTE: Gayatri, Trishtup (same as Trishtubh), and Jagat are metres; 'friends who sit in front' refers to friendly gods who sit at the front of the sacrifice; these verses are not from the Rig Veda.

Agni

1. Agni, is light, light is Agni, Indra is light, light is Indra
    Surya is light, light is Surya.
2. O Agni, turn again with strength, turn you again with food and life:
    Save us again from grief and woe!
3. O Agni, turn again with wealth; sprinkle us from every side, with your own, all-supporting stream!

                                                                    (2.9.2.8)

NOTE: This is not from the Rig Veda; the second and third verses are in the Yajur Veda.

Apah: The Waters

1. Yes, Waters, you bring health and bliss: so help us to have energy.
    That we may look on great delight!
2. Give us a portion of the rasa (dew, rain or divine moisture), the most auspicious that you have,
    Like mothers in their longing love!
3. For you we gladly go to him to whose abode you speed us on,
    And, Waters, give us procreant strength!

                                                                    (2.9.2.10)

Vata

1. May Vata breathe his balm on us, healthful, delightful to our heart:
    May he prolong our days of life!
2. You are our father, Vata, yes, you are our brother and our friend:
    So give us strength that we may live!
3. The store of amrita (divine nectar, the drink of immortality) that laid away yonder, O Vata, in
    your home—
    Give us strength that we may live!

                                                                    (2.9.2.11)

Atharva Veda

In this section, most of the hymns chosen are not related to diseases or healing. For an idea of those, see Chapter 11. In most of the hymns below, Brahma/Brahman is used in neuter form, indicating prayer or spiritual power or exaltation, developing into the later meaning of Brahman, as the absolute.

Prayer for earthly and heavenly success

1. Upon this (person) the Vasus, Indra, Pushan, Varuna, Mitra, and Agni, shall bestow goods (vasu)!
    The Adityas, and, further, all the gods shall hold him in the higher light!

2. *Light, you gods, shall be at his bidding: Surya, Agni, or even gold! Inferior to us shall be our rivals! Cause him to ascend to the highest heaven*

3. *With that most potent charm with which, O Jatavedas (Agni), you did bring to Indra the (Soma) drink, with that, O Agni, do you here strengthen this one; grant him supremacy over his kinsmen!*

4. *Their sacrifice and their glory, their increase of wealth and their thoughtful plans, I have usurped, O Agni. Inferior to us shall be our rivals! Cause him to ascend to the highest heaven!*

(1.9; based on the translation by M. Bloomfield)

A charm to ensure success in gambling
1. *Lord of the World, divine gandharva, only he should be
honoured in the clans and worshipped.
Fast with my spell, celestial God, I hold you. Homage to you!
Your home is in the heavens.*

2. *Sky-reaching, like the Sun in brightness, holy, he who averts
from us the Gods' displeasure.
Lord of the World, may the gandharva bless us, the friendly
god who only must be worshipped.*

3. *I came, I met these faultless, blameless beings; among the
apsaras was the gandharva.
Their home is in the sea—so men have told me—from where they
come quickly here and vanish.*

4. *You, Cloudy! you who follow the Gandharva Vishvavasu, you,
Starry! Lightning-Flasher!
You, O ye Goddesses, I truly worship.*

5. *Haunters of darkness, shrill in voice, dice-lovers, maddeners of
the mind
To these have I paid homage, the gandharva's wives, apsaras.*

(2.2; based on the translation by R.T.H. Griffith)

A charm against fear
1. *As heaven and earth are not afraid, and never suffer loss or
harm,
Even so, my spirit, do not fear.*

2. *As day and night are not afraid, and never suffer loss or harm,
Even so, my spirit, do not fear.*

3. *As sun and moon are not afraid, nor ever suffer loss or harm.
Even so, my spirit, do not fear.*

4. As Brahmanhood and princely power fear not, and never suffer loss,
    or harm,
    Even so, my spirit, do not fear.
5. As truth and falsehood have no fear, nor ever suffer loss or
    harm,
    Even so, my spirit, do not fear.
6. As what has been and what shall be fear not, nor suffer loss
    or harm,
    Even so, my spirit, do not fear.

(2.15; based on the translation by R.T.H. Griffith)

A benediction on homeward-coming cattle

1. Let them come home, the cattle that have wandered, whom Vayu
    has delighted to attend on,
    Whose forms and figures are well known to Tvashtr. These cows
    let Savitr drive within this stable.
2. Let the beasts stream together to this cow pen. Brihaspati who
    knows lead them here!
    Let Sinivali guide the foremost homeward. When they have
    come, Anumati! enclose them.
3. Together let the cattle flow! flow together horses and the
    men!
    Let the increase of grain too flow this way! I offer sacrifice with mixed
    oblation.
4. I pour together milk of cows, with ghee blending strength and
    juice.
    Well sprinkled be our men, as true to me as cows are to their
    herd!
5. Here I bring the milk of cows, here have brought the juice
    of grain.
    Here have our men been brought, here to this house our wives.

(2.26; based on the translation by R.T.H. Griffith)

A prayer for a boy's long and happy life

1. This child, Old Age! shall grow to meet you only; none of
    the hundred other deaths shall harm him.
    From trouble caused by friends let Mitra guard him, as a kind
    mother guards the son she nurses.

2. May Mitra or Varuna the foe-destroyer, cooperating, grant him death
    in course of nature!
    Then Agni, hotr-priest, skilled in high statutes, declares all
    the deities' generations.

3. You (Agni) are the Lord of all animals of the earth, of animals born and to
    be born hereafter.
    Let not his in-breath or his out-breath fail him. Let not his
    friends, let not his foes slay him.

4. Let Dyaus (sky or heaven), the father and let Prithivi, (earth) the mother, cooperating, give you
    death in course of nature,
    That you may live on Aditi's bosom, guarded, a hundred
    winters, through your respirations.

5. Lead him to life, O Agni, and to splendour, this dear child,
    Varuna! and you King Mitra!
    Give him protection, Aditi! As a mother; and all you gods, that his be a
    life of long duration.

                    (2.28; based on the translation by R.T.H. Griffith and M. Bloomfield)

A prayer to secure a husband for a marriageable girl

1. To please us may the suitor come, O Agni, seeking this maid and
    bringing us good fortune.
    Agreeable to suitors, lovely in assemblies, may she be soon
    made happy with a husband.

2. As bliss beloved by Soma, dear to spiritual power (Brahman), and stored by Aryaman,
    With the god Dhatr's truthfulness I work the bridal oracle.

3. O Agni, may this woman find a husband. Then truly King Soma
    makes her happy.
    May she bear sons, chief lady of the household, and blessed, rule beside her consort.

4. As this cave, Maghavan! that is fair to look on, was dear to wild
    things as a pleasant dwelling,
    So may this woman here be Bhaga's darling. Loved by her lord
    and prizing his affection.

5. Mount up, embark on Bhaga's ship, the full, the inexhaustible,
    On this, bring here to us the lover whom you
    Would like to wed.

6. Call out to him, O Lord of Wealth! Make the suitor well-inclined.
    Set each on your right hand, who is a lover worthy of her choice.

7. Here is the bdellium and the gold, the auksha (balsam) and the bliss are
   here;
   These bring you to the husbands, so to find the man whom you
   would have.
8. May Savitr lead and bring to you the husband whom your heart
   desires.
   O Plant, be this your gift to her!

(2.36; based on the translation by R.T.H. Griffith)

NOTE: Maghavan: Indra; Bhaga: (here) good fortune.

A rishi's morning prayer
1. Agni at dawn, and Indra we invoke at dawn, and Varuna and
   Mitra, and the Ashvins two;
   Bhaga at dawn, Pushan and Brahmanaspati, Soma at dawn, and
   Rudra we invoke at dawn.
2. We all invoke strong Bhaga, conqueror in the morning, the son of
   Aditi, the great disposer,
   Whom each who thinks of himself as poor, or as strong and mighty, a king,
   addresses thus, grant you my portion!
3. Bhaga, our guide, Bhaga whose gifts are faithful, favour this
   hymn and give us wealth, O Bhaga.
   Bhaga, increase our store of cattle and horses. Bhaga, may we be
   rich in men and heroes.
4. So may felicity be ours at present, and when the Sun advances,
   and at noontide;
   And may we still, O Bounteous One, at sunset be happy in the
   Gods' protecting favour.
5. May Bhaga truly be a bliss-bestower, and through him, gods,
   may happiness attend us.
   As such with all my might I call and call you; as such be you
   our leader here, O Bhaga.
6. To this our sacrifice may the Dawns incline them, and come to
   the pure place like Dadhikravan.
   As strong steeds draw a chariot may they bring me toward
   Bhaga who discovers treasure.
7. May the kind Mornings dawn on us for ever, with wealth of
   cattle, of horses, and of heroes.

Streaming with all abundance, pouring fatness,
Do preserve us evermore with blessings!

(3.16; based on the translation by R.T.H. Griffith)

Vena

1. *Eastward at first the prayer was generated: Vena disclosed bright*
    flashes from the summit,
    Disclosed his deepest, nearest revelations, womb of the non-
    existent and existent.

2. *Let this Queen come in front, her Father's daughter, found in*
    the worlds for earliest generation.
    For him they set this radiant vault in motion. Let them prepare
    warm milk for him who first would drink.

3. *He who was born as his all-knowing kinsman declares all the*
    deities' generations.
    He from the midst of prayer, his prayer has taken. On high,
    below, spread forth his godlike nature.

4. *For he, true to the law of Earth and Sky (Prithivi and Dyaus), established both*
    the mighty worlds securely.
    Mighty when born, he propped apart the mighty, the sky, our
    earthly home, and air's mid-region.

5. *He from the depth has been reborn for ever, Brihaspati the*
    world's sole Lord and Ruler.
    From light was born the Day with all its lustre; through this
    let sages live endowed with splendour.

6. *The sage and poet truly advances the statute of that mighty primeval*
    god.
    He was born here with many more beside him; they slumbered
    when the foremost side was opened.

7. *The man who seeks the friend of gods, Atharvan the father,*
    and Brihaspati, with worship,
    Crying to him, You are the creator of all! Him, the wise god, self-
    dependent, never injures.

(4.1; based on the translation by R.T.H. Griffith)

To the Rivers, for the cure of heart disease and related illnesses

1. *Forth from Himavant, the Hills of Snow they stream, and meet in Sindhu*
    here or there.

To me the sacred waters gave the balm that heals the heart's
disease.

2. *Whatever rupture I have had that injured eyes or heels or toes.*
   All this the waters, most skilful physicians, shall make well again,

3. *All Rivers who have Sindhu for your Lady, Sindhu for your*
   Queen,
   Give us the balm that heals this ill: this boon let us enjoy from
   you.

(6.24; based on the translation by R.T.H. Griffith)

Prayer for lustre and power

1. *The brilliancy that is in the lion, the tiger, and the serpent; in Agni, the brahmana, and in*
   Surya (shall be ours)! May the lovely goddess that bore Indra come to us, endowed with lustre!

2. *(The brilliancy) that is in the elephant, panther, and in gold; in the waters, cattle, and men (shall*
   be ours)! May the lovely goddess that bore Indra come to us, endowed with lustre!

3. *(The brilliancy) that is in the chariot, the dice, in the strength of the bull; in the wind, Parjanya,*
   and in the fire of Varuna (shall be ours)! May the lovely goddess that bore Indra come to us,
   endowed with lustre!

4. *(The brilliancy) that is in the man of royal caste, in the stretched drum, in the strength of the horse,*
   in the shout of men (shall be ours)! May the lovely goddess that bore Indra come to us, endowed
   with lustre!

(6.38; based on the translation by M. Bloomfield)

Prayer for exemption from the dangers of death

1. *To the 'Ender,' to Death be reverence! May your in-breathing and your out-breathing remain here!*
   United here with (life's) spirit this man shall be, sharing in the sun, in the world of immortality
   (amrita)!

2. *Bhaga has raised him up, Soma with his rays (has raised) him up, the Maruts, the gods, (have*
   raised) him up, Indra and Agni (have raised) him up unto well-being.

3. *Here (shall be) your (life's) spirit, here your in-breathing, here your life, here your mind! We rescue*
   you from the toils of Nirriti (destruction) by means of our divine utterance.

4. *Rise up hence, O man! Casting off the foot shackles of death, do not sink down! Be not cut off*
   from this world, from the sight of Agni and the sun!

5. *The wind, Matarishvan, shall blow for you, the waters shall shower amrita (ambrosia) upon you,*
   the sun shall shine kindly for your body! Death shall pity you; do not waste away!

6. *You shall ascend and not descend, O man! Life and alertness do I prepare for you. Mount,*
   immediately, this imperishable, pleasant chariot; then in old age you shall converse with your
   family!

7. Your mind shall not go thither, shall not disappear! Do not become heedless of the living, do not follow the Fathers! All the gods shall preserve you here!

8. Do not long after the departed, who conduct (men) afar! Ascend from the darkness, come to the light! We lay hold of your hands.

9. The two dogs of Yama, the black and the brindled one, that guard the road (to heaven), that have been despatched, shall not (go after) you! Come here, do not long to be away; do not stay here with your mind turned to a distance!

10. Do not follow this path: it is terrible! I speak of that by which you have not yet gone. Darkness is this, O man, do not enter it! Danger is beyond, security is here for you.

11. May the fires that are within the waters guard you, may (the fire) which men kindle guard you, may Jatavedas Vaishvanara (the fire common to all men) guard you! Let not the heavenly (fire) together with the lightning, burn you!

12. Let not the flesh-devouring (fire) menace you: move far from the funeral pyre! Heaven shall guard you, the earth shall guard you, the sun and moon shall guard you, the atmosphere shall guard you against the divine missile!

13. May the alert and the watchful divinities guard you, may he that sleeps not and nods not guard you, may he that protects and is vigilant guard you!

14. They shall guard you, they shall protect you. Reverence be to them. Hail be to them!

15. Into converse with the living Vayu, Indra, Dhatr, and saving Savitr shall put you; breath and strength shall not leave you! Your (life's) spirit do we call back to you.

16. Convulsions that draw the jaws together, darkness, shall not come upon you, nor (the demon) that tears out the tongue! How shall you then waste away? The Adityas and Vasus, Indra and Agni shall raise you up unto well-being!

17. The heavens, the earth, Prajapati, have rescued you. The plants with Soma their king have delivered you from death.

18. Let this man remain right here, ye gods, let him not depart hence to yonder world! We rescue him from death with (a charm) of thousandfold strength.

19. I have delivered you from death. The (powers) that furnish strength shall breathe upon you. The (mourning women) with dishevelled hair, they that wail lugubriously, shall not wail over you!

20. I have snatched you (from death), I have obtained you; you have returned with renewed youth. O you, that are (now) sound of limb, for you sound sight, and sound life have I obtained.

21. It has shone upon you, light has arisen, darkness has departed from you. We remove from you death, destruction, and disease.

(8.1; based on the translation by M. Bloomfield)

Prana, Breath or Vital Spirit

1. Homage to Prana, to him who has dominion over the universe,

Who has become the sovereign Lord of all, on whom the whole
depends!

2. Homage, O Prana, to your roar, to your thunder and your lightning
flash!
Homage, O Prana, to you and to the rain you send down!

3. When Prana with a thunderous voice shouts his loud message
to the plants,
They straightway are impregnated, they conceive, and bear
abundantly.

4. When the due season has arrived and Prana calls aloud to the plants,
Then all is joyful, yes, each thing upon the surface of the earth.

5. When Prana has poured down his flood of rain upon the
mighty land,
Cattle and beasts rejoice; Now great will be our strength, they cry.

6. Watered by Prana's rain the plants have raised their voices together:
You have prolonged our life, they say, and given fragrance to us
all.

7. Homage to you when you come in with the breath, homage to you when you depart;
Homage, O Prana, be to you when standing and when sitting still.

8. Homage to you at every breath you draw in and send out!
Homage to you when turned away, homage to you seen face to
face! This reverence be to all of you!

9. Prana, communicate to us your dear, your very dearest form.
Whatever healing balm you have, give us thereof that we may
live.

10. Prana clothes living creatures as a father his beloved son. Prana
is sovereign Lord of all, of all that breathes not, and of all that
breathes.

11. Prana is Fever, he is Death. Prana is worshipped by the gods.
Prana sets in the loftiest sphere the man who speaks the words
of truth.

12. Prana is Deshtri, and Viraj; Prana is reverenced by all. He is the
Sun, he is the Moon. Prana is called Prajapati.

13. Both breaths, in and out, are rice and barley, and Prana is called the toiling
ox;
In barley is the in-breath laid, and rice is named the outward breath.

14. The human infant in the womb draws vital breath and sends it out;
When you, O Prana, quicken the babe it springs anew to life.

15. The name of Prana is bestowed on Matarishvan and on Vata, the wind.
    On Prana, past and future, yes, on Prana everything depends.
16. All herbs and plants spring forth and grow when you, O Prana
    quickenest them,
    Plants of Atharvan, Angiras, plants of the deities and men.
17. When Prana has poured down his flood of rain upon the
    mighty earth,
    The plants are wakened into life, and also every herb that grows on ground.
18. The man who knows this truth of you, O Prana, and what supports you,
    To him will all present their gift of tribute in the highest world.
19. As all these living creatures offer you tributes, Prana, so
    shall they bring tribute unto him who hears you with attentive ears.
20. He as an embryo, wanders among the gods; grown; near at hand,
    he springs again to being.
    Having grown, he enters the present and the future, as a father enters the son with mighty powers.
21. As Hamsa (divine swan, mystical word), when he rises up, he leaves in the flood one foot unmoved.
    If he withdrew it there would be no more tomorrow or today,
    Never would there be night, no more would daylight shine or dawn appear.
22. He rolls on, eight-wheeled and single-fellied, and with a
    thousand eyes, forward and backward.
    With one half he engendered all creation. What sign is there to
    tell us of the other?
23. Homage, O Prana unto you armed with a swift bow against the rest,
    In whose dominion is this All of varied sort that stirs and works!
24. May he who rules this varied universe, that stirs and works,
    May Prana, alert and resolute, assist me through the prayer I pray.
25. Erect among the sleepers he is awake, and never lies down himself,
    No one has ever heard that he has been asleep while others slept.
26. You, Prana, never shall be hid, never shall be estranged from me.
    I bind you on myself for life, O Prana, like the waters' germ.

    (11.4; based on the translation by R.T.H. Griffith)

A hymn of prayer and praise to Prithivi or deified Earth
1. Truth, high and potent law (rita), the consecrating rite, fervour (tapas),
   Brahman, and sacrifice uphold the Earth.
   May she, the Queen of all that is and is to be, may Prithivi
   make ample space and room for us.

2. Not over awed by the crowd of Manu's sons, she who has
   many heights and floods and level plains;
   She who bears plants endowed with many varied powers, may
   Prithivi for us spread wide and favour us.

3. In whom the sea, and Sindhu, and the waters, in whom our food
   and corn-lands had their being,
   In whom this all that breathes and moves is active, this Earth.
   assign us foremost rank and station!

4. She who is Lady of the earth's four regions, in whom our food
   and grain-lands had their being,
   supports in each place of breathing, moving creatures, this Earth.
   Grant us cattle with milk that fails not!

5. On whom the men of old before us battled, on whom the gods
   defeated the asuras,
   The varied home of bird, and cattle and horses, this Prithivi
   grant us luck and splendour!

6. Firm standing place, all-bearing, store of treasures,
   gold-breasted, harbourer of all that moves.
   May Earth who bears Agni Vaishvanara, consort of mighty
   Indra, give us great possessions.

7. May Earth, may Prithivi, always protected with ceaseless care by
   gods who never slumber,
   May she pour out for us delicious nectar, may she bedew us
   with a flood of splendour.

8. She who at first was water in the ocean, whom with their wondrous powers the sages followed,
   May she whose heart is in the highest heaven, compassed about
   with truth, and everlasting,
   May she, this Earth, bestow upon us lustre, and grant us power
   in loftiest dominion.

9. On whom the running universal waters flow day and night with
   never-ceasing motion,
   May she with many streams pour milk to feed us, may she
   besprinkle us with a flood of splendour.

10. She whom the Ashvins measured out, over whom the foot of
    Vishnu strode,
    Whom Indra, Lord of Power and Might, freed from all foes
    for himself,
    May Earth pour out her milk for us, a mother unto me her son.

11. O Prithivi, auspicious be your woodlands, auspicious be your hills
    and snow-clad mountains.
    Unslain, unwounded, unsubdued, I have set foot upon the
    Earth,
    On earth, brown, black, ruddy and every-coloured, on the firm
    earth that Indra guards from danger.

12. O Prithivi, your centre and your navel, all forces that have issued
    from your body
    Set us amid those forces; breathe upon us. I am the son of
    Earth, Earth is my Mother. Parjanya is my father; may he
    protect me.

13. Earth on whose surface they enclose the altar, and all-performers
    spin the thread of worship;
    In whom the stakes of sacrifice, resplendent, are fixed and raised
    on high before the oblation, may she, this Earth, prospering,
    make us prosper.

14. The man who hates us, Earth! who fights against us, who
    threatens us with thought or deadly weapon, make him subject to us, as you have done
    before.

15. Produced from you, on you move mortal creatures; you
    support them, both quadruped and biped.
    yours, Prithivi, are these Five human Races, for whom, though
    mortal, Surya as he rises, spreads with his rays the light that is immortal.

16. Together may these creatures yield us blessings. With the honey of
    speech, O Earth, endow me.

17. Kind, ever gracious be the Earth we tread on, the firm Earth,
    Prithivi, supported by (divine) Order, mother of plants and herbs, the
    all-producer.

18. A vast abode you have become, the Mighty. Great stress is on
    you, press and agitation, but with unceasing care great Indra
    guards you.
    So make us shine, O Earth, us with the splendour of gold. Let
    no man look on us with hatred.

19. Agni is in the earth, in plants; the waters hold Agni in them,
    in the stones is Agni.
    Agni abides deep in men; Agni lives in cattle and horses.

20. Agni provides shine and heat in the sky; the spacious air is his, the god's.
    Lover of ghi, bearer of oblation, men enkindle him.

21. *Dark-kneed, clothed with Agni, Prithivi sharpen me*
    and give me splendour!

22. *On earth they offer sacrifice and dressed oblation to the Gods.*
    Men, mortals, live upon the earth by food in their accustomed way.
    May that Earth grant us breath and vital power. Prithivi give
    me life of long duration!

23. *Scent that has risen from you, O Earth, the fragrance which.*
    growing herbs and plants and waters carry,
    Shared by apsaras, shared by gandharvas with that fragrance, make
    me too sweet; let no man hate me.

24. *Your scent which entered and possessed the lotus, the scent*
    which they prepared at Surya's bridal,
    Scent which Immortals of old collected, with that fragrance make
    me sweet; let no man hate me.

25. *Your perfume in women and in men, the luck and light that is in males,*
    That is in heroes and in horses in wild animals and elephants,
    The splendid energy of maidens, with that do unite us, Earth! Let no man look on us with hate.

26. *Rock, earth, stone, and dust, is this Earth, held together, firmly bound.*
    To this gold-breasted Prithivi my adoration have I paid.

27. *We invoke here the firmly held, the all-supporting Prithivi,*
    On whom the trees, lords of the forest, stand evermore immovable.

28. *Sitting at ease or rising up, standing or going on our way.*
    With our right foot and with our left we will not stumble upon the earth.

29. *I speak to Prithivi the purifier, to patient Earth who grows*
    strong through Brahma (spiritual power).
    O Earth, may we rest on you who bear strength, prosperity,
    our portioned share of food, and ghi.

30. *Purified for our bodies flow the waters: we bring distress on*
    him who would attack us.
    I cleanse myself, O Earth, with that which cleanseth.

31. *Earth, let your eastern and your northern regions, those lying*
    southward and those lying westward,
    be propitious to me in all my movements. As long as I walk on the
    ground let me not stumble.

32. *Drive us not from the west or east, drive us not from the north*
    or south,
    Be gracious unto us, O Earth: let not the robbers find us; keep
    the deadly weapon far away.

33. As long as, I look upon you, Earth, with Surya as my friend,
    So long, through each succeeding year, let not my power of
    vision fail.

34. When, as I lie, O Earth, I turn upon my right side and my left,
    When stretched at all our length we lay our ribs on you who
    meet us.
    Do us no injury there, O Earth who furnishes a bed for all.

35. Let what I dig from you, O Earth, rapidly spring and grow
    again.
    O Purifier, let me not pierce through your vitals or your heart.

36. Earth, may your summer, and your rains, and autumn, your winter,
    and your dewy frosts, and spring-time.
    May your years, Prithivi! And ordered seasons, and day and
    night pour out for us abundance.

37. The purifier, shrinking from the Serpent, she who held fires that
    lie within the waters,
    Who gives as prey the God-blaspheming dasyus, Earth choosing
    Indra for her Lord, not Vritra, has clung to Shakra (Indra), to the
    strong and mighty.

38. Base of the seat and sheds (sadas), on whom the sacrificial stake is
    fixed, and the vessels that hold the Soma (havir-dhane)
    On whom the Yajus-knowing priests recite the riks and samans,
    And the other priests (ritvig) are employed so that Indra may drink the Soma juice.

39. On whom the ancient rishis, they who made the world, and with their songs produced the
    cows, the seven worshippers (priests), by the sattra sacrifices and by their fervent zeal (tapas);

40. May she, the Earth, assign to us the opulence for which we yearn,
    May Bhaga share and aid the task and Indra come to lead the way.

41. May she, the Earth, upon whom men sing and dance with varied
    shout and noise,
    Where men meet in battle, and the war-cry and the drum resound,
    May she drive off our foes, may Prithivi rid me of my rivals.

42. On whom is food, barley and rice, to whom these Races Five belong,
    Homage to her, Parjanya's wife, to her whose marrow is the rain!

43. Whose castles are the work of gods, and men wage war upon her plain
    The Lord of Life make Prithivi, who bears all things in her
    womb, pleasant to us on every side!

44. May Earth the goddess, she who bears her treasure stored
    in many places, gold, gems, and riches,

Giver of wealth, may she grant great possessions to us bestowing them
with love and favour.

45. Earth, on whom live people speaking different languages and with diverse customs, according to
their dwelling-places,
Pour, like a constant cow that never fails, a thousand streams
of treasure to enrich me!

46. The snake, the sharply stinging scorpion, lying concealed,
bewildered, chilled with cold of winter,
The worm, O Prithivi, each thing that in the rains revives and
stirs, creeping, do not allow it to creep on us! With all things gracious bless us.

47. Your many paths on which the people travel, the roads for chariots and
wagons to journey over,
on which meet both the good and bad, that pathway may we
attain without a foe or robber. With all things gracious bless us.

48. Supporting both the foolish and the wise, the earth she bears the death
both of the good and evil.
In friendly concord with the boar, Earth opens herself for the
wild swine that roams the forest.

49. All wild forest animals, the animals of the woodlands, the man-eaters,
forest-haunting, lions and tigers,
Jackals (ula), wolves, misfortune, and evil spirits, drive from us, chase the
demons to a distance.

50. Gandharvas and apsaras, kimidins, and malignant sprites,
pishachas all, and rakshasas, these keep you, Earth, far from us.

51. Earth, upon whom the winged bipeds fly together, birds of each various
kind, the swans, the eagles;
On whom Matarishvan, the Wind, comes rushing, rousing the
dust and causing trees to tremble, and flames follow the wind,
back and forth;

52. Earth, upon whom are settled, joined together, the night and
day, the dusky and the ruddy, Prithivi compassed by the rain
about her,
Happily may she establish us, in each delightful dwelling place.

53. Heaven, Earth, and the realm of Middle Air have granted me this
wide expanse
Agni, Sun, Waters, all the gods have joined to give me mental power.

54. I am victorious, I am called the lord superior on earth,
Triumphant, all-overpowering the conqueror on every side.

55. There, when the gods, O goddess Prithivi, named you, spreading your
    wide expanse as you were extending eastward,
    Then into you passed many a charm and glory: you made
    for yourself the world's four regions.

56. In hamlets and in woodland, and in all assembly halls on earth,
    In gatherings, and in meetings, we will speak glorious things of you.

57. As the horse scatters the dust, the people who dwelt upon
    the land, at birth, she scattered,
    Leader and head of all the world, delightful, the trees' protectress
    and the plants' upholder.

58. Whatever I say I speak with honey-sweetness, whatever I behold
    for that they love me.
    Dazzling, impetuous am I; others who fiercely stir I slay.

59. Mild, gracious, sweetly scented, milky, with nectar in her breast,
    May Earth, may Prithivi bestow her blessings, with milk, on me.

60. Whom Vishvakarman with oblation followed, when she was set
    in mid-air's billowy ocean;
    She, a useful vessel, was hidden, when, for enjoyment, she was made manifest to the (divine)
    mothers.

61. You are the vessel that contains people, Aditi, granter of the
    wish, far-spreading.
    Prajapati, the first-born Son of Order (rita), supplies you with whatever you lack.

62. Let your breasts, Prithivi, be free from sickness and disease and let them be produced for our
    advantage.
    Through long-extended life, wakeful and watching still, may we
    be bearers of offerings to you.

63. O Earth, my Mother, set me happily in a place secure.
    Of one accord with Heaven, O Sage, set me in glory and in wealth.

                              (12.1; based on the translation by R.T.H. Griffith)

NOTE: This hymn, in whole or in part, was used in various rituals for establishing the
homestead, propitiating snakes, or for attaining prosperity.

Rohita, a form of Fire and of the Sun
The first six verses of a long hymn of sixty verses.

1. Rise, Mighty One, who lies in the waters, and enter this your
   fair and glorious kingdom.

Let Rohita who made this All uphold you carefully nurtured
for supreme dominion.

2. The strength that was in waters has ascended. Ascend over the
   tribes which you have created.
   Creating Soma, waters, plants and cattle, bring here both
   quadrupeds and bipeds.

3. You Maruts, strong and mighty, sons of Prishni, with Indra for your
   ally crush down our foes.
   Let Rohita, you bounteous givers, hear you, thrice-seven Maruts
   who delight in sweetness!

4. Up from the lap of births, to lofty places, has Rohita, the germ
   of women, ascended.
   Together with these he founded the six realms: seeing his way
   in front here he received the kingship.

5. For you has Rohita obtained dominion, scattered your enemies, become your safeguard.
   So by the potent Sakvari-stanzas let Heaven and Earth be milked to
   yield you all your wishes.

6. Rohita gave the Earth and Heavens their being. There Parameshthin held the cord extended.
   There rests Aja Ekapada. He with his might has established Earth and Heaven.

(13.1; based on the translation by R.T.H. Griffith)

Two hymns to Kala or Time

1.

1. Prolific, thousand-eyed, and undecaying, a horse with seven
   reins, Kala bears us onward.
   Sages inspired with holy knowledge mount him: his chariot
   wheels are all the worlds of creatures.

2. This Kala has seven rolling wheels and seven naves; immortality
   is his chariot's axle.
   This Time brings here all the worlds around us; he, as the primal
   deity, is entreated.

3. On Time is laid an overflowing jar: this we see appearing in many
   forms.
   He carries away from us all these worlds of creatures; they call him
   Kala in the highest heaven.

4. He surely made the worlds of life, he surely gathered the worlds

of living things together.

He was their father, but became their son; no power higher than he exists.

5. Kala created yonder heaven, and Kala made these realms of earth.

By Kala, stirred to motion, both what is and what shall be, grow and expand.

6. Kala created land; in Kala the Sun has his light and heat.

In Kala all created things rest; in Kala the eye sees.

7. In Kala mind, in Kala breath, in Kala name are fixed and joined.

These living creatures, one and all, rejoice when Kala has arrived.

8. Kala embraces spiritual fire (tapas); in Kala is the highest; brahman (spiritual exaltation) in himself.

Yes, Kala, who was the father of Prajapati, is the lord of all.

9. He made, he stirred this universe to motion, and on him it rests.

He, Kala, having now become Brahman, supports Parameshthin.

10. Kala created living things (prajah) and, first of all, Prajapati.

From Kala the self-existing Kashyapa was born, from Kala tapas was born.

(19.53; based on the translation by R.T.H. Griffith)

2.

1. From Kala sprang the Waters, from Kala sprang the regions, Brahman, and tapas.

The Sun rises through Kala, and in Kala sinks again to rest.

2. By Kala freshly blows the wind, through Kala the mighty Earth exists: on Kala rests the mighty Sky.

In Kala, Prajapati produced what is and what is yet to be.

3. From Kala sprang the riks, and from Kala was the yajus born.

They formed in Kala sacrifice, eternal portion for the gods.

4. In Kala the gandharvas and apsaras and worlds abide.

Atharvan and this Angiras in Kala are supreme over heaven.

5. Both this world and the world that is most lofty, the pure worlds and pure intermediate spaces,

Yes, having conquered all the worlds by Brahman, Kala as God Supreme is supplicated.

(19.54; both based on the translation by R.T.H. Griffith)

A NOTE ON THE TRANSLATIONS

In the hymns above, modifications have been made after consulting other translations or the original text, or to modernize the language. The reason for choosing Griffith's (1826–1906) translations as the base for most of these hymns is that, despite belonging to a different era, his work is based on accepted traditions and is still highly regarded. Apart from some modernization in language, there is usually little difference between him and the work of more accepted recent translators. In addition, there are few complete translations in English; most recent translations are of a few selected hymns. Griffith translated all the four Vedas, and thus was in a unique position to understand and compare the texts.

The main sources of these translations are listed below:

Bloomfield, Maurice, trans., *Hymns of the Atharva-Veda*, in F. Max Müller, ed., Sacred Books of the East, vol. 42 (Oxford: Clarendon Press, 1897).

Griffith, R.T.H., trans., *The Hymns of the Rig Veda* (Benares: E.J. Lazarus & Co., 1896).

Griffith, R.T.H., trans., *The Texts of the White Yajur Veda or Vajasaneyi Samhita* (Benares: E.J. Lazarus & Co., 1896).

Griffith, R.T.H., trans., *The Hymns of the Samaveda* (Benares: E.J. Lazarus & Co., 1896).

Griffith, R.T.H., trans., *The Hymns of the Atharva Veda* (Benares: E.J. Lazarus & Co., 1896).

Stevenson, J., *Translation of the Sanhita of the Sama Veda* (London: Oriental Translation Fund of Great Britain and Ireland, 1842).

Keith, A.B., trans., *The Veda of the Black Yajur School* (*Taittiriya Sanhita*) (Cambridge: Harvard University Press, 1914).

GLOSSARY

This book contains a number of non-English words, which are explained within the text. This glossary contains a select list of these words. Unless otherwise mentioned, all words are from the Sanskrit. Sanskrit words can have multiple meanings and connotations. This list provides the meanings that are relevant to this text.

adhvaryu	a Yajur Veda priest
adhyaya	chapter, lesson, or section; also a term for reading or study, particularly of sacred books
agnishtoma	a Soma sacrifice
ahi	a serpent
ahura	a term for a deity in Avestan
aitihasika	legendary; historical; traditional; a traditional historian
anukramani	list, catalogue, or index
anuvaka	saying after; reciting; repeating; passages for recitation
amrita	divine nectar, the drink of immortality
antyeshti	funeral ritual
antyeshti-karika	funeral ceremonies
apri hymns	a class of hymns used in sacrifices and rituals
apsara	a divine nymph
Aranyakas	a class of texts attached to the Vedic Samhitas
aranya	forest
arthavada	explanations
arya	a term meaning 'noble'; used for a group of people in the Rig Veda
asat	untruth, unreality

ashrama	a stage in the life of a brahmana; a hermitage
ashtaka	one-eighth
ashva	a horse
asura	a divine being; in later texts, sometimes demonic
atiratra	a Soma sacrifice
ayas	metal
Brahma	a deity (pronounced Brahmaa)
brahman	a special priest of the Atharva Veda
brahmana	a member of the brahmana caste, the highest of the four castes
Brahman	a term for the Absolute; the ultimate creator and underlying substance of the world
Brahmana	a class of texts attached to the Vedic Samhitas
charana	a group of people who study one particular shakha of any Samhita
chhanda/chhandas	metre
daeva	a deity or a demonic being in Avestan
dakshina	fee or gifts given to a priest; also southern or right side
dana	donations or gifts
danastutis	hymns or parts of hymns, relating to gifts
dasa	a term for a group of people in the Rig Veda; later meant slave or servant
dashat	consisting of ten
dasyu	a term for a group of people in the Rig Veda
dehi	defences consisting of earthworks or dikes
deva	god
dharmashastrika	pertaining to law
durga	fort; literally, difficult to access, impassable, or unattainable
dvadashaha	twelve-day Soma sacrifice
dvija	twice-born, refers to the three upper castes
gana (gaana)	song; singing; a part of the Sama Veda
gana	group, flock, troop
gandharva	a semi-divine being, associated with apsaras
ghata karpara	potsherds, or fragments of a pot
gavidhuka	a type of grass
graha	a vessel, ladle, or cup used to take a portion of liquid out of a larger vessel; also to seize or capture
griha	assistant; servant; house; household; householder
grihya	belonging to a house; domestic; household sacrifices
havirdana	gift of oblation
hotr, hota	the main priest for the Rig Veda

jana	clan or tribe
jyotisha	astronomy and astrology (sciences), essential to fix the right time for ceremonies and sacrifices
kalpa	proper; fit; sacred precept, law, or rule
Kalpa Sutras	a category of Sanskrit texts, relating to ritual
kanda (kaanda)	a section, part, portion, chapter, or division of a work or book
kandika (kaandikaa)	a part or division of a book
karana	an astrological division of the day; there are eleven karanas divided into seven movable and four fixed; two karanas are equal to a lunar day
karika (kaarikaa)	a concise statement in verse, or a book or work containing such statements
khanda	a section of a work, part, or chapter
khandaka	fragment; part or piece; section of a work
khandika	section or part
khila	a supplement to a book, or an additional hymn
kimidin	a class of evil spirits
mandala	a circle; wheel; disk; province; in the Rig Veda, a division of the text
mantra	instrument of thought; a sacred text, prayer, or song of praise; a Vedic hymn; a sacrificial formula
muhurta	a division of time, the thirtieth part of a day; a moment; an instant
nakshatras	constellations through which the moon passes, lunar mansions
neshtri	a priest at a Soma sacrifice
nirukta	uttered; explained; etymological interpretation of a word
nishka	a golden ornament; later, a coin
nivid	proclaim; short formula in a liturgy
pada	a line or quarter of a verse; a word or stem of a noun; a foot
padapatha	a category of texts in which words are arranged in their original form, without following the rules of sandhi
padapathas	word texts
paddhati	a category of texts
panchika	a section of a text containing five adhyayas
parishishta	a supplementary section of a text
parivrajaka	a religious mendicant, a wandering ascetic
parvan	(1) a section, break, pause, or division, particularly of a book, (2) a period or day when the moon changes; a time when the sun enters a new sign; a division of time; a moment
prapathaka	a lecture, chapter, or subdivision of a book
prayoga	a recitation; a sacred text; a connection
pitris	ancestors

pratishakhya	a class of texts on shiksha
pur	fort or rampart or temporary settlement
purodasha	sacrificial cake made of ground rice, placed on receptacles (kapala), offered as oblation
rakshasa	a demonic being
ratha	chariot
Rathantara	the name of a tune mentioned in the Rig, Sama, and other Vedas
rik	a verse
rishi	a sage or ascetic
rishika	a female rishi
sandhi	a conjunction of words, causing a modification of the final and initial letters of the separate words; methods of joining words
saman	a chant
samhita	a collection; compilation, usually of knowledge or hymns in a text
samskara	a sacred or sanctifying ceremony
shakha	literally a branch; in the Vedic context, a recension or school
shastra	hymn of praise; also a weapon
shiksha	phonetics; the science of pronunciation
shrauta	derived from the word 'shruti', that which is heard; refers to sacred tradition, and the three sacred fires
shruti	literally 'that which is heard', hence these texts were 'heard' by the composers, conveyed to them from some divine source
sita	name of a deity, literally 'furrow'
stobha	a sound without meaning that can be used in chanting or singing
stoma	type of verse
stotra	basic unit of verses to be sung
sura	a type of wine
sutra	a short aphorism; a thread or string
svadhyaya	self-study, particularly of the Vedas
svadha	a goddess; and a sacred exclamation, used with offerings to the pitris
svaha	a goddess; and a sacred exclamation, used with oblations to the gods
svara	accent; sound; note (as in music)
tapas	religious fervour; intense religious practices
tithi	a lunar day, the thirtieth part of the lunar cycle, which constitutes a little over twenty-seven days
uktha	types of verse
ukthya	a Soma sacrifice
Upanishads	a class of texts attached to the Vedic Samhitas

upanayana	initiation
uttarayana	the period of the sun's progress to the north
valakhilya	a term for some supplementary hymns in Vedas; also a class of tiny rishis, of the size of a thumb
vamsha	lineage, race, family; a dynasty of kings; a list of teachers; an offspring; a son
vanaprastha	the traditional third stage of life, when the householder's life had been renounced and the person retired to the forest to live the life of an ascetic
vajra	a thunderbolt, particularly Indra's weapon
vara	a day of the week
varga	a group of similar things; a class or separate division; any series or group of words
varna	individual sounds; musical sound or note; order or arrangement of a song or poem; caste; colour; species; tribe
vish (plural vishah)	precise meaning not known but refers to settlement; homestead; house; dwelling; members of a clan; community; tribe; race
vishuvat	equinox; with both sides equal; the central day in a sacrifice
vyakarana	grammar
Vedangas	subsidiary Vedic texts
vidhi	rule; ordinance; statute; precept; law
vritra	a foe or enemy; the name of a demon who may personify drought; he is killed by Indra
yajamana	sacrificing; worshipping; the sacrificer or person for whom the sacrifice is being conducted
yajnika	ritualist; performer of many sacrifices; one well versed in ritual
yajus	a prose or verse mantra recited with a ritual; a sacrificial prayer or formula; religious reverence or veneration
yoga	the main star in a lunar asterism; junction; union; joining; yoking; a philosophical system of uniting with the divine
yoni	in the context of music, of Sama veda, the basic verse; otherwise, the female emblem
yuga	a time period
yupa	the sacrificial post

The definitions here are selected from M. Monier-Williams's *A Sanskrit–English Dictionary* (reprint; Delhi: Motilal Banarsidass, 1973).

SELECT BIBLIOGRAPHY

Abbi, Anvita, 'Tribal Languages', in Braj B. Kachru, et al., eds, *Language in South Asia* (Cambridge, UK: Cambridge University Press, 2008), pp. 153–74.

Akazawa, Takeru and Emöke J.E. Szathmary, eds, *Prehistoric Mongoloid Dispersals* (New York: Oxford University Press, 1996).

Alinei, Mario, 'Towards an Invasionless Model of Indo-European Origins: The Continuity Theory', in M. Pearce and M. Tosi, eds, *Papers from the EEA Third Annual Meeting at Ravenna 1997, Vol. I, Pre- and Protohistory*, BAR International Series 717 (1998): pp. 31–33.

_____, 'Merits and Limits of Renfrew's Theory', in *Origin of European Languages, Vol. 1, The Continuity Theory* (translated from the Italian by S. Kostic, *Meriti e limiti della teoria di Renfrew* of *Le origini delle lingue d'Europa. Vol. I. La teoria della continuità*) (Bologna: Il Mulino, 1996).

Alvar, R.S., et al., *An Introduction to Soma Yagnyas and Vedic Yagnyas in General* (produced for the Vedic Society for Auroville Somayagya 2010 by Samskrti Foundation, Mysore).

Anthony, David, *The Horse, the Wheel and Language: How Bronze-Age Riders from the Eurasian Steppes Shaped the Modern World* (Princeton: Princeton University Press, 2007).

Apte, V.M., *Social and Religious Life in the Grihya Sutras* (Ahmedabad: Virvijaya Printing Press, 1939).

Arvidsson, Stefan, *Aryan Idols: Indo-European Mythology as Ideology and Science*, translated by Sonia Wichmann (Chicago: University of Chicago Press, 2006).

Atre, Shubhangana, *The Archetypal Mother: A Systemic Approach to Harappan Religion* (Pune: Ravish Publishers, 1987).

Aurobindo, Sri, *The Secret of the Veda: With Selected Hymns* (Pondicherry: Sri Aurobindo Ashram, 1998).

_____, *The Integral Yoga: Selected Letters of Sri Aurobindo* (Pondicherry: Sri Aurobindo Ashram, 1996).

_____, *The Synthesis of Yoga* (reprint; Pondicherry: Sri Aurobindo Ashram, 1998).

_____, *The Upanishads: Texts, Translations and Commentaries* (2nd edn; Pondicherry: Sri Aurobindo Ashram, 1981).

Banerjea, J.N., *The Development of Hindu Iconography* (3rd edn; New Delhi: Munshiram Manoharlal, 1974).

Basham, A.L., *The Wonder That Was India* (Calcutta: Fontana and Rupa & Co., 1971).

Barthold, W., *Istoriko-geograficheskii obzor Irana* (Moscow, 1971); translated by S. Soucek, *An Historical Geography of Iran* (Princeton, NJ: Princeton University Press, 1984).

Beja-Pereira, Albano, et al., 'African Origins of the Domestic Donkey', *Science* 304 (18 June 2004): pp. 1781–82.

Bhargava, M.L., *The Geography of Rig Vedic India* (Lucknow: Upper India Publishing House, 1964).

Bhat, D.N.S., 'Retroflexion: An Areal feature', *Working Paper on Language Universals* 13 (1973): pp. 27–67.

Bhattacharji, Sukumari, *The Indian Theogony: A Comparative Study of Indian Mythology from the Vedas to the Puranas* (Calcutta: Firma KLM, 1978).

Bloch, Jules, 'Sanskrit et Dravidien', *Bulletin de la Société de linguistique de Paris*, no. 76 (1924): pp. 1–21.

Bloomfield, M., *A Vedic Concordance* (reprint; Delhi: Motilal Banarsidass, 1996).

——, trans., *Hymns of the Atharva-Veda*, in F. Max Müller, ed., Sacred Books of the East, vol. 42 (1897; reprint, Delhi: Motilal Banarsidass, 2011).

Bodewitz, H.W., *The Jyotistoma Ritual: Jaiminiya Brahmana I, 66–364* (Leiden: E.J. Brill, 1990).

Boethlingk, O. and R. Roth, *Sanskrit Worterbuch*, 7 vols (St Petersburg, 1875; reprint, Delhi: Motilal Banarsidass, 1991).

Boyce, M., *A History of Zoroastrianism*, 3 vols (vol. 1, reprint, Leiden: E.J. Brill, 1989; vol. 2, 1982; vol. 3, with F. Grenet, 1991).

——, *Textual Sources for the Study of Zoroastrianism* (Manchester, UK: Manchester University Press, 1984).

——, *Zoroastrians: Their Religious Beliefs and Practices* (London: Routledge, 1979).

——, 'Priests, Cattle and Men', *Bulletin of the School of Oriental and African Studies* 50, no. 3 (1987): pp. 508–26.

Bronkhorst, Johannes and Madhav M. Deshpande, eds, *Aryan and Non-Aryan in South Asia: Evidence, Interpretation and Ideology*, Harvard Oriental Series, Opera Minora vol. 3 (Cambridge, MA: Harvard University Press, 1999).

Brough, John, 'The Tripartite Ideology of the Indo-Europeans: An Experiment in Method', *Bulletin of the School of Oriental and African Studies* 22, no. 1 (1959): pp. 180–202.

Bryant, Edwin Francis and Laurie L. Patton, eds, *The Indo-Aryan Controversy: Evidence and Inference in Indian History* (London: Routledge, 2005).

Bryant, Edwin Francis, ed., *The Quest for the Origins of Vedic Culture: The Indo-Aryan Migration Debate* (New Delhi: Oxford University Press, 2001).

Caland, W. and V. Henry, *L'Agnistoma: Description complete de la forme normale du sacrifice de soma dans le Culte Vedique*, vols 1–2 (Paris: Ernest Leroux, 1906–07).

Chakrabarti, Dilip K., *Archaeological Geography of the Ganga Plain: The Lower and the Middle Ganga* (Delhi: Permanent Black, 2001).

Chakrabarty, S., *A Critical Linguistic Study of the Pratishakyas* (Calcutta: Punthi Pustak, 1996).

Chatterji, Jagdish Chandra, *Wisdom of the Vedas* (Wheaton, IL: The Theosophical Publishing House, Quest Books, 1992).

Chawla, Jyotsna, *The Rigvedic Deities and Their Iconic Forms* (New Delhi: Munshiram Manoharlal, 1990).

Childe, Gordon V., *The Aryans: A Study of Indo-European Origins* (London: Kegan Paul, 1926).

——, *Prehistoric Migrations in Europe* (Oslo: Aschehaug, 1949).

Christensen, A., *Le Premier Chapitre du Vendidad et l'histoire Primitive des Tribus Iraniennes* (Copenhagen, 1943).

Clutton-Brock, Juliet, *A Natural History of Domesticated Mammals* (2nd edn; Cambridge, UK: Cambridge University Press, 1999).

Dalal, R., *Hinduism: An Alphabetical Guide* (New Delhi: Penguin Books India, 2010).

_____, *The Historical Geography of the Ganga–Yamuna Doab* (unpublished thesis, 1983).

Dandekar, R.N., *Vedic Mythological Tracts* (New Delhi: Ajanta, 1979).

Dani, A.H. and V.M. Masson, *History of Civilizations of Central Asia* (UNESCO, 1992; 1st Indian edn, Delhi: Motilal Banarsidass, 1999).

Danielou, Alain, *The Myths and Gods of India* (Rochester, VT: Inner Traditions International, 1991).

Danino, Michel, 'The Harappan Heritage and the Aryan Problem', in *Man and Environment* XXVIII, no. 1 (2003): pp. 21–32.

_____, 'Genetics and the Aryan Debate', *Puratattva: Bulletin of the Indian Archaeological Society*, no. 36 (2005–06): pp. 146–54.

_____, *The Invasion That Never Was* (Mysore: Mira Aditi, 2001).

Dasgupta, S., *A History of Indian Philosophy*, 5 vols (1922–55; reprint, Delhi: Motilal Banarsidass, 1975).

Dave, K.N., *Birds in Sanskrit Literature* (1985; revised edn, Delhi: Motilal Banarsidass, 2005).

Deshpande, Madhav, M., *Sanskrit and Prakrit: Sociolinguistic Issues* (Delhi: Motilal Banarsidass, 1993).

_____, 'Sanskrit in the South Asian Sociolinguistic Context', in Braj B. Kachru, et al., eds, *Language in South Asia* (Cambridge, UK: Cambridge University Press, 2008) pp. 177–88.

Dey, N.L., *The Geographical Dictionary of Ancient and Medieval India* (New Delhi: Munshiram Manoharlal, 1971).

Diakonoff, I.M., 'Elam', in I. Gershevitch, ed., *The Cambridge History of Iran*, vol. 2 (Cambridge, UK: Cambridge University Press, 1985) p.1ff.

_____, 'On the Original Home of the Speakers of Indo-European', *Journal of Indo-European Studies* 13 (1985): pp. 92–174.

Doniger, Wendy, *The Rig Veda: An Anthology* (Harmondsworth: Penguin Classics, 1981).

Dowson, John, *A Classical Dictionary of Hindu Mythology and Religion* (reprint; New Delhi: D.K. Printworld, 1998).

Drews, Robert, *The Coming of the Greeks: Indo-European Conquests in the Aegean and the Near East* (Princeton, NJ: Princeton University Press, 1989).

Dumezil, G., *Les Dieux des Indo-Européens* (Paris: Presses Universitaires de France, 1952).

_____, *Gods of the Ancient Northmen*, edited and translated by Einer Haugen (Los Angeles: University of California, 1973).

Elfenbein, Josef, 'A Periplus of the Brahui Problem', *Studia Iranica*, no. 16.2 (1987): pp. 215–33.

Elst, Koenraad, *Update on the Aryan Invasion Debate* (New Delhi: Aditya Prakashan, 1999).

Emeneau, Murray B., *Language and Linguistic Area* (Stanford: Stanford University Press, 1980).

_____, *Brahui and Dravidian Comparative Grammar* (Berkeley: University of California Publications in Linguistics, 1962).

Erdosy, George, ed., *The Indo-Aryans of Ancient South Asia: Language, Material Culture and Ethnicity* (Indian edn; New Delhi: Munshiram Manoharlal, 1997).

Fagan, Garrett G., ed., *Archaeological Fantasies: How Pseudoarchaeology Misrepresents the Past and Misleads the Public* (New York: Routledge, 2006).

Farmer, Steve and Michael Witzel, *Indus Valley Fantasies: Political Mythologies, Academic Careerism, and the Poverty of Indus Studies* (talk at Harvard University, 8 October 2010).

Flattery, David S. and Martin Schwartz, *Haoma and Harmaline: The Botanical Identity of the Indo-Iranian Sacred Hallucinogen 'Soma' and Its Legacy in Religion, Language and Middle Eastern Folklore* (Berkeley: University of California Press, 1989).

Feuerstein, Georg, Subhash Kak and David Frawley, *In Search of the Cradle of Civilization* (Wheaton, IL: The Theosophical Publishing House, 1995).

Fortson, Benjamin W., *Indo-European Language and Culture: An Introduction* (Chichester, UK: Blackwell, 2004).

Frumkin, George, *Archaeology in Soviet Central Asia*, no. 6 (Leiden: E.J. Brill, 1970).

Frye, R.N., *The History of Ancient Iran* (Munich: C.H. Beck'sche Verlagsbuchhandlung, 1984).

Fuller, Christopher J., *The Camphor Flame: Popular Hinduism and Society in India* (revised and expanded; Princeton, NJ: Princeton University Press, 2004).

Fuller, Dorian, 'An Agricultural Perspective on Dravidian Historical Linguistics: Archaeological Crop Packages, Livestock and Dravidian Crop Vocabulary', in Peter Bellwood and Colin Renfrew, eds, *Examining the Farming/Language Dispersal Hypothesis* (Cambridge, UK: The McDonald Institute for Archaeological Research, 2003).

Gamkrelidze, T.V. and Vjaceslav V. Ivanov, *Indo-European and the Indo-Europeans: A Reconstruction and Historical Analysis of a Proto-Language and a Proto-Culture*, translated by Johanna Nichols (The Hague: Mouton de Gruyter, 1995).

Ganapati, S.V., *Sama-Veda* (reprint; Delhi: Motilal Banarsidass, 1992).

Gane, Roy, *Ritual Dynamic Structure* (Piscataway, NJ: Gorgias Press, 2004).

Geldner, Karl F., *Der Rig Veda*, Harvard Oriental Series, vols 1–3 (Cambridge, MA: Harvard University Press, 1951).

Gening, V.F., 'Le Champ Funeraire de Sintachta, et le probleme des anciennes tribus Indo-Iranniennes', *Sovetskaya Arkheologiya* 4 (1977): pp. 53–75.

Gershevitch, I., *The Avestan Hymn to Mithra* (reprint; Cambridge, UK: Cambridge University Press, 1967).

Ghirshman, R., *L'Iran et la Migration des Indo-Aryens et Iraniens* (Leiden: E.J. Brill, 1977).

Ghosh, A., ed., *An Encyclopaedia of Indian Archaeology*, 2 vols (New Delhi: Munshiram Manoharlal, 1989).

Ghosh, Abhijit, ed., *Atharvana: A Collection of Essays on the Atharva Veda with Special Reference to the Paippalada Tradition* (Kolkata: Sanskrit Book Depot, 2002).

Gimbutas, Marija, *The Goddesses and Gods of Old Europe* (California: University of California Press, 1974).

Gnoli, Gherardo, *Zoroaster's Time and Homeland: A Study on the Origins of Mazdeism and Related Problems* (Naples: Istituto Universitario Orientale, 1980).

———, *Richerche Storiche sul Sistan antico* (Rome: Istituto Italiano per il Medio ed Estremo Oriente, 1967).

Gonda, Jan, *Change and Continuity in Indian Religion* (reprint; New Delhi: Munshiram Manoharlal, 1997).

———, *Die Religionen Indiens*, 2 vols (Stuttgart: Kohlhammer, 1960–63).

———, *Rice and Barley Offerings in the Vedas* (Leiden: E.J. Brill, 1987).

———, *Selected Studies: Indo-European Linguistics*, Sanskrit Word Studies, vol. 2 (Leiden: E.J. Brill, 1975).

———, *Vedic Literature: Samhitas and Brahmanas* (Wiesbaden: Otto Harrassowitz, 1975).

Gopal, Ram, *The History and Principles of Vedic Interpretation* (New Delhi: Concept Publishing Company, 1983).

Griffith, R.T.H., trans., *The Hymns of the Samaveda* (reprint; New Delhi: Munshiram Manoharlal, 2008).

———, trans., *The Texts of the White Yajur Veda or Vajasaneyi Samhita* (1st edn, 1899; revised and expanded, New Delhi: Munshiram Manoharlal, 1987).

_____, trans., *The Hymns of the Rig Veda* (1896; new edn, Delhi: Motilal Banarsidass, 1976).

Griffiths, Arlo and Jan E.M. Houben, *The Vedas: Texts, Language and Ritual; Proceedings of the Third International Vedic Workshop* (Leiden, 2002).

Griffiths, Arlo and Annette Schmiedchen, eds, *The Atharvaveda and Its Paippaladashakha: Historical and Philological Papers on Vedic Tradition*, Geisteskultur Indiens, vol. 11 (Aachen: Shaker Verlag, 2007).

Hall, T.A., 'The Historical Development of Retroflux Consonants in Indo-Aryan', *Lingua* 102 (1997): pp. 203–21.

Halliday, William R., *Indo-European Folktales and Greek Legend* (Cambridge, UK: Cambridge University Press, 1933).

Harmatta, J., 'The Emergence of the Indo-Iranians: The Indo-Iranian Languages', in A.H. Dani and V.M. Masson, eds, *History of Civilizations of Central Asia, Vol. I, The Dawn of Civilization: Earliest Times to 700 BC* (Paris: UNESCO Publishing, 1992) pp. 357–78.

Hather, John G., *Tropical Archaeobotany: Applications and New Developments* (London: Routledge, 1994).

Haug, Martin, *Essays on the Sacred Language, Writings and Religion of the Parsis* (reprint; Whitefish: Kessinger Publishing, 2004).

Hazra, R.C., *Studies in the Puranic Records on Hindu Rites and Customs* (2nd edn; Delhi: Motilal Banarsidass, 1975).

Heehs, Peter, ed., *Indian Religions: The Spiritual Traditions of South Asia–An Anthology* (Delhi: Permanent Black, 2002).

Heesterman, J.C., *The Inner Conflict of Tradition: Essays in Indian Ritual, Kingship and Society* (New Delhi: Oxford University Press, 1985).

Hemphill, B.E., J.R. Lukacs and K.A.R. Kennedy, 'Biological Adaptations and Affinities of the Bronze Age Harappans', in R.H. Meadow, ed., *Harappa Excavations 1986–1990: A Multidisciplinary Approach to Third Millennium Urbanism* (Madison: Prehistory Press, 1991).

Herzfeld, E., *Zoroaster and His World* (Princeton, NJ: Princeton University Press, 1947).

Hillebrandt, A., *Vedische Mythologie* (Breslau, 1902).

Hinnells, J.R., *Zoroastrianism and the Parsis* (London: Ward Lock Educational, 1981).

Hock, Hans H., '(Pre-)Rig Vedic Convergence of Indo-Aryan with Dravidian? Another Look at the Evidence', in *Studies in the Linguistic Sciences* 14, no. 1 (1984): pp. 89–108.

_____, 'Substratum Influence on Rig Vedic Sanskrit?', in *Studies in Linguistic Sciences* 5 (1975): pp. 76–125.

_____, 'Philology and the Historical Interpretation of the Vedic Texts', in Edwin F. Bryant and Laurie L. Patton, eds, *The Indo-Aryan Controversy: Evidence and Inference in Indian History* (London and New York: Routledge, 2005).

_____, 'Subversion or Convergence? The Issue of Pre-Vedic Retroflexion Reconsidered', *Studies in the Linguistic Sciences* 23, no. 2 (1996): pp. 73–115.

Hock, Hans H. and Brian Joseph, *Language History, Language Change and Language Relationship: An Introduction to Historical and Comparative Linguistics*; Trends in Linguistics, Studies and Monographs 93 (Berlin: Mouton de Gruyter, 1996).

Hopkins, Thomas J., *The Hindu Religious Tradition* (Belmont, CA: Wadsworth Publishing Company, 1971).

Houben, Jan E.M., ed., *The Pravargya Brahmana of the Taittiriya Aranyaka: An Ancient Commentary on the Pravargya Ritual* (Delhi: Motilal Banarsidass, 1991).

Humbach, H., 'A Western Approach to Zarathushtra', *Journal of the K.R. Cama Oriental Institute* 51 (1984): pp. 15–32.

Jarman, M.R., et al., *Early European Agriculture: Its Foundation and Development* (Cambridge, UK: Cambridge University Press, 1982).

Jarrige, J.F., *L'archéologie de la Bactriane ancienne* (Paris: Diffusion de Bocard, 1985).

Jetmar, K., 'Sintasta–Eingemeinsames Heiligtum der Indo Iranier?', *Eurasia Antiqua* 2 (1996): pp. 215–22.

Jordens, J.T., *Dayananda Saraswati: Essays on His Life and Ideas* (New Delhi: Manohar, 1998).

Kachru, Braj B., et al., eds, *Language in South Asia* (Cambridge, UK: Cambridge University Press, 2008).

Kak, Subhash, *The Astronomical Code of the Rig Veda* (revised and expanded; New Delhi: Munshiram Manoharlal, 2000).

Kapoor, Subodh, *Encyclopaedia of Vedic Philosophy*, 9 vols (New Delhi: Cosmo Publications, 2002).

Karambelkar, V.W., *The Atharva Veda and the Ayurveda* (Varanasi: Chowkhamba Krishnadas Academy, 2003).

Keith, A.B., *The Religion and Philosophy of the Vedas and Upanishads* (1st edn, 1925; reprint, Delhi: Motilal Banarsidass, 1998).

———, *Rigveda Brahmanas: The Aitareya and Kausitaki Brahmanas of the Rigveda* (1st edn, 1920; reprint, Delhi: Motilal Banarsidass, 1998).

Kennedy, Kenneth A.R., *God-Apes and Fossil Men: Paleoanthropology in South Asia* (Michigan: University of Michigan, 2000).

———, 'Have Aryans Been Identified in the Prehistoric Skeletal Record from South Asia?', in George Erdosy, ed., *The Indo-Aryans of Ancient South Asia: Language, Material Culture and Ethnicity* (Berlin and New York: Walter de Gruyter, 1995).

Kenoyer, Jonathan M., *Ancient Cities of the Indus Valley Civilization* (Karachi and Islamabad: Oxford University Press and American Institute of Pakistan Studies, 1998).

Kiparsky, Paul, 'Metrics and Morphonemics in the Rig Veda', in M. Brame, ed., *Contributions to Generative Phonology* (Austin, TX: University of Texas Press, 1972).

Kochhar, Rajesh, *The Vedic People* (New Delhi: Orient Longman, 2000).

Koryakova, Ludmila V. and Andrej Epimakhov, *The Urals and Western Siberia in the Bronze and Iron Ages* (Cambridge, UK: Cambridge World Archaeology, 2007).

Krishnamurti, Bh., *Comparative Dravidian Linguistics: Current Perspectives* (Oxford: Oxford University Press, 2001).

———, 'The Emergence of Syllable Types of Stems (C)VCC(V) and (C)VC(V) in Indo-Aryan and Dravidian: Conspiracy or Convergence?', in W.G. Boltz and M.C. Shapiro, eds, *Studies in the Historical Phonology of Asian Languages* (Amsterdam: John Benjamins, 1991) pp. 160–75.

———, *Dravidian Languages* (Cambridge, UK: Cambridge University Press, 2003).

Kuiper, F.B.J., *Aryans in the Rigveda* (Amsterdam-Atlanta, GA: Editions Rodopi B.V., 1991).

Kulke, Eckehard, *The Parsees in India* (reprint; New Delhi: Vikas Publishing House, 1993).

Kuzmina, Elena E., *The Origin of the Indo-Iranians*, Leiden Indo-European Etymological Dictionary Series (Leiden: E.J. Brill, 2007).

Lal, B.B., *The Sarasvati Flows On: The Continuity of Indian Culture* (New Delhi: Aryan Books International, 2002).

Law, B.C., *Historical Geography of Ancient India* (Delhi: Ess Ess Publications, 1976).

Lehmann, Winfred P., *Theoretical Bases of Indo-European Linguistics* (New York: Routledge, 1996).

Lubotsky, A., 'Indo-Iranian Substratrum' (paper at a conference in Tvarminne, Finland, 1998).

Macdonell, A.A., *The Vedic Mythology* (Varanasi and New Delhi: Indological Book House, 1971).

_____, *A History of Sanskrit Literature* (1899; reprint, New Delhi: Munshiram Manoharlal, 1972).

_____, *A Vedic Reader for Students: Containing Thirty Hymns of the Rig Veda* (Delhi: Motilal Banarsidass, 1992).

Macdonell, A.A. and A.B. Keith, *Vedic Index of Names and Subjects*, 2 vols (reprint; Delhi: Motilal Banarsidass, 1995).

Mahony, William K., *The Artful Universe: An Introduction to the Vedic Religious Imagination* (Albany: State University of New York Press, 1998).

Majumdar, R.C., ed., *The Vedic Age* (5th edn; Bombay: BharatiyaVidya Bhavan, 1988).

Mallory, J.P., *In Search of the Indo-Europeans: Language, Archaeology and Myth* (London: Thames & Hudson, 1991).

Mallory, J.P. and Douglas Q. Adams, eds, *Encyclopedia of Indo-European Culture* (London and Chicago: Fitzroy Dearborn, 1997).

Marshall, J., ed., *Mohenjodaro and the Indus Civilization* (London: Arthur Probsthain, 1931).

Masica, Colin P., *The Indo-Aryan Languages* (Cambridge, UK: Cambridge University Press, 1991).

Meier-Brugger, M., M. Fritz and M. Mayrhofer, *Indo-European Linguistics*, translated by C. Gertmenian (Berlin: de Gruyter Textbook, 2003).

Mikhailov, M.I. and N.S. Mikhailov, *Key to the Vedas* (Minsk: Belarusian Information Center, 2005).

Misra, V.N. and Peter Bellwood, ed., *Recent Advances in Indo-Pacific Prehistory* (New Delhi: Oxford and IBH, 1985).

Mole, M., 'La Structure du Premier Chapitre du Videvdat', JA 229 (1951): pp. 283–98.

Monier-Williams, M., *A Sanskrit–English Dictionary* (reprint; Delhi: Motilal Banarsidass, 1973).

Moorey, P.R.S., 'The Hurrians, the Mitanni and Technological Innovation', in Léon de Meyer and E. Haerinck, eds, *Archaeologia Iranica et Orientalis, Miscellanea in Honorem Louis Vanden Berghe* (1989): pp. 273–86.

Müller, Max F., *The Rig-Veda-Sanhita: The Sacred Hymns of the Brahmans, Translated and Explained* (London: Trubner and Co., 1869).

_____, *A History of Ancient Sanskrit Literature* (London: 1860).

_____, ed., *Sacred Books of the East*, including:

    vols 1, 15, F. Max Müller, trans., *The Upanishads*;

    vols 2, 14, George Buhler, trans., *The Sacred Laws of the Aryas*;

    vols 4, 23, 31, J. Darmesteter and L.H. Mills, trans., *The Zend Avesta*;

    vols 5, 18, 24, 37, 47, E.W. West, trans., *The Pahlavi Texts*;

    vol. 11, Julius Eggeling, trans., *The Satapatha Brahmana*;

    vols 13, 17, 20, F. Max Müller and H. Oldenberg, trans., *Vedic Hymns*;

    (reprint; New Delhi, Low Price Publications and D.K. Publishers, 1995).

Nanavutty, Piloo, trans. and commentary, *The Gathas of Zarathushtra* (Ahmedabad: Mapin Publishing, 1999).

_____, *Zarathushtra* (New Delhi: NCERT, 1968).

Nirukta of Yaska, with commentary by Durgacarya (Bombay: Nirnayasagar Press, n.d.).

Nyrop, Richard F., 'Genetics Weaves Tapestry of Indian Heritage', *Focus: News from Harvard Medical, Dental and Public Health Schools* (2009).

Nyberg, H.S., *Die Religionen des alten Iran*, translated into German by H.H. Schaeder (Leipzig, 1938).

Ohala, Manjari, 'Phonological Areal Features of Some Indo-Aryan Languages', in *Language Science* 13, no. 2 (1991): pp. 107–24.

Oldenberg, H., *Die Religion des Veda* (Berlin, 1894).

Olender, Maurice, *The Languages of Paradise: Race, Religion, and Philology in the Nineteenth Century* (Cambridge, MA, and London: Harvard University Press, 1992).

Pandey, Pramod, 'Developments in Indian Linguistics 1965–2005: Phonology', in K.S. Nagaraja et al., eds, *Research Trends in Lexicography, Sanskrit and Linguistics: Proceedings of Seminar in Honour of Professor S.M. Katre* (Pune: Deccan College, 2007) pp. 121–32.

Pandey, R., *Hindu Samskaras* (reprint; Delhi: Motilal Banarsidass, 1994).

Pargiter, F.E., *The Purana Texts of the Dynasties of the Kali Age* (Varanasi: Chowkhamba Sanskrit Series, 1962).

———, *Ancient Indian Historical Tradition* (Delhi: Motilal Banarsidass, 1962).

Parpola, Asko, 'From Archaeology to a Stratigraphy of Vedic Syncretism: The Banyan Tree and the Water-Buffalo as Harappan Dravidian Symbols of Royalty, Inherited in Succession by Yama, Varuna and Indra', in Arlo Griffiths and Jan E.M. Houben, eds, *The Vedas: Texts, Language and Ritual: Proceedings of the Third International Vedic Workshop*, Groningen Oriental Studies, vol. 20 (Groningen: Egbert Forsten, 2004).

———, 'The Coming of the Aryans to Iran and India and the Cultural and Ethnic Identity of the Dasas', *Studia Orientalia* 64 (1988): pp. 195–302.

Pereltsvaig, Asya, *Languages of the World: An Introduction* (Cambridge, UK: Cambridge University Press, 2012).

Pischel, R. and K.F. Geldner, *Vedische Studien* (Stuttgart, 1889–1901).

Plofker, Kim, 'Review of Subhash Kak, The Astronomical Code of the Rig Veda', *Centaurus* 38 (1996): pp. 362–64.

Poliakov, Léon, *The Aryan Myth: A History of Racist and Nationalist Ideas in Europe* (New York: Basic Books, 1974).

Possehl, Gregory L., *Indus Age: The Writing System* (New Delhi: Oxford and IBH, 1996).

———, *The Indus Civilization: A Contemporary Perspective* (New Delhi: Vistaar Publications, 2009).

Pradhan, S.N., *Chronology of Ancient India* (Calcutta: University of Calcutta, 1927).

Prasoon, Shrikant, *Rishis and Rishikas* (Delhi: Pustak Mahal, 2009).

Puri, V.M.K. and B.C. Verma, 'Glacial and Geological Source of Vedic Saraswati in the Himalayas', *Itihas Darpan* 4 (1998): pp. 7–36.

Pusalkar, A.D., 'Authors of the Indus Culture', *Annals of the Bhandarkar Oriental Research Institute* XVIII (1926–27): pp. 385–95.

Radhakrishnan, S., *Indian Philosophy*, 2 vols (New Delhi: Oxford University Press, 1999).

Radhakrishnan, S., et al., eds, *The Cultural Heritage of India*, vol. 1 (1937; 2nd edn, Calcutta: Ramakrishna Mission, 1953–58).

Ramat, Anna G. and Paolo Ramat, *The Indo-European Languages* (London: Routledge, 1998).

Rao, S.R., 'New Light on Indus Script and Language', in B.B. Lal and S.P. Gupta, eds, *Frontiers of the Indus Civilization* (New Delhi: Books and Books, 1984).

Ratnagar, S., *Understanding Harappa: Civilization in the Greater Indus Valley* (New Delhi: Tulika, 2001).

Raychaudhuri, H., *Political History of Ancient India* (Calcutta: University of Calcutta, 1972).

Reich, David, et al., 'Reconstructing Indian Population History', *Nature* 461, no. 24 (September 2009).

Renfrew, Colin, *Archaeology and Language: The Puzzle of Indo-European Origins* (Cambridge, UK: Cambridge University Press, 1987).

Renou, Louis, *Bibliographie Vedique* (Paris, 1931).

_____, *Religions of Ancient India* (1953; reprint, New York: Schocken Books, 1968).

_____, ed., *Hinduism* (New York: George Braziller, 1962).

Roy, Mira, *Family Relations of Some Plants in the Atharva Veda*, National Commission for Compilation of History of Sciences in India (Calcutta: Indian National Science Academy, n.d.)

Saraswati, Chandrasekharendra (Jagatguru Sankaracharya of Kamakoti), *The Vedas* (Bombay: Bharatiya Vidya Bhavan, 1988).

Sarianidi, V.I., *Margiana and Protozoroastrism* (Athens: Kapon Ed, 1998).

_____, 'Recent Archaeological Discoveries and the Aryan Problem', in A.J. Gail and G.J.R. Mevissen, eds, *South Asian Archaeology 1991* (Stuttgart: Franz Steiner Verlag, 1993) pp. 251–64.

Schrader, O., *Prehistoric Antiquities of the Aryan Peoples*, translated by F.B. Jevons (London, 1890).

_____, *Die Indogermanen* (Leipzig, 1911).

Sengupta, S., Lev A. Zhivotovsky, et al., 'Polarity and Temporality of High-Resolution Y-Chromosome Distributions in India Identify Both Indigenous and Exogenous Expansions and Reveal Minor Genetic Influence of Central Asian Pastoralists', *American Journal of Human Genetics* 78, no. 2 (February 2006): pp. 202–21.

Sforza, Luca Cavalli, *Genes, Peoples, and Languages* (New York: North Point Press, 2000).

Sharma, R.S., *India's Ancient Past* (New Delhi: Oxford University Press, 2005).

_____, *Looking For the Aryans* (Hyderabad: Orient Longman, 1995).

Shendge, Malati J., *The Language of the Harappans: From Akkadian to Sanskrit* (New Delhi: Abhinav Publications, 1997).

Sidharth, B.G., *The Celestial Key to the Vedas: Discovering the Origins of the World's Oldest Civilization* (Rochester, VT: Inner Traditions International, 1999).

Singh, M.R., *A Critical Study of the Geographical Data in the Early Puranas* (Calcutta: Punthi Pustak, 1972).

Singh, Upender, *A History of Ancient and Medieval India* (Delhi: Pearson Longman, 2008).

Sontheimer, Gunther D. and Hermann Kulke, eds, *Hinduism Reconsidered* (New Delhi: Manohar, 2001).

Sorensen, S., *Index to the Names in the Mahabharata* (Delhi: Motilal Banarsidass, 1963).

Sparreboom, Marcus, *Chariots in the Veda* (Leiden: E.J. Brill, 1985).

Staal, Frits, *Discovering the Vedas: Origins, Mantra, Rituals, Insight* (New Delhi: Penguin Books India, 2008).

Stein, A., 'Afghanistan in Avestic Geography', *Indian Antiquary* 15 (1886): pp. 21–23.

Stevenson, J., *Translation of the Sanhita of the Sama Veda* (London: Oriental Translation Fund of Great Britain and Ireland, 1842).

Swami Jagdishwarananda and Swami Madhavananda, trans. and commentary, *The Brhadaranyaka Upanisad* (Madras: Sri Ramakrishna Math, 1951).

Szemerenyi, O., *Indo-European Kinship*, in Jacques Duchesne-Guillemin, ed., *Acta Iranica VII* (1997).

Taraporewala, I.J.S., *The Religion of Zarathushtra* (Bombay: B.I. Taraporewala, 1979).

Thapar, R., ed., *Recent Perspectives of Early Indian History* (Bombay: Popular Prakashan, 1995).

_____, *The Penguin History of Early India* (New Delhi: Penguin Books India, 2003).

Thomason, S.G. and T. Kaufman, *Language Contact, Creolization and Genetic Linguistics* (Los Angeles: University of California Press, 1988).

Tilak, B.G., *The Arctic Home in the Vedas* (Poona: Tilak Brothers, 1903).

Trautmann, Thomas R., *Aryans and British India* (New Delhi: Vistaar Publications, 1997).

Turner, R.L., *A Comparative Dictionary of the Indo-Aryan Languages* (1966; reprint, Delhi: Motilal Banarsidass, 2008).

Van de Mieroop, Marc, *A History of the Ancient Near East: ca. 3000–323 BC* (Malden, MA: Wiley, 2004).

Vesci, Uma Marina, *Heat and Sacrifice in the Vedas* (Delhi: Motilal Banarsidass, 1992).

Watkins, Calvert, *The American Heritage Dictionary of Indo-European Roots* (revised and edited; Boston: Houghton Mifflin Company, 2000).

Weber, Albrecht, *History of Indian Literature*, translated by J. Mann and T. Zachariae (2nd edn; London: Trubner, 1882).

Whittle, A.W.R., *Europe in the Neolithic: The Creation of New Worlds* (Cambridge, UK: Cambridge University Press, 1996).

Wikander, O.S., *Vayu. Texte und Untersuchungen zur indo-iranischen Religionsgeschichte* (Uppsala: Lundequist, 1941).

Wilhelm, Gernot, *The Hurrians* (Warminster: Aris and Phillips, 1989).

———, 'The Kingdom of Mitanni in Second-Millennium Upper Mesopotamia', in Jack M. Sassoon, et al., eds, *Civilizations of the Ancient Near East*, vol. 2 (New York and London: Scribner, 1995) pp. 1243–54.

Wilson, H.H., *Rig-Veda Sanhita: A Collection of Ancient Hindu Hymns*, 6 vols (London, 1850–88).

Winn, Shan M.M., *Heaven, Heroes and Happiness: The Indo-European Roots of Western Ideology* (Boston: University Press of America, 1995).

Winternitz, Maurice, *History of Indian Literature*, vols 1–2 (3rd edn; New Delhi: Munshiram Manoharlal, 1991).

Witzel, Michael, ed., *Inside the Texts, Beyond the Texts: New Approaches to the Study of the Vedas*, Harvard Oriental Series, Opera Minora vol. 2 (Cambridge, MA: Harvard University Press, 1997).

Woolner, Alfred C., *Introduction to Prakrit* (2nd edn, 1928; reprint, Delhi: Motilal Banarsidass, 1999).

Yadava, B.N.S., *Society and Culture in Northern India in the Twelfth Century* (Allahabad: Central Book Depot, 1973).

Yarshater, E., ed., *Encyclopaedia Iranica* (Costa Mesa, CA: Mazda Publishers, 1982 onwards); online at www.encyclopediairanica.com.

Zaehner, R.C., ed., *The Hutchinson Encyclopedia of Living Faiths* (4th edn; Oxford: Helicon, 1994).

———, *Hinduism* (2nd edn; Oxford: Oxford University Press, 1966).

———, *Teachings of the Magi* (London: Allen and Unwin, 1956).

———, *The Dawn and Twilight of Zoroastrianism* (London: Weidenfield, 1961).

Zvelebil, Kamil V., *Comparative Dravidian Phonology* (The Hague: Mouton, 1970).

———, *An Introduction to Dravidian Languages* (Pondicherry: Pondicherry Institute of Language and Culture, 1991).

Zvelebil, Marek, ed., *Hunters in Transition: Mesolithic Societies of Temperate Eurasia and Their Transition to Farming* (Cambridge, UK: Cambridge University Press, 1986).

Zysk, Kenneth G., *Medicine in the Veda* (1st Indian edn; Delhi: Motilal Banarsidass, 1996).